D0204633

International Dictionary of Public Management and Governance

International Dictionary of Public Management and Governance

Gambhir Bhatta

Foreword by Des Gasper

M.E.Sharpe
Armonk, New York
London, England

Library of Congress Cataloging-in-Publication Data

Bhatta, Gambhir.
  International dictionary of public management and governance / by Gambhir
Bhatta.
    p. cm.
  ISBN 0-7656-1261-5 (hardcover : alk. paper)
  1. Public administration—Dictionaries. 2. Administrative
agencies—Management—Dictionaries. 3. Management—Dictionaries. I. Title:
Dictionary of public management and governance. II. Title.

JA61.B48 2005

                                      351'.03—dc22   2004025456

Printed in the United States of America

BM (c) 10   9   8   7   6   5   4   3   2   1

Dedicated to the memory of

Lava Dev Bhatta

but for whom I wouldn't be here today doing what I'm doing

Foreword

Good public policy, management, and administration require thinking that is disciplined yet creative, independent yet committed. In his classic study, *Towards a Philosophy of Administration,* Christopher Hodgkinson indicated how administration focuses on the formulation, clarification, testing, communication, and follow-up of evaluative propositions.[1] Strong skills in handling language, logic, and in discussing values are, therefore, essential.

Gambhir Bhatta's formidable dictionary of public management provides a valuable tool for the first part of such work: the giving of close attention to words, and the skilled handling of language. With exceptional energy and patience, he has given a lucid introduction to a large proportion of the technical terms that are likely to confront a public-management specialist. The dictionary is important in several ways.

- The field of public management is a complex intersection that draws concepts and vocabulary from many areas of theory and practice. In such an interdisciplinary field, a dictionary like this can save considerable time for professionals and students, and, even more importantly, gives a basis for thinking further about the complex and competing sources of public management: law, economics, business management and finance, human relations, politics, military planning and strategy, among others.[2]

- The language of public management is dynamic, with the continual entry of new terms and constant evolution of old ones. The injection of concepts from business management, for example, in a series of waves through the twentieth century culminated in the widespread shift in the 1980s and 1990s to a language of "public management" rather than "public administration," and to a whole additional vocabulary of "New Public Management."

- Thinking about word choice is central to the building and testing of arguments that is in turn central in administration and management. Considering alternative possible formulations, as compared to the formulation in a text, helps us to see more clearly and exactly the conclusions which the actual choice of words leads toward, and it helps in

A careful dissection of key concepts is an essential starting point. Consider the terms "public" and "management." "Public" derives from words that referred to adulthood ("puberty," a word connoting the passage to adulthood, reflects the link) and thus to being a member of a political community. It involves a *series* of contrasts with the untrammeled market, with respect to who is considered, not only issues of ownership or profit-orientation. It involves the criteria used, going beyond consideration only of market and market-equivalent impacts; a greater scope of effects considered, concerning both the types of effect and the greater range of affected people considered; a greater range of people to be involved in discussion and decision-making, within an arena for debate of matters of common concern as opposed to an army or a market; and thus overall a broader range of advocated values, including public spirit and concern for others, not only self-interest and (at best) agreement-following. Definitions of "public" and of the field(s) of public policy/public administration/public management reflect contested notions about the functioning and ordering of societies and hence about the proper organization of a political community: notions about the capacity and limits of markets, about the extent of duties to and for others, about the degree of sustainable public-spiritedness, about the capacity of states and of other non-market action, and thus overall about the degree to which non-market action should be legitimated by extension of the label "public."

The term "management" has brought connotations of private-sector know-how, can-do spirit, and delivery of results. The danger of the term in the past quarter century has been the ideology that there is a universally valid "management"—derived in fact from a particular rather narrow vision of Anglo-American private-sector practice—and that it should be imposed on all sectors and all countries: the doctrine of "managerialism" in Christopher Pollitt's terms (1993).[7]

Internationally, there has thus been considerable confusion over the term "public management," with no consistent usage and no consistent differences in usage between it and "public administration." Kettl and Milward's survey of public management revealed many different definitions.[8] In reality, "public management" has been the name adopted by almost any new stream in public administration that reacts against the conventional shape that the field had acquired: state-centered, organization-focused, maintenance-oriented. It is broader than just NPM, some variants of which have been dated private-sector management, imported to discipline a sector that had not always been carefully studied (Pollitt, 1993). By revealing the richness of public management, Bhatta's dictionary helps us avoid adopting oversimplified and overgeneralized packages.

A dictionary of public management needs to be complemented by various methods, including from practical logic, creative thinking and value analysis, and by widely drawn case studies from a variety of contexts and perspectives.[9] A dictionary does not provide these by itself, but Gambhir Bhatta has brought to it an exceptionally rich and relevant range of experience. Born and educated in Nepal; trained in economics and public policy in the United States, and steeped at the distinguished Graduate School for Public and International Affairs at the University of Pittsburgh in William Dunn's extension of practical logic to policy analysis;[10] experienced in a variety of areas in public and development management in countries across four continents, including with the United Nations; an academic for several years at the National University of Singapore; a consultant to public-sector clients in various countries as well organizations such as the Asian Development Bank; and a senior advisor at the State Services Commission in the New Zealand Public Service. He has provided a public-management dictionary for the twenty-first century, a tool for critical, independent, creative public managers. It will be sure to need extension and revision, given such a complex, dynamic and contested field. But it forms an invaluable basis and a noteworthy contribution.

Des Gasper
Dean of Studies
Institute of Social Studies
The Hague, The Netherlands
August 2005

Notes

1. Christopher Hodgkinson, *Towards a Philosophy of Administration* (Oxford: Blackwell, 1978).

2. Mark Rutgers, "Paradigm Lost: Crisis as Identity of the Study of Public Administration," *International Review of Administrative Sciences* 64 (1998), pp. 553–64; Des Gasper, "Interdisciplinarity," in A.K. Giri (ed.), *Creative Social Research: Rethinking Theories and Methods* (New Delhi/Thousand Oaks/London: Sage, 2004), pp. 308–44.

3. Christopher Hood and Michael Jackson, *Administrative Argument* (Aldershot: Dartmouth Publishing Co., 1991). I draw substantially here on my article "Fashion, Learning and Values in Public Management: Reflections on

South African and International Experience," *Africa Development* 27(3) (2002), pp. 17–47, which gives a fuller treatment and detailed illustrations.

4. Christopher Pollitt, "Justification by Works or by Faith? Evaluating New Public Management." *Evaluation* 1(2) (1995), pp. 133–54.

5. For a devastating case study of misapplied NPM, see Nicholas Awortwi: *Fundamentally Flawed: Lessons for Africa from the Delivery of Services in Ghana* (Leiden: Brill, 2004); Nicholas Awortwi, "Getting the Fundamentals Wrong: Woes of Partnerships in Solid Waste Collection," *Public Administration and Development* 24(3) (2004), pp. 213–24. For a general review see Nick Manning, "The Legacy of New Public Management in Developing Countries," *International Review of Administrative Sciences,* 2001, 67(2), 297–312.

6. For one way to integrate these various requirements into an approach usable both for training and professional practice, see Gasper 2002 (note 3 above); also Gasper 2000, "Structures and Meanings—A Way to Introduce Argumentation Analysis in Policy Studies Education," *Africanus* 30(1), 49–72, and Gasper, 2004, "Studying Aid: Some Methods," in J. Gould, and H.S. Marcussen (eds.), *Ethnographies of Aid* (Roskilde, DK: Roskilde University, 2004) pp. 45–92.

7. Christopher Pollitt, *Managerialism and the Public Services: Cuts or Cultural Change in the 1990s?* 2nd ed. (Oxford: Blackwell Business, 1993).

8. Donald F. Kettl and H. Brinton Milward (eds.). *The State of Public Management* (Baltimore, MD: Johns Hopkins University Press, 1996).

9 On practical logic, see notes 3 and 6 above; on creative thinking, see Pradip Khandwalla, *Fourth Eye: Excellence through Creativity* (Delhi: Wheeler, 1988); on value analysis, see for example Christopher Hood's masterful application of "Cultural Theory" in his *The Art of the State* (New York: Oxford University Press, 1998); and for one helpful survey of experiences, see Khandwalla, *Revitalizing the State* (New Delhi: Sage, 1999).

10. William N. Dunn, *Public Policy Analysis: An Introduction* (2nd ed.) (Englewood Cliffs, NJ: Prentice Hall, 1994).

Preface

One staggers under the intellectual weight of pet theories, explanations, ideas and concepts imported to shape up public management theory.

—Barry Bozeman, *Public Management: The State of the Art*

[Public management] has been reactive rather than proactive, open to colonization by marauding theoretical hordes and changing agendas, often driven by outside forces.

—Andrew Gray and Bill Jenkins
"From Public Administration to Public
Management: Reassessing a Revolution?"

These statements above were penned a decade ago, and we can well imagine the explosion of the public management field since then. Which is where, in part, this dictionary comes in. The idea for it goes back at least eight years, when I was busy collating definitions to help students understand various concepts in public management.

Public-management theory is rich in diversity and there has been considerable graft from various fields of study, including economics, political science, sociology, and psychology. Readers will note a fair bit of an economics orientation in the dictionary, not necessarily because it is in keeping with my academic background, but because public management and administration is traditionally considered to be a subset of political science, which itself has involved the incorporation of many ideas from economics.[1] As a matter of fact, the underlying bases of the most significant reforms in public management in recent years (i.e., the so-called new public management) flow directly from microeconomic theory.[2]

The work on public management reaches over many areas, including:

- A substantive focus on the nature and magnitude of public problems (both tractable and wicked ones);

- The nature of the analysis (i.e., conducted in the public domain with competing views and interpretations openly aired);

- A concern with effective and efficient prescriptions and their attempted fair applications across all settings;

- A substantive, and often frustrating, focus on processes as much as on problems; and

- A focus on multi-organizational and network problems.

There have also been some conflicting interactions at play, ranging from the value-neutral prescriptions of efficiency drive to the value-laden and normative dimensions of public-service ethics and codes of conduct.

And that is not where it ends. While public administration tends to deal more with the internal dimensions of bureaucracies (such as budgeting, personnel, etc.), public management brings in concepts such as strategy, policy processes, and governance. Public management is now so rich that it covers practically all areas of inquiry.

Readers need to note several things here:

- All the terms in the dictionary are in use in the relevant literature, or have been applied in practice across different organizations in different jurisdictions (the citations to literature following most of the concepts are not meant to be exhaustive, or, for that matter, even the ones most often cited, but they are to act as entrées to further research for the interested reader);

- The dictionary is written from an international perspective, evident in the frequent references to parliamentary and federal systems of government, for example, as well as to public management in the developed and developing-country context;

- The definitions of the concepts are arrived at primarily from the organizational perspective and the public-policy angle, and they accept, where relevant, the role of metaphor in management and policy languages;

- Terms are often not defined in great detail, as the intention is not so much to provide exhaustive definitions but rather brief explanations of terms, and so depth is sacrificed for breadth; and

- The determination of what to include or not is necessarily rather arbitrary, and so what to some might seem as obvious terms for inclusion may have been omitted.

This dictionary, then, is not meant to be the most definitive source of all terms in public-management and governance parlance, and neither is it a literature review or a historical analysis of developments in public management. It is a collection of terms that students as well as practitioners of contemporary public management are likely to come across in their everyday work.

As with all work of such nature, this dictionary is still a work in progress in many ways. I would appreciate feedback on any aspect of this work for future improvement. Finally, while many individuals have helped in this project, I alone am responsible for all errors and omissions.

Gambhir Bhatta
August 2005

Notes

1. Gary J. Miller, "The Impact of Economics on Contemporary Political Science." *Journal of Economics Literature*, 1997, 35(3), pp. 1173–1204.

2. Donald F. Kettl, "The Global Revolution in Public Management: Driving Themes, Missing Links." *Journal of Policy Analysis and Management*, 1997, 16(3), pp. 446–62.

Acknowledgments

At the time that I decided to undertake the task of writing this dictionary, I was gleefully oblivious of the time and energy it would take to complete it. And as with any venture of this sort, there is never complete satisfaction that the final product is perfect, but the product will benefit from a review by a wider audience now.

This dictionary has been possible because of the support of many individuals and institutions. I would like to thank first the New Zealand State Services Commission (SSC) and, in particular, Jeanette Schollum, who was very supportive. Working at the Commission gave me the intellectual and practical exposure to public management that academicians and practitioners alike can only dream of. For the institutional support in Singapore, The Hague, and Wellington, thanks are due to Professor Des Gasper (Institute of Social Studies, The Hague), Professor Lee Lai To (National University of Singapore), and Professor Gary Hawke (Victoria University of Wellington, School of Government).

Others that I would like to thank are Des for writing the foreword to the book and for diligently reviewing the manuscript, Kripa Sridharan for her hospitality in Singapore, Neil McInnes for the intellectual sparring, and the following reviewers: David Galt (New Zealand Treasury), Clay Wescott (Asian Development Bank), Alex Matheson (then based at OECD), Jon Quah (National University of Singapore), Jeanette Schollum, and Gary Hawke. The anonymous reviewers at the proposal stage were also very helpful. Thanks are also due to Doug Goldenberg-Hart for his support and intervention at a crucial phase of the project; to the copy editor for the diligent work; and to Lynn Taylor, Amanda Allensworth, and Amy Odum at M. E. Sharpe, Inc., for all their patience.

There is a peril in engaging in academic pursuits while not in academia: it eats miserably into family time, and for that I have to apologize to my wife, Bhawana, and our two boys, Ashwin and Adarsh, for being so preoccupied with this project for such a long time, and to whom my efforts and interest must have seen so vain and pointless.

International Dictionary of Public Management and Governance

perceptions of how the other members of the group/team would behave/react. This causes a spiral effect which, if positive, leads to what is known as a bandwagon effect, and, if negative, to inconsistent behavior on the part of team members. See J. Harvey, "The Abilene Paradox: The Management of Agreement," *Organizational Dynamics*, 1974, 17(1), pp. 63–80. *See also* **Bandwagon effect; Groupthink**.

Ability grouping: *See* **Achievement grouping**.

Absolute performance evaluation: A form of performance evaluation where an employee's work is judged against a predetermined but objective standard that has been agreed to by both the employee and the organization. Here, the employee is not evaluated relative to peers. For a rigorous analysis of whether contracts based on such performance evaluation provide first-best incentives to agents, see G. Baker, "Incentive Contracts and Performance Measurement," *Journal of Political Economy*, 1992, 100(3), pp. 598–614. *Cf.* **Relative performance evaluation**.

Absolute threshold: *See* **Perceptual order**.

Absoluteness of accountability: Refers to a situation where every individual in an organization that delegates authority is accountable to an immediate superior—and is the locus for responsibility—for the delivery of results for which the delegation is being made. This is evident in a scalar chain where accountabilities are contained in the hierarchical nature of the organization. *See also* **Scalar chain of authority**.

Absoluteness of responsibility: Refers to the retention of ultimate responsibility by designated managers even though they may delegate authority to those below in the hierarchy. Such absoluteness of responsibility is necessary for proper accountability. The implications of this concept are that managers cannot hide behind the actions of their subordinates when there are lapses in judgment on any particular issue.

Absorptive capacity: The ability of organizations and individuals to assimilate new information and resources and apply them to better fulfill their mandates and roles. The concept has strong implications for the notion of double-loop learning in which organizations use the information contained in performance feedback and begin to reprogram their processes and assumptions. See, e.g., W. Cohen, and D. Levinthal, "Absorptive Capacity: A New Perspective on Learning and Innovation," *Administrative Science Quarterly*, 1990, 35(1), pp. 128–52. *See also* **Double-loop learning**.

Abuse of dominant position: As understood in the public-management context, this concept refers to those practices in which a government (or an agency favored by a government) may engage to maintain or strengthen its leading position. What exactly constitutes abuse will vary from situation to situation and across jurisdictions. For a review of this concept in the context of a governmental agency in regulatory functions, see, e.g., C. Scott, "Organizational Variety in Regulatory Governance: An Agenda for Comparative Investigation of the OECD Countries," *Public Organization Review*, 2003, 3(3), pp. 301–16.

Acceptability threshold: The acceptability threshold determines whether a particular policy alternative is chosen depending upon whether the criteria on which it is evaluated are met. The acceptability threshold may have to be loosened if there are no alternatives that meet the threshold or, conversely, tightened if there is more than one. *See also* **Go/no-go rule**.

Acceptable-level decision rule: *See* **Decision rule**.

Acceptance criteria: Conditions that must be met before any policy alternatives can be accepted. Such criteria normally include staying within budget constraints, if any, and political acceptability, feasibility, and degree of alignment to government objectives.

Acceptance theory of leadership: States that a leader's success is a function of the degree of acceptance of his or her authority by subordinates. In the absence of acceptance, the authority of the leaders tends to be dictated on subordinates. *See also* **Zone of acceptance**.

Accession creation: Refers to the activities in which governments may be engaged toward promoting broad support for improved ethical standards and the inclusion of non-elites in the policy-making process. Access creation is said to be a useful strategy to counter corruption in the public sector. See, e.g., J. Klein, "A Strategic Approach for Donor-Assisted Counter-Corruption Programs," in G. Bhatta, and J. Gonzalez (eds), *Governance Innovations in the Asia Pacific Region: Trends, Cases, and Issues*, Aldershot, UK: Ashgate, 1998, pp. 143–53.

Accommodation: (1) As used in the public-management context, accommodation refers to the extent to which organizational members accept and internalize the external shocks and pressures that bear down on them. (2) The act of finding common ground with those who have opposing views and agreeing to move ahead with a shared understanding. *See also* **Cognitive consonance**

Achievement motive: The desire of an employee to want to do (i.e., achieve) more and for a higher quality of performance. Motivation theorists believe that such a motive needs to be recognized early and encouraged and supported consistently in order that the employee contributes more to the organization, and in that process fulfill the sense of self as well. See D. McClelland, *The Achieving Society*, Princeton, NJ: Van Nostrand Reinhold, 1961.

Acquired-needs theory: A theory of motivation propounded by psychologist David McClelland that states that individuals are driven by three needs: of achievement (to excel in what they do), of affiliation (to get the feeling that they belong to a group), and of power (to be able to control and direct others). See D. McClelland and D. Burnham, "Power is the Great Motivator," *Harvard Business Review*, 1976, 54(2), pp. 100–10.

Acquisition: Refers to obtaining ownership and control of the resources (such as human resources) needed by an organization to fulfill its functions. The costs of obtaining ownership and control are known as acquisition costs, and relate to any acquired asset or program (such as a training program). The actual acquisition costs are specified in a contract between the party supplying the product and the one demanding it.

Across-the-board provisions: Rules, regulations, and processes that apply to all organizations (and all parts of an organization) in a particular area; for example, on retrenchment in an organization. Such provisions, however, have specific criteria that must be met before they can be so applied.

Acting position: A position held by an individual for a temporary period, often until a permanent appointment can be made. Acting positions are often used to provide opportunities to promising individuals to get much-needed senior-management experience. The term acting up is used to denote a development opportunity for an individual in a lower position to temporarily take up a higher position that offers learning opportunities. This form of job elevation is increasingly used in the public sector as a way of developing leadership abilities in promising individuals.

Action-centered leadership: Asserts that there are set activities that a leader can be involved in to motivate and lead a team. These include task achievement, team building, and individual development. This focus on task, team, and individual has remained at the core of much theory on leadership and motivation over the years.

Action group: A group that is created to achieve a specific task or objective. The group disbands upon completion of the task. Membership in the group might come from different levels within an organization, as well as, if necessary, from outside. Action groups are by necessity kept relatively small so that transaction costs are kept to a minimum.

Action learning: Any learning for an individual that takes place by doing (i.e., experiential), has attributes of collaboration, and that reflects on practice as well as lifelong learning. Action learning can be complemented by other forms of individual learning (such as academic work) in order to embed the experiences and give the individual a holistic approach to doing things more effectively. See, e.g., O. Zuber-Skerritt, "The Concept of Action Learning," *The Learning Organization*, 2002, 9(3), pp. 114–24.

Action repertoires: The stock of action that an organization has in response to problems (for example, how to respond to aggressive or critical questioning). Action repertoires are contained in standard operating procedures, and management has the option of employing any action, or mix of action, to address a problem. The range of actions contained in the repertoire is normally a product of individual and joint learning that has taken place in the organizational context, and which has been institutionalized through rigorous knowledge-management practices in the organization.

Action research: Where the researcher meets research subjects in specific tasks and thus reports on them. Action research is focused on empirical "real world" evidence. In action research, practitioners link up with others to share their reflections on any learning opportunity. See, e.g., H. Altrichter, et al., "The Concept of Action Research," *The Learning Organization*, 2002, 9(3), pp. 125–31. For an early discussion of this concept, see also K. Lewin, "Action Research and Minority Problems," *Journal of Social Issues*, 1946, 2(4), pp. 34–36.

Active citizens: Individuals who are actively interested in the affairs of government and who contribute meaningfully to the development of suitable public policy. Active citizens normally form groups in order to maximize their collective voice, but they may act alone as well. The public-policy formulation process is enhanced by active citizens providing meaningful input.

Active listening: A technique used in employee counseling wherein the counselor pays heed not only to factual information but also to employee sentiment. Active listening is facilitated by asking exploratory questions and by encouraging the speaker to further analyze his or her feelings in relation to a subject. For a case-study application of this concept in relation to management, see, e.g., S. Kubota et al., "A Study of the Effects of Active Listening on Listening Attitudes of Middle Managers," *Journal of Occupational Health*, 2004, 46(1), pp. 60–67.

Active misrepresentation: Refers to an extreme form of deception committed by an individual or agent in pursuit of a strategic advantage about planned actions. Active misrepresentation can occur even within an agreement, but this can be considered rational depending upon what the party seeks as the end result. See, e.g., V. Crawford, "Lying for Strategic Advantage: Rational and Boundedly Rational Misrepresentation of Intentions," *American Economic Review*, 2003, 93(1), pp. 133–49.

Active monitoring: Where departments and central agencies (such as a state treasury) work in partnership to regularly and actively monitor management practices and controls in departments to assess their effectiveness. The aim is to facilitate early action where significant risks or deficiencies emerge. Management practices can thus adapt toward effectively addressing perceived vulnerabilities. Active monitoring requires the full cooperation of both governmental departments and central agencies. See, e.g., Treasury Board of Canada Secretariat, *Policy on Active Monitoring*, Ottawa: Treasury Board of Canada, 2001, pp. 1–2.

Active probe: *See* **Active search**.

Active search: Denotes how organizations probe for information and knowledge that will help them determine how best to tackle problems. Active search tends to arise when organizations face critical problems that might jeopardize their core interests. For a discussion of the concept with reference to routine responses of organization in any change process, see, e.g., H. Greve and A. Taylor, "Innovations as Catalysts for Organizational Change: Shifts in Organizational Cognition and Search," *Administrative Science Quarterly*, 2000, 45(1), pp. 54–80. *Cf.* **Passive scanning**.

Activism: Concerted action by groups of citizens toward a particular policy issue. Some examples of activism can include running for political office, gathering signatures for a cause, fund raising, or participating in political demonstrations. The passage by referendum of Proposition 13 in California (in 1978, a tax-revolt law which forced the state government to lower property taxes and to limit future increases) is a classic example of activism in practice. For a case study discussion of activism in practice, see, e.g., J. Barnett and P. Barnett, "'If You Want to Sit on Your Butts You'll Get Nothing!' Community Activism in Response to Threats of Hospital Closure in Southern New Zealand," *Health and Place*, 2003, 9(2), pp. 59–71.

Activity chart: Also known as a Gantt chart, this is a graphic depiction in the form of a timeline of what activity (task) needs to be done when. An activity chart helps management decide how to better facilitate effective allocation of resources for projects and programs. An activity plan is a document that specifies what activity is to be carried out, how it is to be carried out, by whom, and when.

Activity theory: Refers to the process of interactions among individuals in organizations that result in organizational action as well as strategies. There are four interactive components that activity theory considers: (a) organizational structure (which sets parameters around who interacts with whom), (b) the key actors in these structures, (c) the work that these actors do, and (d) the practices and processes through which interaction is made possible. The theory is important in explaining how strategies emerge from the manner in which action is structured in organizations. For a case-study review of how activity theory is used, see, e.g., P. Jarzabkowski, "Strategic Perspectives: An Activity Theory Perspective on Continuity and Change," *Journal of Management Studies*, 2003, 40(1), pp. 23–55.

Activity trap: A situation where employees feel that they are not able to move upward because they are not able to fulfill objectives they set for themselves. Such individuals tend to end up focusing routinely on the activities that are given them rather than on performance that might propel them to better positions. Solutions to the activity trap include job enrichment, rotation, and mobility—experiences that will allow these individuals to tackle new problems. See, e.g., D. Billows, *Managing Cross-Functional Projects*, Denver: The Hampton Group, 2002, pp. 19–21.

Activity variance: Also known as activity variability, this term refers to the difference between two activities in the most time-consuming path (i.e., the path that is likely to take the longest to be completed as used in worst-case scenarios). This allows management to get a better perspective on the completion schedule. Used extensively in project management, the concept is relevant in understanding the variabilities in the completion times of different project configurations. For an analysis of how activity variance may be managed in project settings, see for example G. Gutierrez and A. Paul, "Robustness to Variability in Project Networks," *IIE Transactions*, 2001, 33(8), pp. 649–60.

Actors: In the public-policy context, this term refers to those involved in the policy process. These generally include: (a) adopters—with formal authority to make policies, (b) implementers—with a mandate to give effect to the policy, (c) clients—those whose interests are targeted by the policy, and (d) entrepreneurs—those who think of new ways of solving public problems in the policy-making domain. Note that this last group of policy actors generally comprises those who have access to key parts in the policy-making process. See for example L. Koenig, *An Introduction to Public Policy*, Englewood Cliffs, NJ: Prentice Hall, 1986, p. 141.

Act-utilitarianism: An assertion that any policy action is right if it produces net utility for citizens. It is thus judged on the basis of how it contributes to the general public welfare. For example, giving benefits to unemployed citizens is considered act-utilitarian although it could lead to an incentive not to actively seek employment. For a classic work on this concept, see R. Bales, "Act Utilitarianism: Account of Right Making Characteristics or Decision-Making Procedure?" *American Philosophical Quarterly*, 1971, 8(3), pp. 257–65. For an interesting application of the concept to bureaucrats and the ethical dilemmas they face, see, e.g., W. Gormley, "Moralists, Pragmatists, and Rogues: Bureaucrats in Modern Mysteries," *Public Administration Review*, 2001, 61(2), pp. 184–93. *Cf.* **Rule-utilitarianism**.

Ad hoc committee: A group of individuals who are formally brought together to fulfill a specific task. Such a committee disbands afterward. Ad-hoc committees are generally established to address problems that occur infrequently.

Ad hoc reviews: Unscheduled (i.e., not specified *ex ante*) reviews of a project or program undertaken as a result of some developments that merit closer attention on how they will affect the project or program.

Ad-hoc risk taking: A situation where organizations make decisions affecting core organizational resources and mandates on uncertain opportunities without any strategic considerations.

Adaptability: Refers to the capacity of an individual or organization to adjust a method of operating pursuant to changes in the operating environment. Adaptation can be of several modes: (a) piecemeal adjustment—slight modification of existing practices, (b) recombination—

minor modifications to all the operations so that the combined effect is new, (c) imitation—copying the basic design of a practice evident elsewhere, and (d) prototyping—creating a new design suited to one's own environment. For a discussion of these modes of adaptation, see, e.g., C. Hood, *Administrative Analysis*, Sussex, U.K.: Wheatsheaf Books, 1986, p. 142.

Adaptive agent: An entity (individual or organization) that attempts to fulfill a set of prescribed goals in a dynamic environment by acting upon whatever impulses are generated. Such an agent not only has the ability to sense changes in the environment but also has internal information processing and decision-making capability to deal with them. Basically, the agent adapts depending upon the behavior of those with which it interacts in the environment. One specific type of adaptive agent that is increasingly visible is the "adaptive information agent" that works predominantly in the e-commerce environment. Given the dramatic increase in the use of information in all aspects of organizational work, the role of the adaptive agent has been increasingly affected by the use of information technologies and processes. For a discussion of the concept as it relates to economic theory, see, e.g., J. Holland and J. Miller, "Artificial Adaptive Agents in Economic Theory," *American Economic Review, Papers and Proceedings*, 1991, 81(2), 365–70.

Adaptive behavior: Any behavior of employees or organizations that reflects their ability to adapt to new conditions. Effective adaptive capabilities permit individuals and organizations to react quickly to changes in their environment (or to be proactive in driving such changes).

Adaptive conceptualization: Refers to reorienting concepts used elsewhere to suit the situation/context existing in the environment where a particular policy is formulated. Thus, for example, the concept of gendered development may be recast relative to the specific sociocultural milieu in which policy makers find themselves.

Adaptive configuration: Refers to the steps taken by organizations to optimize effectiveness at the expense of efficiency. As external environments change, organizations need to continually reposition their methods of operating so as to be able to fulfill their mandates (i.e., to be effective). In that regard, efficiency becomes of secondary concern.

Adaptive expectations: These are expectations that result from the extrapolation of recent events into the future. While these may not be entirely valid for rigorous decision making, such expectations form part of what is included in any strategic-planning exercise.

Adaptive implementation: Ensuring that implementation of public policies adapts to changes in the operating environment. This implies that organizations have the adaptive capabilities to locate innovative ways to implement public policies when the external environment undergoes changes.

Adaptive learning: Any learning that takes place in organizations that results from interactions with others in the dynamic environment. If such interactions lead to knowledge about how better to manage organizational processes, or increase the quality of decision inputs, adaptive learning can be said to have occurred. For a brief review of adaptive learning and policy innovation, see, e.g., D. Yencken, "Governance for Sustainability," *Australian Journal of Public Administration*, 2002, 61(2), pp. 78–89.

Adaptive problems: Problems that public-sector organizations face for which no technically correct answer can be determined. An example of an adaptive problem is that of balancing globalization with retention of local culture. *See also* **Wicked problems**.

Adaptive training: Training that is made available to individuals in keeping with the changes in their operating environments such that they are in need of new skills. Adaptive training is then often inherent in customized training. *See also* **Customized training**.

Additionality: When considering the value added of a particular policy or project, the question is asked, "What was achieved which would not have happened without the project?" For example, those who fund projects might wish to know the extent to which project funding generated additional resources from other sources. Additionality has to be defined in the context of the objectives of a particular policy or program. For a practical discussion of how the concept can be used in project analysis, see, e.g., HM Treasury, *Appraisal and Evaluation in Central Government: Treasury Guidance*, London: The Stationery Office, 1997, pp. 61–62.

Additive causality: Refers to establishing cause-and-effect relationships logically and sequentially, from a beginning point to end. The technique takes different people with different frames of reference to the observed results. The concept is useful when exploring the possibility of multiple causality in independent variables. While studies based on statistical techniques provide an adequate basis to study that causality, one of the simplifying assumptions in these techniques is that of additive causality, which means that the effect of each variable is analyzed independent of the effect and value of the rest. To fill that gap, it is considered useful to also conduct a qualitative analysis so that a richer picture of the cause-effect relationships emerges. For a general discussion of the concept and comparative methods of investigation, see, e.g., C. Ragin, *The Comparative Method: Moving Beyond Qualitative and Quantitative Strategies*, Berkeley: University of California Press, 1987, pp. 125–63. *Cf.* **Subtractive causality**.

Additive knowledge: The acquisition of new information that merely substantiates a stock of knowledge that already exists. Thus, for example, if governmental departments report back to central agencies about similarly encountered problems in strategic-planning exercises, then this can be seen as additive knowledge. In this sense, no new knowledge has been added to the stock; rather, existing information has been substantiated.

Adhesion agreement: A proposal in a collective-bargaining process that the more influential party makes to the less influential party on a take-it-or-leave-it basis. Good-faith bargaining, however, discourages such an agreement since it leaves the weaker party with little choice and can lead to an unbalanced relationship between the two parties. *See also* **Good-faith bargaining**.

Adhocracy: Derived from the term "ad hoc," this concept refers to a system whereby powers are delegated to subordinate units based on their specific strengths, areas of specialization, etc. An adhocratic organizational unit refers to the temporary nature of a particular unit within an organization. Such a unit is usually rather small in size, is formed for a particular purpose, and is dissolved afterward.

Adjudication: A public-policy-related action that deals with the management of conflicts and the enforcement of the underlying values of any entity's operating and value systems. See, e.g., J. Bryson and B. Crosby, "Policy Planning and the Design and Use of Forums, Arenas, and Courts," in B. Bozeman (ed.), *Public Management: The State of the Art*, San Francisco: Jossey-Bass, pp. 323–44.

Adjusted case: A situation where an informal settlement between differing parties (such as unions and management) is reached with the understanding that differences between them will be settled out of court.

Adjustive activity: As used in the context of bureaucracies and the environment in which they operate, the term refers to the act of striking a balance between what is directed by the government and what emerges from the adjustment process that various interests engage in, as well as the personal convictions of administrators. See, e.g., E. Redford, *Democracy in the Administrative State*, New York: Oxford University Press, 1969, p. 188.

Adjustive behavior: *See* **Adaptability**.

Adjustive learning: *See* **Organizational learning**.

Administered items: Any policy or program that is a result of legislation, contractual arrangement, or agreement that requires an agency to manage it as specified in the enabling legislation or agreement. The agency that is administering the item has no direct control over its formulation and design, but is required to report on its implementation to an appropriate authority (such as the legislature or a governing board). For example, a United Nations agency may administer funds on behalf of a donor for particular policy priorities (such as community health in selected developing countries).

Administered prices: Prices that are fixed by a governmental agency or any other controlling body rather than determined through market forces.

"Administration as usual" reform approach: Efforts at reforming bureaucracy but with no major accompanying change to either the structure or the process of administration. See, e.g., B. Peters, "Government Reorganization: A Theoretical Analysis," in A. Farazmand (ed.), *Handbook of Bureaucracy*, New York: Marcel Dekker, Inc., 1994, pp. 165–82.

Administration by proxy: *See* **Hollow state**.

Administration lead time: Refers to the time span between when a decision is made to acquire something and when a formal purchase order is placed. Organizations will seek to minimize the lead time simply to ensure that the acquisition decision is not revisited needlessly or that the time-bound quality of the product will not have eroded.

Administration versus management: A public-management distinction that has important implications regarding the role given to governmental departments and other public-sector agencies. Administration refers to the act of implementing, running, or managing a task, policy, or organization, whereas management refers to the search for the optimal use of resources to meet specific objectives. The difference thus lies in the degree of flexibility given to an organization to pursue its mandates. Administration is more process-oriented and is a passive process, while management has connotations of managers taking risks, if necessary, and being involved in active processes to attain set organizational goals. For a good overview of this distinction, see, e.g., L, Kaboolian, "The New Public Management: Challenging the Boundaries of the Management versus Administration Debate," *Public Administration Review*, 1998, 58(3), pp. 189–93.

Administrative accountability: *See* **Accountability**.

Administrative advocacy: Refers to efforts at changing the rulemaking process at any level of government. This can include efforts to influence regulatory issues, advocating—and pushing for more funds for—particular programs or policies, and challenging regulations in courts.

Administrative agency: Any organization (such as a board or a commission) that has been delegated authority by a legislature to provide certain benefits or to conduct specific administrative tasks (such as managing welfare payments). Public employment relations boards are classic examples of administrative agencies. Any legal or formal action that is taken by such a bureaucracy or organization is known as administrative action.

Administrative analysis: Investigation of the manner in which the administrative functions in an organization are carried out for purposes of ascertaining their efficiency and effectiveness. The analysis, if done properly and rigorously, will lead the organization to identify the necessary capability gaps and means of bridging them. Administrative analyses are done at least once a year during the budgeting process to determine the level of funding to be requested.

Administrative audit: The review and appraisal of administrative processes in an organization. The scope of such an audit does not include the programs of the organization but instead focuses on the various processes (such as on human-resource management, financial management, procurement, etc.).

Administrative behavior: The manner in which organizations react to specific situations and their efforts to do so in a rational way. For example, in the face of a public disclosure of an embarrassing fiasco, an organization may seek to blame others or to refrain from public comment. Administrative behavior can be seen as akin to human behavior, but played out in an organizational setting. Herbert Simon's work in this area was the first significant attempt at analyzing administrative behavior in public administration. His work showed how organizations can be understood in terms of their decision processes and how organizational structure, among other things, affects the underlying premise on which organizations make decisions. See his *Administrative Behavior: A Study of Decision-Making Processes in Administrative Organizations*, New York: Macmillan, 1947. For a review of Simon's work, see, e.g., J. Gow, "Decision Man: Herbert Simon in Search of Rationality: A Review of Herbert Simon's Administrative Behavior: A Study of Decision-Making Processes in Administrative Organizations," *Canadian Public Administration*, 2003, 46(1), p. 120.

Administrative bourgeoisie: Refers to the bureaucracy itself appropriating any economic surplus in a country and thus emerging as a ruling class. What enables bureaucrats to engage in such appropriation is their control over rules, processes, and their implementation. This control gives them an opportunity to manipulate the formal requirements to their own ends.

Administrative capacity: The capacity of governmental departments to effectively administer all aspects of a policy. This concept of administrative capacity is slightly different from technical capacity, which has connotations of managerial expertise as well. For a general discussion, see, e.g., M. Turner and D. Hulme, *Governance, Administration and Development: Making the State Work*, London: MacMillan, 1997, pp. 88–91.

Administrative code: Rules and regulations that specify how all facets of the work of governmental administrative departments are to be carried out. *See also* **Code of conduct**.

Administrative conservatorship: When bureaucrats act in a manner that is not opportunistic but is designed to enhance their image as individuals who look after the public interest. A widely discussed work on this concept is that of Larry Terry (see his "Leadership in the Administrative State—The Concept of Administrative Conservatorship," *Administration & Society*, 1990, 21[4], pp. 395–412; the author later expanded this into *Leadership of Public Bureaucracies: The Administrator as Conservator*, Thousand Oaks, CA: Sage Publications, 1995). According to Terry, administrative executives are conservators because they are entrusted with the responsibilities of preserving the integrity of public bureaucracies. He sees this as a legitimate administrative role in relation to constitutional and legal issues. Every now and then, though, public executives are faced with the dilemma of reconciling ethics with efficiency, and how strongly they perceive their role as conservators determines the balance of emphasis they place on one or the other value. *See also* **Administrative stewardship**.

Administrative control: *See* **Administrative discretion**.

Administrative court: A forum where problems and disagreements existing in an administration are heard and dispensed with in line with rules and regulations that have been specified in advance. An administrative court is not a regular court of law, although if there is sufficient degree of misdemeanor or a legal infraction the matter could be thus referred.

Administrative culture: Refers to the values, beliefs, and attitudes held by administrators and bureaucrats at all levels of government. This culture is derivative of the larger political culture since much of what transpires in government administration is shaped by the political orientations of elected leaders. Administrative culture has further subcultures that merit attention; these include: traditional, self-protective, entrepreneurial, guardian, patronage, merit, etc. Discussions of this concept have now been overtaken by a greater focus on two other related ones: organizational culture and political culture. For a good review of the concept, see, e.g., K. Henderson, "Characterizing American Public Administration: The Concept of Administrative Culture," *International Journal of Public Sector Management*, 2004, 17(3), 234–50.

Administrative decentralization: *See* **Decentralization**.

Administrative decision theory: A behavioral theory that asserts that bureaucrats—constrained as they are by the environment and by their own limited capacity—will tend to make decisions that are simply workable and that are usually a product of limited analysis using their own limited judgment rather than relying on tools for rational analysis. *See also* **Bounded rationality**.

Administrative discretion: (1) A bureaucrat's ability to decide whether a particular administrative act is to be implemented, and in what manner. The degree to which the bureaucrat feels he/she has the authority to make independent judgment is termed the zone of discretion or zone of independent judgment. (2) The scope that is given to the administration (usually contained in the leader of the organization or a deputed person) to make binding decisions on behalf of the organization. The debate in administrative discretion is the extent to which organizational leaders should be exhorted to be entrepreneurial or play a mere stewardship role.

from the options available to maximize net benefits) most of the time. As a matter of fact, humans often look for a course of action that is just good enough. This he encapsulated in the term "administrative man." *See also* **Economic determinism**.

Administrative management: Refers to the ways in which organizations should be structured, how their systems should work, and how all aspects of their work should be managed. It is this focus on the administrative aspects of organizations that critics have said leads inevitably to bureaucratic red tape and inefficiencies.

Administrative momentum: *See* **Bureaucratic momentum**.

Administrative morality: Values which administrative organizations demonstrate. Over time, these values have tended to be concentrated around those of responsiveness, efficiency, effectiveness, and neutral competence. A related concept is that of administrative norms, which are principles that organizations have about how administration should be carried out, and how individuals within organizations must adhere to specific rules and regulations. *See also* **Code of conduct**.

Administrative order: A directive (such as on bargaining parameters for unions and management) that comes from an administrative body for organizations to adhere to in the public sector.

Administrative presidency: *See* **Administrative leadership**.

Administrative problem: A term that refers to how organizations should be structured and managed. Not all organizations have the same internal and external environments, and since their mandates differ as well, how their work is mandated is also divergent. The administrative problem thus alludes to the problem of devising appropriate administrative systems for different organizations.

Administrative procedure: Also known as an administrative process, this refers to any process that is in place to run the administration of an organization (including, for example, planning, managing, and monitoring). Administrative procedures tend to be contained in standard operating procedures in organizations so that transaction costs do not rise every time someone in the organization has to consider what needs to get done and how.

Administrative remedy: Seeking to settle an issue by taking recourse to an administrative agency (such as appealing against an administrative decision that has gone against an individual) before taking the matter to court.

Administrative review: An appraisal of how the various aspects of an organization are run (for example, its policies, objectives, and modes of operation). Administrative reviews are in general internally driven, but there are times when external stakeholders (such as a legislature) can also call for such reviews.

Administrative state: A state wherein political authority and mandate for policy actions are contained in the political leadership of the country and where the leadership is characterized by technocratic and bureaucratic competence. In an administrative state, the political arena thus shifts from the citizenry to the bureaucracy. For an example of Singapore as an administrative state, see K. Ho, *The Politics of Policy-Making in Singapore*, Singapore: Oxford University Press, 2000, p. 15.

Administrative stewardship: This refers to the delegation of authority by the citizenry (through their elected representatives) to bureaucrats to act as stewards of the public interest. This means that bureaucrats need to act selflessly and in the foremost interest of the public. The concept also carries the implication that the bureaucrats will have the requisite expertise to be engaged in the functions for which they have been entrusted. *See also* **Administrative conservatorship**.

Administrative support structure: The structure in an organization that supports its core work. This usually includes the: (a) assignment of the administrative functions to the most appropriate level in the organization, (b) determination of a control structure that includes, for example, separation of duties, (c) consolidation of various services required by the organization so that their delivery can be made more efficient, (d) assignment of relevant accountability for the provision of such support, and (e) effective communication at all levels so that other parts of the organization are aware of the nature of the provision of services by the support structure. The term back-office support is used to refer to administrative and clerical assistance that is provided in support of the organization's primary activities.

Administrative tribunal: Any entity (such as a board) that deals with disputes between citizens and public officials or institutions.

Administrative values: The norms that are expected in the administration of policies and in the work of public agencies. Christopher Hood and Michael Jackson identified three clusters of administrative values in any system, which they termed sigma, theta, and lambda values. Sigma values highlight efficiency and effectiveness, theta values focus on fairness and probity, and lambda values give priority to flexibility in the work of the agencies. See C. Hood and M. Jackson, "Keys for Locks in Administrative Argument," *Administration and Society*, 1994, 25(4), pp. 469–88.

Advance funding: Making use of resources that have been set aside for the succeeding year's budget. Advance funding is designed to tidy over resource requirements late in the financial year and there is seen no reason to go for supplemental funding requests.

Advancement, periodic: A move up in the hierarchy for employees resulting from a promotion and which takes place at set intervals. Periodic advancement is not the norm in jurisdictions where career management does not necessarily take place along traditional career paths.

Adverse impact: Any administrative move (such as recruitment) that is to the disadvantage of any minority group. An adverse impact results when the rate of hired minorities is less than 80 percent (or four-fifths) of the majority hired. There is a three-step process that is used to determine adverse impact: (a) the selection rate is first calculated (i.e., the number of majority candidates hired divided by total number of majority candidates that applied), (b) the selection rate for minority groups is calculated in the same manner as in *(a)*; and (c) the rate for *(b)* is divided by the rate for *(a)*. If the impact ratio is less than 80 percent, then adverse impact is said to be evident. For a useful discussion of the concept, see, e.g., C. Lawshe, "Adverse Impact: Is It a Viable Concept?" *Professional Psychology: Research and Practice*, 1987, 18(5), pp. 492–97.

Adverse incentives: Incentives that serve contrarily to the goal set by a particular policy. For example, unemployment benefits at times can be adverse incentives if they discourage recipients from looking for work. It is possible for successive governments (of different political persuasion) to be wedded to one particular policy that produces adverse incentives.

Adverse selection: Also known as the hidden-information problem, this concept refers to the tendency of parties with information that affect other parties to make offers that are then detrimental (for example, someone with illness seeking health insurance). Thus, the concept denotes a "tendency for any contract offered to all comers to be most attractive to those that are most likely to benefit from it" (J. Black, *Dictionary of Economics*, Oxford: Oxford University Press, 1997, p. 6). This implies opportunistic behavior. Adverse selection is not to be confused with mistaken selection (i.e., selecting an individual who is inappropriate for the work for which the selection was made). See, e.g., J. Levin, "Relational Incentive Contracts," *American Economic Review*, 2003, 93(3), pp. 835–47. *See also* **Moral hazard**.

Adverse-inference rule: A rule by which an administrative agency determines that if an organization under scrutiny has withheld information (say in a labor dispute) then it can assume (i.e., infer) that the information is indeed adverse to the organization. The agency, however, should have asked for the information in due time and should have given the organization enough time to respond.

Advice and consent: A governance arrangement where, for example, the executive branch has to seek the advice and consent of the legislature for nominations to judicial posts. This arrangement ensures that there are proper checks and balance in the political system. Advice and consent arrangements can also exist in public-management systems where there is a devolved organizational regime such that public-service departments need to seek the advice of a central agency prior to, for example, engaging in collective bargaining.

Advisory arbitration: *See* **Arbitration**.

Advisory council: A group of individuals who provide advice to an organization on any particular subject matter. The council members are usually drawn from a fairly narrow yet relevant area of expertise, although it is not uncommon to find members who bring in different sectoral perspectives. The council is mandated to provide advice only, not to engage the organization in a directive manner.

Advisory opinion: Solicited expert (agency or individual) opinion. An advisory opinion is designed to secure voluntary compliance without resorting to a consent decree. *See* **Consent decree**.

Advocacy coalition theory: Asserts that actors in policy subsystems form alliances around core values in terms of what they think governments should do. Policy development thus constitutes interaction between different advocacy coalitions and policy makers. For an application, see, e.g., B. Ellison, "The Advocacy Coalition Framework and Implementation of the Endangered Species Act: A Case Study in Western Water Politics," *Policy Studies Journal*, 1998, 26(1), pp. 11–29.

Advocates: A term used by renowned scholar Anthony Downs to denote a type of bureaucrat who has internalized the particular values, norms, and message of an organization and propagates it avidly. Advocates act as lobbyists for the organization and can serve to highlight, for example, the organization's strengths to a legislature and other stakeholders. See A. Downs, *Inside Bureaucracy*, Boston: Little, Brown, 1967, p. 88.

Advocative claim: An assertion that is value laden, and that is used to make a recommendation about a particular policy issue. Advocative claims are normative, and may or may not be based on empirical evidence.

Affected parties: Those which are directly impacted upon by a policy or program in that they are likely to incur compliance costs or are likely to derive benefits. Affected parties can be either of primary nature (i.e., directly affected by the policy or program) or of secondary nature (i.e., indirectly affected and/or affected with a time lag). Cost-benefit analysis of policies and programs tend to normally incorporate only the former since it is much more amenable to quantify the impact there.

Affective commitment: *See* **Organizational commitment**.

Affiliation need: Also called the affiliation motive, this is the desire that individuals in an organization have to be affiliated with others and to belong to a group. A motivation to work stems from such affiliation. The affiliation can take many forms, including simply being around others in a work setting, or working directly with or under others.

Affirmative action plan: A plan prepared by an organization which specifies how it will go about addressing the issue of underrepresentation of gender and minorities within its ranks. The first step in the construction of such a plan is an analysis of an employer's work force in comparison to the relevant job market from which the employer gets its potential pool of applicants. The plan also then includes the objectives and how the specific activities will be undertaken, and by when. Accountability for meeting the plan components lies with the organization. The plan itself is likely to undergo changes as progress on the plan becomes evident or as the external environment changes. For a comprehensive review of the theoretical and empirical economic literature on affirmative action, see, e.g., H. Holzer and D. Neumark, "Assessing Affirmative Action," *Journal of Economic Literature*, 2000, 38(3), pp. 483–568.

Affirmative order: A directive from a governmental agency issued to an employer to end unfair labor practices. The order includes potential penalty provisions given noncompliance. Affirmative orders are issued only after it has been determined conclusively that an employer has not adhered to affirmative action programs mandated by the government.

Affirmative recruitment: Attempts by an organization to recruit individuals who will yield an appropriate representation of minorities in the organization. Ascertaining that representational balance, however, is tricky. *See also* **Recruitment**.

Age discrimination: Unfavorable treatment of an individual based on his or her age. As evidenced in practice, this usually applies to older individuals who may have been retrenched and who are seeking reentry into the workforce.

Agency: (1) The state of being an agent (i.e., one contracted to provide a good or service). (2) An organization, which thus can be of several types, based, for example, on the pressures of external interests: (a) client agencies, (b) entrepreneurial agencies, (c) interest-group agencies, and (d) majoritarian agencies (see J. Wilson, *Bureaucracy: What Government Agencies Do and Why They Do It*, New York: Basic Books, 1989, pp. 79–83). For other categorizations of government agencies, see, e.g., T. Lowi, "The State in Politics: The Relation Between Policy and Administration," in R. Noll (ed.), *Regulatory Policy and the Social Sciences*, Berkeley: University of California Press, 1985, pp. 67–105.

Agency action: A generic term that refers to any action taken by a governmental agency. This can include, for example, rule making, licensing, service delivery, auditing, performance monitoring, and evaluation.

Agency activism: When a governmental agency is active not only in fulfilling its mandate, but also in identifying and targeting new areas for involvement. Excessive agency activism leads to bureaucratic expansion and possible insularity.

Agency behavior: A generic term for how agencies act and react. Such behavior is shaped largely by: (a) the nature of interactions that street-level bureaucrats have with citizens; (b) the collective behavior of public managers responding to pressures from the agency's external environment, including a legislature, control agencies, and others; and (c) the nature of intra-agency interactions among staff members as well as internal processes and organizational culture.

Agency capture: *See* **Going soft**.

Agency competence: Also known as instrumental achievement, this concept refers to the degree to which an organization is able to achieve its mandates with the resources it has at its disposal, including managing human resources to foster economy, efficiency, and effectiveness. Such agency competence often cues the government as to which agency to allocate portfolios to, and how.

Agency costs: Also known as agency loss, there are costs in the form of inefficiency losses resulting from principal-agent problems that occur when two parties pursue different goals despite the presence of a contract. There are generally three sources of agency costs: (a) the expenses that the principal incurs, including monitoring costs, (b) the costs incurred by the agent to act in a manner that conforms to the principal's objectives (this could include, for example, additional reporting and compliance measures), and (c) the residual inefficiency that results because both *(a)* and *(b)* will in themselves demand more attention from both parties. Ways to reduce agency costs include: contestability, complete contracts, and regular interactions between principal and agent. See, e.g., L. Lynn, "Policy Achievement as a Collective Good: A Strategic Perspective on Managing Social Programs," in B. Bozeman (ed.), *Public Management: The State of the Art*, San Francisco: Jossey-Bass, 1993, pp. 108–33.

Agency discretion: The scope and powers for decision making that organizations have been granted by law. This is normally contained in relevant administrative rules and protocols. Such discretion allows organizations, for example, to reallocate funds to different outputs if they better contribute to specified outcomes. There will obviously be limits to such discretion specified in the administrative rules and protocols. See, e.g., R. Calvert, M. McCubbins, and B. Weingast, "A Theory of Political Control of Agency Discretion," *American Journal of Political Science*, 1989, 33(August), pp. 588–610.

Agency fidelity: The degree of adherence of public agencies to the legislative intent of particular policies. The concept is interlinked with agency discretion since it is assumed that even if organizations have the space to make, for example, operational decisions, they will still be geared toward achieving the specified outcomes within parameters of resource use and transparency that is expected of any public organization.

Agency loss: *See* **Agency costs.**

Agency mission: The specific responsibility assigned to a public agency. An agency mission is derived from the agency's mandate as provided by a legislature or any relevant authority. In the organizational strategic-planning processes, mission statements are used to drill down to intermediate objectives and the associated activities that will yield those objectives. A related term is agency-mission valence in which "valence" jectives. A related term is agency-mission valence in which "valence" refers to the positive or negative attractiveness of an outcome. Agency-mission valence indicates the degree of attraction an agency mission may or may not have for employees. Accordingly, the more stimulating the mission to employees, the more the agency will generate support from them.

Agency problem: The problem that a principal faces when an inappropriate agent is selected for delivering specific products, and in observing or judging what that agent does. The problems can mean cost overruns and delays. An agency problem can be minimized in two ways: (a) *ex ante* efforts in ensuring that all selection criteria have been clearly specified and adhered to in deciding to engage an agent, and (b) *ex post* action, by seeking alternative agencies if there is poor performance. *See also* **Principal-agent problem**.

Agency relationship: A contractual relationship between one party (the principal) and another (the agent) where the principal engages the agent to perform some service (such as deliver a product) for a set fee. The underlying premise of agency relationship is that a conflict of interest can emerge between principal and agent since they tend to pursue divergent goals. Such a conflict of interest leads to a principal-agent problem.

Agency repertoires: The range of possible actions that agencies can take in response to disturbances in their environment. Such actions can include, for example, strengthening their audit capacity, agreeing to release documentation toward achieving transparency, etc. The extent to which an agency uses its breadth of available options to deal with a disturbance is largely a function of the resources it can so dedicate, and the style of management in practice. A less risk-averse management team, for example, may take on a more aggressive stance to respond to external pressures. For an application of the concept, see, e.g., E. Clemens, "Organizational Repertoires and Institutional Change: Women's Groups and the Transformation of U.S. Politics, 1890–1920," *American Journal of Sociology*, 1993, 98(4), pp. 755–98.

Agency strategic plan: A statement of the priority directions an agency will take to carry out its mission within the context of statutory mandates and authorizations given to the agency. The plan must be developed with a medium-term outlook (usually five years) and identify infrastructure, capital improvement, and information resources management needs. *See also* **Strategic planning**.

Agency theory: A theory that asserts that interactions among parties in the economic and political domains are essentially contract based. In such interactions, one party seeks a service and the other party delivers it. Such interactions are evident at various levels, for example, between citizens and politicians, between governmental departments and politicians, and between governmental departments and other service providers. Agency theory also assumes that individuals are motivated by self-interest and that they will seek to maximize their own utility even if it means by shirking their responsibilities.

Agency-rationalization policy: A policy of government to ascertain how public agencies should be categorized based on the functions they perform. Not all public agencies will be governmental departments; those for which ministerial involvement needs to be at some distance may well be designated as nondepartmental organizations or as governmental corporations. The endeavor to categorize agencies flows out of agency-rationalization policy.

Agenda: In the public-policy and public-management context, an agenda is an aggregation of issues, i.e., a list of things that need to be addressed by policy makers. There are two types of agenda in the public-management process: (a) systematic agenda (where there is general agreement that some issues merit government attention, such as youth suicide), and (b) a formal agenda (i.e., only those items that are up for active consideration by policy makers at any given time (such as departmental appropriation during budget period). See, e.g., R. Cobb and C. Elder, "Issue Creation and Agenda Building," in J. Anderson (ed.), *Cases in Public Policy-Making*, 2nd edition, New York: Holt, Rinehart and Winston, 1982, pp. 3–11.

Agenda building: Also known as agenda setting, this refers to the process of transforming issues to agenda items for government to address (in some cases, it could also be that some items are deliberately excluded from the agenda). It is normal for issues for consideration in the agenda to go through several iterations of construction and reconstruction before they are formulated in a particular way (this is also known as agenda volatility). Agenda building is generally regarded as the first step in the public-policy process.

Agenda status loss: When an issue drops from being on the agenda for governmental action (either because the issue has resolved itself or support for the agenda item has waned) it is termed agenda status loss.

Agenda status loss can also occur when policy makers decide to postpone consideration of an agenda item until more information can be gathered. For a general discussion of agenda setting and agenda building, see, e.g., T. Romer and H. Rosenthal, "Bureaucrats Versus Voters: On the Political Economy of Resource Allocation by Direct Democracy," *Quarterly Journal of Economics*, 1979, 93(4), pp. 563–87.

Agenda volatility: *See* **Agenda building**.

Agent opportunism: *See* **Contractor opportunism**.

Agent shirking: Refers to a problem that a principal confronts in its relationships with an agent. Rational, utility-maximizing agents have a tendency to exploit contracts to do their jobs in ways that the principal did not intend. Such exploitation is possible because contracts are rarely complete (i.e., rarely will all contingencies be specified in a contract). For a discussion of agent shirking, see, e.g., T. Moe, "The New Economics of Organization," *American Journal of Political Science*, 1984, 28(4), pp. 739–77.

Agility paradox: Agility is the degree to which an organization is capable of being flexible and responsive to deal with a changing environment. Organizational agility is measured, for example, by the amount of time it takes for the organizational leadership to respond to critical reports in the media or the legislature. An agility paradox refers to a situation that organizations find themselves in where, given rapid changes in their operating environment, they need to develop apparently contradictory qualities: flexibility in order to be able to adapt continuously to changes, and stability in order to be able to learn and grow contingent upon such strength. The search for a proper balance between these two attributes means that organizations have to continually reassess their strategies and their frames of reference. For a discussion of the agility paradox, see, e.g., C. Osborn, "Systems for Sustainable Organizations: Emergent Strategies, Interactive Controls and Semi-Formal Information," *Journal of Management Studies*, 1998, 35(4), pp. 481–509.

Agreement: (1) A pact reached between two or more parties to undertake (or not) a particular activity. A legal agreement has the force of law and the concerned parties are thus obliged to adhere to them. (2) An agreement can also refer to the arrangement between unions and management and between an employer and employees.

Aid contract: A contract signed by a donor agency (either a multilateral one, such as the World Bank, or a bilateral one, such as the U.S. Agency for International Development) and a government or group (such as a nongovernmental organization) for the provision of assistance in a particular sector (such as rural agriculture) or for a particular objective (such as eliminating seasonal hunger).

Aid dependence: The condition of a country being dependent on foreign assistance in order to meet its own objectives such that if the resources were to stop flowing in, the state would not be in a position to continue the program. Aid dependence occurs when the state is not able to generate adequate resources of its own and continually looks to foreign donors to secure them. See, e.g., M. Godfrey et al., "Technical Assistance and Capacity Development in an Aid-Dependent Economy: The Experience of Cambodia," *World Development*, 2002, 30(3), pp. 355–73.

Aid tying: Refers to a tie-in that a bilateral donor agency normally insists upon a recipient country while providing financial and technical assistance that requires the recipient to purchase inputs from the donor agency's country. Aid tying is particularly imposed as a condition by the donor if there is considerable domestic pressure in the donor country to curtail assistance to poorer countries. In that case, aid tying serves to channel some of the assistance directly back to the donor country.

Alexithymic: A situation where individuals in an organization display a robot-like adherence to organizational routines which make them immune to learning. See, e.g., M. de Vries, "Alexithymia in Organizational Life: The Organization Man Revisited," in L. Hirschhorn and C. Barnett (eds), *The Psychodynamics of Organizations*, Philadelphia: Temple University Press, 1993, pp. 203–18.

Algedonic evaluation: *See* **Evaluation**.

Alienation: (1) As used in personnel management, alienation refers to a situation where an employee is apathetic to his/her work and the organization, and which begins to adversely affect work performance. If the performance-management system in the organization is robust, such a tendency will have been identified early on, thus allowing for corrective action to be taken promptly. (2) A condition of the nonabsorption of ruling values (i.e., values that govern appropriate behavior in a given context).

Alliance capability: Refers to the capability that organizations have in order to manage alliances with others that operate in the same domain.

This is considered a distinct management capability, and focuses on the absorption of knowledge that is generated in interactions with others and, in that process, enhancing own organizational learning. For a good discussion, see, e.g., J. Draulans et al., "Building Alliance Capability: Management Techniques for Superior Alliance Performance," *Long Range Planning*, 2003, 36(2), pp. 151–66.

Alliance management: Work of an organization centered on maintaining beneficial links with those with which it interacts, and with which it has strong business ties. Alliance management requires considerable relationship management skills on the part of the organizational leadership. See, e.g., J. Quinn, "Outsourcing Innovation: The New Engine of Growth," *Sloan Management Review*, 2000, 41(4), pp. 13–29.

Allocation: Distribution of resources in accordance with some set criteria (for example, the distribution of an appropriation to a budget entity made to lower units such as a program, bureau, or section based on the size of the program). Allocation criteria are frequently reviewed so as to ensure that appropriate levels of funding are constantly maintained for the various programs and entities. A related term is allotment, which refers to the administrative assignment by an agency of a part of an appropriation, allocation, or apportionment to a subdivision of the agency.

Allocative efficiency: Also known as Pareto efficiency, this concept refers to an allocation of resources where no individual's position can be improved without worsening the position of another person. Likewise, a market is characterized by allocative efficiency if it is producing the right goods for the right people at the right price (i.e., if resources are allocated in such a way that they provide the greatest benefit relative to costs). Conversely, allocative inefficiency results when an organization is using resources to produce the wrong output even though cost-effective methods may be in use.

All-or-none bid: A bid put forward by a party in which either the party gets all the items or services listed or none. There can be no partial award on an all-or-none bid. Such a bid will be made if a service provision cannot be divided for purposes of delivery.

Allotment: *See* **Allocation**.

Allowable costs: As used in contract management, the term refers to the costs incurred by an agent that will be reimbursed by the principal, and, in that sense, it is allowable. Expenses such as for air travel to fulfill work requirements could be considered allowable costs.

take on new configurations, which, in turn, result in increased organizational efficiency. See, e.g., B. Arthur, *Increasing Returns and Path Dependence in the Economy*, Ann Arbor: University of Michigan Press, 1994, p. 118.

Annual report: In the public-sector context, an annual report is a report submitted by governmental departments to a legislature at the end of each financial year, citing what was achieved compared to what the department set out in its original plan (such as in a statement of intent). Relevant legislative acts will define the requirements of what must be reported, and in what form. Public-service reformers have tried to make such reports more comprehensive, so as to include not only what was done and delivered, but also the affects that this delivery had on the department itself and externally.

Anonymity: An attribute of those in public service wherein they remain in the background in all matters of work. Such individuals provide the technical expertise that is required for government action while governmental ministers (and other elected officers) front up to the public.

Anorexic organization: An organization that has had its capability minimized, for example, as a result of cutbacks and downsizing, and is no longer able to effectively target work toward attaining its mandates. In such instances, there is a governmental tendency either to amalgamate it with a bigger organization or to let it continue in that fashion until such time that appropriate funds are available to strengthen the organization.

Anticipatory government: A term popularized by David Osborne and Ted Gaebler in the early 1990s which focuses on rethinking what governments do and how they do it. An anticipatory government is focused more on prevention than after-the-fact cure, and in that regard is more proactive in its work. This is reflected, for example, in the work of the police in encouraging and helping communities prevent crime (such as through "neighborhood watch" programs). Osborne and Gaebler's principle sets government toward the solving and prevention of problems in servicing the community as opposed to the mere delivery of services. See D. Osborne and T. Gaebler, *Reinventing Government: How the Entrepreneurial Spirit is Transforming the Public Sector*, Reading, MA: Addison-Wesley Publishing, Inc., 1992, pp. 219–49.

Anti-deficiency act: Refers to an act passed by a legislature to prevent bureaucracies from making financial commitments either in the absence of a relevant appropriation system or that they would not be able to meet, and for which the government would, therefore, be compelled to cover. *See also* **Appropriation**.

Appeal: A request to reconsider a particular decision made by the courts or an administrative tribunal that has gone against a party. In the public service, individuals have the right to appeal a decision that has not gone in their favor. Rules and procedures that govern such an appeal process are generally made transparent and public.

Applicant pool: The total number of applicants for a particular position. Human-resource managers in organizations are interested in ascertaining the size of the applicant pool so that they can get a sense of the coverage of their recruitment efforts. In general, the bigger the applicant pool, the greater the possibility that the organization will be spoilt for choice. *See also* **Spoilt for choice**.

Appraisal: (1) An assessment of the specific aspects of a project or program prior to a decision on funding. Most funding agencies, for example, insist that a proper and independent appraisal be done of any development project before they commit resources. (2) Review of a staff member's performance at work.

Approach-approach conflict: A situation where a choice has to be made between two equally viable alternatives. Which one is eventually selected depends upon the particular composition and relative strengths of the coalition groups that favor each alternative or value.

Appropriate technology: Technology that is suitable to the environment in which it is to be applied, but is not the best available. For example, in less-developed countries, in areas which lack reliable sources of electricity, it would not be appropriate to provide agricultural implements that run on electricity; manually operated ones would be more appropriate.

Appropriation: An act by a legislature that allows governmental agencies to incur obligations and to make payments for specific purposes within the amounts authorized in an appropriations act. Multi-year appropriations refer to funding that is set aside by law for organizations and programs that extend across years. An appropriation limitation is a legal restriction that is evident in the appropriation act that specifies a range (i.e., a maximum and a minimum) of funding levels necessary to meet specified outcomes. Finally, continuing appropriation refers to appropriation made by a legislature that is automatically renewed until amended.

Appropriation, output-based: Funding for a governmental agency based on the specific outputs it is contracted to produce, not the inputs that might be used to produce the outputs. For a discussion of the term (including the difficulties in maintaining such an appropriation system), see, e.g., B. Anderson and L. Dovey, *Whither Accountability?* SSC Working Paper No. 18, Wellington, New Zealand: State Services Commission, September 2003, pp. 5–9.

Approval point: The stage of the decision-making process at which a decision on whether to approve the existing status of a product or policy for further development is made. For example, in the acquisition of a new product by an organization, an approval point may be either at the end of the conceptual stage of the product development (called the initial gate, usually a not-so-rigorous hurdle) or at the end of the assessment stage of the acquisition cycle (called the main gate, usually a rigorous hurdle). For an application of approval points in relation to acquisition, see National Audit Office, *Ministry of Defence: Through-Life Management*, Report by the Comptroller and Auditor General, HC 698 Session 2002-2003, London: The Stationery Office, 2003, p. 36.

Arbitrability: The fact that an issue has been agreed by unions and management to be included in a collective-bargaining agreement, which effectively means that it could be resolved by arbitration if the two parties cannot come to an agreement on how to resolve it. Only those issues that have arbitrability can be brought up in the negotiations for an agreement. An arbitrary decision is when an organization makes a decision that is not based on existing law, standard rules, accepted customs, or even logic.

Arbitration: As used in the context of management-union relationships, arbitration means settling disputes between the two parties through the help of a neutral third party (called the arbitrator) either appointed by government or agreed to in advance by the parties. A decision that emerges from arbitration can be binding (binding arbitration), which both parties must, therefore, honor. A solution that is recommended in a dispute between two parties but is not mandatory for either party to accept it is termed an advisory arbitration. It is merely advisory and designed to move the bargaining process further.

Arbitration clause: Any stipulation in a collective-bargaining agreement that states that any part of the agreement that is in dispute (over either interpretation or application) shall be subject to arbitration. An arbitration clause can be very broad or very specific. Arbitration standards are used in making decisions that serve to mediate conflicts. Such standards generally include: (a) the degree of acceptability by all parties, (b) equity considerations among all parties, (c) public interest and the need to give primacy to it, and (d) the ability of any party to pay if there are financial implications to the decision. Such standards are reviewed by an arbitration tribunal, which refers to the panel of members that are asked to arbitrate in matters of dispute between two parties to a contract.

Architectural knowledge: Knowledge about the specific manner in which an organization's various components are integrated and linked together into a coherent whole. These components include its structural configurations as well as processes and systems, including relational attributes. See, e.g., R. Henderson and K. Clark, "Architectural Innovation: The Reconfiguration of Existing Product Technologies and the Failure of Established Firms," *Administrative Science Quarterly*, 1990, 35(1), pp. 9–30. *Cf.* **Component knowledge**.

Arena: A domain where policies and plans are adopted. Examples include a legislature, a city council, or a marketplace. An arena may be spatial (i.e., a physical location) or nonspatial (for example, transacted electronically). *See also* **Policy arena**.

Arm's-length contracting: A form of contracting where the relationship between principal and agent is characterized by a low level of trust. This form of contracting is characterized by very clear specifications, short-term commitments, pre-agreed prices, and considerable operational autonomy. The purpose of instituting arm's-length contracting in the public sector is to ensure that governmental ministers will not be able to meddle in the operations and planning of the various organizations that are in the public sector but that operate on a commercial basis (not like those in the core public service). An arm's-length relationship, however, does not mean that an organization is not accountable to the legislature; it merely states that ministers will not be able to exert undue influence over the agency's work. See, e.g., P. Cooke and K. Morgan, *The Associational Economy: Firms, Regions, and Innovation*, New York: Oxford University Press, 1998, p. 54. *Cf.* **Obligational contracting**.

Artificial barriers to employment: Limitations such as age, sex, race, or national origin—i.e., anything other than merit—that inhibit an individual from getting productive employment. Affirmative action programs and equal employment opportunity policies are designed to address—and remedy to the extent possible—such artificial barriers to employment.

Ascendancy: Denotes the upper hand that a branch of government has in policy making at any given time, particularly in the United States, where separation of powers has meant that Congress and the president both have a major role in policy making. Hence, for example, the ascendancy of the presidency in initiating and effecting a major social agenda (such as President Lyndon Johnson's "Great Society" program of the mid-1960s) was, in time, replaced by Congress's conservative "Contract with America" in the mid-1990s. See, e.g., L. Koenig, *An Introduction to Public Policy*, Englewood Cliffs, NJ: Prentice Hall, 1986, pp. 81–82.

Ascribed status: A position held by an employee outside the work setting (either in relation to kinships or professional associations). In modern bureaucracies, such an ascribed status is not expected to determine rank in the organization.

Ashby's Law: *See* **Law of requisite variety**.

Asian Miracle: A term denoted to explain the phenomenal growth rates exhibited by countries of the East Asian region prior to 1997 (and beginning from about the mid-1950s). Some of the prominent manifestations (and antecedents) of the "miracle" included: rapid equity growth, macroeconomic stability and export growth, a business-friendly environment, increased human capital, increased savings and investment, open capital markets, and an openness to foreign technology. The term was popularized by the World Bank; for an original description of the Asian Miracle, see *The East Asian Miracle: Economic Growth and Public Policy* (A World Bank Policy Research Report), New York: Oxford University Press for the World Bank, 1993.

Asian values: Term used by proponents of the policies of the advanced countries of Southeast Asia (particularly Singapore and Malaysia) that cite their economic success as being partially a product of a set of common cultural virtues (such as frugality, respect for elders/deference to authority). This concept was often related specifically to Confucian values, but while it was prominent in Singapore, in Malaysia it was distinctly more ambiguous. For a critical analysis of this concept, see, e.g., "Asian Values Revisited. What Would Confucius Say Now?" *The Economist*, 25 July 1998, pp. 23–25.

Assess-assist approach: An approach taken by central and monitoring agencies where they are involved not only in assessing the performance of governmental departments but also in helping them address any problems or outstanding issues that may have been identified in the assessment phase. *See also* **Active monitoring**.

Assessment: (1) A process of testing and validating something; for example, in training, it could be the process of determining competence. In an organizational setting, the term refers to determining the level of performance or of the stock of ability. In employee-performance management, an assessment of competence has four dimensions: (a) the knowledge and understanding required to do a job, (b) the performance indicators that measure such knowledge and understanding, (c) the range of situations that the employee is expected to work in, and (d) the evidence that is collected to determine performance. (2) Denotes the amount of fees an employee pays as a member of a union.

Assessment center: Refers to a series of activities whereby individuals are observed in terms of how they handle real-life, stress-related workplace scenarios as a way to assess how they might handle work of a more demanding nature. This is designed to measure the capability levels of new managerial candidates. The candidates are assessed on their problem-solving and decision-making skills. Such an observation takes place over several days and individuals are put through a fairly rigorous process of observation. Assessment centers are normally used for executives and senior managers, not those lower in the organizational hierarchy.

Asset builder: One of the roles of a legislator as understood in some jurisdictions. The asset-builder role of the legislator implies that he/she is involved in actively championing—or at minimum, supporting—the development of physical and social capital in the country. This role is considered to be one constituent feature of the super-politician. See, e.g., K. Ho, *The Politics of Policy-Making in Singapore*, Singapore: Oxford University Press, 2000, p. 207.

Asset stripping: Also known as asset disposal, this concept implies getting rid of organizational assets (for example, underutilized land or buildings). While asset stripping may reduce an organization's operational cost level (i.e., for maintenance), it could also lead to serious resource erosion in the organization such that outcome attainment becomes compromised. *See also* **Going concern concept**.

Assignable cause: A reason that appears to explain the poor performance of an employee or an organization. Managers are expected to show assignable cause, if applicable, when providing performance evaluation for staff members. This is applicable for both positive and negative evaluations.

Assigned-risk pool: A form of subsidy from the government to the citizens of a particular area wherein it forces private providers to offer subsidized policies to areas that cannot afford a particular service (such as fire insurance). *See also* **Risk pooling**.

Assimilation: *See* **Acculturation**.

Associational capacity: The capacity of an organization to create and sustain cooperation between managers and workers within the organization, and also for getting cooperation from other organizations in its environment. See, e.g., P. Cooke and K. Morgan, *The Associational Economy: Firms, Regions, and Innovation*, New York: Oxford University Press, 1998, p. 9.

Associational engagement: The act of various interested parties coming together to provide collective action on a particular issue/problem. Local authorities, for example, seek to enhance such engagement by encouraging and facilitating voluntary associations to be involved in public policy. An associational group is any group that is formally organized, and which articulates its members' interests over a long time period.

Assumed similarity: Also referred to as false-consensus bias, this term refers to a situation where policy makers assume that either the policy actors or the situation they are dealing with are similar to them or some other given situation. This obviously clouds the manner in which they assume the process will play out and tends to result in suboptimality. For a dated but useful discussion of this concept in relation to group leadership and teams, see F. Fiedler, "Assumed Similarity Measures as Predictors of Team Effectiveness," *Journal of Abnormal and Social Psychology*, 1954, 49, pp. 381–88. *See also* **Projection**.

Assumed situation: *See* **Manifest situation**.

Astroturf feedback: Insincere or uninformed feedback that organizations seek to convey to policy makers through their constituencies about a specific policy. Such uninformed feedback may be delivered if, for example, an organization partly fabricates grassroots feedback on an organization's services or work. For a very good example of this concept in practice, see M. Lord, "Constituency Building as the Foundation for Corporate Strategy," *Academy of Management Executive*, 2003, 17(1), pp. 112–24.

Astroturf organization: Any organization that is set up in such a way as to give the impression that it is a grassroots organization (thus being perceived as one that works for the average citizen) but in reality is set up and directed in other ways (for example, one that is industry-funded and thus caters to industry-particular policy preferences). For an example of its usage, see Commonwealth of Australia, *Senate Hansard, Wednesday, 11 February 2004*, pp. 19795–97.

Asymmetric information: When not all parties possess the same quality or sets of information. Asymmetric information problems can be categorized into: (a) privacy problems (e.g., referring to allocation problems arising from each individual knowing his/her own tastes better than anyone else), or (b) delivery problems (e.g., referring to allocation problems arising from some individuals being more informed than others about the quality of some commodities to be delivered). See, e.g., L. Makowski, and J. Ostroy, "Perfect Competition and Creativity of the Market," *Journal of Economic Literature*, 2001, 39(2), pp. 479–535. *See also* **Bounded rationality**.

Asymmetrical federalism: A system of federated government where there is uneven distribution of powers among states/provinces (i.e., some states/provinces have greater responsibilities or more autonomy than others). Such a situation could be a product of the subjurisdictions themselves opting for lesser autonomy or power. See, e.g., R. Whitaker, "The Dog That Never Barked: Who Killed Asymmetrical Federalism?" in K. McRoberts and P. Monahan (eds), *The Charlottetown Accord, the Referendum, and the Future of Canada*, Toronto: University of Toronto Press, 1993, pp. 107–14.

At-risk pay: That portion of an employee's pay that is payable only when specific performance criteria are met. That portion varies from employee to employee but is usually in the range of 12 to15 percent of total pay. Also some pay is kept "at risk" primarily for top executives who will have been given responsibility for the organization's performance. The concept of "at-risk pay" is rather common now, even in the public sectors of OECD countries.

Attention bottlenecks: Describes a situation where the cognitive capacity of individual policy makers is inadequate to fully grasp the number of policy issues for deliberation. This situation leads to an incomplete consideration of all the issues or all the issues of one particular policy problem. See, e.g., N. Zahariadis, "Comparing Three Lenses of Policy Choice," *Policy Studies Journal*, 1998, 26(3), pp. 434–48. *See also* **Bounded rationality**.

Attitudes: Ways of thinking or beliefs that affect how one behaves. It is relevant to study the attitudes of policy makers in order to understand how and what policies might be forthcoming. Attitudes are commonly divided into three major components: (a) affect: either positive (liking) or negative (disliking); (b) beliefs: which control attitudes; and (c) action tendencies: leaning toward taking certain decisions or (not) supporting certain policies based on attitudes. Actions tend to be determined by the events and atmosphere of the moment, such as the moment just before elections when a voter switches votes. See, e.g., L. Koenig, *An Introduction to Public Policy*, Englewood Cliffs, NJ: Prentice Hall, pp. 338–39.

Attribution: Assignment of a causal link between two variables. This is evident, for example, between *ex ante* specifications and *ex post* observations, taking into account any spurious links that may have entered into the relationships. Thus, for example, policy makers may assign attribution to specific policy impacts after observing changes in the situation that was being addressed by the policy.

Attribution theory of leadership: Asserts that leaders in organizations will determine how best to motivate their staff members by closely analyzing what incentives motivate them to behave and act in a manner that best leads to organizational goal attainment, and then will seek to manipulate those incentives.

Audience-cost theory: Asserts that costs to governments are high when they make commitments that are very visible (such as when they create fiat institutions and are expected to adhere to the commitments that they make publicly). Conversely, if governments make commitments in private (that is, to a much smaller audience and not in public), then the costs of not living up to the stated policies are much lower. For a good discussion of the theory in terms of its application to institutional commitment, see, e.g., S. Lohmann, "Why Do Institutions Matter? An Audience-Cost Theory of Institutional Commitment," *Governance: An International Journal of Policy, Administration, and Institutions*, 2003, 16(1), pp. 95–110.

Audit: An independent and systematic check of the records and accounts of public organizations, usually to make sure that: (a) resources have been used in the manner in which they were intended, (b) the organizations have met the required standards, and (c) they have worked within predetermined parameters. There is a distinction between financial audit (which looks at compliance with relevant regulations) and a performance audit (which is concerned with value-for-money issues of economy, efficiency, and effectiveness). Also, an internal audit is done by someone within the organization, and an external one is done by an independent outsider. Some audit reports are not made publicly available. For an appreciation of the importance of audit, and of audit agencies, in public management, see, e.g., J. Broadbent and R. Laughlin, "Evaluating the 'New Public Management' Reform in the UK: A Constitutional Possibility?" *Public Administration*, 1997, 75(Autumn), pp. 487–507.

Audit risks: Risks that center on errors, which are evident in all organizations. Audit risks are said to have three components: (a) inherent risk (i.e., that errors will indeed occur), (b) control risk (i.e., the organization's risk-management system will not be able to prevent or control such errors), and (c) detection risk (i.e., the risk that any remaining errors will not be detected by the organization's auditors).

Audit standards: Standards that are specified for audits to be considered complete. These normally include general measures of such variables as quality, cost effectiveness, and adequacy of the work done.

Audit strategy: The game plan that an audit agency prepares prior to conducting an audit. The strategy consists of determining all the issues before they are raised, and also includes understanding and preparing detailed reasons and justifications for the positions that the agency is likely to take in the course of its work.

Audit trail: Detailed and verifiable record keeping of transactions so that auditors can follow and keep track of their accuracy and adherence to *ex ante* standards. An audit trail includes methods to minimize audit risks.

Authentication policy: A policy to ensure that users will trust online government through appropriate identification and protection of customers' information. Much of the work around e-government programs in countries has centered on ensuring that there is a secure and reliable authentication policy in place.

Authority system: The manner with which authority is manifest and exercised in organizational settings. The classical view of authority holds that an organization gets its authority only from its stakeholders, i.e., from those that the organization serves. Authority systems can be traditional in nature (as when patrimonial and feudal forms dominate, such as in less-developed countries) or rational-legal (where rationality is inherent in the manner in which means are designed to achieve specific goals, and legality is inherent in authority being exercised by means of a system of rules and procedures). The rational-legal type of authority system is now the most common form in jurisdictions around the world.

Authority-compliance management: *See* **Managerial grid**.

Authorization: The act of giving authority to someone to be involved, for example, in providing specific goods and services to citizens or to incur financial obligations. If the latter, the authorization may either limit the amount of budget authority to be provided to the individual/agency or it may authorize the appropriation of "such sums as may be necessary." An authorizing committee is a committee in a legislature that can author- ize funding for particular policies and programs. And an authorizing leg- islation is an act that permits authorization to agencies. Finally, the domain in which the authorization of funds is made is the authorizing environment. This includes those individuals and procedures (including legislation) that enable the decisions to be made. For a discussion of the authorizing environment, see, e.g., O. Feinstein, "Use of Evaluations and the Evaluation of Their Use," *Evaluation: International Journal of The- ory, Research and Practice*, 2002, 8(4), pp. 433–39.

Automatic review clauses: Provisions in programs that automatically trigger a review process at regular intervals or when the provisions in the program are somehow breached. Automatic review clauses enable over- sight bodies to exercise a regular form of check on a department's work.

Autonomous bureaucracies: Refers to the presence of bureaucratic or- ganizations that have a high degree of autonomy in the work that they do. An autonomous agency is an agency that has been given latitude to run its own affairs (including generating resources) but is still accountable to a legislature for its activities. While it has its advantages, the autonomy over the years can lead to a situation where individual departments begin to develop silo mentalities. For a discussion of the term, see, e.g., C. Knill, "Explaining Cross-National Variance in Administrative Reform: Autonomous Versus Instrumental Bureaucracies," *Journal of Public Pol- icy*, 1999, 19(2), pp. 113–39. *Cf.* **Instrumental bureaucracies**.

Autonomous work group: An independent group of people brought to- gether to complete a task. The group works without supervision and usu- ally has the authority to engage in some personnel-management activities.

Autonomy: When individuals and organizations have been given the right—within certain bounds; for example, on level of resource use, and area of coverage—to make their own decisions on matters that affect them most. This means that they have the freedom and the discretion to manage their own affairs the way they deem appropriate. However, they are held accountable for the results they are expected to produce. At the individual level, autonomy generally provides a higher degree of work motivation to the employee. For a review of the concept in relation to organizations, see, e.g., K. Verhoest et al., "The Study of Organizational Autonomy: A Conceptual Review," *Public Administration and Development*, 2004, 24(2), pp. 101–18.

Autopoiesis: The inherent attribute of an entity to be self-correcting and able to continue maintaining its own organizational identity. Organizations that are characterized by autopoiesis are able to draw on the strengths of their members as well as from the external environment, and change for the better. See, e.g., L. Fitzgerald and F. van Eijnatten, "Chaos Speak: A Glossary of Chaordic Terms and Phrases," *Journal of Organizational Change Management*, 2002, 15(4), pp. 412–23.

Avoidance learning: *See* **Escape learning**.

Award: (1) The act of giving a purchase agreement to a bidder. (2) A reward (such as a bonus) that is given by the organization to employees who have been assessed to have performed well (i.e., exceeded the expectations placed on them in their work).

Awareness training: A type of training where employees are provided information on policies and practices that serve to make them more aware of workplace environments. Awareness training is given in areas such as gender relations, sexual harassment, and workplace safety. Some awareness training can be a legal requirement (such as on antidiscrimination policies of the public sector).

B

Back-channel communication: Any communication (either inside or outside organizational boundaries) that travels through informal rather than formal channels. Back-channel communication can be evident in all phases of the policy-making process, and is particularly used during sensitive negotiations among differing parties.

Backdoor spending: (1) Spending not authorized upfront but which an organization justifies by claiming that it is critical for the completion of its mandate. (2) A situation when an entity within a department makes a purchase for a product or service without going through the central purchasing system or through a public tender. Backdoor spending usually takes place when the value of the purchase is below a certain specified level. A related concept is backdoor authority, which refers to the authority given by a legislature outside the normal appropriations process.

Background expectancies: A term that refers to those assumptions and expectations of individuals that are taken for granted in a given context. For example, a background expectancy of someone who wishes to work in government is that of public-service motivation. See, e.g., T. Bilton et al., *Introductory Sociology,* 3rd edition, London: Macmillan, 1996, p. 654.

Backloaded wage agreement: An agreement where the impact of the payment of higher wages is realized in later years. Such a wage agreement has the potential to be disadvantageous for both the employee and the employer: for the former because the later increases could be effective during a time of worsened economic conditions; for the latter because the wage bill may be unsustainable in the present, especially if near-term economic conditions worsen. The advantage to the employer of such a wage agreement is that it defers the expenditure for a set period.

Back-office support: *See* **Administrative support structure.**

Back-to-back secondments: *See* **Secondment.**

Backup redundancy: *See* **Redundancy**.

Backward integration: Also known as upstream integration, backward integration is evident when an organization produces its own inputs. It can thus better plan for its production process because it has more control over the production and delivery of inputs.

Backward mapping: Also known as bottom-up policy design, backward mapping is a view of the policy-development process that focuses on specific behavior at the lowest stages of the implementation process. It involves identifying the behavior of individuals who are the cause of an undesirable condition, and how the behavior could realistically be changed. See, e.g., R. Elmore, "Backward Mapping: Implementation Research and Policy Design," *Political Science Quarterly,* 1979, 94(4), pp. 601–16.

Bad issues: Issues which lobbyists see as not winnable, i.e., on which it is not considered prudent to spend resources. See, e.g., W. Browne,

Groups, Interests, and US Public Policy, Washington, DC: Georgetown University Press, 1998, pp. 192–208. *See also* **Wicked problems**.

Balanced scorecard: A technique of linking an organization's strategic objectives with various performance measures across a number of perspectives. The underlying assumption of this technique is that there are several domains of an organization's work that need to be considered toward making it more efficient and effective. These include financial (including the views of shareholders for private firms); marketing (i.e., how it is seen by its customers); internal dimensions (including staff development and other organization-specific dimensions); and continuous improvement (i.e., its drive toward innovation and new thinking). The main uses of the balanced scorecard technique are in identifying strategic initiatives, conducting comprehensive performance reviews in the organization, and communicating a strong vision to staff members in the organization. For the original work on the balanced scorecard, see R. Kaplan and D. Norton, "The Balanced Scorecard—Measures that Drive Performance," *Harvard Business Review,* 1992 (January–February), pp. 71–79. For an application of the technique in the public sector, see, e.g., D. Irwin, "Strategy Mapping in the Public Sector," *Long Range Planning,* 2002, 35(6), pp. 637–47.

Bandwagon effect: To get people to do what others are doing. People in general do not want to be left behind and the cumulative effect of others emulating a course of action has a bandwagon effect. It normally has a negative connotation, although enterprising policy makers can see it as an opportunity to push forth pet policies and in doing so may well capitalize on the bandwagon effect. *See also* **Abilene effect**.

Bargaining: The negotiations that take place between two parties where each has a position and each seeks to maximize gains or minimize losses. For example, in employer-employee bargaining, the latter may negotiate for better working conditions, including higher wages. In labor-management negotiations, a union may bargain for increased wages and security of tenure, among others. Any entity that bargains on behalf of employees toward a collective-bargaining agreement is known as a bargaining agent.

Bargaining failures: When parties cannot come up with a mutually satisfactory agreement even though they both may stand to gain from such agreement. Bargaining failures can be due to asymmetric information and the intransigence of one party or another. In such cases of bargaining failures, governments may have the mandate to ask that the parties come to the bargaining table with an independent mediator and negotiate in good faith again.

Bargaining parameters: Conditions that are set by both parties in labor-management relations with regard to how the parties will approach the collective-bargaining process. For example, on the part of a government (as the employer in the public sector), such parameters could include: remuneration policies that are fair but not extravagant, recognition of performance, recognition of the importance of unions in employment security, recognition also of the right of individuals not to be members of a union, etc. The parameters are prepared by a central-government agency and distributed to all public-sector agencies for use in their negotiations with unions.

Bargaining rights: The rights that the law provides to all employees so that they can enter into negotiations with their employers. This can be applied either through unions in collective bargaining or individually in contract negotiations. Negotiations take place within the context of bargaining parameters.

Bargaining strength: The power that each party brings to the process of collective bargaining. Unions have bargaining strength by virtue of the support they receive from employees. Employers have bargaining strength by virtue of the fact that they control the wages.

Bargaining theory of wages: A theory that is used in explaining how wages are set and at what level. In particular, the bargaining theory of wages states that wages are set by: (a) an interaction of demand for, and supply of, labor; (b) the employer's threshold, beyond which it will not acquiesce to a wage agreement; (c) the employees' threshold, below which they will not acquiesce to a wage agreement; and (d) the relative bargaining strengths and the legal bargaining tactics employed by each party in the process. This theory is applicable whether wages are being set by collective agreement or otherwise, i.e., individually.

Barriers to entry: (1) Any factors that limit individuals from public-sector employment. (2) As applied to organizations, the term refers to anything that prevents them from being involved in specific functions. *See also* **Artificial barriers to employment**.

Base points: *See* **Job evaluation**.

Baseline data: Indicators of an organization's current performance level, upon which its future performance will be evaluated. Baseline data also includes information on variables related to the organization's environment that helps the organization to monitor and evaluate its performance. Baseline data results from a baseline study, which is an *ex ante* analysis that describes the existing situation against which future changes and impact will be measured. *See also* **Benchmark**.

Basic skills: (1) Basic literacy and numeracy skills needed for a particular job. They are considered basic because they are integral to any work. (2) Generic skills needed for any job in an office (such as oral comprehension, reading, word processing, teamwork, and telephone skills). The latter reference can also be termed core skills. *See also* **Core competencies**.

Basic training: Training given to new recruits or to those who need basic skills on the job. Not all new recruits, however, need to be provided such training since some may have prior experience.

Beachhead demand: A term used in the collective-bargaining process that refers to a rather unrealistic proposal (for example, a very high/low increase in wages) which one party is sure the other would not accept but which it aims to establish for future negotiations.

Beagle fallacy: This is a basic criticism of incrementalism. A beagle hound has a very good sense of smell but limited eyesight, and thus could miss prey that appears in front of but downwind. Likewise, by only focusing on incremental changes to policies and policy applications, organizations are in danger of missing the broader directions in fulfilling their mandates. *See also* **Incrementalism**.

Bedrock structures: Core socioeconomic and political structures of a society from which policy makers select a potential set of issues and conflicts to address. An example of a bedrock structure may be the intricate and complex system of religion-based community self-help in rural areas. See J. Bryson and B. Crosby, "Policy Planning and the Design and Use of Forums, Arenas, and Courts," in B. Bozeman (ed.), *Public Management: The State of the Art,* San Francisco: Jossey-Bass, 1993, pp. 323–44.

Behavior modeling: The process of showing those in an organization the proper behavior with which to individually interact. Such modeling is usually done by departmental leaders, and subordinates are expected to imitate desirable behavior. This could include, for example, ethical behavior or interactions with customers.

Behavioral approach to management: Refers to a reliance on the belief that paying attention to employees' needs (as manifested in their behaviors at work) yields greater satisfaction among them and, by extension, to greater productivity. Such an approach to management is reflected, for example, in programs such as work-life balance, which takes into consideration the fact that employees will need also to pay attention to their life outside work in order to stay motivated at work.

Behavioral orientation in organizational conflict: Refers to the types of behaviors that may be evident when there are conflicts within and between organizations. These include: (a) competitive (i.e., to win or dominate), (b) accommodative (i.e., satisfying others' needs exclusive of one's own), (c) sharing (i.e., compromising one's own needs), (d) collaborative (i.e., integrating the concerns of others), and (e) avoidance (i.e., indifferent to either party).

Behaviorally Anchored Rating Scales (BARS): A performance evaluation technique where critical incidents related to employee performance are noted and scaled. In this technique, the performance of a staff member is assessed by assigning a number to the judgment that the supervisor makes. Each number then represents a particular behavior that can be observed. BARS requires supervisors to choose from a pre-specified set of behaviors that best describe the employee's performance. The value that BARS brings to employee-performance management is that it helps in identifying which specific area needs to be developed to effectively fulfill occupational responsibilities. When used in conjunction with other management techniques (such as 360-degree feedback), BARS becomes a very practical tool for managers. However, behavioral anchors can be a source of bias as well. If an employee who usually scores high on various performance measures makes a mistake, and the behavior of which is subsequently determined to be an anchor, then the individual will receive a lower rating centered on the particular behavior. This has obvious implications for the motivation level of the individual. See, e.g., K. Murphy and J. Constans, "Behavioral Anchors as a Source of Bias in Rating," *Journal of Applied Psychology,* 1987, 72(4), pp. 573–77.

Belief preservation: Described as a cognitive blind spot and a bias, this concept refers to the general tendency of individuals to cling to preconceived ideas even after being presented with evidence to the contrary. Belief preservation occurs when individuals have formed a strong opinion on a particular issue or problem and it is difficult to get them to change their views. In the management context, this bias counteracts work on evidence-based analysis and can not only jeopardize learning opportunities for the organization as a whole but can also lead to weak organizational action. *See also* **Confirmation bias**.

Belief system: The norms and values that policy makers bring to the policy-making process. Belief systems can be open or closed; the more open the belief system, the more receptive the policy makers are to new information and evidence. The nature of the belief system tends to determine the core nature of policy making. See L. Koenig, *An Introduction to Public Policy,* Englewood Cliffs, NJ: Prentice Hall, 1986, p. 352.

Benchmark: Broad indicators that are used to measure an organization's progress in achieving its mandates. Baseline data and goals are established for each indicator to measure the gap, if present, between what the current position is and where the organization wants to be. A benchmark could include a standard that is practiced elsewhere or a level that an organization has recently reached so as to compare development. A benchmark position is one that is used as a standard to evaluate other positions. See, e.g., A. Kouzmin et al., "Benchmarking and Performance Measurement in Public Sectors: Towards Learning for Agency Effectiveness," *International Journal of Public Sector Management,* 1999, 12(2), pp. 121–41.

Benchmark forecasting: Predicting the future state of an organization or the nature of a problem by relying on benchmark data rather than on intuition. The advantage of benchmark forecasting over intuition is that it is grounded in empirical evidence and thus serves as a more rigorous process of determining what the future might hold. See, e.g., R. Auluck, "Benchmarking: A Tool for Facilitating Organizational Learning," *Public Administration and Development,* 2002, 22(2), pp. 109–22.

Benefit-cost analysis: *See* **Cost-benefit analysis**.

Benign neglect, policy of: When an organization does not pay adequate attention to a particular policy or program. It is not that the policy or program is totally neglected, but is likely diminished. Such neglect may be a function of many variables, including the fact that the appeal of the policy or program may have gradually waned in government. Part of the idea of benign neglect is that intervention is believed likely to cause more harm than good, so the neglect can be quite intentional.

Best fundamentals: Refers to having in place the right conditions that are required for policies to be effective. These include, for example, a capable bureaucracy, transparent processes, robust monitoring and evaluation processes, and effective mechanisms that enable feedback on policy implementation to be considered by policy makers.

Best practice: A term that is designed to refer to practices elsewhere that are considered superior and that have been proven to meet objectives and to contribute to increased welfare objectives. The implicit assumption is that it is good for an organization to know what the best practice is in a particular area of its operations and then try to mimic and/or supplant that. A best-practice methodology is a method of arguing for a particular program or policy because it is considered the best in its field. However, some authors argue that just relying on a collation of best practices—without critical empirical investigation of what is likely to succeed—is inadequate. By that reasoning, even the thesis in the vaunted *Reinventing Government* book by David Osborne and Ted Gaebler fails as it is said to be based merely on the recounting of the experiences of others. See E. Overman and K. Boyd, "Best Practice Research and Post-Bureaucratic Reform," *Journal of Public Administration Research and Theory,* 1994, 4(January), pp. 67–84.

Beta testing: In coming up with new programs, organizations seek to ensure that they are complete in all respects and will first test the complete product in a controlled environment. This is known as beta testing, and it also includes gaining valuable customer feedback on the product. See, e.g., R. Cole, "From Continuous Improvement to Continuous Innovations," *Total Quality Management,* 2002, 13(8), pp. 1051–56.

Bicameral legislature: A legislature in which there are two chambers (often termed upper and lower houses). In some jurisdictions, such as in the United Kingdom, one has more power; in others, such as in the United States, power is more evenly split. *Cf.* **Unicameral legislature**.

Bid: An offer by interested and capable parties to provide particular services sought by an organization. All public bid proposals have to be publicized widely for purposes of transparency. The term bidder of the last resort refers to the party (usually a public-sector agency) that will bid for a particular product if there is none other. In some developing countries, for example, the relevant marketing boards for particular agricultural products (such as paddy and wheat) will be the bidders of the last resort if farmers receive no other bidders for their produce. This is a form of support provided by government to agricultural producers.

Big bang: The view that public-sector reforms should be large packages and should be implemented as quickly as possible rather than in an incremental manner. The scale and pace of change should also be evident at all levels. Public-sector reforms in New Zealand in the late 1980s can be considered as big-bang reforms. For a discussion of the far-reaching changes that took place in the New Zealand public management system, see, e.g., G. Scott, *Public Management in New Zealand: Lessons and Challenges,* Wellington: Business Roundtable, 2001.

Big government: Refers to the increase in the size and role of the government sector in a country during a given period. This can be measured in various ways, although to get a complete picture of just how big a government has become would require looking at several measures. One widely used measure is that of government spending for final goods and services (including transfer payments) as a ratio of the gross national product. Another measure is the level of employment in the government sector. Yet another is the level of revenues a government collects from taxes. A non-quantifiable measure is the level of coercion that a government may exercise over its citizens on matters of various freedoms (such as access to official information, right to protest), or its effective authority over economic decision making and its ability to influence decisions made by corporations and others. See, e.g., R. Rose, *Understanding Big Government: The Programme Approach,* Beverly Hills, CA: Sage Publications, 1984.

Big issues: Issues that dominate the political and public management landscape at any given time. In the 1980s and 1990s, for example, the big issues for many governments were how to streamline their bureaucracies and bring about value-for-money propositions in their activities. The major issues in public management today center on joined-up government services and cost-effective citizen-oriented service delivery. See, e.g., State Services Commission, *Statement of Intent 2002,* Wellington: State Services Commission, 2002, p. 21.

Bilateral contract: An agreement for services sought, and to be delivered, that is made between two parties. Most contractual relationships are bilateral in nature (such as between employers and employees, and between a service provider and an organization). A bilateral contract is contrasted with a unilateral contract. Under a unilateral contract, there is no expectation between the two parties that when one provides a service there will be any expectation of a reciprocal service being provided.

Binding arbitration: *See* **Compulsory arbitration**.

Binding decision: Any compulsory decision; can apply to organizations or individuals. Binding decisions are made by, for example, the legislature for public-sector organizations, and by organizations for employees.

Blanket policies: Policies that apply to all public organizations. In that context, they differ from framework or focused policies (framework policies are broad and rather generic; focused policies are specific and targeted to a very particular area). For a discussion of these terms, see, e.g., R. Lipsey and K. Carlaw, "Technology Policies in Neo-Classical and Structuralist-Evolutionary Models," *STI Review* (special issue on "New Rationale and Approaches in Technology and Innovation Policy"), 1998, 22(1), pp. 31–73. *See also* **Focused policies; Framework policies.**

Blanketing-in: A process of the conversion of posts whereby an elected executive transfers noncareer jobs into the regular public service. By doing so, individuals who hold such posts (i.e., those who were brought in through patronage and not necessarily under the merit system) cannot be removed from their jobs by successive executives.

Blatant resistance: A tactic used by bureaucracies and others to not adhere to policy intent. Other tactics include tokenism and delayed compliance. Blatant resistance may occur for various reasons, including, for example, initial disagreement with the policy intent, and countervailing pressure from citizen groups. See E. Bardach, *The Implementation Game: What Happens After a Bill Becomes a Law,* Cambridge, MA: MIT Press, 1977, pp. 98–124. *See also* **Delayed compliance; Tokenism.**

Blind variation and selective retention: A concept that encompasses some basic principles underlying organizational change and evolution that premises that knowledge can initially only be developed by trial and error. The concept is contained in a three-stage model, which first considers the occurrence of variations in the organization's environment, followed by the consistent selection criteria that organizations employ to retain that part of the variation that enhances their own knowledge, and finally by the employment of a mechanism that preserves and duplicates the positively selected variants. For the original exposition of this concept, see D. Campbell, "Blind Variation and Selective Retention in Creative Thought as in Other Knowledge Processes," *Psychological Review,* 1960, 67(6), pp. 380–400. *See also* **Principle of blind variation**.

Block grant: Also known as special revenue sharing, this term refers to a fixed amount of resources granted from a central government to a local one to be spent on broadly specified activities.

Blue-skies approach: An approach to strategic management in which everything is taken into consideration and an open view is taken of what the external environment looks like. In a blue-skies approach to organizational planning, there is usually a clear sense that there is no commitment to retaining the status quo.

Board: *See* **Board of directors**.

Board independence: The proportion of elected, as opposed to appointed, members in a board. Generally, the greater the number of the former, the better the performance of the portfolio. For example, public pension funds with politically appointed board members usually underperform relative to those with independent boards. For a brief review, see, e.g., A. Ranft and H. O'Neill, "Board Composition and High-Flying Founders: Hints of Trouble to Come?" *Academy of Management Executive,* 2001, 15(1), pp. 126–38.

Board of appeals: A committee of individuals that is mandated to adjudicate the cases (i.e., appeals) that it receives. As the name implies, the board reviews cases and judgments that have previously been heard, or components thereof, and decides whether the original decision should stand.

Board of directors: A group of individuals (the numbers of which can vary) selected to make sure that an organization is well managed. The selection of board members in public-sector organizations can be either through elections or nominations by groups (such as community groups involved in service delivery) or nominated by governmental ministers based upon recommendations from different stakeholders. The board of directors of a public-sector agency is responsible to the legislature although clearly there are times when ministers will try to have a greater say in its affairs. The usual rules governing the functions and other arrangements for boards in private organizations also hold for their counterparts in the public sector. For a discussion of this, see, e.g., E. Ferlie et al., "Corporate Governance and the Public Sector: Some Issues and Evidence from the NHS," *Public Administration,* 1995, 73(3), pp. 375–92.

Board of inquiry: A committee of individuals that is mandated to look at a problematic situation or issue. Unlike a board of appeals, the board of inquiry initiates an original investigation. It does not necessarily have the mandate to pass judgment; it reports its findings and makes recommendations if instructed.

Boiling frog syndrome: *See* **Creeping risk**.

Bona-fide occupational qualification: A qualifier that employers can use in asking, for example, for the ages of candidates for particular positions. While, for example, the Age Discrimination in Employment Act (1967) in the United States prohibits employers from discriminating on the basis of age, such discrimination is legitimate if it can be demonstrated, for instance, that an age criterion is necessary for a position.

Boomerang jobs: A term used to denote when older employees leave the organization as part of a phased retirement program and then re-enter the organization to work limited hours, or to provide assistance in an expert capacity. See, e.g., Corporate Leadership Council, *The Aging Workforce: Retention and Knowledge Management: Literature Review,* Washington, DC: CSC, February 2002, p. 8.

Booster training: Training provided to existing employees to help them learn new ways of doing things. However, there is a clear sense that there was a previous occurrence of training so that the current activity is supplementary in nature.

Bottom line: The most basic requirement that an organization needs to meet (for example, profit maximization in a private firm). A bottom-line mentality refers to a mindset of administrators that focuses on the main thing to be achieved at the expense of any other. While this in itself is not negative, when this mentality crowds out long-term solutions for short-term ones (such as near-term financial success as opposed to long-term capability enhancement), then it is perceived as being a limitation. It is argued that, in the public sector, the financial bottom-line mentality is increasingly being coupled with a political bottom-line mentality (the latter stems largely from unresolved conflicts that are evident in relationships between bureaucrats and governmental ministers, as well as between bureaucrats and a legislature). See, e.g., A. Kakabadse, N. Korac-Kakabadse and A. Kouzmin, "Ethics, Values, and Behaviors: Comparison of Three Case Studies Examining the Paucity of Leadership in Government," *Public Administration,* 2003, 81(3), pp. 477–508.

Bottom-up management: A management style that encourages subordinates and those in the lower hierarchies in an organization to be involved in the management of the organization. Such bottom-up management practices are considered to be empowering to the employees. This term is increasingly associated with others such as "indigenous management" and "community-based management," which is also encapsulated in the term "folk management." See, e.g., C. Dyer and J. McGoodwin (eds), *Folk Management in the World's Fisheries: Lessons from Modern Fisheries Management,* Niwot: University Press of Colorado, 1994.

Boundary conditions: (1) The outer limits to the conditions under which a certain phenomenon can exist. (2) Those activities of a subunit in an organization that relate to the larger organization. Supervisors need to be aware of the boundary conditions in their own subunits so that they can liaise effectively with those outside the sub-unit.

Boundary exchange: The degree to which an organizational subunit's mandate can be transferred to another unit. For example, whereas the evaluation of program staff members may have once been conducted by a corporate human resources department, it may be decided to transfer the responsibility to the office of the program manager.

Boundary permeability: The degree to which an organizational sub-unit's mandate will change depending upon how much external pressure there is to add new requirements to the entity. Managers tend to be very wary of such boundary permeability, not only because it is difficult to manage effectively in a situation of flux but also because unsuspecting managers may tend to get saddled with work that was not originally mandated for their unit.

Boundary setting: A situation where managers empower employees to make decisions within prespecified limits. Such boundaries are set in keeping with the level of authority that has been given to the managers themselves.

Boundarylessness: The degree of openness that organizations exhibit in dealing with others in their environment. In learning organizations, boundarylessness is the norm as organizations seek to maximize their links and interactions with suppliers, stakeholders, and citizen groups. For a cogent analysis of the concept, see, e.g., J. Intagliata, D. Ulrich and N. Smallwood, "Leveraging Leadership Competencies to Produce Leadership Brand: Creating Distinctiveness by Focusing on Strategy and Results," *Human Resources Planning,* 2000, 23(4), pp. 12–23.

Boundary-spanning unit: Any unit in an organization that is used specifically for purposes of dealing with the organization's external environment so as to protect its technical core. For example, an external-communications unit might be created in an organization so that all queries on the organization's activities are channeled through it, thus guarding those in the organization from hostile external questioning. For a review of boundary-spanning operations in public administration, see, e.g., R. Agranoff and M. McGuire, "Multinetwork Management: Collaboration and the Hollow State in Local Economic Policy," *Journal of Public Administration Research and Theory,* 1998, 8(1), pp. 67–91.

Bounded power: (1) Restrictions placed on the exercise of power by managers and administrators. For public-sector managers, such boundedness stems largely from legal and administrative limits placed on the discretion and power to be exercised. (2) The durability of a particular set of organizational values or cultures that make it difficult for change agents to produce changes in performance through reorganization. See J. Olsen, "Modernization Programs in Perspective: Institutional Analysis of Organizational Change," *Governance: An International Journal of Policy and Administration,* 1991, 4(2), pp. 125–49.

Bounded rationality: Also known as limited cognitive competence, this term refers to the type of thinking that yields decisions that are rational in the context of the constraints imposed. The boundedness refers to the parameters or constraints faced by the firm or individual. Bounded rationality is an extremely useful concept in studying decision making and risks, and while it appears suboptimizing, it is not necessarily true that a theory of bounded rationality cannot involve optimization. Organizations are boundedly rational partly because of the limits to managers' cognitive abilities, and this leads to satisficing by organizations in their search for a suitable course of action. See H. Simon, *Administrative Behavior: A Study of Decision-Making Processes in Administrative Organizations,* New York: Macmillan, 1947, pp. 39–41; H. Greve and A. Taylor, "Innovations as Catalysts for Organizational Change: Shifts in Organizational Cognition and Search," *Administrative Science Quarterly,* 2000, 45(1), pp. 54–80. *See also* **Global rationality**.

Bowling-alone thesis: A concept popularized by Robert Putnam's titled article, which focuses on how urban governance in the United States has been adversely affected by a noticeable decline in civic participation. It is interesting to note that when Putnam formulated his bowling-alone thesis, he had also asserted that restoring civic engagement in America would likely be eased by a palpable national crisis. Several years later such a crisis arose, and Putnam's research in the aftermath of September 11 showed that Americans were more than ever receptive to the idea that people of all backgrounds should be full members of the national community. See R. Putnam, "Bowling Alone: America's Declining Social Capital," *Journal of Democracy,* 1995, 6(1), pp. 65–78. *See also* **Social capital**.

Brainstorming: A method of coming up with creative ideas from among group members where the primary objective is to secure as many ideas as possible to address a particular problem. The process of gathering such ideas has to be spontaneous and uninhibited so that all ideas can be tabled and collated. The logic behind brainstorming is that no idea is considered to be unsuitable for initial consideration. See, e.g., A. Mood, *Introduction to Policy Analysis,* New York: Elsevier Science Publishing Co., 1983, p. 31.

Brand: Any name, symbol, mark, etc., that identifies an organization. Some public-sector organizations are now branding themselves as private-sector firms do so that citizens can see—and better relate to—the product/service that is on offer.

Breach of contract: Violation of a contract or collective-bargaining agreement. All such contracts and agreements will have some contingency measures around this. Such a breach usually results from a breach of trust, which is the failure of any party to live up to its obligations, whether contractual or not. For example, a breach of trust may occur if an employee does not carry out duties properly and honestly.

Break-even analysis: An analysis that determines the point at which sales equal total costs. This is a technique which is based on considering production costs as consisting of fixed and variable costs. Fixed costs are for such things as rents and administration, and variables costs are for raw materials, direct labor, etc. Total variable and fixed costs are then compared with revenue from sales to determine at what production level there is neither profit nor loss (i.e., the point at which the business breaks even). With public-sector organizations increasingly adopting private-sector practices, a break-even analysis allows them to better determine the true costs of delivering services.

Break-out procurement: The process of acquiring required goods and services by breaking up large contracts into smaller ones so that smaller businesses may participate in the tender process as well. Break-out procurement is a common tool in jurisdictions where the government is seeking to encourage indigenous business capacity. See, e.g., D. Fourie, "Government Contracting and Official Capacity: Reflections with Reference to South Africa," *Asian Journal of Public Administration,* 1998, 20(2), pp. 233–48.

Bribery: *See* **Corruption**.

Bridge job: Refers to a job that acts as a bridge (or link) to another job that is part of an employee's career plans. Such a bridge job is specifically designed to help an employee move from one job (in which he or she may be currently involved) to another (which the employee seeks in advancement). Bridge jobs are thus a key part of a career ladder, and managers tend to ensure that they are aware of which bridge jobs may be suitable for which employees.

Bridging organization: An entity that can help different agencies link up so that objectives are more effectively attained. For example, when local governments enable voluntary organizations and community groups to work together with them to address specific public problems, they can be considered to be bridging organizations. There may be occasions when such organizations also provide resources (known as bridging finance) to assist others until their regular authorizations are activated.

Broad task assignment: *See* **Task identity**.

Broadbanding: *See* **Task description**.

Brokering: Refers to the act of an entity (such as a public organization) linking different parties by helping them come together to mutually benefit from each other's expertise. For example, central-government agencies in several jurisdictions might help broker secondment opportunities for individuals in different organizations. For application to a developing-country context, see, e.g., T. Hewitt et al., "Seeing Eye to Eye: Organizational Behavior, Brokering, and Building Trust in Tanzania," *Public Administration and Development,* 2002, 22(2), pp. 97–108.

Buddy system: An on-the-job training technique where a trainee individual is assigned to work closely with an experienced individual such that, over time, the trainee will have had the opportunity to gain enough capability to work alone. *See also* **Sitting next to Nellie**.

Budget authority: (1) Any legal authority (such as local government, regional council) that can enter into obligations on behalf of a government or organization. (2) The power to spend resources (or budget utilization) in an organization.

Budget bid: A proposal made by a governmental department to a central financial authority (i.e., a treasury or a finance ministry) for its annual (plus forecasted) budget. Such a proposal will have been preceded by extensive negotiations with the financial authority so that no surprises arise in the legislative process.

Budget blowout: *See* **Cost blowout**.

Budget cap: *See* **Budget constraint**.

Budget constraint: In generic terms, this is a ceiling or a limit to the expenditure. Budget constraints can be either "hard" or "soft." A hard budget constraint is one in which the limits are clearly set and the results of exceeding the limit are serious. A soft budget constraint, on the other hand, is one in which the penalties for breaching the limit are not severe. Many argue that virtually all public-sector organizations operate under soft budget constraints since legislatures rarely punish budget deficits. See, e.g., W. Megginson and J. Netter, "From State to Market: A Survey of Empirical Studies on Privatization," *Journal of Economic Literature,* 2001, 39(2), pp. 321–89. See also J. Kornai, E. Maskin and G. Roland, "Understanding the Soft Budget Constraint," *Journal of Economic Literature,* 2003, 41(4), pp. 1095–1136.

Budget envelope: Also known as a resource envelope, this term refers to the total amount of resources that an organization can have at its disposal in fulfilling its mandates. As applied in practice, such a limit is bounded on the lower side by existing levels of funding, and on the upper side by some factor that takes into consideration the scope of new proposals that a government is willing to entertain for a forthcoming budget period. The size of a budget envelope is also contingent upon budget fungibility, whereupon governmental departments have the ability to shift funds from one program to another, and move surplus funds from one year to the next.

Budget-maximizing behavior: The economist William Niskanen has argued that bureaus wish to maximize the size of their appropriations because bureaucrats are self-interested and they seek to maximize their utility (the assumption being that a larger appropriation yields maximal utility). Niskanen also believed that a legislature has little information on just how much they really should get. See W. Niskanen, "A Reflection on Bureaucracy and Representative Government," in A. Blais and S. Dion (eds), *The Budget-Maximizing Bureaucrat: Appraisals and Evidence,* Pittsburgh: University of Pittsburgh Press, 1991, pp. 13–31. For a rebuttal to Niskanen in the form of an empirical study application, see, e.g., J. Dolan, "The Budget-Minimizing Bureaucrat? Empirical Evidence from the Senior Executive Service," *Public Administration Review,* 2002, 62(1), pp. 42–50.

Budget visibility: Refers to the transparency of expenditures in organizational activities. For example, if organizations cannot easily tell auditors just how much resources they spend in a year on management development opportunities for top executives in the organization, they are said to lack budget visibility.

Budgetary control: (1) A form of control exercised over governmental departments by virtue of being able to manipulate the amount of funding they receive from a legislature. (2) Putting a cap on the level of budget, or spending limits.

Budgeting: Considered a traditional function in an organization, budgeting refers to the practice of estimating—and eventually reconciling—the expenses and revenues for the organization, and preparing a financial plan based upon the organization's objectives. A budget is used as a way of exercising control over bureaucracy (not only through manipulating the level of funding but also the individual line items within the organizational funding scheme). There are two primary approaches to budgeting that can be highlighted: top-down and bottom-up. In the former, the organizational leadership estimates the overall costs and the estimates are passed on to lower-level managers to break down and apportion to the various tasks that need to be done. Because the boundaries are set by senior managers, a budget here does not tend to be inflated. On the other hand, bottom-up budgeting implies that lower-level managers determine the level of resources that will be needed to complete mandated tasks, and all such budget bids are aggregated at the organizational level to arrive at the overall budget. Because bottom-up budgeting stems from an acknowledgment of the actual work to be carried out, budgets derived thus often tend to be more realistic.

Budgeting, traditional: Budgeting that has the following attributes: (a) short-term (i.e., only for a year), (b) incremental (i.e., largely determined by the previous year's limit), (c) input-based (i.e., focusing on the acquisition of inputs rather than the generation of outputs and contributing to outcomes), and (d) line-item based (i.e., not based on outputs but on individual cost items). Given that it is input-based, the government does not—cannot—specify a precise level of services for which the resources are authorized. Traditional budgeting continues to be practiced by governments in many developing countries.

Buffered rationality: A conception of rationality that argues that rather than consider longer-term (and, therefore, more uncertain) scenarios, a shorter term and less fundamental approach, which contains less public risks, is better suited to organizations and should thus be the preferred option for policy makers. One of the first to analyze this concept in depth, H. George Frederickson pointed out that in order to plan the change process in bureaucracy effectively, administrators could rely on the notion of buffered rationality. Frederickson drew heavily on the work of other writers (such as Herbert Simon on rationality and Amitai Etzioni on mixed scanning) to assert that buffered rationality bestows administrators with the opportunity in the short term to put strategic plans into action without being susceptible to the extremes of long-term policy analysis and planning, which tend to be normative and with fuzzy boundaries. What buffered rationality does is give administrators an avenue to be involved in low-risk activities that contribute to some overall objective. See his *New Public Administration,* University: University of Alabama Press, 1980, pp. 58–59.

Buffering: (1) A process of protecting the technical core of an organization such that core activities are not compromised by adverse conditions in the organization's operating environment. (2) Buffering is also used to imply the protecting or shielding of public servants from political pressures. For an example of how a central agency acts as a buffer between the political establishment and politically neutral elements of executive government, see State Services Commission, *Annual Report of the State Services Commission, 2002,* Wellington, New Zealand: State Services Commission, 2002, p. 8.

Build-operate-transfer: The practice of financing private infrastructure and operating a project with the transfer of the ownership right to the public sector at an agreed upon time. Commonly known as BOT, the model is used as a public-private partnership technique wherein a government provides land and other institutional support, and private firms build and operate a facility, eventually transferring ownership to government.

Bureau budgeting: In bureau budgeting, an organization's tasks are costed and then budgeted for, rather than established in an overall amount based on a benchmark, such as an existing baseline. For a discussion of bureau budgeting, see, e.g., J. White, "Entitlement Budgeting vs. Bureau Budgeting," *Public Administration Review,* 1998, 58(6), pp. 510–21. *Cf.* **Entitlement budgeting**.

Bureaucracy: (1) A hierarchical organization relying upon formal authority and rules. The sociologist Max Weber saw government in terms of bureaus, and proposed the most enduring manifestations of a rational bureaucracy (such as their structured nature, hierarchy of decision making, neutrality [impartiality], and technical competence). Weber also argued that as organizations grow bigger, they invariably tend to be increasingly bureaucratized since routinization becomes necessary. The bureaucracy is also seen as an institution of penetration (i.e., when a government relies

Bureaucratic conduct: The behavior exhibited by a bureaucratic organization as reflected, for example, in how it responds to public criticism, legislative demands, and confrontation with other bureaucracies over bureaucratic turf protection. One such conduct is that of bureaucratic maneuvering, where a bureaucracy actively engages in protecting its own turf. A bureaucratic maneuver is planned and is a deliberate attempt to retain whatever powers/resources a bureaucracy has at its disposal.

Bureaucratic discrepancies: When two or more governmental departments do not speak with the same voice on a common policy. This might occur, for example, when there is bureaucratic infighting, which is a situation evident when two or more parties in bureaucracies are struggling to preserve their turf and are not cooperating with each other, even though cooperation would clearly be in the interest of the organization.

Bureaucratic discretion: *See* **Administrative discretion**.

Bureaucratic dramaturgy: When bureaucrats camouflage their lack of any knowledge that is useful to an organization. The concept is related to managerial behavior, and how roles are played out in an organization. It is a social science methodology in organizational analysis, and just like in theater, in organizations too, there are considered to be actors, roles, scenes (i.e., the workplace), and their interactions—as if in a script. Managers use dramaturgy as a behavioral repertoire so that they can better interact with subordinates in accordance with what the particular situation warrants. For a good review, see, e.g., W. Gardner, "Lessons in Organizational Dramaturgy: The Art of Impression Management," *Organizational Dynamics,* 1992, 21(1), pp. 33–46.

Bureaucratic dysfunction: *See* **Bureaucratic pathology**.

Bureaucratic ethos: A concept that refers to a sense of bureaucratic purpose, and the manner in which a bureaucracy proceeds to attain that purpose. This is largely shaped by the structure and the decision-making processes within the bureaucracy. A related concept is bureaucratic socialization, which refers to the manner in which bureaucracies structure their induction processes for new staff members so that they understand the norms that need to be adhered. Another relevant concept in relation to bureaucratic ethos is bureaucratic personality, for it is this that largely tends to determine the ethos that exists in the bureaucracy. The sociologist Robert Merton has written significantly about the existence of bureaucratic personality, and discusses how bureaucracy behaves both during normal times and at times of organizational crises. See R. Merton, "Bureaucratic Structure and Personality," *Social Forces,* 1940, 18, pp. 560–68.

Bureaucratic expansion: The tendency of bureaucracies to increase their size in seeking to enhance their mandates and resources. Bureaucratic fiefdoms can result when the expansion efforts are over-aggressive, or when organizations seek to protect their turf by resisting external influence.

Bureaucratic fiat: *See* **Bureaucratic power**.

Bureaucratic goal displacement: *See* **Goal displacement**.

Bureaucratic impersonality: Max Weber advocated this feature in a bureaucracy because of the existence of formalization and hierarchy in an organization. It is only through bureaucratic impersonality that an organization can work toward fulfilling its mandate effectively. In bureaucratic impersonality, there is a very clear distinction that is assumed to exist between personal and work affairs. This depersonalization is a key characteristic of bureaucratic impersonality. It also ultimately manifests in the emergence of facelessness in bureaucracy. Critics say facelessness implies that citizens are not getting personalized service, while proponents of bureaucratic impersonality argue that this actually facilitates standardization, and serves to minimize discrimination and increase efficiency. See, e.g., J. Martin, K. Knopff and C. Beckman, "An Alternative to Bureaucratic Impersonality and Emotional Labor: Bounded Emotionality at the Body Shop," *Administrative Science Quarterly,* 1998, 43(3), pp. 429–69.

Bureaucratic indigenization: The process of staffing bureaucracies with indigenous populations so that there is a greater balance in ethnic representation in bureaucracies. Bureaucratic indigenization is a policy that was long evident in Malaysia, for example, under its *Bumiputra* (son of the soil) national program.

Bureaucratic lapses: Instances when bureaucracies do not make proper judgments. For example, if an immigration service does not carefully check the papers of an undesirable individual, which results in the person entering the country and posing a danger, then that can be said to be a bureaucratic lapse.

Bureaucratic maneuvering: *See* **Bureaucratic conduct**.

Bureaucratic momentum: Refers to a situation where the work of bureaucracies tends to create more work and where greater attention is placed on processes than on outputs and outcomes. The momentum may result, for example, from a simple decision to have a particular program or policy reviewed, and a particular government agency is tasked with the review. The need for the review might create a committee, which could decide to set up regular coordination meetings with external stakeholders, and that, in turn, might require secretarial and administrative support. In the end, the decision of the review might be the need for instituting a unit within a selected department to monitor the progress of the policy or program (something that another organization may very well be mandated to do but has not been doing so for some reason or another).

Bureaucratic pathology: Refers to infighting and excessively rigid adherence to bureaucratic rules and hierarchy that stifles any new thinking on why a bureaucracy is behaving as it does. This is a dysfunctional and counterproductive aspect of bureaucracy that comes from very formal processes that bureaucracies may have, and which tends to emphasize process over content. One particular pathology that is common is bureaucratic inertia, which is a situation where a bureaucracy is not able to respond to any developments in its external involvement, and is neither able to effectively nor efficiently fulfill its mandate. See, e.g., S. Ott and J. Shafritz, "Toward a Definition of Organizational Incompetence: A Neglected Variable in Organizational Theory," *Public Administration Review,* 1994, 54(4), pp. 370–77. Another dysfunction is bureaucratic insularity, which is a situation in which bureaucracies are removed from the interests of the public, and do not understand the nature of their external environments. One of the first individuals to talk of bureaucratic pathology was the sociologist Robert Merton (see "Bureaucratic Structure and Personality," *Social Forces,* 1940, 18, pp. 560–68). *See also* **Occupational psychosis**; **Professional deformation**; **Trained incapacity**.

Bureaucratic policy making: When bureaucrats are relied on to a great extent to develop policies and not just provide advice to governmental ministers. There are two primary reasons for this: (a) the technical expertise in this area generally lies in the bureaucracy, and (b) because policy continuity is important, there is a tendency to rely on bureaucracies to capitalize on institutional knowledge that exists in bureaucracies. Post-war Japan provides the best example of bureaucratic policy making, where governmental ministers usually deferred to the better judgment of the bureaucrats in matters of policy making in such areas as finance and taxation.

Bureaucratic politics: An organization's attempts to have its policy ideas accepted. Harvard professor Graham Allison posits that bureaucratic politics is one of three lenses that can be used to help explain the choices made by policy makers (the other two being rational actor and organizational process). For an application of this in his classic work, see G. Allison, *The Essence of Decision: Explaining the Cuban Missile Crisis,* Boston: Little, Brown, 1971. There has been much work on its applications elsewhere as well; see, e.g., R. O'Leary, "The Bureaucratic Politics Paradox: The Case of Wetlands Legislation in Nevada," *Journal of Public Administration Research and Theory,* 1994, 4(4), pp. 443–67.

Bureaucratic power: The control that bureaucracies exercise as a result of an expansion of state bureaucracy, and also because the bureaucracy has become professional and possesses technical skills. Excessive bureaucratic power can lead to bureaucratic fiat where decisions that are made by higher authorities in bureaucracies do not tend to be questioned.

Bureaucratic professionalization: The process of developing a bureaucracy that has members with professional knowledge and capabilities, and in which the organization as a whole has a value system based on ethical and professional standards. Bureaucratic professionalization is fostered when there is a fair degree of specialization of functions, and set standards of practice (such as on risk management, unified code of ethics, etc.) are instituted and rigorously followed.

Bureaucratic protest: A term used to denote the opposition that bureaucracies put up when they feel threatened by external forces (such as a legislature). Such opposition could be reflected, for example, in a strong submission to a select committee that a particular measure will have adverse consequences on the bureau's ability to fulfill its mandate. A related concept is bureaucratic resistance, which is a situation where bureaucracies resist a specific external impetus to change their structures, processes, and mandates. The resistance is a result of a bureaucracy's perception that its resource base or power will be diminished or that its value system will be modified. See, e.g., F. Riggs, "Bureaucracy: A Profound Puzzle for Presidentialism," in A. Farazmand (ed.), *Handbook of Bureaucracy,* New York: Marcel Dekker, Inc., 1994, pp. 97–147.

Bureaucratic rationality: Rational behavior exhibited by bureaucracies, which in itself consists of organizational rationality (where bureaucratic action is subsumed under formal legal rules) and systemic rationality (where bureaucracies are driven by meeting societal goals). In addition, the concept of bureaucratic rationality assumes that bureaucracies can generate consensus with their stakeholders. For an application of the concept in relation to a developmentalist state, see G. Koh, "Bureaucratic

Rationality in an Evolving Developmentalist State: The Case of Singapore," in G. Bhatta and J. Gonzalez (eds.), *Governance Innovations in the Asia-Pacific Region: Trends, Cases, and Issues,* Aldershot, UK; Ashgate, 1998, pp. 49–74.

Bureaucratic resistance: *See* **Bureaucratic protest**.

Bureaucratic responsiveness: Bureaucratic responsiveness is evident in two main ways: (a) when governmental agencies reflect, internalize, and carry out the decisions made by governmental ministers and elected representatives in an impartial and value-neutral manner; and (b) when bureaucracies are involved in activities and programs and are addressing the issues that citizens say they face. While intuitively these two pressures should be complementary (after all, elected representatives are to reflect the wishes of their constituencies), in reality, they are often not. This puts a considerable amount of stress on the bureaucracies to balance the pressure points that emanate from both angles.

Bureaucratic secrecy: A tendency of bureaucracies to resist, to the extent possible, the release of any information on how they manage their affairs. The predilection for secrecy could be a function of their sense of insecurity around how such release of information might adversely affect their power and resource base.

Bureaucratic solidarity: A situation where bureaucracies stand up for each other in situations where they feel there are collective interests at stake, and that putting up a joint stance will diminish the chances of an adverse step being taken. Such solidarity could be evident, for example, when two or more organizations decide to agree on joint recommendations on a cabinet-level paper that advises governmental ministers against what they may have professed to do. See, e.g., F. Riggs, "Bureaucracy: A Profound Puzzle for Presidentialism," in A. Farazmand (ed.), *Handbook of Bureaucracy,* New York: Marcel Dekker, Inc., 1994, pp. 97–147.

Bureaucratic turf: Refers to the mandate that a bureaucracy has been specifically given which it seeks to protect against infringement or dilution by others. This tendency to protect its turf (i.e., its area of operations) leads eventually to organizational silos in the public sector. Bureaucratic turf is also evident in the guarding of specific decision rights (such as on agreeing to grant exemptions and licenses) that individual organizations may have which they would not like to cede because it gives them power that can be exercised over others.

Bureaucratization: The process of increasing the size of the bureaucracy, and of making processes extremely administrative. It also denotes an increase in the administrative aspects of how things get done. The term bureaucratization of politics is taken to refer to the process where in enhancing economic development, political development tends to be subsumed, as in Korea in the 1960s and 1970s (see, e.g., B. Kim, "Public Bureaucracy in Korea," in A. Farazmand (ed.), *Handbook of Bureaucracy,* New York: Marcel Dekker, Inc., 1994, pp. 591–602.

Bureaus: Operating entities that are contained within governmental departments—but not necessarily physically located in them. They are responsible for program implementation, and, at times, actual delivery of services. Some bureaus (such as the U.S. Federal Bureau of Investigation) have as high a profile as the government department in which they are located.

Bureaus, life cycle of: An argument has long been made that organizations in bureaucracies tend to go through many stages as they mature. This evolutionary process starts from the initial set up of the organization, and similar to the human lifeline, it develops distinguishing characteristics. Bureaus are generally first susceptible budget wise as they fight for turf and resources, and as they begin to institutionalize their mandates and work processes they become more entrenched. Over time, the bureau might even be able to thwart political challenges for its disestablishment, and it will fight for increased resources. In order to continue to be in operation, bureaus will also seek to reinvent themselves if that ensures their survival. The notion of a life cycle is also applied in the context not only of budget-retention and mandate-expansion activities, but also of the characteristics of the organization itself. For example, a regulatory agency could at first be very focused on the public interest, but over time, and from interactions with those that are regulated, they may come increasingly under the influence of interest groups. This implies that they will come to be interested in maintaining the status quo and be overly bureaucratized. One of the original discussions on this concept was provided by Anthony Downs (see his *Inside Bureaucracy,* Boston: Little, Brown, 1967, pp. 296–309).

Bureau-shaping strategy: A strategy pursued by managers to adjust organizational controls so as to bring about improvements in program results. The strategy informed many of the structural changes that have taken place in public-sector reforms across many jurisdictions. It is argued that such reorganizations are explained as bureau-shaping strategies

C

Cabinet: An executive body that plays a central role in ensuring that a government's policies are pursued. In Westminster systems, the cabinet has collective responsibility to the parliament, which means that if the government loses the confidence of the legislature, then the cabinet is obliged to resign. A cabinet committee is a committee of governmental ministers appointed to consider sector-specific policy proposals prior to full cabinet consideration. For a comparison with the cabinet system in the United States, see R. Moe, "The United States: A Country Study in Organization and Governance," a paper presented at the OECD Governance of State Agencies and Authorities Expert Meeting, Paris, 19–20 April 2001.

Cabinet government: Wherein the executive branch of government consists of individuals who are also members of the legislature, and are responsible to it. The rationale for a cabinet government is that governmental ministers need to be elected representatives (i.e., members of parliament), for their raison d'être to manage portfolios comes from having constituencies. *Cf.* **Congressional government**.

Cabinet minute: A decision reached at a cabinet meeting but which is not necessarily to be legislated. By its inclusion in the official meeting minutes, though, it becomes a requirement for a governmental agency to take it into consideration. While some cabinet decisions have to be routed through parliament, most administrative decisions are effected in cabinet meetings, recorded in the minutes, and are carried out by government agencies. It is possible, however, to have preparatory work on some critical programs started based on cabinet minutes even though they may contain considerable financial implications.

Cabinet responsibility: As applied in the organizational context, this term is used to refer to the agreed behavior among the organizational leadership to encourage debate and discussion regarding any particular policy. The responsibility on the leadership is to ensure that any agreed initiative is upheld in a cohesive and disciplined way. See, e.g., A. Kakabadse, N. Korac-Kakabadse and A. Kouzmin, "Ethics, Values and Behaviors: Comparison of Three Case Studies Examining the Paucity of Leadership in Government," *Public Administration,* 2003, 81(3), pp. 477–508.

Cabinet solidarity: A general convention in government decision making is that all governmental ministers must publicly support the final decisions espoused by the cabinet even if they may have opposed the matter internally in cabinet. If such differences cannot be overcome, then ministers are obliged or may be forced to resign their posts, otherwise they must onward support the policy.

Cabinet-cluster approach: An approach to planning and program management where interagency cabinet clusters (groups of heads of agencies) work together to provide guidance to planning and implementing strategic changes in public policies and programs. Such an approach is generally applied on issues that are complex and that saddle multiple policy areas. For an application, see, e.g., L. Frost-Kumpf et al., "Strategic Action and Transformational Change: The Ohio Department of Mental Health," in B. Bozeman (ed.), *Public Management: The State of the Art,* San Francisco: Jossey-Bass, 1993, pp. 137–52.

Cafeteria approach: Given the general discomfort that the public has with empirical research, there is a consequential tendency to accept research results and form opinions to public policies based on evidence that corroborates own interests while disregarding contrary research. In that sense, selective opinion making is similar to picking and choosing food offered in a cafeteria. See, e.g., P. Edwards-Ham, "The Tension Between Policy Science and Politics: Addressing Cancer Incidence and Environmental Contamination in Michigan," *Policy Studies Journal,* 2001, 29(1), pp. 139–53.

Cafeteria benefits plan: A customized benefits program wherein employees pick and choose the types of benefits they want within a value amount that to which they are entitled. A customized benefits program.

Call center: A service that citizens can access by telephone in order to obtain information on the products, policies, and services that government departments offer. The purported benefits of call centers are that individuals receive service immediately and often outside conventional working hours, and for which they need not visit personally or request in writing. Also, call centers enable organizations to increase efficiency of services by having less skilled personnel, supported by information systems, staff the centers, which frees up skilled personnel to concentrate on more complex matters. However, organizations need to ensure that call centers are fully equipped and that customer-service representatives have all the information required to provide effective services. Government ever, with the "new public management" reforms of the 1980s and 1990s, where lateral entry to the public service was actively encouraged, the concept of the career autonomy of public servants was directly attacked for it meant that there was no guarantee that a public servant's career growth would continue untested.

Career counseling: Providing guidance and counsel to an employee or an individual on how to set a career, change one, and/or move ahead in one. Such advice is provided by a career counselor, and can be provided at any stage of an individual's career; for example, upon entry into the workforce, while considering horizontal movements later on in one's career, or while considering a lifestyle change as retirement age nears.

Career development: Also known as career progression, this concept refers to the movement by an individual along a charted-out career path. Such a movement could be within one organization or involving many. The training and development opportunities that an individual receives/accesses should be aligned with career-development plans. Career development is also a function of career counseling. *See also* **Career counseling**.

Career guidance: *See* **Career counseling**.

Career ladder: Denotes a series of classifications in which an employee progresses into successive levels of responsibility and remuneration. The ladder, however, may not always lead the individual upward. For example, career lattice refers to the horizontal and/or diagonal paths that an individual takes in career-enhancing opportunities. The key feature of a career lattice is that the individual is still moving toward the desired career position, although if the move is horizontal it means that the individual wishes to gain a different set of skills in order to eventually move up the ladder. This movement up the career ladder is known as career mobility, and refers to the movement of an individual from one position to another in line with the career plan that will have been determined jointly by the employee and the employer.

Career lattice: *See* **Career ladder**.

Career management: Giving due regard to the proposed careers of employees. Such career management implies also that both the employer and the employee are actively seeking ways to ensure that the employee is in line to achieve what he or she has set out to achieve. This leads often to a particular specification of the types of competencies and experiences that the employee will need to gain in order to attain the career that has been charted. It is considered to be the responsibility of both parties to manage the employee's career.

Career mobility: *See* **Career ladder**.

Career negotiation: The process between an employer and employee where mutual considerations of interest and requirements are considered and deliberated upon. Such a negotiation would obviously have to benefit both parties. Given the "new public management" reforms of the past two decades, career negotiation with employers is not normally a standard feature in organizations since career-based personnel plans are increasingly discarded for fixed-term based schemes.

Career path: The sequence of jobs and the accumulation of particular experiences that an employee requires in order to attain a specified career. Until the traditional structure of public-sector jobs and careers were de-emphasized, about two decades ago, individuals could be quite sure of their career paths in an organization. Now, however, with open tenure and with movement away from set careers in organizations, the notion of a career path is not very prevalent, although clearly in some traditional government services (such as the diplomatic corps), a career path is still very much the norm. See, e.g., D. Watson and W. Hassett, "Career Paths of City Managers in America's Largest Council-Manager Cities," *Public Administration Review,* 2004, 64(2): 177–84.

Career pattern: Refers to the various jobs that an employee will be involved in which inform where he or she might be headed by way of a career. An irregular career pattern may imply that the employee is not clear about his or her career path. To remedy this, a career-planning process is recommended for such individuals.

Career planning: When employees specify what they would like to do in the career time ahead of them and how they plan on advancing. Career planning requires that the employees look at what their interests are, what skills and capabilities will be needed for the future positions, and how they plan to acquire such capabilities over time.

Career plateau: A situation where an employee has reached the maximum level of achievement in terms of a career. In a career plateau, the employee is not likely to move up to any higher position (at least not in the organization in which he or she may be working). Employees who have reached their career plateau are encouraged to seek other opportunities elsewhere, or seek redundancy from the organization.

Career progression: *See* **Career development**.

Career system: (1) A series of increasingly more responsible positions that an employee can assume over time in an organization. (2) A system whereby recruitment from outside is done only for lower levels and appointment at upper levels is done through promotions and career moves from within the organization. Career systems can be closed or open. If the former, recruitment is not possible from outside the organization; if the latter, then positions can be filled by outsiders as well, provided they meet the merit criteria.

Carnegie theory: A decision theory that asserts that organizational structure plays a key role in the decision-making processes of organizations. The theory further states that organizations need to ensure that their decision-making processes are stable (i.e., not subject to great fluctuations), and that there is thus little conscious deliberation involved in routine guided action. The Carnegie theory provided the intellectual basis for an informal organization theory. Stalwarts of administrative science, such as Herbert Simon, Richard Cyert and James March, were an integral part of the development of the Carnegie theory in the 1950s and 1960s. The theory is named thus because it was first developed at the Carnegie Institute of Technology.

Cascade effect: As a result of the introduction of computers in organizations, managers have begun to devolve more authority since routine tasks are increasingly taken up by computers. This has created a cascade effect of authority to lower levels. Alongside the devolution of authority, the introduction of technology has also usually led to a change in the formal structure of organizations. See, e.g., S. Klatzky, "Automation, Size and Locus of Decision-Making: The Cascade Effect," *Journal of Business,* 1970, 43(2), pp. 141–51.

Case manager: An individual who is in charge of the case of a particular client who has interactions with a governmental agency. Thus, for example, departments that deal with providing assistance to at-risk children will have case managers who deal with individual cases.

Cash accounting: The traditional governmental accounting approach that records transactions when cash is received or paid. With cash accounting, there were opportunities for organizations to pay cash in advance of the delivery of the goods and services, or to hold back bills for a new budget year. This can produce a distorted picture of the commitments that an organization might have made. *Cf.* **Accrual accounting**.

Casual employment: As opposed to staff members on fixed-term employment and ongoing employment, those in casual employment are paid on an hourly rate for no definite engagement period. Also, individuals in casual employment can have their contract for services terminated at very short notice, and they are not normally entitled to the benefits (such as medical) that permanent and temporary employees are.

Casualization of workforce: A process whereby organizations make staff members temporary and casual (i.e., remove them from their permanent payroll). The primary reason why an organization would do this is fiscal stress. Given that regular and full-time, fixed-term positions are eligible for various benefits, organizations have an incentive to contract out work. While this might allow them to cut costs, it does have the long-term effect of eroding an organization's inherent capability since expertise will be developed outside the organization. Even knowledge-management policies that require that contractors share the work-specific knowledge will not ensure the full transfer of expertise to the organization. See, e.g., C. Allan, "Casualization and Outsourcing: A Comparative Study," *New Zealand Journal of Industrial Relations,* 2001, 26(3), pp. 253–72.

Casuals: (1) Casual workers that an organization recruits in order to support the completion of tasks that arise unscheduled. (2) Emergency appointees, such as when heads of public organizations hire followers that have provided political support but are not very qualified. See, e.g., L. Carino, "A Subordinate Bureaucracy: The Philippine Civil Service up to 1992," in A. Farazmand (ed.), *Handbook of Bureaucracy,* New York: Marcel Dekker, Inc., 1994, pp. 603–16.

Catalytic initiative: An initiative that is set in motion by a catalyst (in either the public or the private sector). The catalyst can be a group of firms and may be supported by government. This is most often seen in development processes in regions that are underdeveloped, yet have potential for growth.

Catastrophic failure: Any failure of a system that causes the system to stop functioning. While all systems will have safeguards in place to ensure that a catastrophic failure does not occur, there is always a possibility that one will occur. To deal with the possibility of such a failure, many organizations maintain backup redundancies (i.e., duplicative processes and mechanisms that, in the event of failure, can restore the system).

Category I decision: A decision made by organizations under conditions of certainty, i.e., when the information required to make the decision is readily accessible. Category I decisions are relatively straightforward, although there may be situations when interpretations of the evidence may generate different policy recommendations (for example, if a specific threshold may or may not have been reached before a problem is considered to be critical enough to warrant a particular policy response). Category II decisions, on the other hand, are decisions made by organizations under conditions of uncertainty, i.e., when the organizations do not have access to all information required to make an informed decision. Many decisions in the public sector centered on wicked problems tend to be of the Category II type.

Category II decision: *See* **Category I decision**.

Categorical grant: Any grant that is awarded to a subjurisdiction for a specific activity or purpose (such as for an environmental cleanup after an oil spill). There are different variants of categorical grants: (a) a formula-based categorical grant (or formula grant), where resources are allocated in accordance with some *ex ante* (i.e., prespecified) factors; (b) a project categorical grant, where no formulas are applied but instead funds are allocated in accordance with competitive bids for specific applications; and (c) a formula-project categorical grant, where a combination of *(a)* and *(b)* takes place (i.e., there are *ex ante* formulas to be considered, but the authority making the grants still seeks competitive bids). *See also* **Grants**.

Caucus: A closed meeting of a political party to seek consensus on a policy issue (or issues), and to plan specific actions. Examples of such specific actions could be as integral as selecting candidates or leaders or as routine as ratifying a standard administrative decision. Caucus decisions are usually not made public.

Cause-and-effect diagram: Also known as the Ishikawa diagram (after Kauro Ishikawa of Tokyo University, who developed the technique in 1943) and the fishbone diagram (after how the diagram looks), this is a problem-analysis tool that is used to list systematically all the causes that are attributed to a particular problem. The diagram is helpful in identifying the reasons why something goes wrong. The tool allows an analysis of main and subsidiary reasons why a problem occurs and gives policy analysts an opportunity to go to the underlying causes of policy problems. However, it does not provide cues as to solutions or to which causes are most important.

Caveats: *See* **Exclusion clauses**.

Ceiling: The top level of any price or subsidy or, for example, a contract value, which a contractor is thus not to exceed. Ceilings are sometimes the natural products of capped budgets and, by implication, cannot be negotiated higher (although in reality they often are).

Central agency: Also known as a core executive, this term refers to a central-government body that has broad jurisdiction over the affairs of the public service and that tends to play a coordinating—and in several cases, a directive—role in their management. In general, for example, a prime minister's office (or the cabinet office) and the ministry of finance (or the state treasury) will be central agencies. Central agencies are considered to be "the elite of the elite" government agencies (see M. Brevis, R. Rhodes and P. Weller, "Comparative Governance: Prospects and Lessons," *Public Administration,* 2003, 81(1), pp. 191–210). For a comparison of central agencies across several jurisdictions, see, e.g., O. James, "Business Models and the Transfer of Business-like Central Government Agencies," *Governance: An International Journal of Policy and Administration,* 2001, 14(2), pp. 233–52.

Central clearance: The work done by a core central agency (such as a prime minister's office) in assessing the positions of governmental departments in relation to the elected executive's declared program preferences. This is to ensure that there is a whole-of-government perspective taken in effecting disparate programs.

Central government: (1) The national or highest level of government in a country, taken to mean a government with sovereign powers. (2) Comprises all the agencies (departments and other bodies) of general government that are located at the center or at the national level and that extend over the entire country or jurisdiction. The central government has the authority to dictate to lower levels of government in many cases (such as on how certain functions are to be carried out or how funds are to be spent).

Central overrule: The power of the center (i.e., the national government) to veto (overrule) any decision taken by a lower subjurisdictional unit. Decentralization programs normally have some provision of central overrule embedded in them. This provision is vehemently guarded by the center since it argues that only it has the broad vision and awareness of the entire machinery of government needed to see the possible impacts of decisions taken at lower levels.

Central projection: A projection that is made of the most likely outcome of a series of proposed activities in the development of policies. However, not all risks are considered in making such a projection.

Centrality: A term that refers to the locus of power in an organization and the degree to which someone gets close to the locus. The assertion in centrality is that the closer an individual is to power, the greater the power that is exercised by that individual. For obvious reasons, those with proximity to the locus of power will be in a position to acquire information—and to be heard by senior managers—which enables them to leverage that for acquiring greater power. See, e.g., D. Hickson et al., "A Strategic Contingencies' Theory of Interorganizational Power," *Administrative Science Quarterly,* 1971, 16(2), pp. 216–29.

Centralization: As applied in public management, this term refers to the administrative process concerned with concentrating authority in the center. A centralized decision system thus is a decision-making system where most major decisions are assigned to top leaders, and where those in lower tiers may have some input but are not able to substantively change a decision itself. And a centralist government is one that retains power at the center and does not delegate it to lower (e.g., local) government or subjurisdictional units. See, e.g., D. Porter and E. Olsen, "Some Critical Issues in Government Centralization and Decentralization," *Public Administration Review,* 1976, 36(1), pp. 72–84.

Center of excellence: A concept that draws on the unique strengths that individual units in organizations, or organizations themselves, bring to how they attain their mandates. A center of excellence thus has processes that enable it to manage its own operations as pre-determined, and that should enable it to adapt well to changes in its external environment. Public-sector organizations increasingly work with nongovernmental organizations and others to develop centers of excellence in, for example, service delivery to citizens. For an example of how the concept is applied in a public-sector agency, see, e.g., State Services Commission, *Annual Report of the State Services Commission,* Wellington: 2001, p. 50.

Center of government: A central agency (or a collection of them) whose key task in public management and governance is that of brokerage. This, in itself, refers to the setting up of linkages along the following lines: (a) horizontal (i.e., across ministries and policy areas—for example, linking up public-policy issues related to drug abuse across various agencies), (b) vertical (i.e., from policy formulation to execution—for example, linking up agencies involved in making policies on drug abuse and health with those providing remedial measures), (c) temporal (i.e., across a time horizon—for example, linking up agencies that deal with specific issues over time to ensure their continued participation in the policy process), (d) institutional (i.e., combining administrative and political perspectives—for example, linking up issues in the public sector to the preferences of elected bodies), (e) spatial (i.e., between central and regional/local governments—for example, linking up policies between central government and local governments), and (f) any permutations of the above. For a detailed discussion of the brokerage function of the center of government, see, e.g., OECD, *Aspects of Managing the Centre of Government,* Paris: OECD, 1990, p. 9; see also Review of the Centre, *Report of the Advisory Group on the Review of the Centre,* Wellington: State Services Commission, 2001.

Certainty equivalence: The degree of certainty that an individual or organization considers equal to an activity with risky payoffs. The concept is central to the discussion on rational expectations, and organizational environments (or parts thereof) that are characterized by a high degree of certainty equivalence make it possible for organizations to set and employ decision rules analytically and rationally. See, e.g., J. Hershey and P. Schoemaker, "Probability vs. Certainty Equivalence Methods in Utility Measurement: Are They Equivalent?" *Management Science,* 1985, 31(10), pp. 1213–31. *See also* **Uncertainty discounts**.

Certification: A process of verifying that professional standards related to a particular area/activity have been met (for example, in training). Certified training, then, is training that has been verified as being of a certain standard and which leads to the awarding of a certificate of recognition for the trainee.

Chain of command: A concept that refers to how authority flows in an organization (i.e., downward in a hierarchy; conversely, responsibility flows upward). A chain of command is evident in all organizations, even those that are fairly flat in structure (although a long chain of command generally means that those at the top are quite removed from what occurs at the shop-floor level, say). Chain of command makes it possible to ascertain accountability for organizational action. As such, the chain of command has to be unambiguous. For a discussion of this concept, and how it relates to a perception of empowerment among organizational members, see, e.g., W. Randolph, "Navigating the Journey to Empowerment," *Organizational Dynamics,* 1995, 23(4), pp. 19–32. *See also* **Scalar chain of authority**.

Challenge capacity: A term used to refer to the lack of capability of central and regulatory agencies (such as a treasury) to challenge departments to do better. For example, it has been reported that several countries have found that with managerial delegation, they were left with insufficient challenge capacity to force departmental reallocations of resources (see OECD, *Budget Institutions and Reallocation,* Public Governance and Territorial Development Directorate, GOV/PUMA(2003)2, Paris: OECD, 2003).

Change agent: Any individual that helps in the change process in an organization. The change agent need not necessarily be an individual, but if it is, the person is usually from outside the organization. This provides the opportunity to have someone consider organizational change from an impartial perspective. Change agents that come from within organizations are also termed change masters. These are individuals who are capable of anticipating the nature of changes an organization will need make to continue meeting its mandates effectively. For a discussion of the context in which change agents do their work, see, e.g., M. Doyle, "Selecting Managers for Transformational Change," *Human Resource Management Journal,* 2002, 12(1), pp. 3–16.

Change delivery group: A group created in an organization undergoing rapid change to ensure that there is focus on managing that process effectively. The group is supported by any external change agent that the organization may have recruited. The group is normally tasked with ensuring that the organization's major change programs (since usually there will be more than one aspect of change taking place) are mutually coherent and that they are in alignment with the organization's objective. The group is also charged with ensuring that the change effort is concentrated on those areas of organizational activity that have the highest priority. For an application, see, e.g., National Audit Office, *Ministry of Defense: Through-Life Management,* Report by the Comptroller and Auditor General, HC 698 Session 2002–2003, London: The Stationery Office, 2003, p. 7.

Change management: The system and process of anticipating and dealing with internal and external change pressures that organizations undergo. Because change is usually disruptive, the process needs to be handled with finesse and with a deep understanding of how staff members (including managers) can see the value in changing. Organizations normally bring in outsiders to manage this process.

Change masters: *See* **Change agent.**

Charismatic leadership: Leadership that is based on a leader's personality rather than upon the power that is inherent in a formal position. Research has tended to show that charismatic leadership comprises four dimensions: (a) the energy and determination that the leader exhibits; (b) the vision that the leader has, and is able to convey to organizational members; (c) the challenge and encouragement that the leader gives to members; and (d) the degree of risk-taking behavior that the leader demonstrates. Charismatic leadership, however, is not necessarily considered to be a significant variable in contributing to overall organizational performance. See, e.g., M. Javidan and D. Waldman, "Exploring Charismatic Leadership in the Public Sector: Measurement and Consequences," *Public Administration Review,* 2003, 63(2), pp. 229–42.

Charter: A document that specifies the fundamental governing principles of an organization and broadly specifies how it functions. In some jurisdictions, an organization's charter is used as an *ex ante* document toward determining accountability, i.e., to assess what the organization is expected to accomplish relative to what is planned, and to be thus accountable for any such gaps.

Charter agencies: Agencies that are created as experiments for government management, and if they prove effective, could be incorporated into the public sector. Allowing organizations to serve as charter agencies provides an opportunity for governments to closely assess the extent to which agency functions—that have to be resourced and monitored in much the same way that regular government agencies are—can be made core government ones.

Checklist mentality: A mindset of bureaucrats in which they are almost solely focused on fulfilling explicit rules and regulations, but little else (such as looking at the broader collective interest in the public service). Since everything that is required of agencies cannot be realistically specified *ex ante*, this means that a checklist mentality serves to stifle innovative thinking. See, e.g., S. Goldfinch, "Evaluating Public Sector Reform in New Zealand: Have the Benefits been Oversold?" *Asian Journal of Public Administration,* 1998, 20(2), pp. 203–32.

Checks and balances, principle of: Asserts that in order to ensure that one government body (or jurisdiction) does not acquire absolute power, it is necessary to require that separate governing bodies (or jurisdictions) have equal power. Provisions are then made for restricting power in any one source. In the United States, for example, while the president, as the chief executive officer, has the authority to nominate heads of government departments, their nominations must be approved by the Senate.

Cherry picking: Refers to picking up the best ideas or options from among a series. This is not always considered helpful, however, as it is possible for policy makers, for example, to discard some valuable aspects of prospective policies under the assumption that they are not relevant to their situation. See, e.g., H. de Bruijn, "Performance Measurement in the Public Sector: Strategies to Cope with the Risks of Performance Measurement," *International Journal of Public Sector Management,* 2002, 15(6/7), pp. 578–94.

Chief executive: The highest-level officer of an organization whose responsibility it is to ensure that legislative decisions related to the mandate of the organization are carried out. The chief executive is then held accountable for the results of such agency action. In some jurisdictions (New Zealand, Australia, the UK), that accountability is formalized in a chief executive performance agreement, which is negotiated annually between the chief executive of each government agency and the relevant minister. The agreement, among other things, records any requirements of the chief executive, and serves as the basis for the chief executive's performance review. The chief executive performance review is a process by which the performance of the chief executive of a government agency is evaluated. The process draws on: (a) reviews of the agency's performance related to its mandate, and (b) feedback from the relevant minister, core central agencies, and others (such as external referees).

Chilling effect: Any action or process (such as employment practices) that discourages an individual from exercising his/her right to employment. For example, if the media reports that an organization has a culture of not being friendly to women employees, this may result in a chilling effect on potential female candidates.

Chinese wall: A preventative procedure that organizations follow to ensure that positions or personnel are not compromised as regards areas of potential conflicts of interest. For example, a state treasury may have a policy analyst in a team working on electricity regulation. The final proposal, because it will have financial implications, will revert to the treasury for review. In order that its position not be compromised by one of its staff members being in the policy-formulation team, the organization will put a figurative Chinese wall (e.g., barriers against communication or information flow) around the individual such that there is little scope for that individual to influence in any way the final outcome of the treasury review. For an illustration of how the term is used, see, e.g., House of Commons, Committee of Public Accounts—Minutes of Evidence on "Improving Service Delivery: The Forensic Science Service (HC 523)," Questions 23–24, London: House of Commons, Monday, September 15, 2003.

Choice opportunity: Included in the notion of the garbage-can model of decision making is that of choice opportunity, which is a convergence point for, among others, policy makers with potential solutions looking for problems to solve. This implies a proactive approach to management, and necessitates that others in the organization/system are eager to engage in problem solving. See, e.g., A. Bedeian, *Organizations: Theory and Analysis: Text and Cases,* 2nd edition, New York: The Dryden Press, 1984, p. 119. *See also* **Garbage-can model**.

Choice, theory of: Asserts that any analysis of choice that policy makers employ must address not only the properties of the actor(s) making the choice but also the characteristics of the environment within which the choice is being made. The theory of choice is thus holistic in nature, and, applied in the public-service context, it implies that a whole-of-government approach is taken to policy making. For an original discussion of this concept, see H. Simon, *Models of Man,* New York: John Wiley and Sons, 1957, p. 242.

Citizen administrator: An individual upon whom the responsibilities of being a public-sector administrator are integrated with the obligations of being a private citizen. Framed another way, the concept of a citizen administrator is that the perspective that the administrator takes must be that of the citizen. See, e.g., T. Cooper, *An Ethics of Citizenship for Public Administration,* Englewood Cliffs, NJ: Prentice Hall, 1991, p. 134.

Citizen as customer: A conception of service delivery wherein members of the public who access government services are treated as customers (i.e., as someone purchasing the service), which is designed to make public organizations more susceptible to customer feedback regarding service levels and effectiveness. On the other hand, this implies that, as customers, citizens are excluded from being part of the (public) policy debates regarding the quality and extent of service provision; such decisions are made by politicians and bureaucrats. The important point to note here is that, perceived as customers, citizens might lose certain input into the design, production, and delivery of services. For a discussion of this concept, see, for example, N. Ryan, "Reconstructing Citizens as Consumers:

Implications for New Modes of Governance," *Australian Journal of Public Administration,* 2001, 60(3), pp. 104–09; and P. Larson, "Public and Private Values at Odds: Can Private Sector Values Be Transplanted into Public Sector Institutions?" *Public Administration and Development,* 1997, 17(1), pp. 131–39.

Citizen orientation: The focus of government agencies in serving citizens to the best of their abilities. This prime focus on serving citizens has always been a part of public administration but has been much more in the limelight since the "new public management" reforms of the 1980s and 1990s. For a general review of the concept, see, e.g., E. Vigoda, "From Responsiveness to Collaboration: Governance, Citizens, and the Next Generation of Public Administration," *Public Administration Review,* 2002, 62(5), pp. 527–40.

Citizen report card: A tool used to collect feedback from users on the quality of the services they receive, to rank the service providers on various problems faced (such as excess billing or poor service standards), and to publicize the results in the local media to bring public attention to bear on the quality of service delivery. It is argued that the feedback that is thus provided by the service users is authentic, and that while it does not necessarily focus on the technicalities of the service provision, it does enable the service provider to hear from users on the quality, efficiency, and adequacy of particular services. This provides adequate input for the providers to address any deficiencies that may exist in service delivery. For an oft-cited review of the citizen report card work, see S. Paul, *A Report Card on Three Indian Cities*, Bangalore, India: Public Affairs Centre, 1995.

Citizen review boards: Boards which have members from among the general citizenry, and which review organizations that provide social services for which input from citizens is critical. Such boards are critical to canvassing citizen input, although there are transaction costs in relying on review boards, including time lags, and occasionally, superficial analysis of the issues.

Citizen shops: A distribution method whereby public services are concentrated in one building so as to optimize delivery time. Such "one-stop shops" are now increasingly common in many advanced jurisdictions. For a case study of citizen shops, see, e.g., J. Araujo, "Improving Public Service Delivery: The Crossroads Between NPM and Traditional Bureaucracy," *Public Administration,* 2001, 79(4), pp. 915–32. *See also* **One-stop shop.**

Citizen-participation theory of policy making: The theory alludes to the level of involvement of citizens in the policy-making process and in governance, and asserts that public policy is developed through direct citizen participation in the process. The noted author on community involvement Shelly Arnstein talks of eight levels of citizen participation in policy making, structured in a ladder form with each rung representing a higher gradation of citizens' power in determining the end product: manipulation, therapy, informing, consultation, placation, partnership, delegated power, and citizen control (see S. Arnstein, "A Ladder of Citizen Participation," *Journal of the American Institute of Planners,* 1969, 35(4), pp. 216–24). In reality, poor voter turnout and general apathy tend to counter this notion of active citizen participation. For a case-study application of citizen participation, see, e.g., D. Moynihan, "Normative and Instrumental Perspectives on Public Participation: Citizen Summits in Washington, DC," *American Review of Public Administration,* 2003, 33(2), pp. 164–88.

Citizen's charter: A management innovation brought about in the United Kingdom in the early 1990s whose aim is to raise the standard of public services and to make public agencies more responsive to the needs of the customers they serve. The principle behind the citizen's charter is that of customer empowerment, and that customers have the right to complain if they perceive they have received poor service. Some relevant concepts include information and openness, consultation, courtesy, and value for money. Similar initiatives have been taken in other jurisdictions, such as the "Public Services User's Charter" in Belgium, the "Public Service Charter" in France, and the "Public Service Quality Charter" in Portugal. For a discussion of the basis and impact of citizen's charter, see, e.g., J. Wilson, "Citizen Major? The Rationale and Impact of the Citizen's Charter," *Public Policy and Administration,* 1996, 11(1), pp. 45–62.

Citizens jury: Refers to a mechanism by which policy makers can gauge what average citizens think about a particular issue toward collecting multiple aspects and viewpoints. In a citizens jury, individuals (usually about 18) are randomly selected to consider a particular issue and, after hearing from expert witnesses on all sides, recommend to policy makers how they see the issue being addressed such that all the inputs are given full consideration. The jury is characterized by random selection, representativeness (i.e., jury members are carefully selected to be representative of the public at large), informed (through witness hearings), impartial, and deliberative.

For a review of the concept, see, e.g., G. Smith and C. Wales, "The Theory and Practice of Citizens' Juries," *Policy and Politics,* 1999, 27(3), pp. 295–308.

City management: As jurisdictions around the world begin to decentralize authority, there is an increasing focus on the management of cities (or urban areas) and how public affairs are conducted at the local level. City management normally implies a focus on community-neighborhood relations, citizen-involvement programs, and intergovernmental relations particularly as they relate to financial flows to cities. Land use and zoning, and economic-development strategies also play a large role in city management. The literature shows that there are three models of city management: (a) the mayor-council model (where both parties are elected for a fixed term and where both have equal powers, with the former serving as the executive and the latter as a legislature), (b) the commission model (where the city has several commissions each responsible for a specific function, such as housing, economic development, planning, etc.), and (c) the council-manager model (where the council is elected and the day-to-day affairs are run by a manager that is recruited specifically for implementing council policies). Of these three, the council-manager model is considered to be the most popular. For a good discussion of this, see, e.g., C. Wheeland, "City Management in the 1990s: Responsibilities, Roles, and Practices," *Administration & Society*, 2000, 32(3), pp. 25–281.

Civic culture: The manner in which individuals relate to their polity. Political scientists Gabriel Almond and Sidney Verba distinguish among three types of civic culture: (a) parochial (i.e., largely apolitical), (b) subject (i.e., merely reacting to government policies), and (c) participant (i.e., a more active awareness of government policies). See G. Almond and S. Verba, *The Civic Culture: Political Attitudes and Democracy in Five Nations,* Boston: Little, Brown, 1965. For a further look at the link between civic culture and democracy, see, e.g., E. Muller and M. Seligson, "Civic Culture and Democracy: The Question of Causal Relationship," *American Political Science Review,* 1994, 88(3), pp. 635–52.

Civil service: (1) All civil-employment positions under the jurisdictions of government organizations in all geographic levels (this excludes thus, for example, military-service personnel). (2) The term is also used interchangeably with "public service" in the general literature. One component of the public service is the classified civil service, into which individuals enter by objective testing. The classified civil service is generally free from political pressure, and offers good opportunities for career advancement. For a review of civil-service reforms and governance, see, e.g., M. Dia, *A Governance Approach to Civil Service Reform in Sub-Saharan Africa,* World Bank Technical Paper No. 225, Washington, DC: World Bank, 1993.

Civil service, politicization of: A situation where there is political control over the civil service and bureaucratic apparatus. A move toward depoliticization would see the civil service: (a) develop more neutral competence, and (b) be subject to a system whereby elected representatives would not be able to make appointments at will. For a general analysis of the politicization of the civil service in Africa, see, e.g., M. Balogun, "The Democratization and Development Agenda and the African Civil Service: Issues Resolved or Matters Arising?" *International Review of Administrative Sciences*, 2002, 68(4), pp. 533–56. A reverse process of sorts is evident in civilianizing government and politics. This is a process of, and efforts at, distancing the civil service from military influence (as evident, for example, in Korea). See, e.g., B. Kim, "Public Bureaucracy in Korea," in A. Farazmand (ed.), *Handbook of Bureaucracy,* New York: Marcel Dekker, Inc., 1994, pp. 591–602.

Civil society: Refers to organizations in the nongovernment sector (such as community groups, voluntary associations, and others not attached in any way to government). With the general diminution of the role of government in public life, civil society has stepped in to fill the gap. With respect to helping economic welfare and development in developing countries, multilateral and bilateral donor agencies have now realized that they need to work with civil society in order to provide services to those that miss out on official government programs. Some donor agencies will only provide assistance through civil-society organizations rather than channel the assistance through governmental ministries and departments. For a good review of the role of civil society in a country, see, e.g., R. Belloni, *Building Civil Society in Bosnia-Herzegovina,* Working Paper No. 2, Denver, CO: University of Denver Press, 2000.

Clan: A form of organization that Professor William Ouchi says contrasts with the bureaucracy and with markets in some key respects related to socialization, incentive structure, control, etc. A clan form of organization emerges when organizations socialize individuals but where rewards are given and control is exercised through non-performance-related criteria, such as the number of dependants or seniority of the employee. Tradition plays a big role in the designation of a clan form of organization. See

W. Ouchi, "Markets, Bureaucracies, and Clans," *Administrative Science Quarterly,* 1980, 25(1), pp. 129–41.

Clarifiers (of policy thinking): Individuals who try to clarify the various nuances of public policies so that the public and others can be better informed of what the policies contain. Such clarifiers could be individuals who have credibility in the eyes of the general public or among organizations (such as independent consumer groups). See, e.g., L. Koenig, *An Introduction to Public Policy,* Englewood Cliffs, NJ: Prentice Hall, 1986, pp. 345–46.

Class specification: The process of specifying the duties and responsibilities of particular positions in an employment class, which includes, among others, providing functional descriptions of and defining the minimum KSAs (knowledge, skills, and abilities) needed for the positions. To reclassify is to reassign a position to a different class if the duties and responsibilities of the position undergo changes.

Classification method (of job evaluation): A method of evaluating jobs where a committee first sets up a series of grades along with a functional description of each one, and then assigns a pay-scale range (i.e., minimum to maximum) to them. Such a scale results from matching each job description with a grade description. *See also* **Job evaluation**.

Classified service: *See* **Civil service**.

Clawback: Refers to the act of recouping funds related to an investment, while continuing to seek a return on the investment. For example, the government may decide to spend a certain portion of resources on training and development of potential future leaders of the public service, but it may also decide at the same time to get some of the investment back from departmental budgets as a form of clawback.

"Clear the decks" review procedures: Review procedures that are comprehensive in nature and that look at all possible issues when conducting a review. An output price review and a value for money review, for example, are subject to such review procedures. See, e.g., S. Newberry, "Intended or Unintended Consequences? Resource Erosion in New Zealand's Government Departments," *Financial Accountability and Management,* 2002, 18(4), pp. 309–30.

Clearance points: Refer to the separate, individual locus of decisions that a program must go through before it is considered ready to be implemented. For multisectoral and comprehensive programs, there could be several clearance points depending upon who needs to be mandated and whether any legislative mandates and reviews need to be undertaken. See, e.g., C. Levine, B. Peters, and F. Thompson, *Public Administration: Challenges, Choices, Consequences,* Glenview, IL: Scott, Foresman and Co., 1990, pp. 95–96.

Clearance redundancy: *See* **Redundancy**.

Clearinghouse: (1) An entity that gathers all relevant information and then distributes it to others. For example, the cabinet office in a parliamentary system of government will be the clearinghouse for all information on individual policies. While the term usually denotes work that is merely administrative in nature, in the case of the cabinet office, it is clearly the key to the machinery of government by virtue of its centrality in the policy process. (2) Relates to an organization such that a network can present a single face to consumers while dividing proceeds among distinct producers. The role of the clearinghouse is then to divide receipts among the producers according to some rule.

Clients' advocates: One of three roles of policy analysts in their work wherein they place primary emphasis on their responsibility to the clients that seek the policy (such as elected policy makers). *See also* **Issue advocates; Objective technicians**.

Client-centered organization: An organization that is driven primarily by providing effective services to clients. The performance measure is thus client satisfaction feedback. It is possible, though, that the focus on the core business of such an organization could be diluted (for example, while local health providers may have the delivery of health services as the core business, it is possible that this is lost in the more high-profile—although not necessarily more central—focus on pay and employment equity).

Climber: A term used by the renowned scholar Anthony Downs to denote a type of bureaucrat who is primarily motivated by moving up the organizational hierarchy. This implies, then, that the individual is quite willing to do anything that will enable that climb. See A. Downs, *Inside Bureaucracy,* Boston: Little, Brown, 1967, p. 88.

Cloak of neutrality: Refers to a situation wherein judges are to be neutral in passing judgments on the administrative cases that they hear. However, it has been argued that with the increasing activism of the courts, this cloak of neutrality has been eroded. See, e.g., D. Rosenbloom, *Public Administration and Law,* New York: Marcel Dekker, 1983, p. 223.

e.g., Ministry of Social Development, *He Waka Kotuia: Joining Together on a Shared Journey,* Report of the Community-Government Relationship Steering Group, Wellington: Ministry of Social Development, 2002, p. 65.

Co-equality: A term used to denote judicial courts' increasing activism in the area of administrative action in order to secure, some allege, an equal status with nonjudicial branches of government (i.e., the executive and legislature). Bureaucracies are usually subject to executive and legislative, rather than judicial, oversight. See, e.g., D. Rosenbloom, *Public Administration and Law,* New York: Marcel Dekker, 1983, p. 208.

Coercive centralism: A situation where the center of government exercises considerable power and control over other government departments and subjurisdictional entities, such as local government. Even though the focus and interest on the principle of subsidiarity has not waned, central governments around the world continue to exert a great deal of power over regional and local entities. *See also* **Subsidiarity**.

Coercive deficiencies: A situation that occurs when agencies raise their budget levels before the end of a financial year, and then—by virtue of the fact that they will have to suspend their services if there is no funding—they "coerce" the legislature to make up the deficiencies.

Coercive isomorphism: A step in the convergence process wherein organization and systems in one setting are coerced or forced to incorporate particular forms, policies, and attributes that are in evidence elsewhere. Thus, when the International Monetary Fund, for example, insists on certain types of institutional structures in the finance sector in a jurisdiction, coercive isomorphism can be said to be evident. See, e.g., C. Pollitt, "Convergence: The Useful Myth?" *Public Administration,* 2001, 79(4), pp. 933–47. *See also* **Convergence**.

Coercive power: The ability to coerce others to behave in a certain manner or to do certain things, often under force of threat. For example, organizations that control the funding mechanisms in the public sector can be said to have coercive power over those that seek public funding. In this case, the threat would be the cessation of future funding streams. *See also* **Power**.

Cognitive blind spots: *See* **Belief preservation, Confirmation bias**.

Cognitive consistency: Refers to the identical evaluations of a given situation by two or more entities that are interacting with each other. For example, in organizational networks, it is presumed that the organizations will be consistent in their views of a given problem so that work toward joint outcomes can proceed smoothly. This is not always possible since each entity brings to the relationship its own frame of reference shaped by the context to which it is subject. For a general discussion, see, e.g., P. Monge and E. Eisenberg, "Emergent Communication Networks," in F. Jablin, et al (eds.), *Handbook of Organizational Communication: An Interdisciplinary Perspective,* Newbury Park, CA: Sage, 1987, pp. 304–42.

Cognitive consonance: The state where an individual perceives little inconsistency between what exists and what his/her value systems are. On the other hand, cognitive dissonance refers to the tension that results when individuals are faced with two contradictory situations (one related to their perception of what exists, and the other to the actual situation), and they seek to reduce the tension. People are, for obvious reasons, motivated to reduce high levels of cognitive dissonance. See L. Festinger, *A Theory of Cognitive Dissonance,* Stanford, CA: Stanford University Press, 1962.

Cognitive dissonance: *See* **Cognitive consonance**.

Cognitive resource theory: Stipulates that those leaders who are competent in what they do are so because they are better able to anticipate problems and to find innovative ways of addressing them. The contingency aspect of this theory alludes to the ability of leaders to come up with appropriate solutions depending upon the variance in the nature of the problems.

Cognitive skills: The skills of employees that are related to mental abilities and knowledge. Cognitive skills are considered a core competency and feature highly in any competency lists in organizations since all employees are expected to be knowledgeable of what is required toward effective work conduct.

Co-governance: A concept that is related to network management and how various organizations and individuals interact with each other in order to address particular problems. In co-governance, for example, managers attempt to facilitate cooperation, brokerage, and mediation among others so that problems can be jointly targeted. The concept sits behind much of the recent focus in public management on the collaborative approach to government management and whole-of-government action. For a review of the concept in the context of policy networks in the public sector, see, e.g., E. Klijn, J. Koppenjan, and K. Termeer, "Managing Networks in the Public Sector: A Theoretical Study of Management Strategies in Policy Networks," *Public Administration,* 1995, 73(3), pp. 437–54. *See also* **Culture governance**.

Coherence theory: Asserts that in considering any policy issue or problem, there is a need to incorporate a multiplicity of evidence and explanations so as to better understand how disparate components might be reconciled. Coherence theory thus directs policy makers to look at issues in a holistic manner and to discern connections among the various components.

Collaboration network: A network in which organizations collaborate with other organizations to share external knowledge necessary for effectiveness. Collaboration networks thus offer win-win situations for the organizations concerned. See, e.g., W. Powell, K. Koput, and L. Smith-Doerr, "Interorganizational Collaboration and the Locus of Innovation: Networks of Learning in Biotechnology," *Administrative Science Quarterly,* 1996, 41(1), pp. 116–45.

Collaborative federalism: A system of governance wherein the federal government works together with lower governments (such as state, provincial, or local) to address problems of mutual interest. Collaborative federalism requires that all levels of government develop a trusting relationship with each other.

Collaborative leadership: Leadership wherein those being led are given opportunities to participate in decision-making processes. This participatory style of leadership is particularly useful when team members bring specialized expertise to a group, such that their input in decisions is of value to the whole group. The collaborative leader is expected to be aware and encouraging of this.

Collapsed state: Also known as a failed state, this is a jurisdiction over which a sovereign government has no effective control and in which there is very little or no adherence to the sovereign rule of law. Examples of a collapsed state include Papua New Guinea, Liberia, and Somalia. For a robust review of the issues surrounding failed states, see, e.g., D. Brinkerhoff and J. Brinkerhoff, "Governance Reforms and Failed States: Challenges and Implications," *International Review of Administrative Sciences,* 2002, 68(4), pp. 511–31.

Collective agreement: A written agreement between an employer (represented by management) and workers (represented by unions) that contains the terms and conditions of employment, including wage rates, working conditions, fringe benefits, and a stipulation of how outstanding issues are to be resolved between the parties. Theoretically, collective agreements can be for any period of time, although in practice they rarely are long term since working conditions change rapidly.

Collective bargaining: The process by which various conditions of employment (including wage rates, working conditions, etc.) are negotiated between unions (representing employees) and management (representing the employer). Collective bargaining can be of an integrative or of a pressure-bargaining type. In the latter, there is much more confrontation, and each party comes to the table with different motivations. In the former, there is much more participation, and bargaining starts from the assumption that both parties have common stakes in the organization. Collective bargaining generally has four steps: (a) a determination of who is to do the bargaining, (b) a tabling of the demands of the parties; (c) a negotiation of the demands, including, if necessary, going through an arbitration process; and (d) the administration of the resultant agreement by a set period. For an analysis of the features of collective bargaining in the public sector in New Zealand, see, e.g., Martin, Jenkins & Associates, *Collective Bargaining in the State Sector: Experiences from the Past, Lessons for the Future,* Wellington: Martin, Jenkins & Associates, 2003, pp. 14–19.

Collective consumption service: A service provided by government to all members of a community (such as rural credit facilities for an aquaculture business in a fishing community) or to all members of a particular section of a community.

Collective decision making: Decision-making processes in an organization where all staff members are encouraged to participate, and where consensus is often used to arrive at decisions. While the collective nature of this decision-making process is desirable in its own right, it poses some challenges: it can be a lengthy affair since everyone needs to be engaged, and it can "dumb down" a proposal via the lowest-common-denominator effect.

Collective institutional memory: Refers to the knowledge that resides in any organization and that is manifest in, among others, the organization's archival systems, document management systems, formal and informal networks, and linkages with external agencies such as think tanks, contractors, etc. It is an organization's collective institutional memory that allows staff members to seek solutions to new and to ongoing problems that the organization faces. See, e.g., B. Easton, *The Commercialization of New Zealand,* Auckland: Auckland University Press, 1997, p. 86.

Collective responsibility: The responsibility borne by everyone who participates in a decision to abide by that decision and be responsible for its consequences. In the Westminster system of government, for example, collective responsibility is a doctrine that applies to the cabinet, which is collectively responsible to parliament for its decisions.

Collective system: *See* **Collective bargaining**.

Co-location: A situation when two or more government agencies agree to be located in one site so that they can provide a one-stop venue to citizens to ensure cost effectiveness of service delivery. Co-location is an important part of the push toward joined-up government, which seeks to ensure that citizens are better and more readily served, often via linked or extended interaction points. See, e.g., E. Bardach, *Getting Agencies to Work Together: The Practice and Theory of Managerial Craftsmanship,* Washington, DC: Brookings Institution Press, 1998, p. 138.

Co-management phenomenon: (1) As used in the political context, this is a tendency of elected officials in both the executive and legislative branches to work together to jointly address vexing issues. One particular example of the co-management phenomenon is evident in the United States, where the 1978 Civil Service Reform Act provided the context in which the president and the Congress modified the federal bureaucracy (the president was thus authorized to appoint senior members, the Congress to impose several controls on the bureaucracy). For a good review of the concept, see J. Aberbach, "Sharing Isn't Easy: When Separate Institutions Clash," *Governance: An International Journal of Policy and Administration,* 1997, 11(2), pp. 137–52. (2) As used in a development context, this describes a partnership between the government and different stakeholders (including communities) where resources are employed for development purposes in such a way that the stakeholders have a say over specific resource-use policies. In this regard, co-management is also referred to as collaborative management. See, e.g., C. Sneddon, "Water Conflicts and River Basins: The Contradictions of Comanagement and Scale in Northeast Thailand," *Society and Natural Resources,* 2002, 15(8), pp. 725–42.

Combinatorial explosion: A phenomenon of interpersonal communication and interaction between organizations in networks where an increase in membership yields a greater than commensurate increase in the number of communication channels in a group. For example, when there are only three entities in a network, the number of possible communication channels is three, but if the number of network members is doubled to six, the resultant number of communication channels increases five times, to fifteen.

Command bureaucracy: A form of central control exercised by bureaucracies over those that are more directly involved in providing services to the public. A command and control state system is a system of governance where control over how the economy is run and managed, and how local organizations go about managing their economies, comes from the center (i.e., a power base that is located at the center of government).

Commercial-market strategy: As used in the public-management context, this concept refers to the approach that governments take whereby they subsidize the delivery of certain goods and services to the targeted population by paying the associated bills that clients incur as they access the service from private-sector providers.

Commitment: With regard to employees, three types of commitment are generally evident: (a) affective commitment (i.e., the employee is emotionally attached to the organization and identifies with it), (b) continuance commitment (i.e., the employee is aware of costs associated with leaving an organization—a high continuance commitment is associated with employees believing that staying outweighs the consequences of leaving), and (c) normative commitment (i.e., the sense of obligation the employee has to remain in the organization). See, e.g., J. Meyer and N. Allen, "A Three-Component Conceptualization of Organizational Commitment," *Human Resource Management Review,* 1991, 1(1), pp. 61–89.

Commitment costs: *See* **Committed costs**.

Commitment failure: Refers to a situation wherein democratic governments do not commit to fixed, long-term policies because the desires of voters change and governments have an incentive to be responsive to them. For an economic analysis of the concept, see, e.g., N. Marceau and M. Smart, "Corporate Lobbying and Commitment Failure in Capital Taxation," *American Economic Review,* 2003, 93(1), pp. 241–51.

Commitment problem: A problem related to policy commitment given the impossibility of sovereign policy makers to bind the hands of future governments, which have the power to make, amend, and repeal laws and regulations. This problem can be minimized by legislation that will lead to high political costs associated with amending certain legislation. The commitment problem can also be minimized by delegating responsibility to independent autonomous institutions. See, e.g., K. Yesilkagit, "The

Design of Public Agencies: Overcoming Agency Costs and Commitment Problems," *Public Administration and Development,* 2004, 24(2), pp. 119–28.

Committed costs: Also known as commitment costs, these are funds that governments set aside (or commit) toward meeting costs related to maintaining a policy and fulfilling particular objectives (such as environmental protection) that are long term in nature.

Common-practice criterion: A criterion in ascertaining standards of behavior of organizations where they perceive that failing to adhere to certain practices that may be common in society will be disadvantageous for them. For example, an organization may decide that since others are not adhering fully to the guidelines in, say, a country's resource management act, it too will do the same since it perceives this to be the common practice; otherwise, compliance may result in a position of disadvantage. *See also* **Legality criterion**.

Commons triple: The notion that transactions incorporate three key aspects—order, conflict, and mutuality. Order (i.e., rules of the game) is imposed so that conflict (i.e., how to allocate resources among competing ends) is resolved in order that there may be mutual gain between parties that voluntarily engage with each other. The original work on this concept comes from political economist John Commons (see his "The Problem of Correlating Law, Economics and Ethics," *Wisconsin Law Review,* 1932, 8, pp. 3–26). The economist Oliver Williamson has taken the concept much further in his transaction-costs approach to interactions among policy actors (see his "Public and Private Bureaus: A Transaction Cost Perspective," *Journal of Law, Economics and Organization,* 1999, 15(1), pp. 306–42). *See also* **Transaction-cost approach**.

Communal risk pooling: Refers to the process of aggregating the uncertainty experienced by individuals into a calculable risk for communities and large groups. Thus, for example, a micro-credit program may not be able to specify the probabilities that one particular individual will default on a loan, but taken along with the other members of the community, program administrators may, with greater certainty, predict the rate of loan default in the community as a whole. This makes risk pooling possible, and the probabilities of default generated from the community as a whole is then generally applied on individuals (unless, of course, there is parallel evidence that clearly points to a lower/higher degree of default for a particular individual). For usage of the term, see, e.g., A. Cheung,

"Health Policy Reform," in L. Wong and N. Flynn (eds.), *The Market in Chinese Social Policy,* Hampshire, UK: Palgrave, 2001, pp. 63–87.

Communication channels: The means through which information and feedback flows in an organization or in a policy system. Communication channels can be formal (i.e., institutionalized, such as in public submissions, forums, etc.) or informal (such as in personal connections with policy makers). Communication channels make it possible for citizens to voice opinions on policy issues.

Communication climate: The atmosphere in organizations that permits or hinders the flow of ideas and information. A communication climate can be open (which is solution-oriented, inclusive, and ideas-oriented) or closed (i.e., judgmental, controlling, and stifles new ideas).

Communication nets: A term used to denote the range of structural networks that policy makers have in order to affect a policy. Differently structured nets have different accessibility for participation. See L. Koenig, *An Introduction to Public Policy,* Englewood Cliffs, NJ: Prentice Hall, 1986, p. 47.

Communication networks: Linkages among individuals in organizations, and among organizations in the jurisdiction and abroad, that enable these parties to communicate with each other by sending and receiving information. The networks are formal (as in through computing facilities) and informal (as in through loose associations of individuals from various organizations that are regularly in touch with each other and sharing information). These linkages can be seen along three dimensions: (a) institutional (i.e., when information is exchanged routinely), (b) representative (i.e., when the representative of one organization routinely meets that of another in a formal setting, such as on a cross-agency project), and (c) personal (i.e., when individuals different settings meet informally). For a good discussion of this concept, see, e.g., P. Monge and E. Eisenberg, "Emergent Communication Networks," in F. Jablin, et al (eds.), *Handbook of Organizational Communication: An Interdisciplinary Perspective,* Newbury Park, CA: Sage, 1987, pp. 304–42.

Communication overload: *See* **Information overload**.

Communities of practice: Groups of practitioners who are working on the same theme/sector/issue, but not on the same project, and who are sharing information regularly through formal and informal means. The concept has attained a fair degree of prominence in the literature on organizational learning. See, e.g., J. Swan, H. Scarbrough, and M. Robertson, "The Construction of 'Community of Practice' in the Management of Innovation," *Management Learning,* 2002, 33(4), pp. 477–96.

Community action: Denotes the collective effort of community groups to make an impact on a particular policy at any phase of the policy development and implementation stages. While the concept of community has been prominent in social-policy analysis for some time now, as a policy instrument it is seen as the weakest form. For a review of the term in the public-policy context, see, e.g., D. Rochefort, M. Rosenberg, and D. White, "Community as a Policy Instrument," *Policy Studies Journal,* 1998, 26(3), pp. 548–68.

Community competence: The ability of communities collectively to: (a) collaborate effectively in problem identification, (b) achieve a consensus agreement on goals, (c) work jointly toward those goals, and (d) develop effective conflict-resolution mechanisms. The manner in which issues are collectively confronted by a community determines its level of competence. For a cogent discussion, see, e.g., J. Jurie, "Building Capacity: Organizational Competence and Critical Theory," *Journal of Organizational Change Management,* 2000, 13(3), pp. 264–74.

Community control: A method of citizen participation in which local elected representatives control service delivery, such as education and police protection. That control could be manifest in both administrative and financial domains. See, e.g., N. Fainstein and S. Fainstein, "The Future of Community Control," *American Political Science Review,* 1976, 70 (September), pp. 905–23.

Community development: The process of a community working toward achieving a level of potential that it may have established for itself. There may or may not be external assistance in this exercise, although often there is. Some of the principles that lie at the core of community development are, inter alia, building relationships, involving as many community members as possible, starting small, involving local leadership, seeking to bring in marginalized populations, and employing local solutions to the extent possible. Community development has for a long time been a focus of bilateral and multilateral donors, such as USAID and the United Nations, in their assistance to less-developed jurisdictions. For a practical look at how community development can be approached, see, e.g., *Strategic Framework for Community Development,* Sheffield, UK: Standing Conference for Community Development, 2001, pp. 4–10.

Community governance: Refers to the system of how communities are governed and which institutions play a role in uplifting the status of those in the communities. The term is used to capture the concept of a shift in the purpose and rationale of local governments, and sets a wider role for them.

Community-service obligations: Obligations that a firm or organization has to provide goods and services to communities at reasonable costs. A community-service obligation is in application when, for example, a private firm wins a bid for delivering a particular service (such as long-distance communications) in a jurisdiction but then cannot deny services to some jurisdictional areas on the basis that their servicing it is not profitable.

Comparability principle: *See* **Equal pay for equal work**.

Comparable worth: A concept that refers to the payment of wages to different groups of workers based on the principle that jobs that are deemed to involve roughly the same levels of importance, knowledge, etc., must be compensated equally. For a case-study discussion of the concept, see, e.g., P. Cihon, "Comparable Worth: The Quebec Experience," *Journal of Collective Negotiations in the Public Sector,* 1988, 17(3), pp. 249–55. *See also* **Equal pay for equal work**.

Comparative institutionalism: Refers to a reliance on the varied contexts that decision makers face to explain their action. Different decision makers face different contexts and this affects their frames of reference differently. Their frames of reference will also be shaped by the impact of past experiences, among other things. Comparative institutionalism thus veers away from rational-choice theory in marked ways. For a review of the concept in how development policy making is formulated, see, e.g., M. Grindle, "In Quest of the Political: The Political Economy of Development Policy-Making," in G. Meier and J. Stiglitz, *Frontiers in Development Economics: The Future in Perspective,* New York: Oxford University Press, 2001, pp. 345–80. For a generic discussion, see, e.g., A. Touraine, "An Introduction to the Study of Social Movement," *Social Research,* 1985, 52(4), pp. 749–87.

Comparative risk assessment: Refers to the integration of various sources of information (such as from the public domain, the scientific community, etc.) to ascertain the relative risks of known and hypothesized adverse situations. Such comparative risk assessment helps in reducing weaknesses and uncertainties in problem formulation. See, e.g., M. Arentsen et al., "Institutional and Policy Responses to Uncertainty in

Environmental Policy: A Comparison of Dutch and U.S. Styles," *Policy Studies Journal,* 2000, 28(3), pp. 597–611.

Compatible opening: Liberalization in the economy that is in consonance with the social, economic, and political situations existing in the country such that it is neither too hurried nor too slow. Compatible opening involves partial progress in a number of sectors and is systematic reform that takes place on all fronts. *See also* **Sequencing**.

Compensable factors: Factors that are taken into consideration in the process of job evaluation and in determining the worth of a job. These factors generally include cognitive and other skills, knowledge, level of responsibility, prior experiences, and degree of effort required to get the work done. Compensable factors determine the level of compensation, which is the total remuneration given by employers to employees in return for the work they do. Compensation can be in cash (such as wages and salaries) or in kind (such as fringe benefits, use of vehicle, etc.). The latter is known as a contingent form of compensation. The entire process of the management of the compensation process—including determining the compensable factors as well as the degree of compensation to be set for each job—is termed compensation management. In general, compensation management is related to an organization's financial reward system.

Compensatory power: A form of organizational power where the organization exercises influence over individuals by virtue of its control over compensation. There is a threshold to this power, however, since the legal rights of employees to be rewarded for work done cannot be summarily disregarded by organizations.

Competence-destruction theory: A theory that explains how not all innovations are equally influential; some lead to incremental changes, while a few yield major breakthroughs. The focus of this theory is on the application of technology to the evolution of progress, and it is argued that technological shifts can be competency destroying (or conversely competence enhancing) since they tend to destroy (or enhance) an organization's competence. In general, competence-destruction change emanates from new organizations, and competency-enhancing change from established ones. For some original discussion of the theory, see W. Abernathy and K. Clark, "Innovation: Mapping the Winds of Creative Destruction," *Research Policy,* 1985, 14(1), pp. 3–22. See also, e.g., M. Tushman and P. Anderson, "Technological Discontinuities and Organizational Environments," *Administrative Science Quarterly,* 1986, 31(3), pp. 439–65.

Competencies: The knowledge, skills, and abilities required to perform a given task to an acceptable standard. A related but different concept is competence, which, when used in the broader public-management context, refers either to the expert, objective performance of work (i.e., neutral competence) or to the performance of top officials and bureaucrats doing what the chief executive (such as a president) wants (i.e., responsive competence). For a strong analysis of these two types of competence, see, e.g., J. Aberbach and B. Rockman, "Civil Servants and Policy-Makers: Neutral or Responsive Competence?" *Governance: An International Journal of Policy and Administration,* 1994, 7(4), pp. 461–69.

Competency standards: Levels that are specified for each competency for a job that an employee needs to demonstrate. If an employee cannot demonstrate that competency to a satisfactory degree, his/her employment may be terminated, or the employer may decide to provide the employee with competency-based training, which is training that is specifically geared toward enhancing the competencies of individuals in an organization to a particular standard.

Competing on an equal basis: *See* Level playing field.

Competing rationalities: A situation where bureaucrats are faced with two or more equally logical courses of action but which are in conflict with each other. For example, in national planning, policy makers may find themselves faced with sectoral outcomes that are shaped by various rationalities, all of which are acceptable on their own. These rationalities can include those of bureaucracy (i.e., probity and fairness), of market (i.e., of profit and efficiencies), and of politics (i.e., power acquisition and compromise). Additionally, these rationalities might interact with rationalities imposed by citizens in terms of what they would like to see the planning deliver. Policy makers thus need to be aware of a varied mix of competing rationalities. See, e.g., B. Townley, "The Role of Competing Rationalities in Institutional Change," *Academy of Management Journal,* 2002, 45(1), pp. 163–79.

Competition: Denotes rivalry among different parties in the provision of goods and services to those that demand them. Here, any party that wishes to purchase or sell a specific good or service can choose from among those that are willing to engage in the transaction. The concept is central to the free-market system, and the idea is that competition provides the impetus for people to excel. The concept has also featured prominently in public-sector management in the last two decades as government agencies are increasingly competing with other providers for delivery of services. Competition policies are policies that are designed to facilitate competition. At times, they may also be used to restrict unwanted competition and regulate the market. For a very good analysis of the usage of the concept, see S. Estrin, "Competition and Corporate Governance in Transition," *Journal of Economic Perspectives,* 2002, 16(1), pp. 101–24. *See also* **Managed competition.**

Competition prescription: The argument that: (a) governmental agencies should be operated in business-like ways, with efficiency as their objective; and (b) many governmental functions would be more effective if they were actually run as businesses (i.e., as profit-and-loss ventures). The public-sector reforms in countless jurisdictions in the last decade have been almost wholly based on the competition prescription.

Competition principles: Principles that underpin the conditions in which competition takes place. These include: (a) for the majority of goods and services, markets are more efficient at delivering them to consumers than government; (b) restrictions on competition among service providers in the long run lead to increased net costs to society; and (c) governments need to show overwhelming evidence that such restrictions need to be removed in cases where it is perceived that the marketplace has not efficiently delivered the goods and services.

Competitive adaptation: Refers to a means for resolving the problem presented by the agility paradox (that organizations need to be simultaneously flexible and stable). Applying the concept of competitive adaptation, organizations can achieve a more holistic view of strategy generation (i.e., defining strategies that draw on intelligence gathered from the operating environment), of management controls (i.e., the extent to which organizations can determine how their performance is aligned to the goals they have specified), and of systems development, which provides organizations with the necessary tools to link performance with goals. For a discussion of the concept , see, e.g., C. Osborn, "Systems for Sustainable Organizations: Emergent Strategies, Interactive Controls and Semi-Formal Information," *Journal of Management Studies,* 1998, 35(4), pp. 481–509. *See also* **Agility paradox.**

Competitive benchmarking: When an organization sets *ex ante* specifications of its future performances based on the achievements of its competitors. This is more difficult in the public sector largely because not all public organizations have competitors.

Competitive bidding: Soliciting proposals for the delivery of services and the production of goods from private providers (and governmental agencies, too, if they are interested and consider themselves capable) according to a competitive criteria, often contingent on lowest price. A competitive bidding process is necessary to ascertain who the lowest-cost producer is; however, the party requesting the bids is not necessarily obliged to select the lowest-priced bidder. When competitive bidding is mandatory in determining who gets to deliver a particular service, the term compulsory competitive bidding is used. For a review of relevant issues, see, e.g., D. Grimshaw et al., "Going Privately: Partnership and Outsourcing in UK Public Services," *Public Administration,* 2002, 80(3), pp. 475–502.

Competitive contracting: *See* **Competitive tendering**.

Competitive examinations: Tests that all candidates for public employment must sit through in order to determine their suitability for specific positions. Other than some basic criteria (such as age in some jurisdictions), there are few restrictions on who can sit for the competitive examinations.

Competitive federalism: When there is competition among governments in a federal system in the supply of public policy on emergent public problems. In the United States, the period since the 1980s is generally characterized as competitive federalism, in which the relations between the federal government and the various state and local governments were rather tense. This is largely because the federal government sought to reduce its role in state and local affairs. For a case on the merits of competitive federalism, see, e.g., A. Breton, *Report of the Royal Commission on the Economic Union and Development Prospects for Canada,* Ottawa: Canadian Government Publishing Centre, 1985, pp. 486–526. *Cf.* **Cooperative federalism**.

Competitive interdependency: *See* **Interdependency**.

Competitive neutrality: A situation wherein all competitors (i.e., bidders) for a contract are treated equally, that is, there is neutrality in the competition environment. To ensure competitive neutrality, the rules must apply equally to all parties. *See also* **Level playing field**.

Competitive populism: When public officials, usually candidates for elected office, seek to garner public support by trying to outdo each other in making bold, yet possibly unattainable, promises to citizens. As such, not much thought is given to the specifics of policies or to policy ramifications.

Compliance-related training: Mandatory training that is given to ensure that employees are aware of and can fulfill certain requirements (for example, on legislative mandates and safety standards). Expenses incurred on compliance-related training are considered as compliance costs for planning and accounting purposes.

Component knowledge: Knowledge about the individual elements of a system and the way in which they interact with each other. Component knowledge implies that there is a focus on the details of a particular knowledge experience, and this is considered useful when considering the replication of the experience in a new setting. See, e.g., R. Henderson and K. Clark, "Architectural Innovation: The Reconfiguration of Existing Product Technologies and the Failure of Established Firms," *Administrative Science Quarterly,* 1990, 35(1), pp. 9–30. *Cf.* **Architectural knowledge**.

Comprehensive audit: *See* **Complete audit**.

Compromise: A strategy to achieve policy outcomes that takes into consideration the views of all actors and stakeholders. In coming up with a compromise, it is possible that everyone involved will have to give up something, just as it is possible that there may eventually be a win-win situation for all.

Compulsory advice arrangement: A decision-making procedure where there is a requirement for management to consult with employees before making decisions. This is particularly the case in collective-bargaining agreements where the unions may have been successful in requiring that management seek the advice of employees prior to any decision being taken on employment-related matters.

Compulsory arbitration: Arbitration in which both parties to a dispute are legally required to abide by the decision of an arbiter to whom they submit their demands. Compulsory arbitration is also known as binding arbitration.

Compulsory competitive bidding: *See* **Competitive bidding**.

Compulsory retirement: Refers to the termination of employment of an employee for retirement after a set number of years of service. Such termination is compulsory if the employee reaches a particular age, or has worked at the organization for a given number of years. All organizations will normally have a policy on compulsory retirement, although in jurisdictions such as New Zealand, where there is no mandatory retirement, this does not hold.

Computational strategy: *See* **Decision-making strategies**.

Concentration risk: The risk that emerges when there is a significant presence of institutions in one location, or when many critical functions are concentrated in one institution, and this single-point-of-concentration intensifies the impact of any disruption in systems and processes. For example, finance ministries in many developing jurisdictions have considerable functions concentrated in them, and any failures in the organization would thus be widely diffused. See, e.g., The Monetary Authority of Singapore, *Guidelines on Business Continuity Planning,* Singapore: MAS, 2003, p. 16.

Concept testing: The process of testing an innovative idea before its development. This is considered essential because development costs can be high, especially if the concept does not prove to be viable.

Conceptual skills: The abilities of employees to think in abstract terms and to be able to use appropriate concepts to simplify complex problems and find solutions to them. Conceptual skills are an integral part of any competency sets that are prevalent in all organizations.

Conceptual stretching, problem of: A problem that policy analysts have when they apply situation-specific concepts to dissimilar situations. Thus, for example, concepts of gender in western societies cannot be applied in toto in eastern societies; attempts to do so in a gendered analysis of economic development, for example, is likely to result in inappropriate advice. For an early analysis of the problem of conceptual stretching, see G. Sartori, "Concept Misinformation in Comparative Politics," *American Political Science Review,* 1970, 64(4), pp. 1033–53. *See also* **Adaptive conceptualization**.

Conciliation: The process of getting two sides in a dispute to agree to a compromise, in which the agreement is voluntary (i.e., the process of conciliation, unlike arbitration, does not compel the parties to accept the proposed solution). The conciliation process is facilitated by a conciliator, who is an individual that is tasked with ensuring that the disputing parties negotiate and settle their differences to reach a mutually satisfactory settlement. A conciliator can be imposed by an external entity, such as the government, or agreed to by the disputing parties either before or even during the negotiations.

Concordance principle: A principle in regulation that states that any regulatory approach taken by a government should be in accordance with the political and administrative context in which it will be applied. For example, a government would have take into consideration its administrative capacity when formulating any regulation. See, e.g., K. Turner and H. Opschoor, "Environmental Economic and Environmental Policy Instruments: Introduction and Overview," in J. Opschoor and R. Turner (eds.), *Economic Incentives and Environmental Policies: Principles and Practice,* Dordrecht: Kluwer Academic, 1994, pp. 3–42.

Concurrent power: Power held jointly by multiple jurisdictions, such as on taxation between state and federal governments.

Condign power: A form of organizational power where the organization exercises influence over individuals by virtue of its control over physical domains of work. *See also* **Compensatory power**.

Conditional bidding: A process where a party's bid is conditional on it being eligible to provide the service. Organizations seeking bids will specify upfront the criteria that potential bidders will need to meet before they can place bids. However, they will not necessarily reject a bid outright if all conditions are not met since it is possible that some bidders will specify that, should they be granted the tender, they will ensure that they fulfill the preconditions.

Conditional grant: Any grant that has limitations (i.e., conditions) on how it can be used. Block and categorical grants are such examples, although conditional grants have more stringent criteria for use. *See also* **Grants**.

Conditionality: When external parties impose conditions on what and how certain policies are to be enforced (such as on wage stabilization or use of aid resources). For a case study on conditionality, see, e.g., T. Jayne et al., "False Promise or False Premise? The Experience of Food and Input Market Reform in Eastern and Southern Africa," *World Development,* 2002, 30(11), pp. 1967–85.

Confidence deficit: Refers to the reduction in confidence that citizens have in the bureaucracy, and in the general democratic process, that elected representatives and public officials are not reflecting their wishes. For a discussion of this term in the public-sector context, see, for example, OECD, *Ethics in the Public Service: Current Issues and Practice; Executive Summary,* Paris: OECD, 1997, p. 1. *See also* **Democratic Deficit**.

Confirmation bias: Related to the notion of cognitive blind spots and bias, this term refers to the general tendency in individuals to seek only that information that will confirm a belief that they already have, rather than to have the belief tested by seeking counterevidence. Confirmation bias minimizes the work of the organization as a whole in its search for evidence and in its knowledge management and learning opportunities. It can be addressed by, among others, having individuals question and analyze their a priori assumptions about any particular issue or problem. *See also* **Belief preservation**.

Conflict management: An approach to dealing with conflicts that emerge, or have the potential to emerge, in the organization. The role of managers in conflict management is to ensure that all information is presented to individuals in the organization, and that there are opportunities for discussing all facets of the conflict.

Conflict management and resolution mechanism: Something that helps prepare the involved parties for future conflicts, and provides them with avenues that they can use to resolve those disputes. Such mechanisms are critical, for example, in labor-management relations that are often conflictual. One such mechanism might be, for example, that anytime one party lodges a complaint against the other about any contractual violations, an arbiter will automatically be involved in reviewing the claim.

Conflict of interest: A situation in which a person's private interests are in conflict with the public interest that he/she is entrusted with representing. For example, if a legislator has investments in a certain business, and that business stands to benefit by a particular piece of legislation that he or she is involved in drafting, then there is said to be a conflict of interest. If the legislator in such a situation chooses not to declare this conflict and to abstain from voting, then he/she runs the risk of being accused of unethical conduct.

Conflict resolution: Refers to taking any disagreement among individuals or organizations and ensuring that they are resolved. Many organizations now have the philosophy that a reasonable amount of conflict—and the ability and willingness to talk about it—is good for the organization's health. See, e.g., M. Rahim, "A Strategy for Managing Conflict in Complex Organizations," *Human Relations,* 1985, 38(1), pp. 81–89.

Conflict resolution and sanctioning capabilities: Capacities that actors possess to take to court those who they are in conflict with (or those that they determine have not adhered to specific legislative mandates) and to request the court to sanction their conduct. See, e.g., J. Bryson and B. Crosby, "Policy Planning and the Design and Use of Forums, Arenas, and Courts," in B. Bozeman (ed.), *Public Management: The State of the Art,* San Francisco: Jossey-Bass, 1993, pp. 323–44.

Conformity audit: *See* **Quality-assurance audit**.

Confounded variable: A multidimensional variable with several other variables embedded in it (such as educational level). As such, its meaning and measurement cannot be precisely ascertained. Measurement of a confounded variable is subject to different interpretations and does not necessarily hold in a cross-jurisdictional context.

Confucian dynamism: An organizational value prevalent in those agencies where authority and paternalistic attitudes dominate. The Confucian ethic has been argued for by those who believe in the role of culture in enhancing growth and development. Their argument has been that the Confucian ethic in existence in several East Asian countries explains why they grew so impressively. The ethic puts emphasis on such societal attributes as hierarchy, deference, and stability to explain which conditions facilitate rapid economic growth. For a discussion see, e.g., W. McCord, "Explaining the East Asian 'Miracle,'" *The National Interest,* 1989, 16, pp. 74–82. For one of pioneering work on this concept, see G. Hofstede and M. Bond, "The Confucian Connection: From Cultural Roots to Economic Growth," *Organizational Dynamics,* 1988, 16(4), pp. 4–21.

Congressional government: A form of government where the executive branch is distinct from, and independent of, the legislative branch. The rationale for a congressional government is the separation of powers between the branches of government. This is most clearly evident in the United States federal government where Congress (consisting of the Senate and the House of Representatives) and the executive branch (i.e., the president) share almost equal powers in the governance of the country. Officials who head government departments in the United States are not elected and are instead nominated by the president and approved by the Senate. *Cf.* **Cabinet government**.

Congressional veto: *See* **Legislative veto**.

Conjuncture: Related to the concept of path dependency, this terms refers to the need for several elements to come together in order that an entity can get out of the deterministic scenario implied in a path-dependent policy. Such conjecture offers a window of opportunity to break free from path dependence, but policy makers need to wait for the proper alignment of all relevant elements. See, e.g., D. Wilsford, "The Conjuncture of Ideas and Interests," *Comparative Political Studies,* 1985, 18, pp. 357–72.

Connective capital: Refers to an employee's access to his/her co-workers' knowledge and skills. This concept adds to that of social capital by looking at the dynamic element of how knowledge workers are connecting in organizations. For a discussion of this concept in relation to innovative human-resource planning systems, see, e.g., C. Ichniowski and K. Shaw, "Beyond Incentive Pay: Insiders' Estimates of the Value of Complementary Human Resource Management Practices," *Journal of Economic Perspectives,* 2003, 7(1), pp. 155–80.

Consensual corporatism: A tradition of governance that is a model of deliberation with interest groups, and pragmatic compromise. It is a combination of corporatism (which looks at the relation between the state and organized interest groups) and consensus democracy (which seeks to focus on pragmatic compromise). Consensual corporatism is evident in, for example, the Netherlands—see, e.g., W. Kickert, "Beneath Consensual Corporatism: Traditions of Governance in the Netherlands," *Public Administration,* 2003, 81(1), pp. 119–40.

Consensual imperative: Related to the concept of consensual corporatism is that of consensual imperative, which represents the need for executives to avoid major controversy, and for their need to seek consensus in the resolution of organizational problems. Another related concept is that of consensual validation, which is the validation of any decision or policy by considering whether there is a universal agreement about it in the entity under consideration. Using consensual validation as a criterion for validity ensures that decision makers in organizations take into consideration the views of all concerned parties. *See also* **Legal imperative.**

Consensus: A state of general agreement among all participants in a group. In many organizations, such as the Organization for Economic Cooperation and Development, all decisions are made by consensus, i.e., all the members of the organization have to agree on the decisions that are taken before they are formalized. If no such consensus emerges, then the decision is either shelved or recalibrated to suit the demands of all parties concerned. The consensus method of decision making in organizations has its advantages and disadvantages. It is useful when it is necessary to ensure that the views of all group members are heard and taken into account and that there is thus support for the final decisions taken. On the other hand, reaching consensus on most matters that are complex is not easy, and decision making might be postponed or aborted altogether with a considerable amount of time wasted. A consensus leader is someone who seeks consensus among all parties that have a stake in a particular decision, and that are formally associated to seek solutions to particular problems.

Consent decree: Allows an employer to escape from being sanctioned for not currently adhering to equal-employment provisions in return for a promise that compliance will be honored henceforth. A related concept is a consent order, which is a formal order that is issued by the courts, or by others empowered to do so, that there is voluntary compliance with specific requirements of implementation/timing. Should the compliance not be forthcoming, culpable organizations are forewarned of repercussions. *Cf.* **Advisory opinion**.

Consequence: With respect to risks, a consequence is the outcome of an event that could be either positive (i.e., favorable) or negative (i.e., unfavorable). Consequence analysis is a management technique used to evaluate the progress of ongoing activities where there is focus on measuring the extent to which the outcomes of programs and policies are in alignment with the *ex ante* stated objectives.

Conservative bias: The overriding tendency of bureaucrats to err on the side of caution, and to be tentative in seeking and taking even manageable risks in their work. For how this manifests in development policy making, see, e.g., M. Grindle, "In Quest of the Political: The Political Economy of Development Policy-Making," in G. Meier and J. Stiglitz (eds.), *Frontiers in Development Economics: The Future in Perspective,* Oxford: Oxford University Press, 2001, pp. 345–80.

Conservers: A term used by the noted scholar Anthony Downs to denote a type of bureaucrat whose prime interest is in holding onto their position and power. Such individuals tend to be risk averse since they shun uncertainty. See A. Downs, *Inside Bureaucracy,* Boston: Little, Brown, 1967, p. 88.

Consociational bureaucracy: Refers to a bureaucracy whose basic role is to fulfill its mandate to hold society together. For example, it is generally expected of the public service in a developing country that it will, among other things, be representative of society, and that it will engage key stakeholders such as community groups in the work that it does as a way of binding different elements of society. Such a role is construed to be included in the concept of consociational bureaucracy. See C. Hood, "Paradoxes of Public-Sector Managerialism, Old Public Management and Public Service Bargains," *International Public Management Journal,* 2000, 3(1), pp. 1–22.

Consolidated contract: When several agencies seek the same product or service, it is possible to include the orders in a consolidated contract where there is no separate delivery schedule for each agency. Funds for the contract could also come from a central source. For example, a government supplies office of a country may have a consolidated contract for the delivery of computing hardware that is meant for several government departments, but is channeled through that office.

Consolidated decision package: As used in zero-based budgeting, a consolidated decision package is a report that collates and summarizes all the information contained in individual decision packages that are prepared at lower tiers in the organization.

Consortium grant: A grant awarded to two or more organizations for joint work on a program. Decisions to make consortium grants are contingent upon all the organizations demonstrating that their proposals are financially sound, and that they have ensured that there will be adequate integration amongst themselves so as to achieve the outcomes.

Constant error: *See* **Halo effect**.

Constant-sum game: *See* **Games**.

Constituency building: For an organization, constituency building refers to the process of identifying the groups that support its causes and mandates and on whom it can rely to convey that support to policy makers. Because policy makers are motivated by responding to their constituencies' revealed preferences, constituency building can be a powerful tool for an organization to continue to do what it is doing.

Constituent policies: One of political scientist Theodore Lowi's four functional categories of public policy, constituent policies are those where the government is not likely to force an issue and be instead more apt to let changes be imposed through the environment. Lowi himself provides an example of a government dealing with monopolies by changing the rules protecting their limited liability rather than by regulating their conduct (see T. Lowi, "Four Systems of Policy, Policies, and Choice," *Public Administration Review,* 1972, 32, July–August, pp. 298–310).

Constitutive institution: Public institutions are considered to have a bigger social responsibility than private firms as constitutive or formative contributors to community and society building. They not only need to adhere to simple instrumental (or means-end) rationality, but also model positive behavior and ethical norms. For a discussion of the concept, see, e.g., B. Warner, "John Stuart Mill's Theory of Bureaucracy with Representative Government: Balancing Competence and Participation," *Public Administration Review,* 2001, 61(4), pp. 403–13.

Constitutive outcome: The creation of new goals that a program results in and that become evident once it is being implemented. Constitutive outcomes are not specified *ex ante.*

Constitutive rationality: Refers to a concept that responds to the limitations of relying only on instrumental rationality in the work of the organization. This concept implies that organizations are just as interested in thinking of values of ethics, of normative judgments, and of reasoning about how to constitute something that is valued and ideal. For a discussion of the concept, see, e.g., B. Cook, *Bureaucracy and Self-Government: Reconsidering the Role of Public Administration in American Politics,* Baltimore, MD: The Johns Hopkins University Press, 1996, p. 154.

Constrained budgets: A situation of funding limitations that may adversely affect the successful implementation of public policies. Such constrained budgets may be voluntary (for example, as set by a legislature for a program that has little support) or involuntary (i.e., due to a genuine shortage of funds).

Constrained facet analysis: A technique that permits efficiency analysis of non-enveloped decision-making units. These are units that do not have any predetermined boundary levels of efficiency measurement. As such, performance measurement of the work of such entities tends to be rather fuzzy. The concept is borrowed from applications in the logistics sector and in engineering management.

Constraint: (1) In performance evaluation and review technique, this is a requirement in which an event cannot begin until the preceding event is complete. (2) In organization management, this term refers to any limitation that restricts organizational ability to engage in specific activities. Constraint analysis refers to an analysis done of the constraints faced by an organization such that the inherent components of the constraints are individually studied to see how they inhibit the organization from fulfilling its tasks. Constraint analysis is particularly relevant in a situation where the organization faces a very complex environment and its components are not very well understood. Constraint mapping is a procedure for ascertaining limitations that might adversely affect attainment of policy and program objectives. These limitations include physical, legal, organizational, political, and financial. W. Ross Ashby, noted expert on cybernetics, is one of the pioneers in the study of constraint analysis. See, e.g., his "Constraint Analysis of Many-Dimensional Relations," in N. Wiener and J. Schade (eds.), *Progress in Biocybernetics,* Amsterdam: Elsevier, 1965, pp. 10–18.

Constraint interaction: Refers to any activity that is subject to some limitation (or constraint) such as resources, time, etc. The constraint determines the level of demand, which, in turn, determines how much of the product/service in demand needs to be made available. Constraint interactions can be negative or positive; negative in that the more some individuals demand, the less there is available for others (for example, fossil fuel), and positive in that the more one party spends on it, the more benefits it creates for others (for example, research and development in an industry when the knowledge is made public). See, e.g., C. Manski, "Economic Analysis of Social Interactions," *Journal of Economic Perspectives,* 2000, 14(3), pp. 115–36.

Constructive discharge theory: A theory that states that in cases of constructive discharge (i.e., an employee may appear to leave of his/her own accord whereas in reality the employer had made the conditions of employment very unappealing), the employer is still liable as if there had been a breach of the conditions that safeguards employees from being discriminated against. The burden of proof, however, still rests with the employee to show that the employer had indeed caused the conditions of employment to become unacceptable.

Constructive dismissal: *See* **Constructive discharge theory**.

Constructive pressures: Stress on agencies that have the effect of making them change for the better. A threat of a bankruptcy, for example, is considered to be a constructive pressure since this allows firms to be careful about their investment portfolio.

Consultation: The process of engaging in a dialogue with others that have a stake in a policy or program being developed wherein their views are sought on what such a policy or program should contain and how it should be implemented. Many governments, for example, have instituted requirements that public-sector agencies must consult with labor unions as a government policy on employment and working conditions is being developed. Consultation, however, does not necessarily mean that the parties' feedback will necessarily be incorporated in the final policy.

Consultation charter: *See* **No surprise policy**.

Consultative leader: A leader who actively seeks multiple viewpoints and consults others regularly so as to make a decision that incorporates the views of many. A consultative leader does not necessarily have to adhere to consensus decision making since the essence is to consult with others and hear different views as opposed to necessarily incorporating the different views and opinions.

Consumer watchdogs: Entities (governmental or otherwise) that ensure that products and services meant for public consumption are up to acceptable standards and that any limitations in them are adequately brought to the consumers' attention. Such watchdog agencies, however, are also subject to regulation to some extent to ensure that they remain within certain parameters (such as not to create general panic over some cases in which allegations may not be wholly founded).

Containment: To ensure that an unwanted situation does not spread, but neither should it be directly confronted. As related to organizational change, it refers to the process of understanding and managing individuals' concerns that arise when an organization is undergoing change. In this process, the employer's responsibility is to ensure that employees' concerns are adequately addressed. See, e.g., R. French, "'Negative Capability': Managing the Confusing Uncertainties of Change," *Journal of Organizational Change Management,* 2001, 14(5), pp. 480–92.

Contestability of advice: Different sources of policy advice that ministers can tap into; they are also entitled to require that public servants cooperate with the parties providing such advice. For instance, where private-sector consultants are engaged, public servants are expected to cooperate with them to ensure that the interests of government are enhanced. A related term is continuous contestability, which refers to ensuring that there are different providers that are continually vying for service contracts so as to prevent any bureaucratic capture by a preferred one. Continuous contestability is a very effective accountability mechanism.

Contested consensus: A point where parties involved in interagency collaboration reach a stage where they cannot agree on specific issues. Contested consensus includes those areas where agreement has been reached, and for the rest, a joint decision is taken to "agree to disagree." See

E. Bardach, *Getting Agencies to Work Together: The Practice and Theory of Managerial Craftsmanship,* Washington, DC: Brookings Institution Press, 1998, p. 221. *Cf.* **Sufficient consensus**.

Contextual complexity: Refers to the complex nature of work for leaders regardless of which arena they are involved in. Thus, the context of work of the leader of a nongovernmental organization can be considered to be as complex as that of a governmental department head within the ambit of the environment in which they do their work. See, e.g., R. Brunner, "Teaching the Policy Sciences: Reflections on a Graduate Seminar," *Policy Sciences,* 1997, 39(2), pp. 217–31.

Contextual goals: Goals of organizations that are not primary (i.e., explicitly stated) ones. Contextual goals are objectives that organizations set for which they were not mandated but which emerge from environmental pressures in the process of fulfilling primary goals. Such goals make managers more risk averse since they tend not to be well defined. See, e.g., J. Wilson, *Bureaucracy: What Government Agencies Do and Why They Do It,* New York: Basic Books, 1989, p. 129. *Cf.* **Primary goals**.

Contingency analysis: A method of treating uncertainty that looks at how policy alternatives will change given a change in the environment in which the policy is to operate. This method of analysis is the standard "what-if" analysis that policy analysts conduct wherein they hypothesize consequences if certain conditions were met or unmet. Contingency analysis is different from sensitivity analysis, where the values of the variables are altered to study differing results.

Contingency approach: The contingency or situational approach states that there is no one ideal way to manage, and how different leaders manage in different settings depends upon the specific situation existing in their particular operating environment. Contingency management thus refers to any management style that takes into account the contingency approach, and seeks to develop the capacity for flexibility so that it can respond to environmental pressures in an appropriate manner. As applied to an organizational context, the concept of contingency management implies that there is no one ideal way to organize managerial activities so as to maximize performance. Managerial strategy thus becomes a function of variables such as, for example, organizational culture. See, e.g., R. Vecchio, "A Dyadic Interpretation of the Contingency Model of Leadership Effectiveness," *Academy of Management Journal,* 1979, 22 (September), pp. 590–600.

Contingency clauses: Stipulations contained in all contracts that deal with any unforeseen situations in the administration of the contract. These clauses also make the payment level or the work to be performed conditional upon factors that did not exist at the time of the drawing up of the contract.

Contingency model of leadership effectiveness: Asserts that a leader's effectiveness is based on the contingency aspect of leading individuals, and considers: (a) the powers given to the leader, (b) the structure of the task that the leader's group does, (c) relationships between the leader and those being led, and (d) the organizational context within which the group operates. How these elements are structured and configured will determine how suitable the leader is, further implying whether or not the leader will be effective in that particular setting. Since the setting differs across and within organizations, it is contingent upon the situation. For classic work on this subject, see R. Tannenhaum and W. Schmidt, "How to Choose a Leadership Pattern," *Harvard Business Review,* 36(2), 1958, pp. 95–101. See also A. Ashour, "The Contingency Model of Leadership Effectiveness: An Evaluation," *Organizational Behavior and Human Decision Processes,* 9(3), 1973, pp. 339–55.

Contingency planning: The process of coming up with a plan that accounts for any changes in the operational environment and any contingencies (unknown or uncertain situations) that might emerge. The plan is prepared under conditions of uncertainty although simulation techniques are advanced now and it is possible for an organization to be able to pinpoint probabilities of unfavorable events with a fair degree of accuracy. For a discussion of some lessons in contingency planning for policy making, see, e.g., National Audit Office, *Modern Policy-Making: Ensuring Policies Deliver Value for Money,* Report by the Comptroller and Auditor General, HC 289 Session 2001–2002, November 2001, p. 53.

Contingency theory of leadership: Leadership that is based on incorporating all the factors that are evident in a group setting and that relate to group members. The theory proposes that leadership success is a function of: (a) the degree of formal authority that a leader has, (b) the degree of acceptance of such authority by subordinates, and (c) the degree of task complexity.

Contingent claims contract: A contract that details all the obligations of each party to a contract. However, because of bounded rationality and information asymmetry, it is impossible to specify such a contract completely; hence a contingent claims contract will tend to fail. See W. Ouchi, "Markets, Bureaucracies, and Clans," *Administrative Science Quarterly,* 1980, 25(1), pp. 129–41. *Cf.* **Sequential spot contract; Spot contract**.

Contingent liabilities: Any item that has potential to be a liability for an organization if certain events occur. Contingent liabilities also emerge when other parties in an entity that is jointly owned incur debts. The liabilities are incurred by all the owners since they are jointly and severally liable for any obligations made in the name of the entity. The size of contingent liabilities tends to be rather uncertain, and so cannot be measured *ex ante.* An example of contingent liabilities is when a government gives guarantees for continued-service provision when it has placed, say, infrastructure provision in private hands, or when it guarantees programs to support pension liabilities. Such guarantees are made because private banks may have refused to provide the resources. For a useful discussion of contingent liabilities seen in the context of risks and risk management for governments, see, e.g., C. Lewis and A. Mody, "The Management of Contingent Liabilities: A Risk Management Framework for National Governments," in T. Irwin, et al (eds.), *Dealing with Public Risk in Private Infrastructure,* Washington, DC: World Bank, 1997, pp. 131–53.

Contingent strategies: Political scientist Aaron Wildavsky contended that decision makers tend to act strategically and to push for institutional interests while seeking budgetary approval. Contingent strategies are used to capitalize on any emerging and one-off opportunities to raise funding levels (or retain existing ones). Thus, decision makers may actually make a bold and ambitious proposal in the measured hope that their proposals might well be accepted. For Wildavsky's original work on budgeting, see his *The Politics of the Budgetary Process,* Boston: Little, Brown, 1964. For application to the public sector, see, e.g., A. Fozzard, *The Basic Budgeting Problem: Approaches to Resource Allocation in the Public Sector and Their Implications for Pro-Poor Budgeting,* Working Paper 147, London: Centre for Aid and Public Expenditure, Overseas Development Institute, 2001. *Cf.* **Ubiquitous strategies**.

Contingent workers: Workers who are not permanent members of an organization. For example, experts who are recruited from executive leasing arrangements are contingent workers since they tend to be placed in organizations for short periods of time to address a particular problem, find solutions to them, and then depart.

Continuance commitment: *See* **Organizational commitment**.

Continuing appropriation: *See* **Appropriation**.

Continuing contract: A contract that has no pre-specified term limits and continues automatically year after year. However, it can be terminated if the parties so decide. An advantage of a continuing contract is that it allows the principal and agent to develop useful long-term relationships and synergies, although the danger is of bureaucratic capture.

Continuous budget: *See* **Rolling budget**.

Continuous contestability: *See* **Contestability of advice**.

Continuous improvement: Also known as continuous process improvement, the concept refers to attempts by organizations to strive for zero defects in the goods and services they produce. Continuous improvement is facilitated by flexible labor and capital, by flexible problem-solving processes, and by self-managed teams. In this regard, continuous improvement refers to the never-ending efforts of everyone in the organization to identify problems, their root causes, and the ways to best address them. Solutions that emerge from this analysis could be incremental as well as extensive. Continuous improvement enables an organization to reduce variation in product and service delivery, and to do away with activities that are not adding value. For an oft-cited discussion of this, see M. Aoki, "Toward an Economic Model of the Japanese Firm," *Journal of Economic Literature,* 1990, 27(March), pp. 1–27. *See also* **Zero-defect culture**.

Continuous strategic risk taking: A situation where organizations are continually engaged in seeking new ways of doing things, but strategically and with a fair degree of awareness of their uncertain environments. Such risk taking helps organizations identify and exploit advantages that may be inherent in their environment.

Contract: A legally binding agreement that is made between entities (usually an employer and employee, or between a service provider and an organization that seeks the services) on what and how a service is to be provided and in what time frame. Also included in the contract will be specification of the conditions in which the contract will be valid, and how any problems that may arise will be addressed. A contract authority in an organization has the prerogative to incur contracting costs prior to the funds being appropriated. And contract management refers to the administrative aspects of ensuring that a contract is run according to specifications. This includes monitoring contractual performance, liaising with contractors, and dealing with any others issues (such as payment schedules) that may arise in the fulfillment of a contract. Finally, contract enforcement refers to ensuring that all stipulations in the contract are adhered to. Contract enforcement involves monitoring the process of adherence to the contract.

Contract audit: A review and evaluation of the processes that an organization employs in extending contracts. The audit seeks to ensure that proper protocols have been complied with in contract administration. Such an audit could be regular or ad hoc, internal or independent.

Contract budgeting: A form of budgeting that seeks to establish market-like relationships between public-sector providers and governmental ministers, as reflected in purchase agreements. These purchase agreements are signed between the department head and the relevant responsible minister(s), and specify clearly what the budget levels will be for the department such that the minister(s) may be able to purchase the department's goods and services.

Contract change notification: A notice the principal issues to the agent detailing any changes in a contract that both parties have agreed to, and specifying the supplemental expenditure necessary for the additional tasks, if any. If the purpose of the communication is to merely notify a contract change, then no formal discussions need to take place between the two parties.

Contract management: *See* **Contract**.

Contract of employment: A contract between an employer and an employee to provide certain services in return for compensation. The contract will also contain other relevant information on working conditions, entitlements, and expectations of standards of proper behavior.

Contract schedule: A list of the various products and services an organization is seeking on a continual basis so that contractors may make unsolicited bids for the organization's consideration. For purposes of transparency, such schedules are regularly published and any party that is eligible is able to submit bids.

Contracting costs: All the costs related to negotiating and bargaining, managing relationships, as well as procurement searches and information costs. Such costs include those that are nominal (i.e., the actual amount paid) and opportunity (i.e., the costs of those activities that the organizations had to give up as a result of incurring this cost).

Contracting in: When organizations use internal contractors rather than go to external providers to secure a good or service. For an application of contracting-in work, see, e.g., C. Allan et al., "Casualization and Outsourcing: A Comparative Study," *New Zealand Journal of Industrial Relations*, 2001, 26(3), pp. 253–72. *See also* **Contracting out**, **Reverse privatization**.

Contracting out: Refers to work performed by contractors external to the organization. While this is encouraged if costs considerations are paramount (and if it is more cost effective), contracting-out has often been an area of disagreement between unions and management. In contracting-out, the organization merely transfers the supply or operation of a function to an external party; it does not relinquish program responsibility. Contracting-out can be of two types: arm's-length contracting and obligational contracting. See, e.g., J. Prager, "Contracting Out Government Services: Lessons from the Private Sector," *Public Administration Review*, 54(2), 1994, pp. 176–84. *See also* **Arm's-length contracting; Obligational contracting**.

Contracting within: Refers to the process of entering into performance agreements with those that are already working in the public service. For example, the agreements that departmental chief executives in the New Zealand Public Service sign with the State Services Commissioner can be considered as contracting within. See, e.g., I. Thynne, "Government Companies: Ongoing Issues and Future Research," *Public Administration and Development*, 1998, 18(3), pp. 301–05.

Contractor opportunism: Also known as agent opportunism, this is opportunistic behavior that is exhibited by a contractor when the principal is not perceived to have the capability (or lacks the information) to monitor performance rigorously. At a minimum, this behavior can be reflected in the contractor not fully and accurately completing required reports. See, e.g., D. van Slyke, "The Mythology of Privatization in Contracting for Social Services," *Public Administration Review*, 2003, 63(3), pp. 296–315.

Contractual efficiency: An outcome in the contracting process that results when organizations include a fair balance of risk incidence between themselves and the agent, insist on an open bidding process that encourages new potential contractors to bid, specify contracts that are detailed yet leave some flexibility, and institute appropriate levels of monitoring.

Contractual hazard: Any deficiency and weakness in a contract and its administration that diminishes the probability of the contract being efficiently and effectively enforced. Such hazards include, for example, week intellectual property rights, failures of probity on the part of both the principal and the agent, etc. Both parties incur costs in minimizing contractual hazards, but there may be instances when complex modes of governance are required to do so. For a discussion of the concept, see, e.g., O. Williamson, "The New Institutional Economics: Taking Stock, Looking Ahead," *Journal of Economic Literature,* 2000, 38(3), pp. 595–613. *See also* **Contractual integrity**.

Contractual integrity: Refers to the full and proper administration and enforcement of a contract. Contractual integrity is compromised by existent contractual hazards.

Contractual obligations: Requirements on both parties to a contract to behave/act in set ways. For example, in an employer-employee relationship, the former (as the principal) has an obligation to provide a safe environment within which the latter (the agent) can work. The obligation of the employee is to fulfill the roles accorded to him/her.

Contractual solidarity: Refers to the regulation of exchange behavior between two contractual parties, such as the principal and the agent. Such solidarity can be maintained either based on social norms and etiquette (itself an increasingly discouraged measure these days) or a well-defined and well-enforced legal framework (something that not all governments are capable of putting in place). See, e.g., F. Dwyer et al., "Developing Buyer-Seller Relationships," *Journal of Marketing,* 1987, 51(April), pp. 11–27.

Contractualism: The idea that relationships among parties should be based on explicitly specified contracts such that each party knows what is expected of each other, and is aware that there are penalties (as well as incentives) targeted at the desired (undesired) behaviors.

Contribution analysis: This is a technique that helps in attributing impact with the set of performance measures that are in place in an organization. Policy makers and evaluators often face a problem of trying to ascertain what it is exactly that a policy was able to do. Contribution analysis is used by evaluators to acknowledge the problem being addressed, present the program's logic, identify desired behavioral changes, and track performance over time. Contribution analysis also involves gathering multiple types of evidence to better inform the program and its desired impact. For a discussion of how contribution analysis helps in determining attribution of impact, see, e.g., J. Mayne, *Addressing Attribution Through Contribution Analysis: Using Performance Measures Sensibly,*

Discussion Paper, Ottawa: Office of the Auditor General of Canada, 1999, pp. 6–17.

Control agency: Any agency of government that traditionally serves a control function, such as an audit department, finance ministry, and regulatory commission. Control agencies, by virtue of their mandates, tend to have well-developed monitoring and review capabilities.

Control loop: A managerial control process where performance standards are set, performance-measurement instruments are monitored, where performance itself is measured and compared against a benchmark, and appropriate action is then taken, if necessary. The action could be of three types: (a) continue unchanged if the standards are met, (b) revise the standards in line with observed performance, or (c) take action to correct low performance.

Control on executive: The checks on executive power. In the United States, for example, because of the governmental system of checks and balances, control on the executive branch is exercised by the courts and Congress. However, in New Zealand, for example, there are very limited constitutional checks on the executive.

Control systems: Formal as well as informal routines, procedures, and feedback mechanisms that are used to institute control in organizations. Control systems are also used as constructs to assess how control agencies (such as a state treasury) do their work in relation to governmental departments in centralized as well as devolved public-management systems. The term is also associated with the concept of a "command and control system," which implies that the primary purpose of the system is to ensure that actions by organizations and entities outside the center have little room for variance and flexibility. For a review of the term as it is applied in public-sector management (and particularly 'reinventing government'), see, e.g., T. Lynch and P. Cruise, "Can the Public Sector Leviathan be Reformed? Right Sizing Possibilities for the Twenty-First Century," *M@n@gement,* 2(3), 1999, pp. 149–61.

Controllable costs: Any costs that are incurred by an organization that can be manipulated by managerial action. Maintenance of a clean working environment, for example, is a controllable cost. Controllable costs feature prominently while conducting efficiency audits.

Control-loss problem: A problem that arises when top management goals and outcome intentions are not transmitted effectively throughout an organization, and, in parallel, when top management is not aware of the degree to which these outcomes have been achieved. The economist Oliver Williamson argued that structural reform of such an organization would curtail this problem by providing diminished scope for opportunistic behavior by those further on down the organizational hierarchy. Williamson was of the view that the multidivisional "M" form of organization was better suited to stemming the control-loss problem (see O. Williamson, *Corporate Control and Business Behavior,* Englewood Cliffs, NJ: Prentice Hall, 1970). This concept is contextualized in, e.g., J. Child and S. Rodrigues, "Corporate Governance and New Organization Forms: The Problem of Double and Multiple Agency," *Birmingham Business School Working Paper,* 2003–01, pp. 5–8. *See also* **Double-agency problem**; **Multiple-agency problem**.

Convenience-termination clause: In the contract-negotiation process, the principal may ask for inclusion of the authority to terminate the contract. Such termination will be at the discretion of the principal and will entail settling all outstanding claims that are due the contractor up to that point. There may be any number of reasons why a principal would wish to have a convenience-termination clause incorporated into the contract, including, for obvious reasons, a concern that the agent may not be able to adhere to the contract conditions—thus, the principal would wish to cut its losses before the situation worsened.

Convergence hypothesis: (1) In an organizational context, convergence refers to a meeting point of ideas and approaches to fulfilling mandates. The search for such convergence takes place in various settings, including in formal and informal cross-organizational networks. (2) As applied to organizational culture, the convergence hypothesis states that with increasing industrialization, the influence of economic and technological factors will become stronger than the impact of culture, and that this will lead to some commonality across organizations. See, e.g., R. Common, "Convergence and Transfer: A Review of the Globalization of New Public Management," *International Journal of Public Sector Management,* 1998, 11(6), pp. 440–50.

Convergence model of communication: Stipulates that as people and organizations communicate and interact with each other, they share knowledge that will invariably lead them to become similar in knowledge and attitudes. Convergence itself implies that differences between entities diminish.

Conversational approach: An approach taken by control and monitoring agencies where in the process of collecting information from and giving feedback to departments, they rely more on face-to-face discussions than on documentary reporting. The conversational approach also enables the monitoring agency to tell a richer and more refined story to departments.

Convoluted complexity: A characteristic of a situation that is drawn across various dimensions, and which is difficult to comprehend given its multidimensionality. For a discussion of the term, see, e.g., L. Koenig, *An Introduction to Public Policy*, Englewood Cliffs, NJ: Prentice Hall, 1986, pp. 195–96. *See also* **Wicked problems**.

Cooling-off period: (1) A time period which is allowed for disputing parties (e.g., a union and management) to consider their positions and to give them, and others that may be involved, further opportunity to come to a negotiated settlement. (2) The amount of time an ex-government official has to wait before being allowed to engage in paid professional activity in the private sector that the official may have been regulating while in public sector employment.

Cooperative contracting: Also called negotiated contracting, this is a method of engaging in contracting wherein the bidder and the party that is offering the bid cooperate to finalize the terms of the contract as well as the mode of service delivery. For a general discussion, see, e.g., R. De Hoog, "Competition, Negotiation or Cooperation: Three Models for Service Contracting," *Administration and Society*, 1990, 22(3) pp. 317–40.

Cooperative federalism: One that is based on cooperation between state/provincial governments and the federal government. In the United States, cooperative federalism was in evidence primarily during the period after the Great Depression and after World War II, when large-scale public-works projects were started with federal grants to state and local governments. *Cf.* **Competitive federalism**.

Cooperative organizations: Organizations that are created at the grassroots level, and include communities coming together in cooperation to be involved in activities that seek to enhance their general welfare.

Co-optation: A strategy to achieve policy outcomes by minimizing external opposition. In co-optation, the organization brings in opponents to the policy (e.g., by including them in advisory committees, by letting them co-sponsor a bill in parliament, etc.) and thus absorbs them into its own policy-determining structure. One of the most noted works on co-optation has been done by the sociologist Philip Selznick in relation to the Tennessee Valley Authority (see P. Selznick, *TVA and the Grass Roots,* Berkeley: University of California Press, 1949).

Coordinated decentralization: A seemingly paradoxical principle that basically states that for organizations to better get a handle on their operations, there needs to be coordinated control of their decentralized operations. This stems from the argument that decentralization does not necessarily preclude coordination of activities from the center.

Coordination: Considered a traditional staff function in an organization where managers ensure that different units within the organizations are aware of each other's activities and take them into consideration when engaged in their own work. Coordination failure is a situation where organizations that were meant to be working together to address a common problem fail to coordinate their actions, and a comprehensive response is lacking and/or duplicate responses emerge.

Co-organization: When two or more agencies jointly organize projects either as mandated by law or emerging from the mutual realization that such co-organization leads to more effective work. On the other hand, co-ownership is when two or more agencies own a particular policy domain; for example, dealing with truancy among youths may be a problem that is co-owned by a ministry of youth affairs as well as a ministry of education. Co-responsibility is responsibility that is shared by two parties for a common activity. *See also* **Co-production**.

Coping mechanism: Ways by which individuals and organizations deal with the adverse situations that are evident in their operating environments and that affect their productivity. An overworked employee's coping mechanisms could, for example, be sacrificing family life so as to get work done. One particular coping mechanism is coping by exclusion, which is a strategy for survival whereby the party manages the workload by refusing to take on extra mandates and thus limits the workload. For an example of how this concept is applied, see R. Handerberg, "Organizational Strategy for Coping with External Environments: Reducing Work Load as One Approach," in A. Farazmand (ed.), *Handbook of Bureaucracy,* New York: Marcel Dekker, Inc., 1994, pp. 183–93.

Coping organization: An organization for which neither outputs nor outcomes can be observed (for example, diplomatic services). See J. Wilson, *Bureaucracy: What Government Agencies Do and Why They Do It,* New York: Basic Books, 1989, p. 159.

Co-production: Refers to the process of service delivery by different parties so as to minimize costs and/or improve quality of service. For example, cooperation among a group of citizens may lead to reduced crime in a neighborhood, which also assists the police by enabling them to focus on more serious crimes. Co-production is essential for bureaucracies since it reminds them that they are not the only ones that decide on what and how services need to be provided to citizens. See, e.g., J. Brudney and R. England, "Toward a Definition of the Co-Production Concept," *Public Administration Review,* 1983, 43(1), pp. 55–68.

Core activities: Activities of an organization that are considered central to the organizational goal. For example, one of the core activities of a state treasury is to provide economic advice to government. *Cf.* **Marginal activities**.

Core competencies: (1) Generic skills expected of employees, including, for example, on communication, writing, etc. (2) The area of business in which an organization has maximum expertise; these are factors that set it apart from the competition, if any.

Core executive: *See* **Central agency**.

Core expertise: *See* **Core competencies**.

Core skills: *See* **Basic skills**.

Corporate amnesia: Refers to the loss of institutional memory. This is a result usually of drastic "delayering," whereby senior staff members who constitute the bulk of organizational knowledge are let go without there being any effort to have that knowledge transferred or documented. *See also* **Anorexic organization**.

Corporate bureaucracy: *See* **Market bureaucracy**.

Corporate governance: Refers to the relationships among shareholders, management, and the board of directors on how companies are managed and how they fulfill their various responsibilities. These responsibilities can be in the economic realm (i.e., to generate profits), the social realm (i.e., with deference to generalized societal preferences), and the environmental realm (i.e., in keeping with any environmental standards in place). With increasing reliance placed by governments on tapping quasi-public sector forms of governance and minimizing their direct presence in the economy, corporate governance has taken a higher profile in public-sector management. In general, corporate-governance principles emphasize a distinction between ownership and management, clear corporate objectives (including maximization of employee welfare), specific performance standards that are clearly to be met or exceeded, and rigorous accounting of managerial action. See, e.g., M. Megginson and J. Netter (2001), "From State to Market: A Survey of Empirical Studies on Privatization," *Journal of Economic Literature,* 2001, 39(2), pp. 321–89. For a discussion of the key principles of corporate governance, see OECD, *Governance: Improving Competitiveness and Access to Capital in Global Markets,* Paris: OECD, 1998. *See also* **Governance**.

Corporate management: Refers in general to the introduction of private-sector practices in the public sector. Some of these practices include: performance measurement, increasing focus on results rather than process, and consumer focus. New public management has as its core this notion of corporate management. See, e.g., R. Rhodes, "Different Roads to Unfamiliar Places: UK Experience in Comparative Perspective," *Australian Journal of Public Administration,* 1998, 57(4), pp. 19–31.

Corporate model, interaction based on: Between two agencies, this refers to the mix of informal and formal interorganizational communications. The formality comes from the mandated organization-to-organization interface (such as in the regular heads of agency meeting), and the informality stems from interpersonal links between members of organizations that takes place outside the ambit of official work. See, e.g., M. Emmert, M. Crow, and R. Shangraw, "Public Management in the Future: Post-Orthodoxy and Organization Design," in B. Bozeman (ed.), *Public Management: The State of the Art,* San Francisco: Jossey-Bass, 1993, pp. 345–60.

Corporation: A legal entity that can produce goods and services and engage in market transactions to make profits. A corporation is owned by shareholders who appoint a board of directors that oversee the management of the entity. Corporatization refers to the process of coming up with corporations from what were previously governmental departments or ongoing business concerns. This means that the restructured entity operates on the premise of a commercial enterprise in a competitive environment. The management of the corporation is independent from government (although the government remains a principal shareholder), and accountability relationships will remain in some form with the legislature as well. See, e.g., J. Christensen and T. Pallesen, "The Political Benefits of Corporatization and Privatization," *Journal of Public Policy,* 2001, 21(3), pp. 283–309.

Corrective action: Action taken by management to ensure that performance failures are corrected when they are first evident. This includes ascertaining whether the failure is due to the standards not being attainable (for example, too high, too nebulous, lack of capability) or whether they are being ignored altogether. Corrective action is a subset of corrective maintenance, which is the process of inspecting and taking care of faults and defects as they occur. The idea of corrective maintenance has at its core a control and feedback mechanism that enables the organization to respond to such errors and variances.

Corrective discipline: Discipline that is meted out to employees which gives them ample opportunity to correct their behavior before the organization is compelled to take sterner action. Corrective discipline can take various forms, ranging from verbal warnings to withholding some perks or even salary. *See also* **Progressive discipline**.

Corrective maintenance: *See* **Corrective action**.

Correspondence principle: A principle that states that any new theory that is applied to the understanding of a situation should correspond with the established theory, particularly if it were known to hold in such a situation. *See also* **Law of requisite variety; Principle of self-organization**.

Corruption: Any behavior of individuals with public or private responsibilities which goes against the line of duty and which is aimed at obtaining undue advantages for themselves or for others. Corruption that takes place at lower levels of government, where bureaucrats may seek payment for the decisions they control, is termed entrepreneurial corruption. This is a very broad definition, but examples of corruption can include taking bribes or misusing one's position of public trust. For a study of the determinants of corruption, and what factors explain its variance across jurisdictions, see, e.g., A. Ali and H. Isse, "Determinants of Economic Corruption: A Cross-Country Comparison," *Cato Journal,* 2003, 22(3), pp. 449–66.

Corruption of incompetence: An adverse situation that exists in organizations when they are not able to fulfill their mandates because they lack the required capability and are rendered incompetent. This result is said to be corrupt because, all things considered, agencies must ensure that they remain capable to fulfill their mandates, or else those that rely on them for well being and support suffer needlessly. See, e.g., G. Stahl,

"Ethical Foundations," in A. Farazmand (ed.), *Handbook of Bureaucracy,* New York: Marcel Dekker, Inc., 1994, p. 295–303.

Cosmopolitan-local construct: A concept that refers to a continuum of divergent staff-member roles that can be evident in an organization. At one end are those staff members who can be termed professionals who not only are loyal to the organization but also bring valuable skills and expertise to the organization. At the other end are those staff members who also have a high degree of loyalty to the organization but who exhibit—and bring to the organization—a low level of specialized skills. The former group is termed cosmopolitans and the latter locals. In reality, the divergence is less stark than this. See A. Gouldner, "Cosmopolitans and Locals: Toward an Analysis of Latent Social Roles–I," *Administrative Science Quarterly,* 1957, 2(3), pp. 281–306.

Cost allocation: Apportioning revenues and expenses (including overheads) to output classes to ensure that the full cost of delivery is measured appropriately. How costs are allocated substantially affects the capability of an organization to do its work. While some movement of funds across output classes is expected, persistent underruns or overruns in any output class undermines the confidence of management to successfully carry out its tasks.

Cost analysis: Refers to the analysis of the expenses that are to be incurred in any proposed policy or program. A cost analysis is important so as to know the total resource requirements that will need to be made in order to secure the outcomes that are envisaged. There are several types of cost analysis. A valuation of the monetary costs and benefits of a particular policy or program is contained in a cost-benefit analysis. When costs can be quantified in monetary terms but the benefits cannot, a cost-effectiveness analysis is conducted. Compliance-cost assessment refers to the analysis of costs that are incurred by businesses for complying with regulations and standards. A cost-utility analysis is done when the outputs can be quantified but not valued; and an exchequer cost analysis looks at the expenditure costs and savings to government of a particular policy or program. *See also* **Cost-benefit analysis**, **Cost effectiveness**.

Cost benchmarking: Setting levels for how much departments can charge the government as costs for specific outputs. Such benchmarks may be based on historical trends in the organization, including in regulation, private-sector practice, or practice evident internationally. See, e.g., S. Newberry, "Intended or Unintended Consequences? Resource Erosion in New Zealand's Government Departments," *Financial Accountability and Management,* 2002, 18(4), pp. 309–30.

Cost blowout: A situation where an agency is not able to control its expenses and there is a sudden increase in its costs (resulting, for example, from a heavily funded project, the parameters and assumptions of which were not considered at the formulation stage). A cost blowout does not necessarily mean that the organization is not able to meets its obligations (although it will have a tendency to request supplemental funding from the government). *See also* **Cost containment**.

Cost center: *See* **Responsibility center**.

Cost containment: Managerial efforts to ensure that costs for programs and maintenance are kept to within prespecified limits. When they cannot be contained, cost overruns occur. Cost overruns are excesses in expenditures over and above what had been budgeted. If the cost overruns are excessive, the situation is termed a cost blowout. *See also* **Cost blowout**.

Cost effectiveness: Refers to the desired impact of a particular course of action per unit of cost spent on that particular activity. While efficiency does not necessarily imply effectiveness (and vice versa), relating effectiveness to costs allows the introduction of cost efficiency into the analysis. Cost-effectiveness analysis is done when benefits cannot be measured in the same way that costs can. That is the difference between this concept and cost-benefit analysis. *See also* **Cost-benefit analysis**.

Cost internalization: When external costs of a program are incorporated into an internal cost element structure (i.e., accepted as part of the costs of the program). For example, some permissible costs of the agent in a contractual relationship may be internalized by the principal. Or some losses resulting from deficient financial planning may be considered a cost internalization by the organizational leadership, particularly if the adverse conditions were beyond the organization's control.

Cost overruns: *See* **Cost containment**.

Cost recovery: Enabling an agency to charge for the services it provides so that it can get back the costs of providing such services. The price so charged, however, cannot exceed the unit cost. Cost recovery for public organizations might be in the form of subsidies from government, or user fees, or some other mechanism. If the cost recovery is from a source outside the government, the organization's total budget will reflect this as income earned from other sources.

Cost sharing: When two or more organizations (or units within an organization) decide to share the costs of a particular program. Cost-sharing arrangements are common among international donor agencies that assist less-developed countries in socioeconomic development. A cost-sharing contract is a contract between two parties that have agreed that they will share the costs of a particular activity or project. For example, as per a cost-sharing contract, an organization could agree to reimburse a contractor some allowable costs incurred in research and development for a public good. *See also* **Parallel financing**.

Cost variance: The difference in costs that is evident between what was budgeted for (i.e., *ex ante*) and what was actually incurred (i.e., *ex post*). The smaller the variance, the more accurate the plan, and the less the degree of uncertainty in cost determination. In practically all organizations, such a variance will be minimal, at least on paper, but that is because they have decided to ramp up their expenses in keeping with the level of funds left. In actual fact, cost variances are a fairly regular phenomenon in organizations. *See also* **Hockey-stick effect**.

Cost-benefit analysis: Analysis done to compare the total monetary costs to total monetary benefits of any policy alternative. In the analysis, both costs and benefits are discounted to capture the decline in the value of money over time. The analysis results in a cost-benefit ratio, which gives an indication as to the potential viability of a policy alternative. Here, the opportunity costs of an investment in the activity are often calculated with respect to what net benefits might have been gained by investing in the private sector. A cost-benefit analysis can be tangible or intangible (i.e., directly and indirectly measurable), and primary or secondary (i.e., direct or indirect result of a program and also more or less valued objective). For an excellent review of the background and context of cost-benefit analysis, see, e.g., J. Persky, "Cost-Benefit Analysis and the Classical Creed," *Journal of Economic Perspectives,* 2001, 15(4), pp. 199–208. *See also* **Risk-cost-benefit analysis**.

Cost-overrun contract: One where there is provision for increasing the amount of funding commitment contingent upon the agent demonstrating that cost overruns were unavoidable in the provision of a good or service. Organizations will usually have contingency plans for such expenses, especially when the product or service in question has a volatile market.

Cost-sensitivity analysis: In looking at the financial aspects of decisions and alternatives, a cost-sensitivity analysis allows decision makers to see how different assumptions about various factors impact the final cost levels of specific proposals and alternatives. This then allows decision makers to budget better for resource requirements. *See also* **Sensitivity analysis**.

Cost-utility analysis: *See* **Cost analysis**.

Councilor capture: A form of local government failure where councilors (i.e., elected representatives) are "captured" by professional city/county managers given their ability to control the local policy agenda. For example, bureaucrats can control outcomes by only presenting selected policy alternatives to councilors to vote on. This is possible given the presence of asymmetric information between the two parties. This mirrors the form of capture that occurs at the central-government level as well, and can be viewed in the context of principal-agent relationships. For a discussion of councilor capture, see, e.g., J. Byrnes and B. Dollery, "Local Government Failure in Australia? An Empirical Analysis of New South Wales," *Australian Journal of Public Administration,* 2002, 61(3), pp. 54–64.

Counseling: As used in the employment context, this concept refers to providing advice to individuals on career growth, and other employment-related situations. Counseling is generally private, and face-to-face, and serves to provide emotional support as well to employees.

Counter-expertise: A situation where policy makers on both sides of an issue—using the same policy-related findings—recast their own alternative interpretation of the evidence. Thus, for example, policy makers who wish to decriminalize prostitution may be able to use the same statistics on sexual abuse to show that the profession should not be considered a criminal activity so that prostitutes could more easily report cases of abuse to the police. The notion of counter-expertise is used often in the context of disputing the validity of specific experiments and argumentation and to object to particular claims. It results from the fact that those who dispute a policy claim can always find some aspects of it that allows a counterargument to be made. This is possible also because any number of interpretations and assumptions that have been employed are susceptible to critique. For a contextual review of counter-expertise as it relates to policy analysis, see, e.g., F. Fischer, "Beyond Empiricism: Policy Inquiry in Postpositivist Perspective," *Policy Studies Journal,* 26(1), 1998, pp. 129–46.

Counterfactual: A form of reasoning that looks at the comparison between what is (i.e., actual performance) and what would have been (i.e., if no response had been forthcoming). There are four approaches to doing a counterfactual analysis: (a) before-after, (b) actual-target, (c) with-

without, and (d) comparison of simulations approach. For examples of counterfactual policy analysis, see C. Kirkpatrick and D. Tennant, "Responding to Financial Crisis: The Case of Jamaica," *World Development,* 2002, 30(11): 1933–50.

Counterpart staff: Individuals who are assigned to work along side experts from outside the organization. Usually applied in technical assistance in development projects, the premise in putting in place counterpart staff is that indigenous capability to manage will develop when skills of technical experts are best transferred to local staff members. However, it is not always possible to put in place counterpart staff, and this has been regarded as a serious threat to the efforts of donors to increase national capacity in developing countries. For a good coverage of this issue, see, e.g., D. Rondinelli, "UNDP Assistance for Urban Development: An Assessment of Institution-Building Efforts in Developing Countries," *International Review of Administrative Sciences,* 1992, 58(4), pp. 519–37.

Countervailing risks: *See* **Unintended consequences**.

Country-club management: *See* **Managerial grid**.

Coupling: The process of organizations coming together, either procedurally or in substantive terms, to better address problems that have multifaceted issues. In many public sectors of advanced jurisdictions, government agencies are required to engage in outcome planning with others that share a common mandate with any aspect of the outcome (such as a ministry of social welfare will need to work with the police and prisons to jointly address recidivism).

Cradle-to-grave protection: Protection provided by the state to eligible populations that cover the range of services from childbirth to the time of death. Many countries (even socialist ones, such as China) have begun to remove cradle-to-grave protection to all but a few segments of their populations because of massive costs in providing the services to an ever-increasing population base.

Craft organization: An organization for which outcomes can be observed but not outputs. A typical example is a government department that offers policy advice to government. See J. Wilson, *Bureaucracy: What Government Agencies Do and Why They Do It,* New York: Basic Books, 1989, p. 159.

Craftsmanship theory: A theory put forward by the noted authority on public policy Eugene Bardach to study interagency collaboration. Its central focus is purposiveness and how and why agencies can use opportunities to develop it. Craftsmanship theory is considered by Bardach to be superior to resource dependence theory and network theory of interagency collaboration. For his arguments for this theory, see E. Bardach, *Getting Agencies to Work Together: The Practice and Theory of Managerial Craftsmanship,* Washington, DC: Brookings Institution Press, 1998, pp. 19–51.

Creaming: (1) A process used during the recruitment stage where the eligibility and selection criteria are constructed such that they inherently favor those applicants who are from majority—not minority—groups. (2) Refers to an action by a contractor to quote a higher price for a service than what it actually pays in delivering the service. For a discussion of creaming as a form of market segmentation, see, e.g., E. Savas, *Privatization and Public-Private Partnerships,* Chatham, NJ: Chatham House, 2000, p. 312.

Creative federalism: Relationships among federal and state/provincial governments where both are interested in and capable of jointly formulating intergovernmental programs. In the United States, this form of federalism was largely in evidence during the 1960s and 1970s and is characterized by the formulation of the "Great Society" program where the federal government tried to fight various social ills such as crime and poverty by looking for new and innovative ways to solve them. As before, the federal government provided most of the funding while state and local governments were involved in executing the programs. For a useful discussion, see, e.g., R. Inman and D. Rubinfeld, "Rethinking Federalism," *Journal of Economic Perspectives,* 1997, 11(4), pp. 43–64.

Credible commitment: Steps taken by either the principal or agent in a contractual relationship to ensure that a contract is properly administered and enforced. For a discussion of the concept in relation to transaction-cost economics, see, e.g., See O. Williamson, "The New Institutional Economics: Taking Stock, Looking Ahead," *Journal of Economic Literature,* 2000, 38(3), pp. 595–613. For application in a government context, see, e.g., O. Yap, "Government's Credible Commitment in Economic Policy-Making: Evidence from Singapore," *Policy Sciences,* 2003, 36(3–4), pp. 237–55.

Credit culture: Where individuals and organizations make use of credit sources to meet their resource requirements. While such a culture could be for formal credit (e.g., from banks) or informal (e.g., from moneylenders), it is obviously preferable to encourage the former since transactions in the latter are not legally enforceable. One of the problems identified in developing countries is that the poor people do not wish to access formal credit sources either, usually because none are readily available to them for lack of collateral or that they are too wary of the tight conditions in which credit is extended.

Credit risk: The risk that lenders face when they extend credit to borrowers who cannot show collateral or who represent risky investments. In micro-credit programs, of the type exemplified by the Grameen Bank in Bangladesh, for example, the credit risk is considered to be very low since, notwithstanding the low level of credit, the borrowers (almost all of whom are women) are considered to be very reliable in repayments, not least because there is social and peer pressure to repay.

Creeping expropriation: When a government extracts revenues from multinational corporations and foreign firms by imposing high taxes and tariffs but does not actually nationalize the businesses. Creeping expropriation is used by governments to maximize revenues from non-national firms whilst extending them some incentives to continue to remain in the country. See, e.g., E. Janeba, "Attracting FDI in a Politically Risky World," *International Economic Review,* 2002, 43(4), pp. 1127–55.

Creeping risk: Also known as the "boiling-frog syndrome," this is a progression of adverse consequences or realization of risks that is so gradual, yet persistent, that people get used to it. Creeping risks do not tend to get analyzed during the standard risk-monitoring process unless strategic-planning exercises have flagged them as emerging risks. The current non-planning by several jurisdictions of the emerging demographic changes (whereby there will be an explosion of older workers) in the workplace may be considered an example of a creeping risk. The risk is that existing human-resource practices and work-life balance policies that are geared toward attending to the needs of a younger workforce will no longer be appropriate for an older one, thus leading to motivation problems and issue of qualified staff retention. For a discussion of the boiling-frog syndrome, see, e.g., G. Bhatta, "Organizational Competence and the 'Boiling Frog' Syndrome," *Organisations & People,* 2001, 8(3), pp. 11–16.

Crisis bargaining: Bargaining for a collective agreement that takes place in the context of a deadline for a strike set by the union. While this provides an impetus for both labor and management to come to a mutually satisfactory agreement, it also implies that their relationship was not particularly good to begin with.

Crisis management: Refers to the functions, policies, and frameworks in place in public-administration systems in all jurisdictions which enable governments to respond to the various crises that may beset them. A large part of the crisis-management function deals with rapid-response mechanisms and public communication so as to be able to manage the situation in the immediate aftermath of a crisis. This function has been placed at the forefront of public administration in recent years and governments have had to reorient various aspects of how they deal with crises such as floods, earthquakes, terrorist attacks, etc. For a discussion on the relationship between crisis management and public administration, see, for example, U. Rosenthal, "September 11: Public Administration and the Study of Crises and Crisis Management," *Administration & Society*, 2003, 35(2), pp. 129–43. *See also* **Safety management.**

Crisis theory of decision making: Asserts that policy decisions that are made in the midst of crises are characterized by minimal consultation with stakeholders, and limited consideration of policy alternatives. For an example of crisis theory of decision making in action, see D. O'Sullivan and B. Down, "Policy Decision-Making Models in Practice: A Case Study of the Western Australian 'Sentencing Acts,'" *Policy Studies Journal,* 2001, 29(1), pp. 56–70. *Cf.* **Rational comprehensive theory of decision making**.

Criterion: (1) A rule that allows ranking of various policy alternatives in order of desirability. (2) A normative requirement that must be met in order for the particular action to be taken. (3) A measure of job performance or other work-related behavior compared with a particular benchmark. A criterion-referenced test is one that measures the performance of candidates in relation to the extent to which they have met specified criteria. And a criteria-referenced performance is the performance of an employee, organization, or contractor that is measured on objective criteria. Such criteria are objectively measured (such as turnaround time for products), and are usually agreed upon *ex ante* by all parties. *Cf.* **Norm-referenced performance**.

Criterion problem: Refers to a problem that deals with how policy effects should be measured. When there is only one criterion to be considered, it is termed a scalar-criterion problem; when there are two or more criteria, the term that is used is a vector-criteria problem (or a multivariate or multidimensional criteria problem).

Critical event: (1) As used in performance evaluation and review technique, a critical event is one that has to occur at the designated time in order that the delivery date of the project's activities can be adhered to. Critical events can be rescheduled only if all parties, including the funding agency, give consent. (2) Critical events also imply criticality, which is the point at which any process or event in a system takes on a different structure or characteristic. Criticality is a concept borrowed from thermodynamics, which refers to the phase transitions that are evident when an intervention occurs.

Critical multiplisms: A policy analysis method that is based on triangulation of various sources of data, perspectives, and methods. The concept of critical "multiplisms" is used to add comprehensiveness to the generation of policy-relevant knowledge, and is a key element of evidence-based analysis.

Critical-incident method: A technique that focuses on the critical (i.e., significant) events (incidents) that an employee may have experienced so as to put his/her performance appraisal in proper context. Generally, employees are asked to justify their claims for organizational rewards by specifying how they reacted to the critical incidents which are supposed to be reflective of their work over and above what may have been specified in their job descriptions.

Critical-path analysis: *See* **Critical-path method**.

Critical-path method: A method of planning a project or program that calculates the boundaries of the time frame (i.e., the minimum and the maximum) in which it can be completed. This allows managers to determine which activities should be prioritized to be completed on time. The fundamental concept in the critical-path method is that of dependency— some activities are dependent on other activities being completed first (in which case they have to be done in sequence) while some could be done in parallel.

Crony capitalism: A situation where politicians and senior bureaucrats award contracts for services to family and friends instead of relying on the market to produce the most viable provider of service. A related concept is that of crony statism, which refers to a patronage system where the government systematically seeks to link friends, extended family members, groups, and others with rewards from the state based not on performance but on favors rendered. Such distribution of resources to client networks serves to lead to a corrupt bureaucracy, and is a drain on public resources. For an application of this concept with respect to a developing country and public-sector reforms, see, e.g., J. Cohen, "Importance of

Public Service Reform: The Case of Kenya," *Journal of Modern African Studies,* 31(3), 1993, pp. 449–76.

Cross-cutting approach: Refers to the manner in which a governmental department works with others by collaborating on specific issues. A cross-cutting approach is needed in public-sector governance when, for example, specific policy outcomes are the responsibility of several government departments, when there is need to improve the delivery of services that are complementary, and when policies are complex and multifaceted. For a very good analysis of when and how to be cross-cutting in public-sector governance, see, e.g., Cabinet Office, *Wiring It Up: Whitehall's Management of Cross-Cutting Policies and Services,* London: The Stationery Office, 2000, pp. 15–17.

Cross-functioning approach: As used in the context of developing policies, this refers to working horizontally across different policy makers rather than vertically in a hierarchical manner. Such an approach usually leads to cross learning, which is knowledge gained from interactions across organizations and across sectors. Cross learning is facilitated by formal and informal networks that exist among organizations.

Cross-occupational training: Training that is given to an employee so that he or she is able to perform a task associated with a different occupation. Cross-occupational training is linked to "multi-skilling" given its focus on multiple occupations, and therefore, multiple skills. See, e.g., J. Brickley, C. Smith, and J. Zimmerman, *Managerial Economics and Organizational Architecture,* Chicago: Irwin, 1997, p. G-3.

Cross-subsidization: Refers to the financing of an unprofitable part of a business or government mandate by a more profitable one. For example, in a developing country, the national airline may subsidize air services to rural and remote areas by charging higher fares for its more lucrative routes. For a detailed treatment of this concept, see, e.g., K. Fjell, "A Cross-Subsidy Classification Framework," *Journal of Public Policy,* 2001, 21(3), pp. 265–82.

Crowding effect: Argues that the payment of a reward (particularly monetary) to an individual or agent has the effect of reducing the intrinsic motivation of the party to be involved in other activities (i.e., it crowds out the desire to do something else, particularly if there is no incentive for it).

Cult of personality: As used in a leadership context, this refers to the concentration of power in the incumbent by virtue of his/her personality as opposed to the power being contained in the position that the incumbent holds. The obvious danger with such a cult is that the position is weakened while paradoxically the incumbent is not, and successors tend to have problems of trying to reconcile the two.

Cultural audit: A review of the underlying bases of how things are actually being done in an organization. For all the rules and regulations that exist in an organization regarding how specific processes are to be managed, the employees will have their own perceptions and idiosyncrasies around how they conduct their business. A cultural audit helps the reviewer determine what these underlying bases are so that proper modifications, if needed, may be made. For example, units within the organization, or specific individuals in it, may be hoarding information that may be detrimental to the work of the other units. Business-process reengineering is often based on such a cultural audit. See, e.g., E. Bardoel and A. Sohal, "The Role of the Cultural Audit to Implementing Quality Improvement Programs," *International Journal of Quality and Reliability Management,* 1999, 16(3), pp. 263–76.

Cultural bias: Any predisposition that goes against the underlying beliefs and backgrounds of a particular culture of people. Such a bias can be exhibited by employers (in relation to organizational activities such as recruitment), by employees (in relation to their interactions with each other), or in tests (in relation to measurement of ability).

Cultural capital: The term is drawn from sociology, and is used as an extension to the concept of social capital. It is taken in conjunction with other forms of nonmaterial capital, i.e., human capital and social capital. If human capital is augmented by giving individuals new skills, and social capital is created when interactions and relationships among groups of people alter in ways that facilitate joint and purposive action, then cultural capital is generated when society is able to act in unison so as to attain desired outcomes. All three forms of capital need to be emphasized if societies are to progress holistically. This description of cultural capital in the context of other nonmaterial forms of capital is taken to be akin to understanding systems as focusing on individuals, groups, and societies. The term has been analyzed as applied in different professions (such as economics and accounting). For a useful look at the term, see, e.g., M. Lamont and A. Lareau, "Cultural Capital: Allusions, Gaps, and Glissandos in Recent Theoretical Developments," *Sociological Theory,* 6(2), 1988, pp. 153–68.

Cultural empathy: The willingness to try to understand the reasons why individuals of different cultures act in different ways. With the rise of diversity in the workplace, organizations in all jurisdictions—particularly those in the public sector in light of legislatively mandated requirements— are beginning to consider cultural empathy as part of the required repertoire of an employee's competency sets. Cultural empathy is less of an issue in situations of cultural homogeneity, which, as used in relation to organizations, refers to the similarity of culture across various organizations.

Cultural web: A framework of filtering external developments through an individual's own idiosyncratic way, which is shaped by the value systems the individual possesses. When such developments are filtered throughout the cultural web, the result is always homogenous responses that are aligned with the existing biases that the individuals have. See, e.g., G. Johnson, "Managing Strategic Change: Strategy, Culture, and Action," *Long Range Planning,* 1992, 25(1), pp. 28–36.

Culture breakers: Refers to individuals and programs that are instrumental in deliberately changing the culture of a particular unit or organization. In cross-cutting work in government departments, for example, to demonstrate to others the utility of such an approach may require the selection of some policy issues that straddle various organizations (such as youth suicide) and then concentrated work could focus on it—with support from top leadership in the organization and even governmental ministers—so as to show to others how collaborative work can work in practice. The thrust of such work would be to show that established behavior (for example, on turf protection) could be altered with sustained involvement of various parties across government departments. See, e.g., Cabinet Office, *Wiring It Up: Whitehall's Management of Cross-Cutting Policies and Services,* London: The Stationery Office, 2000, pp. 45–46.

Culture governance: The term has come into usage recently in the context of how governments fulfill their functions either as a regulator or as a provider. The term refers to the fact that in fulfilling their functions, governments should be acutely sensitive to the needs and aspirations of local communities and the voluntary sector. And in contrast to the laissez-faire model of dealing with this sector, the notion of culture governance argues that governments should be in effective partnerships with them, and should serve as an enabling force. In reality, this interpretation of the relationships between government and the voluntary sector can be said to be encapsulated in the generic terms "good governance" and "interactive governance." Because culture governance has strong reference to government and communities working together, it is also associated with the notion of co-governance. For a review of the term, see, e.g., H. Bang, "Culture Governance: Governing Self-Reflexive Modernity," *Public Administration,* 82(1), 2004, pp. 157–90. *See also* **Co-governance.**

Culture-free hypothesis: An assertion that the nature of organizational structure will show similar attributes regardless of which jurisdictional setting is considered. For example, according to the culture-free hypothesis, in any county bigger organizations are likely to be more structured than smaller ones. For a discussion of the hypothesis, see, e.g., D. Hickson et al., "A Strategic Contingencies Theory of Intraorganizational Power," *Administrative Science Quarterly,* 1971, 16(2), pp. 216–29.

Cumulation: The process of taking concepts used in a different setting and reformulating them to be used for purposes other than those originally intended. For an application, see N. Zahariadis, "Comparing Three Lenses of Policy Choice," *Policy Studies Journal,* 1998, 26(3), pp. 434–48.

Current estimated potential: A concept that refers to the highest career point that an individual could reach in the future given what is exhibited in terms of present capability. This concept is used in personnel management systems in certain public sectors in the world (such as Singapore) so as to help organizational leaders engage in succession planning.

Custodial management: Refers to the underlying objective of public servants who consider their responsibility to be the custodians of good public service and of upholding public trust and confidence in their virtues of fairness, probity, and integrity. Altruism thus features strongly in custodial management, as does the value of public interest. The introduction of public choice theory in public service has been responsible for the current diminution of the utility and impact of custodial management in public-management systems around the world. See, e.g., G. Boyne and J. Dahya, "Executive Succession and the Performance of Public Organizations," *Public Administration,* 2002, 80(1), pp. 179–200.

Customer departmentalization: A form of structural design of an organization used when its customers have very different needs and, therefore, it groups activities based on the needs expressed by customers.

Customer empowerment: The concept that citizens (as customers that use government services) should have the power to voice their opinions if they perceive they have received poor service from public agencies. The establishment of the "Citizens Charter" in the United Kingdom, for example, was based on this concept.

Customized training: Training that is tailor-made to suit individuals, groups, or organizations around a particular theme. Customized training is useful when groups of employees in an organization are seeking the same enhancements of skills, as the overhead costs are lower. *See also* **Individualized training**.

Cutback management: Refers to government efforts at downsizing or cutting back on (i.e. retrenching) staff, operations, and administrative costs. However, the term implies that the cutbacks are not done in a random fashion but that there is a strategic approach to doing things more efficiently. Cutback management was common in the 1980s and 1990s across all jurisdictions, and one of the effects of that seems to have been the reduced capacity of public agencies to oversee the work of contracting parties. Public administration theorist Charles Levine was one of the first scholars to use the term (see C. Levine, *Managing Fiscal Stress: The Crisis in the Public Service*, Chatham, NJ: Chatham House, 1980). See also, e.g., R. Behn, "The Fundamentals of Cutback Management," in K. Cameron, et al. (eds.), *Readings in Organizational Decline: Frameworks, Research, and Prescriptions*, Cambridge: Ballinger Publishing Company, 1988, pp. 347–56.

D

Dampened pendulum: *See* **Managerial grid**.

Dangling event: In performance evaluation and review technique, a dangling event is one for which there is no preceding or succeeding events. Even though dangling events do not directly result from an activity, nor do they initiate any, the events themselves will be finite in time, and they will be relevant to the final output or outcome.

Deadweight: The amount of funding that is set aside for a particular project or program that is more than the minimum necessary to bring about the desired program outcomes. A deadweight may not be easy to calculate at the time of program formulation, but it should become evident during mid-term evaluations, for instance.

Deadweight losses: Losses from policies or from interactions among policy actors for which there are no offsetting gains. Policy actors seek to minimize deadweight losses when they are negotiating with others for specific policies, and they will try to ensure that they get something in return for giving up something else. *See also* **Lose-lose alternatives**.

Debarment: As applied to contract management, debarment refers to the blacklisting of contractors because they have not been able to meet performance expectations specified in contracts. Such debarment applies for a given period of time, which is determined by how serious the performance gap is.

Debureaucratization: The process of reducing the number and size of public organizations and of administrative processes within bureaucracies so as to try to make public management and governance more efficient and effective. The assumption here is that reducing the size of the public sector and having a smaller bureaucracy is inherently desirable. For an early discussion of the concept, see, e.g., A. Eisenstadt and N. Shmuel, "Bureaucracy, Bureaucratization, and Debureaucratization," *Administrative Science Quarterly,* 1959, 4(3), pp. 302–20.

Decentralization: When the central government, or the center, cedes some authority and power to lower levels of government. Decentralization can take several forms, including delegation, devolution, and privatization, to name a few. Administrative decentralization refers to giving agencies at the local level the authority to run most of their affairs without having to wait for approval from a central office. Accountability in this case rests with the local agencies (this is not necessarily so in all jurisdictions, however). Political decentralization refers to the same provisions for local governments.

Decentralization theorem: Asserts that all else being equal, decentralization is superior to centralized decision making. That superiority results if there are no known adverse consequences of decentralizing, which ultimately leads to greater societal welfare. The theorem is at the core of the concept of subsidiarity. For a discussion of decentralization in the context of developing countries, see, e.g., P. Smoke, "Decentralization in Africa: Goals, Dimensions, Myths and Challenges," *Public Administration and Development,* 2003, 23(1), pp. 7–16. For the decentralization theorem, see, e.g., W. Oates, "An Essay on Fiscal Federalism," *Journal of Economic Literature,* 1999, 37(September), pp. 1120–49. *See also* **Subsidiarity**.

Decision agenda: A list of policy alternatives from which a particular public policy may be selected. A decision agenda emerges when issues are ready for decisions by policy makers. The establishment of the agenda is a critical task because what gets included in it is what gets discussed in terms of government policies. Hence, policy actors that get to influence the decision agenda wield considerable influence in the policy-making process.

Decision control: The verification and monitoring of decisions in organizations. Control is exercised by management, and generally adheres to organizational hierarchy (i.e., those higher up in the hierarchy tend to have a greater degree of control over what happens in an organization and how it responds to its environment). Some decision latitude may be evident, however, which refers to the amount of control that employees have over their work. A low decision latitude means that there is little control and that most decisions related to their work are made by others.

Decision criteria: The standards that are used to make decisions. For example, the decision criteria around a large-scale transport-infrastructure project might be cost-benefit ratios, level of environmental damage, and degree of nonfinancial impact on stakeholders.

Decision making, time-relaxed: Decision making without any time constraints either in the generation of policy alternatives or in the actual formulation of the final decision. In reality, time-relaxed decision making in public-policy making is not readily evident since complex problems require considerable analysis and discussion, and this is a time-consuming process.

Decision matrix: *See* **Payoff matrix**.

Decision package: As used in the context of zero-based budgeting, a decision package is a document that serves to justify a particular program. Since in zero-based budgeting all programs in an organization need to be annually reviewed for continuation, there can be several decision packages prepared by the organization. The total amount of funds requested for each package cumulated across the organization adds up to its final request for funds.

Decision premise: *See* **Decision rule**.

Decision, programmed: A decision that is taken in the context of a repetitive or routine procedure, something for which the boundaries have already been set. A programmed decision is taken when, for example, a business case goes from a governmental department to the treasury for a consideration of extra-budgetary sources, and the latter subjects the request to its usual and set verification procedures.

Decision regret: *See* **Likelihood of regret**.

Decision rights: Determining who has the authority to make decisions in an organization. Decision rights are exercised by individual parties in areas over which they have the prerogative, given either by legislative mandate or by prior agreement among parties. Public organizations also exercise decision rights generally set by the legislature or by executive orders.

Decision rule: Any rule or principle that assists in making decisions. For example, a decision rule may be that certain organizational actions must be initiated when a problem crosses a particular threshold (such as product defects). A related concept here is that of acceptable level decision rule, which means that an outcome acceptable to the different interests be considered adequate rather than looking for the optimal outcome. Decision rules contain decision premises, which are the underlying values and assumptions that are employed in making decisions.

Decision science: Refers to how decision makers choose among different courses of actions. Decision science also looks at the design of efficient procedures that enable a decision to follow logically from the assumptions and parameters that will have been prespecified. Such parameters include, among others, the uncertainty of the situation, information about consequences, risks, and the revealed preferences of decision makers. *See also* **Satisficing**.

Decision simplification: Making the process of coming up with a decision simpler by disregarding the more risky aspects of a decision. By disregarding them, decision makers do away with the uncertainties that the risks would entail. Disregarding the risks, however, is not an option that organizations should ideally be considering. In its most basic form, decision simplification leads to incrementalism. See, e.g., L. Koenig, *An Introduction to Public Policy,* Englewood Cliffs, NJ: Prentice Hall, 1986, p. 353.

Decision space: Refers to the parameters within which decisions are taken by individuals and organizations. In the public-sector context, some of these parameters include: (a) the political context within which the issue is being debated, (b) the mandates and decision rights that individuals and organizations have been given, (c) the need for public consultations, if required, and (d) the extent to which a whole-of-government perspective needs to be taken (the assumption is that the greater this need, the tighter the decision space).

Decision support system: The term refers to anything designed to support the process of making decisions in organizations. In a knowledge-based decision support system, the organization uses an information base of all the expertise that exists in the organization to help in coming up with decisions. It may also rely on knowledge that exists outside the organization to which it has access (such as independent think tanks).

Decision theory: A body of knowledge on how decision makers choose among alternatives given the possible outcomes. Decision theory can apply to one of three conditions: (a) decision under certainty, where the outcomes of all policy alternatives are clearly known; (b) decision under risk, where each policy alternative will have several outcomes but the probability of occurrence for each alternative can be readily ascertained; and (c) decision under uncertainty, where the probability of occurrence for each alternative cannot be readily ascertained.

Decision tree: A graphical method of showing to decision makers all the risks and information needs that are available to them when considering decision alternatives. The graph shows the various outcomes that can result from alternative courses of action, including providing a balanced picture of the risks and outcomes that are related to each alternative. Decision trees are useful tools to aid in decision making because the various risks and outcomes associated with various options are clearly laid out, and policy analysts can quantify the values of the outcomes to help in selecting the appropriate alternative. For a case-study application, see, e.g., R. Lawrence and D. Deagen, "Choosing Public Participation Methods for Natural Resources: A Context-Specific Guide," *Society and Natural Resources,* 2001, 14(10), pp. 857–72.

Decision unit: As applied in zero-based budgeting, a decision unit is an entity (such as a program) for which budgets are prepared and funds appropriated. The budget at the organizational level then consists of a collation of the appropriations for all the decision units in the organization.

Decision, unprogrammed: A decision that is taken in the context of a new and unstructured environment where there are no prior boundaries set on how to address them. For example, if a disgruntled employee came up with a unique reason for a grievance complaint, the organization would be faced with making an unprogrammed decision on how to respond to that.

Decision-making heuristics: *See* **Heuristics**.

Decision-making opportunities: Opportunities that are available to organizations to consider alternative ways of doing things as a result of an innovation or the introduction of new technology. Thus, for example, a decision-making opportunity arises for an organization where a gender-neutral evaluation tool is introduced which allows organizations to better analyze job characteristics such that gender pay inequity can be better addressed. See, e.g., H. Greve and A. Taylor, "Innovations as Catalysts for Organizational Change: Shifts in Organizational Cognition and Search," *Administrative Science Quarterly,* 2000, 45(1), pp. 54–80.

Decision-making process: The sequence of steps that organizations need to follow in order to make decisions. Public-policy decisions, for example, usually have very complex decision-making processes since there are a multitude of actors and stakeholders involved. Decision making can be of various types, such as incremental (see **Incrementalism**), rational (see **Rational choice**), and consensual (see **Participative management**). A decision-making process can also be sequential or parallel (i.e., decisions on various issues can either be made in sequence, where one follows the other, as in dependent activities, or at the same time on different fronts, when each decision is independent of the others that are being considered).

Decision-making strategy: When organizations engage in decision making, assumptions and preferences of likely results interact to yield particular decisions. For obvious reasons, there is less certainty about some assumptions and preferences, and the matrix that shows their interaction yields four types of decision-making strategies that organizations can employ. When preferences for outcomes are certain, and so are assumptions of cause-and-effect relations, organizations use a computational strategy of decision making where they are confident of likely costs and benefits. Other decision-making strategies that emerge are: compromise (uncertain about outcome but certain about assumptions), judgmental (certain about outcomes and uncertain about assumptions), and inspirational (uncertain about both outcomes and assumptions). See, e.g., L. Ordonez and L. Benson, "Decisions under Time Pressure: How Time Constraints Affect Risky Decision Making Strategies," *Organizational Behavior and Human Decision Processes,* 1997, 71(2), pp. 121–40.

Deconcentration: As understood in the public-management context, deconcentration generally involves a very limited transfer of authority and financial management to local governments. These units are normally outposts of the central government, which maintains control over them, including by staffing them. Deconcentration is considered to be the weakest form of decentralization. *See also* **Decentralization**.

Decoupling: As applied in public management and governance, the term refers to separating functions, accountabilities, and roles of governmental departments. Such decoupling is brought about because of the application of, for example, agency theory, which argues this is necessary in order to avoid bureaucratic capture. Decoupling is evident in four domains of a governmental department work: (a) of commercial and noncommercial functions, (b) of policy and operational functions, (c) of the financer, purchaser, and provider roles, and (d) of ministerial responsibility and managerial accountability. For a discussion of such decoupling in the context of New Zealand (one of the first countries that embarked on this type of reform process), see R. Shaw, "Rehabilitating the Public Service— Alternatives to the Wellington Model," in S. Chatterjee (ed.), *The New Politics: A Third Way for New Zealand,* Palmerston North, New Zealand: Dunmore Press, 1999, pp. 193–203. *See also* **Legislative decoupling; Policy-operations split**.

Decrementalism: To cut staff size, program, mandate, etc. marginally (i.e., a bit at a time). This is in contrast to incrementalism, which means to add marginally. Decrementalism results, for example, when governments begin to have doubts about the utility of an existing program, and wish to send the message that the program may eventually be terminated.

Dedicated funding: Refers to resources that are set aside for a particular program or organization. There are two distinct manifestations of dedicated funding: (a) when organizations cannot use the resources for any other purpose unless authorized to do so by the funding authority itself or as mandated by law, and (b) when the funding authority makes a commitment for a particular level of resources for a set period of time. Such dedicated funding serves to reassure organizations of continued funding for the program as long as they meet the performance specification for the programs.

Dedicated trainer: A party (individual or organization) that is contracted to provide not only the actual training but also the gamut of activities that precede and succeed the particular training. A dedicated trainer is then a party that an organization contracts to help develop skills, and also expects the party to be involved in all other ancillary activities (such as designing, marketing, administration, evaluation, and record keeping).

Deep state: A coalition of all relevant stakeholders in a country working together for the same values. In Turkey, for example, the deep state has been described as one where the army, the security services, and the bureaucracy all work with the collective interest of maintaining the secular nature of the state. See *The Economist,* "Turkey's Generals: Brasshats v. Headscarves," May 3 2003, p. 47.

Deferred wage increase: An increase in wages that takes effect at some point in the future. Deferred wage increases are prespecified, i.e., the levels of increase are known in advance. Collective-bargaining agreements will normally contain provisions for deferred wage increases. Such deferral is both a positive and a negative development for employers in terms of their financial health: negative because the entity may have to incur increased costs at a later date, and positive because future wage costs may prove to be prohibitive and thus the entity may not have to incur a bigger wage bill.

Degradation: Refers to the decreasing ability of an organization to attain some of its mandates, or of any system's decreasing ability to meet prespecified performance standards. Such degradation can occur if there is a persistent lack of attention on increasing (or at a minimum, sustaining) an organization's capability in terms of financial, technological, and human-resource capability. Degradation can also occur if performance standards are set too high for an organization, or if its mandates are too ambitious. If such degradation does not jeopardize the organization or system's core, it is termed graceful degradation.

Degree of default risks: Risks that are inherent in any managerial action that deals with the extent to which an organization may default on its commitments. While not a particularly significant problem for public-sector organizations in terms of "going out of business," it does show the degree to which managers must be aware of the implications of their risk appetite.

Degrees of belief: The assignment of numerical probabilities to what will emerge. The concept of degrees of belief is useful to decision makers since it helps them quantify the odds of a particular alternative of delivering outcomes considering the risks such contains. See D. Ellsberg, "Risk, Ambiguity, and the Savage Axioms," *Quarterly Journal of Economics,* 1961, 75(4), pp. 643–69.

De-identification: Occurs when individuals in the organization feel no connection with it. This could occur, for example, when staff members are not inculcated with—or show little interest in—the organizational mission and values. Temps and short-term contractors are likely to show de-identification tendencies. De-identification is different from dis-identification, where one identifies in opposition to the organization. See, e.g., M. Pratt, "The Good, the Bad, and the Ambivalent: Managing Identification among Amway Distributors," *Administrative Science Quarterly,* 2000, 45(3), pp. 456–93. *See also* **Dis-identification**.

Delayed compliance: A tactic used by bureaucracies and others to not adhere to a policy intent. While this is not frequent in the public sectors of advanced jurisdictions, the same cannot be said of developing countries. Delayed compliance is most obvious when a government is not perceived to have legitimacy in the eyes of the public and the bureaucracy. See E. Bardach, *The Implementation Game: What Happens After a Bill Becomes a Law,* Cambridge, MA: MIT Press, 1977, pp. 98–124. *See also* **Blatant resistance; Tokenism**.

Delayering: (1) Reducing the layers of involvement of public agencies in the provision of services to citizens (i.e., making the services more accessible). (2) Creating a flatter organization by doing away with management tiers. For a good review of this concept, and for case-study applications, see, e.g., C. Littler, "The Dynamics of Delayering: Changing Management Structures in Three Countries," *Journal of Management Studies,* 2003, 40(2), pp. 225–56. *See also* **Corporate amnesia**.

Delegate: (1) Assign power to someone lower in the hierarchy. (2) An individual who is elected to serve in some capacity at a specific function, and who represents a particular organization or group.

Delegated legislation: Decisions and rules made by an executive body by power given (delegated) by a legislature. Delegated legislation enables a legislature to concentrate on essential principles and reduces the time spent on administrative matters. The legislature, however, retains the power to ensure that delegated legislation is not abused.

Delegated spending: Spending powers that are decentralized to regional and local governments. Such delegation contains specific provisions for ensuring that local bodies expend resources appropriately and that they are accountable for their use.

Delegation: The process of giving someone (or some entity, such as local government) the authority to carry out a task or make a decision. The responsibility for the task, however, remains with the person or entity that delegates the authority. An optimum level of delegation is where the total costs of such delegation are minimized. These are costs of dissatisfaction (as reflected in citizen backlash against government for poor service delivery) plus the costs of ineffectiveness (i.e., costs that the organization which delegates the authority incurs in terms of not being able to meet its targets as a consequence of delegating authority). For a discussion of this concept, see, e.g., D. Caron and P. Simard, "Delivery of Government Services: Toward an Optimum Governance Structure," *Optimum, The Journal of Public Sector Management,* 2000, 30(1), pp. 14–21.

Deliberation councils: Bodies created as channels between a state and the domestic private sector, which includes those of government, unions, and business, to deliberate on policies that affect the national economy and that seek consensus decisions on how to move forward. In many jurisdictions in which such deliberation councils have been established (such as Japan, Korea, Malaysia, Singapore), they have been given proposals to review on costly programs and subject the proposals to rigorous analysis. Deliberation councils also give some scope for outside parties (i.e., nongovernmental) to provide feedback on nascent government policies. On how such councils provide flexibility to governments, and on some of their limitations, see, e.g., World Bank, *World Development Report, 1997: The State in a Changing World,* Washington, DC: World Bank, 1997, p. 83.

Delivery problems: Refers to allocation problems arising from some entities being more informed than others about the quality of goods and services delivered. Such problems revolve around the quality, insufficiency, or inefficiency of goods and services delivered to consumers. Delivery problems add substantially to the level of organizational costs in terms of loss of goodwill (in the private sector) and trust (in the case of the public sector).

Delivery system: The manner in which goods and services are delivered to citizens. For example, nongovernmental organizations and voluntary associations could serve as conduits to communities with the required goods and services delivery. Delivery systems in the public sector are increasingly being geared toward ensuring that customers get what they want.

Delphi technique: Developed at the Rand Institute in the United States, this is a method of making a decision in a group setting by arriving at a consensus on a policy alternative. Here, feedback from the first round of judgment is circulated among decision makers for a second, which is again refined until a consensus decision is reached. The technique is iterative and includes the input of all parties.

Delta-type official: A term that denotes a type of government official who has high-level and well-honed capacities to see the organization through turbulent times. A delta-type official focuses on higher-order tasks and on understanding social processes, institutions and their dynamics, and possesses ethical reasoning. The official also has the capability to convey to organizational members such an understanding. See Y. Dror, "Delta-Type Senior Civil Service for the 21st Century," *International Review of Administrative Sciences,* 1997, 63(1), pp. 7–23.

Demand-side moral hazard: *See* **Moral hazard**.

Demerit goods: Also referred to as "merit bad," the term refers to goods that are considered to be intrinsically undesirable to society, independent of the individual revealed preferences of consumers. Examples of demerit goods include alcohol, tobacco, pornography, etc. *Cf.* **Merit goods**.

Democratic deficit: Describes a situation which exists in countries where as a result of the introduction of managerialism in public service, there is evidence of: (a) a weakening of the accountability of the public sector because much of the work is contracted out, (b) a diminution of the spirit of public service, and (c) a hollowing out of the public sector in terms of its participation in the social and economic domains. For a good discussion and case-study application of this concept in a public-management context, see, e.g., M. Kimber and G. Maddox, "The Australian Public Service under the Keating Government: A Case of Weakened Accountability?" *International Journal of Public Sector Management,* 2003, 16(1), pp. 61–74. For a political dimension of the term, see, e.g., P. Aucion and L. Turnbull, "The Democratic Deficit: Paul Martin and Parliamentary Reform," *Canadian Public Administration,* 2003, 46(4), pp. 427–49.

Democratic evaluation: Evaluation where the evaluators seek to ensure that all points of view are included in the exercise, and where evaluators act as brokers of information. In democratic evaluation, a highly participatory approach is emphasized which gives stakeholders an opportunity to eventually carry out their own self-assessment of their situation, as well as follow up on the recommendations on how policies and programs could be made more effective. For its usage in relation to development work, see, e.g., UNICEF, *Democratic Evaluation,* Working Paper No. 3, Bogotá: UNICEF Regional Office for Latin America and the Caribbean, May 1998.

Democratic governance: *See* **Good governance**.

Demonstration grant: A grant given to an organization for the purpose of testing whether a new idea or product is practical and can deliver benefits. Demonstration grants will be sunk costs to the donors if the idea or product ends up being not sustainable.

Department: A governmental agency generally taken to be in the core public service, and which exists to support the elected government of the day with policy advice and operational functions. It implements government's decisions, and carries out executive and regulatory functions. A department's mandates generally emanate from the legislature (i.e., they are statutory), and it must account for its actions to the legislature. Departmentalization refers to the process of grouping work or individuals into manageable units. As used in the machinery of government context, departmentalization also refers to the selection of the departmental form of organizational structure to get some governmental objectives achieved. Departmentalization can be of four types: (a) functional (occurs when an organization groups its activities according to functions; for example, finance, marketing, strategic planning, etc.), (b) product (occurs when an organization groups its activities according to the products it produces; for example, in an insurance company: life insurance, health insurance, property insurance), (c) matrix (occurs when both functional and product departmentalization is undertaken), and (d) territorial (occurs when organizations are broken down according to territories; for example, field offices of government departments in different regions).

Departmental decoupling: Setting up different organizations as a result of bifurcating those involved in helping make policies and those involved in policy implementation. Departmental decoupling was at the core of the "new public management" reforms of the 1980s and 1990s, and served to fragment the public sector considerably. While the decoupling better allowed departments to concentrate on their core business, it also weakened the interconnections between policy and operations. Some advanced jurisdictions have now begun to seriously consider whether they should continue maintaining a decoupling approach.

Departmental performance assessment: Annual review of the performance of governmental departments by a central monitoring agency. The assessment is based on criteria that will have been made known to departments ahead of time. Such a review normally focuses on issues such as departmental capability, statement of intent, and risk-management systems. Its primary aim is to ensure that departments are able to—and do—effectively fulfill their mandates.

Departmental revenue: (1) Revenue generated by a department resulting from its supply of goods, services, rights, or money to other parties. (2) Funds received by a department from the legislature to fulfill its mandate.

Departmental review: *See* **Departmental performance assessment**.

Dependent failure: The error that occurs when a related activity has a failure. Thus, for example, if a social-welfare agency does not effectively target family violence and child abuse, the agency responsible for juvenile crime may also not be able to cope with its caseload, thus increasing the possibility of failures in fulfilling its mandate.

Deployment: When organizational managers use human and financial resources for individual projects/programs for a fixed period of time. They can then be redeployed when the project/program is complete or when other pressing needs emerge.

Depoliticization: (1) A condition wherein citizens do not have all the means necessary—nor often the inclination—to participate in politics and in public discourse, and so the articulation of their political interests is neutralized. (2) To take politics out of consideration while engaging in an activity, such as formulating policy options, or making nominations for senior appointments in government and the bureaucracy.

Deprivileging: Taking away privileges from public servants (such as some fringe benefits). Deprivileging has been used as a way of seeking to reduce the size of the public service since it tends to reduce the incentives that individuals may be considering to join the service. See, e.g., J. Christoph, "A Traditional Bureaucracy in Turbulence: Whitehall in the Thatcher Era," in A. Farazmand (ed.), *Handbook of Bureaucracy,* New York: Marcel Dekker, Inc., 1994, pp. 577–89.

Deregulation: Minimizing or doing away with governmental rules and regulations so that private firms can more freely enter a market for the provision and production of particular goods and services. Deregulation was at the core of the "new public management" reforms of the 1980s and 1990s as politicians began to accept the argument that the government was limiting the full potential for growth in the economy, and that enabling the private sector—and competition—to enter the production and delivery of goods and services better served the needs of citizens. For a jurisdictional review of the concept, see, e.g., F. Cerase, "Japanese Bureaucracy in Transition: Regulating Deregulation," *International Review of Administrative Sciences,* 2002, 68(4), pp. 629–47.

Descriptive accuracy: A richer and more accurate explanation of reality. Descriptive accuracy is useful when considering how outcomes can be predicted by rational choice. Rational-choice theorists tend to minimize the role that descriptive accuracy can play in describing a situation because they are more interested in acceptable approximations rather than descriptively rich characterizations. The economist Milton Friedman, in an early work, argued as much (see M. Friedman, *Essays in Positive Economics,* Chicago: University of Chicago Press, 1953, p. 40).

Design specification: As used in contract administration, this term refers to all the information that a bidder of the product/service specified in a request for proposals must provide for the bid to be considered. Design specifications should be detailed, and should also specify contingencies.

Destatification: The process of lowering the scope of the involvement of a sovereign state in the domestic economy. This could be achieved in several ways, including the contracting out of services previously delivered by the public sector, privatization, etc. Many public management reforms of the last two decades have centered on destatification. For an example of such application to the labor sector in China, see G. Lee, "Labor Policy Reform," in L. Wong and N. Flynn (eds.), *The Market in Chinese Social Policy,* Hampshire, UK: Palgrave, 2001, pp. 12–37.

Destructive competition: Refers to a situation where because of competition in the economy, there is a danger of one entity losing at the expense of another, even though the government would ideally like to see a Pareto improvement (i.e., some entities gaining without others losing). If one entity seeks to enhance its position not by being more efficient and effective but by raising the costs to others, then destructive competition results, which does not necessarily serve the purpose of society as a whole. For a review of the concept, see, e.g., S. Salop and D. Scheffman, "Raising Rival's Costs," *American Economic Review,* 1983, 73(2), pp. 267–71.

Detailed audit: A form of audit where all aspects of an organization's internal control system are reviewed to ascertain that all activities and transactions are legal, mathematically accurate, and conform to applicable standards. While a detailed audit is recommended for all organizations, it tends to be carried out only when some serious problems become evident in organizational processes.

De-unionizing: *See* **Union.**

Development administration: A branch of study in public administration that focuses on the nature of government administration in underdeveloped areas and less-developed countries. The study of development administration reached its heyday in the 1960s when many former colonies become independent countries and began active programs of national development. See, e.g., D. Luke, "Trends in Development Administration: The Continuing Challenge to the Efficacy of the Post-Colonial State in the Third World," *Public Administration and Development,* 1986, 6(1), pp. 73–85.

Development intervention: *See* **Intervention**.

Development learning: (1) Refers to a process of internalizing lessons from observations. This implies that the learner acquires a greater degree of knowledge as a result of the experience or observation. (2) A term used to denote the lessons that development jurisdictions can take from the experiences of more advanced countries. This learning could be of any form, although it is generally understood to be in terms of the policy lessons that other countries can take from those that have already formulated and implemented them. Thus, for example, there was a fair amount of development learning that emerged from the contracting-out initiatives that were undertaken in the United Kingdom and the United States in the 1980s. See, e.g., V. Thomas, "Globalization: Implications for Development Learning," *Public Administration and Development,* 1999, 19(1), pp. 5–17.

Development objective: (1) Also known as a national goal, the term refers to the intended impact at the macro and national level of all programs and projects. (2) As a contract criterion, the government can encourage small businesses to tender for provision of goods and services whereby their bids are adjudicated not only based on price but also on the extent to which they can contribute to the stated development objectives of the government. See, e.g., D. Fourie, "Government Contracting and Official Capacity: Reflections with Reference to South Africa," *Asian Journal of Public Administration,* 1998, 20(2), pp. 233–48.

Development test: As applied in contract administration, this term refers to the assessment of a product (or a service) prototype to ensure that all required processes and subsystems are accurate and functional before a decision is made to proceed with full-scale development or provision.

Development, rights-based approach to: At its core, the rights-based approach to development is a notion that governments have a responsibility to promote a minimum standard of well-being and human development to which all people have a right (including rights of access to the fruits of development). This approach to development introduces the concept of accountability to the provision of services to the population. Accountability is also evident in the duty to provide suitable access to development opportunities to citizens. For a powerful assertion of rights-based development, see A. Sen, *Development as Freedom,* New York: Knopf, 1999. Sen's ideas are incorporated in the United Nations Human Development Report as well (see UNDP, *Human Development Report, 2000,* New York: Oxford University Press, 2000, pp. 19–26).

Developmental state: Refers to a nation-state seeking economic advancement that has a highly capable bureaucracy which is rather autonomous (insulated) from society, and which also makes the substantive decisions to allocate resources to key sectors of the economy. Given its capacity, such decisions are usually successful, and this yields a situation where the state has a very high level of savings, which enables the government to make investments in other areas. The end result of this is rapid industrialization and rapid economic growth. Singapore, South Korea, and Taiwan, among others, can be considered to be good examples of developmental states.

Devolution: A form of decentralization where power is redistributed to a lower government authority. Devolution is most commonly understood to be genuine decentralization. Under devolution, central government exercises little or no direct control over these local units unless over matters of overriding national interest. For a discussion of devolution in the context of the British civil service, see, e.g., R. Parry, "Devolution, Integration and Modernization in the United Kingdom Civil Service," *Public Policy and Administration,* 2001, 16(3), pp. 5–67. *See also* **Decentralization**.

Diagonal communication: The process of transmitting and receiving messages not only up and down the organizational hierarchy but also across different organizational units and divisions. Diagonal communication is a function of the degree to which the organization has network linkages with others, and the intensity of the interactions within the networks.

Dialectical organization: An organization that is responsive to the needs of its clientele. Such an organization is considered to be post-bureaucratic in that it veers measurably from the traditional Weberian notions of an organization. A dialectical organization is characterized by, for example, flexibility, free-flowing communication channels (such as between managers and staff members), and lack of hierarchy. See, e.g., O. White, Jr, "The Dialectical Organization: An Alternative to Bureaucracy," *Public Administration Review,* 1969, 29(1), pp. 32–42.

Differential threshold: *See* **Perceptual order**.

Differential user charge: A fee for services paid by all users but varied to account for their attributes (such as children using bus services will be charged less than adults). Differential user charges are designed to enhance equity, however, instituting controls to ensure that the charges are indeed fair can incur high transaction and compliance costs.

Differentiation: (1) The process of increasing variety, for example, when organizations that provide services to customers alter the mix depending upon the type of demand expressed by them. (2) Also refers to a situation when managers and specialists act differently because both groups are starting from different frames of reference.

Diffusion: The spread of any idea or process beyond where it was first developed or used. Thus, we can speak of diffusion of innovative practices across organizations in different sectors. The diffusion process itself is a function of: (a) the degree of interactions and linkages among organizations in a system, and (b) their absorptive capacity as they try to learn from the innovative practices of others.

Direct costs: Costs allocable directly to a cost center; for example, salaries, wages, and materials. Direct costs help achieve accurate financial measurements of each operation of an organization. They are also much more amenable to measurement than indirect costs. *Cf.* **Indirect costs**.

Direct provider: A party that supplies the good or service directly to customers. States can be direct providers as well as facilitators and regulators. Transaction costs tend to be lower for direct providers since they do not need to go through any other entity in delivering services.

Direct raiding: A situation that occurs when the value of assets under public ownership is below what would be expected. Direct raiding can be a product of the tendency of politicians to misappropriate funds or to be excessively prudent in investment decisions. *See also* **Raiding**.

Direct training costs: Costs that are incurred for inputs such as labor, materials, equipment, and logistics necessary to mount a training program. Such costs are tangible and feed directly to the production or delivery of the training. *Cf.* **Indirect training costs**.

Directive activity: In considering the self-interested behavior of bureaucrats, there is recognition that administrators need external guidance to establish purposes and rules. Such external guidance is termed directive activity. See, e.g., E. Redford, *Democracy in the Administrative State,* New York: Oxford University Press, 1969, p.193.

Dirigisme*:* (1) A particular focus on management and managerial aspects of organizational work. (2) The readiness exhibited by government to enter or intervene in the marketplace and manage a perceived problem of an allocation of resources. *Cf.* **Laissez-faire**.

Dirty-mindedness: Refers to being able to visualize the worst case in terms of what could possibly not go according to plan, and who would have an incentive to contribute to such a situation. This is a useful concept in forward mapping. See, e.g., M. Levin and B. Ferman, "The Political Hand: Policy Implementation and Youth Employment Programmes," *Journal of Policy Analysis and Management,* 1986, 5(2), pp. 311–25. *See also* **Forward mapping**.

Disciplinary action: Action taken by an employer against a staff member subsequent upon the individual violating an organizational policy or rule. Disciplinary action, however, does not normally imply dismissal from the organization, and there is a range of response from the employer, extending from a verbal warning to dismissal (also termed a disciplinary layoff). Any disciplinary action taken against an employee will be in accordance with the disciplinary code, which contains the standards and processes that an organization has in place to maintain discipline at the workplace. All employees will have been given details of the disciplinary code at the time of job entry. Organizations will also usually incorporate a discipline clause in the employment agreement that explains when, how, and why a disciplinary action is likely to be taken against an employee and what remedies the employees may pursue.

Disciplinary procedures: Internal administrative machinery for applying the disciplinary policy to an employee who has been determined to be in violation of some organizational rule or policy. Disciplinary procedures are normally hierarchical (i.e., they start out being fairly informal, such as verbal reminders, and then extend to formal ones such as investigations and disciplinary hearings).

Disclosure: Requirement to show or disclose all information pertaining to all aspects of the work of the organization. This is done to address, among other things, the problem of information asymmetry and that of lack of transparency. Disclosure requirements are embedded in legislative efforts (such as a freedom of information act), which provide access to official information from government agencies. *See also* **Nondisclosure**.

Discourse coalitions: Groups of relevant policy subsystems and policy actors that engage jointly for purposes of better informing policy debates. Discourse coalitions are part of policy communities. They tend to be formed among parties that: (a) subscribe to the same constructs and ways of thinking about a particular policy, (b) form routinized understandings about the issues related to the issue, and (c) assign credibility to some claims and not to others. It is not necessary that the parties have worked together before. For a review of the term, see, e.g., F. Fischer, "Policy Discourses and the Politics of Washington Think Tanks," in F. Fischer and J. Forester (eds.), *The Argumentative Turn in Policy Analysis and Planning,* Durham, NC: Duke University Press, 1993, pp. 21–42.

Discretion, time span of: Refers to the time it takes for an individual's decision to be reviewed. The argument is that the higher one goes in the organizational hierarchy, the greater the time span of discretion. Those in the lower rungs of the organizational hierarchy will have their decisions reviewed immediately for accuracy and effectiveness. The concept is used in determining role complexity of managers. It was first put forward by Elliott Jaques as part of his work at the Glacier Metal Company in London (see his "Preliminary Sketch of a General Structure of Executive Strata," in W. Brown and E. Jaques (eds.), *Glacier Project Papers,* London: Heinemann, 1965, pp. 114–29). See also "Time-Span of Discretion and Human Resources Management. An Interview with Elliott Jaques," *Personnel,* 1977, 54(4), pp. 47–58.

Discretionary budget: Funds that are available to the management of an organization that result from a difference between the monies that it receives from a legislature and what the organization needs to spend at a minimum to produce the required level of outputs. Economist William Niskanen argued that power-hungry bureaucrats have a normal tendency to increase the size of their discretionary budget. See D. Weimer and A. Vining, *Policy Analysis: Concepts and Practice,* 2nd edition, Englewood Cliffs, NJ: Prentice Hall, 1992, p. 133.

Discretionary grant: Any grant awarded by a central government to sub-jurisdictions at its own discretion. The decision rule around such discretion centers on the need to have legislatively specified conditions taken into account whilst making the grant decision.

Discretionary leadership: Refers to the need for leaders in the public sector to be aware of the policy parameters of any required organizational action. Since bureaucrats do not have the luxury of redefining the policy that they implement, being aware of the parameters of action is central to ethical behavior. For a discussion of this term, see, e.g., A. Kakabadse, N. Korac-Kakabadse, and A. Kouzmin, "Ethics, Values, and Behaviors: Comparison of Three Case Studies Examining the Paucity of Leadership in Government," *Public Administration,* 2003, 81(3), pp. 477–508.

Discretionary policy: A policy that emerges from the judgments of policy makers rather than strictly from a reliance on specific rules and procedures. A discretionary policy enables nuances in the policy situation to be measured, and more adaptive policies can emerge as a result. There is a danger, however, that by relying more on the discretion of policy makers, the resultant policies may not be entirely rules based. *Cf.* **Rules-based approach**.

Discretionary spending limits: (1) Any restrictions that are set on the level of discretionary funds that organizations may have access to. Such spending limits are normally specified *ex ante*. (2) Also refers to the limits within which organizations need to remain while spending discretionary funds (i.e., it is not just the level of discretionary funds that are limited but also the manner in which they may be spent).

Discrimination: Treating an individual unequally because of his or her race, color, religion, gender, sexual orientation, disability, age, or country of origin. Discrimination in public-sector employment has been banned in many jurisdictions because it goes against the merit principle, and it limits employment and advancement opportunities to whole groups of people. Also targeted are efforts to prevent retaliation against employees who complain of discrimination. See, e.g., R. Colvin and N. Riccucci, "Employment Nondiscrimination Policies: Assessing Implementation and Measuring Effectiveness," *International Journal of Public Administration,* 2002, 25(1), pp. 95–108.

Dis-identification: When employees identify in opposition to the organization rather than merely feel disconnected (which is termed de-identification). Dis-identification occurs when employees actively involve themselves in sabotaging the work of the organization. This may occur if they perceive some grievance against them by the organization.

See, e.g., M. Pratt, "The Good, the Bad, and the Ambivalent: Managing Identification among Amway Distributors," *Administrative Science Quarterly,* 2000, 45(3), pp. 456–93. *See also* **De-identification**.

Disjointed administrative system: Refers to an administrative system in which organizations are in constant conflict with their external environmental forces, and where they are not able to deal with all the pressures on them. This results in the disjointed nature of their responses as well as their work. A disjointed administrative system can result when bureaucrats are in opposition to elected leaders, as is common in developing countries. See, e.g., R. Khator, "Bureaucracy and the Environmental Crisis: A Comparative Perspective," in A. Farazmand (ed.), *Handbook of Bureaucracy,* New York: Marcel Dekker, Inc., 1994, pp. 195–210.

Disjointed incrementalism: Refers to a situation where an organization applies rationality inconsistently and in a piecemeal fashion. Over time, this results in disjointed incrementalism. Rationality does not mean that there has to be perfect information, just that organizations make choices on the basis of the information they have and can rationally acquire. The problem with most organizations is that they cannot apply this rationality consistently. See, e.g., C. Lindblom, "Still Muddling, Not Yet Through," *Public Administration Review,* 1979, 39(6), pp. 517–26.

Dismissal for cause: A situation where an employer ends the employment contract of an employee for some justifiable reasons, for example, unsatisfactory performance. Such dismissal for cause rarely ends up in court unless the employee can demonstrate that the employer fabricated the cause. *See also* **Redundancy**.

Dispersed strategy: Refers to the fact that in learning organizations, organizational strategies can emerge from anywhere. The traditional method of looking at organizational strategy has been centered on the top management level with strategic planning being a controlled and top-down feature; but in learning organizations, strategizing is a spontaneous process that can have several sources. See, e.g., C. James, "Designing Learning Organizations," *Organizational Dynamics,* 2003, 32(1), pp. 46–61.

Displacement-effect hypothesis: *See* **Displacement / concentration hypothesis**.

Displacement of goals: Refers to a situation where the objectives of organizations are subsumed by a greater focus on the means that are employed to attain the goals. In large bureaucracies, for example, it is said that given their focus on processes rather than results, displacement of goals is often a natural outcome. Strategies to stem displacement of goals in an organization include better planning for management of appropriate outcomes, and ensuring that all employees are imbued with the organizational values and mission.

Displacement/concentration hypothesis: Also known as the displacement-effect hypothesis, this asserts that the trends in growth of government can be attributed to significant events (such as major public-restructuring drives) which at first decrease their size but which after a period of time regain their original strength. It was originally expounded by economists Alan Peacock and Jack Wiseman, and they looked at the reasons for and patterns of increases of government spending over time. For their well-known work, see their monograph on *The Growth of Public Expenditure in the United Kingdom,* Princeton, NJ: Princeton University Press, 1961. For an application of the displacement effect, see, e.g., M. Henrekson, "The Peacock and Wiseman Displacement Effect: A Reappraisal and a New Test," *European Journal of Political Economy,* 1990, 6(2), pp. 245–60.

Dispute resolution mechanism: (1) A system of settling disagreements and disputes in an organization. The system ranges from informal chats with managers to formal court cases. (2) It also refers to the mechanism in place for organizational customers to voice their displeasure at the faulty or inefficient service and how they may go about getting them resolved.

Dissipative structure: An organizational system that exhibits characteristics of being adaptive, with the facility to easily break down an existing structure. Learning organizations, for example, tend to have dissipative structures since that allows them to adapt to the impetus they receive from their environments.

Distance learning: A type of training method where learning is undertaken across distance (i.e., the learner and the trainer are not physically together). Learning via correspondence is an example of distance learning. Advantages of distance learning include ease of learning (for example, at home), and less time commitment. It has its disadvantages too, which include no direct face-to-face interaction with the instructor. As the pressures of work and time—and the perceived demand for continuous learning—mount, distance learning has tended to become more and more appealing, particularly as the electronic dissemination of information and off-site learning has been greatly facilitated by the Internet.

Distinctive competence: (1) The ability of an organization to do better than its competitors. (2) A term used by sociologist Philip Selznick to imply an organizational mission. See P. Selznick, *The Organizational Weapon,* New York: McGraw-Hill, 1957, p. 42.

Distorted markets: When market failures or government interventions distort the relevant market. In distorted markets, price does not act as an effective clearing mechanism between what is demanded and what is supplied. *See also* **Market failure**.

Distributed governance: A term that refers to the idea of greater numbers of public organizations operating with some degree of separateness from core government ministries. With an increase in the number of agencies outside the immediate sphere of influence of elected representatives, distributed governance has taken center stage in public management. See, e.g., OECD, *Distributed Public Governance: Agencies, Authorities, and Other Government Bodies,* Paris: OECD, 2002, pp. 9–31.

Distributed leadership: (1) Refers to the different kinds of leadership that are evident at all levels of the social system. In distributed leadership, decision making is also devolved to lower levels rather than being retained at the center. (2) The concept also implies that governments should serve as enablers in that they should provide and create the opportunities for lower-level leaders to be effective since distributing decision-making abilities into the community is helpful for achieving social outcomes.

Distributional coalitions: Coalitions of interested parties that seek to maximize their share of government funding for specific programs. Distributional coalitions engage in rent-seeking behavior and profit from government subsidies and regulations. Such coalitions have vested interests and they tend to exploit regulations and other mechanisms in place to extract government funding. While the impact of such coalitions can be managed to a great degree in advanced jurisdictions, they can be very debilitating for developing countries. In general, the greater the size of the coalition, the greater the probability of its success. For seminal work on this concept, see M. Olson, *The Logic of Collective Action,* Cambridge, MA: Harvard University Press, 1965. For an application of the concept, see, e.g., H. Schamis, "Distributional Coalitions and the Politics of Economic Reform in Latin America," *World Politics,* 1999, 51(2), pp. 236–68. *See also* **Iron triangle**.

Distributive justice: *See* **Organizational justice theory**.

Divergent thinking: Thinking that veers from the traditional and standard ways of doing things. Fostering divergent thinking is said to be a key ingredient of an innovation culture within an organization.

Divestment: The transfer of planning and administrative functions to voluntary, private, or nongovernmental institutions. Divestiture, on the other hand, is when an organization or government divests (or gets rid of) its assets, for example, as part of a privatization exercise.

Division of labor: (1) Division of an overall task into smaller and smaller units. This has the effect of breaking down complex tasks into smaller units that are more manageable. (2) As applied to organizational structure, it refers to the number of occupational specialties in an organization. Division of work refers to a principle of apportioning work in organizations where specialization allows employees to enhance their expertise and be more productive.

Doctrinal coupling: A situation where politicians are given an opportunity to associate their doctrines to issues that need government attention. Thus, for example, perceived government inefficiency in the United Kingdom in the late 1970s offered the Thatcher government an opportunity to associate its doctrine-based solution (i.e., of managerialism) to the problem. This has been termed a situation where "solutions are attached to problems rather than the reverse." See N. Zahariadis, "Selling British Rail: An Idea Whose Time Has Come?" *Comparative Political Studies,* 1996, 29(4), pp. 400–22.

Doctrine of functional autonomy: Asserts that organizations are continually looking for ways to be independent and to minimize their reliance on the external environment to the extent possible. Engaging in this exercise is beneficial to the organizations since it gives them latitude to respond appropriately to changed conditions in their operating environment.

Doctrine of privilege: The philosophy based on assumptions and attitudes toward clients and employees that it was their privilege that they were being served, rather than their right. The shift in recent decades to the rights of citizens has stood at the core of reforms in public management and policy making.

Domain consensus: The degree of agreement on a set of expectations about what an organization is prepared to do and not do. This is applicable to both members of the organization as well as those outside its boundaries with whom it has any interactions. Domain consensus/dissensus, on the other hand, is the degree to which the organizational domain is generally accepted or disputed and contested in society. The greater the degree of dissent, the less the legitimacy, and the more difficult the environment for the organization in which to function. See, e.g., J. Thompson, *Organizations in Action,* New York: McGraw-Hill, 1967, p. 29.

Dominance: As applied to policy analysis, the term refers to a principle of screening alternatives where policy analysts do not have to consider how to make a trade-off. That is, if policy analysts agree that one alternative (or an approach to generating alternatives) is clearly superior to another, then that alternative (approach) is dominant, and the others can be disregarded. Thus, for example, the transaction-cost approach may gain dominance in arguments for a more relaxed regulatory regime. See, e.g., A. Mood, *Introduction to Policy Analysis,* New York: Elsevier Science Publishing Co., 1983, p. 33.

Dominant coalition: Within the sphere of action of any organization (both internal and external), there will be several coalitions, one of which will always be dominant. This is referred to as the dominant coalition. A dominant coalition is central in ensuring that the organization secures funding, mandate, and space to do its work; thus, organizations have to include them in any decision-making process. The nature of the dominant coalition helps explain the interplay of power and politics in the organization. See, e.g., H. Mintzberg, "Organizational Power and Goals: A Selected Theory," in D. Schendel and C. Hofer (eds.), *Strategic Management: A New View of Business Policy and Planning,* Boston: Little, Brown, 1979, pp. 64–80.

Dominant design: The predominant and most widely accepted way of doing things in an organization. For example, when organizations have settled on one way of using technology in strategic planning and decision making, a dominant design is said to emerge. See, e.g., H. Greve and A. Taylor, "Innovations as Catalysts for Organizational Change: Shifts in Organizational Cognition and Search," *Administrative Science Quarterly,* 2000, 45(1), pp. 54–80.

Dominant strategy: As used in the context of interorganizational dynamics, a dominant strategy is one that is the best for an organization no matter what the other parties employ. Obviously, when two organizations have dominant strategies, then the outcome is stable since neither party has an incentive to change, although this could also very well lead to a stalemate.

Domination of the political-policy process: Describes the eminent role that politics plays in the policy process. This is evident in four ways: (a) special-interest process: by which powerful groups influence government to satisfy their own needs; (b) policy-formulation process: dominated by what the elites perceive as necessary; (c) candidate-selection process: by means of those who are powerful and that have access to candidates; and (d) the ideology process: the dissemination of particular values and beliefs of what should happen and how. See, e.g., L. Koenig, *An Introduction to Public Policy,* Englewood Cliffs, NJ: Prentice Hall, 1986, p. 225.

Donor darling: A country, or the leader of a country, that is highly favored by a donor agency or country either because it shows considerable promise or some broader strategic interest is furthered by the association. For example, in Africa, Uganda's Yoweri Museveni has long been considered to be a donor darling. See, e.g., C. Adams and J. Gunning, "Redesigning the Aid Contract: Donors' Use of Performance Indicators in Uganda," *World Development,* 2002, 30(12), pp. 2045–56.

Dotted-line responsibility: Refers to the obligation to consult with other specified parties but not necessarily to report to them. There are two key observations here: (a) the parties to be consulted will have been specified *ex ante* (i.e., an entity not prespecified will not necessarily be consulted), and (b) all those that have been prespecified will, at a minimum, have an opportunity to engage in the process even though their input may not necessarily be incorporated.

Double majority, principle of: A principle of making decisions in a multilateral organization wherein any decision that is binding on its members must be passed with a majority in two areas: (a) the number of members, and (b) the level of funding such that the decision has to be agreed to by a sufficient number of members that contribute more than 50 percent of the organization's budget (also known as funders' majority). The latter prevents decisions from being hijacked by smaller members that do not collectively contribute substantially to an organization. For a proposal to apply this principle to an international organization, see, e.g., P. Nicholson, *Maximizing the Impact of the OECD: Reorganizing the Committee Structure and Related Matters,* SG(2003)1, Paris: OECD, 2003, pp. 96–97.

Double-agency problem: Refers to a problem that organizations face when different groups of people make strategic and operational decisions (i.e., when there is a disconnect between those who plan and those who implement). The double-agency problem affects many organizational processes including, for example, innovating a new product or service, and where the idea generation part of the strategic process is not well aligned with the testing and implementation part. The problem is also manifest where organizational scale and complexity lead to a distance between managers and those lower down the hierarchy. *See also* **Multiple-agency problem**.

Double-loop learning: Noted organization theorists Chris Argyris and Donald Schon describe double-loop learning as occurring when organizations are able to confront their own basic assumptions and underlying norms on all matters, and are willing to test them publicly to verify their relevance. This differentiates the learning process from simply heeding to the feedback from the external environment. The concept of double-loop learning has its roots in the cybernetic concept of second-order variation whereby organizations are able to not only respond to their environment to return to stability but also to alter the state of stability itself in keeping with what their operating environment dictates. This is the point where the double-loop learning takes place, and the move from the first- to the second-order variation (i.e., the extra learning that takes place) is termed system reflexibility. See C. Argyris and D. Schon, *Organizational Learning,* Reading, MA: Addison-Wesley, 1978, pp. 2–3.

Downshifting: (1) A term that refers to an individual putting more attention on personal and family life and less focus on work itself. (2) Also used increasingly to refer to the interests of older and senior workers in organizations to lower their level of responsibilities and work less as a transition to retired life. See, e.g., State Services Commission, *Facing an Ageing Workforce: Information for Public Service HR Managers,* Wellington: SSC, 2004, p. 13.

Downside risks: Risks that an organization faces at a future date but which are in fact derived in some way from present actions and decisions taken. Risk identification and profiling may or may not be able to adequately account for such risks.

Downsizing: Reducing the size of the organizational workforce as a way of cutting costs. Such reduction is normally planned, and the organizational leadership is generally well tuned as to how and where the cuts need to be made. Downsizing occurs, for example, when the organization is able to outsource some of its functions to private-sector contractors and others. *See also* **Cutback management**.

Downstream innovation interaction: An innovation that emerges from the direct interactions between an organization and its customers. This "near-market point" of innovation is said to be more informed of customer wants than those that take place further upstream in the organization. See, e.g., P. Cooke and K. Morgan, *The Associational Economy: Firms, Regions, and Innovation,* New York: Oxford University Press, 1998, p. 71. *Cf.* **Upstream innovation interaction**.

Downstream integration: *See* **Forward integration**.

Downstream progress: Progress that an organization makes toward the attainment of its mandates because of favorable conditions in its environment. This is in contrast with upstream progress, which relates to outcome attainment under difficult conditions.

Downward communication: Transmitting messages to individuals who are at the bottom of the organizational hierarchy. The term implies that communication is of a one-way flow from top management to staff members, and that there is little scope for feedback.

Downward flow of policy enforcement: While discussing ways in which citizens can influence the decision making of public officials, the downward flow of policy enforcement refers to the passive relationship between policy and the citizens. The passivity of such a relationship implies that citizen input into the policy is near negligible. See G. Almond and S. Verba, *The Civic Culture,* Princeton: Princeton University Press, 1963, pp. 16–18. *Cf.* **Upward flow of policy making**.

Dress down: Refers to a policy of an organization to allow its staff members to dress casually on certain days. The concept originated in the military meaning "not uniform." Organizations use this policy as a way of lessening the stress on employees, and also of presenting a less stern image to the public.

Drift: Refers to the shifts in organizational direction as a result of the formation and reformation of various coalitions within an organization's boundaries. While the nature of such coalition should not necessarily affect the overall direction, it is possible that the organization's dominant coalition at any particular point in time may be able to influence a shift in the way the organization operates. See N. Henry, *Public Administration and Public Affairs,* 6th edition, Englewood Cliffs, NJ: Prentice Hall, 1995, p. 90. *See also* **Dominant coalition**.

Dual accountability: Answerability of a group (usually in cross-departmental projects) to more than one budget holder (i.e., while individuals in the group are accountable to their own managers, they will also be accountable to the superior who is leading the project and who may be from another department or branch of the organization). While this should not normally pose a problem, dual accountability has the potential to complicate the group's relationships with managers as well as others. To avoid that situation, cross-departmental work will normally have very specific stipulations concerning responsibility and accountability.

Dual federalism: *See* **Layer-cake federalism**.

Dual-mode learning institution: An institution that provides both distance learning and face-to-face learning to students. This is designed to facilitate learning for those individuals who are in the workforce and do not have time to physically attend instruction classes.

Dual-track appointment: When an employee is placed on a system of career growth where he/she can alternate between two tracks on the way up. Thus, for example, a bright employee could be working in a department as a finance officer but also be in the elite service as a general manager. *Cf.* **Single-track appointment**.

Dual-career ladder: Also called a parallel-career ladder, this refers to the possibility for technical nonmanagement employees to move up the organizational hierarchy without becoming managers. All other conditions of appointment remain the same as for any employee, however.

Due diligence: Caution that is exercised by organizations when they are purchasing assets. This entails, for example, carefully checking the financial records of the company/asset that is being purchased. Due diligence is in integral part of risk management and managers are specifically required to comply with such provisions.

Due process: A fundamental criterion for administrative adjudications that states that any application of organizational rules must be based upon written guidelines and must be applied fairly to individuals who are accused of improper behavior. While organizations are expected to adhere to due-process stipulations, the burden of proof in cases where it may be lacking generally falls on the party that brings the case for adjudication.

Dumping ground of management: Better known as trashcan management, this term refers to the allocation of any function that appears not to fit anywhere else in the personnel (or human-resources) division. In many organizations, for example, gender-sensitivity training and knowledge management is allocated to this division.

Dutch disease: As applied to foreign aid and aid dependence, this term denotes a situation when a country has massive aid inflows such that it distorts the national economy. In these countries, it is not unusual to find foreign aid constituting up to three-quarters of the national budget. The implication of the concept is that despite the massive resource inflow, the country is not able to better its economy because of inherent systemic weaknesses. See, e.g., M. Godfrey et al., "Technical Assistance and Capacity Development in an Aid-Dependent Economy: The Experience of Cambodia," *World Development,* 2002, 30(3), pp. 355–73.

Duty to bargain: *See* **Good-faith bargaining**.

Dynamic complexity: *See* **Complexity**.

Dynamic consistency: Refers to the ability and incentives of governments to carry out the policy that they say they will. Dynamic consistency presumes, among other things: (a) political will and organizational commitment to the stated outcomes, (b) actions that are consistent with the prespecified outcomes, and (c) ability to reorient processes and systems, if need be, so that outcome attainment is not jeopardized. The key to dynamic consistency is that the judgment is made over time. See, e.g., M. Garfinkel and J. Lee, "Political Influence and the Dynamic Consistency of Policy," *American Economic Review,* 2000, 90(3), pp. 649–66.

Dynamic efficiency: Involves an optimal rate of innovations in firms and organizations to keep up with the changing market (operating) environment. Not all firms (organizations) attain dynamic efficiency, however, as engaging in innovations when competition is intense (or when procedural and systemic rigidity exists in organizations) is expensive. See, e.g., P. Ghemawat and J. R. Costa, "The Organizational Tension between Static and Dynamic Efficiency," *Strategic Management Journal,* 1993, 14 (Winter special issue), pp. 59–73.

Dynamic equilibrium: Denotes a stable situation in an organization that can anticipate and react accordingly to any impetus from its external environment. Dynamic equilibrium is evident in organizations when they are flexible and adept at dealing with change. The point at which organizations attain such equilibrium, however, will differ as they have different operating environments and different internal systems. Also, because organizations are continually adapting and readapting to their operating environments, unexpected outcomes are entirely possible. Thus, all organizations will have in place risk-management strategies that try to get a better handle on these unintended consequences.

Dynamic evaluation: The evaluation of constantly changing systems in organizations. Such changes could be evident in an organization's operating environment, in its internal processes, and in its goals and mandates. In dynamic evaluation, the object of evaluation cannot be specified with any degree of specificity in advance, and it is possible that it is rather loosely framed.

Dysfunction: Any attribute that does not increase the adaptability of an organization or system. Any organizational norm, for example, that insists on absolute and very specific compliance to the rules can be said to be a dysfunction since it does not allow the organization to make judgments on those situations where there may be flexibility in interpreting the rules or when the rules preclude swift organizational action.

E

Early-warning system: Any system in place in organizations that cues them early on when policies are not delivering the results that have been specified. Such a system could include stakeholder feedback, monitoring outcomes, and periodic external review, and are designed to give the organization scope to manage problems early.

Earmarked funds: Funds that have been designated or set aside—but not necessarily committed to—for specific activities and programs. Information on earmarked funds allows organizations to better plan their projected level of activities.

Economic determinism: A doctrine that asserts that human behavior is primarily motivated by economic rationale. Drawing on the doctrine of economic determinism is the concept of economic man, which argues that humans are always seeking the maximum reward at minimum possible cost (i.e., act rationally). The economic man concept can be applied in instances where, for example, managers act on the premise that employees are motivated solely by money and that by manipulating that variable, they can get individuals to be more productive. See, e.g., W. Kern, "Classical Economic

Man: Was He Interested in Keeping Up with the Joneses?" *Journal of the History of Economic Thought,* 2001, 23(3), pp. 353–68.

Economic governance: At the macro level, economic governance refers to how national economies are managed (such as in monetary and fiscal policies, and investment-decision structures). At the micro level, the term refers to the structure of how the production process in organizations is set up. For a discussion see, e.g., P. Cooke and K. Morgan, *The Associational Economy: Firms, Regions, and Innovation,* New York: Oxford University Press, 1998, pp. 170–72. *Cf.* **Political governance**.

Economic man: *See* **Economic determinism**.

Economic problem: The basic problem of how to allocate scarce resources among competing ends. In general, three ways in which such allocation tends to be made can be identified: (a) by love (i.e., voluntarily, as in philanthropic contributions), (b) by trade (i.e., through the market, as in trade between a supplier and those who demand specific goods and services), and (c) by force (i.e., dictated by bureaucrats, as in central planning). Note that the three are not mutually exclusive and they can be in evidence jointly in any economy.

Economic rationalism: While there is no distinct school of thought in economics centered on the concept of economic rationalism, as applied in public-sector management (PSM), it refers to the thinking that has dominated PSM in the last two decades that has at its core the notions of managerialism, downsizing, corporatization, outsourcing and privatization, minimization of transaction costs, and competition as a tool to increase efficiency in the sector. For a comprehensive essay on this subject with application in the Australian context, see C. James, "Economic Rationalism and Public Sector Ethics: Conflicts and Catalysts," *Australian Journal of Public Administration,* 2003, 62(1), pp. 95–108.

Economic risk: *See* **Risk**.

Economically active persons: People that are engaged in production and in productive activities. These are individuals who get paid wages and salaries for their labor, and they are included in the calculation of dependency ratios for those who are not in the workforce.

Economy: The absence of waste, and frugality in minimizing the cost of resources used in the attainment of organizational mandates but without compromising the quality of the products or services delivered. Economy has been a core element of the "value for money" concept. See, e.g.,

J. Broadbent and R. Laughlin, "Evaluating the 'New Public Management' Reforms in the UK: A Constitutional Possibility?" *Public Administration,* 1997, 75(3), pp. 487–507. *See also* **Value for money**.

Economy and efficiency audit: Also referred to as an operations audit, this is an audit that is not concerned with the flow of funds but whether the funds were spent at the least cost to carry out activities required of the organization. The following are some of the considerations that are taken into account when conducting an economy and efficiency audit: (a) ineffective and costly procedures, (b) duplication of work, (c) performance of work that is not tied to organizational mandates, (d) overstaffing given the size of the organizational mandate, (e) accumulation of excess assets, and (f) wasteful use of resources.

E-culture: Refers to the attitudes of employees and managers in an organization toward actively utilizing new knowledge-management (particularly information technology) systems. Creating an e-culture among staff members and organizational leaders, and overcoming their reluctance to utilizing new systems, is a rising concern in many jurisdictions. For a brief review of cross-jurisdictional experiences in enhancing e-culture in the public sector, see, e.g., D. Shim, "Recent Human Resources Developments in OECD Member Countries," *Public Personnel Management,* 2001, 30(3), pp. 323–47.

Effective government, theory of: A theory put forth by H. Rainey and P. Steinbauer that asserts that there are a number of attributes that characterize effectiveness in governments. Those that relate to public management include human-resource development and leadership. They argue that leadership, in particular, is among the most important drivers of governmental effectiveness. See H. Rainey and P. Steinbauer, "Galloping Elephants: Developing Elements of a Theory of Effective Government Organizations," *Journal of Public Administration Research and Theory,* 1999, 9(1), pp. 1–32.

Effectiveness: A measure of how well an organization's outputs contribute to the government's outcomes, and can be seen as meaning "doing the right things." The term is a core element of the "value for money" concept. A related term is efficacy, which refers to the ability to make an impact on intended outcomes. For a discussion of effectiveness with respect to public-management systems, see, e.g., A. Kibblewhite, "Effectiveness: The Next Frontier in New Zealand," *International Public Management Journal,* 2000, 3(1), pp. 79–91. *See also* **Value for money**.

Efficiency: Efficiency is concerned with achieving the lowest cost for a given output at prevailing factor prices (this is the standard interpretation of productive efficiency). In that sense, it looks at doing things right. There are two types of efficiency: (a) technical efficiency (when fewer inputs are used to produce the same level of outputs), and (b) economic or allocative efficiency (when a given level of output is produced at the lowest possible cost). Efficiency, along with economy and effectiveness, is a core element of the value-for-money concept. The efficiency principle asserts that organizations generally seek to cut back on transactions costs. Such costs are evident, for example, in an organization's efforts to monitor, coordinate, and motivate those involved with it in agency relationships. *See also* **Value for money**.

Efficiency agenda: The focus of governments whereby departments are continually being asked to demonstrate in their periodic reporting arrangements how they have enhanced efficiency in their operations. The efficiency agenda thus serves to put the focus on ways to improve accountability of scarce public funds, and to direct the public's attention to any wasteful public spending in/by governmental departments.

Efficiency audit: *See* **Economy and efficiency audit**.

Efficiency dividend: Also known as an efficiency gain, this refers to that portion of the performance of a governmental department that is the result of measures taken to cut costs. In many cases, such efficiency dividends result in the treasury making an expenditure reduction for that department since costs are now lower. Critics argue that the savings resulting from efficiencies should be retained by the departments. For a brief review of efficiency dividends and the experiences of some jurisdictions, see, e.g., GAO, *Managing for Results: Experiences Abroad Suggest Insights for Federal Management Reforms,* GAO/GGd-95–120, Washington, DC: US General Accounting Office, 1995, pp. 49–50. See also, e.g., G. Boyne, "Bureaucratic Theory Meets Reality: Public Choice and Service Contracting in US Local Government," *Public Administration Review,* 1998, 58(6), pp. 474–84.

Efficiency gain: *See* **Efficiency dividend**.

Efficiency, total: Results from an organization altering the machinery for making decisions rather than just the decisions on efficiency drives alone. On the other hand, mixed efficiency refers to altering the mandated objective to suit available resources. In this process, the mandate may be diffused but the original intent still remains. Likewise, pure efficiency is a state where objectives are met at lowest cost to an organization. For a discussion, see, e.g., D. Dillman, "The Thatcher Agenda, the Civil Service, and 'Total Efficiency,'" in A. Farazmand (ed.), *Handbook of Bureaucracy,* New York: Marcel Dekker, Inc., 1994, pp. 241–52.

Egalitarian networks: Networks that have two or more equally effective communication channels. In such networks among organizations, hierarchies do not tend to exist, and interactions among network participants and actors are based on trust and informal agreements (i.e., while there may be standard operating procedures in place, disagreements and conflicts tend to be addressed largely, and initially, through informal channels). *Cf.* **Hierarchical networks**.

Ego network: The composition of an organization's networks, which has three aspects: (a) direct ties (i.e., links with those that an organization relies on for attaining its core mandate), (b) indirect ties (i.e., links with those that an organization does not fully rely on for attaining its core mandate), and (c) structural holes (i.e., any disconnects between an organization and its partners). See G. Ahuja, "Collaboration Networks, Structural Holes, and Innovation: A Longitudinal Study," *Administrative Science Quarterly,* 2000, 45(3), pp. 425–55.

E-government: The use of information and communication technologies (particularly the Internet) as a tool in managing the affairs of government. Principles that govern e-government programs include: (a) they must be citizen-centered and must focus on making government services—and government itself—more accessible to the citizens, (b) they must be able to produce measurable results for citizens, and (c) they must actively promote innovation in the provision of goods and services. The interlinkages in e-government are also evident across three key nodes: (a) government to citizen (G2C), where the focus is on providing a one-stop service to those who wish to access government services; (b) government to business (G2B), where governments try to reduce the burden on private firms and businesses to be involved in the marketplace; and (c) government to government (G2G), where various levels of government (i.e., at the central, regional and local level) seek to together provide more efficient and effective services to citizens.

E-grassroots: The process of using information and communications technology to generate and collect grassroots feedback on specific policy issues and to convey those to policy makers. E-grassroots has been used by politicians to canvass local-level support for their candidacies for public office. For an application, see, e.g., M. Lord, "Constituency Building as the Foundation for Corporate Strategy," *Academy of Management Executive,* 2003, 17(1), pp. 112–24.

Eighty percent rule: Also known as the four-fifths rule, this refers to a rule by which selection of minority members in an organization must exceed 80 percent or more of that of the majority group, otherwise there is said to be adverse impact on minority recruitment. The eighty-twenty rule originally referred to the presence of many that were considered inconsequential and a few that were critical in any system. Increasingly, as applied in work settings, it now means getting 80 percent right and the rest will follow.

Elastic decentralization: Decentralization where the balance of power between two units of government is not rigid and allows for a greater or lower level of central involvement depending upon what purpose needs to be served. This is, then, a much looser application of the decentralization principle and enables national governments to better tune their relationships with local governments. For an application of the term, see, e.g., H. Werlin, "Poor Nations, Rich Nations: A Theory of Governance," *Public Administration Review,* 2003, 63(3), pp. 329–42.

E-leadership: Refers to the kind of leadership that is needed for the pursuit of effective utilization and application of e-business in organizations. Leadership attributes for such a case include, among other things: (a) drive for continuous learning, (b) willingness to take risks, and (c) ability to build and retain talent. Also relevant is the ability to develop and nurture organizational linkages and networks since much organizational learning takes place in that environment. For a discussion of this concept, see, e.g., G. Kissler, "e-Leadership," *Organizational Dynamics,* 2001, 30(2), pp. 121–33.

Elective affinity: A term that refers to a belief system that individuals have through which they evaluate the events around them. Obviously, different individuals and communities have different ways of evaluating such events given that each has a different belief system. It is thus important for policy makers to be aware of such elective affinities of different groups if they are to better target public policies designed to assist vulnerable and marginalized population groups, for example.

Elective dictatorship: A system of government that is described as being based on the dominance of the executive over the legislature, particularly a unicameral parliament elected under a first-past-the-post electoral system (i.e., where the candidate who receives a majority of votes in a parliamentary district thus wins the seat—winner take all). The notion of a dictatorship arises from the perceived lack of restraining power that can be exercised over the government that is formed by the majority party in parliament during its mandate. See, e.g., R. Mulgan, "The Elective Dictatorship in New Zealand," in H. Gold (ed.), *New Zealand Politics in Perspective* (3rd ed.), Auckland: Longman Paul, 1992, pp. 513–32.

Elective politics: Related to patronage, elective politics is evident when successful executive politicians (such as presidents and governors) reward supporters with executive appointments. See, e.g., N. Riccucci and J. Saidel, "The Demographics of Gubernatorial Appointees: Toward an Explanation of Variation," *Policy Studies Journal,* 2001, 29(1), pp. 11–22. *See* also **Patronage**.

Elite: Refers to a controlling group or a minority of people whose preferences regularly prevail over those of others in society. In many jurisdictions, the senior executive service has been critiqued as being elitist since entry into the service is restricted to those few who are considered very bright. Elitism is a doctrine that stipulates that the elites in society should be in leadership positions. For use and a measure of the term, see e.g., R. Gregory, "The Attitudes of Senior Public Servants in Australia and New Zealand: Administrative Reform and Technocratic Consequence?" *Governance: An International Journal of Policy and Administration,* 1991, 4(3), pp. 295–331. *See also* **Governing elites**.

Elite accommodation: A process of coming up with policies that suit the interests of the elites in society so as to co-opt them and stifle any opposition from them. For a discussion of the role of bureaucratic elites in the affairs of less-developed countries, see, e.g., P. Mosley et al., *Aid and Power: The World Bank and Policy-Based Lending,* London: Routledge, 1991, p. 173.

Elite agencies: A term that refers to those select agencies in the public sector that exercise considerable power over other departments. These are normally central agencies (such as the ministry of finance or the treasury, the prime minister's office, etc.). Elite agencies engage in elite circulation, which is a process by which organizations recharge and strengthen themselves by recruiting new and promising leaders from lower levels into policy-making levels or positions of authority. For an example of some of these agencies in jurisdictions around the world, see World

Bank, *World Development Report, 1997,* Washington, DC: World Bank, 1997, p. 83.

Elite theory of decision making: Asserts that policy making is best left to the experts, and characterizes a situation where the locus of decision-making power is vested in some experts or elites. Viewed differently, this relates to a rational decision-making process since neutrally competent decision making is more feasible from technical experts than from others. *Cf.* **Group theory of policy making**.

Embedded autonomy: A situation where the state has the latitude and ability to act independently and at will (i.e., has bureaucratic insularity), but at the same time is quite aware of what society (such as the business sector) is going to be concerned about next. See, e.g., P. Evans, *Embedded Autonomy: States and Industrial Transformation,* Princeton, NJ: Princeton University Press, 1995, p. 50.

Embedded risk management: A system of dealing with risks in organizations whereby there is a continuous attention paid to the risks as opposed to something added on as a result of something gone wrong. In that regard, embedded risk management is similar to quality control systems and internal control systems in organizations. With embedded risk management, risks are managed even without the presence of risk managers and risk-management specialists. The system is centered on the extent to which public-sector managers support and promote risk management, the organizational culture that permits innovation and risk taking and how it deals with failures, the extent to which all staff members are aware of the benefits of effective risk management, and whether the risks associated with working with other organizations have been assessed and managed. For a discussion of embedded risk management in the public sector, see, e.g., National Audit Office, *Supporting Innovation: Managing Risk in Government Departments,* Report by the Comptroller and Auditor General, HC 864 1999–2000, London: The Stationery Office, 17 August 2000, Annex 1.

Emergency management: *See* **Safety management**.

Emic norms: Values of staff members in an organization that are self-perceived and internally driven. These norms are contrasted with etic norms, which are value systems of individuals and organizations that are externally observed, and constitute what the public sees of the organization. See, e.g., C. Fombrun, "Structural Dynamics Within and Between Organizations," *Administrative Science Quarterly,* 1986, 31(3), pp. 403–21.

Eminent domain: The right of a government authority to take private property—suitably compensated (i.e., at market value)—for public use. Governments should have eminent domain so that they can deliver public goods to as wide a constituency as is possible.

Emotional intelligence: Used as a competency requirement for employment, emotional intelligence refers to the ability of individuals not only to express their own feelings and emotions but also to understand those of others with whom they share the workspace. Establishing cooperative relationships with others at work is also considered an emotional intelligence competency. For more on this concept, see, e.g., G. Orme and R. Bar-On, "The Contribution of Emotional Intelligence to Individual and Organizational Effectiveness," *Competency & Emotional Intelligence,* 2002, 9(4), pp. 23–28.

Empire building: As used in the public-management context, this concept refers to the activities of bureaucrats who seek increased mandates for their organizations, greater organizational resources, and greater control over different units and entities in their operational environment. *See also* **Bureaucratic expansion**.

Employability: The state of being able to be employed in other organizations, jobs, and in the future. Employee development programs are now increasingly focused on increasing the individuals' employability rather than just increasing their skills for the current work they do.

Employee development: Any measure targeted at developing staff members' skills and career potential so that they may move up to more responsible positions in the future. *See also* **Training and development**.

Employee entitlements: Benefits that employees are entitled to in the occupations and positions they occupy. Such entitlements can be mandatory (such as annual leave) or discretionary (such as use of official vehicles for personal travel). *See also* **Entitlements**.

Employee involvement: Getting employees involved in organizational decision-making processes. Five levels of such involvement can be ascertained, in order of degree of participation of the employees in substantive decision making: (a) informal (i.e., being told of the decision after it has been made), (b) consulted (i.e., discussed, with an opportunity to provide some feedback but the decision has already been arrived at), (c) given scope to develop (i.e., participate in developing solutions), (d) given input in decision making (i.e., opportunity to influence final decisions), and (e) involved in final decisions (i.e., full partners in reaching final solutions). See C. Donald, T. Lyons, and R. Tribbey, "A Partnership for Strategic Planning and Management in a Public Organization," *Public Performance and Management Review,* 2001, 25(2), pp. 176–93.

Employee-proposed discipline: An approach to workplace discipline that is initiated by employees themselves (usually through a union) and which stipulates the discipline they feel is warranted for infractions that may be committed at work. If management agrees that the disciplinary measures so specified are adequate, then employees and unions cannot consider any resultant action that management might take as contestable (i.e., as something against which there can be complaints). For a review of the concept and a case-study application, see, e.g., K. King and D. Wilcox, "Employee-Proposed Discipline: How Well Is It Working?" *Public Personnel Management,* 2003, 32(2), pp. 197–209.

Employer of choice: A concept that refers to the drive by public-sector organizations to be seen as attractive employers that offer suitable challenges to employees, reward them suitably, and consider their work-life balance as well. The public sector of various jurisdictions has such drivers in place largely to ensure that they continue to attract high-caliber and highly motivated individuals also to public-sector careers. For a case-study discussion of an employer-of-choice program, see, W. Vandenabeele, A. Hondeghem, and T. Steen, "The Civil Service as an Employer of Choice in Belgium: How Work Orientations Influence the Attractiveness of Public Employment," *Review of Public Personnel Administration,* 24(4), pp. 319–33.

Employment-at-will: A contract for employment that can be terminated at any time by either the employer or employee without having to produce any cause for it or having to give a notice to the other party in advance. An employment-at-will is characterized by the fact that it is not set for a specific term, and the employee is aware in advance of its stipulations.

Employment contract: An agreement between an employer and employees that specifies their relationships wherein the employer agrees to reward the employees for work they do in fulfillment of relevant organizational mandates. Some key dimensions of an employment contract include the complexity of the contract, and the frequency of recurrence (i.e., how often it comes up for negotiation). When an employment contract is made for the long term, both the employer and employee commit themselves to each other (i.e., there is bilateral monopoly) and there is less "competition" to gain the upper hand in contract negotiations. See W. Shugart, *The Organization of Industry,* Homewood, IL: Richard D. Irwin, Inc., 1990, pp. 48–54.

Employment modes: Different time-bound types of employment, which include: (a) ongoing (i.e., staff employed on an indefinite basis), (b) fixed term (i.e., staff employed for a finite period of time), (c) casual (i.e., staff paid on an hourly rate for no definite time period), and (d) temporary (i.e., staff hired for a very short period and on a temporary basis for specific tasks).

Employment parity: *See* **Parity**.

Employment protection legislation: Any law or regulation that is related to recruitment and hiring (for example, conditions for using fixed or temporary contracts, and training requirements), and contract termination (for example, redundancy procedures, and severance payments). The objective of the legislation is to ensure that individuals' rights are safeguarded in any employment relationship.

Employment relations: A generic term that refers to all the relationships between employers and employees as specified not only in employment contracts but also as practiced in the organization. This can include human-resource practices, wage negotiation processes, grievance procedures, etc.

Employment testing: Using appropriate measures to assess the knowledge, skills, and abilities of candidates who have expressed interest in being employed in the organization. Employment testing can be done by the organization interested in the candidate or by an outside party after being contracted to provide such service. Regardless of who conducts the tests, however, the tests must be verified as possessing validity.

Empowerment: (1) As used in organizational settings, the term refers to managers sharing power with employees, thus helping in increasing their sense of self-worth and self-efficacy. (2) As used in a governance context, it refers to giving communities and individuals and citizens the opportunities to be involved in shaping policy and in implementing them. Empowerment evaluation occurs when program/project participants conduct their own evaluations and examine issues they themselves bring up. However, use may be made of a trained facilitator who may help in getting participants to raise relevant issues and to marshal them into useful channels. Such empowerment evaluation is said to yield enduring organizational benefits since this invariably leads to a culture of using evaluations. Care should be taken, though, that such a tendency toward self-evaluation does not produce evaluation that merely serves the interests of program staff rather than the customers and stakeholders. See, e.g., D. Fetterman, "Empowerment Evaluation: Presidential Address," *Evaluation Practice,* 1994, 15(1), pp. 1–15.

Emulation: A process of policy transfer wherein policy makers in different jurisdictions base a policy on a model used elsewhere but do not copy all its details. Emulation thus enables those who acquire external experiences to put them into proper context, and make appropriate modifications so as to suit local conditions. For a discussion of this, see, e.g., A. Schick, "Why Most Developing Countries Should Not Try New Zealand's Reforms," *World Bank Research Observer,* 1998, 13(1), pp. 123–31.

Enablement: The process of enhancing self-confidence in subordinates by giving them the means to do their work effectively. This can be, for example, by delegating authority to them, giving them the latitude to learn on their own, and providing them with relevant information. See, e.g., C. Levine, B. Peters, and F. Thompson, *Public Administration: Challenges, Choices, Consequences,* Glenview, IL: Scott, Foresman and Co., 1990, p. 356.

Enabling authority: Any level of government that goes beyond its core task of enabling the private sector to more fully participate in service provision to one that enables voluntary organizations and others to work in partnership to build social capital. The enabling authority thus links these entities to the political opportunity structure inherent in the jurisdiction. See S. Bailey, *Local Government Economics: Principles and Practice,* London/Basingstoke: Macmillan, 1999, p. 270. ***See also* Political opportunity structure; Social capital**.

Enabling environment: Conditions that are conducive to getting something done. An enabling environment, for example, is one where government policies support the actions of individual firms. Such environment is created by, among others, an enabling legislation, which refers to a law that creates an agency or makes it possible for local governments to receive benefits from the central government. An enabling legislation also tends to be permissive and not imperative (i.e., prescriptive).

Encapsulation: The process of keeping organization members so occupied with work that they are deprived of time for nonorganization-related activities. In encapsulation, then, the work-life balance is tilted heavily toward work. See M. Pratt, "The Good, the Bad, and the Ambivalent: Managing Identification among Amway Distributors," *Administrative Science Quarterly,* 2000, 45(3), pp. 456–93. *See also* **Work-life balance**.

Enclaves: Refers to those units that are set up within established governmental departments with a specific mandate to fulfill, and that are resourced disproportionately more favorably so that they can do their work unfettered by resource constraints. Such enclaves also have a considerably higher degree of managerial flexibility and better pay for members. In many countries in Africa, for example, governments have created enclaves so that they can raise tax revenue, or be involved in road maintenance, or any other task that are considered to be of high priority. For a discussion of such enclaves and their limitations, see, e.g., World Bank, *World Development Report, 1997,* Washington, DC: World Bank, 1997, p. 91.

End-of-pipe solutions: Solutions that become evident toward the end point of any process. These are then evident with time lags, and as such can pose a concern to organizations that have to communicate with external stakeholders about the progress of particular programs.

End-evaluation: An evaluation of a policy or program that is done when it is complete as a way to determine the lessons learned, and how any derivative (i.e., follow-up) work should proceed. End-evaluations are both retrospective as well as forward-looking.

Enforceable contract: A contract between the principal and agent that is designed in such a way that it can be easily enforced (i.e., with more certainty but not necessarily with less cost). An enforceable contract is well specified and the enforcement mechanisms are clear and understood by both parties. Such a contract also ensures greater buy-in from the agent since it is transparent. However, as has been obvious in many jurisdictions, there are costs to coming up with enforceable contracts, notably that there is a risk that the nature of the trust that needs to exist between the two parties will deteriorate since an enforceable contract tends to place a premium on a legalistic and more adversarial approach to contracting. For a review of the nature of enforceable contracts in the public sector, see, e.g., OECD, *A Framework for Public Sector Performance Contracting,* PUMA/PAC(99)2, Paris: OECD, 1999, pp. 66–67.

Enforcement action: Any action on the part of an organization (for example, the court) that is geared toward enforcing adherence to applicable rules and regulations, and to inducing specific kinds of behavior. Parties that have the mandate to take enforcement action rely on enforcement mechanisms, which are arrangements to ensure that rules are in fact implemented in the manner that they are supposed to be, and that the laws have been adhered to.

Enforcement mentality: The mind set of bureaucrats in control and regulatory agencies that they need to strictly enforce existent rules and regulations. This mind set encourages them to think of control mechanisms and stifles any chance of flexibility in government agencies that will then tend to have a compliance mentality. Instead, control agencies should focus on encouraging agencies toward voluntary compliance of rules and regulations.

Engendering development: Introducing concepts and analytical tools of gender into the development process. This requires policy makers to re-think their assumptions about how problems and proposed solutions will affect women and consists of three fundamental principles: (a) equality of right must be universal, (b) women must be taken as active agents rather than as passive participants, and (c) there should be no preconceptions of how different cultures exercise choices for women and men. See United Nations Development Program, *Human Development Report, 1995,* New York: United Nations, 1995, p. 2.

Enlightened elite: The top few within the elite ranks in the bureaucracies and government who are in positions to influence policy and who are used as sounding boards for new and innovative ideas. For an excellent discussion of the term, see T. Dye and H. Ziegler, *The Irony of Democracy: An Uncommon Introduction to American Politics,* 9th edition, Belmont, CA: Wadsworth Publishing Company, 1993, pp. 410–11. *See also* **Elite**.

Enterprise government: *See* **Entrepreneurial government**.

Enterprise risk management: An approach to risk management that looks at how to manage risks in an organization holistically, and includes risk identification and assessment as well as risk mitigation. The approach also aligns the various components in an organization that are critical at assessing and managing risks, which include people, technology, and knowledge. Finally, enterprise risk management also accepts the fact that any organization or entity is bound to have failures, and so it tolerates failures up to a point (i.e., provided they do not jeopardize the core tasks of the organization and as long as the costs of guarding against them is less than the costs imposed by the risks themselves). For enterprise risk management to be effective, full commitment from the senior-level organizational hierarchy is required. See KPMG, *Understanding Enterprise Risk Management: An Emerging Model for Building Shareholder Value,* New York: KPMG, 2001, pp. 2–4. *See also* **Risk scanning**.

Entitlement budgeting: Budgeting done on the basis of level of entitlement (i.e., program beneficiaries are entitled to an amount of a budget, and spending is then the sum of the services to be provided). Entitlements are benefits to persons or organizations that meet the eligibility criteria set by law. Government pensions and Medicaid in the United States are examples of entitlements. The key point here is that the recipients need to have met the requirements that have been set. See, e.g., J. White, "Entitlement Budgeting vs. Bureau Budgeting," *Public Administration Review,* 1998, 58(6), pp. 510–21. *Cf.* **Bureau budgeting**.

Entrenched bureaucracy: A bureaucracy that is set in its ways of doing things and is unable or unwilling to take feedback from its internal and external constituents to improve its processes or alter its approach. Entrenched bureaucracies will also find ways to retain a hold over their resources, mandates, and decision-making authority. Bringing in outsiders to senior ranks, and reducing the length of those already in the senior ranks are two usual ways of minimizing the possibilities of an entrenched bureaucracy.

Entrepreneurial corruption: *See* **Corruption**.

Entrepreneurial government: Popularized by David Osborne and Ted Gaebler in the early 1990s, this concept refers to a government that is innovative, problem solving in nature, willing to delegate powers to street-level bureaucrats, responsive to consumer concerns, and willing to cooperate with the private sector in providing services. This concept has been widely used by governments around the world as they have sought to revamp their public sectors. A related term is enterprise government, which refers to an organizational strategy that seeks to make public-sector agencies more enterprising by, among other things, providing incentives for cost containment, and letting consumers have a say in how services should be delivered. Enterprise government is a product of the philosophy that dominated the "new public management" reforms of the 1980s and 1990s. See A. Halachmi, "Entrepreneurial Government: In Theory/In Practice," in A. Halachmi and K. Nichols (eds.), *Enterprise Government: Franchising and Cross-Servicing for Administrative Support,* Burke, VA: Chatelaine Press, 1996, pp. 55–71. For Osborne and

Gaebler's work, see their *Reinventing Government: How the Entrepreneurial Spirit is Transforming the Public Sector,* Reading, MA: Addison-Wesley, 1992.

Entropy: A long term and continuous process that erodes an organization's ability to ascertain and adjust to its environment, thus resulting in its inactivity and disorderliness. Ways in which organizations can stem the process of entropy include being more receptive to feedback from their operating environments, enhancing human-resource capability, and inculcating organizational values and ethos into all staff members. *See also* **Negative entropy**.

Entry: Access to a market or policy domain by a firm or organization that is interested in supplying a particular good or service. In the public sector, this is almost always a function of some legislative move (for example, through primary legislation) to create new entities.

Entry-level training: The training that a newcomer to an organization undertakes. Entry-level training at the upper levels of the organization does not tend to be as structured as for those who are coming in at the lower levels. This is because it is assumed that such senior-level staff members already have most if not all of the knowledge, skills, and abilities (KSAs) required to perform well.

Environmental adaptation: A continuing process for an organization whereby it considers the feedback it receives from those in its operating environment and seeks to amend, if necessary, the ways in which it carries out its business. Such an adaptation allows the organization to better respond to its stakeholders and others. Environmental adaptation is facilitated by environmental feedback, which is information that an organization receives from its environment (i.e., from those that it interacts with and/or those that are impacted upon by the organization's work) regarding its effectiveness of performance. In order for organizations to learn from such feedback, they need to have in place mechanisms whereby such information is actively sourced, collated, and distributed to relevant individuals within the organization.

Environmental contingencies: Refer to sources of uncertainty that an organization faces in its environment. Three levels of environmental contingencies can be usefully identified: (a) general environmental uncertainties (such as in the political sphere and natural calamities), (b) sector-specific uncertainties (i.e., among organizations operating in the same domain, such as that which results from increased competition for the same labor pool of, say, policy analysts), and (c) organizational uncertainties (such as deterioration in labor relations, and opportunistic behavior by managers). See, e.g., K. Miller and H. Waller, "Scenarios, Real Options, and Integrated Risk Management," *Long Range Planning,* 2003, 36(1), pp. 93–107.

Environmental determinism: The belief that an organization's environment fully determines its directions and that, therefore, organizational leaders can do little to shape their environments. A response to the concept of environmental determinism has been strategic-choice perspective. *See also* **Strategic-choice perspective**.

Environmental discontinuities: The changing nature of an organization's operating environment. While some environmental elements of a public organization remain continuous (such as accountability relationships with parliament), others do not (such as developments in academic research that shed light on new managerial thinking). A related concept is environmental turbulence, which refers to changes that take place in the organization's operating environment, and which are difficult to get a handle on because they are very complex and also because the changes are rapid. See, e.g., F. Emery, and E. Trist, "The Causal Texture of Organizational Environments," *Human Relations,* 1965, 18(1), pp. 21–32.

Environmental scanning: Environmental scanning helps organizations to understand the environment in which they operate. Two types of environmental scanning that can be identified are: (a) active search (or active probing, where an organization makes concerted efforts to understand its environment), and (b) passive scanning (where the organization merely does a perfunctory search to confirm existing knowledge). See H. Greve and A. Taylor, "Innovations as Catalysts for Organizational Change: Shifts in Organizational Cognition and Search," *Administrative Science Quarterly,* 2000, 45(1), pp. 54–80.

E-procurement: Using information and communications technology (i.e., electronically) to acquire inputs meant for an organization's production process. E-procurement is fairly recent, and there is still considerable work to be done on standardizing relevant processes and to getting around sticky issues such as online authentication. See, e.g., W. Scacchi, "Redesigning Contracted Service Procurement for Internet-Based Electronic Commerce: A Case Study," *Journal of Information Technology and Management,* 2001, 2(3), pp. 313–34.

Equal employment opportunities: As used in the context of the public sector, this term refers to the fact that all persons, regardless of their race, sex, color, religion, sexual orientation, or national origin should have equal access to public-service employment. The only qualifier in this is that they should possess the ability to do so. In instances where such opportunities are not evident, there are considered two ways of handling the matter: (a) through vigorous enforcement of the relevant laws of the land, and (b) through awareness-enhancing measures for employers to voluntarily provide equal employment opportunities. Many jurisdictions mandate the provisions for—and adherence to—the principles of equal employment opportunities.

Equal pay for equal work: Based on the comparability principle, this concept refers to the assertion that payment for work done should be consonant with the work itself and not the individual doing it, nor to factors unrelated to the work. In the United States, the 1963 Equal Pay Act bans employers from deviating from this principle. See, e.g., L. Sigelman, H. Milward, and J. Shepard, "The Salary Differential Between Male and Female Administrators: Equal Pay for Equal Work?" *Academy of Management Journal,* 1982, 25(3), pp. 664–71.

Equality bargaining: Refers to the type of bargaining that takes place between unions and management centered on trying to ensure that women get paid fairly in relation to men and that the employer is paying attention to issues of discrimination. It is argued that unions—as opposed to individuals—are better placed to engage in equality bargaining and negotiating conditions that benefit women. For a brief description of the role of unions in bargaining and collective coverage in relation to pay equity, see, e.g., *Report of the Taskforce on Pay and Employment Equity in the Public Service and the Public Health and Public Education Sectors,* Wellington: State Services Commission, March 2004, p. 32.

Equifinality, principle of: A principle that stipulates that the final desired state for an organization or any entity may be reached in different ways and which are equally acceptable to the organization's internal and external stakeholders. This principle has wide applications, and is important in the context of organizational action because, in many ways, it allows organizations to veer away from determinism by enabling the search for more applicable and relevant modes of action to attain outcomes. For an original discussion of the principle, see L. Bertalanffy, "An Outline of General Systems Theory," *British Journal for the Philosophy of Science,* 1950, 1(2), pp. 139–64. *See also* **Equipotentiality**.

Equipotentiality: A construct that, as applied in public management, refers to the fact that new organizations that are at early points in their development are undifferentiated to the extent that they have equal potential to develop the expertise they need to support their various functions down the road. By extension, then, organizations learn to respond appropriately to any rewards or sanction they receive early on in their development phase, which leads to the particular culture that they exhibit later on. For the original work on this concept, see L. Bertalanffy, "An Outline of General Systems Theory," *British Journal for the Philosophy of Science,* 1950, 1(2), pp. 139–64.

Equity theory: Asserts that staff members in an organization tend to be motivated not only by the actual compensation and entitlements/benefits they receive but also by the fact that their peers (whom they perceive to be doing the same level of work) receive equitable levels. If that perception is judged not to be valid, then motivation declines, and vice versa.

Equivocality, perception of: Refers to a situation when those in organizations face multiple and conflicting interpretations of the situation that exists. Such a perception results from the fact that the external environment is rarely neatly ordered, and different individuals perceive situations differently. When the changes in the external environment are particularly difficult to interpret, equivocality tends to increase markedly since each individual brings in his or her own schema of how to interpret such events. For a discussion of the term, see, e.g., R. Daft and N. Macintosh, "A Tentative Exploration into the Amount and Equivocality of Information Processing in Organizational Work Units," *Administrative Science Quarterly,* 1981, 26(2), pp. 207–24.

ERG theory: *See* **Hierarchy of needs**.

Erotetic rationality: Refers to a process of reasoned interrogation in organizations (i.e., given that in many cases, information on what is sought, and how it can be measured, is unattainable or incomplete, decision makers need to accept such a situation and start from the a priori assumption that they do not know the relationships between what they want to achieve and how to go about it). Such rationality is central in properly structuring problems, and in setting the proper parameters of the organization's work *ex ante*. *See also* **Rationality**.

Escalation clause: As used in the context of contract administration, an escalation clause is one that is incorporated in a contract that enables the principal to increase the amount of funds available to the agent if and when specified contingencies occur. Escalation clauses are useful when the operating environment of the work that the agent is involved in is fairly volatile and conditions cannot be suitably ascertained *ex ante*.

Escape clause: A clause inserted in a contract between the principal and agent that allows each party to get out of the contract if the situations so warrant. Escape clauses are necessary in contracts since it is difficult to specify all·contingencies in them, and both parties would prefer to be in a position where each may wish to exercise an exit option if conditions so warrant.

Escape learning: Also known as avoidance learning, this term refers to learning that occurs as a result of a measure that reduces or stops adverse stimuli (for example, docking pay for late arrival at work). The learning then results from the drive by an employee to escape sanctions. In terms of motivating employees, this is hardly the most appealing manner in which employers may choose to operate, but used judiciously and sparingly it is rather effective.

Espoused theory: What managers talk about (or espouse) in relation to the degree of openness of communication and participative style of management that should exist in an organization. Every manager has a particular "map" that he/she uses to plan, implement, and evaluate the course of action that has been chosen. However, more often than not, managers are not aware that the map that they use is not in alignment with the theories they espouse. The distinction is not between what is said and what is done, but more between two different theories of action. This is not an unimportant point, for if managers are unaware of the theories that drive their action, it is difficult for them to effectively manage their behavior. The only way they could do this would be to find congruence between their espoused theory and their theories-in-use. See C. Argyris and D. Schön, *Theory in Practice: Increasing Professional Effectiveness,* San Francisco: Jossey-Bass, 1974, pp. 6–7. *Cf.* **Theory-in-Use**.

Esteem needs: *See* **Hierarchy of needs**.

Estimate-to-complete: In performance evaluation and review technique (PERT), the concept of estimate-to-complete refers to the estimated time and costs—at any given point in time—for completion of a program. Estimate-to-go, on the other hand, is a term used in PERT to refer to the estimations of actual costs that would bring about the completion of the remaining requirements of an ongoing activity or program. Such estimation helps managers get a better appreciation of the level of supplementary funding that may need to be sought from the funding authorities.

Estimates of appropriation: A government's statement of the proposed expenses, revenues, if any, and liabilities to be incurred by governmental departments, which is presented to the legislature for approval. "Main estimates" are those that are presented at budget time, while "supplementary estimates" are presented at some other time in the financial year. Departments often use supplementary estimates to seek resources for programs that were not included in the main estimates because a government's financial commitments often become much clearer post budget.

Etatization: The process of increasing the role of the state in public life. This can occur either by an increase in the number of functions set aside for government, or by monopoly control over selected areas of social activity. Both of them, on the other hand, have been generally on the decline in recent times across advanced jurisdictions. See, e.g., G. Caiden, "Getting at the Essence of the Administrative State," in A. Farazmand (ed.), *Handbook of Bureaucracy,* New York: Marcel Dekker, Inc., 1994, pp. 65–78.

Ethics: Standards of conduct and values that are in evidence in public service. Such standards are included in a code of conduct for all public-sector employees to refer to. A relevant term is ethos, which refers to the inherent beliefs, value orientation, and attitudes to work of the employees in an organization. An ethics regime refers to the systems and protocols around how governments seek to enhance the ethics of public service. Two main types of ethics regimes can be identified: (a) integrity based (where the focus is on integrity aspiration, and is rather unenforceable), and (b) compliance based (where the focus is on rules discipline, and, because of the rules, is more enforceable than *(a)*). See, e.g., OECD, *Ethics in the Public Service: Current Issues and Practice,* Paris: OECD, 1996, pp. 59–61. See also, e.g., B. Bass and P. Steidlmeier, "Ethics, Character, and Authentic Transformational Leadership Behavior," *Leadership Quarterly,* 1999, 10(2), pp. 181–217.

Etic norms: *See* **Emic norms.**

Evaluation: Refers broadly to an appraisal of a policy or program's past or ongoing performance, and which assesses how well it is doing in relation to the objectives the program or policy had set for itself. The purpose of the evaluation is to contribute to improved decision making by providing better information to those tasked with managing the policy or program. A key point to note is that the purpose of an evaluation is not necessarily to replace judgments in decision making but to make them more informed in light of evidence that emerges from the review. Evaluation can be of various types: (a) a process evaluation looks at how the program was managed, (b) an impact evaluation looks at accomplishments and results, (c) a formative evaluation is geared toward coming up with recommendations to enhance the performance of the policy or program, and (d) an algedonic evaluation is designed to establish the worth of the policy or program. At times, public opinion is also deemed to be an evaluation in itself. Rules according to which policy actions, programs, policies, etc., are evaluated are known as evaluation criteria. For a review of evaluation in the context of public management, see, e.g., T. Abma and M. Noordegraaf, "Public Managers Amidst Ambiguity: Toward a Typology of Evaluative Practices in Public Management," *Evaluation,* 2003, 9(3), pp. 285–306.

Evaluation, acid test of: A true measure of whether an evaluation is useful or not is the extent to which the evaluation results are used or ignored by those sponsoring the evaluation. Evaluation results are used when the organization takes into active consideration the recommendations contained in the evaluation report and seeks to feed back into the program or policy the relevant amendments that have been recommended.

Evaluation capacity: The capacity of an organization to conduct an effective evaluation that adheres to accepted standards and norms. The capacity should also include active internalization of such standards and not merely the technical expertise for token compliance. See, e.g., World Bank, *Building Evaluation Capacity: Lessons and Practices,* Paper no. 4, Washington, DC: World Bank, 1994. For a discussion of internal evaluation capabilities, see B. McDonald, P. Rogers, and B. Kefford, "Teaching People to Fish? Building the Evaluation Capability of Public Sector Organizations," *Evaluation,* 2003, 9(1), pp. 9–29.

Evaluation cube: An evaluation model that looks at the concept in three dimensions: (a) Where is the locus of control in the evaluation exercise (i.e., who are the people in control whose decisions determine the course of any policy or program evaluation)? (b) Which stakeholders are to be selected for participation in the evaluation? and (c) How extensive does their participation need to be? For an application of the evaluation cube, see, e.g., M. Themessl-Huber and M. Grutsch, "The Shifting Locus of Control in Participatory Evaluation," *Evaluation,* 2003, 9(1), pp. 92–111.

Evaluation, mal-purposes of: Evaluation that is used for purposes other than that of to better inform how a program or policy could be made more effective. Five types of such mal-purposes of evaluation can be identified: (a) eyewash (i.e., to make a policy or program look good by focusing only on its surface attributes), (b) whitewash (i.e., to tidy over program failures by deliberately presenting incomplete or fake evidence); (c) submarine (i.e., to destroy a program by surreptitiously introducing controversial evidence that generates opposition to the program); (d) posture (i.e., to do evaluation merely as a ritual to show the public that the organization is open to scrutiny), and (e) postponement (i.e., to put off attempts to resolve problems by presenting evidence that is inconclusive). See, e.g., E. Suchman, "Action for What? A Critique of Evaluative Research," in C. Weiss (ed.), *Evaluation Research,* Englewood Cliffs, NJ: Prentice Hall, 1972, p. 81.

Evaluation research: The discipline that refers to the theory and methodology of carrying out evaluations, and is centered on a review and investigation of a policy, program, or activity. Such a review results in a normative statement of what ought to happen with the policy or program in order for it to deliver what it set out to do.

Evaluative state: A state where evaluation processes are a routine part of management and a mandatory requirement of government in public management. This is largely seen to be a function of citizen pressure to want better quality of services. See, e.g., M. Henkel, "The New Evaluation State," *Public Administration,* 1991, 69, pp. 121–36.

Evidence-based analysis: The requirement for policy agencies to use evidence to analyze policies and recommend policy alternatives. Increasingly, governments require agencies mandated to provide policy advice to demonstrate that they also provide credible evidence to back up their advice. For "providing evidence" as one of several assessment criteria for good policy advice, see, e.g., Office of the Provincial Auditor, *A Review of the Policy Development Capacity Within Government Departments,* Winnipeg, Canada: Office of the Provincial Auditor, 2001, pp. 39–42. See also I. Sanderson, "Evaluating Policy Learning, and Evidence-Based Policy Making," *Public Administration,* 2002, 80(1), pp. 1–22.

Evolutionary reform: Any reform that is slow and incremental and does not challenge the conventional thinking on how things should be done. There is logical incrementalism in evolutionary reform, and change is cautious and nondisruptive. For an application, see, e.g., R. Jones, "Leading

Change in Local Government: The Tension Between Evolutionary and Frame-Breaking Reform in New South Wales," *Australian Journal of Public Administration,* 2002, 61(3), pp. 38–53. *Cf.* **Frame-breaking reform**.

Ex ante: Before the fact (for example, commitment of policy, targets set, or the specification of what a department is going to deliver for the year ahead and to what standards). *Ex ante* performance documents include departmental estimates, and any prespecified outputs. An *ex ante* evaluation is an evaluation that is done before the implementation of a project or program. This is normally done for large interventions when all parties wish to be certain that they are targeting the right problem and are doing so in an efficient and credible manner. An *ex ante* rate of return to training is the return on training that is calculated based on to-be incurred costs and expected benefits. *Cf.* **Ex post**.

Ex post: After the fact (for example, [non]attainment of targets and performance reporting against the specifications of what a department has achieved over the year in review). Annual departmental reports, as well as audit reports, are good examples of *ex post* documents. An *ex post* evaluation is an evaluation of a project, program, or activity after it has been completed. While an *ex post* evaluation is normally done soon after completion of an intervention, it is not unusual to find this period extended to longer time frames. The intention of an *ex post* evaluation is to assess the impacts and their sustainability, and to draw conclusions for future interventions, if any. An *ex post* rate of return to training is the return on training that is calculated after the training program is completed and after all the financial obligations have been incurred, and is thus based on actual costs and realized benefits. *Cf.* **Ex ante**.

Exception principle: *See* **Management by exception**.

Excessive opening: Liberalization that is hurried and not commensurate with the existing social, economic, and political situation existing in the country. Commentators point out the excessive opening experiences in the 1990s of the Soviet Union (and its subsequent collapse) and the more compatible opening pursued by, for example, China (and its positive impacts) to show that liberalization—both political and economic—needs to be moderated and tuned to the country's situation. *See also* **Compatible opening; Overcautious opening**.

Exchange theory: Asserts that, in general, organizations and individuals inherently wish to engage in transactions with each other so that each party stands to gain from the interaction. This theory helps explain why principals and agents seek to enter into a relationship. It also helps explain the exchange relationship, which is an interaction between two parties that is based on the notion of reciprocity (i.e., if one party respects the operating mechanisms of the other, then it has to be reciprocated). In an equal-exchange relationship, both parties stand to gain from their interactions with each other.

Exchequer cost analysis: *See* Cost analysis.

Excludability: When consumers can be excluded from consuming a good. Excludability can be physical (i.e., if one party has it then it is not possible for another party to have it as well), or legal (i.e., one party has the right to control use of the particular good regardless of whether or not the other party is consuming the good). This legal right over the claim is also known as property right, and is guarded with appropriate legislation in advanced jurisdictions.

Exclusion clauses: Also known as caveats, these are clauses in a contract that refer to instances when certain rules do not apply or when exemptions are granted. While exclusion clauses are a necessary part of any contract, too many such clauses render the contract—and its management—ineffectual.

Excusable delay: As used in contract administration, this term refers to the delay in provision of goods or services due to factors that are outside the control of the agent. Principals will normally allow a reasonable reliance on excusable delay as reason for the late delivery of products and services for which contracts will have already been drawn.

Executive: (1) In the division of government among the executive, legislature, and judiciary, the executive branch of government is involved in implementing the various policies and programs that the legislature passes. In the Westminster system of government, the executive is taken to mean the cabinet of governmental ministers; in the presidential system of government (such as that which exists in the United States), the president is the chief executive officer. (2) As an individual, an executive is anyone who is ultimately accountable to the chief executive of the government department for the effective management of one or more business units/divisions. In that role, the executive will have individuals who will be working for him/her and part of the responsibility is to ensure that these staff members are effectively contributing to the attainment of organizational mandates. An executive action denotes any policy-related decision or action taken by the executive body, i.e., the president or prime minister.

Executive agencies: Also called "Next Steps" agencies, this term refers to the agencies that were created in the United Kingdom in the 1980s as part of the reform of the public service that was initiated by then-prime minister Margaret Thatcher, who wished to shed the public sector of much of the inefficiency and waste that she thought existed. The agencies were created out of a plan to separate the policy and operational aspects of a governmental department's work such that the central (or core) unit was made quite small but focused almost entirely on policy development and providing policy advice to governmental ministers, while the larger chunk of what the department did was hived off into smaller units that were created along private-sector lines (i.e., with a chief executive who was recruited from, if necessary, outside the public service, who was given a fixed-term contract and very specific performance criteria to meet, as contained in a performance agreement). The agency was also kept at arm's length from ministers and from parliament so that political interference in its work was kept to a minimum. This split between policy and operations was picked up quickly by other jurisdictions, and before very long it was considered a key ingredient of any public-sector-reform program. The term "Next Steps" was applied because the recommendation to bifurcate policy from operational organizations was contained in the 1988 report titled: "Improving Management in Government: The Next Steps" (also known as the Ibbs Report, after Robin Ibbs, who led the team). For a case-study application of the work of executive agencies, see, e.g., N. Hyndman and R. Eden, "Rational Management, Performance Targets, and Executive Agencies: Views from Agency Chief Executives in Northern Ireland," *Public Administration,* 2001, 79(3), pp. 579–98. *See also* **Policy-operations split**.

Executive agenda: The programs and policies that the executive branch of government enunciates, some of which that require legislative approval; these will be submitted to the legislature for consideration. The executive agenda takes shape from the time the governing party is vying for power in elections and it releases an election manifesto that lays out its goals and priorities.

Executive appointment: Any appointment made by the president or prime minister in consonance with the statutory right given to him/her as the head of the executive branch of government. An appointment of an ambassador to a country, for example, can be considered to be an executive appointment. Even though generally some executive appointments are made without requiring consultation, others will need to be approved by the legislature.

Executive coaching: Development opportunities provided to senior managers and executives of organizations where they are coached on leadership and management capabilities by outsiders. Coaching includes goal setting, collaborative problem solving, and supervisory involvement, among others. See, e.g., G. Olivero, K. Bane, and R. Kopelman, "Executive Coaching as a Transfer of Training Tool: Effects on Productivity in a Public Agency," *Public Personnel Management,* 1997, 26(4), pp. 461–69.

Executive core qualifications: The list of competencies members of the U.S. Senior Executive Service are expected to possess in order that they can do their work effectively. These competencies are in the broad areas of: leading change, leading people, results-driven, business acumen, and building coalitions and communications. Practically all Organization for Economic Co-operation and Development (OECD) jurisdictions that have a senior public service have specified competencies for their top administrators. For a review of the competencies for senior managers in different OECD jurisdictions, see, e.g., G. Bhatta, "Enabling the Cream to Rise to the Top: A Cross-Jurisdictional Comparison of Competencies for Senior Managers in the Public Sector," *Public Performance and Management Review*, 2001, 25(2), pp. 194–207.

Executive development: Training and developing the capability of organizational leaders to improve their leadership skills. While the focus is on leadership, executive development also concentrates on how organizational managers develop strategies, align operational decisions with the strategies, and execute the decisions. The targeted group for such development consists of top leaders of organizations, but at times can also include those who are on the pathways to leadership positions (as determined by an organization's succession plans). For a comprehensive review of comparative cross-jurisdictional experiences in executive development, see, e.g., M. Maor, "A Comparative Perspective on Executive Development: Trends in 11 European Countries," *Public Administration,* 2000, 78(1), pp. 135–52. *See also* **Management development**.

Executive federalism: A federal process that is characterized by extensive federal-state/provincial interactions at the senior executive level of each jurisdiction (for example, in Canada, this could be at the level of first ministers, departmental ministers, and deputy ministers). Executive federalism permits a closer working relationship among officials at the various levels of government.

Executive nurturing: *See* **Mentoring**.

Executive order: A regulation that is issued by the executive in keeping with authority granted by legislative authorization or in consonance with precedence. Such an order has the force of law and bureaucrats are mandated to adhere to its intent. The legislature has the right to review the granting of the power to the executive to make such executive orders.

Executive oversight: The process of how an executive exercises control over the processes and activities in an organization. This includes how the executive seeks to hold individual managers in the organization to be responsible for their duties and responsibilities. For a discussion, see, e.g., L. LeLoup, and W. Moreland, "Agency Strategies and Executive Review: The Hidden Politics of Budgeting," *Public Administration Review,* 1978, 38(3), pp. 232–39.

Executive power: The power that an executive arm of government has in order to implement the laws and policies passed by a legislature. In the United States, for example, executive power rests with the president who, in turn, exercises this power by delegating authority to subordinate officers. A related concept, executive privilege, is the prerogative of the executive to act in any manner he/she deems fit in specific matters (for example, to withhold information from the legislature).

Executive risk preferences: Preferences toward risk taking shown by organizational leaders. Such preferences need not necessarily be those of the organization as a whole since other considerations may factor into organizational risk preferences. For a discussion see, e.g., S. Chatterjee et al., "Integrating Behavioral and Economic Concepts of Risk into Strategic Management: The Twain Shall Meet," *Long Range Planning,* 2003, 36(1), pp. 61–79.

Exemption: An exception that is made to any rule, regulation, or stipulation. When a party receives an exemption, the party is not expected to be involved in that particular activity or be subject to particular regulation(s) or requirement(s).

Existence value: The value that individuals place on a public good knowing that it continues to exist even if they do not expect to use it at all. This concept is similar to that of option value, and is closely related to that of irreversibility. Both these concepts need to be taken into consideration while appraising a potential project, and they feature in the risk analysis for any proposal. *See also* **Irreversibility; Option value.**

Exit: (1) When providers of goods and services leave the market or policy domain. For example, if a firm cannot compete with others in the market, then it is compelled to cease its operations, and thus is said to exit the market. (2) The disinclination of citizens to voice their opinions on matters of public policy that affect their lives. If all the stakeholders to a policy do not have avenues to give expression to their views (i.e., have voice), then the result is either sabotage or exit. For an original discussion of this interpretation of exit, see A. Hirschman, *Exit, Voice, and Loyalty—Responses to Decline in Firms, Organizations, and States,* Cambridge, MA: Harvard University Press, 1970. See also Hirschman's "Exit and Voice: An Expanding Sphere of Influence," in A. Hirschman, *Rival Views of Market Society and Other Recent Essays,* Cambridge, MA: Harvard University Press, 1992, pp. 77–101. *Cf.* **Voice.**

Exit interview: Also called a separation interview, this is a tool to enable the employer to hear first hand from the employee the lessons of his/her experiences in the organization. The focus of an exit interview is not so much on finding out why the employee has decided to leave the organization, but more on whether there may be insights into how the organization could remedy or make better any aspect of the work or operating environment. The interview is normally conducted by someone from outside the organization to ensure impartiality.

Exogenous expectations: Any expectations of an organization or a government that are taken for granted. In public management, the expectations of incoming governments are taken to be exogenous, and bureaucrats must work with the incoming government on that basis.

Expectancy theory: Asserts that employees are motivated by the results they expect of their efforts. All employees have expectancies regarding outcomes of their actions and if they come true, their motivation increases, and vice versa. The value that is placed on this outcome is termed valence. *See also* **Valence.**

Expectations, management of: The need to ensure that the expectations of individuals and organizations are catered for once a specific program is put in place. If, for example, a major new program for executive development were to be introduced in the public service, then the program formulators would have to ensure that the expectations—unrealistic often—that executives in the public service will have about what the program will do for them need to be managed properly by providing them with accurate information, but also encouraging them to be a part of the program.

Experience-based learning: *See* **Experiential learning.**

Experiential learning: Learning that takes place, and knowledge that is gained, by doing and through valuable experiences. For example, secondments (i.e., placements) of public servants to private companies that are evident in the public services of many jurisdictions are considered an invaluable experiential learning tool. For a case-study application of experiential learning, see, e.g., C. Mainemelis, R. Boyatzis, and D. Kolb, "Learning Styles and Adaptive Flexibility: Testing Experiential Learning Theory," *Management Learning,* 2002, 33(1), pp. 5–33.

Expert power: Refers to the ability of an individual to influence the attitude and behavior of others by virtue of a specialized skill or skills. For example, a staff member with skills in information technology (IT) could bring about a change in the attitude and behavior of a manager toward the use of IT in business management. *See also* **Power**.

Explicit contracts: Formal written agreements (for example, with employees, suppliers) that are enforced by institutions and that can be backed up in a court of law. Explicit contracts, however, do not and cannot specify all the potential contingencies to which the contractual relations might be subject.

Explicit forbearance: *See* **Regulatory forbearance**.

Explicit knowledge: Knowledge that is gained by shared constructs, language, and any other physical and tangible form (such as through books). Explicit knowledge is generally codified (i.e., it is a specified and easily attainable source of knowledge in an organization that can be accessed by staff members). See, e.g., R. Hall and P. Andriani, "Managing Knowledge for Innovation," *Long Range Planning,* 2002, 35(1), pp. 29–48. *Cf.* **Tacit knowledge**, *see also* **Externalization**.

Exposure netting: *See* **Exposure to risk**.

Exposure to risk: The degree to which policies or public organizations could fail to deliver as a result of risks inherent in the public-management system. Some risks for a public-sector organization include passive support from governmental ministers for some policy, change of government, and citizen backlash. To better manage their exposure to risks, organizations usually engage in exposure netting, which is a process of trying to equalize the exposure to risks in one part of the organizational domain with those in another part. This is particularly helpful when organizational leaders perceive that the possibility of both risks materializing are minimal (as happens when the exposures are mutually exclusive).

Expression games: The attitudes, behaviors, and actions of organizations designed to create an impression to outsiders of a high level of competence and commitment to the core beliefs of the organization. This impression helps the organization to retain its preeminent position vis-à-vis other organizations. In the public sector, for example, control agencies (such as the treasury) often engage in expression games to assert their perceived supremacy over other organizations. For a good case-study review of this with respect to the New Zealand Treasury, see J. Wallis and B. Dollery, "Understanding Cultural Changes in an Economic Control Agency: The New Zealand Treasury," *Journal of Public Policy,* 2001, 21(2), pp. 191–212.

Extant situation: *See* **Manifest situation**.

Extension services: Services such as education and training for those who cannot access them through the usual channels (i.e., attendance at a specified time and venue). In many developing countries, for example, governments support agricultural credit-extension services for rural farmers since they cannot access credit readily from private banks.

External bureaucracy: Refers to the group of outside experts that organizations regularly contract with, and the consequent impact they have on the organization (for example, on the organizational culture). It is argued that the behavior of external bureaucrats has aspects of significance beyond the expert knowledge they bring to an organization. See, e.g., C. Alger, "The External Bureaucracy in United States Foreign Affairs," *Administrative Science Quarterly,* 1962, 7(1), pp. 50–78.

External evaluation: Evaluation of a project or program done by someone outside the implementing agency. External evaluation is done to ensure that there is impartiality and an independent perspective. While external evaluations have their advantages, there is also a risk that the external evaluator(s) may not be fully cognizant of the various aspects of the program or policy that would enable a richer and more well-informed analysis.

External locus of control: A belief that a manager has about organizational and work-related outcomes that are products of forces beyond personal control. This leads the organization to succumb to any pressures that emanate from its operating environment because its management collectively perceives that it cannot do anything about such pressures but sustain them.

External recruitment: *See* **Recruitment**.

External training: Training that is delivered by parties that are not part of the organization. External training is normally provided off-site unless there are large numbers of participants in which case the trainer could provide the training in the premises of the organization that is contracting the service.

Externalization: As used in the context of organizational knowledge management, the term refers to the process of transforming tacit knowledge to explicit knowledge. The process is called externalization because it involves taking the knowledge out of an individual and making it available to the others in the organization (i.e., making it explicit). See R. Hall and P. Andriani, "Managing Knowledge for Innovation," *Long Range Planning*, 2002, 35(1), pp. 29–48. *Cf.* **Internalization**.

Externalities: Changes in the conditions faced by an organization caused by the actions of others. It is generally assumed that externalities are exogenous ·variables (i.e., that they are beyond the direct control of the organization in question). The notion of externalities further implies that consent for creating such changes has not necessarily been given by the organization.

Extra-budgetary resource: Funds that are available to an organization whose sources come from outside the regular budget that the funding authority has appropriated. For example, the United Nations has several programs that are largely financed from extra-budgetary resources that have been committed by donor countries that fall outside the ambit of the regular budget that the UN itself approves. Such extra-budgetary resources, however, can be used only for the particular purposes for which they were made available by the donor country.

Extrinsic motivation: Motivation in individuals in organizations that is drawn from some tangible rewards they get as a result of being engaged in that work. Thus, for example, if one works solely for the monetary rewards of a high-paying job, then he or she is said to be extrinsically motivated. For a classic treatment of this concept, see F. Herzberg, "One More Time: How Do You Motivate Employees?" *Harvard Business Review*, 1968, 46(1), pp. 53–62. *Cf.* **Intrinsic motivation**.

F

Facilitative leadership: Also known as servant leadership, this term describes the sort of kinder, gentler leadership that stakeholders prefer to the heroic leader. According to this concept, the manager as facilitator must place focus on these components: (a) corporate responsibility to ensure that staff members participate in decision-making processes to the extent possible, (b) first among equals (i.e., the facilitative leader is one who is alongside the group as opposed to always at the front), (c) team building and focus upon group work rather than individual glory, and (d) empower others and support them in their goals as well. See, e.g., R. Schwarz, *The Skilled Facilitator: Practical Wisdom for Developing Effective Groups,* San Francisco: Jossey-Bass, 1994, pp. 249–60.

Facilitator: A resource person—contracted by an organization—to facilitate (or moderate) various activities such as group interview sessions, workshops, training programs, etc. The facilitator brings in an independent method of working and is not constrained by the norms that the organization may have that may inhibit many employees from contributing freely.

Facilities contract: A contract for the use of organizational facilities by a contractor that the organization has engaged. Such use of facilities is intended to assist the contractor in the performance of the contract. At times, the organization will offer such facilities, although, just as often, the contractor will ask for it in the bid proposal.

Fact-finding committee: A group of people that is asked to come together to investigate a particular problem or issue, collate all the evidence, analyze the relevant information, and then make recommendations on how to address the problem or issue. The committee disbands after it has made its recommendations, although it may be reconstituted—not necessarily with the same membership—if further work is warranted.

Fact-value dichotomy: An assertion that there is a distinction in administration on what the facts are, and what the values of public servants are in dealing with the facts. Also, values cannot be empirically and rationally tested; thus, a decision-making process in the public sector must start from the assumption that some ethical premise is given. This dichotomy also implies fact-value interdependence, which is the distinction between what exists (i.e., the fact) and what normative state (i.e., the value) the organization would like to see as a result of the implementation of a policy or program. See, e.g., H. Simon, *Administrative Behavior: A Study of Decision Making Process in Administrative Organizations,* 3rd edition, New York: The Free Press, 1976.

Factor comparison system: *See* **Factor evaluation system**.

Factor evaluation system: Also called the factor comparison system, this refers to the method of determining all the factors that affect the work in specific occupations in the organization. The system takes into consideration such factors of the occupation as duties and responsibilities; the knowledge, skills, and attributes required; the degree of complexity of the work; the constraints in, and facilitative aspects of, the work environment; the nature and extent of any managerial and/or supervisory effort required, etc. The results of the analysis are then factored into a determination of the compensation levels for the particular positions in the occupations.

Factorial problem: A factorial problem as understood in the public-management context is the degree of rise in complexity in relationships as a result of creating new entities in the public sector. Hence, the larger the number of agencies created for purposes of state sector reform, the more disproportionate the increase in the complexity of their relationships. This complexity generally tends to be underestimated. *See also* **Graicunas' theory**.

Fading: As used in the context of training and development, the term refers to the gradual decline in teaching information that strategically emanates from the training facilitator so that participants develop the confidence to learn on their own.

Fail-safe: Refers to performance failures in one component of the system, but failures not so severe that the system cannot recover or that would otherwise jeopardize overall system performance. A related concept is fail soft, which refers to failures in a system that do not immediately jeopardize the whole system. This allows decision makers to take corrective action in advance of a situation getting critical.

Failed state: See Collapsed state.

Failure-criticality analysis: An analysis done of any program to determine how severe the residual impact of any failures in the system might be. Such failures could be in the form of safety hazards, performance gaps, etc. A failure-criticality analysis allows decision makers to ascertain beforehand their potential responses in the event that something does go wrong in the system.

Failure of invariance: The term refers to the choices made by decision makers that are inconsistent—although they may not necessarily be incorrect—when they are faced with the same situation but in different forms and contexts. According to the concept of failure of invariance, if policy alternative A is preferred to alternative B, and alternative B is preferred to alternative C, rational decision makers will choose alternative A over alternative C. When this does not happen, a failure of invariance can be said to have occurred. See, e.g., P. Bernstein, *Against the Gods: The Remarkable Story of Risk,* New York: John Wiley & Sons, Inc., 1996, p. 275.

Fair employment practices: Activities in human-resource management in an organization that are carried out with no regard for nonmerit factors such as race, color, gender, etc. Public organizations may need to demonstrate to the courts and others (such as the legislature) that they are indeed engaged in fair employment practices at the risk of drawing sanctions. Fair employment practices are based on fairness grounds, which is when a decision in an organization needs to be made on the basis of fairness and equity rather than, say, on cost considerations. *Cf.* **Unfair employment practices**.

Fallacy of unfinished business: Refers to the false belief that organizational leaders may have that a situation or entity that first creates a problem will subsequently be able to adequately address it. This concept is used to argue that technology cannot be trusted to find solutions for the problems it may have created. To continue to adhere to this concept is to ignore the political process of risk. See, e.g., K. Shrader-Frechette, *Science Policy, Ethics, and Economic Methodology: Some Problems of Technology Assessment and Environmental Impact Analysis,* Dordrecht, Netherlands: D. Reidel Publishers, 1985, p. 110.

False-consensus bias: *See* **Assumed similarity**.

False distrust: The belief that a manager has that subordinates are attempting to displace him/her. Such a belief could be based on some incident or on hearsay but is, however, erroneous and serves only to generate ill will among the subordinates.

False negative: A situation that arises when a candidate is excluded from further consideration for recruitment even though he/she is qualified for a particular post. False positive, on the other hand, is a situation that arises when the candidate, who in reality is not qualified for a particular post, is considered further.

Family-friendly policy: *See* **Work-life balance**.

Family rationalization: A term that refers to the reason that employers tend to give to rationalize their decision not to recruit women, i.e., women often quit the workforce for family reasons and so it makes better business sense to recruit men.

Fast track: Refers to a rapid rise upward in the organization. Many organizations, and many public services in jurisdictions around the world, have fast-track schemes in place in order to identify and guide high achievers into rapid upward mobility. The downside of such a scheme is that it may be difficult to manage expectations of those in the fast track, and it also tends to be elitist and rather discriminatory.

Fat work: Refers to work that someone does for which the compensation levels are untypically high considering the typical amount of effort required. A related concept is featherbedding, which refers to any job that requires a minimum amount of effort.

Fault identification and analysis technique: *See* **Potential-problem analysis**.

Fayol's bridge: Also known as the gangplank concept, the term refers to management guru Henri Fayol's notion that communication in an organization at times takes place across hierarchies informally, which actually serves to provide information quickly that would not have been possible had the usual channels of communication (i.e., vertical) been relied on. In reality, despite the presence of hierarchies and formal communication methods in organizations, there is indeed a fair bit of informal and cross-level interaction taking place that is essential in cultivating useful feedback.

Feasibility: A principle of screening policy alternatives. Clearly, if some difficulties and organizational constraints exist in the technical, economic, or administrative domains that will prevent the actual implementation of a policy, then such policy seemingly needs to be rejected. Feasibility studies are studies that are done prior to a project or program being developed so as to assess whether it is feasible, and whether the organization should proceed with getting the technical specifications and other relevant details (including financing considerations). However, merely because a program is feasible does not mean that it will be developed.

Featherbedding: *See* **Fat work.**

Federalism: A system of government where the central government and subjurisdictional ones (such as states and provinces) share power. In reality, however, it is difficult to ascertain the boundaries of where the powers of one end and those of the other begin. U.S. presidents, for example, have long tried to define a federalism that best suits their own political interests, and the states have often sought to resist the federal government's approaches on their jurisdictional power or the handing down of responsibilities without a commensurate increase in resources. See, e.g., R. Agranoff and M. McGuire, "American Federalism and the Search for Models of Management," *Public Administration Review,* 2001, 61(6), pp. 671–81. *See also* **New federalism.**

Federation: A state that is based on the principle of federalism where there is a central federal government and several subjurisdictions (states or provinces). All these parties share power with each other and there is theoretically a clear demarcation as to what falls in the domain of each jurisdiction. Examples of federations are the United States, Germany, Canada, and India.

Fee-for-service basis: Provision of services by charging users a specific amount in order to meet the costs of the service provision. A fee-for-service basis not only allows service providers to ensure that they can recoup some of the costs but also serves to make users feel that they have then some say in the determination of how the service should be provided since they will have paid for the service as opposed to receive it gratis.

Feedback: To provide comments and opinions on any particular proposal or action. Feedback completes the learning cycles in organizations. It can be positive or negative, but either way it helps decision makers fine-tune a policy or program. It can also be intrinsic (for example, the sense that employees themselves get that they are doing a good job or not) and extrinsic (for example, that others in the organization or outside may provide a review of their performance). Feedback mechanisms are ways in which organizations get to hear from clients and customers (such as through feedback surveys). A feedback loop refers to the practice of revisiting the original assertion or program objective based on comments received from internal and external stakeholders and from those outside the policy formulation stage. *See also* **Legitimacy trap.**

Feed-forward learning: Any learning that is initiated by an individual that is then integrated with that of others in the organization, and ultimately feeds forward into group learning and organizational learning. Unlike feedback learning, which has the organization as an inception point, feed-forward learning has a bottom-up orientation. See, e.g., M. Crossan et al., "An Organizational Learning Framework: From Intuition to Institution," *Academy of Management Review,* 1999, 24(3), pp. 522–37. *See also* **Feedback**.

Felt-fair pay: Refers to what staff members in an organization think they and their colleagues in similar-level positions should earn. Any differentials in felt-fair pay then are seen as inequitable by staff members. *See also* **Equity theory**.

Feminization of poverty: A situation that many developing countries find themselves in where an increasing number of those who are poor are women, who are marginalized in economic activity and in accessing resources. Acceptance of the adverse consequences of this phenomenon, and seeking to design policies that embed appropriate responses to the feminization of poverty are the first steps that governments can take to tackle the problem. See, e.g., E. Northrop, "The Feminization of Poverty: The Demographic Factor and the Composition of Economic Growth," *Journal of Economic Issues,* 1990, 24(1), pp. 145–60.

Fenced-off projects: Projects for which a government wishes to maintain separate rules of engagement so that selected parties (such as multilateral firms) might be interested in entering. Governments have a tendency to do this for projects in sectors for which there is a higher risk profile and for which local investments would clearly be inadequate.

Fiat, administrative: When an administrative entity passes a rule that has to be adhered to by others. For example, a regulatory agency may decide to conduct its monitoring and evaluation functions in a particular manner, and all those that are subject to the regulation will be required to adhere to the new requirements. Related to the concept of administrative fiat is a fiat institution, which refers to an institution that is created by government by political fiat. Governments incur political costs if they want to tamper with the work of a fiat institution or do away with it. An exchange-rate regime is an example of a fiat institution. See, e.g., S. Lohmann, "Why Do Institutions Matter? An Audience-Cost Theory of Institutional Commitment," *Governance: An International Journal of Policy, Administration, and Institutions,* 2003, 16(1), pp. 95–110.

Field theory: Developed by organization behavioral theorist Kurt Lewin, this theory asserts that an individual's behavior can be explained by considering the interactions that he/she has with the environment. This is a particularly useful concept in an organizational setting because it partially helps explain how the organizational environment affects the manner in which it conducts business. See K. Lewin, "Behavior and Development as a Function of the Total Situation," in L. Carmichael (ed.), *Manual of Child Psychology,* New York: Wiley, 1946, pp. 791–844. For an application, see, e.g., C. Argyris, "Field Theory as a Basis for Scholarly Consulting," *Journal of Social Issues,* 1997, 53(4), pp. 811–27.

Field training: Training which is provided to employees that is based on the actual working conditions that they face rather than simulated or theory based. Field training could be provided on the job, at the workplace, or in a location outside the workplace. *See also* **On-the-job training**.

Fifty-percent-plus-one rule: A method of making decisions in organizations where any alternative that has the support of half the decision makers plus one more individual is accepted. This is the bare minimum that is needed to attain a majority in decision making.

Final-offer arbitration: Occurs when both disputing parties have placed their final offers on the table and an arbitrator chooses from between them. Both parties to the arbitration will have agreed in advance to abide by the arbitrator's decisions. The fact that final-offer arbitration has to be resorted to implies that the positions of the two parties are still quite far apart. Arbitration allows somewhat of an amicable way of resolving that variance in positions.

Financial accountability: Answerability that public officials have to relevant authorities (including the legislature) on how the financial resources that they were responsible for were spent. Regular audit reports from external and internal auditors will generally show the degree to which the organization has been able to maintain financial accountability over the use of public funds. Such accountability also ensures that the funds have been used for purposes for which they were appropriated.

Financial audit: Review of how the finances of an organization are managed, including whether funds are being used for their stated purposes. Financial management itself is concerned with how the finances of an organization are used and managed in the conduct of organizational business. This includes ensuring that funds are available when they are needed, and are used for the purposes specified.

Financial intermediation: An activity undertaken by an organization (usually a financial institution) to acquire funds to be channeled to borrowers. In serving as an intermediary in this process, the organization ensures that its disbursement process is rigorous and that repayment schedules have been well understood. Financial intermediation is used, for example, in developing countries to make credit available for poor people to become engaged in income-generating activities.

Financial leverage: In the public-management context, this term refers to the leverage that is exercised by one party (for example, a control agency, such as a treasury) through control of another party's budgetary resources. Such leverage is applied to ensure that organizations are properly targeting scarce resources for meeting outcomes that have been articulated by government.

Fire-brigade approach: An approach to decision making where all the energy and attention of management is spent on managing crises, and where calculated long-term problem solving is notably absent. Fire fighting is a rather common phenomenon in organizations, and it requires astute and strategic management to ensure that the organization is also committing itself to thinking beyond the short-term crisis. See, e.g., R. Khator, "Bureaucracy and the Environmental Crisis: A Comparative Perspective," in A. Farazmand (ed.), *Handbook of Bureaucracy,* New York: Marcel Dekker, Inc., 1994, pp. 195–210.

Fire sales: When assets that have come under the control of the government (such as when businesses go bankrupt) are sold at very low prices (in order to entice buyers to purchase). The purpose is also to get rid of the assets at almost any price. Fire sales are in evidence when sellers have critical fund shortages and there are very few buyers; hence, immense markdowns in sale prices are common. For a description of the use of fire sales in East Asia during the Asian financial crisis of the late 1990s, see, e.g., A. Mody and S. Negishi, "Cross-Border Mergers and Acquisitions in East Asia: Trends and Implications," *Finance and Development,* 2001, 38(1), pp. 6–9.

Firm bid: A bid that compels the bidding firm to adhere to the contract in all its specifications, including schedules. A firm bid may result if the organization asking for the bidding does not have any further room for maneuvering and expects the bidder to stay within the specifications laid out during the bidding stage.

First-best solution: The most preferred solution of all that may have been proposed. Obviously, the goal of any organization is to seek to meet the first-best solution.

First customer: *See* **Second customer**.

First-generation reforms: Economic reforms that focus on macroeconomic and broad policies, and in creating the right environmental conditions for an economy to grow. This could include putting in place proper regulatory framework, such as suitable investment and banking regulation. For a general discussion of the concept in light of the issues to be considered while designing subsequent second-generation reforms, see, e.g., V. Tanzi, *The Role of the State and the Quality of the Public Sector,* Washington, DC: IMF Working Paper WP/00/36, March 2000. *See also* **Second-generation reforms**.

First in, last out: Refers to a system of ensuring that employees who joined the organization before others are the last ones to be made redundant. While this concept may appear to safeguard the employment of senior workers in the organization, there are downsides as well, notably that this reduces the mobility of older workers, which makes them less employable (by virtue of the fact that there is little pressure on them to refresh their skills so that they remain employable). For a discussion of this concept in relation to the aging workforce in Sweden, see OECD, *Aging and Employment Policies: Sweden,* Paris: OECD, 2003, p. 10.

First-line manager: A manager who supervises staff members who deal directly with customers. First-line managers play an important role in transmitting valuable customer-specific information up the organizational hierarchy to the leadership.

First-mover advantage: An advantage gained by the first contractor to provide a service, since it has acquired the knowledge specific to the service/organization and can bid more effectively. The inevitable result of first-mover advantage tends to be a situation of "small-numbers bargaining," because the first movers will continue to crowd out others. See, e.g., W. Ouchi, "Markets, Bureaucracies, and Clans," *Administrative Science Quarterly,* 1980, 25(1), pp. 129–41. The converse of this concept is the first-mover disadvantage, which refers to the risks that any party faces when attempting to be at the forefront of the work in a particular area or sector. Thus, for example, first-mover disadvantage applies to those firms that go first in experimenting with new technologies, or with governmental departments that take the lead in trying out new ways of doing things. In dealing with the untried, the risk of failure—and more importantly, of not being able to overcome the failure—often acts as a deterrent. For a discussion of the term in relation to e-government, see, for example, OECD,

*OECD E-Government Flagship Report 'The E-Government Imperative':
Key Issues and Findings,* GOV/PUMA(2003)6, Paris: OECD, 2003.

First-order benefit: A benefit of a program or policy that is direct or
primary. For example, a drug-rehabilitation program will, if managed
effectively, reduce the number of cases of repeat drug users. This is a
first-order benefit; the second-order benefit could be a reduction in the
level of drug-related crimes in the area. *Cf.* **Second-order benefit**.

First-order imitation: *See* **Imitation**.

First-order learning: Refers to merely responding to an existing situation
rather than attempting to make change. How one approaches this determines the selection of appropriate adaptive strategies. In first-order learning, there is no shift in the underlying values and norms of the individuals
and groups, which is akin to single-loop learning. *See also* **Single-loop
learning**.

First-order objectives: Objectives that are taken as overriding, and as
given. For example, according to rational-choice theory, the first-order
objective of a politician is to seek power and to prefer more power to
less. Likewise, the first-order objective of bureaucrats can be said to be
more discretion to less. See, e.g., M. Grindle, "In Quest of the Political:
The Political Economy of Development Policy-Making," in G. Meier and
J. Stiglitz, *Frontiers in Development Economics: The Future in Perspective,* New York: Oxford University Press, 2001, pp. 345–80.

First-order variation: *See* **Double-loop learning**.

First principles: *See* **A priori assumptions**.

Fiscal discipline: Refers to the prudence exhibited by organizations in
managing their finances. Such discipline includes staying within the
bounds of what is specified in the organizational budget, and adhering to
effective and efficient management practices. Fiscal discipline has contained in it adherence to the fiscal envelope, which is the total level of
finances an organization can receive to meet the mandates it has been
given. While budget incrementalism may increase the size of the fiscal
envelope over time, organizations are strongly urged by control agencies
to adhere to the constraints imposed by the envelope.

Fiscal federalism: (1) Refers to the state of fiscal relationships between a
federal or central government and different subjurisdictions. These relationships are characterized by fiscal transfers and decision rights over

areas of intervention on the assumption that some issues and problems are better addressed by the federal government and some by the sub-jurisdictions. (2) Fiscal federalism also refers to the intergovernmental grants-in-aid systems. See, e.g., D. Elazar, "Fiscal Questions and Political Answers in Intergovernmental Finance," *Public Administration Review,* 1972, 32(5), pp. 471–78.

Fiscal illusion: A situation where the actual costs and benefits of government are not accurately seen. For example, in what is known as the flypaper effect, citizens in a jurisdiction may see block grants as gifts but do not also realize that such "gifts" represent added costs to them in the form of higher jurisdictional taxes as the size of governmental expenditures increases. For a discussion of the fiscal illusion in the context of local government, see, e.g., J. Byrnes and B. Dollery, "Local Government Failure in Australia? An Empirical Analysis of New South Wales," *Australian Journal of Public Administration,* 2002, 61(3), pp. 54–64.

Fiscal slack: The cushion in the government's fiscal position that softens the impact of sudden cost increases in public programs. The loss of fiscal slack makes it that much more difficult for government to withstand challenges to maintain programs that rely on fringe funding (i.e., are the first ones to be cut when budgetary pressures rise).

Fiscal stress: As used in the public-management context, fiscal stress refers to the pressures on an organization to manage its operations as a result of budgetary restrictions, yet with no restrictions (or contraction) of its mandate. The stress could also be caused by allocative inefficiencies generated by the organization itself.

Fiscally neutral: When the addition of costs to governmental departments that results from new programs are matched by the decreases in costs that result from doing away with some existing programs such that the net result is the original level of organizational budget. Control agencies insist on fiscally neutral alternatives to new programs such that fiscal discipline is maintained.

Fishbone diagram: *See* **Ishikawa diagram**.

Fishbowl syndrome: The perception that public-sector employees have of working in an environment where they are being observed and critically appraised for every action they take. The fishbowl syndrome can lead to a risk-averse tendency in public servants. See, e.g., S. Washington and E. Armstrong, *Ethics in the Public Service: Current Issues and Practice,* Public Management Occasional Papers, No. 14, Paris: OECD, 1996, p. 23.

Fit and proper, principle of: The principle that organizations need to have proper systems in place in order to be effective. The fit-and-proper principle applies not only to the mandate of the organization, but also to its human-resource capability and its methods of doing things.

Fit-for-purpose organizations: Organizations that are designed in such a way so as to make the most of the operating environment to which they are subject. Fit-for-purpose organizations tend not to have capability shortages (since they are able to balance their resource needs), and are able to secure relevant information relatively easily to stay on track regarding their mandates. See, e.g., M. Goold and A. Campbell, "Fit-for-Purpose Organizations," *Organizations & People,* 2002, 9(3), pp. 12–21.

Fitness-of-character doctrine: A criterion for personnel selection during the early days of the U.S. public service in which men were to be selected for governmental positions based on a determination of their character (i.e., they had to be educated, loyal, of good family background, and represent a balance of geographic interest).

Fixed budget: A budget for an organization that is designed to remain unchanged for the period in which it is prepared. If costs for the organization show a trend that is likely to exceed the fixed budget, then the organization will have to make a request for supplementary funds, scale back its operations, or seek more efficiencies in some operational areas of its business.

Fixed costs: Also called capacity costs, this term refers to costs that are incurred at a particular level regardless of the level of planned production. Thus, fixed costs in a governmental department could include the rent due on premises if the organization did not own its own premises. *Cf.* **Variable costs**.

Fixed-price contract with escalation: In contract administration, such a form of contract enables the contract price to be increased or lowered depending on whether or not specific contingencies become evident. These contingencies will have been specified *ex ante*, and agreed to by both the principal and the agent.

Fixed-price incentive contract: A contract that is characterized by the possibility of adjusting the final price with the agent depending upon how the final negotiated cost compares to the costs that had been targeted. This type of contract is beneficial to both principal and agent because it has the flexibility to consider costs even after *ex ante* specifications.

Fixed-price redeterminable contract: A contract that allows the principal to redetermine the ex *ante* contract price conditional upon performances (including of cost levels) in particular areas to which the principal has expressed concern.

Fixer: A term used by public policy guru Eugene Bardach to denote someone who can help in the policy implementation process. A fixer could be someone who controls resources for the implementing agency and who has the will to push just the right amount of relevant people. See E. Bardach, *The Implementation Game: What Happens After a Bill Becomes a Law,* Cambridge, MA: MIT Press, 1977, pp. 275–77.

Flat organization: Any organization where there are few hierarchies and where there is a narrow span of control. Flat organizations are recently being encouraged because they facilitate effective communication and rapid decision making. *Cf.* **Tall organization.**

Flexibility in government: A concept that refers to a governmental department's capacity to respond effectively to any pressures that its environment may impose. Such a response should not be merely reactive but also proactive in that the department is able to see in advance the nature of changes that will be occurring down the road. For a discussion of the term, see, e.g., G. Peters, *The Future of Governing: Four Emerging Models,* Lawrence: University Press of Kansas, 1996, p. 72.

Flexible benefit package: A package of benefits that an organization offers to its employees whereby they are free to choose which ones they would like to receive. Such a package is beneficial to both parties since it allows only benefits that are to be utilized by employees to be accessed, thus reducing costs for the employer, and it better targets the needs of the employees. Flexible pay is that part of the pay packet of an employee that is variable and could be contingent, for example, on level of individual or team performance.

Flexible work practices: When an employer permits employees to be flexible in some areas related to work. A well-known flexible work practice is flexitime, which is a policy to allow employees to realistically vary the time they start and end work as long as the required hours are met. Flexitime is designed to encourage staff members to reconcile their personal considerations with work requirements, and is centered on the notion of work-life balance. See, e.g., M. Ezra and M. Deckman, "Balancing Work and Family Responsibilities: Flexitime and Child Care in the Federal Government," *Public Administration Review,* 1996, 56 (2), pp. 174–79. *See also* **Work-life balance.**

Flexitime: *See* **Staggered schedule.**

Flexperts: Denotes individuals who have more than one area of expertise (either in associated or separate areas/sectors), and who are flexible in terms of mobility. An organization needs flexperts to fill unplanned shortages in expertise. See, e.g., B. Van der Heijden, "Individual Career Initiatives and Their Influence upon Professional Expertise Development Throughout the Career," *International Journal of Training and Development,* 2002, 6(2), pp. 54–79. *See also* **Footloose experts.**

Flickering authority: The term is drawn from the fact that, in learning organizations, the authority for analyzing issues and for making decision tends to be with those who have access to relevant information related to the particular issue under consideration. Thus, authority could "flicker" from individual to individual in the management structure depending on who is considering what issue. See F. Withington, *The Real Computer: Its Influence, Uses, and Effects*, Reading, MA: Addison-Wesley, 1969, p. 203.

Float: In performance evaluation and review technique, a float is the extra time that is available to program managers to complete a scheduled activity. This is possible when the preceding activity on which this one is dependent may have been completed ahead of schedule.

Floor price: The minimum price an organization is willing to incur in producing goods and services. Determining this lower threshold—and strictly adhering to it—is critical to the financial health of organizations. *Cf.* **Ceiling.**

Fluid participation: A situation where there is a constant movement of policy actors in and out of the different phases in policy choice, which only serves to complicate the negotiation and consultation process.

Flypaper effect: *See* **Fiscal illusion.**

Focused policies: Policies that are designed to encourage certain specific sectors and provide support to firms that are willing to be involved in them. Such policies are generally found in areas that government has highlighted as requiring priority. See, e.g., R. Lipsey and K. Carlaw, "Technology Policies in Neo-classical and Structuralist-Evolutionary Models," *STI Review* (Special Issue on "New Rationale and Approaches in Technology and Innovation Policy"), 1998, 22(1), pp. 31–73.

Folk management: *See* **Bottom-up management**.

Foot in the door approach: A tactic used in bargaining processes where one party gains the confidence of another and gets agreement to several inconsequential proposals as a way of influencing a positive response to a major proposal to be made thereafter.

Footloose experts: Refers to individuals who have expertise in any given area but are not tied to any one project or program and go wherever there are consulting opportunities. See, e.g., M. Turner and D. Hulme, *Governance, Administration & Development: Making the State Work,* London: Macmillan Press, 1997, p. 2. *See also* **Flexperts**.

Forced-distribution method: As used in the context of performance management, this is a method of performance appraisal where there is *ex ante* determination of what proportion of staff members are going to be placed in which performance category. This "forces" supervisors to place staff members in categories that they may otherwise not be located in if no such distribution was enforced.

Force-field analysis: A technique propounded by organization behavioral theorist Kurt Lewin which can be used as a basic procedure for deciding the various factors that impinge on a particular problem faced by an organization, and the intensity of that impact. This is a simple yet powerful technique to assess which factor will affect the desired state and in what manner. See K. Lewin, *Field Theory in Social Science,* New York: Harper & Row, 1951. For application, see, e.g., G. Bhatta, *Contextualizing the Annan Agenda: Reforms at the United Nations,* Singapore: Singapore University Press, 2000, pp. 225–28.

Forecasting horizon: The time period for which organizations make decisions, and which features in their planning assumptions. Depending upon the organization, and the nature of the business, this could be anywhere from three to ten years, for example.

Formal agenda: *See* **Agenda**.

Formal authority: Authority that is associated with assigning decision rights in an organization. Formal authority in a governmental agency stems from the mandate and authority rendered by the legislature or by the executive branch via delegated legislation.

Formal bid: A proposal by a contractor that must be submitted to the contracting office in the prescribed format and in the prescribed schedule.

It is the formal bid that gets reviewed by the contracting office, and not verbal proposals or informal communications that may have been made in advance of the submitted bid.

Formal contract: *See* **Implicit contract**.

Formal corporatism: Refers to an institution where unions and union representatives play a formal role in the governance of public-sector agencies. Despite the setback that unions faced in the 1980s and 1990s in advanced jurisdictions, in many others they have been actively courted back into the management picture. Some countries have signed partnerships for quality agreements with unions so that they become an important player in the public-sector management process. This concept is contrasted with informal corporatism, which enables unions to be involved in management even when it is not formally required. For a discussion of this, see, e.g., J. Christiansen, *Managerial Behavior, Opportunism, and Institutional Reform of the Welfare State,* Paper for the Workshop on The New Public Management, ECPR Joint Sessions of Workshops, Madrid, April 17–22, 1994, Aarhus: Department of Political Science.

Formal organization: Refers generally to the properly specified and structured components of an organization. Formal organizations have written and well-codified standards of operation, and it is possible for outsiders to see how the organization is structured and how its various components interact with each other. *Cf.* **Informal organization**.

Formal rulemaking: A structured process of establishing the rules and modes of operation that applies to organizations and relevant processes that affect interactions among organizations. Some inherent attributes of formal rulemaking include: (a) it has to follow from an agency hearing, (b) it has to have complete records and be supported by evidence, and (c) it should also take into account public input. Given all this, formal rulemaking is very time consuming. Formal rulemaking implies formalization, which, as used in an organizational context, refers to the degree to which procedures are set in writing and codified within the organization. For a review of the impact of formalization on organizational innovation, see, e.g., J. Covin and D. Slevin, "A Conceptual Model of Entrepreneurship as Firm Behavior," *Entrepreneurship Theory and Practice,* 1991, 16(1), pp. 7–25.

Formal training: Training where the purpose and format are pre-specified, the level of training required is determined by an expert, and the training tends to be structured (that is, set in what it offers and how it does so). *Cf.* **Informal training**.

Formative evaluation: Evaluation that is geared toward eliciting recommendations to enhance the performance of a project, program, or policy. Formative evaluation is normally carried out during the implementation phase of the activity rather than at the end. *See also* **Evaluation**.

Formative learning: *See* **Organizational learning**.

Formula grant: Grants imparted from central government to lower jurisdictions where specific proportions of the grant are set aside for formally approved programs and activities. The size of such grants are determined with respect to the application of formulas that will ideally have been rigorously developed and made transparent to all grant recipients *ex ante*.

Forum: A social practice where there is debate on public-policy issues. A forum can include discussion groups, public hearings, conferences, etc., and can be either spatial (i.e., place-bound, such as public hearings) or non-spatial (i.e., non-place-bound, such as television). See, e.g., J. Bryson and B. Crosby, "Policy Planning and the Design and Use of Forums, Arenas, and Courts," in B. Bozeman (ed.), *Public Management: The State of the Art,* San Francisco: Jossey-Bass, 1993, pp. 323–44. *See also* **Arena**.

Forward funding: The practice of making decisions on funding matters that extends beyond the traditional twelve months and incorporate the planned levels of activities in subsequent time periods. Forward estimates are estimates (on a rolling, three-year basis) of future baseline funding requirements. These estimates assume that no policy change will occur, and are designed to add a long-term perspective to the budget process.

Forward integration: Also known as downstream integration, this occurs when an organization does additional work to market its own product. Forward integration also occurs when it uses inputs from its own existing business to produce some good or service. This reduces the need for the organization to depend on other sources for inputs.

Forward mapping: Also known as scenario writing, this concept refers to a view of policy implementation that focuses on the top, from where policy direction stems, and then moves downwards through an organization to define what must occur at each level in order to give effect to—or bring about—that view. *Cf.* **Backward mapping**.

Forward-looking criteria: Criteria that are used by organizations that reflects the capacity of an entity to be involved in some obligations in the future rather than looking at capacity as a function of past performance.

In performance appraisal, for example, forward-looking criteria are used in performance targeting where the focus of the individual is toward the future rather than the past.

Fourth branch (of government): Refers generally to the media (the other three branches being the legislature, executive, and judiciary). See, e.g., J. McKinney and L. Howard, *Public Administration: Balancing Power and Accountability,* Oak Park, IL: Moore Publishing, 1979, p. 411.

Fragile state: A term that is of very recent origin and refers to those countries where there is lack of political commitment and insufficient capacity to develop and implement pro-poor policies. These states normally include those that are at the bottom two quintiles of the World Bank country performance index, and others such as Afghanistan, Liberia, Myanmar, Somalia, and Timor-Leste. Fragile states are now at the forefront of international debate because the costs of failure and of negative spillovers are large. It has been determined that meeting the special needs of fragile states requires the use of a range of instruments in addition to aid—including diplomacy, security and financial measures such as debt relief, and a coherent, whole-of-government approach from international actors. For a discussion of how fragile states can be assisted in the development efforts, see, e.g., OECD, "Senior Level Forum on Development Effectiveness in Fragile States," DAC/Chair(2005)3, Paris: OECD, 2005. *See also* **Collapsed state**.

Frame-breaking reform: Any reform that is not slow and incremental but revolutionary and dramatic, and fundamentally changes the ways in which things have been done. Here, change tends to be rather disruptive within the organization. For an application, see, e.g., R. Jones, "Leading Change in Local Government: The Tension Between Evolutionary and Frame-Breaking Reform in New South Wales," *Australian Journal of Public Administration,* 2002, 61(3), pp. 38–53. *Cf.* **Evolutionary reform**.

Frame of reference: Any set of presuppositions, assumptions, or evaluative criteria that an individual employs to judge a particular issue or problem to determine how he or she should react to it and what course of action should be taken. For example, judging the frames of reference that different stakeholders have about a particular issue helps bureaucrats better understand what elements need to be incorporated in the policy that is finally recommended to governmental ministers.

Framework documents: Contracts that are signed between the government and heads of executive agencies in the United Kingdom that serve as the primary accountability mechanism for the chief executives. Framework documents were revisited periodically to ensure that they reflected the changed operating environment of the particular agency.

Framework legislation: *See* **Framework policies**.

Framework policies: Policies that provide support to particular activities across the entire economy, and are available to any firm or organization involved in the activity. Framework rules govern the basic interactions among economic and political actors, and serve to delineate the "rules of the game." Examples of framework rules include contract laws and labor laws. A related term, framework legislation, refers to the delegation of authority to the bureaucracy to formulate regulations needed to convert legislation into legally binding decisions. See, e.g., R. Lipsey and K. Carlaw, "Technology Policies in Neo-classical and Structuralist-Evolutionary Models," *STI Review* (Special Issue on "New Rationale and Approaches in Technology and Innovation Policy"), 1998, 22(1), pp. 31–73.

Framework setting: A process of determining the dimensions of a particular action to be taken in response to a perceived problem. Framework setting could involve, for example, determining what types of instruments the government can employ to monitor the parties that are involved.

Franchise: As used in the public-management context, a franchise refers to a form of reducing state control over an activity whereby a private firm is given authority by the state to operate a particular business in a particular area or sector.

Free and frank advice: A requirement that the bureaucracy should provide policy advice to governmental ministers that is free and honest. In New Zealand, for example, the performance agreement that is negotiated with the chief executive of a public-service department or ministry by the State Services Commissioner on behalf of the responsible minister contains general requirements for the provision of free and frank advice. See, e.g., S. Goldfinch, "Evaluating Public Sector Reform in New Zealand: Have the Benefits Been Oversold?" *Asian Journal of Public Administration*, 1998, 20(2), pp. 203–32.

Free entry: When those that are interested in entering a market do not meet any hurdles (such as legal restrictions). An example of a legal barrier is monopoly rights enjoyed by a firm that is already in a particular market. Other barriers to free entry can include the difficulty of competing with those that are already in a market who have established their own niche and who have gained the goodwill of customers. The government's role in ensuring that there is free entry in markets is to propound fair rules and to adhere closely to enforcing them impartially. On the other hand, free exit occurs when those that are interested in leaving a market do not meet any hurdles (such as legal restrictions). The legal barrier to exit is evident when, for example, firms have to get permission from government to cease provision of goods and services.

Free exit: *See* **Free entry.**

Free lunch: A term that refers to the advantages that individuals and organizations receive without any disadvantage attached to being involved in a particular policy or program. A "free-lunch" policy package is considered to be Pareto-optimal since everyone is better off without anyone losing out as a result of the policy (discounting the extra costs incurred by the government to manage the policy package). *See also* **Free-rider problem**.

Free market: A market for products and services in which people, firms, and organizations buy and sell voluntarily. In a free market, there is no control exercised by third parties (i.e., the government). However, there will have to be legal regulations (such as on safety, standards, etc.) so as to ensure that all the participants play by the same rules.

Free-rider problem: A problem that arises when individuals have an economic incentive to exploit collective goods without paying for them. Collective goods (or public goods), such as national defense, are jointly consumed, for which it is not feasible to exclude specific consumers. See, e.g., O. Kim and M. Walker, "The Free Rider Problem: Experimental Evidence," *Public Choice*, 1984, 43(1), pp. 3–24. *See also* **Holdout**.

Fringe benefits: Any benefits that employees receive that are supplementary to their wages and salaries. Such fringe benefits can include free or subsidized parking; education allowance for children; airfares, if an employee is from a great distance; study leave; and tuition assistance. In individual employment contracts, as indeed in collective-bargaining agreements, fringe benefits may be a subject of negotiations with the employer by or on behalf of the employees.

Fringe funding: *See* **Fiscal slack.**

Front-line employees: Employees who are in direct touch with customers in the course of providing services. Front-line employees are the organization's interface with its customers, and care is taken to ensure that they project the proper and appropriate image to the public that they serve.

Front loaded: When a greater proportion of costs for programs are incurred early on in the schedule. Front-loaded costs are transparent and customers tend to prefer them since they can see just how much they pay for a particular service.

Full bureaucracies: Refers to organizations whose activities are highly structured and where there is a concentration of authority. The term comes from a typology of organizations first determined by the Aston Group in the UK in the early 1960s (so named after the group of scholars whose research was done while they were connected to the University of Aston). The Group proposed that any organization could be characterized by its degree of specialization of functions, standardization of procedures, formalization of documentation, and centralization (or concentration) of authority. *See also* **Non-bureaucracies; Personnel bureaucracies; Workflow bureaucracies**.

Full funding: Resources that are provided to an organization/program that meet all the costs and all estimated obligations that the organization or program may incur to fulfill the mandate. Provisions of full funding have the advantage of ensuring that any resource uncertainties are minimized, which enables the work to proceed unfettered. The disadvantage is that it commits the funding authority to a level of resources without being certain of the outputs or outcomes. *Cf.* **Incremental budgeting**.

Full training costs: Refers to the total costs of training borne by an organization. This includes not only the actual training-related activities (such as the planning and delivery of the training) but also the back-office support that goes into the provision of the training (such as administrative support, security, catering, etc.).

Full-life paradigm: In the discussion on what development means in different settings, this term refers to the systems and beliefs regarding the ultimate meaning of life that has to be taken into consideration when looking at how to approach enhancing development in a particular setting. For a discussion of this paradigm, see, e.g., D. Goulet, "Development: Creator and Destroyer of Values," *World Development,* 1992, 20(3), pp. 467–75.

Full-time equivalent: A measure of the time put in by a staff member. One full-time equivalent is calculated as one person working full-time (however the term may be defined, though it is normally taken to mean 40 hours per week) for one financial year. Full-time equivalent employment is thus the number of full-time jobs in the organization, which is calculated by dividing the total hours worked by the average hours worked in full-time jobs.

Functional authority: Authority that is given to an individual in relation to the function he or she is involved in. Such an authority then is derived from the particular work assignment. Managers in the human-resource division of an organization, for example, will have functional authority over several personnel-related activities. Functional authority will shift as individuals move around the organization with different portfolios.

Functional classification: The process of subdividing the organization's functions into discrete components so that they can be assigned to individuals with appropriate competencies. Such functional classification is evident in areas such as human-resource management, operations, strategic planning, etc.

Functional departmentalization: A process where the activities of an organization are grouped into separate operations and each one undertakes a distinctive function (for example, marketing, finance, human resource, etc.). *Cf.* **Product departmentalization**.

Functional distance: The gulf between employees (both physical and otherwise) that adversely affects their interactions with each other by not creating the right conditions for them to be so engaged with each other. These conditions include the precise specifications of all the functions in which individual staff members need to be involved. Loosely worded job descriptions, for example, can create functional distance as well as can adversely affect functional leadership.

Functional job analysis: A method of looking at a particular position's requirements by analyzing and measuring the work that is involved in that particular function. Such an analysis helps the organization determine the competencies that need to be demonstrated by the employee who will be involved in the function.

Functional leadership: Refers to a concept that argues that leadership is a product of how individuals are grouped according to the functions they are involved in (and thus how they interact with each other) and not through the attributes exhibited by individuals who are in positions of authority. Deficiencies in functional leadership can lead to, among other things, functional distance. *See also* **Functional distance.**

Functional management: Management of the different functions in an organization that are carried out by specialists who are responsible for those specific functions. A persistent reliance on functional management, however, could lead to what is known as functional myopia, which is when staff members focus on their individual function at the expense of the overall organizational purpose. This leads to a silo view of what is relevant and important for the organization as a whole. At the broader level, this aggregates to a silo view in the public service as a whole.

Functional myopia: *See* **Functional management.**

Functionalism: A principle that organizational careers should be built around, and centered on, functions (such as human-resource management) within the organization. For a discussion of the principle of functionalism, see, e.g., F. Riggs, "Bureaucracy: A Profound Puzzle for Presidentialism," in A. Farazmand (ed.), *Handbook of Bureaucracy,* New York: Marcel Dekker, Inc., 1994, pp. 97–147.

Functionally critical: Any activity or component of a system that is necessary for smooth operations. A functionally critical element jeopardizes the system if it fails to perform to specification. While this is obvious, for example, in technological functions within organizations, there are also other activities in organizations that are functionally critical (such as, say, the payroll system).

Funder/provider/purchaser split: Separation of the roles of a governmental department in relation to its activities on funding, providing, and purchasing public goods and services. Such a split is recommended by those who argue for public-management reforms based on agency theory and public-choice theory. The split refers to the manner in which public agencies' roles in funding and purchasing goods and services is located in organizations that are separate from those that provide them. The assumption is that if these roles are in one single organization, there are greater chances of bureaucratic capture, thus giving providers a competitive advantage. Such a split is evident, for example, in New Zealand, where the Ministry of Health provides funds to the District Health Board that then purchases appropriate goods and services from various providers. Such a split has meant that relationships among various parties are regulated by means of contracts and quasicontracts. A direct and unforeseen consequence of such a split has tended to be that governments have neglected their ownership responsibilities since a large part of the focus has been on getting value for money in the short term. For a discussion of the funder/purchaser/provider split, see, e.g., R. Shaw, "Rehabilitating the Public Service—Alternatives to the Wellington Model," in S. Chatterjee (ed.), *The New Politics: A Third Way for New Zealand,* Palmerston North, New Zealand: Dunmore Press, 1999, p. 196–97.

Funders' majority: *See* **Double majority, principle of.**

Fungibility: Refers to transferability. Fungible grants, for example, are grants whose resources can be used for purposes other than those for which they were first given. And fungible skills are skills of individuals that can be transferred from one position/occupation to another. Related to the concept of multiskilling, fungible skills give individuals the latitude to be involved in different projects and functional dimensions that they can thus use to enhance their career growth.

Fusion process: A process of making individual employee goals mirror those of the organization. Such a process involves ensuring that individuals are aware of—and internalize—the organizational goals, and forms part of the psychological contract between the employer and employee. *See also* **Psychological contract**.

Future-dispute clause: Any clause that is included in a contract that specifies how the parties will handle any future disputes that may arise in the course of contract implementation. Such a clause normally specifies the manner of potential arbitration, which ensures that contingencies will be adequately handled.

Fuzzy logic: Refers to unstructured and rather imprecise responses to environmental stimulus. Thus, instead of a straightforward yes or no (i.e., a binary) response to a pressure, fuzzy logic asserts that organizations will more realistically look for responses that are contained in a continuum of possibilities that range from yes to no. Fuzzy logic thus is concerned with making decisions with imprecise and approximate reasoning; however, it does not facilitate a richer picture of the organization's operational environment.

G

Gain-loss theory of attraction: In the employment context, asserts that if the amounts of employee incentives—both rewards and sanctions—are varied, then there will be a greater impact on employee motivation than if they were static. Thus, according to this theory, vary the incentives given and the impact will be greater motivation on the part of the employee.

Game theory: Helps study how decisions are made when decision makers have different objectives but work in the same environment. The operative assumptions in game theory are: (a) each decision maker has perfect knowledge of the rules of the game and of the opposition, and (b) decision makers are rational (i.e., each will seek to maximize payoff). Game theory has been used in various disciplines including conflict resolution and management science. For a discussion of game theory, see, e.g., K. Hipel and N. Fraser, "Using Game Theory to Model Political Uncertainty," *Peace and Change,* 1988, 13, pp. 118–31.

Games: (1) Games in government with respect to results take on various forms: (a) zero-sum games mean one player's gain is another's loss (a variant here is constant-sum games, where the results do not always cancel each other out to zero but remain at some existing level), (b) positive-sum games have all participants winning, and (c) negative-sum games have all players losing considerably. See, e.g., C. Levine, B. Peters and F. Thompson, *Public Administration: Challenges, Choices, Consequences,* Glenview, IL: Scott, Foresman and Co., 1990, p. 122. (2) Games in bureaucracy with respect to the nature of the game include: (a) the service-delivery game (i.e., resulting from the interaction between street-level bureaucrats and citizens), (b) the public-management game (i.e., from the interaction between street-level bureaucrats and their managers), (c) the policy game (i.e., from the interaction between public managers and political executives), and (d) the social-choice game (i.e., interaction between those who enact the policies and the policy-making executives). See, e.g., L. Lynn, "Policy Achievement as a Collective Good: A Strategic Perspective on Managing Social Programmes," in B. Bozeman (ed.), *Public Management: The State of the Art,* San Francisco: Jossey-Bass, 1993, pp. 108–33.

Gaming the numbers: Refers to a situation where a public organization raises its output in keeping with some performance standard, but the action has little intrinsic value because it is essentially done to meet a particular numerical standard. For example, by turning away difficult cases, and taking in only those cases that it can solve, a public organization is able to increase its output but not add anything substantive to addressing a particular issue. See, e.g., H. de Bruijn, "Performance Measurement in the Public Sector: Strategies to Cope with the Risks of Performance Measurement," *International Journal of Public Sector Management,* 2002, 15(6/7), pp. 578–94.

Gangplank concept: *See* **Fayol's bridge.**

Garbage-can model: Organization theorists Michael Cohen, James March, and Johan Olsen came up with this term to denote that organizations are dumping grounds for various problems and solutions and that decisions are made only if a problem, a solution, the participants, and a choice opportunity simultaneously intersect. Decision making in such cases is conducted under conditions of ambiguity. The formulation goes against the arguments contained in the concept of rationality in decision making. In many ways, this model highlights the phenomenon of solutions chasing problems. See M. Cohen, J. March and J. Olsen, "A Garbage Can Model of Organizational Choice," *Administrative Science Quarterly,* 1972, 17(1), pp. 1–25. For an application of the model in explaining public-sector reforms, see, e.g., J. Aberbach and T. Christensen, "Radical Reform in New Zealand: Crisis, Windows of Opportunity, and Rational Actors," *Public Administration,* 2001, 79(2), pp. 403–22.

Gatekeepers: Individuals/groups whose actions determine what happens to a particular policy demand. Gatekeepers interpret reality and help frame the consequential policy agenda accordingly. There are several varieties of gatekeepers: (a) promoters (those that help place measures on the policy agenda), (b) vetoers (those that could veto any proposal from being included in the policy agenda), (c) concession demanders (those who are opposed to the policy but will support it to gain concession for something they want in return), and (d) neutralists (those that either do not have a view on the proposed policy or are deliberately neutral). See L. Koenig, *An Introduction to Public Policy,* Englewood Cliffs, NJ: Prentice Hall, 1986, pp. 110–11.

Gender-analysis framework: An approach to incorporating gender considerations into any policy or program. The gender-analysis framework is a tool that is widely used in program-formulation activities of governments and donor agencies, and it comprises profiles of women's multiple roles and constraints in family and social life that illustrate the divergences in how their role should be considered in designing appropriate programs and policies. See, e.g., C. Overholt, K. Cloud and M. Anderson, "Gender Analysis Framework," in A. Rao, M. Anderson, and C. Overholt (eds.), *Gender Analysis in Development Planning: A Case Book,* West Hartford, CT: Kumarian Press, 1991, pp. 9–20.

Gender bias: Favoring one gender over the other. Even though not spelled out in detail, it commonly means bias against women. The gender bias is evident in, for example, what is termed gendering, which is the process of divisions resulting as a direct product of subtle biases being made against women. For example, a public sector may be gendered if it was evident that women were concentrated in specific occupation classes and were at the lower end of the salary levels. For a case-study application of gender equity, see, e.g., J. Dolan, "Gender Equity: Illusion or Reality for Women in the Federal Executive Service?" *Public Administration Review,* 2004, 64(3), pp. 299–308.

Gender empowerment: Giving women an opportunity to take active part in socioeconomic and political life. Gender empowerment starts with gender-specific engagement where actions are taken in line with how the two genders view problems differently. For example, on the use of microcredit lending schemes to address poverty, women have a different way of tackling the problem than men, an assertion that is at the heart of the work of the Grameen Bank, which provides collateral-free lending to the poor of rural Bangladesh, mainly to women. See, e.g., United Nations Development Program, *Human Development Report, 2001,* New York: Oxford University Press, 2001, p. 14.

Gendering: *See* **Gender bias.**

General audit: A review of all the activities and funds of an organization. A general audit is not specifically targeted at a particular sector or area of organizational activity, but instead considers the overall work of the organization. *See also* **Audit.**

General-interest reforms: Attempts by governments to adopt policies that are designed to curtail special-interest benefits and bring about radical change toward economic efficiency and/or equity. An example of a general-interest reform is pro-competitive deregulation. For a good discussion of general-interest reforms in the context of public interest, see, E. Patashnik, "After the Public Interest Prevails: The Political Sustainability of Policy Reform," *Governance: An International Journal of Policy, Administration, and Institutions,* 2003, 16(2), pp. 203–34.

General management: (1) A generic term that refers to the overall management in an organization, and to all facets of its work, including finance, strategic planning, marketing, etc. (2) A post below that of the chief executive of the organization, and above those of first-line supervisors. A general management law is any law that regulates the administration of all agencies in the public sector. General management laws are intended to provide uniformity for governmental organizations and governance processes. See, e.g., R. Moe, "The United States: A Country Study in Organization and Governance," paper presented at the OECD Governance of State Agencies and Authorities Expert Meeting, Paris, 19–20 April, 2001.

General systems theory: Refers to the way in which organizations and individuals can view the world around them. The focus in this theory is on looking not so much at the variables in and of themselves but at the interrelationships among them. The key premise in this theory is that organizations are rational and thus that what can be observed in one setting can be reasonably extended to the others as well since all share the same reliance on rationality. Systems theorists thus argue that there are common principles in the operation of all systems and that this enables an interdisciplinary approach with universal application. For the original work on general systems theory, see L. Von Bertalanffy, *General Systems Theory: Foundations, Development, Applications* (revised edition), New York: George Braziller, 1976. See also, e.g., F. Kast and J. Rosenzweig, "General Systems Theory: Applications for Organization and Management," *Academy of Management Journal,* 1972, 15(4), pp. 447–65.

General training: Also referred to as transferable training, this is training that is geared to help the employee not only in the current post/job but also presumably in other posts/jobs that he or she may take up later on. The concept is also related to that of employability. *Cf.* **Specific training**; *see also* **Employability**.

Generative coaching: A process of guiding and coaching staff members where they are assisted to be more self-aware and to critique their own underlying assumptions about all aspects of work and organizational life. Generative coaching allows those being coached to begin to look at their own potential, and at how they can channel that into more productive and rewarding work. See, e.g., K. Murphy, "Generative Coaching: A Surprising Learning Odyssey," in S. Chawla and J. Renesch (eds.), *Learning Organizations: Developing Cultures for Tomorrow's Workplace,* Portland, OR: Productivity Press, 1995, pp. 197–214.

Generative configuration: As applied in the public-management context, this term refers to structuring the organization and organizational processes and protocols such that management seeks to optimize both efficiency and effectiveness.

Generative learning: *See* **Learning.**

Generic capabilities: The core resources or competencies required within all organizations, including, for example, human-resource management and financial management. Similarly, generic skills, also known as basic skills, are skills that can be used in various settings and are not necessarily specific to a particular post, job, or work environment. In practically all organizations, for example, effective communication skills are considered to be generic skills. *See also* **Capability.**

Generic decision making: When organizations follow standard operating procedures in making routine decisions (such as on leave entitlement issues for staff members). Generic decision making and standard operating procedures imply that conditions and attributes that characterize any one setting are similar across all. This is not necessarily universal, which is why generic decision making, in reality, does not always yield the best (i.e., most effective) decisions.

Generic management: Any aspect of management that is applicable and evident in different sectors (such as human-resource management, which is evident in public, private, and nonprofit sectors as well). Some public-service reformers argue that management is similar across all these sectors and so what works in the private sector (such as efficiency drives) should be made a part of public sector management as well. The concept of managerialism stems from this assertion.

Generic policies: Refers to the range of actions that can be taken to tackle policy problems. Generic policies can normally be grouped into five categories, those: (a) establishing rules (to set the rules of the game for all parties), (b) freeing and facilitating rules (to ensure that the rules are being adhered to), (c) using taxes and subsidies (to alter incentives so that potential interventions can be channeled), (d) supplying goods through nonmarket mechanisms (in instances where the market does not have the capability—nor the intention—to do so), and (e) providing insurance and cushion (so that the repercussions of failures are not so severe). See D. Weimer and A. Vining, *Policy Analysis: Concepts and Practice,* 2nd edition, Englewood Cliffs, NJ: Prentice Hall, 1992, p. 144.

Generic skills: *See* **Generic capabilities.**

Geographic distribution: The allocation of posts in an organization based on the countries and regions of origin of applicants. In the United Nations, for example, some recruitment is done on the basis of geographic distribution, whereby candidates from traditionally non- or under-represented countries receive preference for certain positions.

Ghost workers: Identities that are fraudulently cited to bolster staff numbers in an organization so as to gain more funding, and also so as to siphon off resources to individuals. Ghost workers are either dead (and continue to remain on the salary roll) or are manipulators of paychecks. The problem of ghost workers is most acute in jurisdictions where the government does not have effective control over the bureaucratic apparatus. For example, it is reported that "up to 15 percent of PNG [Papua New Guinea]'s 75,000 public servants are 'ghosts'" (see "PNG risk terrorism, financial ruin," *Australian Financial Review,* 12 March 2003, p.18).

Gini coefficient: A measure of income inequality that ranges from 0 for perfect equality to 1 for perfect inequality (however, both extremes are rarely evident). Statistics show that income distribution has tended to be more unequal in Latin America than in other regions. See, e.g., B. Clements, "The Real Plan, Poverty, and Income Distribution in Brazil," *Finance & Development,* 1997, 34(3), pp. 44–46.

Gladiatorial activities: Drawn from political scientist Lester Milbrath's study in political participation, gladiatorial activities refer to the high-end activities that citizens can be involved in to influence governance. Such activities include holding public office, being an active member of a political party, or contributing time and resources in elections. Milbrath also wrote of two other types of activities with respect to political participation: transitional activities (which refer to citizens' middle-order activities; these include becoming an active member of a local organization, or contacting political leaders to provide some feedback on a policy), and spectator activities (which are the low-end activities, including initiating a political discussion, attending an election rally, etc.). See L. Milbrath, *Political Participation,* Chicago: Rand McNally & Co., 1965.

Glass ceiling: Nontangible but real barriers that women and minorities face in an organization in their attempt to move up the organizational hierarchy. Such barriers are placed by the subtle prejudices that male superiors have about the level of contribution and role of women and minorities in the workplace. A glass ceiling is evident, for example, in that the proportion of women in government may have increased, but the promotion of women to senior positions remains low. See, e.g., J. Wanna and P. Weller, "Traditions of Australian Governance," *Public Administration,* 2003, 81(1), pp. 63–94. For a case-study application, see also, e.g., A. van Vianen and A. Fischer, "Illuminating the Glass Ceiling: The Role of Organizational Culture Preferences," *Journal of Occupational and Organizational Psychology,* 2002, 75(3), pp. 315–37.

Glide time: *See* **Staggered schedule.**

Global essay: As used in the context of employee performance appraisal, a global essay is a narrative recap of an employee's performance written by their supervisor. It serves as a summary sheet to the main performance appraisal report, and includes a detailed assessment of the employee's performance for the time period in consideration.

Global public goods: Products whose effects spill across national boundaries (for example, river basins). In such a case, related questions that arise include: which jurisdiction has decision-making authority? Who participates in the decision-making process (for example, governments, the private sector, nongovernmental organizations)? Who ensures that decisions are properly enforced? For an application of the concept of global public goods, see, e.g., D. Kapur, "The Common Pool Dilemma of Global Public Goods: Lessons from the World Bank's Net Income and Reserves," *World Development,* 2002, 30(3), pp. 337–54.

Global rationality: Assumptions about the general existence of rationality in everyday life. Clearly, this is not entirely realistic, and polymath Herbert Simon's concept of bounded rationality was a response to this fact since he argued that global rationality did not approximate observed behavior. See, e.g., H. Simon, "A Behavioral Model of Rational Choice," *Quarterly Journal of Economics,* 1955, 69 (February), pp. 99–118.

Go/no-go rule: Also known as the acceptability threshold, this refers to a rule in policy analysis where a threshold level of acceptability for each criterion is set, and the policy analyst then eliminates all those alternatives that fail to pass any of the thresholds. The one alternative that remains is the preferred alternative. If there are more than one, then the criteria have to be tightened; if there are none, then either the criteria have to be loosened, or new alternatives have to be sought.

Goal: The macroobjective and future state a particular policy or program is expected to achieve, which also consists of the fulfillment of the mission of the organization. A goal is somewhat more concretely stated than a mission statement, and can be stated in terms of, for example, efficiency and satisfaction. Goals are either substantive goals (i.e., related to ends) or instrumental goals (i.e., related to process or means). Instrumental goals enable the attainment of subordinate goals. See, e.g., D. Weimer and A. Vining, *Policy Analysis: Concepts and Practice,* 2nd edition, Englewood Cliffs, NJ: Prentice Hall, 1992, p. 214.

Goal ambiguity: A situation where the organization as a whole, and individual members within, are not clear on what the objectives of the organization are. This is different from confusion surrounding, say, a mandate received from the legislature and refers much more to ambiguities in the intermediate goals of the organization itself.

Goal approach: According to goal approach, an organization exists to accomplish goals; therefore, proponents of this approach say that how effective an organization is should be measured by the extent of goals attainment. The approach has intuitive appeal even in the public-sector context, but in the public sector there are other just as important objectives (such as ensuring transparency) that need to be taken into consideration as well. *Cf.* **Systems-theory approach**.

Goal congruence: *See* **Goal-based system**.

Goal displacement: A situation that arises when the goals of the organization (or individuals) are replaced by instrumental values (i.e., means are valued over ends). For example, those against instituting a system of individual incentives in organizations argue that this would lead to goal displacement because individuals would be more interested in seeking rewards than considering whether their actions lead to organizational goal attainment. See, e.g., S. Kerr, "On the Folly of Rewarding A, while Hoping for B," *Academy of Management Journal,* 1975, 18(4), pp. 769–83.

Goal formulation: The process of determining for the organization what its subsequent goals will be. Goal formulation is a key step in policy and program development for it serves as the basis of determining what happens when and how. This formulation then serves as a part input to the goal-based system of performance appraisal.

Goal independence: When an organization is allowed to set its own goals. This is not normal, but several general oversight bodies (such as an audit office) tend to have a fair degree of goal independence. *See also* **Instrument independence**.

Goal steering: Refers to the activities that, say, central governments engage in to influence the goals and objectives of local governments. The term does not imply any form of regulation or firm pressure to reorient local-level policies and activities, but does refer to the subtle influences that central government can impose on subjurisdictions. For a detailed case study of goal steering in the Danish local government, see, e.g., K. Hansen, "Local Councilors: Between Local 'Government' and Local 'Governance,'" *Public Administration,* 2001, 79(1), pp. 105–23.

Goal-based learning: Learning that is encouraged in individuals in three main ways: (a) learning by doing (i.e., focused on development of skills rather than retention of facts alone), (b) learning from exploration and failure (where there is pressure on individuals to perform), and (c) learning through stories (i.e., individuals get real-life scenarios to help them learn). Goal-based learning is enhanced by support structures such as work improvement teams, and individuals can proceed at their own pace once they attain their prespecified goals. For a review of how goal-based learning is applied in practice, see, e.g., G. Bhatta, "Building Human Resource Competencies and the Training Environment in Singapore's Public Service," *Research & Practice in Human Resource Management,* 2000, 8(2), pp. 101–33.

Goal-based system: A system of management where each employee is given a set of goals and his/her performance is measured based on whether they were achieved. The goals are usually mutually agreed upon between the employer and employee. A goal-based system is less useful for employees if there is no goal congruence (goal congruence is a situation where the goals of the organization and those of the employees are not in alignment, i.e., are not mutually beneficial).

Goal-free evaluation: Evaluation of a program or policy where the focus is on actual outcomes rather than on predicted ones. In goal-free evaluation, the evaluator deliberately refrains from sharing information with the client but instead engages with the target group to discuss the actual impact of the program. See, e.g., T. Hellstrom and M. Jacob, "Knowledge Without Goals? Evaluation of Knowledge Management Programs," *Evaluation,* 2003, 9(1), pp. 55–72.

Goal-setting theory: Asserts that employees perform better if they have been given specific and measurable goals to achieve. An assertion has been made that the degree of difficulty of attaining goals does not necessarily constrain the motivation to achieve them (see, e.g., E. Locke et al., "Goal Setting and Task Performance: 1969–1980," *Psychological Bulletin,* 1981, 90(1), pp. 125–52).

Going soft: Also known as agency capture, this is a situation wherein government workers who work in regulatory agencies go easy on the industries and businesses they are regulating. While this may be largely because they do not possess the capability to effectively monitor and regulate them, it is also likely because there is an expectation of future rewards from those being regulated. See, e.g., S. Kelman, "What Is Wrong with the Revolving Door?" in B. Bozeman (ed.), *Public Management: The State of the Art,* San Francisco: Jossey-Bass, 1993, pp. 224–51.

Going-concern concept: A concept that an organization will continue to function on an ongoing basis, and as such any liabilities and obligations will be met. For an application to a public organization, see, e.g., State Services Commission, *Statement of Intent 2002,* Wellington: State Services Commission, 2002, p. 52.

Golden handcuffs: Refers to the perception that some individuals who are in financially rewarding jobs may have about being bound to continue with the job only because they would lose financially otherwise if they were to quit. The potential for financial loss thus constitutes the "handcuffs" that keeps them continuing with the job that they have.

Golden handshake: Also known as a golden parachute, this term refers to attractive offers from organizations to their staff members that are leaving. While it is understandable for successful organizations to offer a golden handshake, there have been instances of such rewards even in organizations that were in financial trouble. A related term is a golden hello, which refers to attractive offers (such as a signing bonus) to attract individuals that the organization considers are worth recruiting at high costs.

Golden hello: *See* **Golden handshake.**

Golden parachute: *See* **Golden handshake.**

Golden share: A veto power commonly used by governments to vote against certain actions in formerly publicly owned enterprises that are now privately owned. Governments retain a golden share in such enterprises so as to ensure that public interests continue to be considered by the entity. Such vetoes, however, are seldom used.

Goldfish-bowl bargaining: Also called sunshine bargaining, the term refers to all bargaining taking place with full information being transmitted to observers and the public (i.e., it is transparent). The process, as well as the contents, of such bargaining is thus public knowledge.

Good employer, principle of: The principle that an employer should put in place policies that will facilitate employees to do their work well and safely. Good employer provisions refer to putting in place a personnel policy that has necessary provisions for the fair and proper treatment of employees. This includes provisions such as good and safe working conditions, greater commitment to equal opportunity, proper and well understood reward and disciplinary systems, etc. See, e.g., G. Bhatta, "Organizational Competence and the 'Boiling Frog' Syndrome," *Organizations & People,* 2001, 8(3), pp. 11–16.

Good funding practice: Refers to sound basis for funders (for example, central governments) to keep in mind while formulating grants and co-determination policy. One such basis for providing funding is to ensure that the agency receiving the funds has a strong and active field presence in the locales in which it wishes to operate. For an example of the principles of good funding practice, see, e.g., Ministry of Social Development, *He Waka Kotuia: Joining Together on a Shared Journey,* Report of the Community-Government Relationship Steering Group, Wellington: Ministry of Social Development, 2002, p. 67. *See also* **Co-determination**.

Good governance: Taken to mean the systems and processes existent in countries that allow government to encourage policies toward and in: citizen-oriented administration; public participation in decision-making processes; rationalization of state administration, and the active involvement of the private sector in the provision of goods and services; administrative simplification and regulatory reform; and modernizing human-resources management. Public-sector economists and public-policy specialists argue that without good governance, sustained economic performance is not possible. The presence of good governance (where, for example, property rights and contracts are enforced properly by public institutions) is a necessary condition for long-term economic growth. Thus, good governance positively affects growth, which, in turn—all else being equal—alleviates poverty. The principles of good governance revolve around governments and their organizations acting legitimately (i.e., within the bounds of the law), meeting performance standards that have been specified (such as by a legislature), and accounting for actions to legislatures and ultimately to citizens. Given this, good governance is also termed democratic governance (see, e.g., J. Coston, "Administrative Avenues to Democratic Governance: The Balance of Supply and Demand," *Public Administration and Development,* 1998, 18(5), pp. 479–93).

Good management: As used in the context of what is expected of organizational leaders in public service, the concept refers to the requirement that chief executive officers ensure that their organizations are well run, with no management failures that may potentially embarrass responsible ministers. See, e.g., State Services Commission, *Annual Report of the SSC 2002,* Wellington: State Services Commission, 2002, p. 7.

Good model employer: *See* **Good employer, principle of.**

Good practice: An activity or process that has been done particularly well (i.e., it meets the criteria of efficiency, effectiveness, and consumer satisfaction) and which others seek to replicate across organizations and across jurisdictions. See, e.g., State Services Commission, *Statement of Intent 2002,* Wellington, New Zealand: State Services Commission, 2002, p. 46.

Good soldier syndrome: A tendency of an organizational member to go beyond what is normally required of him/her in terms of contributing to the organization. Associated with the concept of organizational citizenship, such behavior represents "employee value added" for which traditional measures (such as meeting output targets) are inadequate. The good soldier syndrome is evident in those who, for example, not only fulfill their mandates but also help others whenever possible and show pro-social behavior. See, e.g., J. Parks, C. Mahoney, and D. Ostgaard, "Can We Predict the Good Soldiers? A Meta-Analysis Review of the 'Good Soldier' Syndrome," Working Paper No. 95–02, Minneapolis: Minnesota–Industrial Relations Center, 1995, pp. 1–34. *See also* **Organizational citizenship**.

Good state: A notion of what and how a state should engage with citizens and provide for their needs and aspirations. In the current reform debate, four major reform traditions that define the good state are evident: (a) public-service reforms that promote organizational effectiveness, (b) reforms that aim to increase efficiency ("most returns for the least cost"), (c) reforms by entrepreneurs to free organizations of undue bureaucratic procedures, and (d) reforms by those who believe in concepts such as citizen participation. For a discussion, see, e.g., R. Stillman, II, "Twenty-First Century United States Governance: Statecraft as Reform Craft and the Peculiar Governing Practices It Perpetuates," *Public Administration,* 2003, 81(1), pp. 19–40.

Good-faith bargaining: Bargaining between labor and management done with good intentions and honesty, and in keeping with the ground rules that may have been predetermined between the two parties. Governments may have in force an act that: (a) requires unions and employers to promote good employment relations and mutual confidence between themselves, (b) sets the environment for individual and collective employment relationships, (c) sets out requirements for the negotiation and content of collective and individual employment agreements, and (d) provides prompt and flexible options for resolving problems in employment relationships. The obligation imposed by governments is also termed the duty to bargain.

Goodness of government: A measure of how well government does its job. This could be measured in several ways, including, for example, its role in enhancing citizen welfare, providing services effectively and efficiently, maintaining proper economic policies, and fostering economic growth. For a concise summary of the measures that serve as good proxies for the goodness of governmental policy, see J. Sachs and A. Warner, "Fundamental Sources of Long-Run Growth," *American Economic Review,* 1997, 87(2), pp. 184–88.

Goodwill: An intangible asset that some organizations have which, unlike in the private sector, provides them with support in terms of any policy that they may pursue. The goodwill could be a product of effective service delivery by the organization to particular communities and regions.

Governance: In general, governance refers to the relationships between governments and citizens that enable public policies and programs to be formulated, implemented, and evaluated. In the broader context, it refers to the rules, institutions, and networks that determine how a country or an organization functions. In terms of how the concept has evolved over time, four types of governance are specified: (a) procedural governance (i.e., the traditional bureaucratic manner of doing things), (b) corporate governance (i.e., governance that is goal driven, and where plans are the primary form of control over managerial action), (c) market governance (i.e., governance that relies on competition, and where contracts are the controls), and (d) network governance (i.e., governance that relies on networks and co-production). For a general discussion of governance in advanced jurisdictions, see, e.g., M. Considine and J. Lewis, "Bureaucracy, Network, or Enterprise? Comparing Models of Governance in Australia, Britain, the Netherlands, and New Zealand," *Public Administration Review,* 2003, 63(2), pp. 131–40. For a discussion of governance in non-advanced jurisdictions, see, e.g., C. Polidano and D. Hulme. "No Magic Wands: Accountability and Governance in Developing Countries," *Regional Development Dialogue,* 1997, 18(2), pp. 1–16.

Governance capacity: Refers to the capability of actors (both public, i.e., government, and private, i.e., firms) to define and shape the various processes that are necessary to produce goods and services that are demanded in society. This capacity is said to be conditioned by many variables, including the regulatory structure in which production takes place and the institutional context that is in evidence in a particular setting. For a discussion of the term, see, e.g., C. Knill and D. Lehmkuhl, "Private Actors and the State: Internationalization and Changing Patterns of Governance," *Governance: An International Journal of Policy, Administration, and Institutions,* 2002, 15(1), pp. 41–63.

Governance infrastructure: Refers to a country's political, institutional, and legal environment that enables the state and nonstate actors (such as nongovernmental organizations) to be engaged in productive activities. Cross-country differences in growth and productivity are said to be a function of a country's governance infrastructure. What the notion of governance infrastructure does not include is human capital and general social capital. See, e.g., S. Globerman and D. Shapiro, "Global Foreign Direct Investment Flows: The Role of Governance Infrastructure," *World Development,* 2002, 30(11), pp. 1899–1919.

Governing elites: Those who play a large role in how a country is governed. There are generally considered to be three types of governing elites: (1) the first governing elite consists of voters who are informed and who take the trouble of participating in public affairs; (2) the second governing elite consists of the elected representatives who are supposed to be the best representatives of the people and who then pass laws that seek to meet the objectives they have been set out to meet in the legislature; and (3) skilled bureaucrats constitute the third governing elite; these are individuals who are expected to be professionally competent yet also neutral and able to implement the laws passed by the legislature. The interaction of these three elites results in what could be considered good governance. *See also* **Elite**.

Government: Refers not only to the entire executive branch of the state but also to the legislature and the judiciary. Also refers to the institutions and processes by which citizens elect representatives, who then make policies on their behalf, as well as to the bureaucrats that implement them. A government is not normally a single monolithic entity, although it is entirely possible for it to be constituted of elites.

Government accountability: The answerability of governmental departments and agencies to the public for their work and for their use of public resources. Such an accounting is done through means such as presenting reports to legislatures, public hearings, and responding to media queries and reports. For elected representatives, the ultimate form of accountability is gaining the support of constituencies during elections.

Government by moonlight: A term used to denote the work of quasi-governmental and nonprofit organizations in the delivery of services that governments have traditionally provided. A related term is government by proxy, which refers to the fact that governments have begun to contract out most of their work to the private sector and nonprofit organizations. See, e.g., D. Kettl, "Government by Proxy and the Public Service," *International Review of Administrative Services,* 1988, 54(4), pp. 501–16. *See also* **Hollow state**.

Government by proxy: *See* **Government by moonlight**.

Government by the market: A notion that the best means of meeting the needs of citizens are represented by a reliance on market systems rather than public bureaucratic systems. Those that adhere to this notion argue that governments should generally scale back their activities by, for example, contracting out delivery of services to the private sector wherever possible. They also argue that public bureaucracies should reorient their own internal systems and administrative processes in accordance with market principles of efficiencies and internal competition. Notions of "government by the market" are contained in such theories as agency theory and public-choice theory. See, e.g., P. Self, *Government by the Market? The Politics of Public Choice,* London: Macmillan Press, 1993, p. ix.

Government corporation: This is generally understood to mean a governmental agency that is mandated to perform a market-oriented public service but which meets all or most of its operating costs from revenues generated from its own enterprise. A government corporation is also at arm's length from ministerial control, although elected representatives clearly do have a measure of influence over it. Some examples of government corporations in the United States include the well-known U.S. Postal Service or the not-so-well-known Legal Services Corporation. See, e.g., R. Moe, "The United States: A Country Study in Organization and Governance," paper presented at the OECD Governance of State Agencies and Authorities Expert Meeting, Paris, 19–20 April 2001, p. 15. For a generic and overarching discussion of these bodies and how they serve as tools of government, see, e.g., I. Thynne, "Government Companies as Instruments of State Action," *Public Administration and Development,* 1998, 18(3), pp. 217–28.

Government failure: The public-choice school describes governmental failure as when the public sector as a whole faces serious difficulties in policy making and implementation, and when governmental agencies fail to achieve their intended outcomes or fail to take action to resolve outstanding issues or problems. Government failure is evident in three main forms: legislative failure, bureaucratic failure, and rent-seeking. See, e.g., B. Dollery and J. Wallis, "Market Failure, Government Failure, Leadership and Public Policy," *Journal of Interdisciplinary Economics,* 1997, 8(2), pp. 113–26.

Government intervention: The involvement of the state in any or all of these activities: (a) providing a good or service, (b) regulating a particular market, (c) mediating disputes between parties, and (d) laying down appropriate rules of the game for market participants to adhere to. Given the breadth of areas that governments could intervene in, their actions—or inactions, as the case might be—sends strong messages to markets about the extent to which governments will seek to influence the economy. *See also* Distorted markets.

Government of bureaucrats: A government wherein bureaucrats hold disproportionate power in that they have considerable influence over what policies are formulated and how they are implemented. A government will tend to cave in to bureaucratic expertise if the bureaucracy has a history of involvement in policy formulation and if it also shows interest in asserting its role. Prior to its amalgamation into China, the former British colony of Hong Kong was considered to be a government of bureaucrats (see R. Khator, "Bureaucracy and the Environmental Crisis: A Comparative Perspective," in A. Farazmand (ed.), *Handbook of Bureaucracy,* New York: Marcel Dekker, Inc., 1994, pp. 195–210).

Government of the day: In looking at the nature and extent of civil servants' duties toward, and relationship with, governmental ministers, it is clear that civil servants fundamentally serve the government of the day, that is, the particular party that has formed the government at any point in time. In that regard, their identity is not separate from the duly elected government. This also means that civil servants need to dutifully follow policy directives that come from the government of the day regardless that such directives may be conflictual from government to government. This is because the role of the civil servants cannot inherently be distinct from that of elected ministers. This does not mean, however, that civil servants have no other duties other than to serve a minister; they have, for example, the duty to act honestly and to obey the law.

Government recognition programs: Programs put in place by governmental agencies so as to reward individuals and groups for work done that is over and above what is required of them. The purpose is to recognize their work so that a demonstration effect can take place. Across jurisdictions around the world, recognition programs have increasingly become a very visible part of public sector work. These recognition programs include granting awards to individuals and groups for specific achievements such as conceptualizing and/or successfully implementing initiatives that lead to, for example, cost savings. The awards usually have some cash component although the focus tends to be on public acknowledgment of the work done. See, e.g., S. Borins, *Government Recognition Programs: A Typology and Analysis,* Occasional Paper of the Institute of Public Administration Canada, Toronto, December 1999.

Government suasion: An instrument that a government has at its disposal whereby it can exert influence to bring about some development that it perceives as necessary (such as the extension of credit facilities to marginalized populations in rural areas). Such persuasion is normally reflected in the introduction of relevant legislation, although it could take less formal forms as well. See, e.g., R. Baggott, "By Voluntary Agreement: The Politics of Instrument Selection," *Public Administration,* 1986, 64(1), pp. 51–67.

Government waste: Any inefficiencies and profligacy inherent in governmental departments and agencies that add costs to the price of the good or service that is delivered to the public. The widespread public-management reforms of the past two decades are a direct result of the perceived intensity of the problem of governmental waste in advanced jurisdictions. See, e.g., W. Stanbury and F. Thompson, "Toward a Political Economy of Government Waste: First Step, Definitions," *Public Administration Review,* 1995, 55(5), pp. 418–27.

Government-sponsored enterprise: Any corporation that is created by government to fulfill public objectives (such as easy access to credit) but is privately owned. While a government-sponsored enterprise receives some privileges that are not normally available to a private firm (such as access to certain funding sources, and the implicit backing of the government), it is also required to promote the government's public-policy objective specific to that sector (an example of a government-sponsored enterprise is the U.S. Federal Home Loan Mortgage Corporation, also called Freddie Mac, that is mandated to provide credit facilities to those that do not have easy access to credit, such as rural farmers).

Governmental activism: A situation where the government plays a very active role in the economy. The development of postwar Japan and Korea is a good example of governmental activism, where Japanese and Korean governments' active policies on steel, coal, machinery, and shipbuilding, among others, fuelled rapid economic growth.

Graceful degradation: *See* **Degradation.**

Graft: When public servants take improper advantage of their positions and public office to make private gain. Thus graft is a form of malpractice, such as corruption. *See also* **Corruption**.

Graicunas' theory: Related to the factorial problem, and raised by Vytautas Graicunas (a Lithuanian who was a Paris-based management consultant), this theory asserts that the number of interactions in a group is far greater than the number of individuals in it. This has important implications for managers in that they have to consider not only the size of their direct span of control but also the associated complexity of interactions among individuals within that span. This is because, with an increase in the span of control, the associated increase in coordination requirements is a geometrical—not an arithmetical—progression. For an original exposition of the theory, see V. A. Graicunas, "Relationship in Organization," *Bulletin of the International Management Institute,* 1933, 7 (March), pp. 39–42. *See also* **Factorial problem.**

Grain of the environment: Refers to the presence of different niches in the environment so that different organizations survive simultaneously. Depending on the number of such niches organizations could either be in direct competition with each other or at separate levels and, therefore, not in direct competition. See, e.g., B. Peters, "Government Reorganization: A Theoretical Analysis," in A. Farazmand (ed.), *Handbook of Bureaucracy,* New York: Marcel Dekker, Inc., 1994, pp. 165–82.

Grameen Bank: A rural micro-credit facility that was established by Professor Muhammad Yunus in 1976 in Bangladesh to provide micro-credits to very poor women in villages so that they could initiate income-generating activities. The word "Grameen" in Bengali means "of a village." While the original area of intervention for the bank was micro-credits, it has now expanded into areas such as fisheries, irrigation, health, venture capital, textiles, among others. As related to the original scope of work, though, the idea of the bank is considered to be a very powerful tool for uplifting the lot of the rural poor. The Grameen Bank has now been replicated in many other countries, including, for example, Malaysia, where the Amanah Ikhtiar Malaysia provides similar services.

Grandfather clause: Refers to any policy that exempts certain categories of individuals from being subject to the standards that the policy institutes. For example, if a policy is laid down in an organization that all policy analysts must have tertiary education, then those analysts that are already in employment in the organization will be exempt from that policy. See, e.g., C. Leman, "How to Get There from Here: The Grandfather Effect and Public Policy," *Policy Analysis,* 1979, 6(1), pp. 99–116.

Grandparenting: *See* **Grandfather clause.**

Grants: Resources that come from central government to state and local governments, or from donor countries and multilateral institutions to developing jurisdictions. Grants can be for specific purposes (as specified by the grantor) or open-ended (i.e., the funds can be used for any purpose the recipient sees fit). Grants-in-aid are any transfer of funds across levels of jurisdictions meant for closely specified objectives and for which there are conditions that apply regarding accountability of usage. Unrestricted grants-in-aid can be used for any purpose without any restriction imposed by the party that has made the grant. Grants-in-kind, on the other hand, refers to the donations of anything that is in surplus in one country to another for purposes of assistance in times of need (such as supplies sent after an earthquake).

Grass roots organization: In public affairs, grassroots generally refers to the efforts of individuals in their capacities as citizens to be involved in some pressing social problem or issue. A grass-roots organization thus operates at the local level and its support comes not from business but from the average citizen. Being at the grass-roots also carries a connotation of carrying some legitimacy in the eyes of other citizens. Grass-roots advocacy refers to getting support for a policy from the ground up (i.e., by cultivating the support of average citizens).

Great-man theory of leadership: A theory that asserts that major ideas are conceived and advanced by those who have exceptional characteristics as leaders. It is argued thus that great men change history. The theory is predicated on the main premise that great leaders are born to lead. See, e.g., L. Nystedt, "Who Should Rule? Does Personality Matter?" *European Journal of Personality,* 1997, 11(1), pp. 1–14. See also, e.g., E. Borgatta, A. Couch and R. Bales, "Some Findings Relevant to the Great Man Theory of Leadership," *American Sociological Review,* 1954, 19, pp. 755–59.

Green harvesting: A term used to denote having access to a pool of very qualified candidates to recruit from. What this means is that governments interested in green harvesting are willing to, and capable of, making offers that act as excellent incentives for high-caliber new entrants into the public-sector workforce. One of the countries that has openly and very successfully practiced green harvesting is Singapore (see, e.g., State Services Commission, *Report on the Regional Conference on "Emerging Issues in Senior Management Development in the Public Sector,"* Occasional Paper 26, Wellington: State Services Commission, 2002, p. 8).

Green paper: A paper put out by the government that discusses a particular theme or issue and which seeks public input and discussion on the subject matter before the government commits itself to introducing related legislation. *See also* **White paper.**

Greiner model: The model stipulates that an organization passes through several successive phases in its maturation, each characterized by a stable period (known as the evolutionary stage) and an unstable one (known as a revolution, i.e., organizational turmoil and change). Organizations tend to have only a narrow range of choices to address the problems that beset them in all the phases of growth, and managers, in particular, are challenged to seek new organizational practices during the revolutionary stage that will help the organizations in the succeeding evolutionary stage. Larry Greiner first talked about this in 1972—see his "Evolution and Revolution as Organizations Grow," *Harvard Business Review,* 1972, 50(4), pp. 37–46.

Gresham's law in public organizations: Using the original Gresham's law as a basis (that bad money drives out good), the Gresham's law in public organizations states that any work in an organization that produces outcomes that can be measured tends to drive out work that produces outcomes that are immeasurable. The implication of this for governments is that, to the extent possible, they need to work toward specifying quantifiable and measurable outcomes. See, e.g., J. Wilson, *Bureaucracy: What Government Agencies Do and Why They Do It.* New York: Basic Books, 1989, p. 161.

Gresham's law of capacity building: Budget expert Allen Schick asserts that in the choice between enhancing the capacity of an organization through the ownership of systems that can produce capability (i.e., "growing your own") and the purchase of such capability, the latter drives out the former. This is symptomatic of government pursuing short-term economic savings at the expense of long-term capability gain in governmental departments. See A. Schick, *The Spirit of Reform: Managing the New Zealand State Sector in a Time of Change,* Wellington: State Services Commission, and the Treasury, 1996, p. 43.

Gresham's law of evaluation criteria: Evaluation criteria that can be easily measured tend to drive out less easily measured criteria. This is so because organizations find it easier to set *ex ante* standards and benchmarks against something that is measurable. See, e.g., D. Weimer and A. Vining, *Policy Analysis: Concepts and Practice,* 2nd edition, Englewood Cliffs, NJ: Prentice Hall, 1992, p. 224.

Gresham's law of managerial gamesmanship: When managers continue to engage in protecting their turf and playing games, what is really at stake tends to be lost and less important games tend to crowd out more significant ones. See, e.g., C. Levine, B. Peters, and F. Thompson, *Public Administration: Challenges, Choices, Consequences,* Glenview, IL: Scott, Foresman and Co., 1990, p. 308.

Gresham's law of oversight: Work and time spent on any activity that has minimal payoffs tends to drive out work and time given to more relevant oversight. This results when audit organizations, for example, do not wish, or do not have the capability, to engage in those oversight activities that are complex, politically sensitive, or require an unacceptable level of resources. See C. Levine, B. Peters, and F. Thompson, *Public Administration: Challenges, Choices, Consequences,* Glenview, IL: Scott, Foresman and Co., 1990, p. 123.

Grievance: An experience that an employee feels, or perceives to feel, that an injustice (such as discrimination) has been done to him/her. When that feeling is given formal expression, it becomes a grievance. Grievance arbitration is any mediation that takes place between, for example, employees and their organization (or labor and management) where the former party has filed a grievance claim.

Grievance adjustment: As used in collective bargaining, this term refers to the process of considering and making decisions on employees' grievances. For a grievance adjustment process to be seen as fair, it must be conducted in a full and timely manner.

Grievance arbitration: *See* **Grievance.**

"Groping along": Describes the experimental process by which organizational leaders perceive opportunities and look for ways to exploit them. This process of exploitation may or may not be made in a rational manner—if the risks are obvious but the rewards are greater, organizations may wish to be tentative about seizing opportunities but still be rational; on the other hand, if no effort is made to assess the level of risks, or consider opportunities strategically, then "groping-along" actions may well not be rational. This is contrasted with a rational way of doing things. See, e.g., R. Behn, "Management by Groping Along," *Journal of Policy Analysis and Management,* 1988, 7(4), pp. 643–63.

Group appraisal: A review of performance done with groups where supervisors, and/or colleagues, jointly evaluate an employee. Performance evaluation obviously becomes a much more complex activity when group appraisal is encouraged in organizations. *See also* **Three-hundred-and-sixty-degree appraisal.**

Group development: The process of like-minded individuals working together on a particular issue or problem to arrive at a joint resolution, and how the group members then go about doing their work. One of the earliest and best known models of group development has been proposed by educational psychologist Bruce Tuckman, who suggests that groups go through four stages of development: forming (i.e., coming together formally), storming (i.e., testing each other, and knowing who stands where), norming (i.e., setting the rules of the game, and establishing levels of commitment), and performing (i.e., when the group is productive). Tuckman later added a fifth stage to this: disbanding upon completion of the work. See B. Tuckman, "Developmental Sequences in Small Groups," *Psychological Bulletin,* 1965, 63(6), pp. 384–99.

Group lending: Extension of credit to groups of individuals who team together (such as in a cooperative) so as to secure credit to run an income-generating activity. Funders prefer group lending because it tends to reduce their risks of defaults, because peer pressure often works in rural credit programs. For an application in group lending in microcredits, see, e.g., B. MkNelly and M. Kevane, "Improving Design and

Performance of Group Lending: Suggestions from Burkina Faso," *World Development,* 2002, 30(11), pp. 2017–32.

Group theory of policy making: A theory that says that policy making is essentially the outcomes of struggle between groups. While it is often compared to the elite theory of policy making, it neglects that groups can be elites too. It also neglects the impact of individuals in the policy-making process. Furthermore, many groups (such as taxpayers) are unorganized and hence their impact in the policy-making process is not readily felt.

Group-incentive pay: A system of bonus payment in an organization that bases employee compensation on overall group performance. With the current focus on matrix organizations and teams, the concept of group-incentive pay makes considerable sense, but one of the problems is how to deal with the inevitable free-rider problem. *See also* **Free-rider problem**.

Groupthink: Refers to a dysfunctional trait in policy making because it gives the illusion that organizational members are certain and agreed about the course of actions to take. This then leads to a shift in risk appetite where decision makers tend to take bigger risks because of the perceived unanimity and certainty. For a good discussion of groupthink in the context of the Abilene Paradox, see, e.g., Y. Kim, "A Comparative Study of the 'Abilene Paradox' and 'Groupthink,'" *Public Administration Quarterly,* 2001, 25(2), pp. 168–89. *See also* **Abilene effect**.

"Growing your own": Organizations have the option of getting capacity either on the spot market or "growing their own." The latter is complex, however, since capability loss (such as in human resources through voluntary departures and redundancies) is always a possibility and also the results are evident only after a long lag. It has thus become very difficult for public organizations to convince legislatures to fund capability-growing initiatives.

Guidelines: Written instructions from agencies (such as regulators) on how organizations and firms are to conduct their business. Guidelines are rules and regulations, procedural manuals, and such, and they translate general legislative intent into more specific prescriptions for administrative action. Guidelines are not laws and, therefore, are not mandatory, but there is an expectation that the public agency will adhere to them.

H

Halo effect: Also known as constant error, this term describes how an initial and/or general impression of any individual, either favorable or unfavorable, affects how the specific characteristics of individuals are judged by those who evaluate their performance. The halo effect is thus something that precludes the observer from seeing the real situation. See, e.g., S. Zalkindand T. Costello, "Perception: Some Recent Research and Implications for Administration," *Administrative Science Quarterly,* 1962–63, 7, pp. 218–35. For an application of the term in the policy-making process, *see* **Illusion**.

Handmaiden-of-government tradition: A form of policy analysis that is based not on theoretical strands but on what practitioners seek in how to handle policy and the policy-making process. The agenda is thus drawn from what government departments want out of policy analysis rather than what is theoretically and intellectually driven. For a generic discussion on the need for rethinking and contextualizing policy analysis, see, e.g., M. Hajer, "Policy Without Polity? Policy Analysis and the Institutional Void," *Policy Sciences,* 2003, 36(2), pp. 175–95. *Cf.* **Ivory tower**.

Hands-off approach: When an authority makes a decision not to intervene too often (or not at all) in the affairs of an organization specifically or of the economy generally. *See also* **Laissez-faire**.

Hands-on training: Any training that gives an individual the opportunity to use or apply an equipment or an idea firsthand, and to experience learning directly. For example, a hands-on training session on the use of information and communication technology in the workplace would include the extensive use of computers and other equipment by learners.

Harassment: In the organizational context, this refers to any unwanted or offensive behavior exhibited deliberately against another individual in the workplace. Such harassment can be verbal (for example, put-downs, obscene emails), social (for example, rumors, public humiliation) or physical (for example, touching, groping).

Hard constraint: A limitation on organizational action that is difficult to minimize. Such a constraint is normally imposed from outside (such as by law). The most common hard constraint an organization faces is that of budget. A hard budget constraint is a situation where an organization is entitled to only certain levels and types of funding. Subnational governments, for example, may have a hard budget constraint imposed on them by the central government in terms of budgetary transfers and their uses. See, e.g., T. Ter-Minassian, "Decentralizing Government," *Finance & Development,* 1997, 34(3), pp. 36–39. *See also* **Budget constraint.**

Hard institution: *See* **Institution.**

Hard pipeline: *See* **Pipeline.**

Hard policy: *See* **Policy.**

Hard value bias: *See* **Value bias.**

Harvard case method: A case method developed at the Harvard Business School that is concerned with problem solving. The method has three primary attributes: (a) it is participative in nature (i.e., it allows all group members an opportunity to be involved), (b) it focuses on the capability of group members to think independently, and (c) it revolves around a particular case that group members dissect to draw lessons for other situations.

Hawthorne effect: Named after the physical location where it was first noticed, the Hawthorne effect refers to the improvement in a production process by virtue of the fact that management is seen as taking an interest in changing employees' working conditions and not necessarily because they are indeed being put into place. The effect was first studied in the Hawthorne experiments. These experiments are widely regarded as the fountain of ideas on the human relations school of management thought, and probably the most widely cited study in this area. The Hawthorne experiments were a series of experiments done between 1927 and 1932 and led by social behavioralist George Elton Mayo in the Western Electric plant in Hawthorne, Illinois. The experiments set out to measure changes in worker productivity and fatigue resulting from changes in working conditions. While the experiments provided a wealth of knowledge about better understanding organizational work life, they did not originally intend to consider the motivations of individuals in a work setting. It was in the results from the experiments that clearly showed how such motivations could be affected. The literature on the experiments, and their interpretations, is large; for some useful discussion, see, e.g., A.Carey, "The Hawthorne Studies: A Radical Criticism," *American So-*

ciological Review, 1967, 32(3), pp. 403–16; see also, e.g., S. Jones, "Was There a Hawthorne Effect?" *American Journal of Sociology,* 1992, 98(3), pp. 451–68.

Hearing: In administrative courts, a hearing can take various forms, the most informal being conciliation. There are also paper hearings (submission of views in writing), oral hearings (opinions and debate), and formal hearings (as in a courtroom).

Hegemonic parliamentary system: A parliament that will pass any bill proposed by the government. See, e.g., F. Riggs, "Bureau Power in Southeast Asia," *Asian Journal of Political Science,* 1993, 1(1), pp. 3–28. The term has been in used in relation to, for example, the system in place in Singapore (see K. Ho, *The Politics of Policy-Making in Singapore,* Singapore: Oxford University Press, 2000, p. 165).

Helicopter trait: Refers to the ability of an individual to see any incident in its broader context but then also to be able to attend to its details. Successful managers are said to have a helicopter trait. For an application, see, e.g., H. F. Kwang, W. Fernandezand S. Tan, *Lee Kuan Yew: The Man and His Ideas,* Singapore: Times Editions, 1998, p. 103.

Herding: A term borrowed from the financial arena to mean the instinct of public-sector organizations to react along the same lines when an exogenous shock hits them; for example, a landmark case in an employment court may lead to all organizations reacting in the same way.

Heresthetics: A political strategy to achieve policy outcomes. Heresthetics are strategies that attempt to gain advantage for one party by manipulating political choice such that other actors in the policy process will want—or are unwittingly forced—to join them. See, e.g., W. Riker, *The Art of Political Manipulation.* New Haven, CT: Yale University Press, 1986, p. ix.

Heroic leader: Assigning the attributes of a hero to that rare individual who can shape history. A heroic leader contrasts with someone who exhibits facilitative leadership. *See also* **Facilitative leadership**.

Herzberg's two-factor theory: Psychologist Frederick Herzberg's formulation of what motivates individuals has been widely accepted as a useful explanation by practitioners. Herzberg asserted that there were certain factors that individuals felt good about in their jobs, and these concerned responsibility and a feeling of achievement. He termed them satisfiers or motivators. Then there were other factors that individuals identified as making them feel bad about their jobs, such as inadequate salary, which Herzberg termed hygiene factors or dissatisfiers. Consequently, poor hygiene factors would make individuals dissatisfied although improving them did not necessarily motivate them, it only removed the dissatisfaction. To effectively motivate individuals, Herzberg asserted that organizations would need to address their feelings of achievement. See, e.g., E. Maidani, "Comparative Study of Herzberg's Two-Factor Theory of Job Satisfaction Among Public and Private Sectors," *Public Personnel Management,* 1991, 20(4), pp. 441–48.

Heterarchy: An organizing principle that focuses on network-based structures as well as on horizontal linkages and teamwork. In a heterarchy, the focus is on the complexity of the organization and on its ordering by looking at the network-based form of organization. For a discussion of the term, see, e.g., P. Cookeand K. Morgan, *The Associational Economy: Firms, Regions, and Innovation,* New York: Oxford University Press, 1998, pp. 39–41. *Cf.* **Hierarchy**.

Heterogeneity: The degree to which diversity prevails among various elements of any entity (for example, an organization). Heterogeneity thus implies the need for organizational leaders to have in place appropriate policies that take into consideration the diverse backgrounds and frames of reference that staff members have. *Cf.* **Homogeneity**.

Heuristics: The rules and routines that determine how decisions are arrived at (generally taken to mean "rules of thumb"). Decision-making heuristics are rules concerning how organizations make decisions that often are reflected in the shared perspectives of organizational members. The heuristics for crafting policy alternatives, for example, are ensuring that all alternatives are mutually exclusive, and that they are within the available resource envelope. See, e.g., H. Greveand A. Taylor, "Innovations as Catalysts for Organizational Change: Shifts in Organizational Cognition and Search," *Administrative Science Quarterly,* 2000, 45(1), pp. 54–80.

Hidden information problem: *See* **Adverse selection**.

Hierarchical bloating: Adding needless hierarchies in an organization so as to accommodate the demand for upward mobility coming from the increased number of personnel in the organization. Hierarchical bloating occurs when succession planning in an organization is not geared toward managing the pressures for mobility that staff members have.

Hierarchical networks: Networks that have only one communication channel. While hierarchical networks have their advantages (including, for example, that there is a set structure to and proper control of the protocols), they also constrain organizations by incurring rather substantial transaction and transmission costs. With increased layers inherent in hierarchical networks, transmitting tacit knowledge across the different layers becomes very time consuming, and there is a danger that the knowledge will be lost in the transmission process. For a discussion of this concept across jurisdictions, see, e.g., A. Innocenti and S. Labory, "Outsourcing and Information Management: A Comparative Analysis of France, Italy and Japan in Both Small and Large Firms," *European Journal of Comparative Economics,* 2004, 1(1), pp. 107–25. *Cf.* **Egalitarian networks**.

Hierarchical participation: A situation where more important policy actors are involved in all decisions but less important actors are involved in only a few. For a discussion of this concept in the context of the multiple streams lens of policy choice, see, e.g., N. Zahariadis, "Comparing Three Lenses of Policy Choice," *Policy Studies Journal,* 1998, 26(3), pp. 434–48.

Hierarchical politics: The interplay of relationships among those in a hierarchical bureaucracy that determines how a policy is implemented. In this respect, one could say that the larger the organization, the weaker the exercise of control (due to the presence of hierarchical politics).

Hierarchy: A generic term that refers to a form of organization resembling a pyramid, wherein individuals are arranged in order of rank. Thus, an executive would be high in the organizational hierarchy and a payroll clerk would be low. See, e.g., E. Jaques, "In Praise of Hierarchy," in G. Thompson et al. (eds.), *Hierarchies and Networks,* London: Sage, 1991, pp. 108–18. *Cf.* **Heterarchy**.

Hierarchy of needs: Psychologist Abraham Maslow propounded this theory of motivation, which looks at the following hierarchy of needs: (a) physiological (such as food, water, shelter), (b) safety (i.e., protection against danger), (c) psychological (such as for love, belonging; also known as social needs), (d) esteem (i.e., a desire for respect from others), and (e) self-actualization (i.e., the desire to realize one's maximum potential. This hierarchy of needs was later refined by psychologist Clayton Alderfer into three types of need: at the basic level, existence needs (such as for survival and reproduction); then relatedness needs (such as through interactions with others); and then growth needs (such as those for personal development and the need for self-respect). This reformulation of the hierarchy of needs is also known as the ERG Theory (from the first three initials of the needs). For Maslow's treatment, see A. Maslow, "A Theory of Human Motivation," *Psychological Review,* 1943, 50, pp. 370–96. For the ERG Theory, see C. Alderfer, *Existence, Relatedness, and Growth: Human Needs in Organizational Settings,* New York: The Free Press, 1972.

High-effort norm: An expectation and a value system in an organization that all employees will put in high levels of effort to contribute to organizational goal attainment. Institutionalization of this particular norm can be one useful way to minimize the free-rider problem. See, e.g., B. MacLeod, "Behavior and the Organization of the Firm," *Journal of Comparative Economics,* 1987, 11(2), pp. 207–20.

High flyers: Individuals in organizations that are very productive and effective and that move up more rapidly than others. While the private sector has always encouraged the provision of more challenging learning opportunities to such individuals, the public sector too has noticed this. Countries such as Singapore and the United Kingdom now have in place mechanisms to identify such high flyers in the public service and develop them further. See, e.g., M. Malone-Lee, "Training the High Flyers: Whitehall Mixes It with Industry," *Personnel Management,* 1986, 18(3), pp. 33–37.

High noon of administrative orthodoxy: The period of the 1920s and 1930s when the "principles of administration" school of thought was predominant. Work in this period came from, among others, management scholars Luther Gulick and Lyndall Urwick. See, e.g., S. Koven, "The Bureaucracy-Democracy Conundrum: A Contemporary Inquiry into the Labyrinth," in A. Farazmand (ed.), *Handbook of Bureaucracy,* New York: Marcel Dekker, Inc., 1994, pp. 79–95. For the original work on such principles, see L. Gulickand L. Urwick (eds.), *Papers on the Science of Administration,* New York: Institute of Public Administration, 1937.

High-performance-cycle theory: This is a meta-theory of motivation that integrates several theories of motivation to explain the relationships between goals, performance, rewards, job satisfaction, and organizational commitment. In that regard, this theory is considered to have superior explanatory power of why individuals are motivated and how that translates into improved performance. The theory was first put forth by industrial psychologists Edwin Locke and Gary Latham in 1990; see their "Work Motivation: The High Performance Cycle," in U. Kleinbeck et al. (eds.), *Work Motivation,* Hillsdale NJ: Lawrence Erlbaum, 1990, pp. 3–25. For a test of the theory, see, e.g., S. Selden and G. Brewer, "Work Motivation in the Senior Executive Service: Testing the High Perform-ance Cycle Theory," *Journal of Public Administration Research and Theory,* 2000, 10(3), pp. 531–50.

High-reliability organizations: Refers to those organizations that are specifically designed to perform efficiently under conditions of extreme stress (for example, hospital emergency systems, nuclear power produc-tion, etc.). The basis of the work of high-reliability organizations lies in the interplay among various potential limitations and failures, including technical failures and human limitations. High-reliability organizations are characterized by, among others, resiliency, strong organizational cul-ture, deep peer support networks, and an all-encompassing safety culture. For a discussion of its application, see, e.g., T. LaPorte and P. Consolini, "Theoretical and Operational Challenges of 'High-Reliability Organiza-tions': Air-Traffic Control and Aircraft Carriers," *International Journal of Public Administration*, 1998, 21, pp. 847–52.

Higher-level review: A review of supervisory decisions with the purpose of helping to minimize errors or inconsistencies in a manager's decisions. In such a review, what is targeted is whether managers have justified their decisions with their immediate superiors.

Hiving off: The process of parceling out parts of organizational functions to those outside its structure. With the rise of "new public management" and its consequent focus on delegation of authority away from central agencies to departments, hiving off has been a recurring theme in the public sector. This has generally allowed departments to focus on policy tasks while hiving off routine operational matters. It has also enabled these departments to better align their recruitment policies to suit their mission. For application in a country setting, see, e.g., M. Painter, "Public Administration Reform in Vietnam: Problems and Prospects," *Public Administration and Development,* 2003, 23(3), pp. 259–71. *See also* **Contracting out**.

Hockey-stick effect: An effect that is usually in evidence in organiza-tions where managers find spare money left in the budget and tend to spend it without sufficient control (because failure to do so will mean the funds will have to revert to central authority). If this effect were to be graphed, the shape of the spending curve would show an increase in the latter part of the year (hence the hockey-stick effect). The direction of the curve can go the other way as well, because managers may have had a higher level of spending during the course of the year and then realize that they need to drastically cut back in the final months. See, e.g., R. Moleand A. Parkinson, *The Capable Manager: Budgeting and Performance,* Milton Keynes, UK: The Open University, 1994, p. 25.

Hold-harmless clause: A stipulation in any legislation that those who receive government funds at present do not receive lesser amounts down the road if a new formula were to be put into use. This clause then ensures that should there be any reductions in the future on government funding, beneficiaries do not lose out if they remain eligible.

Holdout: Refers to the problem of someone withholding agreement on the specifics of a policy. A holdout problem thus implies a barrier to action. A holdout is evident, for example, when unanimity is required for a particular action to proceed but one individual or group refuses to agree to the measure unless it obtains an unreasonably large share of the benefits of group activities. The problem is the counterpart to free riding (where parties go along with the policy because they do not have to pay any costs for it). *See also* **Free-rider problem**.

Holdover officials: Government officials from the previous administration. While most will have left voluntarily upon the end of the tenure of the individual who appointed them, a few may be asked to continue. See, e.g., F. Riggs, "Bureaucracy: A Profound Puzzle for Presidentialism," in A. Farazmand (ed.), *Handbook of Bureaucracy,* New York: Marcel Dekker, Inc., 1994, pp. 97–147.

Hollow state: Also termed administration by proxy; this is a situation when a government activity is contracted out and subcontracted to the point that a vacuum has been created where its role was once pronounced. For example, the central government may wish to provide health services but will give resources (i.e., contracts) to subjurisdictions that will, in turn, bring in (i.e., subcontract) private or third-party providers to actually deliver the services. This hollows out the core of the public sector since its involvement becomes extremely limited. See, e.g., H. Milward, "Implications for Contracting Out: New Roles for the Hollow State," in P. Ingraham et al. (eds.), *New Paradigms for Government: Issues for the Changing Public Service,* San Francisco: Jossey-Bass, 1994, pp. 41–62.

Homeostasis: Refers to balance and dynamic self-regulation; that is, the ability of an organization to maintain its essential attributes even when faced with unexpected external and internal disturbances. A homeostatic equilibrium is reached when an organization finds its niche in an uncertain environment; that is, it has identified what it needs to do, and when and how, in order to deal with any environmental pressures such that it continues to remain stable. See, e.g., M. Hannan and J. Freeman, "The Population Ecology of Organizations," *American Journal of Sociology,* 1977, 82(5), pp. 929–64. *See also* **Dynamic equilibrium.**

Homogeneity: A principle of administration that maintains that the major functions of an organization should be grouped together according to two criteria: (a) the objective sought, and (b) the process used. The homogeneity principle also asserts that a single plan of action is good for any organization. *Cf.* **Heterogeneity.**

Horizon problems: Related to the concept of a psychological contract, horizon problems are incentive conflicts when owners and employees have different time horizons and act accordingly in their relationships with each other.

Horizontal accountability: The answerability that entities (individuals and organizations) have to their peers with whom they may have formal network relationships. This notion of horizontal accountability is in stark contrast to the traditional notion of vertical accountability. At a time when networked governance is increasingly evident across jurisdictions, horizontal accountability has become an increasingly relevant concept to describe the relationships that individuals and organizations have with others. See, e.g., M. Considine, "The End of the Line? Accountable Governance in the Age of Networks, Partnerships, and Joined Up Service," *Governance: An International Journal of Policy, Administration, and Institutions,* 2002, 15(1), pp. 21–40. *Cf.* **Vertical accountability.**

Horizontal communications: Communications that take place among those at the same level in the organizational hierarchy. Because they are at the same levels, there are greater possibilities that informal communication channels will emerge as well.

Horizontal conflict: Refers to tensions and conflicts that exist between bureaucratic units of an organization when both are at similar hierarchical levels (for example, between policy and operations as opposed to between policy and the office of the chief executive).

Horizontal fast track, theory of: Asserts that in order to identify, track, and properly target high achievers in an organization, it is necessary for talented employees to be moved around from task to task so that they gain the widest extent of knowledge of the organization and its environment. This is expected to produce individuals who are not only aware of what the organization needs but also how best to start acquiring it.

Horizontal federalism: Refers to the relationships among states/provinces (such as the administration of public parks that span such jurisdictions) in a federal system. Under horizontal federalism, subjurisdictions need to recognize the actions of other such governments.

Horizontal integration: The merger of two or more public-sector organizations that are similar in orientation (i.e., either policy-based or service-delivery ones). Horizontality here is used to denote the idea of working together across agencies. *Cf.* **Vertical integration.**

Horizontal job loading: A situation where an employee's scope of work is increased but does not include higher responsibilities. Used as a job-enlargement technique, horizontal job loading provides employees the scope to be doing different tasks than what they would normally be doing, and this could serve as a good training ground for future career growth. See F. Herzberg, "One More Time: How Do You Motivate Employees?" *Harvard Business Review,* 1968 (reprinted in the *HBR,* 2003 [January], pp. 87–96). *Cf.* **Vertical job loading**.

Horizontal management: Refers generically to the management of programs that are delivered by more than one organization. The concept is related closely to those of networks, joined-up government, and policy alliances. For a review of the concept, and what it means for how governments can enhance cross-agency coordination, see, e.g., M. Sproule-Jones, "Horizontal Management: Implementing Programs across Interdependent Organizations," *Canadian Public Administration,* 2000, 43(1), pp. 93–109.

Horizontal organization: An organization whose hierarchy has a wide span of control at the top (i.e., between the chief-executive level and the first level of managerial positions). This attribute emerges when organizations place emphasis on reducing hierarchies at the top of the organizational structure.

Horizontal work group: A work group wherein members possess more or less the same rank and level of knowledge and skills. For a discussion of its application, see, e.g., R. Iverson and D. Buttigieg, "Antecedents of Union Commitment: The Impact of Union Membership Differences in Vertical Dyads and Horizontal Workgroup Relationships," *Human Relations*, 1997, 50(12), pp. 1485–1510.

Hot-stove principle: Asserts that an organization's disciplinary system— not unlike a hot stove—should give a clear signal (i.e., a warning) of adverse consequences if not heeded. Likewise, it should also affect (i.e., "burn") anyone that does not heed the warning.

Housekeeping agency: An administrative unit in an organization that is charged with providing administrative services and support to the other units in the organization. An example of a housekeeping agency is the human-resource division of any government agency.

Howl meter: The degree to which there is a public outcry when a government or bureaucracy does something that is wrong and/or wasteful. This invariably leads to a bias toward playing it safe, and its most obvious impact is in encouraging the selection of the alternative that consists of doing nothing. See, e.g., R. Mack, *Planning on Uncertainty: Decision Making in Business and Government Administration,* New York: Wiley-Interscience, 1971, pp. 130–31.

Human capital: (1) An individual's competencies that he/she brings to the job. (2) Taken collectively, human capital refers to the total knowledge, skills, and abilities of the organization's members. Given the increasing realization that human capital is central to the ability of an organization to attain its mandate, the issue of investment in human capital has recently been much in the limelight. This refers to expenditures made on human resources in the organization to develop the competencies of the employees. It also includes investments made in employee wellness, training, etc. that contribute to the enhancement of human capital. The fungibility of human capital refers to the extent to which human capital can be moved around in an organization (such as among different divisions during the time of restructuring). For an analysis of the importance of human capital, see, e.g., L. Hendricks, "How Important Is Human Capital for Development? Evidence from Immigrant Earnings," *American Economic Review,* 2002, 92(1), pp. 198–219.

Human development: Refers to the creation of an environment where individuals can develop to their full potential and lead lives according to their own needs and interests. The concept of human development is based on principles such as equality and equity, health and well-being, and partnership among government, civil society, and business. See, for example, UNDP, *Human Development Report, 2001,* New York: Oxford University Press, 2001, p. 9.

Humanization: A trend in public administration that was first in evidence in the 1940s, and which focused on the needs of employees as individuals, and thus with the human side of organization. The focus on work-life balance that has now become central draws its impetus from the concept of humanization. A related concept, humanistic ethic, denotes a value evident in the leadership of an organization that, among other things, treats employees as assets and values their commitment to the organization. For a discussion of humanization, see, e.g., C. Ascher, "Trends of a Decade in Administrative Practice," in C. Hawley and R. Weintraub (eds.), *Administrative Questions and Political Answers,* Princeton, NJ: D. Van Nostrand, pp. 245–55. For a review of humanization as a driver of change, see, e.g., L. Wise, "Public Management Reform: Competing Drivers of Change," *Public Administration Review,* 2002, 62(5), pp. 555–67.

Human-resource development: The generation and enhancement of human resources needed to fulfill the necessary objectives, whether of an organization or a country. Human-resource development involves all phases of human-resources management, including recruiting and appropriate development.

Human-resource forecasting: The process of determining the level of human resources that will be needed in the future to help fulfill organizational objectives. Such a forecast considers the demand for and supply of labor in the workplace, including factoring in any external variables that might affect the nature and size of the organization.

Human-resource management: The process by which all facets of the human resources in an organization are managed. This includes areas such as recruitment, training, performance evaluation, motivation, discipline and sanctions, etc. The term is increasingly replacing "personnel management" in usage since people in organizations are "resources" more than just personnel. For a review of how this concept ties in with organizational outcomes, see, e.g., C. Truss, "Complexities and Controversies in Linking HRM with Organizational Outcomes," *Journal of Management Studies,* 2001, 38(8), pp. 1121–49. For a good review of the concept in the public sector, see, e.g., M. Gowing and M. Lindholm, "Human Resources Management in the Public Sector," *Human Resource Management,* 2002, 41(3), pp. 283–95.

Human-resource movement: Focuses on individuals and groups working in organizational settings seeking to understand the extent to which organizations are able to meet their mandates, and how supervisors should manage their employees in that process. The human-resource movement is said to be founded by Elton Mayo, and draws from the Hawthorne experiments.

Human-resource planning: The systematic process of determining the level and type of human resources that will be needed at a future date, and determining measures to acquire them. Human-resource planning is a complex process, and it is an integral part of the overall corporate and budgetary planning procedures since there are cost and utilization implications of all human-resource planning measures. Human-resources planning models are those that help organizational leaders forecast future manpower, and consequential financial, requirements in the organization. The models include supply and demand considerations in the internal and external environments, and also presume the existence of adequate information on which to base the analysis.

Hurdles method in budgeting: A feature of the budgetary process evident in many jurisdictions where governmental departments must meet specific standards and thresholds before they can receive budgetary and operational flexibility.

Hybrid organization: *See* **Quasi-autonomous executive agency**.

Hybrid rulemaking: While both formal and informal rulemaking are at extremes, hybrid rulemaking allows organizations to generate rules rather more easily on various organizational dimensions, but it also requires that they provide stringent documentation of the rationale for such rules. See, e.g., C. Levine, B. Peters, and F. Thompson, *Public Administration: Challenges, Choices, Consequences,* Glenview, IL: Scott, Foresman and Co., 1990, p. 175.

Hygiene factors: *See* **Herzberg's two-factor theory**.

I

Ideal bureaucracy: Max Weber's concept of a bureaucracy that pursues rationality. This is the intellectual basis upon which much of the groundwork on organizations and bureaucracies has been based. The ideal bureaucracy, according to Weber, exhibits attributes such as organized hierarchy, adherence to set rules and regulations, and specialization. For a discussion, see, e.g., M. Waters, "Collegiality, Bureaucratization, and Professionalization: A Weberian Analysis," *American Journal of Sociology,* 1989, 94(5), pp. 945–72.

Identification: A process of aligning one's goals and values with those of an organization's. Those who identify with the organization they work in are thus regarded as being more committed. An organization is interested in ascertaining the degree to which its staff members exhibit identification, and also to determine how best to foster (if it does not exist) or maximize identification. *See also* **Psychological contract**.

Idiosyncratic risk: Any risk in an organization that is not related to any other. This means that the causes and effects of a particular risk can be isolated, thus allowing organizations to diversify risk so as to net out losses and gains. This type of risk is also organization specific. For a discussion of idiosyncratic-risk measures in relation to assets and the management of portfolios, see, e.g., A. Richards, *Idiosyncratic Risk: An Empirical Analysis, with Implications for the Risk of Relative-Value Trading Strategies,* IMF Working Paper 99/148, Washington, DC: IMF, 1999.

Ill-defined problems: *See* **Wicked problems**.

Illusion: In policy making, when decision makers have a wrong perception of the policy problem, an illusion is created. A common source of illusion in public-policy making is the misperception of the decision makers of the seriousness (or lack thereof) of a particular problem. A halo effect of the policy leader also creates an illusion. When policies are formulated in an environment where there is illusion, clearly the right problems are not being addressed or the existence of appropriate conditions for successful policy implementation is exaggerated. Either way, the policy fails to yield the desired outcomes.

Imitation: When organizations copy others that they perceive are innovative in some way that is relevant to their work. It is imitation that transmits innovation across organizations. The concept of first-order imitation is imitating specific policies of others without analyzing their content specificity to the environment that the imitator faces. Thus, a first-order imitation tends to be rather superficial. A second-order imitation is one where an organization copies an underlying decision process from another source that can be adapted to multiple areas. See, e.g., J. Westphal, M. Seidel and K. Stewart, "Second-Order Imitation: Uncovering Latent

Effects of Board Network Ties," *Administrative Science Quarterly,* 2001, 46(4), pp. 717–47. *See also* **Adaptability; Information diffusion.**

Immutable expenditure ceiling: Refers to that organizational budget amount that cannot be increased in any condition. Budget ceilings can sometimes be breached if the situation so warrants (for example, if some exogenous factor adversely affects the expenditure patterns of an agency). An immutable expenditure ceiling means that the government will not be budged on the expenditure level allocated. Such a ceiling is used as a way of inducing government departments to work within set parameters since there is no room for renegotiation on the allocations.

Impact: A consequence or result that reaches beyond the direct purpose of an action. An impact can be positive or negative (i.e., favorable or unfavorable), of primary or secondary long-term effects (i.e., immediate or distant), direct or indirect, and intended or unintended. It could also be a combination of any of these. Some impacts are difficult to operationalize, and, as such, pose a constraint to appropriate policy formulation.

Impact analysis: *See* **Impact evaluation.**

Impact evaluation: An examination of the extent to which an organization is able to achieve the impact (i.e., effect) that has been specified. Here, the focus of the evaluation is on gauging the impact of the program rather than merely the processes with which the impacts were attained. For a case-study application of impact evaluation, see, e.g., M. Boyle and J. Willms, "Impact Evaluation of a National, Community-Based Program for At-Risk Children in Canada," *Canadian Public Policy,* 2002, 28(3), pp. 461–81. *See also* **Evaluation.**

Impact lag: *See* **Lag.**

Impact ratio: As used in the employment context, an impact ratio refers to the proportion of those who are offered employment in an organization to those who represent the group with the highest selection rate. An impact ratio helps in determining adverse impact in employment decisions in an organization. *See also* **Adverse impact.**

Impact theory of discrimination: A theory of discrimination that focuses more on the impact rather than on the intent of specific administrative action and employment practices to ascertain whether or not discrimination has indeed occurred. If the consequences are negative, regardless of how noble the intent might have been, then clearly the organization has engaged in employment discrimination.

Imperfect information: Information that either is not available to everyone (because, for example, of limited access) or is inadequate in the first
place. Despite the current emphasis on evidence-based analysis in policy
development, the existence of imperfect information means that policy
formulation will continue to be less than ideal. For a case study, see, e.g.,
M. Neiman and S. Stambough, "Rational Choice Theory and the Evaluation of Public Policy," *Policy Studies Journal,* 1998, 26(3), pp. 449–65.
See also **Evidence-based analysis ; Information asymmetry**.

Imperial bureaucracy: A bureaucracy acting in a manner that is arro-
gant and does not show much concern for citizens' welfare. Bureaucrats
can get to that state when excessive administrative and regulatory conditions are imposed on an activity. A rent-seeking bureaucracy is a
manifestation of an imperial bureaucracy.

Imperial executive: When the executive arm of government (for example, the cabinet) acts in a manner that does not seek to be conciliatory
toward other branches of government (i.e., the legislature and the judiciary). In all systems of government, an imperial executive emerges when
those in the executive branch presume that a political mandate, either for
the individual leader or for the party itself, means that they can push
ahead with their agenda at all costs. By contrast, a legislature in a country
may seek to assert its power on the other branches of government (in the
United States, the term for this is an imperial congress; see, e.g., K. Nos-
sal, "The Imperial Congress: The Separation of Powers and Canadian-
American Relations," *International Journal,* 1989, 44[4], pp. 863–83).

Imperial judiciary: Denotes that in addition to the active involvement of
the courts in various areas of public policy, there is a conception that
judges are not particularly concerned about the impact of their perceived
intrusion into the business of the other branches of government. See, e.g.,
R. O'Leary and J. Straussman, "The Impact of Courts on Public Management," in B. Bozeman (ed.), *Public Management: The State of the Art,* San
Francisco: Jossey-Bass, 1993, pp. 189–205. *See also* **Judicial activism**.

Impersonality: A trait that Max Weber identified as existing in an ideal
bureaucracy, wherein members carry out their functions in an impersonal
manner (i.e., do not permit personal views to affect judgment).

Implacement: The process of using the services of an external resource
person to counsel someone who has performed poorly in an organization.
Introducing an external person in this intervention facilitates the counseling process because it confers impartiality.

Implementation gap: A perceived gulf between what actually transpires as a result of organizational action and what was intended in the first place. Program evaluation helps identify such gaps and ways to address them. *See also* **Lag**.

Implementation lag: *See* **Lag**.

Implicit contract: Shared understandings between parties that are not formalized (i.e., that are largely based on trust and are not drawn in a contract). Implicit contracts are often enforced by existing moral codes and social mores. Since formal contracts need specify all circumstances to be effective (which would be difficult to negotiate), implicit contracts tend to arise at times.

Implicit forbearance: *See* **Regulatory forbearance**.

Implied powers: Any power conferred on an entity that is not explicitly stated but that can be inferred largely based on the interpretation of the powers that, for example, are expressed by the courts.

Impossible trinity proposition: An assertion that an authority cannot implement three related but contradictory policies at the same time. An example from economics is when a government cannot simultaneously have a fixed exchange rate, free capital mobility, and an independent monetary policy (at least one has to be abandoned). See, e.g., R. Mundell, "A Theory of Optimal Currency Areas," *American Economic Review,* 1961, 51(4), pp. 657–65.

Impoverished management: *See* **Managerial grid**.

In-basket exercise: A technique used in training senior managers of organizations that simulates real-life issues that managers face (i.e., those that appear in their in-trays on a daily basis). Training facilitators then evaluate how the managers respond to those simulated issues.

Incentive: Anything that spurs individuals/organizations to accomplish something. An incentive wage plan, for example, encourages employees to be more productive. Incentive instruments are of four types: (a) material (or extrinsic, tangible rewards), (b) solidary (or intangible satisfaction, such as friendship), (c) purposive (i.e., something that taps an employee's idealism), and (d) task (i.e., that increases the fulfillment that one gets from completing a task). Incentivization refers to linking incentives to performance in accordance with prespecified standards. Incentivization is a key component of the "new public management."

Incentive coefficients: Weights that an employee's compensation plan attaches to the various tasks that the employee is assigned. The weights then determine the level of incentives that the employee is entitled to depending on which tasks were completed to the pre-specified threshold.

Incentive contract: A contract that specifies the details of the terms and conditions of a bonus. Incentive contracts have incentive structures built into them. An incentive structure refers to the manner in which an incentive wage plan works, including the decision rules around when it becomes applicable.

Incentive funds: Funds that are earmarked by funding authorities to serve as incentives to organizations/employees for action in specified areas and in a specified manner. Only a small proportion of a total program budget, however, is usually set aside, if at all, as incentive funds.

Incentive-based rules: Rules that have incentives attached to them so that organizations can be encouraged to adhere to set rules. Such incentives may include reductions in fees paid if certain rules are adhered to. It is generally argued that while incentive-based rules are relatively easily designed, even in less-developed countries despite their weak legal and supervisory infrastructure, their enforcement is weak.

Incidence of training: The extent to which employees (either individually or in groups) in an organization receive some form of training. Using incidence of training as an organizational performance measure has its weaknesses, though, because it does not actually distinguish who has received the training, nor what learning level was achieved.

Incident analysis: Analysis of specific incidents in an organization's environment to assess their impact on organizational goals, activities, and intervention logic. Incident analysis is conducted usually while monitoring the organization's activities. For applications, see, e.g., State Services Commission, *Statement of Intent 2002,* Wellington, New Zealand: State Services Commission, 2002, p. 24.

Incidental learning: Also called latent learning, this concept refers to any learning that emerges from situations where individuals are exposed to various opportunities that can enhance their knowledge and skills. Even though there is no formal instruction here, incidental learning is considered a very powerful method of imparting the required knowledge and skills to individuals in organizations as it provides an element of realism in the learning process. The knowledge so gained is also considered to be much more practical to the individuals and the organizations.

Incidental revenues: Revenues that are generated by agencies in the course of their business (such as from fees and penalties) but do not constitute their revenues for operating purposes (which come from budget appropriations) and as such are not critical (i.e., they are incidental) to the operation of the agency.

Inclusiveness: Refers to the fact that policy makers must take as full an account as possible of the impact of the policy they are formulating on different groups in society. Incorporating inclusiveness in the policy development process not only enables policy makers to ensure policy fairness but also gives them a more holistic view of the policy and its likely impacts. The main advantage of this is that it reduces the possibilities of unintended consequences. A usual way of ensuring inclusiveness is to ensure that as many stakeholders as possible have an opportunity to contribute to policy development. For a discussion of this term in the context of policy making, see, e.g., Cabinet Office, *Professional Policy Making for the Twenty First Century,* Report by Strategy Policy Making Team, London: UK Cabinet Office, September 1999, pp. 44–49.

Income-generating activities: Any activity (usually small in scale) that enables individuals and poor families to generate increased income. Examples of income-generating activities include any small-scale business activity that yields goods and produce that can be sold in the market for monetary gain. Many donor agencies have at one time or another contributed meaningfully to supporting programs of income-generating activities in less-developed countries.

Incomplete contract: A contract that does not specify every potential scenario under all possible contingencies. Incomplete contracts tend to be the norm in principal-agent relationships, because in reality not all possible contingencies can be ascertained at the time contracts are agreed upon.

Incomplete information: A situation where parties do not have access to all possible information (either because it does not exist, is unknown, or because of lack of access). Incomplete information leads to bounded rationality since it constrains decision makers' knowledge of what exists. *See also* **Asymmetric information**.

Incremental budgeting: The securing of resources for an organization or program that, in doing so, focuses on marginal (i.e., incremental) changes (either an increase or a decrease) in the annual budget. For an original perspective on this concept, see A. Wildavsky and A. Hammon, "Comprehensive vs. Incremental Budgeting in the Department of Agriculture," *Administrative Science Quarterly,* 1965, 10(3), pp. 321–46. *Cf.* **Full funding**.

Incrementalism: A term coined by economist and political scientist Charles Lindblom to denote a process whereby policy changes take place one step at a time (i.e., incrementally), and where the focus is on minimizing costs rather than maximizing benefits. Lindblom termed this "muddling through" and argued that given bounded rationality, this was a more realistic—although cautious—way of ensuring policy changes. There is a fair degree of truth to this: public-policy making is bound to be incremental and with only small deviations because of the multitude of actors, complexity of policy problems, requirement of openness of debate, and information asymmetry, as well as information gaps. Still, there is nothing "muddling" about incrementalism; the process is quite rational and logical (hence the term "logical incrementalism"). See C. Lindblom, "The Science of 'Muddling Through,'" *Public Administration Review,* 1959, 19(2), pp. 79–88. *See also* **Partisan mutual adjustment**.

Indefinite delivery contract: Any contract that does not specify a durational limit on the delivery of goods and services; that is, the contracted party is expected to continue to provide them for an indefinite period. This arrangement allows both parties to maintain reliable provision of goods and services, and without having to devote possibly considerable time or resources in renegotiating contracts.

Indenture: A written agreement between an individual and an organization that formalizes an apprenticeship arrangement. Some apprenticeships, however, are based on oral agreements.

Independent agency: An agency that is outside the controls of an executive department. It is still subject to the law, just as agencies that are located within governmental departments are. The head of an independent agency reports to the executive, and is accountable to the legislature.

Independent evaluation: An evaluation carried out by someone external to the organization that is implementing a project or program. An independent evaluation is done so as to increase the credibility of the particular evaluation. Independent evaluations of government programs are necessary elements of a transparent governance system.

Independent failure: Any failure in a system that is not caused by another failure or shortcoming elsewhere in the system. In that sense, independent failures are more amenable to targeted and localized control than those that are dependent because the latter require more coordinated effort. *See also* **Primary failure**.

Independent regulators: Institutions that are not affiliated with a governmental agency, and are authorized to regulate an economic sector, such as electricity or gas. Such authorization comes from a legal provision made by a legislature, although usually such regulators will be responsive' to both the executive and the legislature. This dual responsiveness has been termed "plural executive leadership." See R. Moe, *The United States: A Country Study in Organization and Governance,* Paper presented at the OECD Governance of State Agencies and Authorities Expert Meeting, Paris, 19–20 April, 2001, p. 12.

Independent risks: Risks that are inherent in projects and programs wherein they occur separately. This means that the adverse effects of one are not related to those of the others. An argument is generally made that, to the extent possible, producers of goods and services should not be protected from independent risks by governments; this task should be left to the private sector.

Indexing: A system where salaries and other payments to individuals are automatically adjusted for costs of living, proxied by the rate of inflation.

Indirect costs: Also known as overhead costs, these are costs that cannot be ascertained to result from a specific activity and apportioned to it in an economically feasible way. Administrative costs in an organization, for example, are indirect costs.

Indirect raiding: Describes a situation where those who are entrusted with public funds spend available surpluses inefficiently. Indirect raiding, however, is rather difficult to ascertain, and managers tend to get away with making unproductive expenditures. For a good discussion of the concept, see, e.g., N. Davis, *Governance of Crown Financial Assets,* Treasury Working Paper 98/2, Wellington: The Treasury, 1998. *Cf.* **Direct raiding**.

Indirect training costs: Costs of providing training that cannot be apportioned specifically to a given cost object in an economically feasible way. *See also* **Indirect costs**.

Indirect wages: Compensation received by employees for work performed that is non-financial in nature (such as a good working environment in an organization, which could be manifest in a family-friendly policy the organization follows).

Individual agreement: Refers to a formal agreement between an organization and a staff member. The terms and conditions of an individual agreement, by definition, vary from employee to employee unlike in a collective agreement where uniform terms and conditions apply to those who are subject to the collective bargaining agreement.

Individual development plan: A plan prepared and regularly updated by an employee in conjunction with his/her supervisor. The plan charts the way forward for the employee in terms of development experiences, including work assignments and any other learning opportunity that will enable the employee to enhance his/her knowledge, skills, and abilities.

Individual development training: Training provided to employees not only for work-related skills but also for individual development (for example, for stress management, financial skills, etc.). This component of the training, however, is not a substantial part of the total training package for the employee. In the elite Administrative Service of Singapore, for example, individual development training constitutes about 40 percent of the total training time for a senior public servant.

Induction training: Also known as orientation training, this is training that is given to a newcomer to the organization that is designed to familiarize the employee with the organization's rules and regulations and an initial introduction to the organization's culture.

Industrial relations: A system of relations between workers and management centered on how work is done in an organization. As used in everyday language, the meaning of this term is extended to the system of relationships that exists between management and unions.

Inequity theory: Asserts that inequity would exist if an employee perceived or had confirmed that his/her compensation was at the same level as someone who was doing less and/or working less hard. Unless it is addressed, such an employee is inclined to do less relative to his/her colleagues.

Influence costs: Costs that are incurred by employees when they engage in nonproductive activities to influence decisions. Such costs could be measurable (as in staff downtime) and immeasurable (as in the loss of goodwill of managers and peers).

Influence peddling: Refers to selling one's influence in government to get something done. The influence is largely drawn from previous experience in government or the public sector (although it could be based on personal contacts and networks as well). Note that influence peddling is not the same as information peddling, where a party is only selling information but may or may not have any influence over the agency. *See also* **Revolving door.**

Informal corporatism: *See* **Formal corporatism.**

Informal organization: Refers to relationships and interactions among employees in an organization that develop spontaneously and are outside formal rules and protocols. The early twentieth-century Hawthorne Experiments showed conclusively that workers looked for an outlet for their emotions with others whom they felt shared similar sentiments. Such interactions did not necessarily mirror formally laid down ones.

Informal rule making: Also termed notice-and-comment proceedings, informal rule making refers to the public being informed of a proposed rule, and their comments sought. The responsible agency, however, is not mandated to consider them in the final specification of the rules. See, e.g., N. Eisner, "Agency Delay in Informal Rulemaking," *Administrative Law Journal,* 1989, 3(1), pp. 7–52.

Informal sector: The collection of economic activities that take place outside the formal control of government. This means that these activities are not subject to official regulations regarding taxation, credit controls, employment regulations, workplace safety, etc. Informal sector activities are unincorporated and usually small-scale in operation, although, taken together, the sector can be quite substantial.

Informal training: Any training that is provided to individuals that is not structured (i.e., it can be organized in an ad hoc manner depending upon the needs expressed by the individual), and that does not have a formal learning plan (although specific learning objectives will have been specified in advance). *Cf.* **Formal training.**

Informality: A situation where formal mechanisms of governance do not exist (such as well-established contracts that govern relationships between principals and agents). Countries such as New Zealand succeeded in embarking on ambitious public-sector reform programs partly because there were strong informal norms and control mechanisms in place. Jurisdictions that lack this find it difficult to mimic the experiences of countries such as New Zealand in seeking reform. See, e.g., A. Schick, "Why Most Developing Countries Should Not Try New Zealand's Reforms," *World Bank Research Observer,* 1998, 13(1), pp. 123–31.

Information aggregation: A situation where organizations pool their stock of information and information-gathering mechanisms together to minimize risks that they might face individually in the absence of such aggregation. Information aggregation requires uniform database, protocols, and a joint understanding that information will be shared freely. See, e.g., B. Chowdhry, M. Grinblatt, and D. Levine, "Information Aggregation, Security Design, and Currency Swaps," *Journal of Political Economy*, 2002, 110(3), pp. 609–33.

Information asymmetry: A situation where not all parties have equal access to information. This notion is embedded in all of the activities of government and of the market, and explains why individuals, firms, and governments behave in the manner that they do. The notion of information asymmetry is also related to the nature of uncertainty evident in the real world and can be seen as existing across time and space (i.e., an organization which knows less than another has a greater risk potential [the "space" asymmetry], and both bear a greater degree of risk tomorrow instead of now since they do not know what lies ahead [the "time" asymmetry]). One particular application of the term is in what the economist Joseph Stiglitz calls the "political economy of information," that is, how information affects political processes and collective decision making; for clearly not all parties to the process have the same level of access to information. See J. Stiglitz, "Information and the Change in the Paradigm in Economics," *American Economic Review*, 2002, 92(3), pp. 460–501.

Information decay: The phenomenon of gaps in information as it is diffused throughout an organization or a system. As information decay sets in, managerial decision making tends to move from a rational basis to a more nonrational one, where subjective judgments tend to dominate. See, e.g., H. Greve and A. Taylor, "Innovations as Catalysts for Organizational Change: Shifts in Organizational Cognition and Search," *Administrative Science Quarterly*, 2000, 45(1), pp. 54–80.

Information diffusion: A process by which any information spreads within an organization or a system. The speed of the diffusion is a function of how closely those who hold the information guard its access. See, e.g., P. Cooke and K. Morgan, *The Associational Economy: Firms, Regions, and Innovation*, New York: Oxford University Press, 1998, p. 211.

Information elite: (1) A term coined to denote those professionals with expertise in computer-assisted analysis and use of information and communication technologies. See, e.g., C. Levine, B.G. Peters, and F. Thompson,

Public Administration: Challenges, Choices, Consequences, Glenview, IL: Scott, Foresman and Co., 1990, pp. 381–82. (2) Also refers to those who have continual access to privileged information in the government decision-making machinery.

Information hierarchy: (1) A situation that is created when the flow of information is not uniform across all levels of an organization or across all spheres of society. (See, e.g., E. Welch and W. Wong, "Public Administration in a Global Context: Bridging the Gaps of Theory and Practice Between Western and Non-Western Nations," *Public Administration Review,* 1998, 58[1], pp. 40–49.) (2) At a broader level, and in the context of knowledge management, this is also known as the knowledge hierarchy and knowledge pyramid. This hierarchy extends at the first instance from data to information, then to knowledge/understanding, and finally to wisdom. There is also a temporal aspect to this hierarchy, with information aging rapidly and knowledge having a longer time span and permanence.

Information impactedness: Refers to a situation where, among parties interacting with one another, one has more and/or better information or knowledge about the interaction, and thus an advantage. The party that does not have that advantage will often have to go to great effort or expense to get access to the information. See, e.g., O. Williamson, *Markets and Hierarchies: Analysis and Antitrust Implications,* New York: Free Press, 1975, p. 14.

Information integrity: When parties that access and use information that others provide are satisfied that it is accurate and relevant. Information integrity is critical to decision making since the right information will help an organization frame its decisions better.

Information overload: A problem that results from too much information (much of it of marginal value) coming into the organization. Such an overload invariably has the effect of clouding the determination of judgment regarding what is important. Thus, an information-overload problem leads to a situation where organizations are not able to respond effectively to the information they are receiving. A paradoxical result of an information overload is that managers then tend to use less information rather than more in their decision-making processes.

Information peddling: *See* **Influence peddling**.

Informativeness principle: As used in the context of compensation plans and performance appraisals, this principle argues that, to the extent possible, an employee's compensation plan should ideally include carefully specified performance indicators that provide adequate information to the employee of what to expect for the degree of effort that he/she puts into the job. If such indicators have been mutually agreed upon, then the information contained in the plan is useful to the employee in associating performance with rewards. See, e.g., J. Brickley, C. Smith, and J. Zimmerman, *Managerial Economics and Organizational Architecture,* Chicago: Irwin, 1997, p. G-5.

In-house training: Training provided within an organization to its employees (although the organization may at times bring in external participants). In this form of training, resources from within the organization are used although, again, external providers may also be brought in. In addition, it is usually held on-site, but in situations where the nature of training (or the number of participants) warrants it, it could be held off-site as well.

Initial gate: *See* **Approval point**.

Initial training: (1) Training that is required to be proficient in a particular job. (2) Training that is provided to new employees. *See also* **Induction training**.

Initiating structure: Refers to organizational behaviors that result from the organization's specific roles, responsibilities, and control mechanisms that lead to a particular leadership style. In a central-government control agency, for example, the initiating structure leads to a type of leadership that is different from that evident in one where the organization deals with citizens on a day-to-day basis. See, e.g., R. House, A. Filley, and S. Kerr, "Relation of Leader Consideration and Initiating Structure to R and D Subordinates' Satisfaction," *Administrative Science Quarterly,* 1971, 16(1), pp. 19–30.

In-kind financing: Also known as an in-kind match, this term refers to financing provided by a party not in the form of funds but in the form of products and other means of support. In-kind financing is usually provided by poor governments to show their support to development projects that are largely financed by bilateral and multilateral donors.

Innovation: New approaches, inventions, and the application of creative new ideas. In a public-service context, for example, an innovation may be a new way of delivering services to citizens in remote areas. Two models of public-sector innovation are usually cited in the literature: (a) the planning model, wherein public entrepreneurs move an innovative idea systematically; and (b) the groping model, wherein public entrepreneurs search uncertainly for a general direction of change, and experiment tentatively with various initiatives as they arise. For a discussion of the applications of innovation models in the public-sector context, see, e.g., K. Manley, *Innovation in the Public Sector,* A study prepared for the Queensland Innovation Council, Brisbane, Australia, January 2001, pp. 13–14.

Innovation capacity: The ability of organizations to be innovative in their work. There are several variables that affect innovation capacity, including: (a) availability of resources, (b) the nature of the information-processing system, (c) extent of public support for governmental flexibility, and (d) ability to develop behavioral patterns to institutionalize innovative policies. See, e.g., R. Merritt, "Innovation in the Public Sector: An Introduction," in R. Merritt and A. Merritt (eds.), *Innovation in the Public Sector,* Beverly Hills, CA: Sage Publications, 1985, pp. 9–16.

Innovation deficit: A term that is used to denote the difference between what a deliberate policy on enhancing innovation emphasizes and what is actually seen in practice. The policy may, for example, place emphasis on trying to get public-sector agencies to seek novel and innovative ways to provide service delivery in remote areas of the country. For a discussion of the term, see, e.g., P. Cooke and K. Morgan, *The Associational Economy: Firms, Regions, and Innovation,* New York: Oxford University Press, 1998, p. 96.

Input: Monetary and nonmonetary resources (such as staff time and salaries) used to produce outputs. The level of demand for services may also be considered an input since it helps determine what and how much should be produced.

Inside-initiation model: A model of agenda setting where policy initiatives come from elites. Where it is allowed, public involvement and articulation is negligible, as the elites are convinced that they are in the best position to offer the best solutions to problems. See, e.g., R. Cobb, J. Ross, and M. Ross, "Agenda Building as a Comparative Political Process," *American Political Science Review,* 1976, 70(1), pp. 126–38. *Cf.* **Outside-initiative model**.

Inspirational strategy: *See* **Decision-making strategy**.

Institution: (1) While the term could refer to an organization, it is broadly defined to be inclusive not only of organizations like households and firms but also of, for example, the legal framework, social rules within which all activities take place in society. A hard institution refers to a collection of organizations, such as governmental agencies and banks, which are part of what is known as an institutional milieu in the public-management system. This is contrasted with soft institutions that refer to the norms and conventions (such as natural clustering among economic agencies) that dictate how networks and interactions take place among organizations. Soft institutions also form a part of the institutional milieu in any society. (2) Refers to the rules of the game governing contractual relationships between parties that wish to interact with each other. Institutionalism refers to the notion that institutions play a large role in the effect of public policies, and the belief in the primacy of institutions as a way to understand how public actions are done and how citizens' demands are aggregated. For an analysis of the role of institutions, see, e.g., T. Besley and A. Case, "Political Institutions and Policy Choices: Evidence from the United States," *Journal of Economic Literature,* 2003, 41(1), pp. 7–73.

Institution building: Refers to the process of building the capacity of institutions (both organizations as well as systems) such that they assist in attaining the goals the government has set. As used in the context of technical assistance to developing countries, this term has tended to refer to developing: (a) particular organization(s) that possess the technical capability and the mind-set to initiate and sustain change; and (b) appropriate systems that facilitate the work of the institutions.

Institutional ageism: Refers to the fact that discrimination against older workers in the workplace is a product not only of individual prejudice, but also of institutionalized, social prejudice in the labor market and economy. This is not necessarily true in all societies, however. In countries such as Japan, Singapore, and Korea, where age is venerated, institutional ageism is less of a problem than in Western societies. For a discussion of the concept, see, e.g., A. Walker and P. Taylor, "Ageism vs. Productive Ageing: The Challenge of Age Discrimination in the Labor Market," in S. Bass et al. (eds.), *Achieving a Productive Ageing Society,* London: Auburn House, 1993, pp. 61–80.

Institutional analysis: A review of the role that institutions play in the policy-making process. An institutional analysis first involves identifying all the organizations and processes that could have an impact on, or be influenced by, a policy. Then the nature of that impact or influence needs to be assessed. Policy makers need to be aware that not all institutions bear the same characteristics or the same level of impact on a policy.

Thus, an institutional analysis prior to policy recommendation is considered necessary.

Institutional capacity: The capacity of government institutions to enforce the rules of the game to ensure that there is a level playing field, and to regulate economic and administrative activity in its own jurisdiction. This capacity of government is different from its technical capacity. A related term, institutional competence, refers to the capability of organizations that emerges from the human and social capital that they possess. In the public-sector context, the competence is also a product of the mandate that institutions have been given by a legislature. See, e.g., M. Grindle, *Challenging the State: Crisis and Innovation in Latin America and Africa,* Cambridge: Cambridge University Press, 1996, p. 8. *See also* **Technical capacity**.

Institutional catalyst: Any institution that serves as the focal point to make or force desired change. The institution could be a select committee, a governmental ministry, or any other party. An institutional catalyst has, or is perceived to have, an appropriate mandate to play such a role.

Institutional commitment: Refers to the commitment expressed by the government to an institution that it creates by fiat. The commitment is in evidence only when there are costs to be paid by governments in doing away with such institutions or in tampering with their work. Still, all governments would like to have in place the option of being flexible in the degree of commitment they give to a particular institution. See, e.g., S. Lohmann, "Why Do Institutions Matter? An Audience-Cost Theory of Institutional Commitment," *Governance: An International Journal of Policy, Administration, and Institutions,* 2003, 16(1), pp. 95–110. *See also* **Fiat institution**.

Institutional competence: *See* **Institutional capacity**.

Institutional development impact: The impact that any intervention has regarding the strength of the country's institutional arrangements. Such strength may be evident in, among others, the stability of the institutions, in the proper alignment of the institutions' mandates, or in the manner in which they carry out their work.

Institutional discrimination: Discrimination that is evident across the organization even though there was no overt intention of the organization to discriminate against any individual or group. Such discrimination could occur as a result of a policy that an organization institutes that has the unintended effect of treating someone (or a group) differently.

Institutional economics: A strand of economics that places primary emphasis on the role that institutions play in the economy. It is the reliance on the principles of institutional economics that has served as the conceptual basis for the creation of executive agencies in jurisdictions around the world. *See also* **Institution**.

Institutional elites: Refers to those (relatively few) in any jurisdiction who are instrumental in policy making. These normally include finance and other governmental ministers, chief executives of the biggest industries and businesses, union leaders, etc. For an application of this concept in the context of public-sector reforms, see, e.g., S. Goldfinch, "Remaking New Zealand's Economic Policy: Institutional Elites as Radical Innovators, 1984–1993," *Governance: An International Journal of Policy and Administration,* 1998, 11(2), pp. 177–207.

Institutional inflexibility: When governments cannot redesign and reorient their institutions to deal with some changes in their environment. This inflexibility is evident, for example, when rural farmers cannot get access to formal credit regardless of the need for it that may have been recognized by government.

Institutional isomorphism: A term used to denote fundamental changes in the institutional settings that results from innovation. A risk in innovation is that organizations attempting it risk losing legitimacy. The innovation may well set in motion a process leading to institutional isomorphism. See, e.g., M. Arndt and B. Bigelow, "Presenting Structural Innovation in an Institutional Environment," *Administrative Science Quarterly,* 2000, 45(3), pp. 494–522.

Institutional knowledge: Knowledge that is gained by an organization collectively (i.e., the sum of expertise and knowledge that exists in the employees of the organization). Those who have been in the organization for some time will be more aware of the historical context and background of much of what may be happening in an organization. *See also* **Institutional memory**.

Institutional malleability: The ease with which state institutions can be changed (either legally through parliament, for example, or managerially through internal action). The degree of institutional malleability has some impact on institutional reforms since such reforms require institutions to take on different roles.

Institutional memory: Knowledge that exists in organizations that is cumulative and that resides not only in the documentation and the record-management system of the organization but also in the minds of the staff members. Not all knowledge gained is recorded, and some valuable information resides in individuals. If staff turnover is high, then there is a danger that valuable knowledge will be irretrievably lost. For a discussion of the importance of institutional memory in knowledge creation and sharing, see, e.g., J. Walsh and G. Ungson, "Organizational Memory," *Academy of Management Review,* 1991, 16, pp. 57–91.

Institutional milieu: An environment that comprises both "hard" institutions (like government agencies) and "soft' institutions (i.e., social norms and conventions) that determine how organizations and others interact with each other. See, e.g., P. Cooke and K. Morgan, *The Associational Economy: Firms, Regions, and Innovation,* New York: Oxford University Press, 1998, p. 9. *See also* **Institution**.

Institutional rationality: The rationality that bureaucrats employ to address the tension between what is demanded of an organization and what is practical. That gap could arise due to several factors, including incompatible mandates, unrealistic expectations, and incomplete information.

Institutional reform: Changes that are made to institutions (organizations and processes) so that they can have more impact. Thus, such reform effort is extensive and encompasses changing the rules of the game as well. Institutional reform is generally reflected in any of the following: adoption of innovative policies, termination of strategic programs, major public-sector reorganizations, and constitutional reengineering. See, e.g., S. Goldfinch and P. t'Hart, "Leadership and Institutional Reform: Engineering Macroeconomic Policy Change in Australia," *Governance: An International Journal of Policy, Administration, and Institutions,* 2003, 16(2), pp. 235–70.

Institutional transformation: As economies grow and become more complex, the need for different types of institutions to manage the economy increases. Hence, for example, a country with small-scale income-generating activities and micro-credit programs may be forced to look at more complex institutions to manage growth in the formal credit market. This also implies that institutional transformation is associated with change in cultural values. Privatization, for example, has been said to be a manifestation of institutional transformation. See, e.g., M. Veenswijk and J. Hakvoort, "Public-Private Transformations, Institutional Shifts, Cultural Changes, and Altering Identities: Two Case Studies," *Public Administration,* 2002, 80(3), pp. 543–55.

Institutional utilitarianism: In considering what—and how—goods and services may be produced and delivered in an economy, this concept refers to giving primacy to the role of institutions to ensure the distribution rather than to the choice of goods and services themselves. See, e.g., D. Weimer and A. Vining, *Policy Analysis: Concepts and Practice,* 2nd edition, Englewood Cliffs, NJ: Prentice Hall, 1992, p. 97.

Institutional veto points: Sources of where a veto to a policy proposal could come from (for example, the veto-wielding U.S. president if the proposal has already passed Congress, or a governmental minister if the proposal has not yet reached parliament). See, e.g., J. Blankenau, "The Fate of National Health Insurance in Canada and the United States: A Multiple Streams Explanation," *Policy Studies Journal,* 2001, 29(1), pp. 38–55. *See also* **Veto**.

Institutionalized clientelism: A new form of the traditional pattern of authority wherein patron-client relationships are dominant, and in which citizens rely on social institutions and their leaders to receive services (such as, for example, clan-based networks in rural areas). See, e.g., A. Walder, *Communist Neo-Traditionalism: Work and Authority in Chinese Industry,* Berkeley: University of California Press, 1986, p. 8.

Institutionalized policy arena: Forum and structured environment (such as in the legislature and town hall meetings) where formal debates over policies take place.

Instructed delegate: Any representative who acts according to the expressed preferences of his/her constituencies or those whose interests he/she is mandated to safeguard, rather than his or her own. For a good review of how issues around instructed delegates, constituencies, and representational linkages work, see, e.g., P. Hurley and K. Hill, "Beyond the Demand-Input Model: A Theory of Representational Linkages," *Journal of Politics,* 2003, 65(2), pp. 304–26.

Instrument independence: The latitude that an organization has to select and use a particular policy instrument in response to a problem. Hence, for example, a federal civil-service commission could have instrument independence on performance evaluations and job descriptions, while the goal determination could be done, for example, by the prime minister's office. Instrument independence requires that there be no political interference. *See also* **Goal independence**.

Instrumental achievement: *See* **Agency competence**.

Instrumental bureaucracies: Bureaucracies that are not independent from government (i.e., they are used as instruments by government to fulfill mandates). Governmental departments are the archetype instrumental bureaucracies. See, e.g., C. Knill, "Explaining Cross-National Variance in Administrative Reform: Autonomous Versus Instrumental Bureaucracies," *Journal of Public Policy,* 1999, 19(2), pp. 113–39. *Cf.* **Autonomous bureaucracies**.

Instrumental goal: *See* **Goal**.

Instrumental rationality: Looks specifically at the relationships between means and ends (i.e., are the means that have been selected likely to lead to the ends that have been determined?). Thus, being instrumentally rational implies that the appropriate means have been selected to get to the end, which is considered to be predetermined and given. In that regard, instrumental rationality is aimed at maximizing the chances of success (i.e., in the most efficient way) to attain a policy goal that has already been set. See, e.g., M. Friedman, *Dynamics of Reason.* Stanford, CA: CSLI Publications, 2001, p. 54. *Cf.* **Substantive rationality**.

Instrumental value: *See* **Value**.

Instrumentality: A measure of the probability that an individual places on a relationship between the amount of effort (and, thus, performance) and the likelihood of certain outcomes, such as rewards. The greater the degree of causation of the two, the greater the degree of instrumentality.

Intangible objective: An objective of an organization that cannot be directly measured (such as, for example, reasserting its status among peers). An intangible objective could be termed a second-order objective for the organization.

Intangible rewards: Rewards that employees get that are not tangible (for example, job satisfaction from having completed a major project successfully). Organizational leaders and managers need to take into consideration intangible rewards as well as tangible ones in seeking to motivate employees.

Integrated contracting: Contracting arrangements which require organizations to determine the specific nature of their relationships with contractors, assess which contractor is best placed to take the lead in delivering the product or service for the organization, and specify the right balance between reliance on a long-term relationship or a highly specified performance agreement, or both. Integrated contracting veers from the traditional mode of contracting between organizations and suppliers, in which there was a reliance on a high degree of specification and performance reporting, and in which organizations were often separately contracting with the same supplier, often for a relatively small amount of business.

Integrated performance system: Refers to a performance management system that, for example, a central agency uses in monitoring the performance of governmental departments. The integrated performance system consists of: (a) a performance planning process, (b) an *ex ante* performance specification, and (c) an *ex post* performance report. These three documents taken together give a holistic picture of what is expected of the department and what it delivers against the specifications. For a detailed discussion see, e.g., State Services Commission, *Improving Accountability: Developing an Integrated Performance System,* Occasional Paper No. 11, Wellington: State Services Commission, 1999.

Integrated rural-development approach: An approach to tackle rural poverty where development interventions are made not only in one sector (such as health) but also in a combination (such as health, education, income-generating activities, etc.). The assumption here is that since poverty is multidimensional, targeting only one sector is not effective.

Integrated service delivery: Refers to the provision of services to the public that is not done in isolation from other related providers. For example, police work against youth offenders may be handled in conjunction with interventions by organizations responsible for social welfare as well as for remedial schooling and job apprenticeships.

Integrative decision: Any decision that is taken by an organizational leadership that incorporates input from first-level managers. An integrative decision thus has a greater likelihood of reflecting the actual state of affairs than any other method of decision making. For a case-study application of integrative decision making, see, e.g., L. Leung and W. Cheung, "An Integrative Decision Methodology for Designing and Operating an Air-Express Courier's Service Network," *Decisions Sciences*, 2000, 31(1), pp. 105–27.

Integrity-based ethics regime: A system of governance where the enhancement of ethics in the public sector is largely facilitated by the integrity expected of public servants themselves rather than by a formal set of rules and directives, which tend to be coercive. Monitoring the integrity-based ethics regime, however, is more difficult.

Intellectual capital: The assets of an organization that consist of three other types of capital: human (the basis of which are the people of the organization, and the collective knowledge, skills, abilities they bring), structural (i.e., the forms and processes that exist in an organization), and relationship (i.e., the interactions among organizational members as well as with external stakeholders. See, e.g., M. Sarkar et al., "The Influence of Complementarity, Compatibility and Relationship Capital in Alliance Performance," *Journal of the Academy of Marketing Science,* 2001, 29(4), pp. 358–73.

Intelligence function: As used in an organizational context, an intelligence function relates to gathering and analyzing information and presenting it to management so that more informed decisions can be made. While the intelligence can be sourced by anyone in the organization, it tends to be housed institutionally in the knowledge-management unit.

Intelligent accountability: Accountability that strikes a sensible balance among costs, risks, and control in governmental departments. By not merely focusing on control and accountability, governments enable departments to be better suited to work toward the desired outcomes. See, e.g., B. Anderson and L. Dovey, *Whither Accountability?* Working Paper No.18, Wellington: State Services Commission, 2003, pp. 15–16.

Intended bargaining process: If relations between labor and management are good, both parties will make clear to the other in advance of the collective bargaining process how they plan on approaching the negotiations. This pre-bargaining process generally includes information sharing on how the costs of negotiations are to be met, the roles advocates and others in the bargaining process are to take, and what agreements are required on external and internal communication, among others.

Intended outcomes: Refers to what effect the government intends its outputs to have on society. An inherent assumption is that government intentions are in alignment with the stated purposes of its activities. When they are, such as those formulated in laws or policies, the intended outcomes are plainly evident to citizens. *See also* **Unintended distortions**.

Intended rationality, principle of: Asserts that people are goal-oriented and that they make conscious decisions designed to meet those goals. However, such goal realization is often not fully possible because of the complexity of the environment they operate in and/or because of their lack of requisite cognitive ability. The principle is useful in studying the goal-behavior tendencies in individuals, and is the cornerstone of Herbert Simon's views on bounded rationality. See, e.g., B. Jones, "Bounded Rationality and Public Policy: Herbert A. Simon and the Decisional Foundation of Collective Choice," *Policy Sciences,* 2002, 35(3), pp. 269–84.

Intensity of training: The extent to which a particular training session is used in an organization. This is measured in two ways: (a) the amount of time the employees of an organization spend on training (measured as, for example, number of hours per week), or (b) the number of employees who participate in any particular training session (measured as, for example, a ratio of total number of employees).

Interaction: Relationships and involvement among various actors in the policy-making process and in governance. Such interactions are evident, for example, between political executives and career civil servants, between the executive and the legislature, and between citizens and public servants, among others.

Interaction influence analysis: A technique used in organizations to observe the dynamics of interactions between the leadership and staff members so that areas for improvements can be identified. One area where this is evident is in the analysis of how staff members give feedback to organizational leaders when they do not understand or disagree with directives.

Interactional justice: *See* **Organizational justice theory**.

Interagency collaboration: Joint activity by two or more agencies intended to increase public value. The study of interagency collaboration has focused on several areas, including organization strategy, resource acquisition, learning and innovation, and organizational networks. See E. Bardach, *Getting Agencies to Work Together: The Practice and Theory of Managerial Craftsmanship,* Washington, DC: Brookings Institution Press, 1998, p. 8.

Interdependency: Refers to the linkages that exist between actors such that the functional overlap affects the degree of goal attainment of one or both actors. Where the actions of one actor interfere with those of another, it is labeled competitive interdependency, and the reverse of this is symbiotic interdependency. In the former, conflict is the norm (and one actor tends to benefit at the expense of another), and in the latter, cooperation results, which tends to benefit both actors. For a good discussion of the term, see, e.g., M. Fenger and P. Klok, "Interdependency, Beliefs, and Coalition Behavior: A Contribution to the Advocacy Coalition Framework," *Policy Sciences,* 2001, 34(2), pp. 157–70.

Interest arbitration: Refers to mediation efforts by an arbitrator to decide what the proposed agreement between two disputing parties will contain. Both parties to the dispute will have already signaled their intent to agree with the mediated result. See, e.g., I. Helburn and R. Rodgers, "Hesitancy of Arbitrators to Accept Interest Arbitration Cases: A Test of Conventional Wisdom," *Public Administration Review,* 1985, 45(3), pp. 398–402.

Interest group: Any group that lobbies government on behalf of the interests of its members. Such lobbying may take the form of, for example, working to elect officials who are sympathetic to their cause, or making donations to election campaign funds. Interest-group liberalism asserts that since private interest groups have increasingly taken on a major role in shaping public policy, and since private providers have been more actively involved in what used to be traditional government domains, the government has tended to be weak and not very capable of effective long-term planning. This is because it ends up just managing interests rather than taking the lead. For the classic work on this concept, see T. Lowi, "Public Philosophy: Interest Group Liberalism," *American Political Science Review,* 1967, 61(1), pp. 5–24.

Interest-based bargaining: A bargaining technique where the parties start by putting forward a statement of their interests rather than their proposals. They will then seek to agree on the criteria of acceptability to be used for an evaluation of alternatives that are consistent with their stated interests. A mutually acceptable agreement is then reached when the acceptability criteria are applied to the various alternatives and the one that best meets the criteria is selected. The advantage of incorporating this form of bargaining is that it allows both the parties to get what they want from the negotiation process, but it does presume that there is a fair amount of trust between them. *Cf.* **Position-based bargaining**.

Interest-group liberalism: *See* **Interest group**.

Interest-group politics: The interactions and domains within which interest groups operate. Four types of interest-group politics can be distinguished: (a) client politics (where an interest group is in support of an agency's own goals), (b) entrepreneurial politics (where an interest group is against an agency's own goals), (c) interest-group politics (where two or more interest groups conflict over an agency's goals), and (d) majoritarian politics (where there is no important interest group focusing on an agency's goals). See, e.g., J. Wilson, *Bureaucracy: What Government Agencies Do and Why They Do It,* New York: Basic Books, 1989, p. 76.

Intergovernmental contracting: When responsibility for service production is transferred to other units of government (such as from state/provincial government to local government).

Intergovernmental transfer: *See* **Transfer**.

Interim: The time period between which events or processes can occur. Thus, for example, an interim agreement is one reached in order to defer a strike action called for by a union and to give the negotiating parties (labor and management) more time to reach a conclusive agreement. An interim evaluation is an evaluation of ongoing development activities, and usually takes place mid-term in the implementation period or at the end of a distinct phase of a policy or program. Interim evaluations will typically focus on operational activities, but will also take a wider perspective and possibly give some consideration to long-term effects. An interim review is a review of a program done during the gap in a program (such as between activity phases).

Interinstitutional externalities: The impacts on other organizations of the actions of any one agency. Such externalities can be positive or negative, and are important considerations in determining whether the quality of the public sector will improve or not. See, e.g., V. Tanzi, *The Role of the State and the Quality of the Public Sector,* IMF Working Paper WP/00/36, Washington, DC: International Monetary Fund, p. 16.

Interjurisdictional compacts: Refers to agreements that two or more countries, or jurisdictions such as states and provinces, share in relation to the operation of joint programs of mutual interest. Thus, several provinces, for example, could have a compact on how best to use the water resources that they may share (such as a lake or river).

Interior solution: *See* **Two-corner solution**.

Interlocking directorate: Related to corporate governance, the term refers to a situation where one person sits on the board of directors of two or more companies. In public corporations, interlocking directorates can be avoided by legal provisions. A large part of the problem that was evident in the Asian economic crisis of the late 1990s was centered on the existence of interlocking directorates in the largest companies of many countries.

Intermediate institutions: Institutions (such as local government) that are neither the first point of contact with the public, nor the farthest (i.e., at the apex of the government policy formulation process). For a discussion of intermediate institutions, see, e.g., P. Cooke and K. Morgan, *The Associational Economy: Firms, Regions, and Innovation,* New York: Oxford University Press, 1998, p. 101.

Intermediate outcomes: Outcomes that contribute to the attainment of overall governmental outcomes. In most cases, the work of public organizations attains intermediate outcomes, which taken together with those of other organizations will lead to the attainment of governmental outcomes.

Internal alignment: The relationship and interactions among the various divisions of an organization that lead to a more coordinated approach to what the organization has to accomplish overall. Thus, even though one division can continue, for example, with a blue-skies approach while others are tied down with day-to-day operational activities, they still need to communicate on coordinating their work.

Internal audit: An independent review of one division in an organization. Internal audits are quite adequate to ensure that there is process and results accountability at the organization. In relation to risk management, internal audits are used to give independent assurance about the way in which risk is controlled in an organization, See, e.g., HM Treasury, *Management of Risk: A Strategic Overview,* London: Treasury, January 2001, p. 12. *See also* **Audit**.

Internal benchmarking: Setting standards in an organization using best-practice indicators from within the various components of the organization. This is useful in scenario planning if no relevant benchmark indicators can be ascertained in the external environment.

Internal bureaucracies: The administrative apparatus within a bureaucracy (so, for example, a governmental ministry will have several internal bureaucracies that are centered on finance, strategic planning, etc.). *See also* **Bureaucracy**.

Internal compass: Term used to denote that government bureaucrats are committed and have values and ethos of their own. This guides their behavior independent of external checks on them. It can be argued that an integrity-based ethics regime facilitates the emergence of behavior that is guided by an internal compass. See, e.g., C. Levine, B.G. Peters, and F. Thompson, *Public Administration: Challenges, Choices, Consequences,* Glenview, IL: Scott, Foresman and Co., 1990, pp. 191–92.

Internal consultancy: Services sought by one organizational division from another in a manner similar to contracting outside the organization. The major difference here is that there is no formal service agreement, although some guiding principles will have been agreed in advance by the heads of the different branches and by the organizational leadership.

Internal contracting: Formalized contractual relations between two parties in an organization. For example, a performance agreement between the chief executive of a government department and the public service commissioner that specifies an attainment of particular targets could be considered an internal contract.

Internal control: Refers to the measures that an organization will have in place to ensure that all organizational processes and rules are adhered to. An organization's internal control system consists of the following components: (a) the assessment of risk, (b) control environment and control activities, (c) information processing and protocols around the use of information, and (d) monitoring activities. In reality, most organizations have both formal and informal internal control systems. For a concise description of the various categories of internal control, see, e.g., HM Treasury, *Management of Risk: A Strategic Overview*, London: Treasury, January 2001, pp. 10–11.

Internal evaluation: An evaluation done by an entity within the agency that is implementing a particular project or program. Internal evaluations are encouraged when there is confidence that such evaluation can be done impartially and rigorously. However, internal evaluations risk being perceived as neither thorough nor transparent.

Internal governance failure: A situation where organizational leaders, including those in government, seek to maximize their own welfare at the expense of the organization or government. These lead to organizational costs, and inefficiencies result. For a cogent discussion of internal governance failure, see e.g., A. Vining, "Internal Market Failure: A Framework for Diagnosing Firm Inefficiency," *Journal of Management Studies,* 2003, 40(2), pp. 431–57.

Internal insurance: (1) Originally referred to the fact that a sufficiently large entity (like a public sector) might have risks which are sufficiently distributed and varied for there to be no gain from an external insurance contract compared with simply paying for losses as they occurred. (2) Also refers to the fallback position that employees have when they are engaged in risk-taking within the context of their own work. Just as organizations need to take up insurance against external risks, so too do they need internal insurance to encourage innovation in the workplace. A forgiving culture for the first failure is an example of internal insurance.

Internal labor market: Refers to a situation where an organization has a recruitment pool from within its own ranks. In an internal labor market, there are few points of entry for outsiders, and generally, such points of entry happen to be at the lower rungs of the organization. This means that positions at the upper end tend to be filled by internal promotion or movement from within divisions of the organization.

Internal locus of control: A belief that an employee has that his/her own actions, rather than external sources, determine the outcomes.

Internal market failure: A situation when there are inefficiencies in the manner in which units within organizations interact with each other. Such interactions can be likened to markets existing outside the organization. For a discussion of internal market failures, see, e.g., A. Vining, "Internal Market Failure: A Framework for Diagnosing Firm Inefficiency," *Journal of Management Studies,* 2003, 40(2), pp. 431–57.

Internal marketization: A new form of managerialism in which the market-like properties that are evident in an organization's external environment are developed internally, such as by instituting internal contracting arrangements. Thus, for example, in looking at the questions of effective property rights and incentives within organizations, an internal market perspective is developed.

Internal monitoring: Monitoring of activities and programs by an internal part of the organization rather than by some party from outside.

Internal policy advice: Policy advice that comes from sources within governmental departments. Such sources include policy shops in operational organizations as well as those in core bodies such as the office of the chief executive officer within the departments.

Internal promotion: The promotion to a higher position of someone already within a particular unit or division of an organization. Traditional civil-service practices were to rely on internal promotion to manage succession in an organization. However, with the increasing disuse of the tenure system, senior positions in organizations are also being filled by lateral entry (i.e., entry from outside the organization). While this may bring new blood and fresh ideas into an organization, it also may serve to demotivate those within an organization who were overlooked or who now face increased competition.

Internal rate of return to training: As in standard cost-benefit analysis, this is the rate of return on training where discounted costs equal discounted benefits. While it is easy to define the term, it is, in practice, very difficult to measure the internal rate of return since few organizations are able to quantify the benefits of the training given to employees.

Internal recruitment: *See* **Recruitment**.

Internal review: Any assessment that is done internally in the organization. Such a review could be for a varied range of purposes, including, for example, determining the facts around a particular procedural omission, or ascertaining the extent of a particular problem in employee morale.

Internalization: As used in the context of employees in an organization, the term refers to the process whereby they understand and accept the values and norms of the organization and apply them in their work. See, e.g., R. Hall and P. Andriani, *"Managing Knowledge for Innovation,"* *Long Range Planning,* 2002, 35(1), pp. 29–48. *Cf.* **Externalization**.

Internship: An assignment that an individual does in an organization for a brief period of time, usually as part or immediately upon completion of an academic program. The purpose of the internship is to provide to the individual an appreciation of how things are done in practice, and it offers the individual an opportunity to see firsthand the application of concepts that are discussed in books. The organization that offers the internships also benefits by being able to showcase itself to potential candidates its appeal as a future employer of choice. At a minimum, it allows the organization to complete some tasks at low cost and with motivated individuals. The intern also benefits by being able to gain experience, exposure, and academic credit in the process. Internships are usually unpaid.

Intervention: Refers to any step taken to bring about a desired result. For example, a government may intervene in the marketplace if there are imperfections in the economy, including, for example, situations of monopoly. Development intervention refers to any activity (project or program) that will facilitate and enhance economic development in a country. For a discussion of the term in relation to policy analysis see, e.g., J. Stewart and R. Ayers, "System Theory and Policy Practice: An Exploration," *Policy Sciences,* 2001, 34(1), pp. 79–94.

Intervention logic: Also known as program logic, this term refers to the web of cause and effect that shows how a given set of interventions or outputs contributes to outcomes. It is obvious that only robustly constructed program logic will enable an organization to fulfill its mandates effectively. For a practical guide on how to develop the intervention logic in program formulation, see, e.g., K. Baehler, "Intervention Logic: A User's Guide," *Public Sector,* 2002, 25(3), pp. 14–20. *See also* **Outcome line**.

Interventionist state: A sovereign state that shows a clear predilection for involving itself in the provision of goods and services, and in shaping how resource allocations among competing ends should be effectuated. There is clearly a large role for public bureaucracies in an interventionist state.

Intra-agency accountability: Accountability that is expected of different divisions within an organization in terms of fulfilling whatever is expected of them. Generally, jointly developed performance measures are the primary means of intra-agency accountability.

Intrinsic motivation: Motivation in individuals in organizations that is drawn from the work itself and not from tangible rewards that individuals might receive as a result of being engaged in that work. Thus, for example, if one works for a voluntary agency to help the marginalized segments of the population, then he or she is said to be intrinsically motivated. For a discussion of intrinsic motivation with respect to the behavior of agents, see, e.g., K. Murdock, "Intrinsic Motivation and Optimal Incentive Contracts," *RAND Journal of Economics,* 2002, 33(4), pp. 650–71. *Cf.* **Extrinsic motivation**.

Intrusion power of organizations: The power that organizations have either mandated by law or developed through administrative procedures, whereby they can seek, and expect to receive, information from others. Thus, for example, a central-government agency has the intrusion power to ask all governmental departments to report back on the sizes of contracts issued to companies owned by minority groups.

Inverted appraisal: The review of the performance of supervisors by subordinates (part of what is known as 360-degrees appraisal). While this notion of inverted appraisal is gathering increasing appeal in jurisdictions around the world, there are still problems around its usage, primarily that of the disinclination of superiors to accept that subordinates can be impartial when appraising their performance. In some societies where rank is important (such as those in East Asia), this valuation technique is important (such as those in East Asia), this valuation technique appears to be a long way off still.

Investment center: *See* **Responsibility center.**

Invisible foot: In response to the notion of an invisible hand in the marketplace that will bring about equilibrium in the demand and supply of goods and services, the idea of an "invisible foot" is that there are individuals and groups in society who tend to protect themselves from competitive market forces. Often, this is a function of the use of political rationality, which tends to dominate decision-making scenarios.

Invisible hand: Economist Adam Smith's classic term used to denote the marketplace (i.e., the interaction of demand and supply) without government intervention in the provision of goods and services in society. The notion of an invisible hand is at the heart of the free enterprise system. In the 1990s, this came to be accepted by many policy makers as the solution to the problems of how economies were to be managed and services provided to citizens. *See also* **Visible hand**.

Invitation to tender: *See* **Request for proposal.**

Iron cage: A concept used in the context of how organizations tend to be structured in limited ways or formats rather than in the free format one would expect given the complexity of their environments. This was evident, for example, in the "new public management" reforms of the 1980s and 1990s, where the "next steps" type organizational form tended to be evident in most advanced jurisdictions. See, e.g., P. DiMaggio and W. Powell, "The Iron Cage Revisited: Institutional Isomorphism and Collective Rationality in Organizational Fields," *American Sociological Review,* 1983, 48(2), pp. 147–60.

Ironclad oath: Also called an ironclad contract, this term refers to the antiunion tactic that employers used in the past to deter employees from joining a union. Employees were obliged to take an oath to that effect as a precondition for employment.

Iron law of oligarchy: Asserts that, given its very nature, and the inherent structures in every organization, there is bound to be a situation where there are a few leaders and a multitude of people who are led. There are two components to this law: (a) this just-described tendency emerges despite the presence, if any, of practices such as employee feedback; and (b) as the drive for organizational survival takes hold, the organization tends to become more conservative in its approach and orientation. For a good discussion, see, e.g., W. Cassinelli, "The Law of Oligarchy," *American Political Science Review*, 1953, 47(3), pp.773–84.

Iron rectangle: *See* **Iron triangle**.

Iron rice bowl: Refers generally to any "reward" (such as lifetime employment, guaranteed employment, or even social protection) that an individual is guaranteed by an institution, but usually the state. See, e.g., N. Flynn, I. Holliday, and L. Wong, "Introduction," in L. Wong and N. Flynn (eds.), *The Market in Chinese Social Policy*, Hampshire, UK: Palgrave, 2001, pp. 1–11.

Iron triangle: Strong coalitions of three actors—interest groups, governmental agencies, and legislative bodies—at all levels of government that are engaged in influencing the share of funding that goes to specific programs. The notion of an iron triangle is derived from economist Mancur Olson's path-breaking work on distributional coalitions (see, e.g., C. Levine, B. Peters and F. Thompson, *Public Administration: Challenges, Choices, Consequences,* Glenview, IL: Scott, Foresman and Co., 1990, p. 128). To these three actors, some have added a fourth—the courts—to form what has been termed an iron rectangle. See, e.g., R. Melnick, "The Politics of Partnership," *Public Administration Review,* 1985, 45(Special Issue), pp. 653–60. *See also* **Distributional coalitions**.

Irreversibility: A concept that is relevant in considering the risks underlying particular policies where expenditures and effects are not reversible (i.e., they cannot be undone). An example of irreversibility is deterioration of environmental quality as a result of a decision to proceed with a particular infrastructure project. Projects with irreversible effects could rule out other possibilities down the road, and resources set aside for such projects could have high opportunity costs. For this reason, irreversibility should feature prominently in any risk assessment of policies and programs. *See also* **Option value**.

Ishikawa diagram: Also known as the fishbone diagram, this term was named after Kaoru Ishikawa, who pioneered it in the 1960s in his work on quality management processes. The diagram, which is also known as the cause-and-effect diagram, shows all the causes (potential or real) that yield a particular effect. The causes can be seen as inputs and the effect as output. The causes are presented in the diagram according to their level of perceived importance to the entity that is developing the diagram with reference to a particular organization or issue under consideration (the big bones in the diagram depict major causes, while the smaller bones show the factors that are likely to cause the major factors). The diagram helps in identifying the root causes of particular problems along with the relative importance of each cause.

Issue: Any undesirable situation that needs to be addressed. An accumulation of issues creates an agenda. An issue definition is the determination of the nature and type of an issue that organizations have to face in the course of fulfilling their mandates. Issue definition is relevant whenever it is necessary to understand the operating environment of the organization. See, e.g., Y. Jeon and D. Haider-Markel, "Tracing Issue Definition and Policy Change: An Analysis of Disability Issue Images and Policy Response," *Policy Studies Journal,* 2001, 29(2), pp. 215–31.

Issue advocates: Refers to one of three roles of policy analysts wherein they champion a particular interest (such as the environment or victims of crime). The other two roles are clients' advocates and objective technicians. Issue coalitions refer to the coming together of individuals and organizations that share similar views on the nature of a particular policy problem, what the issues are, and how they should be addressed. Public-sector organizations are said to be more effective at getting issues in the public agenda (and in that process also presumably increasing their own mandates) if they can create and facilitate issue coalitions with those inside and outside government. *See also* **Issue networks**.

Issue coalitions: *See* **Issue advocates**.

Issue diagnosis: Ascertaining the nature and dimensions of a particular issue that needs to be addressed by government. The diagnosis includes, among others, finding out about the attributes of the issue, its depth of incidence, and what scope for action exists.

Issue expansion: A situation where the parameters of a particular issue begin to be expanded so that all the dynamics and all sides of the issue are considered. Issue expansion is almost entirely dependent upon public acceptance so that there is support for its altered state. An issue expander is a policy actor (such as a legislator) whose role is to bring to the open all facets of a particular issue. In some cases, the bureaucracy can play this role. For an example of Singapore, see, K. Ho, *The Politics of Policy-Making in Singapore,* Singapore: Oxford University Press, 2000, p. 122.

Issue fatigue: The disinterest that sets in when a particular issue has been in the public domain for longer than what the public can tolerate. For example, during the 1980s and 1990s aid to developing countries for poverty reduction was characterized by issue fatigue.

Issue initiator: A policy actor that plays a central role in getting attention placed on an issue that merits policy action from government. That role can be played either unwittingly (such as intense public attention on a report that analyzes an issue) or knowingly (such as, for example, a predetermined release of research findings on the costs of a controversial program just prior to the budget debate). See, e.g., D. Palumbo, *Public Policy in America*, New York: Harcourt Brace Jovanovich Publishers, 1989, pp. 37–43.

Issue monopoly: When government is successful in maintaining interest in one particular issue such that it is addressed extensively. The disadvantage of this is that the particular issue takes away a disproportionate share of resources that could have been placed on other equally (or more) important issues. Issue monopoly also keeps the public from placing attention on other pertinent issues and could lead to issue fatigue.

Issue networks: Refers to the product of interactions among public-interest groups that have considerable expert knowledge and that are continually engaged in shaping and re-shaping the dimensions and interpretations of issues and how particular issues are viewed. Invariably for each potential issue, there will be a network of individuals that will support or oppose it. For a general discussion of the term, see, e.g., H. Helco, "Issue Networks and the Executive Establishment," in A. King (ed.), *The New American Political System*, Washington, DC: American Enterprise Institute, 1978, pp. 87–124. *See also* **Issue coalitions**.

Issue paper: A paper prepared by policy analysts that summarizes the issues related to a particular problem. The issue paper serves as a basis for policy analysis and recommendations of appropriate policy options.

Issue-attention cycle: The cyclical process of the public focusing attention on one issue such that a particular issue goes from being unnoticed, although evident, to extensively considered and then "discarded" for another seemingly more important or relevant one. The noted scholar Anthony Downs identified five steps in this cycle: pre-problem stage, alarmed discovery and enthusiasm to resolve it, recognition of costs, decline of public interest, and post-problem stage. See A. Downs, "Up and Down with Ecology—The Attention Cycle," *Public Interest*, 1972, 28(1), pp. 38–50. For an application of the term, see, e.g., J. Blankenau, "The Fate of National Health Insurance in Canada and the United States: A

Multiple Streams Explanation," *Policy Studies Journal,* 2001, 29(1), pp. 38–55.

Item veto: *See* **Line-item veto**.

Iterative process: A method of conducting policy analysis wherein the review process to generate the policy recommendation is repeated continually with new and emerging evidence so that the desired result is eventually arrived at. The purpose of the iterative process is to ensure that as more and more iterations are carried out, the desired result should be more and more evident.

Ivory tower: A term used to describe the nature of work that takes place in academia that is theory-driven, and critics argue not really practical and suitable for government to put into action. *Cf.* **Handmaiden-of-government tradition**.

J

Jawboning: Any pressure that emanates from outside the workplace in order to make disputing parties change their behavior and positions in order that the broader societal and national interests are not compromised. Thus, for example, the prime minister of a country might intervene to let labor and management of a particular industry know that their inability to settle their dispute is detrimental to the national interest.

Job action: Any action taken by employees to get their employer to accede to a concession made by them. A strike, for example, is a job action.

Job analysis: The process of breaking down specific tasks for specific jobs, and determining the associated requirements by way of qualifications (i.e., knowledge, skills, and abilities). Job analysis is used by organizations to make decisions regarding recruitment, managerial load, compensation, and training needs for employees. For a case-study application of job analysis, see, e.g., J. McKillip, "Case Studies in Job Analysis and Training Evaluation," *International Journal of Training and Development*, 2001, 5(4), pp. 283–89. *See also* **Job factors**.

Job brokering: Refers to the process of enabling job seekers to link up with organizations that seek potential candidates. The process of matching individuals that possess specific knowledge, skills, and abilities with jobs that require them is termed job placement.

Job classification: Grouping jobs based on particular criteria, usually the level of difficulty of the job. The job classification/evaluation method is a method of determining how jobs are to be grouped together, for example, by the level of difficulty of the job; the level of knowledge, skills, and abilities; and experiences needed. This classification is then used to determine the total worth of the particular job.

Job content: Refers to the totality of duties and responsibilities of a specific position, including the reporting and accountability arrangements. A related term is job scope, which refers to the range of work outlined for a position. In that regard, it also alludes to the relative complexity of particular tasks.

Job definition: *See* **Job description.**

Job depth: Measure of latitude that an employee is given to make decisions related to the work he/she is performing. In an organization, generally, greater job depth is found the higher up one moves in the hierarchy.

Job description: Also known as a job definition, this is a formal statement of what a job requires (in terms of the work to be done, and what knowledge, skills, and abilities are required for it). A job description is used in recruitment, training, and performance evaluation of employees.

Job design: A process by which various aspects of a job (such as its contents and relationships) are specified. Such a design is done in a manner that allows the attainment of the needs of both the employee and the organization as a whole. Every now and then, when the conditions and context of specific jobs change, they are suitably amended, a process termed job redesign.

Job dilution: *See* **Job fragmentation.**

Job enlargement: Refers to adding more but similar duties to the workload of the employee, that is, increasing the output demand on employees (thus making a job structurally bigger).

Job enrichment: A form of employee motivation where organizations allow employees to use more of their judgment to resolve matters related to their work. In job enrichment, organizations also vary tasks such that employees are given more responsibility. This is also known as vertical loading and allows individuals to get a sense of job fulfillment, which managers use as a motivating measure. See, e.g., F. Herzberg, "One More Time: How Do You Motivate Employees?" *Harvard Business Review*, 1968 (reprinted in the *HBR*, 2003 [January], pp. 87–96).

Job evaluation: A method of ascertaining the worth of a job. Two of the most sought after outcomes of job evaluation are: (a) consistency of internal pay equity, and (b) competitiveness of pay within the external market. Organizations also use market conditions to determine compensation levels. See, e.g., D. Figart, "Equal Pay for Equal Work: The Role of Job Evaluation in an Evolving Social Norm," *Journal of Economic Issues*, 2000, 34(1), pp. 1–19. *See also* **Job size**.

Job exchange: Also referred to as a stretch assignment, this is a process of moving employees around different jobs as a way of transmitting new experiences and thus enhancing their competencies. Job exchanges are possible when different units within an organization (or different organizations themselves) see benefits in such. *See also* **Job rotation**.

Job factors: Variables that are taken into consideration while analyzing any job. These normally include the task to be done and the context in which it is to be done; its complexity; the knowledge, skills, and abilities needed to perform the duties of a specific job; personal relationships; accountability; and span of control.

Job fragmentation: Also known as job dilution, this refers to breaking up specific requirements of a job so that different parts can be done by different individuals or so that the same employee can better manage the work by making it discrete and manageable. Job fragmentation may be done, for example, if it is determined that the employee is not able to efficiently fulfill all the tasks expected of him/her, or if the job itself becomes more and more specialized, as happens in technology-related work.

Job loading: Refers to a process of assigning greater and/or more varied duties and responsibilities to a particular job so as to provide the employee who performs the job an opportunity to enhance his/her on-the-job knowledge, skills, and abilities, and to provide greater motivation. Job loading can be of two types: (a) horizontal job loading (i.e., adding new tasks at the same level of responsibility), and (b) vertical job loading (i.e., adding new tasks with greater responsibilities, and, therefore, more scope for a sense of personal self-worth and achievement). See F. Herzberg, "One More Time: How Do You Motivate Employees?" *Harvard Business Review*, 1968 (reprinted in the *HBR*, 2003 [January], pp. 87–96).

Job lock: The inability of an individual to quit a particular job for fear of losing the benefits that are associated with it. A job lock then implies that the individual is motivated by extrinsic factors alone. *See also* **Golden handcuffs.**

Job mobility: The process of moving employees around different parts of the organization doing work at the same responsibility level. Job mobility can also be initiated by employees themselves, particularly if they see opportunities for career growth as a result of being mobile.

Job pairing: *See* **Job sharing.**

Job placement: *See* **Job brokering.**

Job range: The tasks of a particular job that the employee is expected to perform. While some jobs have a narrow range (such as clerical support), others have a much broader one (such as providing the overall direction of the organization's work).

Job ranking: The most basic method of job evaluation in which all the jobs in an organization are ranked subjectively in accordance with how they are perceived to be relevant and important to the organization. One of the criteria in job ranking is normally the degree to which a particular job is considered critical to the core competence of the organization. *See also* **Job evaluation.**

Job redesign: *See* **Job design.**

Job restructuring: Changing the nature of tasks that are required as part of a job. Employers will need to continually restructure jobs because change will take place in the operating environment. These may include: (a) the mandate has expanded or contracted or shifted, (b) the individuals they hire bring multiple skills and managers would like thus to expand their roles, and (c) the manner in which the mandate is fulfilled changes due to the introduction of new techniques and technology. See, e.g., W. Pasmore, "Overcoming the Roadblocks in Work-Restructuring Efforts," *Organizational Dynamics*, 1982, 10(4), 54–67.

Job rotation: When an employee moves horizontally through different jobs in an organization, that is, does dissimilar work but work that is at the same responsibility level. Job rotation is encouraged as a way of giving employees different experiences in an organization so as to enhance their skills.

Job satisfaction: The pleasure that an individual gets from knowing that he/she has done particularly well at work. Job satisfaction is different across individuals. In general, an individual's performance leads to the attainment of some outcomes that ultimately lead to job satisfaction, but this remains a difficult concept to operationalize. See, e.g., E. Locke, "The Nature and Causes of Job Satisfaction," in M. Dunnette (ed.), *Handbook of Industrial and Organizational Psychology*, Chicago: Rand McNally, 1976, pp. 1297–1349.

Job scope: *See* **Job content**.

Job security: Protection of a job that is accorded to some employees. This means that there are safeguards against demotion and discharge that are not based on poor performance or some violation of organizational policies. With the wide-reaching extent of reforms in the public-management sector across many jurisdictions, and in particular in human-resource management, job security has become less of a pre-occupation of employers of late.

Job sharing: Also known as job pairing, the term refers to the sharing of a particular job by two individuals. This means that the individuals either divide the total number of hours to be worked and perform the same tasks or spend distinct periods separately on the job. While job sharing is a way of ensuring employment continuity for individuals, it does require that both be subject to the same performance evaluation criteria.

Job size: The measurement of the level of requirements for a particular job. Job size consists of three elements: (a) know-how (i.e., the sum total of all the skills needed to do the job well, including technical know how, managerial know-how, and human-relations know-how), (b) problem solving (i.e., the thinking required to reason and arrive at conclusions, including the freedom to think, and level of thinking challenge), and (c) accountability (i.e., the answerability for actions, including the degree of freedom to act, and the size and type of impact). Job size is one determinant of the level of compensation in the organization (the others being affordability of the organization, historical compensation levels, etc.).

Job specialization: A situation where an individual performs only specific tasks but is an expert at doing them. It is obvious that job specialization tends to enhance labor productivity; however, it is also possible that such specialization tends to restrict the individual's possibilities of employment mobility given the narrow range of skills that will have developed as a result of the specialization. On the other hand, employers have an incentive to encourage job specialization since with the consequent disaggregation and desegregation of tasks (which yield job specialization in the first place) there is less danger of loss of proprietary knowledge should one specialist leave the organization.

Job specification: *See* **Position.**

Joined-up government: An ideal condition wherein agencies collaborate with each other to provide services to the public, which minimizes the transaction costs for them, particularly if they need to be in touch with several governmental departments to resolve a particular problem. A joined-up government requires strong networks and that these networks work with one another for shared outcomes. For an attempt at an application of the concept, see, e.g., Cabinet Office (United Kingdom), *Modernizing Government,* London: Her Majesty's Stationery Office, 1999, cm 4310. For an analysis of the issue, see, e.g., G. Mulgan, "Joined Up Government in the United Kingdom: Past, Present, and Future," *Canberra Bulletin of Public Administration,* 2002, 105 (September), pp. 25–29.

Joint evaluation: Evaluation that is done by different agencies coming together for the purpose of reviewing an organization, a program, or a policy. For example, donor-funded projects and programs will normally have a party from the donor agency, the national government, and the program management team in any evaluation group. Results from the joint evaluation are normally deemed credible because of the presence of different parties in the group.

Joint monitoring: As applied in the context of central agencies and governmental departments, joint monitoring refers to the collaboration between monitoring agencies in the collection and analysis of information about departments. It is generally assumed that such collaboration leads to improvements in the monitoring agencies' ability to advise governmental ministers and to reductions in the compliance costs for departments in dealing with multiple agencies.

Jointness of supply: *See* **Nonrivalry.**

Judgmental strategy: *See* **Decision-making strategy.**

Judicial activism: Denotes the increasing involvement of the courts in public affairs (particularly in that of governmental departments), and where they have interpreted their oversight function too aggressively. This judicial influence has led some to conclude that policy implementation has become "judicialized." See, e.g., R. O'Leary and J. Straussman, "The Impact of Courts on Public Management," in B. Bozeman (ed.), *Public Management: The State of the Art,* San Francisco: Jossey-Bass, 1993, pp. 189–205.

Judicial independence: A situation where neither the executive nor the legislature can unduly influence the recruitment of judges and of the operations of the judiciary branch of government. Judicial independence is considered important if there is to be an effective check on the powers of government.

Judicial review: A court review of an agency's administrative action. The courts can also, because of judicial review, declare as unconstitutional any such action by the executive branch or the legislature.

Judiciary: The judiciary is the system of law courts that exists in a country, and is one of the three branches of government (along with the legislature and the executive). It is the judiciary that interprets the laws and makes decisions on the legality and validity of laws passed by the legislature if there is a challenge.

Jurisdictional externalities: Any resource or good that crosses political boundaries (renewable resources such as rivers are a good example of jurisdictional externalities). Because jurisdictional externalities are related to the ownership rights of different jurisdictions of the same resources (or the part that is within their boundaries), and yet the exercise of that right is to a large extent contingent upon the actions of other jurisdictions, there is a need for a cross-jurisdictional coordination of efforts to manage the resources. See, e.g., G. Brown, "Renewable Natural Resource Management and Use without Markets," *Journal of Economic Literature*, 2000, 38(4), pp. 875–914.

Jurisdictional fragmentation: The separation over who has authority over what as evidenced either between organizations (such as the U.S. State Department and the Pentagon) or between levels of government (such as between the U.S. federal and state governments). A useful discussion of this concept is given in the introductory chapter in David King's *Turf Wars: How Congressional Committees Claim Jurisdiction*, Chicago: University of Chicago Press, 1997; see also, e.g., B. Jones, F. Baumgartner, and J. Talbert, "The Destruction of Issue Monopolies in Congress," *American Political Science Review*, 1993, 87(3), pp. 657–71.

Just-in-time approach: A concept borrowed from the private sector that looks at how best to supply raw materials and inputs when they are needed in the production process so that storage and other costs are minimized. As applied in public-sector organizations, a just-in-time approach is increasingly being used to explain the tendency to cut staff size and instead rely on the spot market to acquire capability to get something done. This just-in-time approach may fix the short-term aspect of goal attainment but underestimates the long-term costs of not having in-house capability that may be more cost effective for the organization. See, e.g., J. Atkinson, "Flexibility or Fragmentation?" *Labor and Society*, 1987, 12(1), pp. 87–105. *See also* **Make-or-buy decision**.

K

Kepner-Tregoe model: A model of organizational decision making and problem structuring (named after the two management consultants, Charles Kepner and Benjamin Tregoe, who developed it) that comprises the following four major components: (a) situational appraisal, (b) problem analysis that results from the situational appraisal, (c) decision analysis (based on the nature of the problem identified), and (d) potential-problem analysis. This last component (potential-problem analysis) provides a strategic perspective and also introduces some form of rationality into the decision-making process. For their original model, see C. Kepner and B. Tregoe, *The Rational Manager: A Systematic Approach to Problem Solving and Decision-Making*, New York: McGraw-Hill, 1965.

Key competencies: *See* **Basic skills**.

Key priorities: Also known as key results areas, key priorities (for example, a trusted public service, or better health outcomes for disadvantaged groups) are the main objectives that an organization will focus on in the medium term (i.e., up to three years). The priorities will be of high impact and be strategically significant that will contribute, wherever possible, to one or other of the government's key goals. See, e.g., A. Matheson, "Governing Strategically: The New Zealand Experience," *Public Administration and Development*, 1998, 18(4), pp. 349–63. *See also* **Strategic results areas**.

KITA: Stands for "kick in the ass" attempts at motivating employees. Motivation theorist Frederick Herzberg used the term to show that such attempts (both physical and psychological) could be negative (such as through strong criticism) or positive (such as through substantial monetary rewards for good performance). See F. Herzberg, "One More Time: How Do You Motivate Employees?" *Harvard Business Review*, 1968, 46, pp. 53–62 (reprinted in the *HBR*, 2003 [January], pp. 87–96).

Kitchen cabinet: An informal cabinet that consists of the president's or prime minister's closest and most trusted advisors. The term was first used in relation to the informal cabinet that U.S. president Andrew Jackson turned to for advice and political support.

Kitemark: As used in training, this term refers to an indication of quality of training provision measured by: (a) the training process utilized; (b) the qualification attained by the trainees; and (c) the amount of expenditure spent on the training provision. See OECD, *Manual for Better Training Statistics: Conceptual, Measurement and Survey Issues,* Paris: OECD, 1997, p. 252.

Knock-on effects: Follow-on impact from changes in one particular variable as a result of some organizational action. Almost all organizational action has knock-on effects and they generally tend to have the potential to be uncontrollable. Such effects could be either positive (such as on motive to return to the workforce as a result of a hand-out during lean times) or negative (such as continued dependence on the hand-outs). Policy analysts need to be on the lookout for such effects in the analysis they perform on new policy proposals.

Knowledge assets: Different knowledge strengths that an organization can possess in the pursuit of organizational objectives. Such knowledge assets can be considered to be of four categories: (a) experiential (i.e., the collective judgment and know-how of employees), (b) conceptual (i.e., explicit manifestations of organizational brand, customer relationships, stakeholder management, etc.), (c) systemic (i.e., product specifications, strategic plans, etc.), and (d) routine (i.e., the organization's daily routines). See, e.g., R. Bodle, "Mobilizing Tacit Knowledge," *Organizations & People,* 2001, 8(3), pp. 2–10.

Knowledge capture: The process of documenting the knowledge that an organization already possesses so that others in the organization—and in some cases, outsiders as well—can readily access it in its entirety. Unless there are well-designed document-management systems, including policies that are designed to ensure that such records are kept, knowledge capture will be weak and the organization will lose valuable stock of knowledge for future use.

Knowledge gap: The difference between what an organization needs to know (or access) to fulfill its mandate effectively and what it currently does. Such knowledge gaps can be of two types: (a) gaps to do with process issues (such as inefficient management systems that are reflected in budget bids), or (b) gaps to do with content issues (such as weak policy advice that is tendered to governmental ministers). Such gaps can be filled either by revamping the operational base of the organization or by recruiting from outside to acquire the competencies needed to fill the content gap. See, e.g., R. Hall and P. Andriani, "Managing Knowledge for Innovation," *Long Range Planning*, 2002, 35(1), pp. 29–48.

Knowledge hierarchy: *See* **Information hierarchy**.

Knowledge migration: Also known as knowledge transfer, this is the process of passing information and knowledge from one entity (individual or organization) to another. Just as with any other transfer mechanism, there is a danger here that some knowledge will be lost or discarded in the transfer process unless knowledge systems in the organization are rigorous (such as the accurate documentation of all aspects of development of a particular product or service).

Knowledge organization: An organization that produces and uses knowledge as part of its operations. Knowledge in an organization can be of two types: (a) component knowledge (which focuses on the individual element under inspection, i.e., at the individual or unit), or (b) architectural knowledge (which looks at the collective aspect of the component knowledge). For a discussion of these types of knowledge, see, e.g., R. Henderson and K. Clark, "Architectural Innovation: The Reconfiguration of Existing Product Technologies and the Failure of Established Firms," *Administrative Science Quarterly*, 1990, 35(1), pp. 9–30.

Knowledge pool: *See* **Policy knowledge pool**.

Knowledge pyramid: *See* **Information hierarchy**.

Knowledge sharing: The process of disseminating information and knowledge inside and outside the organization. Knowledge management adds value to the organization when it is shared widely so that others can add to the stock of knowledge that exists on any particular issue. Broadscale introduction of information technologies in the workplace helps in the sharing process, but what is also important is that organizations have policies that encourage such sharing, and just as critical, that employees internalize this predilection for sharing knowledge with others.

Knowledge spillover: Refers to a situation where there are no restrictions on the flow of knowledge (information) between organizations and other parties. Such spillovers can be either intergenerational (i.e., temporal) or interjurisdictional (i.e., spatial). Knowledge spillovers lead to the problem of free riding because those benefiting from the knowledge once it is gained do not pay any charges. For a cogent review of this concept, see, e.g., J. Eeckhout and B. Jovanovic, "Knowledge Spillovers, and Inequality," *American Economic Review,* 2003, 92(5), pp. 1290–1307.

Knowledge spiral: A notion that refers to the process of ever-growing knowledge that is generated from interactions between, say, operational managers and academic researchers. Each group feeds off the other (e.g., the researcher could be based in an organization or the manager could be attached to an academic institution for a period of time) and the knowledge so gained enhances their ability to better understand and address organizational problems. See, e.g., I. Nonaka and N. Konno, "The Concept of 'Ba': Building a Foundation for Knowledge Creation," *California Management Review,* 1998, 40(3), pp. 40–54.

Knowledge transfer: *See* **Knowledge migration**.

Knowledge worker: The management theorist Peter Drucker used the term to denote someone who works professionally with the knowledge he/she has gained from education and prior experiences and who also generates and utilizes relevant knowledge. Knowledge workers take responsibility for mastering their work and for sharing that knowledge/learning so gained with others in the organization. They also continually update their skills base, and in that process help their organization adapt to new environments.

L

Labor hoarding: Another term for overstaffing. If organizations can afford the added payroll expenditure, they will continue to keep the extra staff in the event that their turnover rate becomes high. Labor hoarding is particularly evident for occupations for which the supply of labor is constrained. This can arise due to various reasons, including deliberate government policy to restrict intake in institutions producing graduates in certain occupations. Labor hoarding can be a rational decision, similar to paying an insurance premium.

Labor mobility: The ease of movement of workers across jobs and occupations as well as geographic locations. Labor mobility in an economy denotes that there is flexibility and openness in a labor market. Labor mobility is evident in the public sector in the same manner as in the private. However, a particular variance here is deliberate policies that governmental agencies charged with managing the public service may institute that actively encourage staff members, particularly at the senor level, to be mobile in the public service as well as beyond. This mobility is considered useful in providing opportunities to those with the potential for leadership positions to enhance their repertoire of competencies.

Lag: In the public-policy context, a lag is the difference in time between the formulation of a policy and its implementation, including its ultimate impact. This is termed a policy lag, which refers to the period between a particular event that merits a policy and the impact of the policy. Inherent in policy lags are three other types of lags: (a) recognition lag (the time it takes for policy makers to recognize the state of a situation), (b) implementation lag (the time it takes for policy makers to act once they recognize a situation as requiring action), and (c) impact lag (the time it takes for the full impact of the policy). In general, changes in policy and policy structure generally take place with long lags, because it takes a considerable amount of time to push through major change in the public-policy domain.

Laggard organizations: Organizations that are reluctant to adopt new operational methods. Laggard organizations are generally characterized by a low level of innovation capacity and insufficient internal drive to adapt readily to new environments. Laggard organizations also lack the capacity to use existing institutional knowledge to improve their internal administrative processes. For a case-study application, see, e.g., R. Kanter, "Can Higher Education 'Evolve'? Mastering the Challenges of Change," in M. Devlin, R. Larson, and J. Meyerson (eds.), *The Internet and the University,* Boulder, CO: Educause, 2003, pp. 39–80.

Laissez-faire: Originally taken to mean the desirability of the respective, somewhat autonomous, roles of government and business in society. As used in the public-administration and management context, this refers to the hands-off style of management and a considerable devolution of decision-making authority. In the public-sector reforms of the mid-1980s in New Zealand, for example, there was a freeing up of the central control that was exercised in the management of the senior executive service, and Public Service departments were also given a free rein to manage their own human resources. This laissez-faire approach to departmental management has its advantages and disadvantages, but on the whole it has given departmental chief executives more incentives and authority to manage their own affairs without the undue imposition of a central agency. *Cf.* **Dirigisme.**

Last in, first out: A method in human-resource management and cutback management whereby the last person to be hired is normally the first one to be fired in the event of layoffs. This is generally the standard position that unions take in the collective-bargaining process with management.

Latent learning: *See* **Incidental learning.**

Lateral entry: Also known as an open career, a lateral entry is the appointment of an individual from outside the organizational hierarchy, which means that the individual will not have to move through the ranks of the organization. Lateral entry is taken as a form of competition since careerists within the organization will not necessarily be automatically guaranteed upward mobility. While lateral entry has its advantage in that it introduces an element of external competition to the appointment process, it also tends to demotivate those within the organization who may feel that their opportunities for advancement have been reduced. *See also* **Internal promotion.**

Lateral job movement: *See* **Lateral entry.**

Lateral team: Task forces that are created whose members come from different parts of an organization although generally from approximately the same level in the hierarchy. Lateral teams allow for the introduction of various approaches to determining the solutions to organizational problems and to doing things differently. Lateral teams are the most appropriate when organizations have to deal with complex problems requiring varied solution mixes. *See also* **Horizontal work group.**

Law of bureaucratic assimilation: Asserts that the time it takes for an idea to be internalized in governmental departments depends very much on the number of agencies that are needed to have the idea adopted. The argument is that the greater the number of agencies that have to buy into a particular idea, the greater the chances that the bureaucratic interests of some will collide, thus making it difficult for the idea to be assimilated. *See also* **Factorial problem.**

Law of critical junctures: Asserts that because policy making is generally characterized by uneven developments (i.e., a policy does not always smoothly transition itself; there are bound to be delays as well as rapid transformations along the way), there are considered to be several critical junctures in the formulation of a policy. It is at these critical junctures that the dimensions, speed, and attributes of a policy could undergo substantive change. One such critical juncture, for example, is when a draft policy recommendation is first exposed to relevant stakeholders. For a discussion of the concept of critical junctures, see, e.g., D. Richards and M. Smith, "How Departments Change: Windows of Opportunity and Critical Junctures in Three Departments," *Public Policy and Administration,* 1997, 12(2), pp. 62–79.

Law of decreasing coordination: Asserts that the larger any organization becomes, the poorer is the co-ordination among its actions. This is so because the increase in the number of components compounds the interaction problem substantially. *See also* **Factorial problem**.

Law of diminishing control: Similar to the law of diminishing returns in economics, this law states that the larger an organization becomes, the weaker is the control over its action exercised by those at the top. This law is also evident in the span of control dimension. For a case-study example of this law, see J. Cohan, "'I didn't know and 'I was only doing my job': Has Corporate Governance Careened out of Control? A Case Study of Enron's Information Myopia," *Journal of Business Ethics,* 2002, 40(3), pp. 275–99.

Law of effect: States simply that what will be learned/avoided by individuals are those things that provide satisfaction/nuisance. The law of effect is a basic concept in human learning, but has important cues for how employees internalize organizational values. See, e.g., D. Dennett, "Why the Law of Effect Will Not Go Away," *Journal for the Theory of Social Behavior,* 1972, 2(2), pp. 167–87.

Law of emulation: Asserts that in government, as elsewhere, if one branch has a resource for policy making then another branch must have one as well. Organizational rivalry as well as turf battles characterize the law of emulation, which could lead eventually to organizational dysfunction. See L. Koenig, *An Introduction to Public Policy,* Englewood Cliffs, NJ: Prentice Hall, 1986, p. 82.

Law of genesis of structure: Asserts that as a result of any regular communication among organizational entities, there emerges a social structure among such entities that is a function of the regularity of communication. How fast such a structure is created depends upon: (a) how complex the communication is, (b) how many entities are involved in it, and (c) how quickly messages are relayed back and forth.

This law is helpful in describing the emergence of an organizational culture and how the culture is conveyed to organizational members.

Law of immediate reinforcement: In training, this law states that learning in participants is likely to be enhanced if reinforcements (i.e., rewards) are made at the point of incidence of learning, that is, at the moment of evidence of learning. This positive reinforcement (i.e., stimulus), it is argued, enables participants to better internalize the learning.

Law of imperfect control: The noted scholar Anthony Downs' assertion that it is not possible to control the behavior of a large organization. Also, in large organizations, because of their multiplicity and complexity of relationships and processes, organizational leaders are not entirely able to be on top of all organizational action. See A. Downs, *Inside Bureaucracy,* Boston: Little, Brown, 1967, pp. 143–45.

Law of primacy: As used in the context of training, this law asserts that whatever participants learnt first is likely to remain with them as ingrained learning. A related concept is the law of recency, which, as used in the context of training, asserts that learning that is recent is likely to be retained the most by individuals. This tells trainers how they need to structure their programs to maximize relevant learning in participants. See, e.g., N. Miller and D. Campbell, "Recency and Primacy in Persuasion as Function of the Timing of Speeches and Measurements," *Journal of Abnormal and Social Psychology,* 1959, 59(1), pp, 1–9.

Law of recency: *See* **Law of primacy**.

Law of regulatory models: Asserts that a regulatory system must contain a model of that which it is regulating so that its characteristics can be internalized in the regulatory system. This allows the system to be dynamic enough to help explain the regulated entity/industry. For example, if a particular industry is undergoing rapid transformation, then a regulatory system for that industry should be constructed such that its composition and structure can alter at a moment's notice. *See also* **Law of requisite variety**.

Law of requisite constraint: Asserts that every organization should have sufficient knowledge about its environment so that it will know what will not lead to correct action in order not to have to do things time and again. A related concept is the law of requisite knowledge, which says that in order to deal with all possible scenarios, an organization would have to have adequate knowledge so that the search for the correct choice is made with some degree of confidence rather than blindly. Such knowledge could come from prior experience with similar cases (such as economic crises from around the world or from the same jurisdiction in previous years), the expertise that is resident in the system itself, the reliance on expertise from the spot market, or elsewhere.

Law of requisite knowledge: *See* **Law of requisite constraint**.

Law of requisite variety: Also known as Ashby's law, this law states that for appropriate regulations of an entity/industry to occur, the regulator must have as much as—or maybe even more—variety than what is being regulated. Ashby asserted that in active regulations, variety is needed to manage variety. The implications are that those involved in regulatory functions need to maximize internal variety to be prepared for any contingency. See W. Ashby, "Requisite Variety and Its Implications for the Control of Complex Systems," *Cybernetica,* 1958, 1(2), pp. 83–99. *See also* **Law of regulatory models**.

Law of unintended consequences: States that each policy action creates new problems, which, in turn, can be solved only by coming up with more policies. This leads to a spiral of government activity that feeds onto itself. For an example, see K. Ho, *The Politics of Policy-Making in Singapore,* Singapore: Oxford University Press, 2000, pp. 17–18.

Law of the situation: States that in those times when organizations and groups face adverse situations, there should be more emphasis on reading cues from the situation and what knowledge can be generated than on who should be giving orders and who should merely follow. See, e.g., M. Follett, "The Giving of Orders," in H. Metcalf and L. Urwick (eds.), *Dynamic Administration: The Collected Papers of Mary Parker Follett,* New York: Harper & Brothers Publishers, 1940, pp. 50–70.

Layer-cake federalism: Also known as dual federalism, this is the traditional view of federalism wherein there is no interaction between the various layers of governments in a federal system, and each layer of government performs its functions more or less separate from the other. However, in modern times, layer-cake federalism has waned in practice.

Lead agency: The agency that is leading work on a particular cross-agency program. Such lead work involves coordinating the input of various members of different agencies and preparing the final report of the program. Lead agencies for particular pieces of work are determined in several ways, including the extent to which the relevant governmental minister is able to either retain or divest ownership of the particular issue.

Leadership: Generally described as the exercise of authority over others. Such exercise of authority can be evident in several dichotomous ways, for example, formal versus informal (i.e., as mandated by law or organizational procedures vs. traditional acceptance), and directive versus coordinating (i.e., dictating to others as opposed to considering others' views as well). The concept of leadership has been well described in the literature; for an early but enduring discussion, see P. Selznick, *Leadership in Administration,* New York: Row, Peterson, and Company, 1957. For an updated and comprehensive review of leadership theories in application in the public sector, see M. Van Wart, "Public-Sector Leadership Theory: An Assessment," *Public Administration Review,* 2003, 63(2), pp. 214–28. *See also* **Transactional leadership**; **Transformational leadership**.

Leadership, contingency theory of: A theory that argues that the notion of leadership needs to be viewed from the perspective of what the context is in which a particular form of leadership is exercised. Thus, one type of leadership evident in one jurisdiction/situation is not similar to the same exercised in another jurisdiction/situation.

Leadership ecology: A concept that refers to a situation where leadership is made to be a valued mode of organizational behavior. This means that organizational leaders at all levels are active in motivating others, to mobilize them for action. See, e.g., R. Fulmer and J. Keys, "A Conversation with Peter Senge: New Developments in Organizational Learning," *Organizational Dynamics,* 1998, 27(2), pp. 33–42.

Leadership grid: *See* **Managerial grid.**

Leadership networks: Necessary for policy change and policy leadership, these networks are designed to place network members in key stages of the reform process so that there is collective momentum regarding the reforms. See, e.g., J. Wallis and B. Dollery, *Market Failure, Government Failure, Leadership and Public Policy,* Houndmills, Basingstoke: Macmillan, 1999, p. 116.

Leadership role constellation: Refers to the degree of complementarity that may exist in any group of leaders in an organization. The greater the leadership role constellation, the easier to push through organizational change. See, e.g., J. Denis, A. Langley, and M. Pineault, "Becoming a Leader in a Complex Organization," *Journal of Management Studies,* 2000, 37(8), pp. 1063–99.

Lean and mean organization: An organization that is better suited to fulfill its mission because: (a) of a reduced workforce (hence with no or little overcapacity), (b) of an increase in its human-resources skills, and (c) it is better targeted toward its goals.

Learned behavior: Organizational members—as human beings—will all have developed behaviors that follow patterns that have been learned. Those behaviors that prove to be favorable will be replicated and those that do not will be discarded (or at least put away until a suitable opportunity emerges in which to apply them). Managers need to be aware of such learned behaviors of staff members so that they may be better able to channel organizational responses to them.

Learned implementation: Refers to the process of learning that is generated when policies are actually implemented. Two key components of learned implementation are: (a) knowledge generation as a function of the actual operations (as opposed to lessons drawn, for example, from the experiences of others), and (b) the implication of a feedback process that is in place which ensures that the lessons so learned are fed back into the policy generation stage. Learned implementation is more evident where policy directives are ambiguous and bureaucrats need to learn a range of new and detailed techniques to implement them effectively. See, e.g., J. Schofield, "A Model of Learned Implementation," *Public Administration,* 2004, 82(2), pp. 283–308. *See also* **Policy learning**.

Learned routines: Refers to the behavior of individuals (and collectively, organizations) involved in set ways of doing things and in carrying out functional activities. These activities could include anything from processing applications and permits to strategizing and adapting to environmental pressures. Such learned routines, if positive, become a key component of organizational capability; if negative, they serve to debilitate the organization. For a cogent analysis of learned routines and organizational capability, see, e.g., A. Chandler, "Organizational Capabilities and the Economic History of the Industrial Enterprise," *Journal of Economic Perspectives,* 1992, 6(3), pp. 79–100.

Learner analysis: Before providing any training, trainers will first analyze the competencies, backgrounds, and learning objectives of all participants. This is what learner analysis refers to. It is a useful exercise since it provides an appropriate backdrop to the work of those providing the training. It also serves as a useful benchmark against which to measure the learning that is hoped to be instilled in the trainees.

Learning: A process of acquiring knowledge and then using that knowledge to adapt to new ways of doing things. Learning implies changes in behavior and greater efficiency in doing things, and in this sense it means much more than merely acquiring new information. Learning can be of several types, but three that are relevant in the public-sector context include: generative learning, routine learning, and strategic learning. Generative learning is when employees are encouraged to see the organization's "big picture" so that they themselves know where and how they fit into the organization vis-à-vis its mandates. Once that organizational purpose is ingrained in their thought processes, collective learning is facilitated, wherein systematic problem solving and trying out new ideas becomes more of a norm. Routine learning is when organizations take feedback from their operational environment and make changes to their routine (i.e., in their day-to-day operations). Finally, strategic learning is when organizations take feedback from their environments and seek to fundamentally align the organization in consonance with what they see as the new realities of their environments. For a discussion of how learning can take place in organizations, see, e.g., C. James, "Designing Learning Organizations," *Organizational Dynamics,* 2003, 32(1), pp. 46–61. *See also* **Selective learning**.

Learning by doing: Where an employee learns and develops new competencies by doing and being exposed to actual job situations rather than through formal instruction. *See also* **Experiential learning**.

Learning circle: Refers to a group of employees (normally small in number) in an organization who enhance their learning of the work by engaging in critical discussions of work-related tasks. A learning circle is a key component of a quality circle.

Learning organization: An organization that focuses on enhancing learning and new ways of doing this in its operational and strategic environments. A learning organization changes the way it does things based on evaluations of its experiences. See, e.g., R. Teare and R. Dealtry, "Building and Sustaining a Learning Organization," *The Learning Organization,* 1998, 5(1), pp. 47–60. *See also* **Double-loop learning**; **Organizational learning**.

Learning spillover: *See* **Knowledge spillover**.

Least-cost governance framework: A framework that draws from the ideas of transaction-cost economics in considering how the costs of governance could be minimized in a jurisdiction. These include, for example: (a) a credible commitment from the executive to fulfill its functions efficiently, (b) contracting out of provisions of all goods and services that can be performed by private providers and at least costs, (c) enforcement of existing regulations to ensure adherence to the rules of the game, and (d) the residual work to be performed by the public service with strict accountability to the legislature. For a discussion of this concept in relation to the management of asset portfolios by governmental agencies, see, e.g., N. Davis, *Governance of Crown Financial Assets,* Treasury Working Paper, 98/2, Wellington: The Treasury, 1998, pp. 11–12.

Legal imperative: A requirement of administrators and governmental officials to obey the law as well as the formal interpretations of it as may have been made by courts and other judicial organs. *See also* **Consensual imperative**.

Legal inconsistency, problem of: When the intent of two or more laws conflict with each other, or when old laws (that are still on the books) conflict with new ones. Such a situation obviously creates confusion among citizens and among those organizations charged with implementing the laws. For an analysis of this problem, see, e.g., V. Tanzi, *The Role of the State and the Quality of the Public Sector,* IMF Working Paper, WP/00/36, Washington, DC: International Monetary Fund, March 2000, p. 10.

Legal rationality: *See* **Rationality.**

Legality criterion: A criterion in ascertaining behavioral standards that states that the laws of a country (and other associated rules of an organization) are adequate to serve as the basis on which the actions of organizations can be judged correct and ethical. This means that the organization is more inclined to give priority to adhering to legality than to morality. This could be evident, for example, when organizations stick to the letter of the law and thus meet the minimum required of them legally without doing anything more to enhance their social responsibility to the communities that they serve. *See also* **Common-practice criterion**.

Legislative action: Any step taken by a legislature that affects how governance is carried out in a jurisdiction. A legislative action can include, for example, the passage of a law, the determination of a budget, the formulation of a policy, or the receipt of reports from government departments (particularly as they relate to how funds have been spent). Some actions (such as budget determination) have to be accepted by the executive as well (in some jurisdictions), but generally, legislative action is contained within the realm of the legislature itself.

Legislative activism: An active and aggressive legislature that is keen to pursue its own agenda in public-policy matters. Such activism is possible where the separation of powers between branches of government (such as in the United States) facilitates an environment for the legislature to be active. See, e.g., R. Pilon, "Legislative Activism, Judicial Activism, and the Decline of Private Sovereignty," *Cato Journal,* 1985, 4(3), pp. 813–33.

Legislative agenda: The programs and policies that the legislature announces, some of which require executive approval as well. The legislative agenda is set by the party or parties (if they are in coalition) that hold the majority of seats in the legislature.

Legislative audit: An audit by a specialized body within a legislature of a governmental activity that uses public funds. A legislative audit is considered to be more independent than a regular audit because the executive itself is not conducting its own audit. It also serves as a form of legislative scrutiny, which is the review that the legislature (either collectively or through specific committees) undertakes to ensure that governmental departments and others are keeping to their accountabilities.

Legislative decoupling: The separation of accountabilities for outputs and outcomes as mandated by law. Such legislative decoupling is evident, for example, when departmental heads are made responsible for outputs (i.e., goods and services) and governmental ministers are made responsible for outcomes (i.e., the results that are effected by the outputs). The purpose of legislative decoupling is to ensure that ministers are kept away from directly intervening in the affairs of the departments so that they are better able to fulfill their mandates. Ministers may set policy parameters and monitor departments, but may not influence them. See, e.g., R. Shaw, "Rehabilitating the Public Service—Alternatives to the Wellington Model," in S. Chatterjee (ed.), *The New Politics: A Third Way for New Zealand,* Palmerston North, New Zealand: Dunmore Press, 1999, p. 198–201.

Legislative intent: Refers to the purported real meaning of a particular law as interpreted by those executing it and those determining its legality. Since legislative intent is not determined by the original framers of the law, there is potential for a fair bit of difference in the interpretation of a particular law, which inevitably creates stress and tensions among rival advocates.

Legislative oversight: The various methods by which a legislature (either collectively or through specific committees) monitors the work of governmental departments so as to ensure that laws are executed in the manner and spirit in which they were formulated. Legislative oversight also includes the determination of whether departments have spent the resources appropriated to them in the manner and for the purposes that were specified *ex ante*.

Legislative scrutiny: *See* **Legislative audit.**

Legislative veto: Refusal by the legislature to accept an executive or administrative action. There are constraints around applying the legislative veto, however. In the United States, for example, the Supreme Court in 1983 invalidated Congress's legislative veto authority over executive action, declaring it unconstitutional.

Legitimacy: Receiving support from the public for a particular policy where the support is based on the premise that the entity formulating such policy has taken the public interest as a primary consideration. Legitimacy is said to be "granted" when: (a) the policy conforms to established rules, (b) the rules can be justified by reference to beliefs shared by the general public, and (c) there is evidence of consent by subordinates. See, e.g., D. Beetham, *The Legitimation of Power,* London: Macmillan Education, Ltd., 1991, p. 16.

Legitimacy deficit: A situation that arises when decisions (for example, policies) that legal entities make are considered to be inappropriate for some reason or other (but primarily because they are not considered to be made with the public interest at heart). See, e.g., D. Beetham, *The Legitimation of Power,* London: Macmillan Education, Ltd., 1991, p. 209.

Legitimacy of policy actions: Refers to public acceptance of policy actions made by a particular legal entity. Such legitimacy must be based on one (or more) of three foundations: (a) legality, (b) tradition (i.e., fitting the general patterns of past practice), and (c) charisma (and, therefore, more amenable for a lawmaker to accept the policy action being proposed). Such legitimacy comes from legitimate power, which is power based on legitimate sources, such as election to public office, or a manager's formal position in an organizational hierarchy. See, e.g., L. Koenig, *An Introduction to Public Policy,* Englewood Cliffs, NJ: Prentice Hall, 1986, p. 230.

Legitimacy trap: Refers to the rejection by an organization of a valuable learning opportunity because the impetus emanates from a source the organization considers not legitimate (i.e., not valid). For a discussion of the concept and organizational learning, see, e.g., C. Zietsma et al., "The

War of the Woods: Facilitators and Impediments of Organizational Learning Processes," *British Journal of Management,* 2002, 13(September), pp. S61-S74.

Lesson drawing: Studying other management practices and determining how one can learn from them. Lesson drawing is a key feature of contemporary policy making. The following are seen as some forms of lesson drawing: emulation (i.e., applying the essence rather than the details), hybridization (i.e., combining substantive elements of one institution with that of another), and inspiration (i.e., to give ideas on something different but in the same area). See R. Rose, "What Is Lesson-Drawing?" *Journal of Public Policy,* 1991, 11(1), pp. 3–30.

Level playing field: The concept that all competitors must be able to compete on an equal basis. An uneven playing field (i.e., one that discriminates) has deep implications for costs, and, therefore, the final price that is charged to customers. It is the government's responsibility as the final regulatory authority in the economy to ensure that the rules are applied equally.

Leverage points: Specific points in a policy-development process when those with little power can use a given situation/forum to make their voices heard. Thus, for example, public hearings serve as leverage points for citizens and citizen groups to affect the nature and content of a specific public policy under consideration.

Liability of adolescence: A concept that suggests that younger organizations can survive for some time with risks of failure largely because they will have had some stock of goodwill among legislators and citizens at the time of establishment. That survival rate, however, begins to diminish as organizations grow into adolescence. Liability of obsolescence argues that failure rates in organizations tend to increase with age as they become inertial and cannot align themselves to their ever-changing environments. For a general discussion of both these concepts, see, e.g., A. Henderson, "Firm Strategy and Age Dependence: A Contingent View of the Liabilities of Newness, Adolescence, and Obsolescence," *Administrative Science Quarterly,* 1999, 44(2), pp. 281–314.

Liability of newness: A theory of aging in organizational ecology which asserts that younger organizations—by virtue of their newness and, therefore, lack of sufficient organizational knowledge and learning—are generally hesitant to try anything innovative in their routines unless they adopt an innovation from elsewhere. See, e.g., J. Baum, "Liabilities of

Newness, Adolescence, and Obsolescence: Exploring Age Dependence in the Dissolution of Organizational Relationships and Organizations," *Proceedings of the Administrative Science Association of Canada,* 1989, 10(5), pp. 1–10.

Liability of obsolescence: *See* **Law of adolescence**.

Liability of senescence: Asserts that organizations with high overhead costs and unsustainable burdens of accumulated rules and routines will be less efficient. Thus, a liability of senescence results from dysfunctional organizational capabilities, which, in turn, tend to increase with organizational age. See, e.g., D. Barron, E. West, and M. Hannan, "A Time to Grow and a Time to Die: Growth and Mortality of Credit Unions in New York City, 1914–1990," *American Journal of Sociology,* 1994, 100(2), pp. 381–421.

Liability rules: Rules that organizations need to institute in order that employees are clear as to what the liabilities of their actions are. For example, a code of conduct—if it clearly specifies the actions that will result—is considered to have liability rules on employees' ethical-behavior requirements. See, e.g., L. Sacconi, "Codes of Ethics as Contractarian Constraints on the Abuse of Authority within Hierarchies: A Perspective from the Theory of the Firm," *Journal of Business Ethics,* 1999, 21(2/3), pp. 189–202.

Liberalization: The process of making free (i.e., opening) the process of production and the distribution of goods and services in an economy. Under a policy of liberalization, governments open up markets to competition and relax rules that limit the participation of various actors (such as foreign entities) in domestic markets. Liberalization in the public-management context refers to devolving authority from central-government agencies to line departments and local bodies.

Licensing: Refers to the granting of legal permission by a government to an entity to produce or distribute a good/service. Licenses will usually specify only what can be produced and are often accompanied by various restrictions (such as the level of prices that can be charged, or as regards product-quality standards). There will usually be a charge involved in granting such a license. All licenses will have to be renewed periodically. This allows the government to ensure that other agencies or firms also get an opportunity to be involved in producing/distributing the good or service.

Life-cycle theory: Any theory that traces how entities (such as organizations, businesses) grow and mature, and what characteristics they exhibit in the life cycle. In economics, this theory states that consumers base their decisions on expectations of income and expenditure over the whole of their lives. Relatedly, the life-cycle theory of leadership asserts that the type of leadership that is exhibited in any given situation is contingent upon the task maturity level of organizational members. The concept of task maturity is critical in judging whether the leader should be directive or facilitative.

Lifelong learning: Learning that occurs at various stages of an employee's career in the organization. The assumption here is that learning does not end once an employee reaches a higher level in the career, let alone at the end of attendance at educational institutions.

Lifers: Refers to those staff members who remain for life in an organization, and who will not, indeed who cannot, contemplate a career outside the organization. The related concept here is that of lifetime tenure, which means secured employment in an organization (or public service, generally) until retirement. While there are still some public sectors around the world that have retained lifetime tenure for public-sector workers, increasingly organizations are replacing it with fixed-term tenure where continuance of employment is contingent upon satisfactory performance.

Lightning rod: An organization or individual that takes the criticisms of a particular policy failure. Such criticisms are most useful at the initial stages of a policy implementation so that the organization can get valuable feedback on how the policy should proceed further.

Likelihood of regret: A decision criterion that looks at the degree of probability that there will be considerable difference between the eventual outcome of a decision and the anticipated one. The greater is the variance, the greater the likelihood that the decision will be regretted. Decision makers will thus opt to go for that particular policy decision that will produce for them the lowest variance between *ex ante* specifications and hypothesized *ex post* observations. See, e.g., D. Weimer and A. Vining, *Policy Analysis: Concepts and Practice,* 2nd edition, Englewood Cliffs, NJ: Prentice Hall, 1992, p. 235. *See also* **Decision regret**.

Limit of absolute discrimination: Refers to the maximum distinctions that an individual can discern of the influences in the operating environment (i.e., the domain within which he/she works) beyond which confusion reigns and unreliable transformation takes place. For example, it is said that the human mind can remember only about seven or so values at a time. Compelling it to do more is bound to lead to errors in retention. This concept is relevant in considering the notion of bounded rationality. *See also* **Bounded rationality**.

Limited cognitive competence: *See* **Bounded rationality**.

Limited competition: A situation where the providers of goods and services compete for market share under certain restrictions placed on them by government in order to ensure that, for example, other smaller providers have reasonable opportunity to compete. Limited competition might also entail competition to particular areas and sectors, for instance.

Limited contingency: While an organization is affected to a considerable degree by the environment in which it operates, it is also true that when external management influences affect an organization, the organizational culture will be able to modify the impulses only to a limited extent. This limited contingency concept goes a long way in explaining how, for example, quality-control mechanisms or structural governance arrangements have tended to be similar across diverse jurisdictions in the area of public-sector management reforms. See, e.g., R. Vengroff, M. Ndiaye, and M. Lubatkin, "Culture and Management: Are Western Management Styles Transferable?" in A. Farazmand (ed.), *Handbook of Bureaucracy,* New York: Marcel Dekker, Inc., 1994, pp. 253–63.

Limited government: The idea of having a smaller-sized government in place, one that does not intervene in all areas and one that operates within very tightly defined boundaries. Reform efforts in the public sectors of practically all jurisdictions, and particularly under the rubric of "new public management," have centered on limiting government (by reducing the scope of governmental intervention in many parts of the economy, as well as by reducing its absolute size). See, e.g., S. Haber, "Introduction: The Political Economy of Crony Capitalism," in S. Haber (ed.), *Crony Capitalism and Economic Growth in Latin America: Theory and Evidence,* Stanford, CA: Hoover Institution Press, 2002, pp. xi–xxi. *See also* **New public management**.

Limited-term contract: A contract of employment for individuals that is for a set period of time. Renewal of the contract is not automatic and is contingent upon satisfactorily meeting *ex ante* performance standards.

Line: Traditional term to denote the lower ranks of an organization, usually in staff functions such as human resources and accounts. There are several different applications of the term to consider: a line manager refers to a person with supervisory roles in an organization, but who supervises employees who are directly providing services to clients. Line authority refers to the authority that a manager has to allocate tasks—and more importantly, resources—to employees in an organization. Finally, a line ministry is usually understood to mean a governmental agency that is involved in implementing policies of the government (as opposed to, for example, an agency that provides policy advice to governmental ministers on the strategic content of public-management directions).

Line functions: *See* **Staff functions**.

Line-item budgeting: A type of budgeting where the focus is on manipulating the inputs to the production process. In line-item budgeting, particular focus is placed on individual items that constitute the organization's input to the work it does. Thus, for example, the appropriation of budget funds is made according to categories (or budget item lines) such as salaries and wages, travel, equipment, and so forth.

Line-item veto: Refusal by the executive to accept a bill not necessarily in its entirety but in relation to particular line items. This is normally applicable in the case of budgets where a veto-wielding president, for example, may not be satisfied with one (or several) individual inclusions for funding. However, not all executives have the authority to exercise a line-item veto; that is, they must either accept the whole of the budget or reject it in toto. In the United States, for example, the Supreme Court in 1998 declared the executive line-item veto unconstitutional because it violates a requirement related to how legislation is to be framed and passed. *See also* Veto.

Line-staff conflict: Refers to the disagreement that arises when there is a presumption that line managers know more about service provision and interaction with consumers than front-line staff. While it is tempting to say that in the newer form organizations of today, such line-staff conflicts—and indeed the distinction itself—is not very likely, this is not entirely true. For a discussion of this conflict in the broader dimension of human-resource management, see, e.g., P. Wright et al., "Comparing Line and HR Executives' Perceptions of HR Effectiveness: Services, Roles, and Contributions," *Human Resource Management,* 2001, 40(2), pp. 111–23.

Linking pin: A term used by management expert Renesis Likert for a group leader (since the linking pin connects working groups within the organization). Usually, the individual will be a group leader in one team and a group member in the other, although it is not uncommon for him/her to hold superior positions in both. See R. Likert, *New Patterns of Management,* New York: McGraw-Hill, 1961, pp. 113–16.

Lippitt-Schmidt model: Related to the notion of how organizations grow, the Lippitt-Schmidt model says that organizations go through three stages of development: birth, youth, and maturity. The model's explanatory power comes from the fact that, not unlike parenting, this has relevance to the type of management strategies needed to see the organization through a particular phase. See G. Lippitt and W. Schmidt, "Crises in a Developing Organization," *Harvard Business Review,* 1967, 45(6), pp. 102–12.

Load shedding: (1) Eliminating marginal programs so that the funding level that an organization has received is better reconciled. (2) An act that allows the role of the government in the economy to be diminished. This can occur either systematically (by specifying what should be the domain of the private sector) or gradually (by restricting resources and allowing standards to drop to low levels, thus encouraging market development). The term originated in the context of a system of electricity distribution, which features the ability to discard some customers to bring demand within supply limits, but not the ability to auction limited supply. See, e.g., J. Merriam, "Privatization and Debureaucratization: A Comparative Analysis of Bureaucratic Alternatives," in A. Farazmand (ed.), *Handbook of Bureaucracy,* New York: Marcel Dekker, Inc., 1994, pp. 319–29.

Lobbying: Any activity that is designed to influence policy makers in favor of the interests of specific groups. The act of lobbying is seen in a negative light although not all lobbying activity is as such (for example, some lobbying is for informational purposes alone). See, e.g., D. Austen-Smith and J. Wright, "Theory and Evidence for Counteractive Lobbying," *American Journal of Political Science,* 1996, 40(2), pp. 543–64.

Local autonomy: Granting local governments the discretion and freedom to make and implement policies in specific areas. With the current focus on citizen-oriented services, local autonomy is encouraged since contact with citizens is much more evident at that level.

Local government: A unit of government that is not sovereign in that its powers are delegated from either the central government or state/provincial government. Resources for local governments come from a mixture of central-government funding and from taxes levied locally (such as on refuse collection). They also have discretion to formulate and implement some policies, and usually administer central policies.

Laws that are made by local authorities are termed by-laws, and they are derived from laws that have already been passed by national or state/ provincial legislatures.

Local policy: *See* **Policy culture**.

Local purchase: Any purchase made by an organization from within the area where it is located.

Local rationality: Rationality exhibited by a subunit in an organization to deal only with the problems that beset it. Taken collectively for the organization as a whole, however, it is possible that these local rationalities can be mutually inconsistent (i.e., what appears rational for one subunit may not only be nonrational for the others, but the entire organization's response may prove to be nonrational). See, e.g., G. Antonelli and C. Bicchieri, "Game-Theoretic Axioms for Local Rationality and Bounded Knowledge," *Journal of Logic, Language and Information,* 1995, 4(2), pp. 145–67.

Local service contracting: Contracting for services that takes place at the local government level. For a review of the evidence and a discussion of several relevant hypotheses, see, e.g., G. Boyne, "Bureaucratic Theory Meets Reality: Public Choice and Service Contracting in US Local Government," *Public Administration Review,* 1998, 58(6), pp. 474–84.

Localistic cooptation: Refers to management's effort to isolate individuals from interacting with colleagues so that they retain loyalty to their own division. This is entirely plausible, especially if turf battles are being fought inside an organization. For a review of the concept of co-optation, see, e.g., G. Bertocchi and M. Spagat, *The Politics of Co-optation,* CEPR Discussion Paper, No DP2156, London: Centre for Economic Policy Research, 1999.

Locality pay increases: Increases in salaries that take place only for a given number of sectors (in the economy) or units (in organizations). Such increases may be necessary if, for example, employers realize that the salaries for particular groups within the organization are not in keeping with the general trends evident elsewhere. In order, then, to stem the potential outflow of skilled staff, they may decide to resort to locality pay increases.

Logic of cost and efficiency: The manner in which management looks at the issue of problems in worker-management cooperation. Elton Mayo, in the Hawthorne experiments, argued that management tends to be more concerned with the difficulties of a situation than with sentiments around it. The logic of sentiment, on the other hand, is the manner in which employees look at their own work and how they perceive problems of worker-management cooperation. Mayo argued that workers tend to have emotion-based attitudes on such issues.

Logical framework: A management tool that provides an organization with a comprehensive view of its activities. It includes information on intervention design; inputs, outputs, and outcomes and their causal relationships; indicators; and assumptions around how activities will yield desired effects. For a critical review of the logical framework, see, e.g., D. Gasper, "Evaluating the 'Logical Framework Approach': Toward Learning-Oriented Development Evaluation," *Public Administration and Development*, 2000, 20(1), pp. 17–28.

Logical incrementalism: A situation where decisions build upon each other continually in response to unique situations such that while the process is incremental, it does cope with the complexity that is faced. This is different from disjointed incrementalism, where there is no sense of building logically on prior decisions. See, e.g., J. Quinn, "Strategic Change: Logical Incrementalism," *Sloan Management Review*, 1978, 20(1), pp. 7–21. *See also* **Incrementalism**.

Logrolling: Refers to compromises that legislators tend to arrive at when, to please many, they package together unrelated proposals. See, e.g., D. Weimer and A. Vining, *Policy Analysis: Concepts and Practice*, 2nd edition, Englewood Cliffs, NJ: Prentice Hall, 1992, p. 320. *See also* **Pork-barrel spending**.

Lordstown syndrome: A situation where low productivity levels in organizations are attributable to the negative perceptions of employees, who believe they are required to perform what is termed "monotonous and dehumanizing work." Lordstown, Ohio, in the United States, is the site of the General Motors assembly plant where this was first noticed. See *Business Week*, "The Spreading Lordstown Syndrome," March 4, 1972.

Lose-leave style (of policy leadership): A style of leadership wherein leaders who consider a particular conflict unwinnable opt to disregard it while they are considering policy alternatives. The style of leadership that is evident here is one of avoidance: because the leader sees a conflict as hopeless, there is a tendency to avoid disagreement, including abstaining from taking sides in disagreements. For a discussion of how managers deal with conflicts with others in an organizational setting, see, e.g.,

M. Rahim, "A Measure of Styles of Handling Interpersonal Conflict," *Academy of Management Journal,* 1983, 26(2), 368–76.

Lose/lose alternatives: Also known as super-malimum alternatives, these are alternatives, which, if selected, lead to the worst expectations of all parties concerned. See, e.g. S. Nagel (ed.), *Handbook of Public Policy Evaluation,* London: Sage Publications, 2002, p. 25. *Cf.* **Super-optimum alternatives**.

Loser hare: A term used to denote something that is done quickly but is done wrong. For example, it is argued that the current clean-air policy in the United States was pushed through in a hurry but that it is flawed because of the conflict-oriented litigant-style of politics evident in the country. For a good discussion of this concept in relation to environmental policies, see, e.g., L. Lundqvist, *The Hare and the Tortoise: Clean Air Policies in the United States and Sweden,* Ann Arbor: University of Michigan Press, 1980. *See also* **Winner tortoise**.

Lower participants: Term used by the noted sociologist Amitai Etzioni to refer to individuals in positions of lower rank in the organization. See A. Etzioni, *A Comparative Analysis of Complex Organizations: On Power, Involvement, and Their Correlates,* New York: The Free Press, 1961, p. 12. For application of the term, see, e.g., D. Mechanic, "Sources of Power of Lower Participants in Complex Organizations," *Administrative Science Quarterly,* 1962, 7(3), pp. 349–64.

Lowest responsible bidder: A bidder who is awarded a contract because his/her bid is lower than that of other bidders, but he/she is still considered to have submitted a responsible and realistic bid.

M

Machine bureaucracy: Refers to the archetypal Weberian-type bureaucracy where some or all of the following attributes can be expected to be found: (a) primacy of written rules and protocols that dictate how organizational actions should be undertaken and staff behavior regulated, (b) a hierarchical structure with differentiated functions, (c) impersonal relationships among staff members, and (d) reliance on competencies as a standard of both internal and external recruitment. See, e.g., H. Mintzberg, *Structure in Fives: Designing Effective Organizations,* Englewood Cliffs, NJ: Prentice Hall, 1983, p. 163.

Machinery of government: (1) Generally refers to the organizational structure of the executive branch and the allocation of functions to public-sector organizations. (2) It also refers to the organizational and policy processes that make governments work.

Macho meritocracy: A term used in relation to polities such as that in Singapore where the selection process for even governmental ministers is meritocratic and focused on expertise and qualifications. This has an objective of eliminating candidates who are self-interested. The term was coined by the noted academician Ezra Vogel; see "A Little Dragon Tamed," in K. Sandhu and P. Wheatley (eds.), *Management of Success: The Moulding of Modern Singapore,* Singapore: Institute of Southeast Asian Studies, 1989, pp. 1049–66.

Macroculture: The overriding culture inherent in an organization. For example, at a treasury, we can talk of a macroculture of control whose primacy determines the various other subcultures in the organization. See, e.g., E. Abrahamson and C. Fombrun, "Macrocultures: Determinants and Consequences," *Academy of Management Review,* 1994, 19(4), pp. 728–55.

Macro-level prescriptions: Also known as regime-level prescriptions, these are prescriptions for reforms that address broad parameters that affect a reform process. Thus, for example, a macro-level prescription to reform the senior civil service could be the introduction of new legislation that provides more power to a civil-service commissioner to initiate bolder initiatives on senior management development.

Main estimates: *See* **Estimates of appropriation.**

Main gate: *See* **Approval point.**

Mainstream: The process of bringing issues and policies as a common and accepted approach. The term has been used largely in conjunction with the inclusion of women and those with disabilities in public affairs and in decision-making roles. Accordingly, mainstreaming implies that there is a comprehensive and enabling legislative framework, independent review and monitoring and evaluation mechanisms, and, very importantly, a cultural climate that accepts the presence of women and those with disabilities in such roles. For an application of the concept in relation to those with disability and mainstream-supported employment programs, see, e.g., P. Crothall, *Mainstream in Context*, Working Paper No. 10, Wellington: State Services Commission, 2000, pp. 10–12.

Maintenance of effort: Funding authorities will at times insist that in order for a potential recipient to be awarded a grant, the recipient demonstrate that it has maintained a particular level of relevant program expenditures (as a proxy for its commitment and effort). Such an insistence is captured by the term maintenance of effort.

Maintenance of standards clause: A provision in a collective-bargaining agreement that the employer will maintain the conditions of employment unless changes need to be made, at which point negotiations with unions will have to proceed.

Maintenance review: A review that is done periodically of all the employment positions in an organization with a view toward contemporizing all classifications and position descriptions. Maintenance reviews are carried out fairly regularly, particularly in organizations whose mandates, administrative processes, or technologies are constantly evolving.

Make-or-buy decision: The choice that organizations face when they must increase their capacity to fulfill functions (i.e., skills) in order to attain their mandates. The choice is whether the needed skills should be purchased in the market (i.e., readily available expertise contracted for a set period, usually at a rather high price) or nurture capability from within the organization by developing staff members who may not possess the skills but who possess such potential. See, e.g., B. Lyons, "Specific Investment, Economies of Scale, and the Make or Buy Decision: A Test of Transaction Cost Theory," *Journal of Economic Behavior and Organization*, 1995, 26(3), pp. 431–43.

Mal-leaders: Mal-leaders are mal-adjusted managers. These are individuals who do not possess the inherent attributes of good leaders (two of the most basic being task competence and interpersonal skills). While there is no clear-cut and across-the-board definition of who is and who is not a mal-leader (most managers may exhibit some characteristics of a mal-leader at some point or another), we can talk of them as being in a continuum from those who are ineffective but do not mean any harm to others to those who are ineffective but seek to harm others. For a discussion of this continuum, and other types of mal-leaders, see M. Whicker et al., "Mal-Leaders and Organizational Decline," in A. Farazmand (ed.), *Handbook of Bureaucracy*, New York: Marcel Dekker, Inc., 1994, pp. 149–63.

Maladjusted worker: A staff member who has not been able to internalize the organization's norms and value system and is often in violation of organizational roles and protocols. Maladjusted workers tend to be eased out of an organization unless they are sanctioned for disciplinary reasons, in which case the separation is much more abrupt.

Maladministration: Refers to the work of organizations that is characterized by inefficiency, ineffectiveness, and dishonesty, and denotes an organization that has lost the trust of the citizens it is mandated to serve. Maladministration is said to occur when a public body does not act in accordance with a rule or principle that is binding on it. Such rules and principles for a public organization can include, for example, acting promptly, paying due diligence to evidence presented, listening to all stakeholders and parties, and acting in a transparent manner. Ombudsmen can give a ruling of maladministration against an agency if their review determines that the agency did not act in accordance with principles. This judgment is made following a quasi-judicial review and is considered to be a stern warning that the agency needs to review its processes. For a description of the concept in relation to the European Ombudsman, see, e.g., K. Heede, "Enhancing the Accountability of Community Institutions and Bodies: The Role of the European Ombudsman," *European Public Law,* 1997, 3(4), pp. 587–605.

Malicious compliance: A dysfunctional situation where an individual shows overt support for a particular policy but is busy trying to subvert it covertly.

Manage by agreement: A tendency of public-sector departmental managers to focus only on the provisions inherent in their agreements (such as a purchase agreement) so that while they manage their department's resources efficiently and in a focused manner, they tend to be discouraged from doing anything that is outside the purview of the agreement. This tendency leads them to cease to be innovative. See, e.g., A Schick, *The Spirit of Reform: Managing the New Zealand State Sector in a Time of Change,* Wellington: State Services Commission, and The Treasury, 1996, p. 48. *See also* **Manage by checklist.**

Manage by checklist: A tendency of public-sector departmental managers to comply with a "checklist" of things they need to do pursuant to their agreements, and it discourages them from pursuing anything that is not specifically included in their performance agreements. This tendency leads them to cease to be innovative and merely to "manage by agreement."

Managed competition: When government allows competition among agents in the marketplace for the production and distribution of goods and services but still institutes rules to ensure that such competition is not without regulation. This may be necessary, for example, when the government wishes to ensure that there are no artificially raised profit levels for firms as a result of market action.

Managed costs: *See* **Controllable costs**.

Management: The process of administering an organization, which includes the following activities: (a) developing organizational strategy and long-term plans, (b) regulating and coordinating the organization's production process, and (c) interacting with staff members to get them to engage in achieving desired organizational goals. The noted social psychologist Renesis Likert classified management as of four types: the exploitive authoritative (where fear and threats are used), the benevolent authoritative (where rewards are also used and the subordinates' views are at times heard), the consultative type (where subordinates can have a fair degree of influence on how organizations are managed), and the participative type (where full use is made of group participation in organizational actions). See R. Likert, *New Patterns of Management,* New York: McGraw-Hill, 1961, pp. 226–31. (Later on in his career, Likert also talked of a fifth type of management in which the authority of hierarchy would no longer be evident.)

Management audit: A review of an organization's operations, procedures, and other arrangements so as to determine if proper managerial processes are in place and how well they function. Management control refers to the influence and control that managers exercise to ensure that all organizational actions and processes are geared toward the attainment of organizational goals.

Management board: An organizational form that brings together managers from various divisions within an organization and ensures that there is horizontal communication across the divisions. This horizontal-management idea ensures that a silo mentality in organizations is minimized.

Management by contract: The process of fulfilling organizational mandates by contracting out large parts of the work rather than do it in-house. When the organization itself is involved in fulfilling all aspects of the mandate, the term management by hierarchy is employed to denote the hierarchical method of getting something done. Management by contract can be evident in internal contracts, competitive tendering, or contracting out. For a good review of the term, see, e.g., R. Almqvist, "'Management by Contract': A Study of Programmatic and Technological Aspects," *Public Administration,* 2001, 79(3), pp. 689–706.

Management by exception: (1) Frederick Taylor, the father of scientific management, termed this the exception principle, and used it to refer to subordinates reporting to their superiors only those events which merited the latter's attention. (2) Used in the context of cost controls, this refers to concentrating only on those instances where significant variances are evident between *ex ante* specifications and *ex post* observations.

Management by hierarchy: *See* **Management by contract**.

Management by objectives: An approach to managing work, popularized by management guru Peter Drucker based on his work with others at General Motors and General Electric. In this approach, organizational goals are disaggregated into results expected of individuals over a set period of time. Some principles of MBO include objectives that are specific, participative decision making, and ample feedback. For Drucker's original work, see his *The Practice of Management,* New York: Harper & Row, 1954; for an application, see, e.g., W. Kretlow and W. Holland, "Implementing Management by Objectives in Research Administration," *Journal of the Society of Research Administrators,* 1988, 20(1), pp. 135–41.

Management by walking around: Refers to managers not necessarily relying just on formal reporting mechanisms to know what is happening in the organization, but that they physically circulate to see firsthand what employees are doing in their work areas.

Management charter: *See* **No-surprise policy**.

Management control: *See* **Management audit**.

Management deficit: Refers to the lack of managerial capability of an organization to address the myriad of problems it faces. The capability gap is not so much the lack of resources as it is the structural bias of an organization to take on more than it can deliver. If organizations make decisions that they do not have the capability to implement, then a management deficit is said to exist. For an example of application of this concept to the European Union, see L. Metcalfe, "Reforming European Governance: Old Problems or New Principles?" *International Review of Administrative Sciences,* 2001, 67(3), pp. 415–43.

Management development: Also called executive development, this term refers to enhancing the skills of managers to be able to manage in an organization. While the components of such a development program may be discrete, the term itself is loosely used, and can refer to a variety of interventions that can be taken to develop the managerial cadre. For a cogent analysis of the term, see, e.g., C. Mabey, "Mapping Management Development Practice," *Journal of Management Studies,* 2002, 39(8), pp. 1139–60.

Management organizations, ideal types of: Sociologist Tom Burns posits that there are two ideal types of management organizations that can be seen as being the ends in a continuum along which all organizations can be placed. At one end are the mechanistic types of organizations that closely resemble the Weberian rational-legal bureaucracy. At the other extreme are organic types of organizations that are quite suited for unstable environments and where there is less formal structure, and communication across all levels is encouraged. See, e.g., D. Pugh and D. Hickson, *Writers on Organization,* 4th edition, Middlesex, UK: Penguin Books, 1989, pp. 41–44.

Management prerogative: *See* **Management rights**.

Management responsibility, doctrine of: Refers to the precepts around how and to whom managers in public organizations need to be responsible. Stemming directly from the realization that administrative discretion is essential in better delivering organizational outcomes, the doctrine of managerial responsibility involves considering concepts of procedural and outcome-oriented accountability, value-based and ethical reasoning, and rationality, among others. For an application of the doctrine of managerial responsibility, see, e.g., A. Bertelli and L. Lynn, Jr., "Managerial Responsibility," *Public Administration Review,* 2003, 63(3), pp. 259–68.

Management rights: Also known as management prerogative, these refer to the rights given to managers to exercise control over, and give direction, to the organization. In collective-bargaining processes, for example, it is considered part of management rights that organizational leaders can decide which specific policies they wish to pursue in order to make the organization more effective. Management rights are not subject to the bargaining process.

Management science: Also known as operations research, this refers to an approach to management that relies on the application of scientific methods to solve problems that managers face. One such area of management science that has been particularly helpful has been risk analysis in organizational strategic planning.

Management theory jungle: A term used to describe the plethora of management theories that sprouted when the rigorous and analytical study of management was just beginning to grow. Management theorist Harold Koontz, who coined the phrase, identified six major schools (those centered on or drawing from: management process, empiricism, human behavior, social system, decision theory, and mathematics). See H. Koontz, "Management Theory Jungle," *Journal of the Academy of Management,* 1961, 4(3), pp. 174–88.

Management threshold: A term that denotes the level beyond that which an individual is not able to go because of capability failures. This level then becomes a plateau, and the individual tends to stay in this particular position for a long time. *See also* **Peter principle**.

Management versus administration: *See* **Administration versus management**.

Management, contingency approaches to: A view that managerial practices depend upon all factors that are at play in the organization's environment at any given point in time. How these factors are taken into account varies between those that argue for a more traditional approach to management (i.e., through control and coordination) and those that assert that flexibility and adaptability is needed. Regardless of which approach is taken, it is obvious that given the changing environment within which an organization operates, the most effective management style is a function of the particular situation as it exists at any point in time. For a good review of the concept, see, e.g., V. Govindarajan, "A Contingency Approach to Strategy Implementation at the Business-Unit Level: Integrating Administrative Mechanisms with Strategy," *Academy of Management Journal,* 1988, 31(4), pp. 828–53.

Manager, roles of: The most widely cited work on the roles of a manager is the work of the noted management theorist Henry Mintzberg, who postulated ten managerial roles that can be grouped into three areas: interpersonal, informational, and decisional. This stems from an assertion that the work of managers is fragmentary in nature and that they perform a wide variety of roles. For a fuller discussion of the ten managerial roles, see H. Mintzberg, "The Manager's Job: Folklore and Fact," *Harvard Business Review,* 1975, 53(4), pp. 49–61; see also L. Kurke and H. Aldrich, "Mintzberg Was Right! A Replication and Extension of the Nature of Managerial Work," *Management Science,* 1983, 29(8), pp. 975–84.

Managerial accountability: *See* **Managerial autonomy.**

Managerial autonomy: The degree of freedom given to managers to ensure that they do their work without interference. In return for autonomy, managers are expected to be closely accountable for the results. The notion of managerial autonomy is contained in the motto "let managers manage," which public-sector reformists have used to argue for managers' accountability and overall performance. Managerial accountability refers to the answerability of managers for their decisions and actions to their superiors in the organization hierarchy, and of organizational leaders to the board, if there is one, and/or to the legislature.

Managerial discretion: *See* **Administrative discretion.**

Managerial entrepreneurship: Refers to those properties that enable organizational performance to be enhanced, including effectively attaining mandates, ensuring efficiency, and reducing bureaucratic procedure. Managerial entrepreneurship is a hallmark of the "new public management." For a good review of the concept, as well as a case-study application, see, e.g., M. Moon, "The Pursuit of Managerial Entrepreneurship: Does Organization Matter?" *Public Administration Review,* 1999, 59(1), pp. 31–43.

Managerial gamesmanship: An aspect of administrative life where managers engage in strategizing consistent with generic politics. Such politics are seen, for example, in matters of securing more resources for one's branch at the expense of others, and resisting the mobility of one's human resources to other branches. See E. Bardach, *The Implementation Game: What Happens After a Bill Becomes a Law,* Cambridge, MA: MIT Press, 1977, pp. 51–55.

Managerial grid: Also called leadership grid, this is a tool used by business management experts Robert Blake and Jane Mouton to look at the issue of leadership from the perspective of concern for people and concern for production. The grid has two axes, with different coordinates representing different styles of leadership. For example, a high concern for people but a low one for production yields a style of leadership that Blake and Mouton term "country-club management." The other styles of leadership that emerge from the grid are: impoverished management (low concern for production and for people), authority-compliance (high concern for production but low for people), team management (high concerns for both production and people), and middle-of-the-road management (where there is equal concern for people and production). The lattermost leadership style is also called "dampened pendulum" because there is a tendency to move marginally around the happy medium. See R. Blake and J. Mouton, "Overcoming Group Warfare," *Harvard Business Review,* 1984, 62(6), pp. 98–108.

Managerial pragmatism: A concept that denotes the introduction of practical realities in the application of managerial techniques adopted from other environments. For a review of managerial pragmatism, with reference to Commonwealth jurisdictions, see, e.g., M. Kaul, "The New Public Administration: Management Innovations in Government," *Public Administration and Development,* 1997, 17(1), pp. 13–26.

Managerial rent-seeking: *See* **Rent-seeking behavior.**

Managerial revolution: A dramatic change that is now evident in the fact that control over firms and organizations is increasingly being exercised by professionals with technical administrative expertise. The same trend can be seen to some extent in public-sector organizations, where it is felt that increasingly managers, and not political leaders, control organizational direction.

Managerial risk aversion: *See* **Risk aversion.**

Managerial slack: A term that refers to the absence of managerial efficiency wherein an organization faces no competition. This is manifest in, for example, lack of motivation, and tendency toward greater risk aversion. This is particularly evident in transitional economies, where only recently has there been a shift from central-planning systems to managerial entrepreneurialism. For a general discussion, see, e.g., S. Djankov and P. Murrell, "Enterprise Restructuring in Transition: A Quantitative Survey," *Journal of Economic Literature,* 2002, 40(3), pp. 739–92.

Managerialism: A term that denotes the adoption by the public sector of private-sector management practices. The assumption under managerialism is that management is a generic activity and that, therefore, the attributes and methodology of managing in the private sector should be replicable in the public sector. The public-sector reforms evident in many jurisdictions around the world since the 1980s have been based on the principle of managerialism, and are evident, for example, in the introduction of competition and managerial devolution in the public sectors. Furthermore, reliance on the concept of managerialism (which is argued to be neutral and objective) has also meant that efforts have been made to reduce the impact of political influences on the operations of governmental departments. For a discussion of the term in relation to its evidence in several jurisdictions, see, e.g., M. Maor, "The Paradox of Managerialism," *Public Administration Review,* 1999, 59(1), pp. 5–18. *See also* **New managerialism; Policy-operations split.**

Managing government, models of: The questions that elected representatives and others have posed for a long time include: How exactly should governments be managed? How should the activities of the public sector be managed so that the stated objectives of the government can be attained? The noted management theorist Henry Mintzberg, in a very powerful and well-cited analysis, has talked about five ways in which governments should be managed. These include: as a machine bureaucracy dominated by rules and standards; as a network characterized by flexibility and interactivity; as a performance control, where business characteristics are introduced in the public sector; as virtual government which extends the performance-control model and makes governments nonvisible to citizens; and as normative control, where the focus is on the attitudes of the individuals who work in the public sector (thus relational contracts tend to replace explicit written contracts). See H. Mintzberg, "Managing Government, Governing Management," *Harvard Business Review,* 1996 (May–June), pp. 75–83.

Mandarin bureaucracy: A bureaucracy that is staffed only by careerists who have been recruited on merit. A mandarin bureaucratic system is one that is hierarchical in nature, has limited entry and is meant only for high-potential candidates (as measured usually by their educational qualifications and experience), and that has a set career path. France, Singapore, and Japan are considered to be prime examples of jurisdictions that have a mandarin bureaucracy.

Mandate: As understood in the public-management context, the term refers to the wishes of constituents expressed to elected representatives who, through the legislature, direct public-sector organizations to get involved in particular activities and provide services as sought by constituents. The term mandate space is used to denote the shared understanding among politicians and administrators about what it is that the bureaucracy should be doing. See, e.g., P. Daffern and A. Wyatt, "Beyond the Checklist: Towards an Integrated Policy Impact Methodology," *International Review of Administrative Sciences,* 2001, 67(4), pp. 663–72.

Manifest situation: Refers to one of various situations that exist in any organization at any one time. The manifest situation is what is formally displayed and described by the organizational hierarchy in its reports and publicity material about what the organization is and does. This is contrasted with three other situations: the assumed situation (for example, as perceived by individual employees in the organization), the extant situation (that is, what actually exists), and the requisite situation (that is, what would need to be in place in order to fulfill the relevant organizational mandates).

Manifest/latent function: Drawing from organizational sociology, this term refers to functions of organizations that are evident at two extremes, i.e., those that are manifest (obvious) and those that are latent (hidden). There are three such dimensions of organizational behavior: (a) between publicly stated (i.e., manifest) purposes and the actual ones (i.e., latent), (b) between purposes of organizations that citizens are aware of (i.e., manifest) and not aware of (i.e., latent), and (c) between intended effects (i.e., manifest) and unintended ones (i.e., latent).

Manpower planning: *See* **Human-resource planning**.

Marble-cake federalism: As opposed to layer-cake federalism, where there is an almost total separation evident among the various levels of governments in a federal system, in marble-cake federalism there are cooperative relationships among levels of government. Marble-cake federalism is evident, for example, in any local program that is funded by the state but whose guidelines come from the federal government.

Marginal activities: Activities that organizations engage in that are not part of their core business, and are clearly at the margin. For example, a central-government policy agency may be involved with relevant academic institutions as marginal activities.

Marginal costs: Refers to the extra costs that are incurred for every extra unit of production of a good or service. This concept is important for public administrators in managing the resource flow into organizations from a legislature. The concept is also useful in looking at managerial strategies in organizations. In an environment where many decisions are made incrementally, marginal analysis is used overwhelmingly to support assertions and to make claims on resources. In marginal analysis, the focus is on the margin (i.e., the positive effect of the next product or service purchased or sold). The concept has been used in various ways in public administration, including by the parliament in the United Kingdom in authorizing government departments to charge up to a certain percentage (10 percent) of the marginal costs of locating and providing information that is being sought under the Freedom of Information Act. For a discussion of the concept in relation to marginal analysis and public administration, see, e.g., J. Erik Lane, "Will Public Management Drive Out Public Administration?" *Asian Journal of Public Administration*, 1994, 16(2), pp. 139–51.

Marginal effectiveness: *See* **Effectiveness**.

Marginal employees: Refers not only to those staff members who contribute the least to the organization's mission (largely because of the nature of their work) but also to those who have been tagged as poor performers. See, e.g., C. O'Reilly and B. Weitz, "Managing Marginal Employees: The Use of Warnings and Dismissals," *Administrative Science Quarterly,* 1980, 25(September), pp. 467–84.

Market: An interaction of willing buyers and suppliers to exchange goods and services for a price. A market can be in equilibrium or disequilibrium depending upon whether the demand for or supply of goods and services are equal. A market may exist at any geographic level (i.e., local, regional, national, or international), and increasingly also in cyberspace (i.e., a virtual market). Market forces refer to the demand for and supply of goods and services without the intervention of governments. This does not preclude the government being one of the purchasers or sellers. Marketization refers to the creation of market mechanisms of resource allocations to replace bureaucratic ones. A marketization strategy is one that helps create/develop a market (such as enabling public agencies to rely less on grants but more on generating own resources).

Market analogs: Wherein the implementation of policies is designed to imitate the private sector. This means that features of the market are replicated to the extent possible in the public sector, even if it requires governmental action. For a description and application of the term, see, e.g., R. Hula, "Introduction: Market Based Public Policy," *Policy Studies Review,* 1986, 5(May), pp. 583–87.

Market bureaucracy: Also referred to as the corporate bureaucracy, this concept refers to the creation of business units within public-sector organizations that are created along the lines of private-sector firms. Generally, this covers a style of bureaucracy where the management culture is focused on outputs, efficiency, and cost effectiveness, and where performance is measured and rewarded as in private firms.

Market discipline: Subjecting the organization to the mechanisms of the market as well as to the measures that determine success or failure (such as profitability). Just as private firms discipline themselves in relation to what the markets will tolerate, market discipline refers to public organizations doing the same.

Market economy: Refers to an economy where decisions on allocation of resources are determined by market forces independently rather than by command from the government. The benefits of a market economy are that the prices of goods and services will, more often than not, more accurately reflect their true costs.

Market exposure: The degree to which an organization is subject to the same market pressures as private-sector firms. Governments will modulate this degree of exposure in the case of state-owned companies and others depending upon how they perceive these companies can successfully withstand market forces.

Market failure: A situation where the market does not promote efficiency in the allocation of resources by firms, and where market prices are not the true barometer of social costs and benefits. This occurs when the market does not exhibit characteristics of being Pareto efficient. Invariably, a situation of market failure increases the likelihood of remedial governmental intervention. See, e.g., W. Ouchi, "Markets, Bureaucracies, and Clans," *Administrative Science Quarterly,* 1980, 25(1), pp. 129–41.

Market forces: *See* **Market**.

Market governance: *See* **Governance**.

Market infiltration: When market-like tendencies become increasingly introduced to previously nonmarket sectors. Such infiltration takes place through the use of market instruments, which are tools, such as competition, that governments use in order to create market conditions in nonmarket areas. For an application, see, e.g., N. Flynn, I. Holliday and L. Wong, "Introduction," in L. Wong and N. Flynn (eds.), *The Market in Chinese Social Policy,* Hampshire, UK: Palgrave, 2001, pp. 1–11.

Market matrix form: An organizational form that is of recent origin, which mixes the matrix form (with team membership from across organizational divisions) with market features such as requiring matrix team leaders to bargain to procure resources internally.

Market segmentation: A technique that allows an organization to understand how its market (or customer base) is structured toward better understanding how the needs of stakeholders differ in each segment. Not all benefit seekers, for example, share similar characteristics, and knowing how their needs differ enables social-service organizations to provide more targeted—and, therefore, more effective—services. This notion of market segmentation is applicable in the public sector as well. See, e.g., G. Bhatta, "'It's the Identification, Stupid': Profiling Senior Public Service Managers for Training and Development," *International Journal of Training and Development,* 2002, 6(2), pp. 98–111.

Market testing: A managerial reform in government that involves placing an activity for the provision of goods or delivery of services open for competition from internal and external bidders. The primary benefit of this is that the provision of goods and services will most likely be more cost effective and of higher quality. For a review of the issues related to market testing, see, e.g., J. Newman, "'What Counts Is What Works?' Constructing Evaluations of Market Mechanisms," *Public Administration,* 2001, 79(1), pp. 89–103.

Marketing mix: A concept borrowed from the private sector to denote the elements that an organization needs to keep in mind while marketing its products or services. These are: price, product, place, process, service, and promotion. With public organizations increasingly compelled to behave like private firms in many jurisdictions, the marketing mix is a useful concept to help explain how they could better market their services.

Marketization: *See* **Market.**

Market-like mechanisms: Any mechanism that is introduced to create markets where none existed before. These markets do not have all the attributes of a market for goods and services as exists generally, but they do serve to encourage competition, and thus efficiency, to some extent. Examples of market-like mechanisms include customer satisfaction guarantees, contracting out non-core agency functions, and developing mechanisms wherein citizens can hold agencies accountable for service quality.

Market-management capability: The capability that governmental agencies have to manage markets. This includes, for example, properly regulating banks, investment flow, etc. Weakness in this area contributes to making the economy vulnerable to destabilizing market shocks.

Marriage-bureau functions: Functions that serve to link one set of activities with others. An example of such functions are referral services for welfare and child care for families with low income who avail of governmental services because they have been so identified and referred by specialized agencies. For a discussion of such functions of intermediary institutions, see, e.g., P. Cooke and K. Morgan, *The Associational Economy: Firms, Regions, and Innovation,* New York: Oxford University Press, 1998, p. 101.

Mass media: Refers to the popular press (print, electronic, and broadcast media) that reports on governmental activities to the general masses. In all advanced countries, the mass media plays a very strong role in checking the perceived excesses of governments and public-sector bureaucracies. For an example of the mass media and its subordinate role in the agenda-setting process in Singapore, see K. Ho, *The Politics of Policy-Making in Singapore,* Singapore: Oxford University Press, 2000, pp. 133–34.

Matching funds: Money provided by a party (or the recipient party) to match a contribution made by another entity. Matching requirements are stipulations that one party (such as a local government) is obliged to equal the contribution made by another party (such as the federal government). A matching grant is a fixed portion of the resources given by the central government to local governments to match the level of resources generated by the latter. The level could be unit for unit or some other fixed level.

Material incentives: Refers to extrinsic or tangible rewards to employees to motivate them toward achieving certain performance goals. Examples of such incentives are performance bonuses, gifts, etc.

Materiality concept: The concept that there are some transactions for which organizations do not need to account to auditors and/or the legislature because they are not significant (or material) enough to affect costs nor mandates. What constitutes that materiality is contingent upon whether or not the same result would have been evident had that transaction not taken place. The application thus varies according to situation.

Matrix accountability system: A situation where a worker in an interagency collaborative assignment is based outside his/her home agency but reports to the home agency supervisor as well as to the leader of the interagency project. In this arrangement, then, managers across agencies have relationships, although they will be interacting with each other through said employee. See, e.g., E. Bardach, *Getting Agencies to Work Together: The Practice and Theory of Managerial Craftsmanship,* Washington, DC: Brookings Institution Press, 1998, p. 120.

Matrix departmentalization: Increasingly, due to the complexity of organizational tasks, matrix departmentalization has been the norm as organizations combine the various other forms of departmentalization. The focus here is on coordinating the efforts of others in other teams. This form, also called the matrix diamond, combines the product and functional approaches to departmentalization and is considered to be the most flexible of the various types of organizational structures.

Matrix diamond: *See* **Matrix departmentalization**.

Maximal implementers: Those that do the utmost that is required of them to implement a public policy. This could include making the necessary structural and legislative changes to ensure that the policy is implemented. Minimal implementers, on the other hand, are those that do the minimum that is required of them to implement a public policy. The minimal implementers ensure that they do not disturb the existing arrangements but still come across as being seen to have fulfilled what was required of them. See, e.g., G. Gianakis and G. John Davis, "Reinventing or Repackaging Public Services? The Case of Community-Oriented Policing," *Public Administration Review,* 1998, 58(6), pp. 485–98.

Maximax strategy: A strategy where policy makers seek to find the maximum benefit associated with each possible alternative action, and then choose the action that is associated with this maximum of maxima (i.e., select the alternative that provides the maximum payoff). A maximin strategy is one where policy makers first determine the minimum gains associated with each policy alternative and then choose the alternative that produces the maximum of these minimum gains. On the other hand, a minimax strategy is a strategy in analyzing policy alternatives wherein policy makers first determine the maximum loss for each action and then choose the least (i.e., minimum) of the maximum losses.

Maximin strategy: *See* **Maximax strategy**.

Maximum entropy: This concept is based on the premise that when estimating the probability distribution of a particular eventuality, decision makers should select that distribution which leaves them the largest remaining uncertainty (i.e., the maximum entropy) consistent with their constraints. That way they will not have introduced any additional assumptions or biases into their calculations.

Maximum feasible participation clause: A stipulation in the aid received by subjurisdictions from elsewhere which requires that the recipients themselves document that they have fully cooperated with any such stipulation. The clause is designed to demonstrate to the donor that the recipient has done what it could to meet any requirements that may have been specified as a condition for receiving the aid.

Maximum-likelihood criterion: As used in organizations, this term refers to decision making under conditions of uncertainty where an organization does not take into consideration any other probability of outcome but the one that is the most likely and then searches for actions that produce the optimal result consequent upon the most likely event. The optimal result here refers to either maximum benefit (regardless of cost) or minimum cost (regardless of benefit).

Meaning-making rights: As used in performance measurement, this concept refers to the rights that an entity possesses to assign particular meanings to performance standards achieved. It is important to determine who has the right to interpret differences in performance for a particular variable. The argument is that the greater the distance between an entity producing figures and the one interpreting it, the greater the scope for misreading the results. For a discussion, see, e.g., H. de Bruijn, "Performance Measurement in the Public Sector: Strategies to Cope with the Risks of Performance Measurement," *International Journal of Public Sector Management,* 2002, 15(6/7), pp. 578–94.

Means test: A test to see what means are available to citizens who seek a particular subsidy or governmental service (for example, the governmental department that is mandated to provide income support to needy and eligible citizens may require recipients to show what other sources of income they have, and only upon verification of the response would the assistance be rendered).

Means-end analysis: Also known as a root approach, this concept is related to that of the rational comprehensive model of policy analysis. The basic idea that underlies the means-ends analysis is that the decision maker knows what the ends are and then systematically and rationally goes about identifying the most logical and cost-effective way of attaining the ends. However, as is obvious, in reality such a rational approach is rarely possible, and what usually transpires is that decision makers end up looking at successive improvements rather than seeking to attain the optimum solution. See, e.g., C. Lindblom, "The Science of Muddling Through," *Public Administration Review,* 1959, 19(2), pp 79–88. *See also* **Rational-comprehensive model**.

Means-end rationality: *See* **Instrumental rationality**; *see also* **Misplaced means and ends syndrome**.

Mediation: Refers to any effort by a neutral and independent third party to help settle a dispute between two parties. The mediator can only advise, and the parties are not mandated, unlike in arbitration, to accept any decision or suggestion resulting from the mediation. A mix of mediation and arbitration is known as med/arb, which is a process that attempts to mediate between two parties, and if differences persist, then arbitration is sought in order to have the issues resolved in a binding manner.

Mega-departments: Governmental departments that are big in scope, although not necessarily in size (i.e., staff size). The Ministry of Finance in some countries, for example, has several portfolios (such as tax, budgeting, financial advice) that generally are spread out among different departments in other jurisdictions.

Memorandum of understanding: An agreement negotiated between two or more parties that is formalized in a document that sets out the basis of the relationship among them. The memorandum will have some principles about how the relationship will be maintained, and the obligations of the various parties. A memorandum of understanding is only that—an agreement about the understanding that parties may have reached amongst themselves—thus it is not prescriptive. It is worth noting that governmental departments usually subscribe to MOUs among themselves, and not via contract—a relic of the old idea that each department is merely an extension of a governmental minister, and ministers are parts of a collectively responsible unit, not distinct entities.

Mentoring: Refers to a more experienced individual helping out a less experienced colleague in work-related issues such as by serving as a role model, teacher, or counselor as a means to aiding the latter's professional and/or personal development. The concept of mentoring is broader than management, and is qualitatively different from formal training, since it is characterized by an ongoing relationship between the two individuals. Mentoring can be formal (for example, as part of a formalized mentoring scheme) or informal (yet still organized and structured). Mentoring is often used in conjunction with the term "coaching," but there are fundamental differences between the two. See, e.g., D. Henderson, "Enlightened Mentoring: A Characteristic of Public Management Professionalism," *Public Administration Review,* 1985, 45(6), pp. 857–63. *See also* **Coaching**.

Merit bad: *See* **Demerit goods**.

Merit goods: Goods that are considered to be intrinsically desirable or valuable to society, independently of the revealed preferences of the consumer. Such goods have value but no direct market price. Examples of merit goods include the arts, museums, etc. *Cf.* **Demerit goods**.

Merit increase: *See* **Merit system**.

Merit system: A system of recruiting and promoting the best and most qualified individuals based solely on merit (skills, knowledge, and attributes). A merit system will have several attributes, including: (a) recruitment from all segments of society; (b) fair and equitable treatment for all; (c) equal pay for work of equal value; (d) high standards of integrity; (e) retention of those who perform well, developing those who need development, and terminating those who do not perform well; and (f) protection of employees against reprisals for lawful disclosures of information. A merit pay system is a system of compensation in place in organizations where employees are given increases in their salaries based on work-related performance, and as measured against *ex ante* specifications. This is also known as a merit increase. While such salary increases are not fixed, there are always caps placed on how large the increments can be.

Meritocracy: *See* **Merit system**.

Meta-analysis: An analysis that is done using a technique that combines the evidence that is found in various other studies. Such a combination of research evidence allows the analyst to carefully sift through all relevant information to make informed judgments about the subject matter under investigation.

Meta evaluation: The term is used for an evaluation designed to aggregate findings from a series of evaluations. It can also be used to denote the evaluation of an evaluation; that is, to judge its quality, the criteria used, and/or assess the performance of the evaluators.

Method of active participation: Refers to the manner in which change agents and external facilitators seek to encourage the participation of all stakeholders and actors in a particular program or activity. In this scenario, the change agent is no longer the only expert whose knowledge is decisive in determining the action to take. Instead, those who are to be affected by the particular program are given an opportunity to contribute ideas and suggestions. Only those actions that have had the input and acceptance of the stakeholders are then selected. Such a method of active participation is characterized by equality (i.e., all participants have equal opportunity to raise concerns and ideas) and transparency (i.e., all the results are presented to all participants).

Methodological rationality: Focusing on ensuring that the bureaucracy does things methodically and in a rational manner. This focus on rigorous methods assumes that the desired end is an acceptable goal and that bureaucrats thus need only seek to find the most cost-effective way of attaining it. *See also* Rationality.

Micro lending: Loans of small amounts usually given to poor rural households, largely for income-generating activities. While the amount of credit may be small, there are still very well-designed criteria around standards of business proposals and credibility of repayment. Micro lending is a popular feature in the rural economies of developing jurisdictions, and one of the most noted of such endeavors is the Grameen Bank of Bangladesh. See, e.g., A. Groetz and R. Sen Gupta, "Who Takes the Credit? Gender, Power and Control Over Loan Use in Rural Credit Programs in Bangladesh," *World Development,* 1996, 24(1), pp. 24–64.

Micro-level prescriptions: These are prescriptions for reforms that focus not on broad parameters but on agency-specific factors such as organizational mission and technology. For a discussion, see, e.g., J. Thompson and S. Fulla, "Effecting Change in a Reform Context: The National Performance Review and the Contingencies of 'Microlevel' Reform Implementation," *Public Performance & Management Review,* 2001, 25(2), pp. 155–75.

Micromanagement: Paying attention to minute details. Managers are usually exhorted to ensure that they keep on top of developments in the workplace, but they should avoid dictating that they sign off on all decisions or that every development be reported to them as it occurs.

Middle management: The intermediate level in a management hierarchy in an organization that bridges the gap between the staff and the senior organizational leadership. Middle managers can be supervisors, but not necessarily. Their role is important because they transmit appropriate feedback both top/down and bottom/up. For a discussion of the role that middle managers can play in enhancing ethics, see, e.g., R. Hubbard, "People: Hearts and Minds—Towards Rebirth of the Public Service Ethic," *Public Administration and Development,* 1997, 17(1), pp. 109–14.

Middle-of-the-road management: *See* **Managerial grid.**

Midterm evaluation: An evaluation of a project or program that is carried out toward the middle of the period between implementation and closure. The purpose is to ensure that the project or program is on track in terms of delivering what it intends.

Milestone: Also called an event, this term refers to an activity that is completed within a given period of time. A milestone thus implies a measurable product or result.

Mimetic adoption: When other organizations adopt innovations already tried out elsewhere. Because it is not firsthand, mimetic adoption can be said to be a limited form of organizational learning. Nonmimetic adoption, on the other hand, implies that organizations have gone through that process of experimenting for themselves. See, e.g., H. Greve and A. Taylor, "Innovations as Catalysts for Organizational Change: Shifts in Organizational Cognition and Search," *Administrative Science Quarterly,* 2000, 45(1), pp. 54–80. *See also* **Mimetic isomorphism.**

Mimetic isomorphism: When an organization—in response to the uncertainties in its operational environment—models itself after organizations that it considers to be successful. While mimetic isomorphism implies that organizations do not have to reinvent the wheel, it also means that there may not be a considerable level of knowledge generation since the organization does not experiment for itself. See, e.g., M. Mizruchi and L. Fein, "The Social Construction of Organizational Knowledge: A Study of the Uses of Coercive, Mimetic, and Normative Isomorphism," *Administrative Science Quarterly,* 1999, 44, pp. 653–83. *See also* **Convergence hypothesis.**

Minimal implementers: *See* **Maximal implementers**.

Minimal policy goal: The most basic objective of a policy. For example, in many developing countries a minimal policy goal is to ensure that there are adequate legal and institutional bases on which to mount public-sector reform.

Minimalist state: An argument that the role of the state should be minimal and should be restricted to facilitating the management of explicit contracts, to providing a proper environment for the private and nongovernmental sectors to provide goods and services, and to basically play a monitoring role. The idea of a minimalist state has been championed by neo-liberal thinkers and by international financial institutions. See, e.g., V. Tanzi, *The Role of the State and the Quality of the Public Sector,* IMF Working Paper, WP/00/36, Washington, DC: IMF, March 2000, p. 3.

Minimax strategy: *See* **Maximin strategy**.

Ministerial autonomy, principle of: Argues that central agencies in devolved public-management systems cannot dictate the manner in which they would like to see policy implementation to other governmental departments. Ministerial autonomy prevents these agencies from acquiring ministerial portfolios. For a discussion of this concept in relation to maximizing policy coherence across government, see, e.g., OECD, *Building Policy Coherence: Tools and Tensions,* Public Management Occasional Papers No. 12, Paris: OECD, 1996, p. 25.

Ministerial cultures: *See* **Ministerial individualities**.

Ministerial individualities: A term used to denote that while collectively governmental ministers may act in certain expected ways, each minister brings to the portfolio his/her own way of looking at issues and norms of behaviors. Thus, bureaucrats need to be in tune with the ministerial individualities that will affect how they carry out their work. Bureaucrats also need to be aware of different ministerial cultures, which refer to the more or less common levels or planes of ministerial work and behavior that are evident across a group of ministers. While ministers may have unique individual attributes, it is argued that they also share some commonalities, which is evident in their approach to: (a) their colleagues, particularly those who are junior to them, (b) the depth of their portfolios, (c) those who work with them, and (d) the job itself. See, e.g., P. Chabal, "Do Ministers Matter? The Individual Style of Ministers in Programmed Policy Change," *International Review of Administrative Sciences,* 2003, 69(1), pp. 29–49.

Ministerial responsibility: A principle in the Westminster system of government where cabinet ministers are individually responsible to the legislature (i.e., parliament) for the actions of the departments in their portfolio, and collectively responsible to the legislature for the actions of the executive branch of government. This is why if the government loses a vote of confidence in parliament, it is duty bound to resign, upon which a general election usually follows. For a review of accountability in the context of ministerial responsibility, see, e.g., P. Aucoin, "Independent Foundations, Public Money, and Public Accountability: Whither Ministerial Responsibility as Democratic Governance?" *Canadian Public Administration,* 2003, 46(1), pp. 1–26.

Misconduct: A situation where an employee does not behave as per the public-service code of conduct. Minor misconducts may not be investigated, but major ones are subject to scrutiny not only by the employee's organization but often also by external actors (such as audit agencies).

Misplaced bureau: Generally, bureaus performing similar functions are located in the same governmental department, but there are times when, due to political pressures, for example, a bureau will be located in a different department. The problem with having a misplaced bureau is that it may not be championed by the departmental leadership, and its interests may tend not to be well protected, although on the positive side it may enjoy a considerable level of administrative autonomy. For examples of misplaced bureaus, such as the U.S. Maritime Administration, see, e.g., R. Moe, *The United States: A Country Study in Organization and Governance,* paper presented at the OECD Governance of State Agencies and Authorities Expert Meeting, Paris, 19–20 April 2001.

Misplaced means and ends syndrome: Refers to a situation wherein organizational leaders focus on wanting to be liked by staff members rather than fulfilling the prerogatives of management (i.e., they substitute the ends, i.e., managing the organization, by the means, i.e., being liked). This is a dysfunctional environment and leads to a situation such as that evident in the Abilene effect. See, e.g., M. Harvey et al., "The Abilene Paradox after Thirty Years: A Global Perspective," *Organizational Dynamics,* 2004, 33(2), pp. 215–26. *See also* **Abilene effect**.

Missing contingencies: Contracts that are not complete will not have all contingencies specified. Missing contingences result because the parties to a contract will realize greater costs for writing very specific contracts, and enforcing them, compared with the low probability that they will indeed arise. For a discussion of the concept, see, e.g., R. Posner, *Economic Analysis of Law,* 3rd edition, Boston, MA: Little Brown, 1986, p. 92.

Mission budgeting: This is a predecessor to output budgeting, and refers to budgeting tied specifically to the end purpose of the organization's program. This demonstrates to a legislature what specific objectives will be met by what outlay of resources.

Mission drift: Refers to the gradual process of an organization not being able to stay within sight of its mission. Mission drift can be caused by various factors, including lack of management capacity, failure to enforce accountability mechanisms on contractors, and goal divergence between stated policy and actual implementation.

Mission statement: Refers to the organization's clearly stated overall purpose, that is, its raison d'être. A mission statement lets others know for what the organization exists. All organizational strategic-planning processes start from a reiteration of the organization's mission statement.

Mix of policies: *See* **Package of policies**.

Mixed efficiency: *See* **Efficiency, total**.

Mixed scanning: Sociologist Amitai Etzioni proposed mixed scanning to get around the weaknesses of the rational-comprehensive method as well as of incrementalism in decision making. Mixed scanning adopts different strategies to problems depending upon how they present themselves to policy makers. What is rational in one case may not be rational elsewhere, so mixed scanning selectively combines elements of rationality and incrementalism. How much of each are chosen depends upon the specific problem faced by the policy maker. See A. Etzioni, "Mixed Scanning: A 'Third' Approach to Decision Making," *Public Administration Review,* 1967, 27(2), pp. 385–92.

Modeled behavior: Behavior that is exhibited by managers which reflects what they encourage in their staff members. Thus, for example, adherence to the high standards of ethics that the organization may have specified for all senior staff members would send a strong message to other organizational members about expected behavior.

Modular training: Training that is provided in discrete forms where each form/unit is fully contained in terms of learning objectives. For example, training on project management may be offered sequentially by modules that consist of: problem definition, design, management, and evaluation. The modules may be offered in one session (if the content is not heavy or difficult) or in various sessions that span any length of time.

Momentum building: Signifies a developmental sequencing process where one success or event leads to more of the same in increasing levels. In inter-agency collaboration, for example, any success is taken to represent an impetus to create further success. Public policy guru Eugene Bardach argues that momentum is typically built through enthusiasm effects (where one party is eager to mimic the success of another), bandwagon effects (where many parties see benefits in mimicking successful activity), consensus effects (where two or more parties reach agreement on a way forward), and trust effects (where one party is sure of, i.e., trusts, the actions of the other and mimics them). See E. Bardach, *Getting Agencies to Work Together: The Practice and Theory of Managerial Craftsmanship,* Washington, DC: Brookings Institution Press, 1998, pp. 276–77. *See also* **Platforming**.

Monitoring: A term usually employed in conjunction with evaluation, but there is a difference between the two. Both are key parts of the project cycle, but monitoring focuses on an ongoing review and tracking of activities to steer a project toward the desired state, whereas evaluation focuses on a review done at a particular point in time in the project cycle. A monitoring system is often put in place to ensure that proper monitoring takes place. Monitoring includes a mandate for such intervention, a determination of the resources and monitoring rights, and relevant protocols about how programs/organizations are to be monitored. It has been reported that monitoring contractors' performance is often the weakest link in the entire process of privatization (see, e.g., General Accounting Office, *Privatization: Lessons Learned by State and Local Governments,* Report to the Chairman, House Republic Task Force on Privatization, Washington, DC: US Government Printing Office, GAO/GGD-97-48, p. 17).

Monitoring agency: Any organization charged with monitoring the performance of other organizations or programs in various areas. A monitoring agency is given a mandate to collect relevant information and to make recommendations on how activities should be adjusted to achieve the desired end state. This mandate may come from legislation or by executive order. It could also emerge from agreement among organizations and groups that decide to voluntarily subject themselves to monitoring by a particular organization that may or may not be a part of their group.

Monitoring problem: Public-choice theory postulates that any contracting process generates a monitoring problem because alternative costs are generated by the bidding process, and the organization that tenders the bid, and that manages the contract, needs to incur costs associated with monitoring the contract as well.

Monitoring rights: Determining whether the contractual obligations of another party have been met. These rights enable an organization to assess if and how programs are being managed according to any *ex ante* specifications.

Moon and ghetto problem: A way of arguing about the capabilities of governments that says that if they can be successful in placing a man on the moon, then there should be no reason why they cannot solve the everyday problems that are inherent in society, such as extreme economic inequality. See, e.g., R. Nelson, "Intellectualizing About Moon-Ghetto Metaphor—Study of Current Malaise of Rational Analysis of Social Problems," *Policy Sciences,* 1974, 5(4), pp. 375–414.

Moral hazard: Describes behavior when agents do not bear the full cost of their actions and are thus more likely to take them. As applied to the governance realm, moral hazard refers to the fact that, in the eyes of public-sector organizations, there is always a last resort (i.e., the government) to turn to that will extricate them from bad decisions. For a well-cited discussion of this concept, see K. Arrow, "Uncertainty and the Welfare Economics of Medical Care," *American Economic Review,* 1963, 53(5), pp. 941–73.

Moral leadership: Leadership that is exercised which promotes goals that are universally beneficial to society. A moral leader is one who is able to lead social action by virtue of the courage of his/her convictions that what is being attempted is socially desirable. A related concept is moral suasion, which refers to a situation where the government tries to persuade a particular form of action by giving strong arguments in its favor (for example, in encouraging community action against a social ill, such as domestic violence). See, e.g., M. Whicker et al., "Mal-Leaders and Organizational Decline," in A. Farazmand (ed.), *Handbook of Bureaucracy,* New York: Marcel Dekker, Inc., 1994, pp. 149–63.

Moral suasion: *See* **Moral leadership**.

Motivation: Motivation can be considered to be made up of three components: (a) direction of action—what an individual chooses to do when presented with alternatives; (b) intensity of action—the strength with which the individual proceeds in the direction that has been chosen; and (c) persistence of effort—the staying power of behavior, or how long the individual will continue to expend the effort. There are several well-cited theories of motivation, including Maslow's hierarchy of needs, and Herzberg's two-factor theory. Factors that motivate individuals to work include: money, prestige, working conditions, a sense of service, vocation, etc. See, e.g., K. Chung, *Motivational Theories and Practices,* Columbus, OH: Grid, Inc., 1977.

Motivational dynamic: In considering the relationship between an individual's identity and the organization, it is usually the case that there is a big difference between the individual's current self and an ideal self that he/she hopes to be. This difference is contained in the concept of a motivational dynamic since trying to bridge that gap is what motivates the individual. See, e.g., M. Pratt, "The Good, the Bad, and the Ambivalent: Managing Identification Among Amway Distributors," *Administrative Science Quarterly,* 2000, 45(3), pp. 456–93.

Motivation-hygiene theory: *See* **Herzberg's two-factor theory**.

Muddling through: Economist and political scientist Charles Lindblom's assertion that decision makers tend not to be able to make decisions ideally (i.e., using all the information that may be available, considering all policy options, and taking the broader and long-term view), but that they lurch from one decision to another (i.e., muddle through), making small adjustments which do not have long-term consequences. Having said that, Lindblom was quite aware that radical change could still be possible through several smaller decisions. See C. Lindblom, "The Science of Muddling Through," *Public Administration Review*, 1959, 19(2), pp. 79–88.

Multicriteria decision making: A perspective of public-policy analysis wherein analysts consider several criteria for each decision-making situation, and there is an emphasis on seeking relations between goals and alternatives to choose the best alternative. See, e.g., S. Nagel (ed.), *Handbook of Public Policy Evaluation*, London: Sage Publications, 2002, p. 105.

Multicentering: The process of delegating authority and decision-making competence to local governments as well as to other service providers, independent parties, voluntary associations, etc. This encourages the rise of multiple centers of delivery competence and competitive pressures. For a case-study application of this concept, see, e.g., K. Hansen, "Local Councilors: Between Local 'Government' and Local 'Governance,'" *Public Administration*, 2001, 79(1), pp. 105–23.

Multidimensional criteria problem: *See* **Criterion problem**.

Multifinality: *See* **Open system**.

Multilevel governance: A term that refers to the system of governance as reflected in the European Union, where numerous distinctly independent territorial units come together for purposes of determining joint action. The term is used less in relation to the system of governance that is evident within a jurisdictional setting (as in federal-state relations in Australia or the United States) and more in the context of the complexity of policy making and accountability relationships among different states. While in multilevel governance there will be constitutional and/or institutional arrangements concerning how their relationships are structured (for example, in terms of interjurisdictional commerce, etc.), the hierarchical order of institutions is such that local or regional bodies can bypass the nation-state level and interact with the supranational body to pursue their policy interests in the international arena. For a look at multilevel governance in relation to the European Union, see, e.g., A. Benz "Two Types of Multilevel Governance: Intergovernmental Relations in German and EU Regional Policy," *Regional and Federal Studies,* 2000, 10(3), pp. 21–44.

Multiple accountabilities disorder: A phenomenon that arises when multiple and conflicting perceptions of accountability of public servants and public organizations by different stakeholders diminish organizational effectiveness. The ideas underlying it have long been in evidence in the public sectors across all jurisdictions. For a good review and application of the term, see, e.g., J. Koppell, "Pathologies of Accountability: ICANN and the Challenge of 'Multiple Accountabilities Disorder,'" *Public Administration Review*, 2005, 65(1), pp. 94–108.

Multiple award: Granting a contract for different parts of a product to two or more bidders because it may not be practical to have only one entity engaged in the work. For example, one bidder may be strong in one aspect of the work and the other in the rest, in which case the principal could maximize effectiveness and efficiency by parceling out the tender.

Multiple streams: A policy lens that is used at the systematic level of analysis and which views policy choice as a collective output that results from the interactions of multiple factors. It is a particularly useful lens to use when the environmental structure is unstable and the goals of the various policy actors are ambiguous (as one would expect in sensitive subject matters such as teenage pregnancy). See, e.g., N. Zahariadis, "Comparing Three Lenses of Policy Choice," *Policy Studies Journal,* 1998, 26(3), pp. 434–48.

Multiple veto points: A situation where there are many parties that can effectively block the passage of rules, regulations, bills, etc. For a brief explanation of how this works, see, e.g., C. Campbell, "Juggling Inputs, Outputs, and Outcomes in the Search for Policy Competence: Recent Experience in Australia," *Governance: An International Journal of Policy and Administration,* 2001, 14(2), pp. 253–82. *See also* Veto.

Multiple-agency problem: A problem that arises when there are several agency relationships (such as those evident in formal organizational networks). The problem arises because each agency brings to the table its own framework for participation in such networks, and because all the agencies need to rely on each other in order to effect the outcomes that problems of interactions develop. As such, role conflict is a rather common manifestation of the multiple-agency problem, as is the complexity of relationships. *See also* **Factorial problem.**

Multiskilling: Training employees in a range of skills such that they are better able to perform a range of tasks. This is beneficial not only to the employee (who develops competencies in different areas that will be useful for career growth) but also to the employer (which can utilize multi-skilled employees to different activities in the organization). Multi-skilling facilitates multitasking, which refers to staff members being engaged in more than one task as part of their portfolios. Multitasking implies that the staff members are being given an opportunity to develop new skills or use ones they may already have.

Multitask principal-agent model: A problem that arises when what the principal (for example, the employer) wants the agent (for example, the employee) to do is multidimensional and where not all dimensions are measurable. The multitask principal-agent problem argues that in such a situation placing incentives on activities that can be measured (or observed) alone can be dysfunctional. When the principal is concerned with both the observable and the unobservable activities of the agent, but compensates only based on the observable ones, the agent will naturally be inclined to put more effort into this set of activities. As applied in the workplace, then, the problem is for employers to get employees to do useful work throughout, rather than work hard at a single task. See, e.g., J. Brickley, C. Smith, and J. Zimmerman, *Managerial Economics and Organizational Architecture,* Chicago: Irwin, 1997, p. G-6.

Multi-year appropriations: *See* **Appropriation.**

Must objective: Refers to a target that is critical for the organization to attain. A must objective is contrasted with a want objective, which refers to a target that is not a part of the organizational mandate and is not necessary for organizational survival but which the leadership wishes to pursue for other purposes (for example, to cultivate goodwill among stakeholders). The tension between a must and a want objective is usually resolved through internal planning and managerial processes such that fulfillment of organizational mandates are not compromised. However, such resolution generally depends upon the ability of senior management to put organizational priorities in proper perspective, not always a given.

Mutual goal setting: A process of interaction between the employer and the employee where as part of the employee's performance appraisal, goals that are suitable to both parties are developed. Mutual goal setting encourages commitment from the employee for the goals. Such goal setting can be evident at organizational levels as well, in which case working together with other organizations to determine mutual goals is obvious.

Mutual recognition: An instrument that governments use in order to reduce the barriers for integration in a particular area or sector. For example, two countries may decide that they will mutually recognize the standards that each jurisdiction applies in certifying skills levels of particular occupations that are characterized by increasing mobility (i.e., individuals in these occupations have incentives to be physically mobile because of opportunities in other jurisdictions). An example of a mutual recognition is the Trans-Tasman Mutual Recognition Arrangement in place between Australia and New Zealand.

Mutual rating: *See* **Peer rating**.

Mutualism: A process where organizations interact with each other and influence the direction each takes. This leads either to organizational mortality or to organizational aggregation. Mutuality refers, in general, to mutual dependence between two parties, and to rights and responsibilities with respect to each other. Partnerships between organizations become enduring when mutuality leads to benefits for both. For a good review of the term, see, e.g., J. Austin, "Strategic Collaboration between Nonprofits and Businesses," *Nonprofit and Voluntary Sector Quarterly,* 2000, 29(1), pp. 69–97. See also J. Baum and J. Singh, "Organizational Niches and the Dynamics of Organizational Mortality," *American Journal of Sociology,* 1994, 100(2), pp. 346–80.

N

Narrative policy analysis: A form of policy analysis that also looks at the underlying, and often overlooked, stories and narrations of particular policy problems as a way of coming up with better policy alternatives. Narrative policy analysis is particularly useful when a policy situation is very complex and there are no cut-and-dry solutions evident. The analysis provides a richer picture to policy formulators so that they have a more holistic perspective of the policy issue or problem being addressed. See, e.g., T. Kaplan, "The Narrative Structure of Policy Analysis," *Journal of Policy Analysis & Management,* 1986, 5(4), pp. 761–78.

National competency standards: Standards for competencies that are set across the board for given jobs in a range of occupations. Such standards are regularly updated to ensure that the competencies being assessed are current. For the public sector, the standards are set by either a governmental agency or a government-appointed body.

National Performance Review: The review initiated by President Clinton in the early 1990s in the United States, which identified changes (both generic and specific) that were defined as required to improve the efficiency and effectiveness in federal government departments. The review was focused on agency-level structures, processes, and, more importantly, belief systems. The literature on this subject is vast; but relevant materials can be found in: D. Osborne and T. Gaebler, *Reinventing Government: How the Entrepreneurial Spirit Is Transforming the Public Sector,* Reading, MA: Addison-Wesley, 1992; US National Performance Review, *Creating a Government That Works Better and Costs Less: The Report of the National Performance Review,* Washington, DC: US Government Printing Office, 1993; and J. Thompson, "Reinventing as Reform: Assessing the National Performance Review," *Public Administration Review,* 2000, 60(6), pp. 508–21.

Nationalization: When a privately owned and operated business is taken over by government and made into a public agency. Those who oppose nationalization cite its potential inefficiency and costliness because it often leads to overcentralization, and those who support it argue that coordination is enhanced when industries are under one source of control. While the pace of the nationalization of industries and businesses has slowed down considerably in recent years, it continues to remain a potentially powerful tool for a central government to manipulate the production and distribution of goods and services in the national economy. See, e.g., N. Long, "Resource Extraction Under the Uncertainty about Possible Nationalization," *Journal of Economic Theory,* 1975, 10(1), pp. 42–53.

Natural attrition: The rate at which the staff size in an organization diminishes without any external shock (such as, for example, layoffs due to funding cuts by the legislature). The rate of natural attrition signals to organizational leaders how they should target their entry-level and mid-level recruitment campaigns. It is easier to plan for natural attrition in jurisdictions where a mandatory retirement age is in effect; in those that do not (such as New Zealand), employers are often unable to plan around the decision space of older workers to retire at a particular age.

Natural soldiering: Frederick Taylor, the father of scientific management, used this term to explain how low output could result when workers were not able to stifle their inherent instinct to take it easy and put in only the bare minimum to their work. The term "soldiering" was taken by Taylor to refer to laziness and loafing. See F. Taylor, *The Principles of Scientific Management,* New York: Harper Bros., 1911, pp. 5–29. *Cf.* **Systematic soldiering**; *see also* **Theory X**.

Needs analysis: Refers to analyzing the deficiencies an individual or organization experiences, and determining the approaches that might give cues on how to meet the identified deficiencies. Needs analysis is an assessment of needs, which is a management function that looks at the gaps between what is needed and what exists in order that, ultimately, the relevant goals may be attained. It is particularly useful in training because it allows a proper stock-take of what exists and where the gaps are so that the training program can be targeted to achieve the desired objectives.

Needs hierarchy: As propounded by the noted psychologist Abraham Maslow, there are five types of human needs, and they are organized into a hierarchy as follows: physiological needs (such as air and water) at the bottom, followed by safety needs, affiliation needs, ego needs, and finally self-actualization needs. Only when the lower ones have been met will the higher one be addressed. See A. Maslow, "A Theory of Human Motivation," *Psychological Review,* 1943, 50, pp. 370–96.

Negative capability: Capacity to live with and to tolerate ambiguity. Negative capability implies an ability to learn and to work within the uncertainties of organizational environments. The term also refers to the capability not to act in situations of uncertainty—this means generating fresh insights into how to respond and then doing so with a much greater awareness of the environment. This is a rather important capability to possess for organizations since it implies that in situations of external uncertainty, they have the presence of mind not to come up with knee-jerk reactions. For an application, see, e.g., R. French, "'Negative Capability': Managing the Confusing Uncertainties of Change," *Journal of Organizational Change Management,* 2001, 14(5), pp. 480–92. *Cf.* **Positive capability**.

Negative entropy: Refers to the tendency of an organization to create appropriate conditions to ensure continued operation despite adverse pressures from its operational environment. The term explains how organizations aim to regulate their behavior and orientation (by coming up with new protocols, for example) in anticipation of internal and external influences. Negative entropy is evident in an open system.

Negative externality: Also called third-party effects, this term refers to the adverse effects borne by one party of actions taken by another. For example, pollution caused by a particular industry is a negative externality to those who are affected by it. When the cost associated with a negative externality is effectively attributed to the agent behind the externality (through, for example, government action), then the externality can be said to have been "internalized." *See also* **Spillover effects**.

Negative slack: In project planning, a negative slack occurs when the latest end date of an activity is later than the earliest start date of a successive activity (thus the project has to be accelerated by the time differential between the end date and the start date of the respective activities).

Negative-sum games: A form of managerial gamesmanship where all players lose considerably (i.e., leave with less of whatever they were seeking, for example, money, prestige, goodwill, than what they began with). Wars are obvious examples of negative-sum games because wealth is destroyed on all respective sides. *See also* **Games**.

Negotiate in good faith: The understanding in employment relations is that both parties to the debate (i.e., management and unions) will try their best to agree on a solution. Negotiating in good faith then ensures that both parties retain an open mind about the offers and counter offers made. At times, such good faith is ensured at the bargaining table by an external mediator.

Negotiated contracting: A method of engaging in contracting wherein the bidder and the bidding party negotiate the terms of the contract and the mode of service delivery. In negotiated contracting, there is only one bidder that has been invited by the organization (based on pre-qualifications) to submit a bid. For a general discussion of various models of contracting, see, e.g., R. De Hoog, "Competition, Negotiation or Cooperation: Three Models for Service Contracting," *Administration and Society,* 1990, 22(3) pp. 317–40. *Cf.* **Competitive contracting**; **Cooperative contracting**.

Negotiated grievance procedure: All collective-bargaining agreements between labor and management will have a grievance procedure that results in final and binding arbitration in cases where either party claims a grievance against something that has been agreed *ex ante*. The protocols of such a procedure will have been agreed during the collective-bargaining phase (and if it has tended to work satisfactorily in the past, then the parties will let it remain).

Negotiation: The process of discussing or bargaining to reach an agreement. In the collective-bargaining process, for example, negotiations take place between representatives of labor and management where they discuss proposals to eventually hammer out an agreement that is acceptable to both parties. Negotiations take place whenever two or more parties have divergent views. For a discussion of the role and impact of negotiations in policy making, see, e.g., K. Holzinger, "Negotiations in Public Policy-Making: Exogenous Barriers to Successful Dispute Resolution," *Journal of Public Policy,* 2001, 21(1), pp. 71–96. *See also* **Bargaining**.

Neo-managerialism: Refers to the notion that public administrators must be entrepreneurs as well. By extension, this implies—under the "new public management"—that citizens will have a rather passive role, and that values such as fairness and justice will be subsumed by efficiency and economy. For a cogent analysis of the concept, see, e.g., L. Terry, "Administrative Leadership, Neo-Managerialism, and the Public Management Movement," *Public Administration Review,* 1998, 58(3), pp. 194–200.

Nepotism: Refers to the practice of awarding positions in an organization to family members by those who hold office. The presumption here is that nepotism is negative in that those individuals brought into the posts do not have the merit (i.e., the knowledge, skills, and abilities) required to fulfill the responsibilities. But that need not necessarily be so. What is more of a problem, however, is that there will have been no process of competition for awarding such positions.

Net present value: Value of resources obtained by discounting for the future (at a specific level, expressed as a percentage) all costs and revenues for a particular project or program. The fundamental premise behind this concept is that money is worth less at a future date than at present. *See also* **Risk-adjusted NPV**.

Net public benefit test: As applied in public-sector management, this refers to the test that needs to be conducted when the government wishes to preserve a restriction on competition in a particular sector. If it can be demonstrated that the benefits to the community as a whole of continuing to maintain the restrictions outweigh the costs (derived from freeing up the market), then the government will continue to impose the restriction. Across jurisdictions, this is usually evident when considerations are given to social-welfare and equity issues, policies relating to ecologically sustainable development, etc.

Network closeness: Refers to the concept of network cohesion, which focuses on the extent to which a network can influence the organizational and policy processes. Such cohesion can occur both through loose linkages among relevant parties and through more formal institutionalized structures. In both situations, cohesion or closeness requires that there be considerable mutual recognition of, and collaborative relationships with, the parties that are part of the network. For a good discussion of this concept, see, e.g., J. Forrest, "Networks in the Policy Process: An International Perspective," *International Journal of Public Administration,* 2003, 26(6), pp. 591–607.

Network governance: *See* **Governance**.

Network organization: Also called a service implementation network, a network organization is a relatively new organizational form. It is characterized by extensive interactions (both formal and informal) among its clientele and stakeholders. However, not all networked organizations are equally integrated with each other. For a good discussion, see, e.g., M. Landau, "On Multiorganizational Systems in Public Administration," *Journal of Public Administration Research & Theory,* 1991, 1(1), pp. 5–18.

Network theory: As applied to interagency collaboration, network theory explains how such cooperation can occur, can be sustained, and can create value for all parties. The actors in an interagency production network are organizations, not individuals, although clearly individuals will shape the way in which the network operates. Network theory also states that networks across organizations can be either coercive (i.e., relies on authority and is mandated) or beneficent (i.e., relies on trust and integrity). See, e.g., S. Newberry and P. Barnett, "Negotiating the Network: The Contracting Experiences of Community Mental Health Agencies in New Zealand," *Financial Accountability and Management,* 2001, 17(2), pp. 133–52.

Network, factorial effects of: Effects of networks that progressively get more complex as the size of the networks grow. For an application, see, e.g., L. Dovey and B. Anderson, *Whither Accountability?* SSC Working Paper No. 18, Wellington: State Services Commission, 2003, p. 11.

Neutral competence: A belief that politics and administration must be kept separate. This is a direct response to the abuses of patronage, and the term "neutral competence" is used to denote the technical competency and merit of civil servants rather than their functions. Adherence to this leads to reliance on bureaucrats' neutral expert role, which is a role played by public servants wherein they are expected to provide their expertise without regard to the political orientation of the government they work for. See, e.g., J. Hart, "Central Agencies and Departments: Empowerment and Coordination," in B. Peters and D. Savoie (eds.), *Taking Stock: Assessing Public Sector Reforms,* Montreal: McGill-Queen's University Press, 1998, pp. 285–309. *See also* **Responsive competence**.

New federalism: A new interpretation of state-federal relations that many U.S. presidents have made during their tenure. Under President Ronald Reagan, for example, there was emphasis on easing regulations on business. Other significant elements of new federalism were those of: (a) contracting out (i.e., reducing the scope of work of the public bureaucracy), (b) cutbacks in federal spending, and (c) local governments having to do more with less resources. *See also* **Federalism**.

New managerialism: A philosophy that is closely aligned with the widespread public-sector reforms of the 1990s and later. Ingrained in new managerialism is the fundamental belief of the supremacy of markets and competition over bureaucratic hierarchy. Efficiency is enhanced when there is competition for an organization's products and services, and, therefore, the argument that new managerialism makes is that organizations should be subject to competition. See, e.g., M. Vickers and A. Kouzmin, "New Managerialism and Australian Police Organizations: A Cautionary Research Note," *International Journal of Public Sector Management,* 2001, 14(1), pp. 7–26.

New political economy: The new thinking on how governments behave in relation to the economy. The argument is that all parties in this (including citizens, politicians, and bureaucrats) use the authority of government to press home advantages for themselves. Citizens use political influence to get access to benefits that are allocated by government; politicians use resources to purchase popular support; and bureaucrats use their positions of authority for personal reward. For a good review of the term, see, e.g., D. Rodrik, "The Positive Economics of Policy Reform," *American Economic Review,* 1993, 83(2), pp. 356–61.

New public administration: A movement that questioned the traditional focus on value neutrality and sought to encourage public administration and administrators to be more involved in instituting changes. This movement—in the 1970s and early 1980s—was to have some measure of impact in the rise of what is now referred to as the "new public management." See, e.g., H. Frederickson, "Comparing the Reinventing Government Movement with the New Public Administration," *Public Administration Review,* 1996, 56(3), pp. 263–70.

New public management: The type of public-management system that has been in evidence in practically all developed jurisdictions since the 1990s. New public management (NPM) has three components: (a) marketization (i.e., introducing market competition into public-sector production), (b) disaggregation (i.e., decoupling policy and executive functions), and (c) "incentivization" (i.e., linking incentives to performance). The argument was simple: the public sector was inherently inefficient because it did not allow for incentives along the lines provided to firms operating in the marketplace, and there were constraints (such as operational interferences from elected representatives) imposed on public managers that needed to be removed. The term is generally attributed to public-management guru Christopher Hood (see his "A Public Management for All Seasons?" *Public Administration,* 1991, 69(1), pp. 3–19). For the application of NPM at the local level, see, e.g., K. Hansen, "Local Councilors: Between Local 'Government' and Local 'Governance,'" *Public Administration,* 2001, 79(1), pp. 105–23. For a review of the application of NPM in developing countries, see, e.g., N. Manning, "The Legacy of the New Public Management in Developing Countries," *International Review of Administrative Sciences,* 2001, 67(2), pp. 297–312.

New public service: A proposition that the primary role of the public service is not just "steering rather than rowing," but actually serving. That is, the public servant should be actively involved in helping citizens better articulate their demands, engage and inform them, and ultimately serve them better. This ideas goes beyond the argument that the noted writers Osborne and Gaebler made about the public service steering the economy. See R. Denhardt and J. Denhardt, "The New Public Service: Serving Rather than Steering," *Public Administration Review,* 2000, 60(6), pp. 549–59.

Newness: A development that depicts a change in the existing pattern of how organizations are involved in doing their work. The newness is a function of several variables, including changes in an organization's external operating environment (such as a shift in its mandate upon a change in government), application of new technology on existing organizational processes, change in management style upon leadership shuffles, etc. See, e.g., H. Greve and A. Taylor, "Innovations as Catalysts for

Organizational Change: Shifts in Organizational Cognition and Search," *Administrative Science Quarterly,* 2000, 45(1), pp. 54–80.

Next-steps agencies: *See* **Executive agencies**.

No-bid response: A response made by an organization to a request for proposal (RFP) that states that no bid will be made. A no-bid response is desirable since it prevents the organization from being blacklisted—by virtue of not responding to a RFP—from submitting future bids.

Noblemaire principle: A principle used in determining the level of salaries at the United Nations. The principle is derived from the recommendations of the Noblemaire Committee, which in 1921 proposed that the salaries of the professional staff be based on those of the best-paid civil service in the world. At that time (for the then League of Nations), the comparator was the British civil service, and since the creation of the United Nations, the comparator has been the U.S. federal government (although the UN's International Civil Service Commission argues that the best paid civil service is now that of Germany's). See, e.g., G. Bhatta, *Reforms at the UN: Contextualizing the Annan Agenda,* Singapore: Singapore University Press, 2000, pp. 52–53.

Noise: As used in the context of decision making in organizations, this refers to any undesired information that decision makers receive from a communication channel and which is not intended to be part of the main message. Noise is inherently a subjective concept since it depends upon the perception of the receiver that the information that it is receiving is not useful.

Nominal group technique: A technique used in group decision making where brainstorming, round-robin feedback, individual voting on priority ideas, etc., are employed to generate discussion and seek consensus on what decisions to take. As the name implies, the technique centers on getting collective group input into decisions.

Nonaccountability, space of: The domain within which public agencies tend not to be accountable for their actions. Such a situation arises when there are two principals, such as the central government and local government. The accountability challenge for governments is to ensure that such nonaccountability space is as minimal as possible by clarifying the respective responsibilities of the principals.

Nonassociational (latent) group: Refers to any group that is not formally organized but which has the potential to be so, particularly if it is properly mobilized. Many community-level groups in less-developed countries can be considered to be nonassociational.

Nonbureaucracies: Refer to organizations that are not highly structured and that do not have a high concentration of authority. The term comes from a typology of organizations first determined by the Aston Group in the United Kingdom in the early 1960s (so named after the group of scholars whose research was done while they were connected to the University of Aston). The group proposed that any organization could be characterized by its degree of specialization of functions, standardization of procedures, formalization of documentation, and centralization (or concentration) of authority. *See also* **Full bureaucracies**; **Personnel bureaucracies**; **Workflow bureaucracies**.

Noncompete provision: A provision that is inserted in some employment contracts which stipulates that individuals that work for the organization will not be allowed to seek employment with competitors upon termination of their contract. This restriction is for a specified period of time, usually a year.

Noncompetitive procurement: Getting goods and services for the organization without open competition among potential contractors to provide the same. A noncompetitive procurement normally takes place when the amount of the potential contract does not exceed a certain threshold and the organization is allowed to select a contractor without open competition.

Noncompliance: When an organization is found to have not complied with, or diligently followed, standard policies or requirements made of them in respect to, for example, financial policy. Noncompliance can draw sanctions, particularly if they are serious enough to disrupt programs and policies.

Nonconformance analysis: An analysis that is conducted to determine why a product or service did not conform to *ex ante* specifications. The analysis helps ascertain how problems can be remedied so that the required product or service standards can be met.

Noncooperation: A situation that exists when two parties (such as principals and agents) do not cooperate with each other even though a binding contract may demand such cooperation. In such a situation, a third party (for example, a regulatory agency, or a mutually acceptable entity) may initiate procedures to terminate the contract.

Non-core activities: Activities of an organization that are not central to the primary organizational goal. For example, a training agency may also be involved in generating resources by renting out its premises to others for various uses. That, and activities related to managing that activity, would be a non-core activity. *Cf.* **Core activities**.

Nondecisions: A term that denotes that policy makers tend to exclude in their agenda the demands of various groups that might disrupt the established way of doing things (hence, when lawmakers refuse to include the issue of aboriginal rights in a policy agenda, say, they are, in effect, coming up with nondecisions).

Nondirective counseling: Counseling given to employees, not by dictating to them the preferred course of action, but by trying to understand what their own needs are and how they may go about acquiring a possible solution, which they will need to seek for themselves.

Nondisclosure: When organizations do not make public their actions or the information they hold. Such nondisclosure leads to problems of moral hazard and adverse selection because those outside the organization will have to make decisions under conditions of information asymmetry. All government organizations will be subject to specific disclosure requirements, and an incidence of nondisclosure can be easily identified by someone requesting information from a government department (particularly through a freedom of information, or an official information act, request). *Cf.* **Disclosure**.

Nondiscretionary action: An administrative action, normally prescribed by law, that an organization has to undertake (i.e., it does not have discretion not to undertake it). Reporting on adherence to equal employment opportunity is an example of nondiscretionary action in governmental departments.

Nonemployee: Someone who is not paid wages or salaries by an organization but is associated with the organization by virtue of, for example, being a director of the organization, or on pension from the organization.

Nonexclusiveness: Refers to the fact that if something is available to one party, it is then available to all. *See also* **Public goods**.

Nongovernmental organization: Any organization that is independent of government and has a core function of primarily humanitarian or co-operative, rather than commercial, objectives. Such organizations have proliferated in the last two decades and they are active in practically all jurisdictions. Not all nongovernmental organizations (NGOs) are genuine, however, or have genuine motives (there are also termed "astroturf" or phony NGOs; see J. Switzer, "Influencing Environmental Policy in Rural Communities: The Environmental Opposition at Work," *Policy Studies Journal*, 2001, 29(1), pp. 128–38). For a broad overview of NGOs and other partners in development, see, e.g., D. Hulme and M. Edwards, "NGOs, States, and Donors: An Overview," in D. Hulme and M. Edwards (eds.), *NGOs, States, and Donors: Too Close for Comfort?* New York: St. Martin's Press, 1997, pp. 3–22.

Nonmimetic adoption: A process whereby an organization comes up with a new routine or process by experimenting itself rather than merely copying what others may have already done. *Cf.* **Mimetic adoption**.

Nonoccupational specific training: Training that is generic and not tied to any specific occupation (such as supervision, project management, computing, etc.).

Nonprofit federalism: A term used to describe the phenomenon of a federal government increasingly using nonprofit organizations to provide services. See, e.g., M. Wyszomirski, "Lobbying Reform and Nonprofit Organizations: Policy Images and Constituent Policy," *Policy Studies Journal*, 1998, 26(3), pp. 512–25.

Nonprofit organizations: Organizations whose primary business objective is to provide services to customers rather than to maximize profits. Such organizations are considered an alternative mechanism for providing collective services. An argument is made that the more homogenous a society is, the less scope there will be for nonprofit organizations to operate in (largely because there is expected to be a greater similarity of citizens' preferences). Nonprofit organizations are said to be characterized by several vulnerabilities, including institutionalization (i.e., the tendency to formalize everything) and goal deflection (i.e., giving more focus to means over ends). See B. Weisbrod, "The Future of the Nonprofit Sector: Its Entwining with Private Enterprise and Government," *Journal of Policy Analysis and Management*, 1997, 16(4), pp. 541–55.

Nonrivalry: Also called jointness of supply, this refers to the fact that the consumption by one does not diminish the supply of the good being potentially available for others. *See also* **Public goods**.

Nonroutine problem solving: When organizations do not employ the standard protocols to address and solve emergent problems. Nonroutine problem solving is a capability that all organizations cherish, but the danger is that without standardization, organizations will not be able to minimize the cost of employing such nonroutine protocols.

Nonsolution: Refers to the fact that when a policy is formulated, it may not be a solution, and may, in fact, end up aggravating the problem. For an example of the application of the concept in relation to the highway repair bill in the United States, see L. Koenig, *An Introduction to Public Policy,* Englewood Cliffs, NJ: Prentice Hall, 1986, pp. 114–15.

Nonsubstitutability: Refers to the nonreplaceability of a group's activities in an organization. A group can gain more power if it has more nonsubstitutability (i.e., no one can do what it does). In such a situation, the group will have an incentive to retain its unique capabilities and mandate, and there is thus a danger that it will not be willing to disseminate its knowledge widely in the organization, thus minimizing organizational learning. See, e.g., D. Hickson et al., "A Strategic Contingencies' Theory of Interorganizational Power," *Administrative Science Quarterly,* 1971, 16(2), pp. 216–29. *See also* **Centrality**.

Nonsystematic risk: A risk that is evident in all the projects/programs of the organization, but where there is no one factor that is causing variance in their performance. *Cf.* **Systematic risk**.

Nontransferable training: *See* **Specific training**.

No-redundancy policy: An organization's explicit policy statement that it will not lay off employees (i.e., make them redundant) in the event of restructuring or loss of business or mandate. Should such restructuring indeed take place, the organization will attempt to place the affected employees elsewhere within the organization or outside it.

Normative commitment: *See* **Organizational commitment**.

Normative isomorphism: A step in the convergence process where organizations and systems in one jurisdiction copy from others whose value systems they wish to incorporate. Such copying is largely evident in the area of professionalization as resulting from uniform training and exposure to on-the-job learning experiences in different settings. Normative isomorphism may also result from the work of professional institutions in a jurisdiction that apply the same standards as those in other jurisdictions. As organizations increasingly begin to interact with others both physically and in cyberspace, such normative isomorphism becomes more and more commonplace. For a discussion of this concept, see, e.g., C. Pollitt,

"Convergence: The Useful Myth?" *Public Administration,* 2001, 79(4), pp. 933–47. *See also* **Convergence hypothesis**.

Normative policy analysis: A form of policy analysis that considers the values of policies rather than the causes and consequences. Given its focus on values—which, by definition, vary across individuals and groups—normative policy analysis tends to generate much more debate in the policy arena.

Normative risk: A risk for organizations that arises when specific risk-management techniques become institutionalized elsewhere in the system and there is pressure to adopt them, otherwise the perception is that the organization will be at a disadvantage. The concept is thus taken in the context of the work of other organizations and how and whether it is applied there.

Norm-referenced performance: Measurement of an employee's performance in relation to that of others in the organization. The norms are thus fairly standard across employees, who will generally have had an opportunity to review their determination. *See also* **Criteria-referenced performance.**

No-surprise policy: A mutual policy that two or more parties have whereby each will let the other know of emergent issues so that no party is taken by surprise when particular policy decisions are made. Such a no-surprise policy is normally in place among central agencies of governments so that emergent policy decisions are shared before they are forwarded to governmental ministers. Within an organizational setting, a no-surprise policy takes the form of: (a) a management charter, which specifies what employees can expect from their managers; and (b) a consultation charter, which specifies how employees will be consulted in the development of human-resource policies.

Nothing job: Refers to a job that an employee performs only for purposes of securing wages, and from which the employee does not derive any intrinsic reward.

Notice-and-comment consultation: A method of public consultation on a policy document whereby a governmental department first puts up a notice by way of informing the public about what the policy is, and then also allows a certain time period to allow citizens and others to comment. Such an arrangement does not mean that the agency will need to incorporate every comment made regarding the policy document, but it does provide an opportunity for broad-based feedback (which means not only those who are directly affected by it but also others). For a notice-and-comment consultation to be effective, it has to be widely circulated with effective mechanisms to capture the feedback received. See, e.g., S. Balla and J. Wright, "Interest Groups, Advisory Committees, and Congressional Control of the Bureaucracy," *American Journal of Political Science,* 2001, 45(4), pp. 799–812. *Cf.* **Targeted consultation**; *see also* **Regulatory negotiation**.

Notice-and-comment proceedings: *See* **Informal rule making.**

Not-in-my-backyard philosophy: The attitude that stakeholders have about wanting a particular service (such as drug-rehabilitation clinics) but not in their neighborhoods. The philosophy gives rise to the particular problem of how and where to situate the production and delivery of services, and how to ensure support from all stakeholders. For a review of the concept in relation to how it may be resolved, see, e.g., E. Feinerman, I. Finkelshtain and I. Kan, "On a Political Solution to the NIMBY Conflict," *The American Economic Review,* 2004, 94(1), pp. 369–81.

Nous capability: Also termed street skills, this concept refers to the ability that public servants are expected to possess which enables them to be sensitive to the nuances of public-sector work, primarily their interactions with politicians, and to know what to say when and how to handle relationships with nonbureaucratic actors. See, e.g., C. James, "Rankin Case Raises Governance Issues," *New Zealand Herald,* 11 July 2001, p. A15.

No-wrong-door principle: A principle in e-government and application of information and communication technologies where customers have choices in the method of interacting with government and they can do it through any of several ways. For example, feedback on a particular government policy or service may be provided through the Internet, by mail, e-mail, fax, phone, or physically visiting a governmental site. All these options will be provided to the user at the time he/she accesses a particular information base on government services.

O

OB (out-of-bound) markers: Issues that are too sensitive to be discussed in public. For example, the issue of race relations is an OB marker in

Singapore because there is fear that it could destabilize or jeopardize public order. See, e.g., K.L. Ho, *The Politics of Policy-Making in Singapore,* Singapore: Oxford University Press, 2000, p. 186.

Objective: Refers to a statement of accomplishment that is to be achieved in the short term. Objectives are derived from goals, which, in turn, are derived from mission statements (i.e., are long term). Objectives in programs are generally disaggregated between intermediate and overall ones. The intermediate objectives are those that collectively lead to the attainment of the overall one.

Objective performance measure: A measure that is used in evaluating the performance of employees or organizations that is objective and can be easily quantified (such as, for example, an increase in annual sales).

Objective quality evidence: Refers to evidence collected on the attainment (or nonattainment) of an objective that is derived from verifiable and robust measurements.

Objective responsibility: A term used to describe the responsibility of bureaucrats to carry out the will of the government regardless of whether they agree with policy. This is the political neutrality aspect of public service. The parallel aspect of objective responsibility is subjective (or psychological) responsibility, which refers to the conscience that individual public servants have and that they feel they must adhere to. For an early discussion of these types of responsibility, see, e.g., F. Mosher, *Democracy and the Public Service,* New York: Oxford University Press, 1968, p. 7.

Objective technicians: One of the three roles of policy analysts in their work where they hold analytical integrity as their fundamental value. Objectivity is demanded of these individuals in light of the increasing use of evidence-based analysis in public-policy analysis.

Objectives mapping: A technique in policy analysis used to map objectives and their relationships to relevant policy alternatives. An objective tree is a representational result of objectives mapping. Such mapping exercise helps analysts better understand the eventual hypothesized impact of the various policy alternatives that are under consideration. These effects ideally will be centered on the stated outcomes (i.e., goals) of the government.

Objectivity convention: The convention of using reliable facts/evidence to value an organizational asset. With public-sector organizations being asked to better account for their assets, this convention provides a rigorous basis for determining an organization's financial capability. It also enables governments to make more credible decisions toward increasing agencies' capacities.

Obligated position: A position in an organization to which an employee has a legal right to return. For example, when an employee leaves the organization on long-term study leave sanctioned by the organization, his/her position can be said to be obligated. However, an obligated position can be filled by someone else while the employee is absent.

Obligational contracting: A form of contracting where there tends to be a high degree of trust and considerable sharing of information between the principal and agent. Such a form of contracting leads to long-term mutual dependence between the two parties. See, e.g., P. Cooke and K. Morgan, *The Associational Economy: Firms, Regions, and Innovation,* New York: Oxford University Press, 1998, p. 54. *Cf.* **Arm's-length contracting**.

Occam's Razor: *See* **Principle of parsimony**.

Occupational hazard: A danger that an employee faces that is evident at his/her workplace, and that is directly associated with the work that is being performed. For example, an inspector at a governmental agency mandated to clean up hazardous waste has an occupational hazard of being exposed to toxic elements.

Occupational licensure: Refers to the regulation of occupations (such as medicine and law) and the behavior of members within these various occupations. Sanctions that emerge from occupational licensure—such as, for example, being barred from practicing one's occupation for a set period—are powerful means of ensuring that members of the occupation adhere to professional ethics and standards. *Cf.* **Self-regulation**.

Occupational obsolescence: Refers to employees not generating new knowledge or skills in their professions. Such obsolescence means that the individual's knowledge, skills, and abilities are not augmented to keep up with the new responsibilities and/or operational environment. All organizations will have some form of professional-development training programs that seek to address such occupational obsolescence.

Occupational overuse syndrome: Also called repetitive strain injury, this term refers to discomfort caused by muscle fatigue as a result of over-using one particular body part (such as looking at the computer screen for a long time every day). Organizations will normally have programs to help staff members deal with such a syndrome.

Occupational parity: *See* **Parity**.

Occupational prestige: An intrinsic reward that an individual may perceive from his/her occupation. Such prestige is entirely ascriptive, and, because it depends upon perception, varies from individual to individual.

Occupational psychosis: Refers to the fact that employees, as a result of their day-to-day tasks, develop unique preferences and value systems that are specific to their particular occupations. This will alter when the individual moves to another occupation (such as, for example, from academia to a governmental bureaucracy). Occupational psychosis is relevant to consider when ascertaining, for example, how employees may value intrinsic rewards differently across occupations.

Occupational socialization: Refers to a process through which an employee internalizes the values that are associated with a particular occupation. Thus, for example, when someone makes a career move and goes from academia to governmental service, the occupational socialization process will provide that the predisposition toward academic freedom changes toward a much more neutral competence orientation.

Occupational-specific training: Training that is specific to an occupation (such as computer programming, accountancy, etc.).

Okun's leaky bucket: Named after economist Arthur Okun, whose work focused on the trade-off governments are forced to make as they seek to enhance income equality in society. His view was that for every increase in the level of equality, some level of output would be sacrificed since incentives to work and invest would tend to diminish, and the administrative costs to manage governmental programs would increase. For a cogent review of the concept, see, e.g., R. Haveman, "The Big Trade-Off: Fundamental Law or Red Herring?" in S. Nagel (ed.), *Handbook of Public Policy Evaluation,* London: Sage Publications, 2002, pp. 7–12.

Old boys' network: A term that refers to the informal links which individuals that share a similar background (such as the same school) use to help others. The network has the effect of excluding others who do not share the same values and ethos that arise from similar backgrounds.

Ombudsman: A public official who normally holds a statutory position and who is mandated to investigate—in a neutral manner—complaints made by individuals about the activities and decisions of public agencies as it affects them. See, e.g., L. Hill, "The Ombudsman Revisited: Thirty

Years of Hawaiian Experience," *Public Administration Review,* 2002, 62(1), pp. 24–41.

One-stop shop: A term that denotes one location where citizens can go to in order to get services from governmental agencies. Such a location will either include the presence of governmental agencies that provide the service or will consist of an entity that will channel service requests to appropriate agencies. It could be, for example, that citizens who change addresses and wish to inform various governmental agencies could do so at one particular agency site, or a foreign investor who wishes to invest in a particular country could address all related procedure via one governmental agency.

One-time support: Resources that are provided to an organization on a single occasion to meet a financial requirement not expected to repeat itself. For example, one-time funds may be given to organizations when they need to make up the difference in wage contributions to pension funds subsequent to a legislative change to a new scheme. Ongoing support, on the other hand, is support that one party provides another (for example, a central agency may provide ongoing support to a governmental department in its strategic planning processes). Monitoring agencies that prescribe to the assist and assess approach will also accord ongoing support to departmental chief executives.

Onion model: This model of crisis decision making is part of the psychoanalytic tradition of looking at organizational dynamics. The model argues that organizations, in relation to their approach and preparedness for crises, can be looked at in the context of strategy, structure, assumptions, and core beliefs/values. These involve multiple layers that interact together and that result in an organization being on a continuum from crisis-prone to crisis-prepared. In this model, the strategy and structure are the outer layers, and assumptions and core beliefs are the inner ones. While it is relatively easy to manipulate the outer layers of the model, unless fundamental changes were brought about in the assumptions and beliefs/values of the organization, it would still not be better able to avert and handle crises. For an application of the model, see, e.g., Z. Sheaffer and R. Mano-Negrin, "Executives' Orientations as Indicators of Crisis Management Policies and Practices," *Journal of Management Studies,* 2003, 40(2), pp. 573–606.

On-the-job training: Training given to employees while in their workplace and doing their jobs. This could also refer to development that results from training that is part of regular work (such as from job rotation). The key point is that such training must be part of a work mode whether done in-house or outside.

Opaque measure: A policy measure which citizens cannot readily ascertain the specific policies, authority, or practice thereof. It is difficult, then, for the public to assess the monetary and social costs of such policies. Usually in public management, the first two (i.e., who makes the decision, and how they do so) are relatively easy to determine, but the true costs of policies are generally hard to calculate. *See also* **Policy measure**.

Open bid: When bids are permitted by any party that has the perceived capability to deliver the services required. An open bid year refers to the time period when governmental agencies do not require every service provision opportunity to be subject to an open bid (for purposes of minimizing administrative costs). Hence, at frequent intervals (say, two to three years), they will ask for open bids to be submitted by interested and capable parties to register their interest in providing the services. A selection of these will then be kept on as preferred providers.

Open career: *See* **Lateral entry**.

Open-ended agreement: A collective-bargaining agreement where there is no set time limit. The agreement will hold until one party wishes to reopen negotiations. Likewise, an open-ended contract is a contract where there is no termination date, either for employment or for delivery of goods and services.

Open-ended reimbursement grant: A grant awarded to subjurisdictions in the form of reimbursement given to them for local expenditure on specific projects that have the support of the granting authority as well. An open-ended matching grant is a grant where there is no cap on the total subsidy the local government can receive from the central government in terms of a matching grant.

Open-ended program: Any governmental program for which the legislature has set no ceiling on the amount of funding that is made available. Medicaid support in the United States is a good example of an open-ended program.

Open game: Any management game in which the participants (for example, the employer and employees) know how the other party will respond to any move. The process of setting collective bargaining agreements in organizations where labor-management relations are excellent can be considered to be an open game.

Open learning: Learning that is possible with ease of access and with no restriction on time and place. The pace of learning must also be flexible such that an individual can take his or her own time. There is no requirement for coaching on a regular basis although it is generally assumed that there will be someone for the individual to refer to should there be need.

Open policy window: *See* **Window of opportunity**.

Open recruitment: When an organization decides to seek candidatures for a particular post from individuals outside the organization. The purpose of seeking an open recruitment is to ensure that the net for qualified candidates is more widely cast. While there are administrative costs associated with this, the benefits may easily outweigh the costs. *See also* **Recruitment**.

Open-market purchase: When an organization decides to procure goods or services from the spot market rather than from a bidder who has responded to a request for a proposal. An open-market purchase is usually higher in costs but may be advantageous for the organization in that it is then not tied to one supplier.

Open-office plan: Where employees are not given rooms for offices but where they work in open spaces. The plan is characterized by an absence of interior walls and enclosed space, and is designed to facilitate camaraderie and the sharing of knowledge among employees.

Open system: (1) An organization that has extensive interactions with its environment, which includes other organizations, stakeholders, the legislature, and the general public, as well as any external rules, regulations, and protocols that the organization must adhere to. Organizations get mandates and feedback from the open system, and need to respond to them by either reorienting their internal processes or reconfiguring their production process. (2) Wherein the final state that the organization is headed toward is not dependent on initial conditions (i.e., the final state may be reached from different initial conditions and in different ways; this is also called equifinality). For more on the second interpretation of open system, see, e.g., L. Bertalanffy, "An Outline of General Systems Theory," *British Journal for the Philosophy of Science,* 1950, 1(2), pp. 139–64. *Cf.* **Closed system**.

Operating environment: The context in which an organization conducts its business. This includes not only the internal environment in the organization but also the external one. The operating environment, for example, for an immigration department may include pressure from some legislators to be more selective in accepting migrants, legal challenges by refugee organizations to existing and planned legislation on immigration, etc. See, e.g., State Services Commission, *Statement of Intent 2002,* Wellington: State Services Commission, 2002, pp. 8–9.

Operating frameworks: Basic rules and ways of doing things that allow an organization to operate (or fulfill mandates) in a particular way. Many governmental organizations will, for example, have stakeholder consultations as a primary operating framework.

Operational audit: A review of the operations of the organization. The audit looks at the activities and processes of the organization, and how any problems inherent in them could be better addressed. A related concept is operational control process, which is any management process that is designed to ensure that the operations of the organizations are carried out according to specifications efficiently and effectively. This involves planning and scheduling activities, and monitoring and taking any corrective action should *ex ante* specifications not be adhered to.

Operational decision: A decision that is concerned with the day-to-day operations and planning of the organization, as opposed to a strategic decision that considers the organization's long-term perspectives. An operational decision should ideally be a subset of the strategic plan of the organization so that all organizational actions contribute collectively to broad outcomes that the organization is mandated to help achieve.

Operationalization: The process of coming up with measurable indicators for any variables under consideration. This could be in relation to: (a) performance targeting where measures of performance need to be rigorously specified, or (b) identifying benchmarks for organizations to be aware of as they go about their business.

Operations audit: *See* **Economy and efficiency audit**.

Operations management: Processes that are geared toward the development and use of an effective and efficient operational system. Implicit in operations management are operations performance processes, which refer to a structured and formalized way of doing things and that are related to how routine operations are performed. Because of this routine nature, operations performance processes tend to be repetitive.

Operative learning: *See* **Organizational learning**.

Operative personnel: *See* **Operators**.

Operators: Also known as operative personnel (or rank and file), this term describes front-line deliverers of public services, and those who do not have any supervisory responsibility. For a discussion of how operators deal with task difficulty, see, e.g., J. Bohte and K. Meier, "Structure and the Performance of Public Organizations: Task Difficulty and Span of Control," *Public Organization Review,* 2001, 1(3), pp. 341–54.

Opportunism: The possibility for individuals and organizations to behave in an opportunistic manner that will maximize their own welfare. Thus, for example, contractors may see and seek to exploit opportunities to go around the specificities of a binding contract (also called agent opportunism). Opportunism affects all aspects of organizational life, including the efficacy of performance contracts, since it is inherent human nature. A related concept here is optimizing behavior, which is behavior exhibited by individuals and organizations in a way that maximizes their own interests or gives them the best results possible with the information and resources they have on hand. When optimizing is not complete, suboptimizing occurs. See, e.g., K. Conner and C. Prahalad, "A Resource-Based Theory of the Firm: Knowledge versus Opportunism," *Organization Science,* 1996, 7(5), pp. 477–501.

Opportunity costs: The costs of using resources for one purpose as measured in terms of alternatives lost as a result. The concept of opportunity costs is a key economic concept on costs and is used primarily in determining which project/policy to invest resources in.

Opportunity sets: The number of choices that an individual or organization has in relation to a possible course of action, subject to constraints of time and budget. In a public-service organization, the constraints also include the degree of political support (the equivalent in a private-sector firm would be support from the executive board).

Optimal contracts: Contracts that can be clearly specified and fulfilled, and where the scope for opportunism is negligible. The likelihood of optimal contracts can be increased if the behavior of each party can be monitored and measured by the other, which in itself cannot be in equal fashion since one party (such as the principal) will tend to have more access to such resources than the other (such as an agent). Optimal contracting is also evident when the subjective evaluation of the performance of the agent (by the principal) is agreed to by the agent. See, e.g., W. MacLeod,

"Optimal Contracting with Subjective Evaluation," *The American Economic Review,* 2003, 93(1), pp. 216–40.

Optimistic time estimate: As applied in performance evaluation and review technique, this term refers to the amount of time that project planners assume will be needed to complete a particular project under optimum conditions (i.e., when all conditions are fully and satisfactorily met). An optimistic time estimate does not, however, mean that this is the quickest completion time.

Optimizing behavior: *See* **Opportunism**.

Option to extend: As applied in contract administration, this term refers to the choice that both the principal and the agent wish to incorporate in their contract such that when specified criteria are satisfied, the contract is extended for a mutually agreed time period. This option gives both parties an opportunity to assess each other's behavior, and to ascertain whether the contractual relationship is beneficial and should be continued. A related concept is option to renew, which allows both principal and agent to renegotiate the terms of the contract to account for any changes in the situation under which the original contract was prepared.

Option value: The value that individuals place on a policy alternative that offers them the option of consuming something even if they may never do so. For example, the public may be ready to pay extra costs to preserve a nature reserve that they do not visit but possibly might do so if they had an option. See, e.g., B. Weisbrod, "Collective Consumption Services of Individual Consumption Goods," *Quarterly Journal of Economics,* 1964, 78(3), pp. 71–77. *See also* **Existence value**; **Irreversibility**.

Organic system: Conditions in an organization that render it able to operate in changing environments. The characteristics of an organic system include, among others, the ability to assess and reassess the macro operating environment and how that affects organizational tasks; open communication and consultative leadership style, so as to better facilitate the alignment of these tasks and available expertise; and ad hoc authority and control regimes since a rapidly changing operational environment requires fleet-footed responses. In an organic system, organizations also tend to attach less weight to hierarchy.

Organigram: Also known as organization chart, an organigram refers to the structure of an organization as reflected in a hierarchical representation.

Organization: As used in public management, an organization is an agency that is created with set structures and processes and that is mandated to fulfill some functions of the state. An organization will have rules and procedures that govern how decisions are taken, and how it goes about fulfilling its tasks. For a review of the types of organization in the public sector, see, e.g., P. Aucoin, "Independent Foundations, Public Money, and Public Accountability: Whither Ministerial Responsibility as Democratic Governance?" *Canadian Public Administration,* 2003, 46(1), pp. 1–26.

Organization, cultural dimensions in: Resulting from the seminal work done by social psychologist Geert Hofsteede, the cultural dimensions of an organization can be seen as consisting of: (a) the power-distance dimension (i.e., the extent to which the culture encourages superiors to exercise power), (b) the uncertainty-avoidance dimension (i.e., the ease with which organizations deal with new developments), (c) the individualism dimension (i.e., the extent to which individual considerations dominate group-centered ones), and (d) the masculinity dimension (i.e., where performance and ambition are preferred over quality of working life, good employer relations, etc.). See, G. Hofsteede and M. Bond, "The Confucian Connection: From Cultural Roots to Economic Growth," *Organizational Dynamics,* 1988, 16(4), pp. 4–21.

Organization development: The process of ensuring that the capacity of an organization to be involved in problem solving is sustained over time. There are many ways in which such capacity can be enhanced, including by emphasizing a collaborative work culture and teamwork. In organizational development, the assumption is that personnel in the organization will be willing and able to make the changes in mind-set that are necessary to make the organization more effective in its work. For a useful, although a bit outdated, discussion, see, e.g., W. French, "Organization Development: Objectives, Assumptions and Strategies," *California Management Review,* 1969, 12(2), pp. 23–34.

Organization image: Refers to how an organization is viewed by its personnel and by outsiders. A favorable image implies increased legitimacy of stakeholders to the organization or the policy it manifests. See, e.g., P. Bansal and W. Bogner, "Deciding on Economics, Institutions and Context," *Long Range Planning,* 2002, 35(3), pp. 269–90.

Organization life cycle: Describes the process of how all organizations go through several life stages, including introduction (normally by mandate in the public sector), growth (where they accumulate increased resources and functions), maturity, and decline. Not all organizations go through this cycle, however; for example, governmental departments will always continue to be in business since their mandates (such as monitoring and controlling) cannot be terminated (although some parts may be transferred to other governmental organizations, the voluntary sector, or to the private sector).

Organization man: Any individual that accepts and internalizes the norms and values exhibited by the organization with which he/she is affiliated. This includes, for example, adherence to hierarchical decision making, acceptance of superior authority, and instrumental rationality. Social philosopher William Whyte is one of the most noted authors to have discussed the concept (see his *The Organization Man,* New York: Simon & Schuster, 1956). For further discussion, see, e.g., D. Randall, "Commitment and the Organization—The Organization Man Revisited," *Academy of Management Review,* 1987, 12(3), pp. 460–71.

Organization, technical core of: The basic work activities of an organization that are at the heart of what the organization does. Thus, for example, a small policy unit at the central-government level will have a technical core of providing policy advice on a particular sector to the executive branch of government, or the parliamentary counsel office will have a technical core of drafting legislation.

Organization, thickness of: Denotes a situation where an organization's activities, networks, and knowledge and skills base rise as a result of deliberate action. Indicators of thickness are evident in factors such as occupational specialization, organizational density, and degree of collaboration between organizations and research centers such that collective knowledge is shared. The thicker the organization, the more immune it tends to become to termination. Sunset legislation is one way of dealing with the thickness of organizations. See, e.g., H. Kaufman, *Time, Chance, and Organizations,* Chatham, NJ: Chatham House Publishers, 1985, p. 141.

Organizational accountability: The answerability of organizations to a legislature for the resources they have been given and the objectives that are expected of them. Such accountability is often specified in law (for example, a public-service commission may by law be accountable to parliament on how the merit principle is applied in the public service).

Organizational aggregation: The process of two or more organizations joining hands as a way of dealing with the pressures that emanate from their operating environment. Such an aggregation could, for example, be a decision to pool their energies to address a particular problem (also known as organizational alignment), or it could be something more tangible where the organizations decide to merge altogether. Organizational aggregation in the public sector is a product of a political decision, whereas in the private sector market conditions determine this phenomenon. For a discussion of the concept, see, e.g., T. Powell, "Organizational Alignment as Competitive Advantage," *Strategic Management Journal,* 1992, 13(2), pp. 119–34.

Organizational aggregation, density model of: A model that focuses on the dynamics of competition to explain the number of organizations that exist in a system. Basically, the model asserts that as the number of organizations grows, there is inevitably competition for scarce resources, which invariably leads to the "death" of some organizations or some of them may opt to aggregate (i.e., band with others) to retain some of their presence. See, e.g., J. Baum and J. Singh, "Organizational Niches and the Dynamics of Organizational Mortality," *American Journal of Sociology,* 1994, 100(2), pp. 346–80.

Organizational alignment: *See* **Organizational aggregation**.

Organizational architecture: Generally, refers to three protocols that are evident in any organization: (a) the assignment of decision rights within the organization, (b) the methods of rewarding employees, and (c) the structure of systems to evaluate the performance of both individuals and organizational units. See, e.g., J. Brickley, C. Smith, and J. Zimmerman, *Managerial Economics and Organizational Architecture,* Chicago: Irwin, 1997, p. G-7.

Organizational attraction: The appeal that an organization exhibits to potential candidates who show an interest in being a member of the organization. Such an appeal could be manifest in: (a) its reward structures (such as level of remuneration), (b) its perceived power (such as by virtue of being a central-government agency), or (c) in its working environment (such as if flexitime were possible). See, e.g., T. Judge and D. Cable, "Applicant Personality, Organizational Culture, and Organizational Attraction," *Personnel Psychology,* 1997, 50(2), pp. 359–94.

Organizational autonomy: The independence that an organization needs in order to be able to make decisions on how best to manage its affairs and achieve its mandates. Such autonomy is restricted in traditional public-service departments, while agencies at arm's length from governmental ministers tend to have more organizational autonomy. For a good review of the concept, see, e.g., K. Verhoest et al., "The Study of Organizational Autonomy: A Conceptual View," *Public Administration and Development,* 2004, 24(2), pp. 101–18.

Organizational behavior: (1) The behavior that organizations exhibit (for example, in responding to criticism in the media). (2) The human behavior, attitudes, and performance within an organizational setting. Organizational behavior modification is a process of manipulating the organization's reward and sanctions system to change the behavior of employees.

Organizational boundaries: The parameters (both physical and otherwise) within which organizations operate. With the increasing use of contractual relationships for long periods of time, organizational boundaries are beginning to shift and become blurred since both parties to the contract get more opportunities to interact with—and be influenced by—each other. Ideally, the boundaries should not be impermeable and organizations should be able to learn from their external environment.

Organizational change: The process of internal reconfiguration in an organization such that it is better able to manage the resources it has at its disposal to attain its objectives. While organizational change can be disruptive to the established rules and protocols, and to employees' understanding of what is expected of them and how they operate, it is necessary to ensure that the organization is continually able to respond to pressures from its operating environment. Such a response can be facilitated either by an external change agent or by the organizational leadership itself. See, e.g., B. Schneider, A. Brief, and R. Guzzo, "Creating a Climate and Culture for Sustainable Organizational Change," *Organizational Dynamics,* 1996, 24(4), pp. 7–19.

Organizational character: A term used by early organizational theorists such as Philip Selznick to denote the unique and distinctive identity of an organization. Such an identity is said to be a product of various variables, including methods of work, organizational norms and value systems, and operating environment. For a discussion of this concept in a cross-jurisdictional setting, see, e.g., A. Som, "Building Sustainable Organizations through Restructuring: Role of Organizational Character in France and India," *International Journal of Human Resources Development and Management,* 2003, 3(1), pp. 2–16.

Organizational citizenship: The degree to which the employees in an organization internalize its value systems and consequently feel an integral part thereof. Behavior that denotes a high degree of organizational citizenship includes, for example, going beyond what the particular role requires, helping others, volunteering for extra work or to fill in for someone else, and upholding marginal organizational rules even when it is inconvenient. For a case-study application of the concept, see, e.g., G. Murphy, J. Athanasou, and N. King, "Job Satisfaction and Organizational Citizenship Behavior: A Study of Australian Human-Service Professionals," *Journal of Managerial Psychology,* 2002, 17(4), pp. 287–97. *See also* **Good soldier syndrome.**

Organizational climate: The environment that exists in an organization, which affects how employees work and how their interactions with each other are structured. Considerations of the climate include factors such as physical working conditions, the degree of adherence to rules, communications with managers, and behavior of organizational leaders.

Organizational clout: The wherewithal and power that an organization will have accumulated over time to ensure that it has the means at hand to attain its objectives in the manner that it sees fit. Organizational clout, not unlike individual power, stems from sources such as access to resources, legal mandates regarding decision rights, proximity to political power, among others. In general, central agencies in government, by virtue of their mandates, have a greater degree of organizational clout than other public-sector organizations.

Organizational cluster: *See* **Organizational aggregation**.

Organizational cohesiveness: The degree to which disparate divisions of the organization as a whole are united in the work that they do, and to which staff members feel that they are an integral part of the organization. The cohesiveness is reflected in, for example, the manner in which the organization responds as one to external demands (i.e., speaks with one voice), and in how the organizational climate is conducive to work.

Organizational commitment: Refers to the extent to which an employee identifies with the organization that he/she is working for, and the degree to which the individual is involved in, and attached to, the organization. Three elements of organizational commitment can be identified: (a) affective commitment (i.e., commitment as a result of feeling good about the organization), (b) continuance commitment (i.e., commitment that results from the perceived losses if the employee were to leave the organization), and (c) normative commitment (i.e., commitment that is drawn from an alignment of the goals of the organization and of the employee). See, e.g., H. Angle and J. Perry, "An Empirical Assessment of Organizational Commitment and Organizational Effectiveness," *Administrative Science Quarterly,* 1981, 26(1), pp. 1–14.

Organizational competence: The ability of an organization to refine and coordinate its internal routines as well as put in place mechanisms to ensure that it is capable of maximizing the use of the individual competencies of employees to attain organizational objectives. Organizational competence is also evident when organizations show an ability to deal effectively with their operating environments, including dealing with any adverse developments. See, e.g., J. Sorensen and T. Stuart, "Aging, Obsolescence, and Organizational Innovation," *Administrative Science Quarterly,* 2000, 45(1), pp. 81–112.

Organizational complexity: The complexity in the rules, protocols, and operations of an organization that is driven largely by, among other things: (a) increased interdependencies among employees, (b) divisions internally and with other stakeholders externally, and (c) changes in technology that affect how organizational operations are run. See, e.g., M. Emmert, M. Crow, and R. Shangraw, "Public Management in the Future: Post-Orthodoxy and Organization Design," in B. Bozeman (ed.), *Public Management: The State of the Art,* San Francisco: Jossey-Bass, 1993, pp. 345–60.

Organizational conflict: Conflict that exists between groups and individuals within an organization (such as over decision rights regarding perceived domains) as well as between organizations (such as in who has exclusivity over which mandate). As with any form of conflict, it is not accurate to say that all conflicts are negative; some organizational conflicts, if treated properly, serve to make organizations stronger.

Organizational culture: Explicit and implicit expectations of behavior within the organization (including, for example, how employees are rewarded, controlled, and allowed to express themselves). Organizational culture is shaped in many ways, for example, by the predispositions of members, the technology in use in the organization, and the situational imperatives with which the organization must cope to give it a distinct way of responding to its operating environment. Organizational culture is also evident at three different levels: (a) the tangibles (i.e., that which is physically evident), (b) the norms and values, and (c) the basic assumptions on which the organization operates. Public organizations are generally categorized as possessing a process organizational culture where feedback (such as from citizens) is slow or nonexistent and where the risks of termination are low. See, e.g., E. Schein, *Organizational Culture and Leadership,* 2nd edition, San Francisco: Jossey Bass, 1992. For a case-study application of organizational culture in the public-sector context, see, e.g., A. Driscoll and J. Morris, "Stepping Out: Rhetorical Devices and Culture Change Management in the UK Civil Service," *Public Administration,* 2001, 79(4), pp. 803–24.

Organizational Darwinism: The basic idea that only those organizations that are relatively more efficient and effective will survive. While this may be apt in the private-sector context, it is generally argued that in the public sector, organizational terminations are not common and so this concept does not apply wholly to public-sector organizations.

Organizational decline: The diminution of power and appeal of an organization. Such a decline is generally marked by falling productivity and low employee morale. See, e.g., W. Weitzel and E. Jonsson, "Decline in Organizations: A Literature Integration and Extension," *Administrative Science Quarterly,* 1989, 34(1), pp. 91–109.

Organizational democracy: Refers to the manner in which organizations need to function so as to better harness the knowledge and learning opportunities that exist for staff members. In an organizational democracy, the need for continual innovation means managers must be open and trusting of their staff members, and give them certain autonomy (i.e., space) to do their work. Because organizational democracy also has implications for networks with others, how external stakeholders add value to the work of the organization is critically analyzed. For a good analysis of this concept, see, e.g., D. Butcher and M. Clarke, "Organizational Politics: The Cornerstone for Organizational Democracy," *Organizational Dynamics,* 2002, 31(1), pp. 35–46.

Organizational density: The number of organizations performing similar functions. Organizational density in the public sector is controlled by legislative action and political will rather than by market forces.

Organizational design: The process of planning and structuring an organization in such a way that its functions and operations contribute optimally to its mandates. Such design can be manifest either in the physical layout of the organization or in the functional and decision-making reconfiguration of its various divisions (i.e., whether it has a flat structure or is hierarchical with various levels of decision making). Whichever it is, the main implication of organization design is that of manipulability. See, e.g., H. Mintzberg, "Organization Design: Fashion or Fit?" *Harvard Business Review,* 1981, 59(1), pp. 103–16.

Organizational design triangle: A situation existing in an organization where three features are evident: (a) centralization (i.e., decision making in a hierarchical fashion), (b) decentralization (i.e., where lower levels in the organization can make their own decisions regarding operational matters and where not every decision needs prior approval), and (c) teamwork (i.e., cooperation among individuals, horizontally and vertically).

Organizational design, L-form of: The learning form of organizational design focuses on structuring the organization in such a manner so as to facilitate learning across the organization. Such learning comes from interactions with others, which is why in the L-form, multidivisional teams tend to be the norm. In that sense, L-form organizations are characterized by a lack of boundaries. See, e.g., C. James, "Designing Learning Organizations," *Organizational Dynamics,* 2003, 32(1), pp. 46–61.

Organizational design, M-form of: The multidivisional form of organization design has been the traditional way in which organizations have been structured. In this design, divisions within organizations form silos, with a management structure planted across the top. The M-form focuses on specialization and efficiency, although their silo nature means that divisions tend to remain isolated from one another. See, e.g., P. Cooke and K. Morgan, *The Associational Economy: Firms, Regions, and Innovation,* New York: Oxford University Press, 1998, pp. 39–41.

Organizational design, N-form of: In contrast to the M-form of organizational design, this refers to the network form, which is based on heterarchy. See, e.g., P. Cooke and K. Morgan, *The Associational Economy: Firms, Regions, and Innovation,* New York: Oxford University Press, 1998, pp. 39–41. *See also* **Heterarchy.**

Organizational diagnosis: Refers to the methods in use that helps assess whether organizations have the capacity to meet their mandates. While organizational diagnosis can take place at any time, it is often done when substantial mandate change is being considered, such as, for example, when governments consider the merger of public organizations. See, e.g., M. Beer and B. Spector, "Organizational Diagnosis: Its Role in Organizational Learning," *Journal of Counseling and Development,* 1993, 71(6), pp. 642–50.

Organizational distance: The degree of removal of an organization from the stated needs of the clientele it is mandated to serve. When an organization focuses more on strengthening its own position rather than on re-orienting its products and services to suit the needs of its client base, then organizational distance is said to exist. The distance is measured, for example, by the amount of time it takes for the organization to respond to stated demands from the public (for example, in doing away with a procedure that impedes quick access to services).

Organizational domain: Refers to an organization's: (a) operating locations; (b) primary and secondary functions and activities, clients and customers; and (c) rules and protocols concerning how it operates. As a general rule, the more complex and extensive an organization's mandate, the greater its organizational domain.

Organizational ecology: The environment within which an organization operates. In the public sector, for example, this is characterized by, among other things, accountability to the legislature, transparency of process, adherence to the merit principle, and principles of fairness and equal treatment. The ecology also incorporates the organization's stakeholders, and the protocols that organizations have to engage them. A related concept is that of organizational environment, which refers collectively to those conditions that affect how an organization operates. Organizations have several ways of dealing with their environment, including by: (a) rapidly exploiting new opportunities and immediately addressing disturbances by asserting their positions, and (b) strengthening organizational processes to secure their standing. See, e.g., B. Peters, "Government Reorganization: A Theoretical Analysis," in A. Farazmand (ed.), *Handbook of Bureaucracy,* New York: Marcel Dekker, Inc., 1994, pp. 165–82.

Organizational economics: Determination of work of personnel by targets and income-generation requirements rather than by rules, regulations, and internal processes. In that regard, organizational activity is said to be governed by economic-rational principles and less by traditional legal-rational ones. See, e.g., T. Moe, "The New Economics of Organization," *American Journal of Political Science,* 1984, 28(4), pp. 739–77.

Organizational environment: *See* **Organizational ecology**.

Organizational evolution: The change that organizations go through in time, but not necessarily devoid of deliberate management action. In this regard, organizational evolution may be seen as an effort by organizational leadership to take the agency "to the next level." This is manifest in two ways: (a) micro-evolution, which refers to upgrading management capability (such as in strategic planning), and (b) macro-evolution, which refers to identifying new competencies for the organization as a whole (for example, in finding new and more effective ways of engaging citizens). See, e.g., M. Tushman and E. Romanelli, "Organizational Evolution: A Metamorphosis Model of Convergence and Reorientation," in B. Straw and L. Cummings (eds.), *Research in Organizational Behavior,* Greenwich, CT: JAI Press, 1985, pp. 171–222.

Organizational failure: At the extreme, this refers to the inability of an organization to fulfill its mandate. In general, it means the inability of the organization to deal with an emergent problem to the satisfaction of its stakeholders. Organizational failure could result from any number of factors, including absence of resource planning, self-interested managerial behavior, and nonadherence to established safety standards. For an example of an application of the concept, see, R. Frank and M. Gaynor, "Organizational Failure and Transfers in the Public Sector: Evidence from an Experiment in the Financing of Mental Health Care," *Journal of Human Resources,* 1994, 29(1), pp. 108–25.

Organizational functioning, model of: States that in all organizations there has to be both appropriate differentiation as well as adequate integration in order that they deal effectively with their external environment. This stems from the assertion that all organizations internally develop some degree of differentiation in their work, which leads to differences in internal management culture, and which will eventually need to be integrated otherwise they risk losing coherence. This model provides important cues to practitioners on the need to find the right balance between differentiation and integration.

Organizational goal: The objective that an organization is mandated to achieve. It is useful to distinguish between the official goals (i.e., the publicly stated mandate in the public-sector organization and the business mission in the private firm) and the operative goals (i.e., goals that are actually pursued). *See also* **Manifest/latent function**.

Organizational health: Leadership guru Warren Bennis developed this idea to refer to the degree to which an organization is able to understand, and get a better handle on, the intricacies of the various situations it faces. Such situations can be: (a) manifest (i.e., what is formally displayed and described by the organization in its reports and publicity materials), (b) extant (i.e., what actually exists), (c) requisite (i.e., what would need to be in place in order to fulfill the relevant organizational mandates), and

(d) assumed (i.e., as perceived by employees in the organization). An organizational health audit is a periodic check that is done of all the processes and systems in an organization to ensure that they remain accurate and effective. It is normally carried out internally, although an external auditor may be used. For a discussion of organizational health, see, e.g., C. Argyris, "Organizational Health and Executive Development," *Advanced Management,* 1959, 24(12), pp. 8–11.

Organizational heartland: Refers to the core of the organization (i.e., the nucleus or heart of the organization). Managers generally tend to expand organizational functions and staffing so that when cuts need to be made, the core (heartland) can remain protected (by cutting marginal functions and laying off marginal staff members). See B. Peters, "Government Reorganization: A Theoretical Analysis," in A. Farazmand (ed.), *Handbook of Bureaucracy,* New York: Marcel Dekker, Inc., 1994, pp. 165–82.

Organizational humanism: Refers to an approach of making the work environment in organizations more humane. The main argument in organizational humanism is that treating employees humanely leads to greater organizational efficiency and helps promote organizational evolution because employees then tend to better internalize change. See R. Denhardt, *Theories of Public Organizations,* Monterey, CA: Brooks/Cole, 1984, p. 92.

Organizational hypocrisy: Refers to the existence of multiple and conflicting norms and value systems in organizations. This multiplicity of norms is manifested, for example, in discrepancies in what organizations say and what they do, and in how organizational leaders engage different stakeholders in different manners. For a case-study application of the concept, see, e.g., T. Huzzard and K. Ostergren, "When Norms Collide: Learning Under Organizational Hypocrisy," *British Journal of Management,* 2002, 13(special issue), pp. S47-S59.

Organizational identification: The process of employees internalizing the values and norms of the organization by which their goals are in alignment with those of the organization. Identification, however, is different from commitment, and while employees may share the same goals, this does not necessarily mean that they are committed to fulfilling them. For a case study of organizational identification, see, e.g., M. Pratt, "The Good, the Bad, and the Ambivalent: Managing Identification among Amway Distributors," *Administrative Science Quarterly,* 2000, 45(3), pp. 456–93.

Organizational identity: Refers to that which uniquely characterizes an organization (i.e., something that is distinctive about it). Organizational identity enables an organization to maintain continuity of its value system and culture, and it is this that enables it to replenish itself in terms of external support, including recruitment of human resources. For a discussion of organizational identity and organizational success, see, e.g., D. Giola, M. Schultz, and K. Korley, "Organizational Identity, Image, and Adaptive Instability," *Academy of Management Review,* 2000, 25(1), pp. 65–81.

Organizational incompetence: (1) Denotes a situation where an organization is not able to effectively attain its mandates. (2) The inability, or lack of willingness, exhibited by an organization to learn from its environment (including its failures). Organizational incompetence stems from many sources, including organizational inertia, which is a state where organizations cannot and/or will not change in keeping with the changes in their environment. There is a circular effect between organizational incompetence and organizational inertia where one situation leads to, and compounds, the other. See, e.g., S. Ott and J. Shafritz, "Toward a Definition of Organizational Incompetence: A Neglected Variable in Organizational Theory," *Public Administration Review,* 1994, 54(4), pp. 370–77. See also M. Hannan and J. Freeman, "Structural Inertia and Organizational Change," *American Sociological Review,* 1994, 49(2), pp. 149–64.

Organizational inertia: *See* **Organizational incompetence**.

Organizational information availability: Refers to the ready availability of relevant information to the organizational leadership so as to facilitate better decision making. Such information results from the formal and deliberate efforts of management to monitor its operating environment, and to channel the information so gained into proper processing protocols (i.e., to make sense of the information). It is argued that organizational information availability enhances vigilant issue interpretation. For a case study, see, e.g., B. Kuvaas, "An Exploration of Two Competing Perspectives on Informational Contexts in Top Management Strategic Issue Interpretation," *Journal of Management Studies,* 2002, 39(7), pp. 977–1001.

Organizational justice theory: Asserts that employees perceive fairness in organizations as consisting of justice in three areas: (a) distributive (i.e., whether they see justice in the way rewards are distributed among fellow workers), (b) procedural (i.e., fairness in the way organizational processes are applied), and (c) interactional (i.e., how they are treated by the organizational leadership). For a review of the essentials of this theory, see, e.g., J. Paterson, A. Green, and J. Cary, "The Measurement of Organizational Justice in Organizational Change Programs: A Reliability, Validity, and Context Sensitivity Assessment," *Journal of Occupational and Organizational Psychology,* 2002, 75(4), pp. 393–408.

Organizational learning: Refers to the process of how organizations take cues from their internal and external environments and use the knowledge so gained to improve their work. Organizational learning can be of four types: (a) "reinventive" (i.e., when organizations question and replace old knowledge and information with new ones), (b) formative (i.e., when organizations create new schemas to provide new interpretations to existing knowledge and information), (c) adjustive (i.e., when organizations acquire new shared information and update existing schemas), and (d) operative (i.e., when the existing schemas within organizations are reaffirmed and validated—this form of learning tends to take place in stable environments). For an analysis of these types of organizational learning, see, e.g., D. Gnyawali and A. Stewart, "A Contingency Perspective on Organizational Learning: Integrating Environmental Context, Organizational Learning Processes, and Types of Learning," *Management Learning,* 2003, 34(1), pp. 63–89. For a review of the various definitions of organizational learning, see, e.g., N. Bontis, "Managing an Organizational Learning System by Aligning Stocks and Flows," *Journal of Management Studies,* 2002, 39(4), pp. 437–69.

Organizational loyalty: *See* **Good soldier syndrome**.

Organizational maintenance: Refers to the process of ensuring that an organization has adequate resources so as to fulfill its functions. Organizational maintenance is an issue that is at center stage primarily during budget rounds since organizations need to justify their bids for resources then. See, e.g., J. Wilson, *Bureaucracy: What Government Agencies Do and Why They Do It,* New York: Basic Books, 1989, p. 181.

Organizational memory: *See* **Institutional memory**.

Organizational mission: Refers generally to the goals of an organization. Organizational mission statements tend to be broadly stated, which leaves room for the organization to be flexible in how it approaches its work. A mission statement helps formulate the organizational strategic intent, which, in turn, enables specification of the tactical actions necessary to achieve the mandates.

Organizational mortality: Literally, the death of organizations (i.e., the termination of organizational mandates). In general, organizational mortality in the public sector is less evident than in the private sector because of the absence of strong market pressures. See, e.g., J. Baum and J. Singh, "Organizational Niches and the Dynamics of Organizational Mortality," *American Journal of Sociology,* 1994, 100(2), pp. 346–80.

Organizational myopia: Refers to a situation where an organization tends to be focused too narrowly on one particular objective or sub-objective and disregards the other facets of its work and/or is unable to take different perspectives in fulfilling its mandates. Thus, for example, an organization could end up focusing on minimizing low-level operational inefficiencies (such as responding to a customer complaint within one working day) at the expense of tasks that are at a higher but as important level (such as strategic planning for task alignment). See, e.g., D. Johnson and G. Macy, "Using Environmental Paradigms to Understand and Change an Organization's Response to Stakeholders," *Journal of Organizational Change Management,* 2001, 14(4), pp. 314–34.

Organizational niche: Refers to the level at which an organization is placed depending upon its mandates, productive capacities, and consequential resource requirements. Depending on their organizational niches, different organizations face different pressures from their operating environments. For example, central-government departments are in a different niche than line organizations and consequently face a greater degree of pressures from the political establishment. For a general discussion of the concept, see, e.g., J. Baum and J. Singh, "Organizational Niches and the Dynamics of Organizational Mortality," *American Journal of Sociology,* 1994, 100(2), pp. 346–80.

Organizational obesity: A term used to refer to the personnel bulge in the middle-management levels in an organization. If internal mobility and promotions become increasingly constrained, then over time, a large group of managers will cluster around the middle of the hierarchy thus unbalancing it. Such a bulge leads to a lack of agility as middle managers—not seeing viable options to move up rapidly—begin to lose the vision and the broad outlook needed for leadership positions.

Organizational politics: A process whereby individuals use informal (and sometime formal) tactics to gain the upper hand in organizational matters. This is evident, for example, when a manager circumvents standard operating procedures to get more operating resources, or when an individual staff member aligns himself/herself to a particular manager and denigrates others. See, e.g., B. Mayes and R. Allen, "Towards a Definition of Organizational Politics," *Academy of Management Review,* 1977, 2(4), pp. 672–78.

Organizational power: The ability of organizations to compel employees and others to respond in set ways. Organizations are generally considered to have access to three primary instruments of power: (a) condign power (i.e., physical, as in determination of the working environment), (b) compensatory power (i.e., economic, as in reward structures), and (c) conditioned power (i.e., belief, as in values and norms). See, e.g., D. McKevitt and A. Lawton, *Public Sector Management: Theory, Critique, and Practice,* London: Sage Publications, 1994, p. 272.

Organizational process: Refers to the various activities and procedures in an organization. Some examples of organizational processes are internal communications, managerial decision making, and training and development. Organizational processes are one of three lenses that can be used to help explain the choices made by policy makers (the other two being rational actor, and bureaucratic politics). The organizational process paradigm asserts that the behavior of organizations can be understood better if they are seen as large units that have standard patterns of behavior rather than as rational actors that make deliberate choices in the production of outputs and in the attainment of their objectives. See, e.g., D. Welch, "The Organizational Process and Bureaucratic Politics Paradigms: Retrospect and Prospect," *International Security,* 1992, (17)2, pp. 112–46.

Organizational psychoanalysis view: Argues that a study of the organization's covert and unconscious processes need to be considered and dealt with in order to discourage staff members from using existing frames of reference to continue with "business as usual" in their work. The organizational psychoanalysis view thus considers both the rational and nonrational dimensions of individuals' behavior in organizations. For a review of the concept in relation to rational-technical approaches to change in organizations, see, e.g., D. Anderson and J. White, "Organizational Psychoanalysis in Public Administration," *American Review of Public Administration,* 2003, 33(2), pp. 189–208.

Organizational pyramid: A term that refers to the hierarchical nature of organizational structure with power and control limited at the top. There are far more members of an organization at the bottom and progressively fewer as one moves up the hierarchy, hence the shape of a pyramid. In an organizational pyramid, those below are responsible to those at the top and the leadership is accountable for the actions of the organization.

Organizational reengineering: A fundamental rethinking and redesign of an organization in response to pressures from its operational environment. Such reengineering usually takes the form of substantially altering organizational protocols and methods of work, and at times there is also an expansion—and contraction—of organizational mandate (such as when a cabinet decides to give a related time-bound function to a particular organization that is in some way related to the organization's broad mission).

Organizational renewal: Revamping of organizational mandates, operating procedures, and resources so that the organization can do its work more effectively. Organizational renewal can be enhanced, for example, by endeavoring to break out of the status-quo mode, taking on multiple perspectives to any problem situation, encouraging employees to be positive in responding to change situations, encouraging them to be interested in activities and developments that are only tangentially related to their field of study and work, and creating ad hoc task forces and cross-functional teams to stimulate new ideas on ways of fulfilling the same mandates. See, e.g., B. Leavy, "Strategic Renewal: Is Disruptive Revolution Unavoidable?" *Strategic Change,* 1997, 6(5), pp. 283–98.

Organizational routine: A term that refers to the regular and predictable behavior of organizations. Such routine is a product of the formalization of specific rules and regulations as well as operating protocols that staff members and outsiders are expected to adhere to. For a very good discussion of the concept, see, e.g., M. Feldman and A. Rafaeli, "Organizational Routines as Sources of Connections and Understandings," *Journal of Management Studies,* 2002, 39(3), pp. 309–31.

Organizational slack: A term coined by noted organizational theorists Richard Cyert and James March to denote the excess of resources at the disposal of a coalition within an organization required to make side payments. Organizational slack is significant in the coalition process of goal formation. In the process of dealing with coalitions, the organization will have resources available that are in excess of total payments necessary to maintain the contributions of coalition members. This slack allows an organization to deal with demands from coalition members that exceed expectations or the norm. In that sense, it serves as a cushion to successfully adjust to various internal and external pressures that the organization may face. For an original exposition of the term, see R. Cyert and J. March, "Organizational Factors in the Theory of Oligopoly," *Quarterly Journal of Economics,* 1956, 70(1), pp. 44–64.

Organizational social capital: Just like societies, organizations too can generate social capital, which in this case are networks and shared values that allow different divisions within an organization to cooperate with and help each other. The formation of organizational social capital is facilitated by a clear organizational mission and by inculcating appropriate values in staff members. See, e.g., L. Prusak and D. Cohen, "How to Invest in Social Capital," *Harvard Business Review,* 2001, 79(6), pp. 86–93.

Organizational social responsibility: The responsibility that an organization needs to demonstrate toward the society at large and not only to the mandate-specific clientele that it deals with on a continuing basis. This concept is more applicable in the private sector, where firms are encouraged to think of their responsibilities to society (such as on minimizing pollution) at the same time that they focus on increasing the profit margin. For an application of the term, see, e.g., D. Johnson and G. Macy, "Using Environmental Paradigms to Understand and Change an Organization's Response to Stakeholders," *Journal of Organizational Change Management,* 2001, 14(4), pp. 314–34.

Organizational socialization: A process whereby newcomers to an organization learn the values and beliefs of the groups to which they belong. Such socialization can be either implicit or explicit, formal or informal. Rarely is the socialization process dramatic (although the military may well serve as an exception); often the process is subtle and evolutionary. Over time, the newcomers will get a good sense of how things work in the organization, and what is and is not expected of them.

Organizational structure: The formal pattern of how an organization's personnel and jobs are grouped. The formal organizational structure can be analyzed by looking at degrees of specialization of roles, standardization of procedures, and centralization of authority. See, e.g., C. Fombrun, "Structural Dynamics Within and Between Organizations," *Administrative Science Quarterly,* 1986, 31(3), pp. 403–21.

Organizational subculture: Any culture that is evident within an organization's dominant culture. Organizational subcultures are not easy to identify and individuals can be members of more than one subculture. For example, within a process-dominant culture (i.e., a bureaucracy), subcultures can be found in computing services, secretarial support, etc.

Organizational turf: Drawing from some pioneering work done by political scientist Matthew Holden in 1966, this concept has been widely used to denote the tendency of organizations to retain their mandates and to guard their work and their domains of influence. Further to this, organizational turf enhancement tends to become a key preoccupation for organizational leaders who would like to expand their areas of intervention so that they can increase their influence in the public sector. The concept has a pejorative connotation generally, and implies that organizational leaders are more interested in protecting their particular area than keeping in mind the broader goals that the government wishes to pursue. See, e.g., M. Holden, "'Imperialism' in Bureaucracy," *American Political Science Review,* 1966, 60(4), pp. 943–51.

Organizational values: The norms that organizations exhibit in their everyday work. Some agencies, such as a finance ministry, for example, seek to exhibit organizational values that are characterized by control, direction, and rigor of analysis given their focus on maintaining tight control over how resources are spent and how they are budgeted for.

Organizations, survival tactics of: Refers to how organizations seek to maintain survival in the face of pressures for their dismantling. Such survival tactics could include seeking the support of important groups (including legislators and persons of prestige and influence), directly appealing to the public, and compromising on some marginal functions.

Organized anarchies: Situations that occur when an organization has the following attributes: (a) the preferences of its members, as well as of the organization itself, are rather ambitious; (b) the organization tends to work by trial and error rather than by set procedures; and (c) there is what is known as "fluid participation," i.e., which member is involved in what activity is constantly changing. Obviously, not all organizations are anarchies, but most of them will tend to exhibit some of these attributes at times. See, e.g., M. Cohen, J. March, and J. Olsen, "A Garbage Can Model of Organizational Choice," *Administrative Science Quarterly,* 1972, 17(1), pp. 1–25.

Organized complexity: A situation existing in an organization where the mandates, protocols, and interrelationships among the various entities produce fairly complex relationships but they are still organized (i.e., there are deliberately manipulated so as to avoid any unplanned interactions that might jeopardize the organization's capacity to work towards its mandates). In contrast, organized simplicity refers to the linear relationships among the various elements and protocols in an organization where the interactions among the entities do not create complex relationships.

Organized simplicity: *See* **Organized complexity**.

Orientation training: *See* **Induction training**.

Outcome: The results government seeks to achieve in order to meet the needs of the public. An outcome is an impact on, or the consequence for, the public of the outputs/activities of the government. In common usage, however, the term is often used more generally to mean results, regardless of whether they are produced by governmental action or other means. A related term, outcome of interest, refers to the ultimate goal that is being sought in response to a problem, not necessarily one that is feasible (see, e.g., T. Sefton, "Economic Evaluation in the Social Welfare Field: Making Ends Meet," *Evaluation,* 2003, 9(1), pp. 73–91). *See also* **Intended outcomes**.

Outcome evaluation: A thorough review of the outcome of a governmental activity compared with its intended (or *ex ante* specified) outcome. Often, outcomes cannot be measured directly because of complexity, time lags, and influences not under governmental control; thus, outcome evaluation must typically take account of a variety of indicators.

Outcome line: A chain of events with cause and effect relationships that ultimately lead to some outcome. What constitutes the outcome line then becomes necessary to determine in order to realize the overall objectives of a program. *See also* **Intervention logic**.

Outcome measure: An indicator of the actual impact of a program as measured by program results such as service quality, effectiveness in achieving goals, and degree to which the need for services is being addressed. For a discussion of performance management that is outcomes-based, see, e.g., C. Heinrich, "Outcomes-Based Performance Management in the Public Sector: Implications for Government Accountability and Effectiveness," *Public Administration Review,* 2002, 62(6), pp. 712–25.

Outcome risk: The risk that a government faces that its intended outcomes will not be achieved, and that unintended outcomes will result. The risk is easy to see since outcomes are not only attributable to governmental action; other variables (such as adverse weather) can also influence outcomes.

Outcome of interest: *See* **Outcome**.

Output: Discrete service or product (including policy advice) produced by departments and purchased by the government. Outputs are potentially largely controllable by governmental departments and are measurable either quantitatively or qualitatively. Thus, outputs can be used for performance management more easily than outcomes (since the latter focus on states of being rather than tangible products). Outputs contribute to the achievement of outcomes.

Output agreement: An agreement between a governmental minister and a governmental department concerning the outputs to be delivered by the department and the basis on which it is to be paid for the delivery of those outputs. Since the outputs are costed in the departmental budget, an output agreement is prepared annually. The agreement specifies the various output classes sought from the department. Output classes, on the other hand, are groups of outputs that an organization is expected to produce which are to be purchased as a package (i.e., together, either because they share the same characteristics or because they lead to one particular outcome). The process of coming up with output classes is known as output specification, which is the way of describing output classes for appropriation purposes. Such a specification includes both the description and the projected performance required of them (usually in terms of quantity, quality, timeliness, cost, and location of delivery).

Output-based management: The inclusion of output-based information in management planning, reporting, budgeting and performance measurement, as opposed to the use of traditional input-based measures such as, for example, amount of money spent on training.

Output budgeting: *See* **Output steering**.

Output class: *See* **Output agreement**.

Output-focused officers: Also known as place managers, these are individuals who work in place-management programs and who are charged with identifying underlying causes to problems and to seek innovative solutions to long-standing area-specific problems. These officers are also expected to help form broad coalitions of willing partners and keep them energized to take joint action. See, e.g., J. Mant, "Place Management as an Inherent Part of Real Change: A Rejoinder to Walsh," *Australian Journal of Public Administration,* 2002, 61(3), pp. 111–16.

Output price review: A fundamental review undertaken by governmental departments to assess their efficiency. Such reviews do have the risk of a reduction in future funding as well as a rise, thus it makes it likely that only departments that are confident of a positive result will want to go through and seek a review. Generally, only those departments that are in fiscal distress will seek, or be singled out for, an output price review. See, e.g., M. Petrie and D. Webber, *Review of Evidence on Broad Outcome of Public Sector Management Regime,* Wellington: The Treasury, 1999, p. 8.

Output specification: *See* **Output agreement**.

Output steering: Refers to manipulating the levels and types of outputs that a governmental department produces so as to meet certain outcomes that the government wants. The impact of output steering is evident in output budgeting, which is the budgeting process that links resource allocation to outputs to be delivered and/or produced by an agency. The price of inputs is thus factored into the budget that the agency receives. See, e.g., H. de Bruijn, "Performance Measurement in the Public Sector: Strategies to Cope with the Risks of Performance Measurement," *International Journal of Public Sector Management,* 2002, 15(6/7), pp. 578–94.

Outreach: A process of systematically reaching out to beneficiaries and those who show interest in one's work. For example, the Organization for Economic Co-operation and Development has an outreach program with several countries (such as China) that is designed to help both parties share knowledge on public-management practices.

Outside-initiative model: Asserts that in the process of agenda formation in the public sector, the impetus for the inclusion of a particular issue comes not internally from the bureaucracy/executive or other branches of government, but from outside (i.e., groups external to government who engage in generating public support for such inclusion). For a cogent review of this concept with reference to the inside-initiation model, see, e.g., R. Cobb, J. Ross, and M. Ross, "Agenda Building as a Comparative Political Process," *American Political Science Review,* 1976, 70(1), pp. 126–38. *Cf.* **Inside-initiation model**.

Outsourcing: Moving an activity that was originally done within an organization to a source outside it. The accountability, however, for the activity still rests with the party that offers the contract, particularly in the case of a governmental department which is answerable to the legislature for its resources and for effective delivery of services for which it was given the mandate. It is relevant to note that with outsourcing, the government can revert the activity to state control more readily than if the activity has already been privatized. Examples of outsourcing include the Australian Commonwealth Employment Services and the Australian government's IT (information technology) program to private service providers. For a comparative review of outsourcing, including the skills needed to manage such provisions, see, e.g., A. Kakabadse and N. Kakabadse, "Outsourcing in the Public Services: A Comparative Analysis of Practice, Capability, and Impact," *Public Administration and Development,* 2001, 21(5), pp. 401–13.

Overadvocacy trap: When wrong solutions are recommended because the wrong problem has been formulated. An overadvocacy trap occurs, for example, when multiple sources of evidence are not considered, and when not all the dimensions of a policy problem have been take into account.

Overcapacity: Refers to a situation where an organization has a greater workforce than is required to fulfill its mission effectively. Organizations tend to use this overcapacity as slack to help them out in lean times. There are costs to maintaining overcapacity, however, including opportunity costs for more effective resource use.

Overcautious opening: Liberalization that is very slow and cautious. Proponents argue that liberalization should be commensurate with the existing social, economic, and political situation in a country, and should be neither too rapid nor very protracted. *See also* **Compatible opening**; **Excessive opening**.

Overhang: Funds for a program or an organization that have been budgeted for but not yet spent. The greater the overhang, the less considered the organization's capability to deliver. This is based on the premise that the organization is not able to usefully expend the funds it has been apportioned.

Overhead costs: *See* **Indirect costs**.

Overload: A situation where the public sector in practically all jurisdictions in the 1960s and 1970s was saddled with more mandates than it could handle as public expectations of what governments should do for them ballooned. This invariably led to the public sectors growing unwieldy, ineffective, and ungovernable. The corresponding reaction to that phenomenon in the 1980s and 1990s was downsizing and a general retraction of public-sector interventions.

Oversight: The power of one party (such as the legislature or a regulatory agency) to review the activities and processes of an organization. *See also* **Legislative oversight**.

Oversight paradox: The increase in the number of legislative bodies to oversee governmental agencies in some jurisdictions has resulted in a situation where for every entity that attempts to discipline an agency there is another one ready to come to its defense. This is termed the oversight paradox for while it increases oversight of a governmental body, it also means that there is proliferation of such bodies. See, e.g., C. Levine, B. Peters, and F. Thompson, *Public Administration: Challenges, Choices, Consequences,* Glenview, IL: Scott, Foresman and Co., 1990, p. 121.

Oversimplification: A common pitfall in policy making, oversimplification occurs when policy makers tend not to put in proper perspective all the issues that could affect a particular policy. This may be a result of a lack of information or of reasoned analysis, but it could also very well be one of a tendency to push through policies that appear to address a problem in the short term. See, e.g., L. Koenig, *An Introduction to Public Policy,* Englewood Cliffs, NJ: Prentice Hall, 1986, p. 320.

Ownership: As used in the public-management context, the term refers to ownership of enterprises by government. Discussions of the public-management model in various countries often refer to governments exercising an ownership interest, on behalf of citizens, in the public sector. This has tended to revolve around four elements: (a) strategic alignment (i.e., whether a department's outputs contribute to governmental outcomes), (b) organizational capability (i.e., whether a department has the capability, now and in the future, to deliver its outputs), (c) public-service integrity (i.e., whether public servants are behaving in ways, and to standards, that the public has a right to expect), and (d) long-term cost effectiveness (i.e., whether the prices being paid for the department's outputs are optimal in the long run).

Ownership agreements: Agreements between the government and departments/agencies (in the form of charters and performance statements) that specify the target financial and nonfinancial performance that is expected of them. As an owner, the government should fully exercise its right to demand this of departments and agencies.

Ownership/purchase model: *See* **Purchase/ownership model**.

Oxbridge bias: An erstwhile preference in the British Civil Service for recruiting individuals who attended either Oxford or Cambridge universities, which were considered to produce the best university graduates in Britain. This Oxbridge elitism is, however, being reduced through open recruitment and the wider use of experts. See, e.g., M. Bevier and R. Rhodes, "Searching for Civil Society: Changing Patterns of Governance in Britain," *Public Administration*, 2003, 81(1), pp. 41–62.

P

Package of policies: When government introduces several—but related—policies at the same time to address a particular problem. The government may wish to introduce a package of policies for various reasons, including ensuring that any negative side effects from any one policy are minimized (or at least absorbed and hidden from the public eye). Also, by introducing a package of policies, governments hope that some of the policies in the package will have a certain impact, which may not be the case if policies were formulated singly. *See also* **Policy bundling**.

Paired-comparison system: A method of employee evaluation where supervisors simultaneously compare two employees on several criteria, such as behavior, performance attributes, and other traits. The purpose is to be able to gain a relative perspective of employee performance as measured at the same point in time.

Parallel career ladder: *See* **Dual-career ladder**.

Parallel case review: A technique used in multisectoral project planning that includes a roundtable meeting of line staff from various agencies involved in a case that cuts across different sectors. A key product of the meeting is a plan (derived consensually rather than by majority vote) on how to proceed as regards a particular multisectoral problem/task (including who will lead the project and how reporting to various stakeholders will be done). For an example of the application of a parallel case review, see E. Bardach, *Getting Agencies to Work Together: The Practice and Theory of Managerial Craftsmanship*, Washington, DC: Brookings Institution Press, 1998, pp. 69–70.

Parallel financing: When two or more funding agencies jointly provide resources to a common program in which the resources are separately administered (i.e., the resources are managed by the respective agencies).

This allows agencies more control over resource utilization and degree of compliance with any financial regulations they themselves may have in place. *See also* **Cost sharing**.

Parallel organization: Refers to the flat/hierarchical and matrix-type organization that is linked vertically as well as horizontally with others. A parallel organization is an alternative to the traditionally hierarchical structure of organization. For an example, see A. Shani and B. Eberhardt, "Parallel Organization in a Health Care Institution," *Group and Organization Studies,* 1987, 12(2), pp. 147–73.

Parallel processing capacity: The ability of individuals and organizations to process (or focus on) more than one issue at a time. This capacity enhances the organization's grasp of complex environments and the ability to come up with policies that more accurately reflect the actual situation on the ground. *Cf.* **Serial processing capacity**.

Parastatal institutions: Agencies that are not subject to direct governmental control but are still considered to be in the public sector. Parastatal institutions could be involved in any number of sectors. For example, the World Bank seeks to address problems of urban poverty often through the use of municipal development funds, which are parastatal institutions that lend to local governments for major investment projects. Other examples of parastatal institutions include the International Union for the Conservation of Nature.

Pareto efficiency: Comes from the work of the Italian economist Vilfredo Pareto that refers to a situation wherein one more person cannot be made better off without someone else being worse off. If someone is indeed made better off at the expense of another, then the loss in welfare is known as deadweight welfare loss (or is a measure of allocative inefficiency). See J. Stiglitz, "Information and the Change in the Paradigm in Economics," *American Economic Review,* 2002, 92(3), pp. 460–501, on why Pareto efficiency cannot be attained in a situation of information asymmetry. *See also* **Allocative efficiency; Pareto optimality.**

Pareto's principle: A principle that states that a small percentage of events and variables causes the most change. The Italian economist Vilfredo Pareto made this assertion in 1906 in relation to the unequal distribution of wealth in Italy (20 percent of the population owned 80 percent of the country's wealth). As applied in management, however, it was the quality-management guru Joseph Juran who, in the late 1940s, talked of the "vital few and trivial many" and asserted that 20 percent of the defects are responsible for 80 percent of the damage (implying that managers need to concentrate on the few things that are problematic since they would cause the most damage). *See also* **Eighty percent rule**.

Parity: In generic terms, this means equivalency. The term is applied in various settings. For example, employment parity is reached when the constituent parts of a population are proportionally reflected in an organization. Other examples of parity include occupational parity (i.e., when the proportion of protected groups in an organization in all occupations mirrors the proportion in labor-market composition), and wage parity (i.e., when the salary level of one group of employees in the same employment classification is equal to that of employees in other classifications). As applied in a management context, the parity principle states that the power given to any leaders of organizations should be commensurate with their responsibilities. This balance between power and responsibilities is important as it ensures that managers are able to fulfill their roles and functions with adequate power to enable them to deliver what is expected of them. Public-management reform centered on the accountability of public-sector leaders is based on such a parity principle.

Parkinson's law: An assertion originally made by the historian Cyril Parkinson that "work expands so as to fill the time available for its completion." In recent times, however, the assertion has been applied in other settings as well (for example, that generally as organizations increase in size, the number of staff needed for administrative support increases more than proportionately). As originally described by Parkinson, this occurs due to two forces: an inherent tendency of bureaucrats to multiply subordinates rather than competitors for their roles; and bureaucrats make work for each other. See C. Parkinson, *Parkinson's Laws and Other Studies in Administration,* Boston: Houghton Mifflin Co., 1957. For an interesting application of the law, see, e.g., L. O'Toole and K. Meier, "Parkinson's Law and the New Public Management? Contracting Determinants and Service-Quality Consequences in Public Education," *Public Administration Review,* 2004, 64(3), pp. 342–52.

Parliament: Refers to a legislative body comprising members usually chosen by an electorate. A national parliament is sovereign—and, therefore, supreme—and makes binding laws (i.e., laws that are applicable to all). In some parliamentary systems, there are two chambers (a bicameral legislature, for example, the House of Commons and House of Lords in the United Kingdom), and in others, such as in New Zealand, there is only one (a unicameral legislature). The business of parliament is conducted through various parliamentary committees and public management is channeled through the appropriate committees. A parliamentary system refers to a system of government where there is a fusion of legislative (i.e., the legislature) and executive (i.e., the government) relations, also known as the Westminster system. In a parliamentary system of government, the leader of the government usually holds that position by virtue of his or her party's majority in parliament. As such, when a government loses the confidence of the parliament (i.e., in a vote), it is obliged to resign from power.

Parliamentary question: A question that is put to governmental ministers by a member of parliament that requires a written or verbal reply. Usually it is the opposition (i.e., nongovernmental) members of parliament who pose questions. A parliamentary question is an important way for the opposition to scrutinize the work of the government. However, rules for parliamentary questions can be quite rigid. Generally, they can be asked only of ministers and must pertain to matters within the minister's portfolio. Of the total allotted number of parliamentary questions that can be asked in any parliamentary session (twelve in the case of New Zealand, for example), individual parties are assigned a share depending upon their level of representation in the legislature. *See also* **Question time**.

Parliamentary scrutiny: Refers to any review that parliaments conduct on any matter that pertains to the public sector. Such scrutiny is publicly announced and opinions and views are sought from various sources. The scrutiny could take place in public forums (such as committees and public hearings) as well as outside the public eye (such as informal consultations between specialists and parliamentarians). Upon completion of the review, a report is also prepared, which, however, may or may not be made public in its entirety, depending upon the nature of the subject matter under investigation.

Parochial civic culture: *See* **Civic culture**.

Parochialism: Having a narrow view (for example, restricted to the local environment) of any public-policy issue. Parochialism results from cultural distinctions between—and exclusionary practices of—insiders and outsiders in any public-policy setting. Since like-minded individuals tend to come together more than those with differing views, this "likes-attract" feature leads to rather homogenous networks and a rather restricted view of the policy under consideration. See, e.g., S. Bowles and H. Gintis, "Optimal Parochialism: The Dynamics of Trust and Exclusion in Networks," SFI Working Paper No. 00–03–017, Santa Fe, NM: Santa Fe Institute, 2000.

Participant civic culture: *See* Civic culture.

Participation constraint: A clause in a contract that prevents breaching by the principal. This provides a measure of certainty to the agent that the contract will be enduring.

Participative leadership: One that allows employees to participate in organizational matters, including decision-making processes. This type of leadership is considered to be empowering as employees are given the opportunity to express and to act on ideas that help fulfill organizational mandates. Participative leadership is reflected in participative management, which is a style of management that enables employees to be involved in day-to-day organizational administration. See, e.g., E. Lawler, "Participative Management Strategies," in J. Jones, B. Steffy, and N. Bray (eds.), *Applying Psychology in Business: The Handbook for Managers and Human Resource Professionals,* Lexington, MA: Lexington Books, 1991, pp. 578–86.

Participatory evaluation: A form of evaluation where representatives of the stakeholders and other parties are brought together to conduct or to be included in an evaluation. This enhances the credibility of the evaluation since the stakeholders themselves will have been able to assess a project's or program's success. On the other hand, a significant disadvantage of a participatory evaluation is that the stakeholders could bring their biases with them to the evaluation process and skew the results. See, e.g., M. Themessl-Huber and M. Grutsch, "The Shifting Locus of Control in Participatory Evaluations," *Evaluation,* 2003, 9(1), pp. 92–111.

Participatory policy analysis: A method of enhancing citizen participation in decision making that ultimately has the effect of better informing the policy process. In stakeholder-participatory policy analysis, individuals who have vested interests in a policy issue are empowered to participate by providing advice to policy makers on the issue at hand. For case studies of participatory policy analysis, see, e.g., D. Haight and C. Ginger, "Trust and Understanding in Participatory Policy Analysis: The Case of the Vermont Forest Resources Advisory Council," *Policy Studies Journal,* 2000, 28(4), pp. 739–59; and D. Durning, "Participatory Policy Analysis in a Social Service Agency: A Case Study," *Journal of Policy Analysis and Management,* 1993, 12(2), pp. 297–322.

Participatory research: Research conducted where the researcher commits to fully being involved in the lives of the subjects being studied. The main advantage of this research method is that it allows the researcher to see the underlying complexities and dynamism of the subjects being observed. The disadvantage is that the researcher may be affected by the subjects and suffer a loss of the impartiality that is required for objective research.

Particularism: The general tendency to apply a specific policy in a specific situation to a limited number of clients. Because particularism does not have an outward scope, its utility in lesson drawing is minimal. On the other hand, it does enable a better appreciation of how specific policies serve specific interests. See, e.g., B. Kim, "Public Bureaucracy in Korea," in A. Farazmand (ed.), *Handbook of Bureaucracy,* New York: Marcel Dekker, Inc., 1994, pp. 591–602.

Partisan mutual adjustment: A term coined by economist and political scientist Charles Lindblom to describe a situation wherein a policy maker makes choices based on his/her own beliefs and goals but is dependent on the support of other participants; hence the process of mutual adjustment among all parties. In partisan mutual adjustment, different parties negotiate positions, and some sort of compromise is then sought among the various stated positions. The focus here is on incrementalism, because in the process of negotiating positions, the only mutually acceptable position tends to be incremental to the one that was negotiated from. See C. Lindblom, *The Intelligence of Democracy,* New York: The Free Press, 1965, pp. 3–9. For an analysis of the concept in relation to specific policy contexts, see, e.g., I. Lustick, "Explaining the Variable Utility of Disjointed Incrementalism: Four Propositions," *American Political Science Review,* 1980, 84(2), pp. 342–53. *See also* **Incrementalism.**

Partnership: As used in public management, this term refers to the process of seeking out and linking with one or more parties with whom an organization can be involved in addressing particular problems that are commonly shared. Parties that collaborate in such a venture are called partners; for example, nongovernmental organizations can be considered effective partners of government. The principle that guides how two or more agencies work together to address a problem jointly faced by the organizations is called the partnership principle. For a partnership principle to be useful, broad guidelines on the operational dimensions of the partnering arrangement need to be made clear at the outset. An excellent analysis of the concept of partnership at the level of central government is provided in E. Loffler, *Managing Accountability in Intergovernmental Partnerships,* PUMA/RD(99)4/Final, Paris: OECD, 1999, pp. 7–30. *See also* **Public-private partnerships.**

Partnership model: As used in the context of interactions between parties, the partnership model envisages replacing the contractual relationships inherent in the principal-agent model with negotiated partnership agreements drawn from the mutual considerations of the parties. In this case, the focus is not so much on the priorities of the purchaser alone but of the stakeholders in the transaction. The governance of such relationships is then based on collaboration, although it cannot really be a partnership of equals. For a discussion of this, see, e.g., R. Shaw, "Rehabilitating the Public Service—Alternatives to the Wellington Model," in S. Chatterjee (ed.), *The New Politics: A Third Way for New Zealand,* Palmerston North, New Zealand: Dunmore Press, 1999, pp. 187–218. *Cf.* **Principal-agent relationship**.

Part-time employment: Working less than full time; part-time employment is not generally the norm and is often a product of negotiation between employer and employee. An individual who works for less than the standard time that full-time employees work is called a part-time employee. In several jurisdictions, such as the Netherlands, it is mandatory for organizations to consider the requests of all employees who seek part-time status. Those individuals who are in part-time employment are not normally entitled to the full benefits of full-time employment.

Party platform: The collection of policy statements that a political party issues prior to elections and that specifies its various programs of action, including its philosophies and how it views particular issues. The party platform serves as a basis for policy intent.

Passive nondiscrimination: A situation where an employer treats employees alike but wherein there is no evidence of the employer reaching out specifically to minority groups. In a passive nondiscrimination situation, it cannot exactly be said that discrimination has occurred, and, therefore, no sanctions can be applied against the employer. *See also* **Affirmative action plan**.

Passive scanning: A form of environmental scanning conducted in the latent stage of a problem-solving exercise (i.e., when there is no substantive problem that is jeopardizing the organization's work) to assess the nature of its environment. Here, the organization is not actively seeking to determine the attributes of the various factors that impact on its mandate. *Cf.* **Active search**; *see also* **Environmental scanning**.

Pass-through: (1) A process whereby regional (for example, state, provincial) governments channel funds that come in the form of grants from the central government to local (for example, municipal) governments. A pass-through is necessary in situations where there are too many sub-level government bodies for the central government to administer on an individual basis. (2) Also refers to the process of cost increases being passed into end prices.

Paternalism: A practice of governing or managing in a manner akin to a father dealing with his children (i.e., by taking care of their needs but giving them virtually no responsibility). Paternalism has an inherent as-sumption that the government acts in the best interests of the citizens, though without seeking their input and often ignoring any revealed pref-erences. For an excellent discussion of the concept, see J. Wilson, "Pater-nalism, Democracy, and Bureaucracy," in L. Mead (ed.), *The New Paternalism: Supervisory Approaches to Poverty,* Washington, DC: Brookings Institution Press, 1997, pp. 330–44.

Path analysis: A statistical technique used to test consequences of pro-posed causal relations among a set of variables. The proper specification of these variables is key, otherwise inaccuracies result. Path analysis yields values that are termed path coefficients, which show researchers how important the various direct and indirect paths to the dependent vari-able are. For a discussion, see, e.g., A. Duane and R. Hauser, "The De-composition of Effects in Path Analysis," *American Sociological Review,* 1975, 40, pp. 37–47.

Path dependence: Also known as a state-determined system, this is the assertion that the historical pattern of any development in any area or sector plays a central role in determining the pace of future change in that area or sector. Path dependence is used to argue that what decision a party makes at one stage will result in certain consequential follow-on effects in time. See, e.g., D. North, *Institutions, Institutional Change, and Economic Performance,* Cambridge: Cambridge University Press, 1990, p. 94. For a case-study application, see, e.g., I. Greener, "Understanding NHS Reform: The Policy-Transfer, Social Learning, and Path-Dependency Perspectives," *Governance: An International Journal of Policy, Administration, and Institutions,* 2002, 15(2), pp. 161–83. *See also* **Conjuncture**.

Path-goal theory of leadership: A theory that explains how leaders set a path that employees can follow in terms of the work they do. This is de-signed to ensure that employees are aware of their objective and ultimately of the achievement thereof. For a discussion of the path-goal theory of leadership, see, e.g., R. House, "Path-Goal Theory of Leadership: Lessons, Legacy, and a Reformulated Theory," *Leadership Quarterly,* 1997, 7(3), pp. 323–52.

Patronage: A practice of staffing government positions with supporters. The term is derived from the assertion that "to the victor go the spoils." There are two types of patronage appointees: (a) retainers—those who are able to retain their jobs in government on a contract basis when the government changes, and (b) transients—those who are forced out when government change occurs. In theory, at least, patronage serves to protect the public from the potential abuses of a group of nonaccountable public servants. See, e.g., S. Koven, "The Bureaucracy-Democracy Conundrum: A Contemporary Inquiry into the Labyrinth," in A. Farazmand (ed.), *Handbook of Bureaucracy,* New York: Marcel Dekker, Inc., 1994, pp. 79–95. *See also* **Spoils system.**

Patron-client relationships: A superior-subordinate relationship that exists between a party (the patron) that has the wherewithal to provide services and favors (such as employment) and a party (the client) that relies on such provision of services. Patron-client relationships are said to be particularly manifest in less-developed societies. For a discussion of such relationships in transitional economies, see, e.g., S. Appold and D. Phong, "Patron-Client Relationships in a Restructuring Economy: An Exploration of Inter-Organizational Linkages in Vietnam," *Economic Development and Cultural Change,* 2001, 50, pp. 47–76.

Pattern matching: When policy makers compare the information they have and are receiving with their own recollections of their experiences and use that analysis to discern similarities between the current situation and what existed. While pattern matching is helpful in some cases, it can lead to distortions in decision making. See, e.g., K. Lorenz, *Behind the Mirror: A Search for a Natural History of Human Knowledge,* New York: Harcourt Brace Jovanovich, Inc., 1977, p. 114.

Pay comparability: When employers use the market as a source of comparing the level of pay they are offering to their own employees, which may lead to pay-level adjustments.

Pay compression: Refers to a situation where the pay bands of employees are similar. This situation invariably implies that a job of a lesser value to an organization is being paid at a rate similar to a job of a greater value. One obvious cause of pay compression is when employees are eligible for pay supplements (such as overtime pay) but supervisors are not.

Employees that are at the job with the greater value may feel that pay compression is not treating them fairly. See, e.g., S. Barr, "Davis Outlines Plans for Revamping Pay System, Structure of Government," *The Washington Post,* March 11, 2003, p. B02. *Cf.* **Pay inversion.**

Pay criteria: The basis on which pay is given to employees. In the public sector, pay criteria can be generally regarded as being contained in three ways: (a) representativeness (i.e., that generally the lifestyle of the public servant should be representative of that of the average citizen), (b) alimentation (i.e., in order to deter corruption among public servants, they should be paid at a level that would keep them from want/deter bribery), and (c) market (i.e., that the public servant should be paid what the market would pay for the particular sets of skills he/she brings to the job). The three criteria are not necessarily mutually exclusive, although practice across jurisdictions varies considerably. For a discussion of the criteria, see, e.g., R. Gregory, "Getting Better but Feeling Worse? Public Sector Reform in New Zealand," *International Public Management Journal,* 2000, 3(1), pp. 107–23.

Pay equity: A demand of employees that employers give equal pay for work requiring equivalent levels of skills, effort, and responsibility. In many jurisdictions, pay disparity based on age, gender, race, or other nonmerit-related factors is prohibited. There are two sides to the issue of pay disparity: those that argue for labor-market mechanisms to determine the level of pay, and those that argue for more deliberate efforts to bring about pay equity. The former is focused on the value of efficiency, while the latter concentrates on the value of social equity. See, e.g., Y. Abraham and M. Moore, "Comparable Worth: Is It a Moot Issue?" *Public Personnel Management,* 1995, 24, 291–314. See also, e.g., M. Gunderson, "Male-Female Wage Differentials and Policy Responses," *Journal of Economic Literature,* 1989, 27(1), pp. 46–72.

Pay-for-knowledge system: A system for setting the remuneration level of a particular job by the knowledge, skills, and abilities required for the job rather than the nature of the work that is to be done.

Pay inversion: When a job of a lesser value is at a pay rate higher than a job of a greater value (i.e., pay inversion is a situation where some subordinates are paid more than their supervisors). There are similar issues around pay inversion as around pay compression. *Cf.* **Pay compression.**

Pay restructuring: Changes that are made to the amount, type, and manner of remuneration in an organization. Pay restructuring includes reconsidering the existent pay bands in the organization. It results from different sources: for example, from new and revised collective-bargaining parameters, from changed market conditions, and from shortages in the labor market. Pay restructuring for some public-sector agencies must be approved by the legislature (such as for the Senior Executive Service in the United States), while for others, such as those organizations where collective-bargaining agreements yield a pay restructuring need, they will have such delegated authority.

Payments in kind: Staff members of organizations receive cash or cash-equivalent (for example, check) payment as a matter of course. However, in some instances, and in several developing jurisdictions, payments in kind are also made to employees. Such noncash payment (such as specific amounts of food items every month) is a flexible way to compensate staff members since employers do not have to make payments in cash only. In developing countries, this is sometimes seen as a way to get around a liquidity crunch; also, employees at times find payments in kind more practical and useful than cash.

Payoff function: An analytical tool that is used in rational-choice decision-making processes where policy makers first specify the policy alternatives, then assign weights to them according to preferences expressed by clients (usually the government). In addition to preferences, other weights used are information requirements and environmental constraints. The alternative with the best net benefits (i.e., benefits less costs) will be recommended. A payoff matrix (also called a decision matrix) is a technique that policy makers use to ascertain the respective costs and benefits of a particular policy alternative. It has to be noted that some of the costs and the benefits will have proxy measures as contingencies.

Payoff matrix: *See* **Payoff function**.

Payouts: Payments that are made to staff members to have their employment contracts terminated. While payouts provide a convenient way out for employers to get rid of troublesome staff members and those that they consider not suitable for employment, payouts can be criticized for their lack of transparency.

Payroll system: Refers to the arrangements that an organization has in place to pay employees their salaries and wages. This could include direct deposits into bank accounts or the issuance of checks. Additionally entered into the payroll system is information on leave taken, performance evaluation, and other variables that have a monetary implication.

Peak-period pricing: A way of charging higher fees to users upon the consumption of a service when demand is at its highest. By pricing a service higher during peak periods, there is a general downward pressure on demand, thus rendering demand more manageable.

Peer accountability: Refers to the accountability that is imposed on staff members by their peers. This form of accountability is an important concept since of all the parties that are associated with a staff member's performance (such as customers, clients, superiors, contractors, etc.), it can be argued that peers have a better awareness and appreciation of the effort and diligence that a colleague puts into the job. For practical purposes, however, it is difficult to measure peer accountability because peers do not always have knowledge of the larger organizational picture. See, e.g., E. Bardach, *Getting Agencies to Work Together: The Practice and Theory of Managerial Craftsmanship,* Washington, DC: Brookings Institution Press, 1998, p. 144. *See also* **Peer review**.

Peer evaluation: *See* **Peer rating**.

Peer rating: Also called mutual rating, this term refers to a performance-appraisal process that allows colleagues to rate individual employee performance. Peer rating is part of the 360-degrees performance evaluation where an employee provides a self-rating (zero degree), and is rated by superiors (ninety degrees), by peers (180 degrees), and by subordinates (360 degrees). Peer rating is useful only if the selection of peers is relevant. While there are obvious advantages to having an employee's peers evaluate his or her performance, the disadvantages include the introduction of personal biases from colleagues that may not relate to merit.

Peer review: A process whereby policy analysis and research work is subject to outside review by individuals or a qualified panel. Many public-sector agencies in jurisdictions around the world order peer reviews on important papers before policies are submitted to the legislature. Peer review is extremely useful in the policy advice stage. Since policy alternatives that are likely to be recommended to the executive need to have been analyzed extensively, it is useful to have them peer reviewed prior to such recommendation. See, e.g., Cabinet Office, *Professional Policy-Making for the Twenty First Century,* Report by Strategy Policy-Making Team, London: UK Cabinet Office, September 1999, pp. 63–64.

Penalty clause: In contracts, it is usual to include a penalty clause that specifies the conditions upon which a penalty will be levied upon the contractor. A penalty clause allows the principal to be satisfied that there are mechanisms in place that compel the agent to deliver a quality product/service on time, and the agent, in turn, knows precisely what needs to be done to avoid being penalized. The penalty clause thus informs the parameters of the principal-agent relationship.

Penetrative capacity: The ability of organizations to reach out to their constituencies, especially if they have spatial-based branches (such as in regions). Some only have superficial capability to engage their constituents. For a discussion of the penetrative capacity of governments, see, e.g., M. Kamrava, "The Politics of Weak Control: State Capacity and Economic Semi-Formality in the Middle East," *Comparative Studies of South Asia, Africa, and the Middle East,* 2002, 22(1&2), pp. 43–52.

Pension: Funds set aside by employees during their employment for use in retirement. In many situations, the employer contributes a matching (or greater) proportion to the pension fund. However, this is not a mandatory benefit; i.e., an employer does not necessarily have to have pension arrangements in place for employees—it is up to the employee to make such arrangements. There are several issues concerning pensions that merit attention, including: vesting and portability (i.e., entitlement to the accrued portion of the funds and carrying the benefits earned in one agency to another when changing employment), and defined benefit and defined contribution (i.e., predictability of benefits upon retirement based on several factors, and determination of actual benefits received by the success of how well the contributions were managed). Pensions are now almost entirely public transfers; private arrangements result in superannuation rather than pensions. See D. Klingner and J. Nalbandian, *Public Personnel Management: Contexts and Strategies,* 4th edition, Englewood Cliffs, NJ: Prentice Hall, 1998, pp. 143–45.

People skills: Skills expected of staff members toward developing and maintaining relationships with other people, including with their colleagues at work, external customers, and anyone else they might engage through their employment. Such skills are also contained in the competency of interpersonal communication and team building and includes the ability to, for example: (a) develop professional relationships of trust and confidence, (b) negotiate and consult effectively, (c) develop equitable partnerships, and (d) influence others, that is, persuade, convince, or impress others toward winning support for a particular policy or position.

Perceptual defense: A term that refers to perceptual distortion, and to the fact that when confronted with something that is inconsistent with a stereotype already held by a person, he/she selectively perceives the evidence in such a manner that eliminates or minimizes the inconsistency. Hence, the distorted perception protects the individual's stereotypes. See, e.g., S. Zalkind and T. Costello, "Perception: Some Recent Research and Implications for Administration," *Administrative Science Quarterly,* 1962, 7, pp. 218–35. *See also* **Stereotyping**.

Perceptual distortion: *See* **Perceptual defense**.

Perceptual error: When policy makers perceive a problem or its ramifications incorrectly, or when they overlook or misinterpret the facts. Perceptual errors inevitably lead to policy distortions. For a succinct description of the term, see, e.g., G. Mead, "Perceptual Error," in C. Morris, et al. (eds.), *The Philosophy of the Act*, Chicago: University of Chicago, 1938, pp. 154–58.

Perceptual order: Policy makers obviously prefer that perceptions be orderly, reliable, and consistent so that it is easier to define and address a policy problem. However, if a policy maker is overly committed to a particular perceptual order, it becomes difficult to recognize changes in the environment. Two relevant terms here are absolute threshold and differential threshold, which highlight the level of stimulation a policy maker would need in order to recognize changes in the environment. See, e.g., L. Koenig, *An Introduction to Public Policy,* Englewood Cliffs, NJ: Prentice Hall, 1986, p. 309.

Perceptual synthesis: A process wherein organizational managers independently carry out analyses related to an organizational action (such as the decision to innovate) and then share their subjective perceptions. This process provides managers with a common language with which to communicate their tacit knowledge regarding the challenges inherent in the action. See R. Hall and P. Andriani, "Managing Knowledge for Innovation," *Long Range Planning,* 2002, 35(1), pp. 29–48. *See* **Tacit knowledge**.

Perceptual uncertainty: When policy makers are uncertain of the scope of a recommended policy option; they have no frame of reference to begin to perceive the full import of the problem to be addressed. The invariable result of this phenomenon is to ask officials for further information toward reducing the uncertainty. See, e.g., H. Courtney, J. Kirkland, and P. Viguerie, "Strategy Under Uncertainty," *Harvard Business Review,* 1997, 75(6), pp. 66–81.

Perfect foresight: In the policy-making arena, perfect foresight tends to imply that policy makers have deep knowledge of the future state of a particular policy issue and work toward devising appropriate policies that help to attain such a future state. Clearly, this is a normative situation because perfect policy foresight is not plausible.

Performance agreement: A contract that sets out the achievement expectations of employees and the standards of their performance. The agreement generally provides a basis for monitoring, reviewing, and managing performance. Performance agreements undergo amendments, refinements, and updates during an individual's tenure of employment. For a brief review of and lessons in establishing performance agreements from senior managers in different jurisdictions, see, e.g., GAO, *Managing for Results: Experiences Abroad Suggest Insights for Federal Management Reforms,* GAO/GGd-95–120, Washington, DC: US General Accounting Office, 1995, pp. 38–43.

Performance ambiguity: A term that denotes a problem in organizations where not all employees share an understanding of what is required. This ambiguity is managed by encouraging intensive formal and informal socialization among the various operating units. See, e.g., W. Ouchi, "Markets, Bureaucracies, and Clans," *Administrative Science Quarterly,* 1980, 25(1), pp. 129–41.

Performance appraisal: A formal method wherein an employer assesses the performance of a staff member and makes relevant judgments regarding reward or sanction. Some performance appraisals require feedback from external stakeholders, such as that for public-sector chief executives, for example, since such positions are high profile and the impact of their work is extensive. A related concept, performance evaluation, is a formal assessment of the performance of an employee or program to determine whether performance criteria have been met. To be useful, a performance evaluation needs to be done at regular intervals. For a discussion of the various methods of performance appraisal, see, e.g., D. Klingner and J. Nalbandian, *Public Personnel Management: Contexts and Strategies,* 4th edition, Englewood Cliffs, NJ: Prentice Hall, 1998, pp. 282–92.

Performance bond: A monetary guarantee that the successful bidder makes upon winning a contract so that the principal is more confident that the bidder has an incentive to complete the contract as per agreement. Levels of performance bonds differ depending upon the type of contract and its value.

Performance contract: An agreement (usually prepared annually) that is reached between two parties (for example, the employer and employee, or the principal and agent) on what the employee or agent will do and in what manner. A performance contract will also specify how the employee's or agent's performance is to be measured. Some reasons why performance contracts are not always effective include: (a) the possibility of opportunistic behavior (or opportunism) on the part of both the agent and the principal, (b) limited communication between the two parties, and (c) promises made but not properly enforced. For a good discussion of performance contracting, and its application in government, see, e.g., M. Petrie, *Synthesis Paper on Performance Contracting,* PUMA Management Committee, PUMA/RD(99)5, Paris: OECD, Public Management Committee, March 1999, pp. 18–27.

Performance criteria: Standards against which the performance of an employee or program is measured. To be effective, performance criteria need to be specific, realistic, and measurable. They should also be set in advance (i.e., specified *ex ante*). Performance criteria also denote targets that, if not met, would call into question their fundamental viability, including triggering a decision to terminate. For an application with respect to aid programs, see, e.g., C. Adams and J. Gunning, "Redesigning the Aid Contract: Donors' Use of Performance Indicators in Uganda," *World Development,* 2002, 30(12), pp. 2045–56. *Cf.* **Structural benchmark**.

Performance development: Any program that is jointly developed by employees and employers to enhance the former's performance potential. An employee wellness program, which gives access to staff members to various ways of improving mental and physical well-being, is a good example of such a program since it allows employees to benefit to the extent that their own performance is enhanced, and the employer can be satisfied that the employees are focusing on something that is helpful to them as well.

Performance efficiency index: The ratio between what employees are doing and the performance standard. There are two items of importance here: (a) the operational and measurement techniques used to determine performance, and (b) the subsequent action that results from a calculation of the index such that the gap between performance and criteria is properly addressed. The measurement issue is not trivial, as any nonrigorous method will not be acceptable to all parties. Performance agreements then need to specify very clearly how performance is to be measured in the first place.

Performance evaluation: *See* **Performance appraisal**.

Performance failure: The inability of an individual or program to attain predefined targets. Performance failure is determined, in the first instance, as the gap between the *ex ante* specifications and the *ex post* evidence. Once the gap is identified, its severity is ascertained by looking at which specific aspects of the performance are the gaps most conspicuous. If they are in key areas in which the organization has placed emphasis (for example, in effectiveness over efficiency), then a situation of performance failure is said to have occurred. Such a failure has the potential effect of leading to adverse consequences including termination of employment or of the program. Performance failures are then direct results of performance gaps.

Performance goal: A target level of performance that is specified in advance. It is ideally expressed as a tangible, measurable objective (*ex ante*), against which actual achievement can be compared (*ex post*). Performance goals can be either outcome or output goals.

Performance indicators: Certain features or empirical evidence used to measure the performance of an employee or program. Performance indicators are designed to show how well, or poorly, an individual or program is performing against preset goals. Because not all outputs or outcomes can be readily measured, there tends to be a fair degree of subjectivity in some of the performance indicators. In general, though, these indicators refer to the quantity, quality, timeliness, and cost attributes of outputs for which performance targets are set and monitored. Performance indicators may also apply to other aspects of performance, such as effectiveness.

Performance information: Evidence about performance (including any critical incidents) that is collected and used systematically. Such information may be quantitative or qualitative, or a mix of both. Its usefulness is strengthened by applying standards against which the current performance is measured; these standards can include past performance, other comparators (including programs, agencies, etc.), or level of *ex ante* specifications that allow valid judgments to be made about the current performance. Performance information collected during the monitoring process is investigated in greater depth in an evaluation. *See also* **Critical-incident method**.

Performance management system: A system of information specification, monitoring, assessment, evaluation, and reporting of the performance of individuals, programs, or agencies. To be useful, such a system should be integrated with corporate management so that appropriate action, if any, may be taken subsequent to a performance appraisal. A performance management system has to be carefully managed as any perception of its weaknesses will serve to undermine confidence in it and delimit its effectiveness for employees and the organization, or both.

Performance measure: A quantitative or qualitative indicator used to assess performance either of an agency or of an employee. Performance measures related to economy, efficiency, and effectiveness include: (a) workload and productivity ratios, (b) time targets, (c) utilization rates, and (d) unit-cost indicators. Workload and productivity ratios are used to measure the quantity of useful work performed by employees over time (for example, number of immigration entries processed per hour at a border-crossing checkpoint). Time targets are used to measure the amount of time taken to complete a defined task. Utilization rates measure to what degree a service is used (for example, occupancy rates in public hospitals). Unit-cost indicators measure the actual cost of delivering a defined unit of service. Several criteria can be determined to come up with performance measures: target focused, benchmark comparative, and learning. The first two apply to targets and benchmarks that are set, and performance is compared against them. The third is more iterative in nature, and implies that considerable feedback loops are inherent in the measures as it seeks to determine the level of knowledge and learning that an agent retains because of the activities the agent has completed in the period in which performance is measured. For issues surrounding the adoption of performance measures in public organizations, see, e.g., P. Julnes and M. Holzer, "Promoting the Utilization of Performance Measures in Public Organizations: An Empirical Study of Factors Affecting Adoption and Implementation," *Public Administration Review,* 2001, 61(6), pp. 693–708.

Performance paradox: Refers to a situation where the presence of performance indicators do not necessarily adequately measure overall organizational performance. This paradoxical situation tends to result when, for example, employees put all their energies on meeting specified output levels without necessarily affecting the outcome performance of the organization. For a good review of the concept, see, e.g., S. Thiel and F. Leeuw, "The Performance Paradox in the Public Sector," *Public Performance and Management Review,* 2002, 25(3), 267–81.

Performance pay: Refers to pay increases that are directly attributable to individual (or sometimes team) performance assessed by evaluation. Hence, it excludes pay increases resulting from promotions, or from formal career path growth. It also excludes allowances that are attached to conditions such as hazardous working conditions and overtime work. Performance pay is difficult to justify and has come under increasing attack over how it is applied across the organizational level on a fair basis.

Performance ratchet: *See* **Ratchet effect.**

Performance rating: As used in human-resource management, this refers to assessing an employee on a scale for his/her performance level. There are two different systems used to ascertain such a rating: person based or performance based. In the person-based rating system, the evaluator compares the employee with others, or on an absolute standard, and determines an appropriate value depending upon where he or she assumes the particular employee is situated. While this is easy to design and implement, it can be unfair to the employee since personality characteristics are often, though not always, unrelated to job performance. In the performance-based rating system, each employee's behavior is measured against previously established behavioral norms and standards. Research has found that this latter method of performance rating produces better goal clarity and goal commitment in employees. See A. Tziner, R. Kopelman, and N. Livneh, "Effects of Performance Appraisal Format on Perceived Goal Characteristics, Appraisal Process Satisfaction, and Changes in Rated Job Performance: A Field Experiment," *Journal of Psychology,* 1993, 127(3), pp. 281–91.

Performance review: *See* **Performance appraisal.**

Performance specification: Stating clearly what is required of an individual or organization in order to meet set targets. Performance requirements are usually mutually set by supervisor and employee. For an excellent discussion of this concept in the broader context of organizations and governments, see, e.g., A. Schick, *The Performing State: Reflections on an Idea Whose Time Has Come but Whose Implementation Has Not,* GOV/PUMA/SBO(2003)17, Paris: OECD, 2003, pp. 1–22. *See also* **Performance agreement.**

Performance standards: Requirements for certain results or outcomes that are clearly prespecified. They are used to describe results-based regulations and do not prescribe specifications, and as such do not tend to stipulate how the agencies or employees are to comply with the regulations. Performance standards need to be continually updated and employees need to be aware of them. *See also* **Performance criteria.**

Performance targets: Precise standards to be achieved against each performance measure. Targets should present clear and quantified measures against which agencies and employees can assess output performance. Targets are expressed in absolute number, percentage, or ratio terms, and represent the minimum acceptable requirement. For performance management systems to be effective, the employees and the employer need to have agreed to performance targets.

Performance-based organization: This is the American version of the British "Next Steps" agency that the Clinton administration attempted to create as part of its National Performance Review reform exercise. In that, a performance-based organization was to focus on service delivery without being subject to political interference (such as in executive appointments made by the president). The performance-based organization initiative, however, has not been as successful as the Next Steps initiative. See, e.g., J. Thompson and S. Fulla, "Effecting Change in a Reform Context: The National Performance Review and the Contingencies of 'Microlevel' Reform Implementation," *Public Personnel and Management Review,* 2001, 25(2), pp. 155–75.

Performance-based program budgeting: Budgeting that links performance levels with specific funding amounts; as such, consideration of outputs is important. This form of budgeting considers how well an agency is achieving its goals using the money it has been given. It identifies specific reasons for funding requests, considers evidence of past performance, and reviews various program comparisons. It offers managers flexibility to reallocate resources, and consequent to that, provides rewards for achievement or sanctions for failure.

Permanent appropriation: Long-term funding for a public program, though for a fixed period; that is, the funding does not need regular legislative approval. A permanent appropriation saves the legislature valuable time by having to make a consideration only once for a given period. However, the danger is that, for whatever reason, a flawed funding decision will compound in time.

Permanently failing organizations: Public organizations that continually fail to meet their mandates but continue to operate because government is too weak to terminate them. Permanently failing organizations are generally understaffed and underresourced. They also invariably have a workforce that is not motivated, and internal relationships, as well as external ones, are generally in disarray. For the most well-known work on this concept, see M. Meyer and L. Zucker, *Permanently Failing Organizations,* Newbury Park, CA: Sage Publications, 1989.

Permissive leadership: A type of leadership that allows members to participate in organizational matters in the manner they see fit. Permissive leadership is based on participatory and consensus-seeking principles. The underlying premise of permissive leadership is that organizational action is better informed if many are involved in the process.

Personal power: Power that an individual secures by virtue of his/her personal qualities and personality. Personal power may or may not involve resource power, unless the individual is able to use their personal power to secure an elective position.

Personal-rank system: *See* **Rank in person**.

Personnel administration: An all-encompassing term that refers to the organizational functions of ministering personnel. This includes recruitment, remuneration, training and development, evaluation, etc. The term is often used interchangeably with "personnel management," but there are important differences (personnel management is more concerned with the broader issues of human-resource management; personnel administration is more technical in application).

Personnel bureaucracies: Organizations that are highly structured and in which the work is mostly related to personnel matters, such as recruitment and placement. A good example of a personnel bureaucracy is a public-service commission in countries where there is centralized recruitment for public-sector employment. *See also* **Full bureaucracies; Non-bureaucracies; Workflow bureaucracies**.

Personnel management: *See* **Personnel administration**.

Personnel planning: *See* **Human-resource planning**.

Personnel ratio: The number of full-time employees involved in personnel administration as a portion of the total number of employees in the organization. This ratio is an indicator of the level of overhead and back-office support costs.

Personnel selection: *See* **Recruitment**.

Person-organization fit: A situation where an individual's knowledge, skills, and abilities—and the orientation and value system he/she brings to an organization—are considered to be appropriate to the organization's mandate and value system. *See also* **Psychological contract**.

Person-role conflict: A tension that arises when the requirements expected of an employee conflict with the individual's personal values. A person-role conflict contributes to lack of motivation and may lead either to the person either leaving the organization or subverting its goals.

Perverse incentives: Incentives that do not encourage the desired behavior in economic agents and consumers. Thus, for example, welfare support could serve as a perverse incentive if it discouraged recipients to actively seek employment.

Pessimistic time estimate: In performance evaluation review technique, this concept refers to the assumption that an activity will be completed at the last possible moment (i.e., under the least favorable conditions).

Peter principle: A satirical principle that states that employees who are competent will be promoted up the hierarchy but eventually to a job that is beyond their capabilities, where they will remain. In other words, as expressed by Laurence J. Peter, "In a hierarchy every employee tends to rise to his level of incompetence." See L. Peter and R. Hull, *The Peter Principle: Why Things Always Go Wrong,* New York: Morrow, 1969. For an interesting discussion of the principle, see also E. Lazear, "The Peter Principle: A Theory of Decline," *Journal of Political Economy,* 2004, 112(S1), pp. S141–S163.

Phased implementation: Implementation of policies and programs in a staggered manner. Phased implementation can be either because of limited resources or to assess the impact before implementing a policy or program elsewhere. If the latter, the idea is to select a representative set of sites (i.e., a pilot testing) so that a full range of problems can be encountered early on.

Phased liberalization: A process of making an economy freer in stages. Evidence exists that phased liberalization is less stressful on a society in terms of the economic transition that is experienced. For a contextual discussion of this in relation to Chinese social policy, see, e.g., L. Wong and N. Flynn (eds.), *The Market in Chinese Social Policy,* Hampshire, UK: Palgrave, 2001, 138–50.

Phased retirement: A tool increasingly being used in workforce planning whereby employees are encouraged to retire in stages, such as in reducing the number of hours worked per week leading up to retirement, job sharing, or working from home. As the number of older workers increases in a workforce, employers need to think about the dual situation of having a sizable portion of the workforce retire concurrently and the need to retain institutional knowledge in a manner that will continue to benefit the organization. For a discussion of the concept, see, e.g., A. Rappaport, R. Maciasz, and E. Bancroft, "Exit Stage, Rightfully: Phased Retirement in the Spotlight," *WorldatWork Journal,* 2001, 10(4), pp. 30–36.

Physiological needs: The most basic level of personal motivation as identified in the psychologist Abraham Maslow's hierarchy of human needs. Physiological needs include food, air, water, and shelter. See A. Maslow, "A Theory of Human Motivation," *Psychological Review,* 1943, 50, pp. 370–96.

Picket-fence federalism: Refers to the vertical linkages that exist among different levels of government, and, in particular, of the bureaucratic specialists who are involved in intergovernmental programs. This interaction yields connections between the layers of government that resembles a picket fence, hence the term.

Picking-winners policy: A deliberate policy by governments to focus only on those sectors, industries, etc. that are more viable and that show signs of being (or are already) successful and that can deliver desirable results. This invariably leads to a situation where a few sectors or organizations are targeted at the expense of others. Rationally, such a policy makes considerable sense, but some argue that this should not always be so since it tends to marginalize those who are already disadvantaged in society (see, e.g., United Nations Development Program, *Human Development Report, 2001,* New York: Oxford University Press, 2001, p. 5).

Piecemeal adjustment: *See* **Adaptability**.

Pilot testing: When a policy first goes through a test of being tried out on a select group of people (areas, etc.) that are representative of the final population on whom the policy would be applicable. Piloting thus refers to introducing a program in a phased manner.

Pipeline: In project planning, a pipeline refers to the developmental process of a project toward implementation. A hard pipeline project is one for which funding has been approved but is not yet accessible (for example, because of other administrative requirements yet fulfilled). A soft pipeline project is one that is being developed in its initial stages and which may or may not have received funding approval.

Place management: Refers to programs used by government at all levels to improve outcomes in economically depressed areas through integrated measures involving a multisectoral and a multiorganizational approach. In place management, for example, community renewal will be attempted by bringing in all concerned parties (such as local government, businesses, community and civic leaders, and central-level representatives in the locale) under one framework to work together. It is a form of joined-up government at the local level. See, e.g., P. Walsh, "Improving Government's Response to Local Communities—Is Place Management an Answer?" *Australian Journal of Public Administration*, 2001, 60(2), pp. 3–12.

Place managers: *See* **Output-focused officers**.

Placement in ineligibility status: Barring a party from providing contracting services until the party proves that it has resolved the issue(s) that caused it to be declared ineligible.

Plain-language laws: Laws that require contracts to be written in straightforward and simple language. Plain-language laws are designed to increase ease of comprehension for consumers and to address the problem of information asymmetry.

Plank: A plank denotes any of the principles that are spelled out in a political party's platform. Such planks are the bases on which particular policies are developed. For example, one such plank could be the primacy of the market—rather than government—to provide economic benefits to the public.

Planned economy: Also called a command economy, this term refers to an economy in which the goals, priorities, production schedules, and prices are set by the central government. A planned economy is characteristic of socialist societies, where the public good is to be enhanced by the governmental manipulation of economic forces. However, as history has shown, planned economies are rarely as prosperous or as efficient as those that practice free enterprise.

Planning: (1) A systematic step-by-step process of doing things for which *ex ante* and *ex post* specifications have to be prepared and monitored regularly. (2) The process of working out what a department needs to achieve, how it should go about achieving that, and what that achievement will thus take. Planning is considered a traditional staff function in an organization. The sequence of planning that takes place on a regular level is known as a planning cycle. Such cycles are normally for one year (such as annual plans) and five years (such as five-year plans). A related term is planning horizon, which refers to the period of time for which a plan is considered.

Planning-programming-budgeting system (PPBS): An extended version of program budgeting that is concerned not only with inputs and outputs but also with effects and alternatives. It was first developed by the U.S. Department of Defense in the 1950s, and concerns the: identification of objectives, determination of what measurable outputs contributed to those objectives, specification of activities that would yield those outputs, and considerations of the costs of implementing the activities (for multiple years). It was also assumed that in the process of preparing all of the above, the organization requesting budget funds would have conducted a cost-benefit analysis of other alternatives. Much of outcome-based budgeting shares similar bases with PPBS.

Platform knowledge: The current level of knowledge that exists in an organization. It also refers to the knowledge on which the organization builds target knowledge (i.e., the desired state). See, e.g., R. Hall and P. Andriani, "Managing Knowledge for Innovation," *Long Range Planning,* 2002, 35(1), pp. 29–48. *See also* **Target knowledge**.

Platforming: A technique that fosters interagency collaboration, and includes individual acts of collaboration between agencies that represent a firm basis on which to continue and deepen the collaboration. See E. Bardach, *Getting Agencies to Work Together: The Practice and Theory of Managerial Craftsmanship,* Washington, DC: Brookings Institution Press, 1998, p. 305. *See also* **Momentum building**.

Player-manager syndrome: When a newly promoted manager cannot divorce himself/herself from thinking in terms of his/her previous position instead of as a manager. This has a dual effect: either it reduces the individual's effectiveness as a manager or it enables the individual to be that much more aware of the conditions in which the staff members continue to do their work.

Plural executive: Refers to a committee that exercises the executive functions of an organization. A plural executive is usually preferred in situations where the organization does not yet have a permanent chief executive installed. This is also known as plural leadership.

Plural executive leadership: *See* **Independent regulators**.

Pluralism problem: Pluralism is the underlying belief that people pursue their own overriding interests through government and other institutional means. This is the dominant premise for making policy decisions, and it incorporates bargaining and negotiations among competing interests. A pluralism problem is a problem that is evident in all jurisdictions because there is a tendency for public-sector agencies toward differentiation (i.e., going their own way) rather than integration (i.e., working together collaboratively) largely due to the fact that there are political and institutional pressures on them. The differentiation trend leads ultimately to so-called silo mentality in organizations. See E. Bardach, *Getting Agencies to Work Together: The Practice and Theory of Managerial Craftsmanship,* Washington, DC: Brookings Institution Press, 1998, p. 11. *See also* **Silo mentality**.

Pluralist policy making: Policy making that is characterized by the presence of multiple actors with multiple (and often times, poorly framed) policy preferences, and by policy-making processes that are complex and subject to frequent disruptions given differences between competing parties. For a classic analysis of the nature of pluralist policy making, see T. Lowi, *The End of Liberalism: The Second Republic of the United States,* 2nd edition, New York: W.W. Norton & Company, 1979.

Pluralistic evaluation: A form of evaluation that accepts that there can be several judgments about any single performance, and that it is thus necessary to incorporate multiple assessments in evaluations. For a review of the advantages of such evaluation, see, e.g., H. de Bruijn, "Performance Measurement in the Public Sector: Strategies to Cope with the Risks of Performance Measurement," *International Journal of Public Sector Management,* 2002, 15(6/7), pp. 578–94.

Pocket veto: In U.S. federal lawmaking, a pocket veto is a de facto veto that is exercised by the president by not signing into law a legislative bill. Presidents are known to exercise pocket vetoes if they wish not to favor a particular bill, and if they wish not to have Congress attempt to override a formal presidential veto. *See also* **Veto**.

Point-factor job evaluation: A method of job evaluation and pay setting that is among the most widely used in contemporary organizations. This method determines factors that measure job worth (such as skills and responsibility), weights them according to significance, specifies levels for each job-worth factor to capture the range of work that could be done, and then establishes pay ranges for benchmark positions based upon which the pay for other positions will be determined. The benchmarking is normally done by a neutral third party. This job-evaluation method is valued for its reliability and objectivity. See D. Klingner and J. Nalbandian, *Public Personnel Management: Contexts and Strategies,* 4th edition, Englewood Cliffs, NJ: Prentice Hall, 1998, pp. 114–15.

Polarization: Profoundly divergent positions taken in the development of public policies. In the public debate on the use of public funds for abortion, for example, there is clear polarization of views around the issue for and against. Such polarization stems, for example, from an inflammatory stand taken by one party that is then reciprocated by the other. A related term is that of polarity, which refers to the tendency of an individual to be at any one end of an issue. As applied in an organizational setting, it refers to the tendency of employees to be pulled to extreme views on how, for example, organizational processes should be conducted.

Policy: Generally taken to mean a statement of a governmental goal. A hard policy refers to a policy that is controversial and unpopular and that has a high probability of generating discontent; and a soft policy refers to one that is essentially supported by the public and for which there are no, or few, related intractable issues.

Policy abstraction: A state in the policy-development process wherein the policy sought has yet to be implemented. A policy can be represented at different levels, from policy abstraction (such as declaring that the government is intent on "enhancing the welfare of citizens") to specific policy goals (such as "decreasing the youth suicide rate in the country by X percent over Y number of years").

Policy action: Activities that result during the implementation stage of a particular policy. There are generally two types of policy actions: (a) regulative policy action, which is designed to ensure compliance with procedures and standards; and (b) allocative policy action, which requires proper allocation of inputs among various activities that give effect to the policy. Policy adjustments refer to amendments made to a policy to account for changes in the environment or to rectify policy shortcomings (for example, a government changing its income transfer policy to block a loophole prone to abuse).

Policy advice, quality of: Advice given to governmental ministers by public-sector officials should be subject to certain quality standards to ensure accuracy of scenarios and available alternatives. The quality of policy advice is normally ascertained in two ways: (a) as measured by ministerial feedback, and (b) through internal quality-assurance procedures. Some criteria used to measure the quality of policy advice rendered to ministers include: (i) Is the purpose clearly stated and does it address all questions raised? (ii) Have all the assumptions been stated, and is the reasoning logical and supported by evidence? (iii) Is the evidence accurate?

(iv) Has an adequate range of options been considered, and benefits-costs and likely consequences assessed? (v) Has there been consultation with interested parties and their viewpoints considered and incorporated, if necessary? (vi) Have all problems of implementation, technical feasibility, timing, and such been considered and stated? (vii) Is it effectively summarized and free of errors (i.e., what is the presentation style)? See, e.g., Department of Labor, *Guide to Excellent Policy Advice,* Wellington: New Zealand Department of Labor, 2001, pp. 26–27. For some practical pointers on how to provide good-quality policy advice, see, e.g., R. Butterworth and N. Horne, "Policy Advice: A Practical Perspective," *International Journal of Public Sector Management,* 2003, 16(3), pp. 219–29.

Policy advocates: *See* **Policy analysts**.

Policy agenda: Refers to the major contemporary issues that inform and craft a government's decision making. The policy agenda could spring from various sources, including the executive, the legislature, public-interest groups, media, and major external events. The policy agenda can be looked at in two respects: as a governmental agenda (i.e., issues that are being considered) and as a decision agenda (i.e., issues for which decisions are pending). See J. Kingdon, *Agendas, Alternatives, and Public Policies,* 2nd edition, New York: HarperCollins, 1995, pp. 3–4.

Policy ambiguity: An unresolved state of policy specification that could be intentionally thus because many difficult, but essential, issues have been disregarded thus rendering the policy vague. Paradoxically, policy ambiguity increases the scope of adoption because there is room for everyone to read what they wish into the policy situation and how the measure might be best able to address what they want.

Policy analysis: Analysis done to determine the likely effects of a policy under consideration. A good policy analysis will be: client oriented, value based, rigorous in systematic research, and rational (including an extensive search for, and analysis of, alternatives). However, the rigor of policy analysis conducted in governmental departments may at times be found wanting. For a discussion, see, e.g., Office of the Provincial Auditor, *A Review of the Policy Development Capacity Within Government Departments,* Manitoba, Canada: Office of the Provincial Auditor, 2001, p. 6.

Policy analysis, branch technique: *See* **Successive limited comparisons**.

Policy analysis, root approach: *See* **Rational-comprehensive theory of decision making**.

Policy analysts: Individuals who conduct policy analysis and help make recommendations to policy makers. Policy analysts can have different roles: (a) as policy experts (i.e., with technical expertise in specific sectors), (b) as policy advocates (i.e., actively pursuing a particular policy), or (c) as policy troubleshooters (i.e., "fixing" problems related to a policy's implementation or practice). See, e.g., C. Snare, "Windows of Opportunity: When and How Can the Policy Analyst Influence the Policymakers During the Policy Process," *Policy Studies Journal,* 1995/1996, 14(3/4), pp. 407–30.

Policy arena: (1) Where all aspects of a particular policy are played out during the formulation stage. (2) The political and administrative environment in which policy issues are considered.

Policy argumentation: The process of using factual statements and own interpretations as well as value orientations to make a case for or against a policy. Policy argumentation is an integral part of developing policy alternatives. See, e.g., G. Majore, *Evidence, Argument, and Persuasion in the Policy Process,* New Haven, CT: Yale University Press, 1989, p. 63.

Policy autonomy: When a party (a bureaucracy, a subjurisdiction of government, etc.) has the authority to make policies without interference from other parties. Policy autonomy is highly valued because it allows policies to be made that are suitable to a party's own needs and circumstances. The concept implies policy discretion, which is the amount of flexibility, authority, and freedom that a policy-making entity has in order to formulate relevant policies. Much of the autonomy enjoyed by public bureaucracies has been sharply curtailed in the contemporary trend in public-management reform, which have bifurcated the policy and operations roles of organizations (as evidenced in the creation of Next Steps agencies in the United Kingdom in the 1990s).

Policy balance: A situation where an incoming government administration facilitates the general continuation of previous governmental policy. This is often done to reduce the shock that a sudden change in policy might impose on the public. For a case-study application of sudden policy reform in New Zealand, see, e.g., S. Newberry, "Intended or Unintended Consequences? Resource Erosion in New Zealand's Government Departments," *Financial Accountability and Management,* 2002, 18(4), pp. 309–30.

Policy bias: A situation that arises when a policy favors one area, sector, or group over another. Policy bias tends to result, for example, when one group of policy advocates dominates a policy.

Policy broker: A policy actor who brings together different parties and viewpoints to facilitate timely policy making. A policy broker need not be an independent third party, although impartiality and evidence-based (i.e., technically rational) analysis helps in the brokering role.

Policy bundling: The process of putting together different policies for purposes of getting them passed by a legislature. Such policies could be similar in nature or dissimilar; in case of the latter, the aim may be to get an unpopular policy passed by bundling it with more agreeable ones.

Policy by analogy: A term that refers to the perceptions by policy makers about an analogy between a policy being considered and one implemented in another jurisdiction. While such may give policy makers a better frame of reference on a policy and its implications, it may distort their reasoning because the condition in which the policy elsewhere was implemented will, in all likelihood, be different. Thus, for example, developing policies on public-management reforms along the lines of the so-called new public management will be different in, say, New Zealand and Mongolia. Similarly, the International Monetary Fund's insistence on applying the same stabilization policies in Brazil and Mexico as in Thailand and Indonesia can be termed policy by analogy. See, e.g., L. Koenig, *An Introduction to Public Policy,* Englewood Cliffs, NJ: Prentice Hall, 1986, pp. 318–19.

Policy capacity: (1) The ability of a policy shop to formulate and recommend quality policy advice to policy makers. (2) The capacity of a government to ensure that its policy decision-making process is well structured and efficient, including ensuring that it is able to benefit from stakeholder feedback and engagement. The concept of policy capacity is used in conjunction with policy competence in referring to a country's capacity to formulate and implement well-designed plans and policies. See, e.g., C. Campbell, "Juggling Inputs, Outputs, and Outcomes in the Search for Policy Competence: Recent Experience in Australia," *Governance: An International Journal of Policy and Administration,* 2001, 14(2), pp. 253–82. See also C. Polidano, "Measuring Public Sector Capacity," *World Development,* 2000, 28(5), pp. 805–22.

Policy chain: A link that exists between policy decisions made at the central and the local levels (including at the household level), and their impact on production, consumption, and investment. Along that link, policies undergo differences in orientation at three intervals: (a) when the policy is delivered, (b) when it is being transmitted, and (c) when the household makes a decision. See, e.g., A. Zezza and L. Llambi, "Meso-

Economic Filters Along the Policy Chain: Understanding the Links Between Policy Reforms and Rural Poverty in Latin America," *World Development,* 2002, 30(11), pp. 1865–84.

Policy change: A change in policy that emerges from emergent realities in an environment, and which adhere to three types of logic: (a) situational (i.e., a change determined by an emerging situation), (b) instrumental (i.e., is technically feasible), and (c) normative (i.e., is something that has to be done in the broader interests of society). For a taxonomy of policy change, see, e.g., R. Durrant and P. Diehl, "Agendas, Alternatives, and Public Policy: Lessons from the US Foreign Policy Arena," *Journal of Public Policy,* 1989, 9(2), pp. 179–205.

Policy circles: The domain in which discussions and debate centered on a particular policy are located. For example, the policy circle for regulatory policies could consist of business lobbies, regulatory agencies, and policy wonks in central agencies.

Policy coherence: The familiar state of synergies between related policies in any particular area such that they jointly reinforce the thrust of a government in adequately addressing an issue. Such policy coherence also relies on links between the public sector and nongovernmental actors in supporting the achievement of a governmental objective. Policy incoherence, on the other hand, refers to a situation wherein two or more related policies—or the various elements of one particular policy—do not jointly reinforce the thrust of a government in adequately addressing an issue. See, e.g., OECD, *Policy Coherence,* GOV/PUMA(2003)4, Paris: OECD, 2003, p. 2. *See also* **Policy consistency**.

Policy commitments: Promises made by any of the parties involved in the formulation and implementation of a policy to the policy. Policy commitments can be explicit or implicit. If they are clearly stated in a document, they are explicit; if they have only been vocalized, then they are implicit.

Policy communities: Groups of individuals (i.e., specialists in particular sectors) and organizations that share an interest in a particular public policy. Such interest may be manifest in the discourse of policy details, or in their advocacy for, or opposition to, the policy. Individuals in policy communities and policy communities themselves can be inside or outside government, or both. See J. Kingdon, *Agendas, Alternatives, and Public Policies,* 2nd edition, New York: HarperCollins, 1995, p. 117.

Policy complexity: The degree of intricacy that exists in a policy. For example, any policy to enhance innovation in a public sector has a high degree of complexity since there are numerous issues and stakeholders to take into account. See, e.g., D. Dolowitz and D. Marsh, "Policy Transfer: A Framework for Comparative Analysis," in M. Minogue, C. Polidano, and D. Hulme (eds.), *Beyond the New Public Management: Changing Ideas and Practices in Governance,* Cheltenham, UK: Edward Elgar, 1998, pp. 38–58.

Policy conflict: Conflict that arises when two or more policies are focused on disparate objectives. Thus, while a tax-incentives policy may be in place to encourage foreign companies to invest in a country, stringent rules on the repatriation of profit may discourage foreign investment. *See also* **Policy inconsistency**.

Policy consistency: Refers to a situation where the intent of a range of policies formulated to address a particular issue is uniform over time. Policy consistency thus refers to the process of ultimately ensuring that policy objectives are delivered and that they are not contradictory. For example, if a government has undertaken to tackle corporate-governance problems in a particular manner, then unless circumstance dictated, it should adhere to its committed policies. *Cf.* **Policy inconsistency**.

Policy consultants: Individuals and firms that provide policy advice to governments when called upon. Governments usually rely on third-party sources to verify and triangulate the policy advice they get on difficult issues. This competition for policy advice is said to increase the credibility of advice that governments ultimately receive. Policy consultants can include think tanks, academic institutions, and research institutions, among others.

Policy content: The individual specifications of a policy. Good policy content has several attributes, for example, clear specification of the desired outcome; assumptions made explicit; adequate stakeholder consultation; proper specification of performance standards; and specific and rigorous accountability arrangements. See, e.g., A. Ranney, "The Study of Policy Content: A Framework for Choice," in A. Ranney (ed.), *Political Science and Public Policy,* Chicago: Markham Publishing Co., 1968, pp. 3–22.

Policy contradiction: *See* **Policy inconsistency**.

Policy convergence: The harmonization of policy across different jurisdictions. Often, in federal systems, such as in Canada, the United States, and Australia, policies on the same issue are likely to be different across the states or provinces (for example, on the nature and degree of regulating a particular industry). Policy convergence is about ensuring that jurisdictional differences are eliminated or minimized.

Policy conversion: *See* **Policy translation**.

Policy credibility: (1) A term that refers to the degree of citizens' trust that a governmental policy will serve to enhance the public welfare. (2) The acceptance by the public of a particular policy or of a particular institution that makes the policy. This is considered to be one of the positive attributes an organization needs to possess in order to perform well.

Policy criteria: Criteria against which the policies recommended to government are evaluated. There are many such criteria but the most relevant ones include: (a) quality (are they rigorous, logical, accurate, and backed by evidence?), (b) timeliness (are they relevant for the problems that are evident at a particular point in time?), (c) cost (are the recommended policies the most cost efficient?), and (d) political feasibility or practicality (do they account for the political opposition that may exist?).

Policy culture: The environment that surrounds the policy-making process. Such a culture could be one wherein policy actors are keen to be involved in the determination of public policy. Local policy culture refers broadly to the surroundings in which local bureaucrats (for example, municipal zoning authorities) do their work. See, e.g., R. Khator, "Bureaucracy and the Environmental Crisis: A Comparative Perspective," in A. Farazmand (ed.), *Handbook of Bureaucracy,* New York: Marcel Dekker, Inc., 1994, p. 199.

Policy cycle: The range of steps that policy makers need to take in order to formulate policies. These include agenda setting, problem definition, policy formulation, implementation, and evaluation. While this is the rational model in action, the garbage-can model says that the cycle does not necessarily conform to this serialization. For a general review of the term, and a case study, see, e.g., S. Everett, "The Policy Cycle: Democratic Process or Rational Paradigm Revisited?" *Australian Journal of Public Administration,* 2003, 62(2), pp. 65–70. *See also* **Garbage-can model**.

Policy debates: The process of a formal discussion of the pros and cons of a particular policy or of alternative policies being contemplated by government. Formal policy debate is not limited to the exclusive confines of the legislature, although that is where decision-making authority generally rests; debate also occurs in forums outside the government setting (such as in think-tank publications and in the popular media).

Policy decentralization: The degree to which subjurisdictions (such as states and provinces) are given the freedom to make policies in what is normally the central government's domain. Generally, it is felt that the more heterogeneous the subnational jurisdictions, the more policy decentralization there needs to be. See, e.g., K. Strumpf and F. Oberholzer-Gee, "Endogenous Policy Decentralization: Testing the Central Tenet of Economic Federalism," *Journal of Political Economy,* 2002, 110(1), pp. 1–36.

Policy decision point: The entity or forum where public policies are formally made (normally in legislatures but also in the executive branch, such as the cabinet).

Policy decision making: The manner in which policy decisions are made. There are several modes of policy decision making: (a) "technical" or "elite," which involves using expert knowledge to select the most appropriate means to achieve a specific policy outcome; (b) "economic," which involves taking into consideration the monetary gains or losses in pursuing a particular policy; (c) "political," which looks at what political benefits can be accrued—and which costs may be incurred—as a result of opting for a particular policy; and (d) "participatory," which considers the level of participation of relevant stakeholders in the process. See, e.g., C. Matheson, "The Premises of Decision-Making Within the Australian Public Service," *Australian Journal of Public Administration,* 1997, 56(1), pp. 13–24.

Policy deliberation: The act of deliberating on or debating a particular policy problem. The range of discussions that takes place in the course of formulating policies includes not only those at the political level (for example, in cabinet or in the legislature), but also in the bureaucracy (for example, from where the policy paper was first prepared upon orders of the relevant minister) and in the public consultation process. *See also* **Policy argumentation**.

Policy departure: The act of reversing, amending, and/or abandoning a policy. A policy departure could result from several factors, including changes in the policy environment, pressures from groups opposed to the policy, and citizen backlash. *See also* **Policy change**.

Policy design: The parameters, composition, and configuration of individual policies being formulated by government. The nature and mode of a policy design has a substantial impact on the prospects of its passage in the legislature. A component of policy design is the policy-development process, which considers all manner of policy elaboration, from problem identification to agenda building to final policy specification. Given the scope of work, numerous actors are involved in any policy-design process.

Policy dialogue: Discussions of specific policy issues and how a particular policy should be shaped. The discussions can be formal (such as in select committee hearings in the legislature) or informal (such as in conversations between ministers in the lobbies of the legislature). While it is the legislature that ultimately makes the policies, policy dialogue also takes place among other participants in the policy-development process.

Policy diffusion: Refers to a process of a policy being considered and adopted in other jurisdictions. Policy diffusion generally takes place through a process called pragmatic acculturation. See, e.g., D. Rodrik and S. Mukand, "In Search of the Holy Grail: Policy Convergence, Experimentation, and Economic Performance," National Bureau of Economic Research Working Paper, No. 9134, 2002; for an application, see, e.g., J. Quah, *Singapore's Model of Development: Is It Transferable?* Working Paper No. 7, Department of Political Science, National University of Singapore, 1997, pp. 20–22. *See also* **Pragmatic acculturation**.

Policy dilemma: When the government is torn between two or more policies in addressing a particular problem (such as focusing on management development based on potential versus existing capability in senior executives). Policy dilemmas are often subject to vigorous debate prior to the determination of a final decision.

Policy direction: Incremental policy measures that suggest a larger, cumulative intent. For example, raising an income-tax rate may indicate the direction of a government's fiscal policy. In that regard, policy direction implies policy intent.

Policy discourse: The totality of policy debate, dialogue, interest articulation, and negotiation that takes place in the formulation of public policy. See, e.g., P. Sabatier and H. Jenkins-Smith, "The Advocacy Coalition Framework: Assessment, Revisions, and Implications for Scholars and Practitioners," in P. Sabatier and H. Jenkins-Smith (eds.), *Policy Change and Learning: An Advocacy Coalition Approach,* Boulder, CO: Westview, 1993, pp. 211–36.

Policy disputes: Disagreements between two or more parties on any aspect of, or indeed the whole of, a policy. Not all policy disputes get resolved. Policy disputes can be evident at any stage of the policy-making process, although those played out in the legislature are often the most visible. Settlements of policy disputes where both parties gain what they seek are known as win-win solutions.

Policy distance: A term that is used to denote the differences that inevitably arise in assigning a particular meaning to any policy element. Given the diversity of stakeholder backgrounds, interests, and revealed and unrevealed stated preferences, policy distance is a rather common phenomenon.

Policy distortions: Unintended and negative changes to a particular policy that result when a policy is being implemented. Policy distortion can result from the impact of variables that were not considered in the development stage, or from conflicting objectives presented by government after a particular policy has been formulated. For example, a policy of enhancing the skills of the unemployed is distorted if the government does nothing to encourage those who are unemployed to seek retraining. See, e.g., S. Pradhan, "Improving the State's Institutional Capability," *Finance & Development,* 1997, 34(3), pp. 24–27.

Policy domain: *See* **Policy envelope**.

Policy drivers: Variables that contribute to policy impact. In the public-policy domain, such drivers can generally include: political leadership, fiscal and economic position, public expectations, public-service leadership, etc. See, e.g., C. Scott, "Policy Analysis and Policy Styles in New Zealand Central Agencies." Paper delivered at the Public Policy Network Conference, Wellington, January 31, 2003.

Policy effects: *See* **Policy impact**.

Policy elasticity: The range of flexibility in a policy in terms of what it seeks to achieve. The more elastic the policy, the greater the probability that some or all of the components will be deliverable. But too much elasticity, on the other hand, could make it unclear as to what specifically is to be delivered and who shall be accountable.

Policy element: (1) Any particular specification of a policy, such as a goal or sets of a goal, options, or events which stakeholders consider in order to justify a particular policy. (2) A component of a particular policy, such as accountability agreements inherent in a governmental policy on pay and employment equity.

Policy entrepreneurs: Refers to those individuals in policy-making positions who have the ability to give a policy high profile, who can ensure that the legislature gives it high priority, and who are then able to see that the policy is approved. Policy entrepreneurs are innovators, and the term "policy innovator" refers to an individual who is able to bring in novel policy concepts, new ways of understanding and doing things, and new approaches to addressing recurring problems. For an application, see, e.g., Y. Jeon and D. Haider-Markel, "Tracing Issue Definition and Policy Change: An Analysis of Disability Issue Images and Policy Response," *Policy Studies Journal,* 2001, 29(2), pp. 215–31.

Policy envelope: The range of issues that are considered to be relevant to a particular policy. Because policies can be complex, policy makers first seek to determine the policy envelope to ascertain what should and should not get considered in the development of a particular policy. A related term is "policy domains" (or policy parameters), which refer to the boundaries around which all relevant matters related to a particular policy are played out. Such boundaries incorporate a broad category of policy-relevant agents, policy actors, and policy issues. See, e.g., State Services Commission, *Annual Report of the State Services Commission, 2002,* Wellington, New Zealand: State Services Commission, 2002, p. 20.

Policy environment: *See* **Policy system**.

Policy error: *See* **Policy failure**.

Policy evaluation: A detailed assessment done to ascertain whether a policy is (or has been) working or not. A typical policy evaluation looks at whether and how the outputs of the policy have resulted in, or contributed to, the policy impact or performance, i.e., the extent to which a policy output has accomplished its assigned goals. A policy evaluation has several attributes: (a) it focuses on values and judgments regarding the desirability of the policy; (b) such values are results of actions taken in the implementation of the policy (i.e., there is fact-value interdependence); (c) the evaluation is backward looking, and occurs *ex post* (i.e., after actions have been taken); and (d) claims that result from policy evaluation can be regarded as ends as well as means. Criteria used for policy evaluation include: (i) effectiveness (did the policy achieve what it intended?), (ii) efficiency (did it achieve the policy with least cost?), (iii) adequacy (was it adequate to resolve the problem it was addressing?), (iv) responsiveness (did it address the problem?), and (v) appropriateness (was it relevant to the problem being addressed?). For a review of the features of good policy evaluation as applied in governmental departments, see, e.g., National Audit Office, *Modern Policy-Making: Ensuring Policies Deliver Value for Money,* Report by the Comptroller and Auditor General, HC 289 Session 2001–2002, November 2001, p. 59.

Policy evolutionist: An individual involved in the policy-making process but who favors gradual policy change as a way of bringing about the desired results. A policy revolutionist, on the other hand, favors drastic policy changes to achieve the desired results. L. Koenig, *An Introduction to Public Policy,* Englewood Cliffs, NJ: Prentice Hall, 1986, p. 142.

Policy experts: *See* **Policy analysts**.

Policy failure: The lack of success of a particular policy to achieve its stated outputs and outcomes. Such failure results from, among other things, policy errors, which refer to the wrong policies being developed and/or the implementation of the policy being weak or faulty.

Policy feedback: The process of putting back into the policy process feedback that is received from the public and other stakeholders. While there are formal channels for the soliciting of policy feedback (such as deliberation councils in Singapore), in many jurisdictions there are often none in place.

Policy flexibility: The degree of resilience that is evident in a policy to deal with contingencies. Most policies will usually have a fair degree of flexibility in-built so that the policy will continue to remain valid even in slightly different circumstances.

Policy formulation: The act of preparing and coming up with a policy. This spans the gamut of activity from agenda setting to final deliberations in the legislature, after which a policy is considered to have been formulated. See, e.g., C. Matheson, "Policy Formulation in Australian Government: Vertical and Horizontal Axes," *Australian Journal of Public Administration,* 2000, 59(2), pp. 44–55.

Policy formulation, counsel model of: A model of coming up with a policy that encourages dialogue among the various policy actors in which the role of the policy analyst is to frame the issues and the alternatives in such a way that the policy makers can address all outstanding issues fairly and with equal consideration. See, e.g., B. Jennings, "Policy Analysis: Science, Advocacy, or Counsel?" in S. Nagel (ed.), *Research in Public Policy Analysis and Management,* vol. 4, Greenwich, CT: JAI Press, 1987, pp. 101–30.

Policy fragmentation: Refers to the state of diffusion of policy-making and policy-implementing abilities and rights between levels of government (such as federal versus provincial); between agencies at the same level of government (such as at the central or national level); and among public, private, and nonprofit organizations. This fragmentation makes a cohesive approach to any policy very difficult to bring about. See, e.g., J. Koschinsky and T. Swanstrom, "Confronting Policy Fragmentation: A Political Approach to the Role of Housing Non-Profits," *Policy Studies Review,* 2001, 18(4), pp. 111–27. *See also* **Policy coherence.**

Policy framework, rules-based: *See* **Rules-based approach.**

Policy framing: Identifying the parameters (i.e., the boundaries) of a specific policy at the developmental stage. A policy frame refers to a particular understanding about what the problem is that is under investigation and for which a policy is being sought to address it, and what might be appropriate to deal with it.

Policy fundamentals: The basics that can be expected from government in response to the emergence of a particular problem, and in the management of ongoing concerns and issues. For example, in order to encourage foreign direct investment into a country, the policy fundamentals that would be required would include strong financial institutions, enforceable contract law, and transparency in the corporate sector, among others.

Policy game: A type of game that is evident in a public bureaucracy that results from, for example, the interaction between public managers and political executives. Policy games tend to be standard fare in the policy-development process as different actors and stakeholders jockey for position, and as each tries to understand where the other parties stand on the issues and how they might eventually react to the policy. See, e.g., L. Lynn, "Policy Achievement as a Collective Good: A Strategic Perspective on Managing Social Programs," in B. Bozeman (ed.), *Public Management: The State of the Art,* San Francisco: Jossey-Bass, 1993, pp. 108–33.

Policy goals: The objectives that a particular policy is seeking to attain. While such goals should be very clearly specified, they can be left deliberately vague so that some degree of flexibility is possible during the implementation stage. Policy goals can also be strategic or tactical. The former refers to objectives that are related to targets and final goals, while the latter are related to instruments and operating targets. *See also* **Policy ambiguity.**

Policy guidance cluster: Refers to a loose and changing association of individuals at high levels of government (i.e., at the ministerial level) that interact on a regular basis to ensure that government agenda is being properly targeted. The composition of the cluster varies according to the policy problem under consideration. The cluster does not resemble a departmental structuring, and is kept fairly loose so as to draw on the strengths of many individuals. See, e.g., R. Mascarenhas, "Building an Enterprise Culture in the Public Sector: Reform of the Public Sector in Australia, Britain, and New Zealand," *Public Administration Review,* 1993, 53(4), pp. 319–28.

Policy harmonization: When different policies that deal with the same sector or issue are brought into alignment so as to eliminate discrepancies (for example, higher taxes and tougher regulation and enforcement). Policy harmonization could include revisiting existing policies with a view to substantially changing them if that leads to a better alignment of different but related policies.

Policy image: A term that refers to a new understanding of a particular problem that government wishes to address. The understanding is a result of either the emergence of new evidence or new interpretation of existing evidence. For a case study of the policy images of gun laws, see, e.g., M. Godwin and J. Schroedel, "Policy Diffusion and Strategies for Promoting Policy Change: Evidence from California Local Gun Control Ordinance," *Policy Studies Journal,* 2000, 28(4), pp. 760–76.

Policy impact: The degree to which a policy has the desired effects on the targeted group or area or final outcome. Policy impacts, however, can be intended or unintended, and are often difficult to measure. For an attempt at such measurement, see e.g., P. Daffern and A. Wyatt, "Beyond the Checklist: Towards an Integrated Policy Impact Methodology," *International Review of Administrative Sciences,* 2001, 67(4), pp. 663–72.

Policy implementation: The act of putting into practice a public policy. The implementation of a policy is at times done by a separate agency than the one that formulated it. Since it is much easier to set goals than to put them into action, implementation considerations tend to be less accounted for than the other processes in policy development. Policy implementation can be either programmed (i.e., focused on a thorough review of all aspects of program implementation with emphasis on structured processes) or adaptive (i.e., focused on allowing initial plans to be adjusted as the implementation proceeds with emphasis on feedback and iteration). The effective implementation of a policy is said to suffer when there are uninformed actors. One well-known problem in policy implementation is the presence of bureaucratic competitors. For a good review, see, e.g., S. Giacchino and A. Kakabadse, "Successful Policy Implementation: The Route to Building Self-Confident Government," *International Review of Administrative Sciences,* 2003, 69(2), pp. 139–60.

Policy incoherence: *See* **Policy coherence**.

Policy inconsistency: Not being uniform in commitment to the policies that are formulated to address a problem; and also not adhering to the selected policy over time. For example, a government may decide that the best way to deal with family violence is through prevention, then change direction and address the problem in a different manner. A related term is policy contradiction, which refers to a conflict not only in the specific policy being pursued to address a problem but also to how the particular policy is implemented. For a good case study of policy contradictions, see, e.g., W. Kay, "Problem Definitions and Policy Contradictions: John F. Kennedy and the 'Space Race,'" *Policy Studies Journal,* 2003, 31(5), pp. 53–68. *Cf.* **Policy consistency**.

Policy independence: A situation wherein institutions have freedom and leeway to make and set policy. For example, in many countries, the central bank has policy independence to manipulate the monetary supply, and this takes place without the involvement or intervention of the executive branch or the legislature.

Policy inertia: The inability of decision makers to swiftly and effectively address policy issues, and the low probability that the policy direction taken will yield objectives. Such inertia could be a function of several variables, including, for example, the complexity of the policy issue, and lack of government capability to initiate novel solutions to address persistent and vexing problems.

Policy initiation: The process of formulating a policy that begins with a perception of a problem for which a policy to address is deemed desirable. The policy initiation process also includes issue identification, i.e., identification of a problem's context, determination of policy goals, and specification of suitable policy alternatives. A policy initiator is an agent that gets an issue included on a government's policy agenda. For an application of this role as played by legislators, see, e.g., K. Ho, *The Politics of Policy-Making in Singapore,* Singapore: Oxford University Press, 2000, p. 93.

Policy innovation: Any policy that brings something new, including to the process of making policy itself. Successful policy innovations have four attributes: (a) they are highly visible to all policy actors and other stakeholders; (b) they clearly represent a departure from past practice and thinking; (c) they tend to have longer-lasting impacts than policy responses to crises, although a policy innovation could have as its genesis a crisis; and (d) they are proactive. See N. Polsby, *Political Innovation in America: The Politics of Policy Initiation,* New Haven, CT: Yale University Press, 1984, p. 8.

Policy innovators: *See* **Policy entrepreneurs**.

Policy instrument: A policy measure that gives effect to public policies. Policy instruments can be opaque (difficult to identify) or transparent (identifiable and clearly manifest). Policy instruments—which include, for example, regulation, incentives, autonomy, price ceilings, price floors, etc.—can be coercive, with penalties assessed for infringements.

Policy integration: Refers to the creation of institutions and policy tools that allow actors to respond positively to pressures to enhance performance. Policy integration is more successful when existing policy processes (such as standing committees or mandatory central-agency monitoring) as well as traditional policy tools (such as budgeting and regulations) are manipulated.

Policy intent: *See* **Policy direction**.

Policy intervention: Responding to problems by developing appropriate policies. Interventions are often instigated by policy advocates in convincing policy makers that something needs to be done to address a particular problem. The degree of policy intervention contemplated by government is a function of, among other things, pressure from lobby groups, resource availability, legal provisions, etc.

Policy issue: A subject matter over which there may or may not be disagreement among different groups about how to address it. A cross-cutting policy issue is one that spans across several sectors and thus becomes even more complex to address, not least because it requires several organizations to come together and jointly work on it. An example of a cross-cutting policy issue is that of youth suicide, in which government agencies such as the ministry of health, department of youth and family services, and the police all need to work together.

Policy knowledge pool: An agglomeration of knowledge resources in an organization and related to a particular sector (such as information technology project management) into a cohesive unit such that it can be utilized by anyone in the organization wishing to collect evidence, share ideas, and draw upon expertise for a particular policy. Such a knowledge pool is usually part of an organization's quality assurance process, and can include a resource centre to serve the needs of policy makers as well as a cross-departmental research and evaluation function (see, e.g., UK Cabinet Office, *Professional Policy-Making for the Twenty-First Century,* Report by Strategic Policy-Making Team, London: Cabinet Office, 1999, pp. 40–42).

Policy leadership: Taking the lead role in making policy. In democracies, policy making is a domain determined by citizen demands as much as by the drive of political leaders. The notion of policy leadership can be seen in two dimensions: (a) horizontal (such as the differences in policy leaders, i.e., the legislature, executive, judiciary), and (b) vertical (i.e., hierarchical, with those lower exhibiting leadership in their own sub-jurisdictions and over their own policy domains).

Policy learning: Lessons that are derived from the application of policies and the manner in which such learning is fed back into the policy-development process. Generally, however, there is a time lag in the feedback process, and this yields, in most cases, a continuation of the policy regardless of the negative impact in practice. See, e.g., B. Deacon, B.I. Holliday, and L. Wong, "Conclusion," in L. Wong and N. Flynn (eds.), *The Market in Chinese Social Policy,* Hampshire, UK: Palgrave, 2001, pp. 138–48. *See also* **Learned implementation**.

Policy legitimation: The act of making a particular policy adhere to set rules and procedures and also be acceptable to all or most of the public (i.e., granting legitimacy, for example, by legislative approval). In the newly industrializing countries of Southeast Asia in the decades since the 1970s, policy legitimation invariably meant "delivering the goods and improving the economy," which constituted the main performance criterion by which the ruling government's legitimacy was judged. See, e.g., B. Chua, *Communitarian Ideology and Democracy in Singapore,* London: Routledge, 1995, p. 188.

Policy lenses: Frameworks, both theoretical and experiential, that policy actors use in the process of developing policies. Hypotheses that are generated from various lenses are contrasted to assess which have more explanatory power and which are more relevant. For a classic study of policy lenses in application, see G. Allison, *Essence of Decision: Explaining the Cuban Missile Crisis,* Boston, MA: Little, Brown, 1971. See also, e.g., N. Zahariadis, "Comparing Three Lens of Policy Choice," *Policy Studies Journal*, 1998, 26(3), pp. 434–48.

Policy levers: The different tools and techniques policy makers have at their disposal to give effect to a particular policy. Thus, for example, the interest rate is a policy lever that a central bank can manipulate in order to give effect to its monetary policy. *See also* **Policy instrument**.

Policy linkage: When two or more policies are linked in such a way that the gains of one may or may not be complemented by the other. For example, as a result of GATT (the General Agreement on Trade and Tariffs), certain cross-border tariff barriers may have fallen, but the domestic policy of some GATT-signatory countries has created secondary trade barriers (such as labor standards, competition policy, etc.). In this sense, there is policy linkage, but one is not complemented by the other. See J. Ederington, "Trade and Domestic Policy Linkage in International Agreements," *International Economic Review*, 2002, 43(4), pp. 1347–67.

Policy maintenance: Refers to the need for governments to be highly adaptive to change so as to uphold policy effectiveness. Accordingly, governmental departments need to ensure their ability to (a) continue providing a service even when the unexpected occurs (i.e., it should maintain service delivery), (b) review policies in keeping with any changes in the environment to remain relevant, and (c) terminate policies if they are not delivering desired outcomes. For a discussion of the concept in practice, see, e.g., National Audit Office, *Modern Policy-Making: Ensuring Policies Deliver Value for Money*, Report by the Comptroller and Auditor General, HC 289 Session 2001–2002, November 2001, p. 53.

Policy makers: Individuals who are involved in formulating and developing policies. These are formally legislators, although the meaning of the term has now expanded to include others (such as bureaucrats who provide advice on policy alternatives and who analyze policy options). Policy makers bring their own points of view to a problem. These may be a product of many factors, but when they dominate rational ways of making policy (such as, for example, relying on evidence-based analysis) then a bias will have entered the policy-making process. *See also* **Nondecisions**.

Policy making, cognitive infrastructure of: Composed of an organized system of constructs that are used in the policy-making process and that may or may not be subject to shared understandings among policy makers. Examples of such an infrastructure include organizational learning, problem structuring, and stakeholder consultations.

Policy making, style of: The manner in which individuals, groups, policy advocates, and legislators go about building agendas and making policies. For example, in a presidential system of government, the style of policy making tends to be integrative (i.e., it is the president who provides the strategic direction to policy making) because the legislative branch tends to be fragmented given that each legislator brings his or her own unique approach and view to a policy problem. See L. Koenig, *An Introduction to Public Policy,* Englewood Cliffs, NJ: Prentice Hall, 1986, p. 75.

Policy management: Generally refers to a process of identifying and assessing needs and priorities, analyzing capability, mobilizing and allocating resources to meet them, establishing appropriate policies to put them into action, and developing evaluation frameworks related to the range of policy work that needs to be done. The view of the policy-making process that elected officials have will obviously be different from that of governmental departments and the officials therein.

Policy mandate: The overlapping support given to the government of the day by citizens for formulating or developing a particular policy. The mandate is thus for the policy alone and not necessarily for the whole of the government agenda, particularly if the government of the day consists of coalition parties in which there is always a possibility of policy disagreement. The majority party in the coalition may end up saying that it is willing to continue with the policy.

Policy mapping: A method of looking at the different dimensions of a particular policy, including its different components, and identifying which stakeholder is advocating which particular dimension of the policy. It enables policy makers to identify the space within which there might be room for agreement. For an application, see, e.g., A. Gray et al., *Policy Change in a Context of Transition: Drug Policy in South Africa 1989–1999,* Centre for Health Policy, School of Public Health, University of the Witwatersrand, South Africa, July 2002. *See also* **Policy translation**.

Policy measure: Specific policies formulated to address particular problems. Policy measures can be categorized as either opaque or transparent. Opaque policy measures are those where it is difficult to discover what they are, who decides, what they cost, and what is their basis; by contrast, transparent policy measures are clearly delineated.

Policy modifier: Any event or activity that triggers changes in the manner in which a policy is specified or how it is actually implemented is termed a policy modifier. Policy modifiers can be ad hoc in nature (such as spontaneous opposition to a particular policy), or systematic and well planned (such as an openly stated policy stance of a minority party in a coalition government that challenges the majority party's own policy). Policy modifications, then, are changes made to policies once they are formulated. This could be due to feedback received upon implementation or to a change of heart on the part of government.

Policy momentum: Movement created by a successful policy in one jurisdiction or sector that creates the opportunity for such or similar policy to be developed in another jurisdiction or sector. For example, the privatization policies of the United Kingdom in the 1980s created a policy momentum for such policies in other countries. Momentum generally stems from the following effects: (a) when the success that some agencies generate excites others through networks; (b) when agencies copy what they see others doing successfully; (c) when the number of agencies increase as the particular innovation begins to be accepted; and (d) when agencies copy a policy because they feel they will get similar results. See E. Bardach, *Getting Agencies to Work Together: The Practice and Theory of Managerial Craftsmanship,* Washington, DC: Brookings Institution Press, 1998, pp. 276–77.

Policy neglect: When a government—deliberately or otherwise—does not focus on a particular problem, and neglects to develop appropriate policies to deal with it. Some reasons for policy neglect could be resource scarcity; lack of understanding of the problem, or of the consequences of leaving the problem unaddressed; and lack of consensus among stakeholders on how to proceed, and their refusal to contribute jointly to problem resolution.

Policy networks: Formal (i.e., institutionalized) and informal (i.e., ad hoc and/or noninstitutionalized) contacts between and among policy makers and those who are in key positions to influence policy. Policy networks exist across several policy domains and consist of several policy communities. For a taxonomy of policy networks, see, e.g., M. Howlett and M. Ramesh, "Policy Subsystem Configurations and Policy Change: Operationalizing the Postpositivist Analysis of the Politics of the Policy Process," *Policy Studies Journal,* 1998, 26(3), pp. 466–81.

Policy order: The perceived correct and theoretically pure approach to policy making as called for by, for example, the rational-choice theory of decision making. For a discussion of policy order called for by rational models, and its counterpart of democratic norms, see, e.g., M. Neiman and S. Stambough, "Rational Choice Theory and the Evaluation of Public Policy," *Policy Studies Journal,* 1998, 26(3), pp. 449–65.

Policy outputs: (1) The tangible results of a policy that are consequential and measurable. (2) The outputs produced by an agency that is mandated solely with providing policy advice.

Policy oversight: Ensuring that policies are implemented in the manner and with the intent that they were formulated. Such an oversight role is played by all three branches of government—the executive, through day-to-day control over the bureaucracy; the legislature, through periodic sessions with bureaucrats where the latter explain their decisions and update legislators on progress; and the judiciary, through recourse to judicial reviews of executive action.

Policy paradigm: A policy paradigm is considered to be a dimension of a policy regime and shapes the way particular problems are defined, what solution set exists, and how they can be applied. A policy paradigm evolves from the joint contribution of work from practitioners, academicians, researchers, interest-group leaders, and others. For a good discussion of the concept, see, e.g., C. Wilson, "Policy Regimes and Policy Change," *Journal of Public Policy,* 2000, 20(3), pp. 247–74. *See also* **Policy regime**.

Policy paralysis: Refers to a stalemate that is reached in policy formulation because of: (a) irreconcilably divergent views on a policy, and/or (b) a lack of political will on the part of government to tackle a particularly difficult issue. Such a stalemate leads to inaction on the part of government, which invariably worsens the problem situation. For an illuminating case study of policy paralysis, see, e.g., Q. Beresford et al., "The Salinity Crisis in Western Australia: A Case of Policy Paralysis," *Australian Journal of Public Administration,* 2001, 60(4), pp. 30–38.

Policy parameters: *See* **Policy envelope**.

Policy participation: Allowing all stakeholders of a particular policy to have a say in its definition and final construction of the policy itself. In some cases, there may be legal provisions to ensure such participation (such as seeking and incorporating the feedback of unions in the development of policy).

Policy planning: Using systematic processes and techniques to formulate and achieve desired policy outcomes. This includes specifying what needs to be addressed, how it should be done, and how it needs to be implemented. See, e.g., J. Bryson and B. Crosby, "Policy Planning and the Design and Use of Forums, Arenas, and Courts," in B. Bozeman (ed.), *Public Management: The State of the Art,* San Francisco: Jossey-Bass, 1993, p. 324.

Policy position: The stance taken by government (or other actors) vis-à-vis any issue that needs to be addressed. While ideally policy positions should not shift in the short run, in reality they do with the emergence of new scenarios.

Policy preferences: The perceived desirability of each policy element. Sometimes policy preferences are explicitly expressed, but often they are not (largely because preferences, once stated, tend to be constraining). Generally, political parties will have voiced their policy preferences in an election manifesto; at times, though, policy preferences change as parties come into office either because the promises were not well reasoned or because coalition-building reduces the scope of their own policy preferences and forces compromise. See, e.g., D. Dolowitz and D. Marsh, "Policy Transfer: A Framework for Comparative Analysis," in M. Minogue, C. Polidano, and D. Hulme (eds.), *Beyond the New Public Management: Changing Ideas and Practices in Governance,* Cheltenham, UK: Edward Elgar, 1998, pp. 38–58. *See also* **Policy element**.

Policy problem: Any undesirable situation in society that merits the formulation of a public policy to address it. A condition is regarded as a policy problem when either a sizable number of people perceive themselves as being negatively affected and seek government involvement in its amelioration or when a few policy advocates and policy entrepreneurs define a problem in such a way that the government perceives it as something for which a policy needs to be determined. Not all problems in society merit a formal public policy, this being the essence of the argument of those who argue for a diminution of the role of government in public life.

Policy reform, crash-through approach to: An assertion that in reforming the public sector, it is preferable to push through reforms aggressively rather than to spend time promoting the potential benefits of such reforms. However, this runs the risk of alienating citizens if not done properly, and reform fatigue can set in rather rapidly. For a contextual discussion of this approach to policy reform, see, e.g., S. Goldfinch and P. 't Hart, "Leadership and Institutional Reform: Engineering Macroeconomic Policy Change in Australia," *Governance: An International Journal of Policy, Administration, and Institutions,* 2003, 16(2), pp. 235–70. *See also* **Reform fatigue.**

Policy regime: The set of policies and policy-making dimensions that are needed for a particular policy area. For example, the policy regime for regional economic development would have several policies centered on different aspects of the problem of spatial economic underdevelopment, such as tax disincentives for industry set-ups, regional transport bottlenecks, narrow credit markets, etc. For a good analysis of the concept, see, e.g., C. Wilson, "Policy Regimes and Policy Change," *Journal of Public Policy,* 2000, 20(3), pp. 247–74.

Policy research: (1) A term that refers to work done on the relationships and interactions among several variables that reflect social problems and, more importantly, that can be manipulated by public policy. (2) A search for evidence-based reasoning in the formulation of public policies. For a discussion of why agencies tend to do poor policy research, see, e.g., S. Elkin, "Political Science and the Analysis of Public Policy," *Public Policy,* 1974, 22(3), pp. 399–422.

Policy response: The actions of a government in constructing a policy to address an emergent issue. For usage of the term, see, e.g., Y. Jeon and D. Haider-Markel, "Tracing Issue Definition and Policy Change: An Analysis of Disability Issue Images and Policy Response," *Policy Studies Journal,* 2001, 29(2), pp. 215–31.

Policy responsibility: The task of formulating policies in response to public perceptions of problems. With the acceptance of the principle of subsidiarity, policy responsibility has shifted increasingly to lower levels of government, although in the eyes of the citizens, governments (at all levels) are still responsible for remedying wrongs when policy problems emerge or persist.

Policy reversal: A situation when public policies are changed and/or reversed either by one government or by succeeding ones. For example, Singapore's family-planning policy in the 1960s and 1970s of two children per family was reversed in the 1980s after proving too successful, and families were given governmental incentives to have more children. The difference between policy reversal and policy termination is that, in the latter, the policy itself is halted, whereas in the former, the government goes back on the policy. For an application, see, e.g., P. Larmour, "Policy Transfer and Reversal: Customary Land Registration from Africa to Melanesia," *Public Administration and Development,* 2002, 22, pp. 151–61. *See also* **Policy termination**.

Policy review: A formal (and long-term) assessment of the effectiveness of a governmental policy. A policy review is normally done to determine the following: (a) the value-for-money of a particular policy, (b) public perceptions of the policy, and (c) if the policy needs to be amended. While policy reviews can be held internally by departments, it is generally considered more effective to have an external source conduct the review. For a discussion of how policy reviews add to the strength of policy making in government departments, see, e.g., National Audit Office, *Modern Policy-Making: Ensuring Policies Deliver Value for Money,* Report by the Comptroller and Auditor General, HC 289 Session 2001–2002, November 2001, p. 55.

Policy revolutionist: *See* **Policy evolutionist**.

Policy risk: (1) An issue that could jeopardize the successful implementation of a public policy. (2) A more fundamental risk in the public sector that is also termed strategic risk. See, e.g., G. Scott, "Managing Operational and Policy Risks at the Centre of Government," in J. Yeabsley and A. Sundakov (eds.), *Risk and the Institutions of Government,* Wellington: Institute of Policy Studies and NZIER, 1999, pp. 14–34.

Policy shifts: Changes that are evident in policies from one period to another. While it is normal to expect some policy shifts when governments change, these shifts can also arise within the term of a single government. For an example of the usage of the term with respect to policy shifts in the health sector in China, see A. Cheung, "Health Policy Reform," in L. Wong and N. Flynn (eds.), *The Market in Chinese Social Policy,* Hampshire, UK: Palgrave, 2001, pp. 63–87. *See also* **Policy Reversal**.

Policy shop: A policy-advice agency or a unit within a governmental department that provides advice on policy related to the particular sector in which the agency operates. In the context of a policy-operations split, policy shops tend to be inherently small in size and are restricted almost wholly to providing policy advice to chief executives (internally) and to ministers (externally). A policy unit is a small division within a policy shop that is tasked with supporting the agency's core competence in providing quality advice to government. For a discussion of the key charac-teristics of a high-performing policy unit, see, e.g., State Services Com-mission, *High Fliers: Developing High-Performing Policy Units,* Occa-sional Paper No. 22, Wellington: State Services Commission, 1999. See also, e.g., G. Bhatta, "Evidence-Based Analysis and the Work of Policy Shops," *Australian Journal of Public Administration,* 2002, 61(3), pp. 98–105.

Policy signal: A sign indicative of a government's policy direction. For example, to denote that a government is keen on establishing a new or different way of managing its relationship with public-sector trade un-ions, it may first float the idea (through, for example, a cabinet minute) that every public-sector agency must sign a "partnership for quality" memorandum of understanding with all relevant unions.

Policy simulation: (1) Related to policy evaluations, policy simulation refers to modeling a mixture of policies in order to determine the most appropriate course. (2) Also refers to simulating a policy so as to test its likely impact. For an application, see, e.g., J. Nugent and C. Sarwa, "The Three E's—Efficiency, Equity and Environmental Protection: In Search of 'Win-Win-Win' Policies: A CGE Analysis of India," *Journal of Policy Modeling,* 2002, 24(1), pp. 19–50.

Policy slippage: A situation when the policy that was introduced in re-sponse to a particular issue begins to lose its effectiveness and relevance. Governments need to make policy adjustments to address slippage.

Policy specification: The final product that emerges from the policy-development process. A policy specification details what a particular pol-icy is, what specific issues it seeks to address, and how it would do so (i.e., its intervention logic).

Policy stance: A stand taken by policy leaders toward a policy in devel-opment, which could be any one of: (a) supportive or oppositional; (b) prejudicial, in holding on to long-held but erroneous views on the policy; (c) superficial, or inconsiderate of numerous aspects of the relevant pol-icy; and (d) evasive, either in a purposely vague manner or through igno-rance of the respective positions. Any particular policy stance taken by policy leaders need not be permanent; with new information or interven-tions from various sources, stances may reasonably change. See, e.g., L. Koenig, *An Introduction to Public Policy,* Englewood Cliffs, NJ: Pren-tice Hall, 1986, p. 41.

Policy statement: The announcement of a policy that a government seeks to implement. A policy statement could be formal (such as made in a president's inaugural address, or in a speech convening a parliamentary session) or informal (as a minister's response to media questioning). A policy statement can also be positive or prescriptive. A positive policy statement (also called a normative policy statement) contains facts and no value propositions. On the other hand, a prescriptive policy statement presents policy intentions, which is a value proposition.

Policy stream: A term that is used in relation to the policy-making process to denote where options are considered and where a decision is made. A policy stream usually consists of a select set of alternatives that have been presented to policy makers for final consideration. A policy sub stream, on the other hand, refers to a group of actors that are actively involved in the policy-development process. Such involvement can be formal or informal. See J. Kingdon, *Agendas, Alternatives, and Public Policies,* 2nd edition, New York: HarperCollins, 1995, p. 3. For a case-study application of policy sub streams, see, e.g., B. Ellison, "The Advocacy Coalition Framework and Implementation of the Endangered Species Act: A Case Study in Western Water Politics," *Policy Studies Journal,* 1998, 26(1), pp. 11–29.

Policy system: The environment in which all aspects of a policy are played out. This includes how public problems are perceived, defined, and alternative solutions identified and analyzed; how opted policy is recommended; and how it is debated in the legislature.

Policy termination: Ending a particular policy, either because it has served its purpose, is unsuccessful, or is undesired. For a case-study application of the issues around policy termination, see, e.g., J. Frantz, "Political Resources for Policy Terminators," *Policy Studies Journal,* 2002, 30(1), pp. 11–28. *See also* **Policy reversal**.

Policy time lag: *See* **Lag**.

Policy transfer: The process by which knowledge of ideas, etc. is transferred. Such transfer can be either voluntary (as when different jurisdictions proactively adopt the policies that are evident elsewhere) or coercive (as when international financial institutions compel governments to enforce a particular policy). Coercive policy transfer is also known as conditionality. See D. Dolowitz and D. Marsh, "Learning from Abroad: The Role of Policy Transfer in Contemporary Policy-making," *Governance: An International Journal of Policy and Administration,* 2000,

13(1), pp. 5–24. For an application of policy transfer, see, e.g., K. Jacobs and P. Barnett, "Policy Transfer and Policy Learning: A Study of the 1991 New Zealand Health Services Taskforce," *Governance: An International Journal of Policy and Administration,* 2000, 13(2), pp. 185–213.

Policy translation: The transformation of a policy from one level of representation to another (such as from abstraction, i.e., from broadly stated goals to implementation). Such translation usually takes place at the bureaucratic level to begin with, then is endorsed or amended at the political level. By the time the policy proposal goes to the legislature for debate, the translation is complete, notwithstanding the fact that it could go through more translations in the legislature.

Policy troubleshooters: *See* **Policy analysts**.

Policy unit: *See* **Policy shop**.

Policy venture: Refers to any new area in which government intends or is compelled to come up with a public policy. A good example is that of genetic cloning or genetic modification.

Policy venues: Places where public policies are formally debated and considered. In jurisdictions where the same policy can be debated in multiple venues (such as in the United States, for example, in Congress, in state legislatures, and in local jurisdictions), political activists and advocates can seize upon any one of those venues in which to push their agenda. For a case study on the impact of policy venues on policy making, see M. Godwin and J. Schroedel, "Policy Diffusion and Strategies for Promoting Policy Change: Evidence from California Local Gun Control Ordinance," *Policy Studies Journal,* 2000, 28(4), pp. 760–76.

Policy window: Refers to an opportune moment that policy makers might await or take advantage of to introduce proposals for a new policy. As old problems are pushed out by new ones for public attention (for example, as reflected in media coverage), policy makers may wait for an appropriate condition to arise before introducing certain legislation. Windows close when policy makers feel their concerns have been sufficiently addressed or, conversely, are not addressable at that particular time. See J. Kingdon, *Agendas, Alternatives, and Public Policies,* 2nd edition, New York: Harper Collins, 1995, p. 20.

Policy-making process: The process of making policies, which generally contains four phases: (a) focusing attention on a particular issue, including properly specifying its parameters; (b) seeking alternative solutions to the issue; (c) debating the alternatives; and (d) making and formalizing the policy decision. The policy-making process is evident at three levels: (i) at the grassroots level, for example, community and local government; (ii) within policy subsectors, such as rural maternity health; and (iii) at the national level, such as in a national parliament. The policy-making process in the public sector is inherently political because of the exercise of political and legislative leadership, the role of the bureaucracy in analyzing and framing policy options, and the involvement of the public.

Policy-operations split: A division of the roles of government agencies between providing inputs toward policy making and policy implementation. Those that advocate the role of elected officials to make policies, and that of unelected bureaucrats to implement them argue that the split is necessary so that public policies can more accurately reflect the wishes and demands of citizens. Just as important, those arguing for a policy-operations split maintain that such a split will ensure that departmental policy advice to governmental ministers is not captured by those that deliver services, and that ministers will not thus be compelled unknowingly to favorably resource the delivery priorities of the departments. The risks of such a split, however, are that there then tends to be little interface between policy and operations, and the policies recommended to ministers may not accurately reflect ground-level realities. The Next Steps agencies in the United Kingdom and Crown entities in the New Zealand public sector are good examples of a policy-operations split in government. For a discussion of the policy-operations split in New Zealand, see, e.g., R. Shaw, "Rehabilitating the Public Service—Alternatives to the Wellington Model," in S. Chatterjee (ed.), *The New Politics: A Third Way for New Zealand,* Palmerston North, New Zealand: Dunmore Press, 1999, pp. 193–95. *See also* **Executive agencies**.

Policy-relevant knowledge: Knowledge that informs policy during the formulation stage. Such knowledge comes from various sources, including cross-jurisdictional evidence, policy makers' own experiences, literature research, and other heuristic measures. See W. Dunn, *Public Policy Analysis: An Introduction,* 2nd edition. Englewood Cliffs, NJ: Prentice Hall, 1994, p. 22

Political access: Access by governmental department leaders and senior officials to politicians and decision makers beyond their respective ministries. Such access is shaped not only by a department's mandate (for example, finance, foreign affairs, defense) but also by the personality of department leaders. The greater is the political access of a department, the greater its scope of influencing public policy, and especially of those matters that are within its own mandate.

Political accountability: *See* **Accountability**.

Political advisers: Individuals who give advice to politicians (usually to governmental ministers) on all matters of public policy. Political advisors were not key players in the policy-making process until recently, when, in the context of the UK, for example, Prime Minister Tony Blair increased by manifold the number of political advisers serving the prime minister's office, and who increasingly supplant advice that traditionally comes for the bureaucracy.

Political agency problem: A problem in governance that is created when the number of principals is very high and the number of agents is very low. The problem then manifests in a lack of coordination in contracting with agents. For example, when governments seek to centralize power, the principals (i.e., the citizens) are many and those who are in central government (i.e., the agents) are few, and the argument is that the contract between them is not as efficient as when there is one agent per locality (i.e., when there is decentralization). For a discussion on this in relation to decentralization, see, e.g., P. Bardhan, "Decentralization of Governance and Development," *Journal of Economic Perspectives,* 2002, 16(4), pp. 185–205.

Political agenda: As with policy agenda, a political one refers to those matters of public concern to which politicians (and those who are involved in advising them) are aware and mindful of. See J. Kingdon, *Agendas, Alternatives, and Public Policies,* 2nd edition, New York: HarperCollins, 1995, p. 3.

Political appointees: Individuals who are appointed to public-sector positions by political incumbents and thus do not normally go through the usual channels of merit selection and competition. Political appointees tend to leave their posts when the political incumbency changes (with some exceptions). *See also* **Transients**.

Political assessments: (1) An appraisal of the political dimensions of any public policy. (2) The term also refers to the practice of employees paying yearly fees (or assessments) in return for continued employment. This practice has been discontinued in advanced jurisdictions but is still evident in many developing countries.

Political capability: The capability of a government to respond to citizens' demands, mediate conflicting interests inherent in society, and ensure that policies that emerge are as inclusive as can be. This capability issue does not relate to the ability of the bureaucracy to deliver on policies per se because the bureaucracy generally does not have a political attribute. See, e.g., M. Grindle, *Challenging the State: Crisis and Innovation in Latin America and Africa,* Cambridge: Cambridge University Press, 1996, p. 44.

Political capital: The goodwill that an actor (an individual, organization, political party, or even a government) has in the political arena. Usage of the capital involves, for example, getting others to support one's own position on various issues.

Political culture: Refers to habits, perspectives, and modes of belief of individuals and communities that together influence how they govern themselves and manage their affairs. Such habits and perspectives are in themselves products of history and how the particular society has evolved over time. This notion of political culture is relevant to public management because it highlights the environment in which public-policy making is conducted. See, e.g., D. Elazar, *American Federalism: A View from the States,* New York: Crowell, 1984, p. 110.

Political decentralization: *See* **Decentralization**.

Political economy: Refers to the interactions of political motivations in economic policies. Political economy studies the natural laws that explain how wealth is produced and distributed. Philosophers such as Adam Smith and Karl Marx made fundamental contributions to the study of political economy. For a concise description, see, e.g., G. Saint-Paul, "The 'New Political Economy': Recent Books by Allen Drazen and by Torsten Persson and Guido Tabellini," *Journal of Economic Literature,* 2000, 38(4), pp. 915–25. For a discussion of political economy in the context of countries that are undergoing transition, see, e.g., G. Roland, "The Political Economy of Transition," *Journal of Economic Perspectives,* 2002, 16(1), pp. 29–50.

Political governance: (1) Refers to the structure of organizations and how they are managed. (2) As understood in the context of how a country is managed, it refers to the work of government. Thus, for example, when donor agencies seek to affect the political governance of developing countries, they are seeking to affect the political incentives of governments to achieve desired outcomes. This could include donor assistance to formal institutions such as an electoral commission, parliament, the media, and support to supreme audit agencies. For an example of a discussion of political governance, see P. Cooke and K. Morgan, *The Associational Economy: Firms, Regions, and Innovation,* New York: Oxford University Press, 1998, pp. 168–70. *Cf.* **Economic governance**.

Political hazard: As used in the context of policy making, this refers to the uncertainty that is generated by the manner in which political institutions work (such as, for example, from a deadlock in parliament over a particular issue). See, e.g., W. Henisz and A. Delios, "Uncertainty, Imitation, and Plant Location: Japanese Multinational Corporations, 1990–1996," *Administrative Science Quarterly,* 2001, 46(3), pp. 443–75.

Political impetus: A term that refers to the political drive that sustains policy making. An impetus may result from various sources, including, for example, the election of a new government or the onset of a major problem that necessitates governmental response.

Political interference: When governmental ministers and politicians intervene in the workings of a public-sector organization (such as when ministers insist on certain things being done in a particular way). Autonomous agencies are created to minimize the incidence of political interference in the work of governmental agencies.

Political market: A domain where the competition is for the authority to form government, effect policy, command resource allocation, and administer the public service. See, e.g., M. Grindle, "In Quest of the Political: The Political Economy of Development Policy-Making," in G. Meier and J. Stiglitz, *Frontiers of Development Economics: The Future in Perspective*, Oxford: Oxford University Press, 2001, pp. 345–88.

Political neutrality: A principle applicable in the public service which states that public servants must be free of political interference, and that they must serve the government of the day in a way that ensures not only that they maintain ministerial confidence but also that they are able to establish the same impartial relationship with succeeding ministers. This is, however, very difficult to maintain as there are always pressures on public servants to respond directly to the specific interests of ministers and other politicians. For a good application of the principle, see State Services Commission, *Annual Report of the State Services Commission, 2002,* Wellington: State Services Commission, 2002, p. G-3.

Political opportunity structure: Refers to those aspects in a jurisdiction's political environment that facilitate networks and collective action among various stakeholders, including citizen groups, voluntary associations, local businesses, and political parties. Such aspects could include available forums for public discussions, mandatory requirements to consult widely, and guidelines on how collective action could be fostered. Political opportunism refers to the actions of a government that are driven toward getting votes and that maximize political expediency. Such political opportunism can exist in policy makers as well. For a discussion of the concept, see, e.g., S. Tarrow, *Power in Movement,* Cambridge: Cambridge University Press, 1994, pp. 85–86.

Political overhead theory: *See* **Bureaucratic accountability**.

Political receptivity: The degree of support received from the political establishment for particular policies. While politicians are responsible for formulating policies, they often rely on what emerges from different parts of society in making their agenda. Some issues (such as campaign finance reform in the United States) are ignored, while others (such as the idea of a family commission in New Zealand) are picked up for further consideration.

Political risk: *See* **Risk**.

Political stream: A stage in the policy-making process when a policy problem reaches the political arena. Included in this stream are the interactions among institutions and the policy makers who ultimately decide policy. Unlike in the policy stream, however, the environment in this stream is much more fluid and any external event (such as public mood swing over a particular issue) is likely to cause variance in the inclination toward a policy. See J. Kingdon, *Agendas, Alternatives, and Public Policies,* 2nd edition, New York: HarperCollins, 1995, p. 17.

Political will: The willingness of governments to initiate and sustain unpopular but necessary reforms in the face of significant political costs and risks. For a case study of why and how lack of political will, among other ills, can lead to a failure in the performance of public-management systems in developing countries, see, e.g., H. Zafarullah and A. Huque, "Public Management for Good Governance: Reforms, Regimes, and Reality in Bangladesh," *International Journal of Public Administration,* 2001, 24(12), pp. 1379–1403.

Politicization of policies: Refers to imparting any public policies with a political character. For example, if a public-policy issue (such as school prayer in public schools) becomes divided along political-party lines, with each party refusing to take into account any other view, then a politicization of the policy is said to be evident.

Politico-bureaucratic networks: A system of linkages between the political establishment and the bureaucratic structures evident, for example, in ex-bureaucrats becoming politicians (through membership of a political party) and ex-politicians taking up bureaucratic positions (such as directorships in the boards of public agencies). This results in a nexus of relationships between the bureaucracy and the political establishment. For a case study, see K. Ho, *The Politics of Policy-Making in Singapore,* Singapore: Oxford University Press, 2000, pp. 143–78.

Politics-administration dichotomy: Refers to the belief that public administration should be free from the influences of politics, i.e., that the execution (implementation) of public policy should be objective and unbiased rather than a political exercise. For a cogent review of the issues around this dichotomy, see, e.g., K. Hansen and N. Ejersbo, "The Relationship Between Politicians and Administrators—A Logic of Disharmony," *Public Administration,* 2002, 80(4), pp. 733–50. *See also* **Political neutrality**.

Pooled interdependencies: As used in the context of organizations, this term refers to a situation whereby the individual components (i.e., units) in an organization do not need to interact with other units in order to accomplish their individual goals. However, in order for the whole organization to succeed, these individual units will need to pool together. *See also* **Reciprocal interdependencies; Sequential interdependencies**.

Pork-barrel ethic: Where one legislator does not question the merits of another's project in return for the same treatment. Pork-barrel spending refers to item expenditures, seemingly unwarranted, amended to a larger bill in a quid pro quo among legislators for the bill's support. *See also* **Log-rolling**.

Portability: The ability to transfer benefits (such as health insurance) from one job to another. Unions have long advocated this issue because workers thus do not have to forfeit entitlements if they change jobs.

Portable skills: Skills that are transferable, such as concerns, for example, computing, teamwork, and supervisory skills. Portable skills are usually generic skills, and are also related to the concept of employability because workers with portable skills enjoy greater mobility in the job market. *See also* **Fungibility**.

Portfolio approach: As applied to the management of public goods, this term refers to the provision of goods and services whereby some are completely contracted out and some are not. The exact mix will depend upon how the government of the day sees which services should be retained for delivery by the public sector and which should be contracted out. See, e.g., P. Larson, "Public and Private Values at Odds: Can Private Sector Values Be Transplanted into Public Sector Institutions?" *Public Administration and Development,* 1997, 17(1), pp. 131–39.

Portfolio management: (, for example, a minister that has the portfolios of education and public service would need to ensure that attention to those areas were balanced 1) As used in public governance, portfolio management refers to ensuring that the mix of areas of responsibility that a minister has are managed properly. Thus appropriately. A related concept is a portfolio review, which is an evaluation of selected areas under the purview of ministers. Portfolios could cover several sectors, and in a portfolio review all would be evaluated to see how better coordination could be achieved. Portfolio reviews are normally endorsed by cabinet to give the exercise some importance. (2) As used in business, portfolio management refers to ensuring that the mix of stocks and other forms of assets are carefully monitored to yield the greatest return to investors. Here, a related concept—portfolio optimization—occurs when the best mix of different assets is brought about to yield the highest return to investors. See, e.g., KPMG, *Understanding Enterprise Risk Management: An Emerging Model for Building Shareholder Value,* New York: KPMG, 2001, p. 5.

POSDCORB: An acronym coined by the noted administration specialist Luther Gulick to refer to the following functions of a chief executive: planning, organizing, staffing, directing, coordinating, reporting, and budgeting. Gulick adapted the concept from the functional analysis work done by management scholar Henri Fayol. Gulick argued that following from this classification, an organization itself *may* (emphasis his) be structured along POSDCORB lines. See L. Gulick, "Notes on the Theory of Organization: With Special Reference to Government in the United States," in L. Gulick and L. Urwick, *Papers on the Science of Administration,* New York: Institute of Public Administration, 1937, pp. 1–45.

Position: (1) A stance taken by policy makers and politicians on a particular policy. (2) An employment status that has specific responsibilities. Position analysis is the examination of all positions in an organization with the purpose of determining what is entailed of the positions and what competencies and levels of skills are needed for each. This is a fundamental task in planning personnel management. Position classification is the process of putting into groups the various positions based on similarities of several variables, including functions, competencies needed, and level of responsibilities, among others. Finally, position specification is a detailed summary of the activities attached to a job, its monetary value, and the necessary qualifications required to do it effectively.

Position analysis: *See* **Position**.

Position-based bargaining: A bargaining technique where the parties start by putting forward their proposals rather than a statement of their interests. Such proposals, in the eyes of the party putting them forward, are the preferred solutions. This method of bargaining is more conflict oriented than interest-based bargaining, although the parties are still required to justify their proposals in terms of how they advance their own interests. *Cf.* **Interest-based bargaining**.

Position classification: *See* **Position**.

Position evaluation: *See* **Job evaluation**.

Position management: A process of analyzing, determining, and assigning positions in an organization such that its mission can be effectively accomplished. It involves the determination of positions needed, followed by specification of the required competencies. It also includes the process of ensuring that the right people staff the right positions. An organization will take a fresh look at its position management system regularly to reflect the changes that are evident in the market in general and in the internal structure of the organization in particular. For example, the organization may manage a position by bringing about a position transfer, which is when an employee is transferred from one position to another within the same organization. Such a transfer could be the result of a restructuring or an opportunity created for the employee to gain broader experiences.

Position specification: *See* **Position**.

Position transfer: *See* **Position management**.

Positive capability: As used in organizational psychology, this term refers to the ability of an organization (i.e., senior individuals in organizations) to act decisively in the face of uncertainty. See, e.g., R. French, "'Negative Capability': Managing the Confusing Uncertainties of Change," *Journal* *of Organizational Change Management,* 2001, 14(5), pp. 480–92. *Cf.* **Negative capability**.

Positive externalities: *See* **Social costs**.

Positive policy statement: *See* **Policy statement**.

Positive recruitment: A situation where an organization makes an active effort to attract worthy candidates. For example, in light of the low levels of minorities in its senior civil service, the United Kingdom Cabinet Office has come up with a plan to market itself to minorities so that they are encouraged to seek opportunities in the public service. See UK Cabinet Office, *Bringing in and Bringing on Talent,* London: Cabinet Office, 1999.

Positive slack: In project planning, positive slack is a state where there is time between the end date of the preceding activity and the start date of the succeeding one. This slack allows organizations to have some breathing space if problems emerge with the preceding activity.

Positive-sum games: A form of managerial gamesmanship where all participants win (i.e., go away with more of whatever they are seeking— for example, money, prestige, goodwill—than what they came in with). Positive-sum games, however, implicitly assume trust among the players. *See also* **Games**.

Post-audit: *See* **Pre-audit**.

Post-bureaucratic organization: An organization where the internal structure and dynamics are very different from those articulated by traditional theorists. Post-bureaucratic organizations tend to be, among other things, less hierarchical, more employee friendly, and less rules based. They are also active in encouraging collective action, continuously improving processes, and seeking feedback. See, e.g., C. Heckscher, "Defining the Post-Bureaucratic Type," in C. Heckscher and A. Donnellon (eds.), *The Post-Bureaucratic Organization,* London: Sage, 1994, pp. 14–62.

Post-contractual information problem: A problem that arises because of information asymmetry after a contract has been negotiated. The key assumption here is that a party has an incentive to deviate from the contractual specifications if it believes that the other party has little information about whether the contract was indeed honored. *See also* **Moral hazard**.

Post-purchase regret: A term that alludes to the regret that is expressed by the principal once a purchase has been made from a contractor. This is possible because of the existence of information asymmetry at the time of the purchase decision wherein the principal did not fully ascertain the capabilities of the contractor to deliver as per specification. *See also* **Winner's curse**.

Posturing: Where policy makers compete for public attention with respect to a specific policy. Posturing is a common phenomenon during the initial phases of policy formulation, but tends to diminish once negotiations start among competing parties (such as politicians, political parties, etc.). However, even when agreement may have been reached on a certain policy, politicians may continue to posture so as to demonstrate dedication to their constituents or cause.

Potential compensation, principle of: An assertion in cost-benefit analysis that if gainers could potentially compensate losers then any change in the status quo could be determined as an optimal solution. Whether compensation is actually made or not is immaterial for purposes of ascertaining the validity of the principle.

Potential-problem analysis: An analysis that seeks to determine the future state of a problem and its potential impact. Potential-problem analysis is related to the strategic thinking of policy development. *See also* **Scenario planning**.

Power: The ability to influence or command the behavior of others. The source of power of a person in an organization comes from controlling access to information, persons, and instrumentalities (such as resources). There are several types of power, such as reward power (to provide rewards so that others will have an incentive to behave accordingly), and coercive power (compel others to behave in a particular manner), among others. See, e.g., D. Mechanic, "Sources of Power of Lower Participants in Complex Organizations," *Administrative Science Quarterly,* 1962, 7(3), pp. 349–64.

Power, faces of: As seen in the public-policy context, this concept refers to the different facets of power as becomes evident in the policy-making process. The first and most visible level, the "first face," is power/ability that is used to resolve outstanding issues in the policy-making process; the "second face" is power/ability that is exerted to control the policy agenda; and the "third face" is the power/ability to control the policy preferences of other actors. For a review of the concept, see, e.g., C. Brunner and P. Schumaker, "Power and Gender in the 'New View' Public Schools," *Policy Studies Journal,* 1998, 26(1), pp. 30–45.

Power game: A game that is played between unequal groups within an organization where players select different strategies to further their own interests. Those in subordinate positions, for example, may have defensive strategies and withhold their ready acquiescence to authority, while superiors may have a strategy of divide and rule. However, depending on what is at stake, players may not go all out to play the game.

Pragmatic acculturation: A process of policy diffusion which takes place in three steps: (a) once a particular policy problem is identified, evidence is gathered on how it has been framed in other jurisdictions; (b) experts from outside are invited to provide professional opinions; and (c) the ideas are calibrated to the specific situations existing in the particular jurisdiction, and then a policy decision is reached. See S. Quah, "Confucianism, Pragmatic Acculturation, Social Discipline, and Productivity: Notes from Singapore," *APO Productivity Journal,* 1995, p. 55.

Pre-audit: A check of the suitability of the proposed financial transactions (i.e., before being registered) and systems in place in an organization. This is to ensure that the organization uses the right financial framework in its operations. Post-audit, on the other hand, is an audit of resources spent (i.e., after being registered).

Pre-award survey: An assessment that is done of the bidders that have expressed an interest in providing a particular product or service to a purchaser. In a pre-award survey, the purchaser may opt to evaluate the capabilities of those bidders that look likely to be strong contenders for winning the bid.

Prebendary bureaucracies: Bureaucracies where individual members enhance their salaries by accepting contributions (such as gifts) from users of services. These are not really considered to be bribes but neither are they considered to be an element of the formal salary package. Prebendary bureaucracies continue to exist in most underdeveloped countries. See F. Riggs, "Bureaucracy: A Profound Puzzle for Presidentialism," in A. Farazmand (ed.), *Handbook of Bureaucracy,* New York: Marcel Dekker, Inc., 1994, pp. 97–148.

Pre-bid activities: Activities that need to be undertaken before a bid is prepared and announced. Such activities include feasibility studies, planning, and needs assessment, among others.

Precautionary principle: Asserts that if policy makers do not know the probability of outcomes of the policies that they are recommending (which is likely to be the case more often than not), they should try to use a strategy that minimizes the maximum potential harm. The principle is widely used in environmental science, but is useful to explain decision making in the policy-making arena as well. For a discussion, see, e.g., M. Adams, "The Precautionary Principle and the Rhetoric Behind It," *Journal of Risk Research,* 2002, 5(4), pp. 301–16.

Precedence relationship: A relationship between two activities where one precedes the other; in that sense, the second activity is dependent on the first. If the first one is delayed for some reason, then the schedule for the second is pushed back as well. *See also* **Critical-path method**.

Precision policies: Policies that are precisely targeted at specific sectoral areas or groups of individuals. While well-designed macro policies are essential, their impact is limited if they are not accompanied by policy interventions that are targeted to specific micro-level problems. Thus a macro policy of poverty reduction may set the right environment, but unless specific policies on, for example, agricultural credit extension in rural income-generating activities are developed, a poverty-reduction policy is less likely to have much impact. See, e.g., A. Zezza and L. Llambi, "Meso-Economic Filters Along the Policy Chain: Understanding the Links Between Policy Reforms and Rural Poverty in Latin America," *World Development,* 2002, 30(11), pp. 1865–84.

Precision targeting: A term borrowed from the private sector that refers to offering products and services tailored to individual need. Given the variance in customer demands, even within particular customer niches, precision targeting tends to be rather resource heavy. *See also* **Precision policies**.

Pre-commitment: A situation where the agent can only make its intentions credible by binding itself *ex ante* to a proposed course of action with the principal. The extent of pre-commitment costs that are eventually realized by the agent depeYnds upon the extent of variation between *ex ante* specification and *ex post* observations and feeding that information into the next round of agency commitments.

Pre-contractual information problems: Problems that both the principal and the agent face after a contractual relationship has been established due to information asymmetry present at the time the contract was negotiated. *See also* **Adverse selection**

Predatory government: A government that extracts resources for the benefit of its own supporters and thus does not enhance the welfare of the citizenry. By virtue of its actions, then, it tends to prey on the weaker segments of society (i.e., the poor, the disenfranchised, and the marginalized).

Predictability: A state of affairs that results from laws and regulations that are clear and uniformly enforced. Statutes need to be clear so that there is no ambiguity as to what is being required; and they need to be uniformly enforced so that citizens see impartiality. Lack of predictability obviously makes it difficult for firms to soundly make business-related decisions. Predictability is one of the basics for good governance as regarded by international financial and development institutions.

Predictive capability: The ability to make valid predictions about a future condition. Rational-choice theorists assume, for example, clarity of preferences and then go on to predict outcomes based on the conditions inherent in the preferences. If a decision is rational, then their argument is that the outcome can be predicted with a fair degree of accuracy.

Predictive efficiency: The number of performance predictions that turn out to be accurate as a proportion of those made. This is a relevant measure as it allows informed judgments to be made about how, for example, an employee's future performance can be predicted, which can thus be used meaningfully in any career-planning dialogue with the employee.

Preferential access: When one party is granted priority access to certain resources (such as bank credit). In Malaysia, for example, native Malays (*bumiputras*) were for a long time given preferential access to public-sector employment and admission to public educational institutions.

Preliminary design review: An assessment of the specifications of a particular product that is meant to ensure that the design is in accordance with requirements. Preliminary design reviews are necessary to bring about lower levels of costs in the actual design and delivery of the particular good or service.

Premature termination: Ending an employment relationship or a program before the completion of its tenure. While there could be many reasons for such termination, it often results from problems that have surfaced which jeopardize successful implementation/continuation, and when it is considered more cost effective to end the employment/program than to continue.

Premium pay: Pay that is given over and above that for regular work. This includes payment for work during holidays or in working in hazardous conditions, for example. The extent of premium pay is, at times, specified in statutes.

Preproduction inspection: An examination by the purchaser of a prototype of a product that is sought so that any decisions on changes can be made before production begins.

Prequalification of bidders: The evaluation of vendors (their qualification and capacity) toward assessing bid eligibility. The purpose of prequalifying bidders is to save time when a contract needs to be issued and the purchaser does not wish to receive more proposals than it can reasonably handle. Such a prequalification exercise, however, is done (or refreshed) regularly (annually, in some cases) so that newer vendors may have the opportunity of consideration.

Preraiding: A situation where the public sector is likely to overcommit against the surplus resource it expects to receive over time. Pre-raiding is a problem because resources tagged for use for one purpose (such as contributions to an investment fund) could be more elastic than other items of governmental expenditure, particularly during times of fiscal stress. See, e.g., N. Davis, *Governance of Crown Financial Assets,* Treasury Working Paper 98/2, Wellington: New Zealand Treasury, 1998, pp. 4–6.

Preselection: The process of identifying and recruiting someone prior to conducting a standard recruitment process. Such preselection could result because of pressures to recruit that individual or because of some other motive, but it can make the entire process suspect.

Prescriptive policy statement: *See* **Policy statement.**

Pressure group: Any group that is organized to influence government toward certain policy measures. The group may seek to influence government through any of several means, such as information campaigns, demonstrations, active lobbying, etc. *See also* **Interest group.**

Prevailing wage: The average wage offered to employees in a particular occupation. Such a prevailing wage serves as a benchmark for organizations on which to base their own compensation packages. Across jurisdictional boundaries, this is practiced in relation to prevailing wages in a comparator country with steps taken to equalize for cost-of-living differentials, currency exchange rates, etc.

Preventive discipline: Refers to actions by management in seeking to preclude breaches of discipline by, for example, making all employees aware of the organization's disciplinary policies. In cases where an employee files a complaint against the employer for wrongful dismissal, it would help the employer's defense to demonstrate that it had engaged in preventive discipline at the start of the process.

Preventive mediation: In collective-bargaining processes, a mediator may be appointed early on in the process (i.e., prior to a bargaining conflict) in an attempt to prevent conflicts from emerging and to keep the process moving toward an agreement.

Price agreement: An understanding that is reached regarding the price a purchaser will pay a vendor for a product or service. A price agreement— especially if it is for a product whose prices are constantly changing— will tend to be for a shorter duration so that the vendor can negotiate a different price when the situation so demands.

Price competition: As used in the context of contract administration, this term refers to the competitive selection of a vendor based solely upon the criterion of price. While price usually serves as a primary criterion in evaluating bids, organizations may look at other factors (such as, for example, if the fulfillment terms are reliable).

Price protection: Refers to an agreement between contractual parties for a fixed price level even if prices should rise or fall after the contract has been signed. Both situations require that the vendor and the purchaser accept any "loss" that may accompany any change in price after the contract signing. The potential loss is compensated by the fact that there is a fair degree of certainty in the contract.

Price rebate: As used in contract administration, the term refers to a reduction in the cost specified in the contract allowed to the vendor when the contract has been fulfilled. Such rebate is contingent upon the contract being successfully executed, and when all other contractual conditions have been met.

Price regulation: The policy of setting prices of specific goods and services by a governmental agency. Under price regulation, either a price range is set (i.e., the maximum and minimum) to provide cues to providers of goods and services, or guidelines are developed, for example, on the magnitude of price increases. Both elements of price regulation are periodically reviewed by the relevant governmental agency. A related concept is price-cap regulation, which is regulation that sets a ceiling on the price that can be charged by an industry. Price-cap regulation can give an industry the incentive to be efficient since any gains in productivity (given a price cap) yields greater profits.

Primary decision: As applied in the public-policy context, a primary decision is one that is taken by policy makers to address a particular problem. While such a decision broadly covers how the problem will be addressed, it does not go into specifics. *Cf.* **Secondary decision**.

Primary failure: Refers to any failure in a system that initiates other subsequent failures. A primary failure need not be a significant one; in fact, in the first instance, the failure may only be marginal (for example, a national organization may not take very seriously a call for help from a social worker in a regional office, which eventually could lead to some very adverse consequences for the organization). *Cf.* **Secondary failure**.

Primary goals: Goals of organizations that dominate their work. Almost all governmental organizations have multiple goals that they pursue in tandem, although clearly some will be primary. *Cf.* **Contextual goals**.

Primary legislation: Refers to a proposed new act of the legislature, which is termed a bill until it is enacted. Governments use primary legislation to pass new programs and functional/structural arrangements in pursuit of the outcomes they will have specified in advance. Given the procedural nature of the exercise, it generally takes considerable time to pass primary legislation. *Cf.* **Secondary legislation**.

Primary uncertainty: Uncertainty that arises from acts of nature and unpredictable societal change. This uncertainty greatly influences the degree to which contractual arrangements between a principal and agent can be specified in detail. When uncertainty is high (such as in long-term arrangements), contracts are often relational and make use of binding arbitration as an enforcement mechanism. On the other hand, low levels of uncertainty (for example, spot contracts, where the existing levels of availability and capability are clearly evident) allow tightly specified mechanisms to enforce contracts.

Prime contract: A contract that is awarded for a major project to a contractor who is to provide all aspects of the project. A prime contract thus has only one contractor, although this does not preclude the possibility of subcontracts, particularly if the contractor faces changed conditions and is not able alone to deliver on the specified product or service.

Principal: A party that contracts out agents and that is authorized to enter into contract with a service provider and, therefore, one who seeks the services of an agent.

Principal item: As used in contract administration, this term refers to something that is the most important in terms of resource implications, and, as such, requires detailed analysis of its cost implications and other factors.

Principal opportunism: A term used to denote the opportunistic behavior of the principal in a contractual relationship. For example, in the relationship between a government minister and the chief executive of a government department (where the minister is the principal), it is possible that he/she could sacrifice the long-term interest of the public-service department (such as in capability enhancement) for the short-term attainment of a goal. Indeed, this is a concern that has been raised in jurisdictions where a strong contractual relationship exists between the government and departmental chief executives. For a discussion of this in the case of New Zealand, see S. Goldfinch, "Evaluating Public Sector Reform in New Zealand: Have the Benefits Been Oversold?" *Asian Journal of Public Administration,* 1998, 20(2), pp. 203–32.

Principle of asymmetric transitions: *See* **Principle of self-organization**.

Principle of blind variation: The principle states that because not all organizational action will have had the benefit of previous experience (i.e., hindsight), trial-and-error tests should be conducted so as to inform otherwise "blind" decision making as regards an action and its results.

Principle of competence: *See* **Principle of participation**.

Principle of events of low probability: (1) An assertion that the fundamental basis of a system should not be compromised just to accommodate some developments that have a very low probability of coming true. The principle thus discounts the possibility of the incorporation of measures that are designed to address such contingencies. (2) The principle also has implications for decision making in organizations with respect to incorporating the feedback of stakeholders. According to this principle, the organization should not compromise something that has the broad support of most stakeholders just on the assumption that a small minority might not be satisfied. See, e.g., R. Machol, *System Engineering Handbook,* New York: McGraw-Hill, 1965, pp. 1–7.

Principle of incomplete knowledge: A principle that asserts that the use of a policy model is inherently incomplete in knowledge since it cannot possibly replicate a real event. This is similar in many ways to the uncertainty principle, which states that the information any entity can get from its environment is necessarily limited. *See also* **Bounded rationality**.

Principle of interaction: States that all else being equal, the greater the interaction between two entities, the greater the similarity in their attitudes. This is a relevant concept in considering the nature of organizational networks and the learning processes inherent in interactions among public agencies involved in producing joint outcomes. This principle is complemented by that of reflected exclusivity, which states that the extent of knowledge sharing between two entities is related to the level of interaction between them and with others as well. For a review of these two principles, see, e.g., D. Krackhardt and D. Brass, "Intra-Organizational Networks: The Micro Side," in S. Wasserman and J. Galaskiewicz (eds.), *Advances in Social Network Analysis: Research in the Social and Behavioral Sciences,* Thousand Oaks, CA: Sage, 1994, pp. 207–29.

Principle of least effort: An assertion that, all else being equal, a system will opt for the easier decision when it comes to either trying to adapt to the environment or trying to change it. *See also* **Zipf's law**.

Principle of parsimony: Also known as Occam's Razor, this principle asserts that in the organizational change and restructuring process, entities should not be multiplied needlessly. In other words, if options exist, then the simplest one should be preferred.

Principle of participation: A principle that states that the participation of citizens is critical to the governance of societal affairs. A related concept is that of the principle of competence, which states that the participation of those citizens in society who are the most qualified/competent (however defined) should be as great as possible. This allows a greater weight to be given to those who are directly affected by a particular governmental action.

Principle of reflected exclusivity: *See* **Principle of interaction**.

Principle of selective retention: A principle that states that organizations generally tend to retain stable systems while discarding unstable ones. This appears to be rather obvious, except that if organizations are to capitalize on opportunities, then they may also wish to take into account unstable ones as well. As applied in the learning context for individuals, the term also refers to the tendency of individuals to retain only certain aspects of an issue or problem. Such selective retention necessarily diminishes the rigor of policy and decision making.

Principle of self-organization: States that every entity involved in change will develop protocols that will enable it to adapt to its environment. Note that this does not mean that the entity will necessarily maximize its interactions with the environment, just that it will find its own acceptable level of interaction. See, e.g., W. Ashby, "Principles of the Self-Organizing System," in H. von Foerster and G. Zopf (eds.), *Principles of Self-Organization,* Oxford: Pergamon, 1962, pp. 255–78.

Principle of suboptimization: States that optimizing each sub-system of a larger system will not necessarily lead to improvements in the system as a whole. The "tragedy of the commons" is considered a good example of the application of the principle of sub-optimization (because individuals tend to maximize their own gains without regard for others). For a discussion on how this principle provides the basis for a link between organizational structure and the policies adopted, see R. Machol, *System Engineering Handbook,* New York: McGraw-Hill, 1965, pp. 1–8.

Principle of subsidiarity: A principle that states that problems are best solved at the level at which they arise and little utility is added by referring them to higher authority. The principle is being increasingly incorporated into decentralization programs around the world. As applied in the European Union, higher levels of authority appear only in matters of coordination or dispute resolution. See, e.g., G. Majone, "The Credibility of Community Regulation," *Journal of Common Market Studies,* 2000, 38, pp. 273–302. *See also* **Management by exception**.

Principle of supportive relations: Asserts that, in all relationships within the organization, if staff members view an experience as supportive then it contributes to their sense of self-worth. This principle serves as one of the bases of the establishment of an informal organization. See R. Likert, *New Patterns of Management,* New York: McGraw-Hill, 1961, p. 103.

Principle of the humble elite: An assertion that while elitism is not necessarily good, experts need to be involved in some public functions. Having said that, the elites then need to be humble enough to explain their decisions to the public and to be ready to hear their views. This is particularly relevant in policy-making areas where the subject matter tends to be complex (such as genetic engineering, which has great potential for human welfare but which is also fraught with complex ethical issues).

Principal-agent problem: Conflicts of interest that emerge between principal and agent when, and if, they pursue different goals. This results in inefficiency losses called agency costs. Conflicts of interest arise when both parties seek to maximize their own utilities and each seeks to use the information asymmetry that characterizes their relationship to its own advantage. See, e.g., J. Coats, "Applications of Principal-Agent Models to Government Contracting and Accountability Decision-Making," *International Journal of Public Administration,* 2002, 25(4), pp. 441–61.

Principal-agent relationship: A contract under which one party engages another to perform some service on its behalf. The party that seeks the service is called the principal and the other the agent. Such a principal-agent relationship can be seen not only between governmental agencies and service providers (i.e., contractors) but also between citizens and the public-sector bureaucracy. In this case, the citizens serve the role of the principal and the bureaucracy the agent, and the agent can be expected to behave inefficiently when, for example, there are surplus resources at its disposal. One of the original persons to focus on the principal-agent relationship was the economist Stephen Ross; see his "The Economic Theory of Agency: The Principals Problem," *American Economic Review (Papers and Proceedings),* 1973, 63(2), pp. 134–39. For a review of the limitations of the use of principal/agent solutions to reduce agency costs in the public sector, see, e.g., OECD, *A Framework for Public Sector Performance Contracting,* PUMA/PAC(99)2, Paris: OECD, 1999, pp. 58–59. *Cf.* **Partnership model**.

Principled negotiation, model of: A model of contract negotiations that addresses the problem of managers who oppose outsourcing because they fear loss of control, loss of authority, conflict, etc., and who, when finally engaged, negotiate in an adversarial manner. The principled negotiation model requires that managers and service providers discuss their concerns, exchange views, and seek to come to a mutually beneficial agreement so that they can both realize benefits.

Principles of management: The principles that scholar Henry Fayol propounded regarding management in an organizational setting, which included: (a) specialization and division of labor; (b) authority with corresponding responsibility; (c) discipline; (d) unity of command; (e) unity of direction; (f) subordination of individual interest to the general; (g) fair levels of compensation to staff; (h) centralization; (i) scalar chain/line of authority; (j) order (i.e., each employee is able to see where he or she fits into the organization); (k) equity and fairness; (l) stability of tenure; (m) initiative at all levels; and (n) *esprit de corps* in order to build team harmony. For a concise discussion of Fayol's principles of management, see, e.g., D. Pugh and D. Hickson, "Henry Fayol," *Writers on Organizations,* 4th edition, London: Penguin Books, 1989, pp. 85–89.

Principles of organization: The operating rules of how organizations are to be structured. These principles generally include, for example, legitimacy (the building block of an organization), division of work, span of control, authority (and the associated notions of lines of command), responsibility and accountability, coordination, etc. For a general discussion, see, e.g., J. Kallinikos, "The Social Foundations of the Bureaucratic Order," *Organization,* 2004, 11(1), pp. 13–36.

Prioritized bidder: While governmental agencies will ask for bids when seeking to contract out, they will also have a list of prioritized bidders drawn from past experiences and their history of offers made. In certain cases, it may be that, as mandated by law, a minority-owned business enterprise must be considered a prioritized bidder.

Priority consideration: Emphasis that is placed on the recruitment of people from segments of society who may have been unlawfully excluded from employment in the past. As used in the context of affirmative action, it refers to giving priority to those who may have been discriminated in the past by virtue of their race and color.

Priority-based budgeting: *See* **Zero-based budgeting**.

Priority-setting mechanism: The process by which an organization sets its priorities. Normally pressures for such determination comes from external stakeholders, but it is in the budget process that the mechanism is most manifest. The composition of the budget will then largely reveal the priorities set by the organization.

Prismatic society, theory of: A conceptualization of a developing society where modern and traditional influences merge to create a myriad of societal relationships that do not conform to the standard norms of the modernization process. The theory posits a society that is a fusion of many old and new social structures. The development sociologist Fred Riggs, who is credited with the term, also said that given the uniqueness of each developing society, the study of public administration has to be viewed in terms of the particular situations existing in each. See F. Riggs, *Administration in Developing Countries: The Theory of Prismatic Society,* Boston: Houghton Mifflin, 1964.

Prisoner's dilemma game: A game where the optimal behavior of a player depends on the behavior of another player. In the absence of communication or mutual confidence, each will choose behaviors which result in a poorer outcome for both than could have been secured had they cooperated. Thus, the maximization of gain for both players is possible only when they work together. For an application of the term in a public-management case setting, see, e.g., L. Lynn, "Policy Achievement as a Collective Good: A Strategic Perspective on Managing Social Programs," in B. Bozeman (ed.), *Public Management: The State of the Art,* San Francisco: Jossey-Bass, 1993, pp. 108–33.

Privacy problems: (1) Resource-allocation problems arising from each individual knowing his/her own tastes better than anyone else. (2) Problems that governmental agencies need to be aware of when dealing with confidential information on citizens. This includes, for example, ensuring that extraneous confidential information is not inadvertently released when a request for official information is fulfilled pursuant to a freedom-of-information act.

Private good: A good or service whose benefits are exclusively received by one individual (a meal in a restaurant is an example of a private good). Two key characteristics of a private good are: (a) what is known as rivalry, i.e., what one individual consumes cannot be consumed by someone else; and (b) that a particular person has exclusive control over the good or service and may choose to do whatever he/she wants with it. *See also* **Excludability**.

Private ordering: Refers to the efforts of two parties that seek to be engaged in a transaction to design incentives and governance structures that will enable them both to meet their needs. Private ordering is related to concepts of agency theory and incomplete contracting. See, e.g., O. Williamson, "The Theory of the Firm as Governance Structure: From Choice to Contract," *Journal of Economic Perspectives,* 2002, 16(3), pp. 171–95. *Cf.* **Public ordering**.

Private sector: A term that generically refers to: (a) firms, enterprises, and businesses that produce goods and services for public consumption and that charge for such consumption; and (b) the principle by which private ownership is encouraged, and where markets and competition determine the level and type of production. Characteristics of the private sector include, among others: (i) the importance of contracts to determine the relationships between parties that provide funds and those that use them, (ii) the existence of regulatory frameworks to sustain those contractual arrangements, and (iii) the existence of competition to provide incentives to invest funds efficiently. While the first characteristic does not normally tend to be an area of government intervention, the latter two are very much so. See, e.g., Development Assistance Committee, *DAC Orientations for Development Cooperation in Support of Private Sector Development,* Paris: OECD/DAC, 1994, p. 4.

Privatization: Refers broadly to the deliberate sale by government of public assets to the private sector. Some key objectives of privatization include: raising revenue, reducing governmental interference in the economy, and introducing competition in the economy. While there are many ways to privatize, the literature points to four key ones: (a) by returning previously private property, such as land and manufacturing plants, to their original owners or their heirs—called restitution; (b) by selling public property either through direct sales of assets or through shares issued to interested citizens; (c) by distributing freely—or at nominal cost—vouchers which citizens can then use to bid for shares in state-owned enterprises; and (d) by contracting out services that were formerly provided by governmental agencies. When done in a poorly regulated setting, privatization has a risk of producer capture of value because of information asymmetry and other problems. See, e.g., W. Megginson and J. Netter, "From State to Market: A Survey of Empirical Studies on Privatization," *Journal of Economic Literature,* 2001, 39(2), p. 321.

Privatization, Machiavellian: Refers to privatization that is used as a strategic policy to retain power by the authority that wishes to privatize. The concept is with reference to the Italian political philosopher Niccolò Machiavelli. For a good discussion of this term, see, e.g., B. Biais and E. Perotti, "Machiavellian Privatization," *American Economic Review,* 2002, 92(1), pp. 240–58.

Pro forma: Latin for "as a matter of form." As used in an organizational setting, it refers to the standard way in which any organizational action needs to be done. For example, a letter of agreement for an external contractor could be done as per pro forma (i.e., as done before for other contractors and to follow the same routines).

Proactive bureaucracy: A bureaucracy that initiates measures to shape its environment rather than simply reacting to developments in the environment. What this means in practice is that bureaucratic leaders may seek to pre-empt developments, and by effectively using their political access to governmental ministers, for instance, they seek to influence ministerial consideration. Obviously, this is not easy because public-sector organizations have their mandates set by the legislature, which is less malleable. In that sense, the proactive nature of bureaucracies seems limited to how they do things rather than what they do.

Probability: The likelihood of occurrence. The probability of an outcome is the ratio of a favorable outcome to the total opportunity set. The term is central to the study of risks, and it is relevant to talk of the likelihood of the occurrence of risks (i.e., probability) and the impact that such likelihood will have to determine risk severity. This interplay between likelihood and impact constitutes the core of risk analysis.

Probity: Refers to integrity, honesty, fairness, and good faith. Employees in the public service are expected to act with honesty and probity.

Problem analysis: An assessment and review that is done of a problem. Problem analysis consists of three stages: (a) clear understanding of the problem, (b) choice and explanation of relevant policy goals and limitations, and (c) choice of appropriate method of solution. See D. Weimer and A. Vining, *Policy Analysis: Concepts and Practice,* 2nd edition, Englewood Cliffs, NJ: Prentice Hall, 1992, p. 206.

Problem definition: Explaining the nature of a particular problem. Such articulation—if it is done rigorously—assists in narrowing the alternatives for consideration toward solving the problem. There are several key elements to the process of problem definition, including the: (a) identification of a condition that merits governmental response, (b) collection and presentation of evidence to justify targeting the problem for governmental action, (c) explanation of the causes of the condition, and (d) articulation of a set of alternatives that would remedy the perceived problem. Generally, how a policy problem is defined depends on the values that policy makers bring to the process and the comparisons that they make, including the manner of the comparison. For an application, see, e.g., D. Houston and L. Richardson, "The Politics of Air Bag Safety: A Competition Among Problem Definitions," *Policy Studies Journal,* 2000, 28(3), p. 486.

Problem formulation: The process of identifying a problem, including describing the problematic situation as currently exists, specifying the resources—including time—available to address the problem, and developing the criteria that need to be satisfied to successfully address the problem. Problem formulation is an important activity in the policy-making process because how a problem is formulated determines which solutions are sought.

Problem intervention: The involvement of an agency or program in an attempt to address and solve a particular policy problem. Such involvement has to be timely, relevant, technically robust, and of a sufficient scale that it can be reasonably expected to solve the problem. See, e.g., E. McGregor, "Toward a Theory of Public Management Success," in B. Bozeman (ed.), *Public Management: The State of the Art,* San Francisco: Jossey-Bass, 1993, p. 182.

Problem reduction: The disaggregation of a problem that may be intractable to a series of sub-problems that are easier to tackle. Hence, the problem of rural poverty, for example, may be disaggregated into the lack of formal credit mechanisms, and insufficient access to the local markets, among others things.

Problem solving: A process of identifying the correct problem to be addressed, collecting the relevant data related to that particular problem, analyzing the data, and recommending a relevant solution. Problem solving also includes testing the proposed solution so that it can be used repeatedly for similar problems as they arise.

Problem stream: A stage in the policy-making process where attention is given to a particular problem. In the problem stream, numerous stakeholders have a say in defining the problem and in setting its parameters. See, e.g., J. Kingdon, *Agendas, Alternatives, and Public Policies,* 2nd edition, New York: HarperCollins, 1995, pp. 3–4. For an application of the term, see, e.g., J. Blankenau, "The Fate of National Health Insurance in Canada and the United States: A Multiple Streams Explanation," *Policy Studies Journal,* 2001, 29(1), pp. 38–55.

Problem structuring: The process of outlining the various disparate parts of a problem (particularly a complex one) in such a manner so as to discern their interlinkages and causal relationships, if any. Problem structuring follows problem perception and problem identification, and is a key step in coming up with viable strategies to address a perceived problem.

Problem transformation: A situation where the nature of the problem shifts—either by design or otherwise—from what it was originally perceived. For example, a particular problem of youth suicide in a community might be identified more fundamentally as a problem of substance abuse. Such transformation can make the problem easier or more difficult to address, depending upon its complexity.

Problem-centered organizational system, principle of: Refers to the focus of an organization on problem resolution as opposed to only on program delivery. This is done largely by integrating planning and budgeting processes such that outputs delivered is not the major yardstick of the organization's performance, that being, rather, the extent to which the organization's activities affect the resolution of the problem. See M. Emmert, M. Crow, and R. Shangraw, "Public Management in the Future: Post-Orthodoxy and Organization Design," in B. Bozeman (ed.), *Public Management: The State of the Art,* San Francisco: Jossey-Bass, 1993, p. 359.

Problematic preferences: Preferences expressed by actors in the policy-making process that are not properly informed. Such problematic preferences serve to make the policy-making process more complex.

Procedural analysis: Analysis of procedures by breaking a task down to its constituent parts and then reviewing each part and how they interconnect. Procedural analysis is useful when routine tasks go wrong and there is need to find out why and whether the failure affected other procedures.

Procedural governance: *See* Governance.

Procedural justice: *See* **Organizational justice theory**.

Procedural leadership: The leadership and ability exhibited by political executives to influence the process of organizational decision making (i.e., setting the rules of the game). It is generally thought that the greater the mandate political executives believe they have from their constituencies, the more they will show appetite to change the rules of the game. Such rules of the game could include deciding on who is to be involved in organizational decision-making processes and how participation in such processes should be devised. *See, e.g.,* R. Andeweg, "A Model of the Cabinet System: The Dimensions of Cabinet Decision-Making Processes," in J. Blondel and F. Müller-Rommel (eds.), *Governing Together: The Extent and Limits of Joint Decision-Making in Western European Cabinets,* London: Palgrave Macmillan, 1993, pp. 23–42.

Procedural organization: An organization for which outputs—but not outcomes—can be readily observed (for example, a central agency that provides policy advice on the machinery of government issues or an agency that monitors occupational health and safety in government organizations). A procedural organization has formal rules, and its raison d'être comes from adhering to set processes and procedures. See J. Wilson, *Bureaucracy: What Government Agencies Do and Why They Do It,* New York: Basic Books, 1989, p. 159.

Procedural rationality: When individuals and organizations use some form of reasoning, or a deduction process, to address and solve problems. Behavior is procedurally rational when it results from appropriate deliberations. See, e.g., J. Dubra and E. Ok, "A Model of Procedural Decision Making in the Presence of Risk," *International Economic Review,* 2002, 43(4), pp. 1053–80. *See also* **Rationality**.

Procedural rights: The rights that all citizens are entitled as concerns the procedures to which public officials and bureaucrats must adhere. Such procedural rights—if adhered to and enforced vigorously—guard the public from arbitrary actions of public officials.

Process: The system or "the way of doing things." Processes exist in all institutionalized settings and organizations and cover all areas of organizational action, such as planning, service delivery, risk management, resource allocation, training and development, employee sanction, etc. The process of making policies, for example, includes, among others, legislative debate. For a basic review of the concept of process management, see, e.g., R. Bawden and O. Zuber-Skerritt, "The Concept of Process Management," *The Learning Organization,* 2002, 9(3), pp. 132–38.

Process consultation: A process by which external stakeholders provide information to—and consult with—an organization to help it better understand the context in which it is fulfilling its mandate. Such process consultation is useful to the organization because it offers an external perspective on the organization's environment, and also because it better prepares the organization to justify its own stance on any number of issues that it faces in the course of fulfilling its mandate. See, e.g., E. Schein, *Process Consultation Volume II: Lessons for Managers and Consultants,* Reading, MA: Addison-Wesley, 1987, pp. 18–38.

Process evaluation: A methodological approach to examining and assessing how an organization implements its activities, with reference to management practice and organizational systems. In the public sector, how an organization goes about fulfilling its mandate is just as important as what it does. In that regard, a process evaluation seeks to measure the extent to which an organization is able to achieve its mandate according to the respective guidelines. See, e.g., S. Murphy and J. Dowling, "The Rush to Measure Outcomes: Process Evaluation and Return on Investment," *The Public Manager,* 2002, 31(2), pp. 39–42.

Process intervention: As used in the context of organizational development, process intervention refers to changing the basis of how employees behave so that any planned intervention (such as, for example, a restructuring) can proceed smoothly.

Process reengineering: *See* **Business-process reengineering**.

Process tracing: A technique used by policy analysts to chart the progress of a particular policy over time. This allows analysts to gain a deeper understanding not only of what actually happened but also who the policy actors were, how their thinking evolved and/or changed during the course of events, and how the final outcomes can be usefully explained. See, e.g., A. George and T. McKeown, "Case Studies and Theories of Organizational Decision Making," in R. Coulam and R. Smith (eds.), *Advances in Information Processing in Organizations* (Volume 2), London: JAI Press, 1985, 2, pp. 21–58.

Producer capture: The process wherein public organizations come to be run in the interests of those who work in them rather than in the public's. For example, a regulatory agency could tend to identify, over time, with the industry it regulates to the point where it defends rather than polices the industry. This can occur not only due to problems of information asymmetry between the two parties but also because regulatory bodies often recruit individuals from related industries, especially if such relevant expertise is hard to come by. Over time, this could lead to a situation where the agency becomes more and more sympathetic to the industry. See, e.g., The Treasury, *Government Management: Brief to the Incoming Government,* Wellington: The Treasury, 1987, pp. 75–77. *See also* **Privatization**.

Product departmentalization: Where the activities of an organization are grouped based on related product markets. Product departmentalization facilitates better product management, which is concerned with ensuring that all aspects of the product-delivery process (ranging from generation of ideas to providing feedback) are better managed. *Cf.* **Functional departmentalization**.

Product testing: Ensuring that the product or service that an organization is to provide is adequate. Product testing gives an organization a measure of confidence about the efficacy of a particular program or policy when it is eventually applied across the board or brought to the market.

Production organization: An agency whose objectives can be precisely specified *ex ante* and against which any progress can be clearly measured, including as regards outputs and the extent to which the objectives are being met. For application in two U.S. governmental agencies, the

Social Security Administration and the Internal Revenue Service, see J. Wilson, *Bureaucracy: What Government Agencies Do and Why They Do It*, New York: Basic Books, 1989, p. 11.

Productive efficiency: Efficiency that is enhanced by lowering production costs (i.e., increasing productivity). In terms of public management and governance, arguments have been made that the decentralization of authority to local jurisdictions improves governance and public-service delivery by increasing productive as well as allocative efficiency. To bring this about, however, there is also need to ensure that such devolution of functions take place in a proper institutional environment, where local jurisdictions have the authority (political, administrative, as well as financial) and the resources to fulfill their mandates. For a discussion of this term in relation to public-sector downsizing, see, e.g., D. Jeon and J. Laffont, "The Efficient Mechanism for Downsizing the Public Sector," *The World Bank Economic Review,* 1999, 13(1), pp. 67–88. *Cf.* **Allocative efficiency**.

Productivity: In simple terms, productivity refers to the degree of efficiency with which work is done. That is, it measures the ratio of inputs to the outputs that result. Such inputs could be either single (as in labor or capital) or joint (as factors of production taken together). Productivity can also be measured at various levels (i.e., at the individual, unit, firm, industry, sector, or national levels). However, looking at productivity merely from the perspective of efficiency is not enough. Productivity should also be aligned to the value of effectiveness, i.e., to how well the program (or employee) is able to increase the quality of the output.

Productivity improvement: Any step taken to ensure that the productivity of the organization is increased. Such an improvement in productivity is evident at three levels: (a) internal to the organization (i.e., its structure and processes as evident in steps such as consolidation of services, streamlining in operating procedures, etc.), (b) in the use of technology to improve how work is done (for example, in using updated software to accomplish more complex tasks), and (c) in personnel-related activities (for example, in changing its incentive structure, flexi-work arrangements, etc.).

Productivity measurement: An assessment of the degree of productivity that is evident in the work of an individual, sub-unit, or in the organization itself. Productivity measurement in any setting is difficult, but in the public sector, where notions of efficiency, effectiveness, and impact are often difficult to operationalize, it becomes that much more problematic. With the focus in public management now increasingly on outcomes (away from inputs), productivity measurement is central to assessing whether an organization is indeed able to deliver on its mandate. However, as long as it is difficult to operationalize the various variables that constitute productivity, it will be difficult to come up with a completely sound measurement tool. See, e.g., W. Ostrom, "The Need for Multiple Indicators in Measuring the Output of Public Agencies," *Policy Studies Journal,* 1973, 2(Winter), pp. 85–92.

Professional bureaucracy: A bureaucracy that is characterized by, among other things: (a) highly trained people with professional skills, (b) well-functioning rules and protocols, (c) a focus on efficiency and effectiveness in organizational work, and (d) standards of values and ethics that earn it the trust of those it serves.

Professional deformation: Refers to a form of organizational dysfunction and a negative aspect of bureaucracy. The term is used in conjunction with other concepts, such as trained incapacity and organizational psychosis, to denote a state where organizations are ambivalent and do not conform to the traditional Weberian notions of precision, reliability, and efficiency. For a concise description of these terms, see, e.g., R. Merton, *Social Theory and Social Structure,* Glencoe, IL: Free Press, 1957, pp. 195–206. *See also* **Occupational psychosis; Trained incapacity**.

Professional values: Norms regarding the individual professions that organizational members bring to their work. For example, professional values that policy analysts bring to their work include those stemming from their roles as: (a) objective technicians (thus holding analytical integrity as the fundamental value), (b) clients' advocates (thus placing primary emphasis on their responsibility to their clients, such as elected policy makers), and (c) issue advocates (thus championing a particular interest, such as the environment or victims of crime). See H. Jenkins-Smith, "Professional Roles for Policy Analysts: A Critical Assessment," *Journal of Policy Analysis and Management,* 1982, 2(1), pp. 88–100.

Profiling: (1) As used in the context of human-resource management, this term is associated with the notion of competency profiling. Competency profiling is a method for identifying the specific competencies (i.e., skills, knowledge, attitudes and behavior) of an employee necessary to fulfill a particular role in the organization. Every organization has a different competency framework and so competency profiling can vary considerably across organizations. Competency profiling is necessary because it helps the organization to match the right competencies with the right roles. (2) Profiling is also a technique that develops a behavioral pattern of an unknown criminal offender. The term race profiling denotes the practice of police in the United States, for example, in targeting African Americans for traffic stops because their assumption is that African Americans are more likely to engage in criminal activity.

Profit center: *See* **Responsibility center**.

Profit-padding regulation: A type of regulation that limits competition among financial institutions. This is evident, for example, when a regulator seeks to disincline commercial banks from taking undue risks. In some way, there is merit to this since too much competition force banks to take greater risks. For an incisive analysis of this term, see, e.g., T. Hellman, K. Murdock, and J. Stiglitz, "Liberalization, Moral Hazard in Banking, and Prudential Regulation: Are Capital Requirements Enough?" *American Economic Review,* 2000, 90(1), pp. 147–64.

Program administration: The administration of any organized set of activities that are related in their orientation to a common goal and for which there is a sizable amount of funds allocated for the achievement of that goal. The term program administration is a rather generic one that refers to the process of managing a program. This includes a gamut of tasks ranging from maintaining program records to ensuring the proper attainment of program objectives. For an example of the use of the term, see DANIDA, *Evaluation Report: Mixed Credit Program,* Copenhagen: Evaluation Secretariat, Ministry of Foreign Affairs, Denmark, 2002.

Program budgeting: The process of determining and securing resources for a particular program. Program budgeting also refers to the manner in which expenses are incurred—and financial accountabilities determined—in program delivery. The program budget includes only those expenses that are directly related to the execution of program activities. These include staff wages, administration and logistics costs, contracting services costs, etc., as well as any incoming revenue (or funding) stream. For an example of the issues around program budgeting in an organizational setting, see World Health Organization, *Evaluation of WHO's Strategic Budgeting and Planning Process: Report of the Director General,* Document No. EBPDC8/2, Geneva: WHO, 2001. *See also* **Budgeting**.

Program evaluation: Evaluation of an entire program, done normally at its end, although it will have been continuously monitored. Program evaluation measures program performance and reports on the comparisons with what was expected. Program evaluation can be goal based, process based or outcome based in orientation. In general, six different aspects of a program are usually evaluated: (a) Do all the stakeholders of the program have access to the services? (b) Are the needs of stakeholders being met? (c) What is the quality of the services offered? (d) What is the overall impact of the program on the problem being addressed? (e) Did the program provide all this in a cost-effective manner? (f) Does the program have scope for replicability in other settings? For many programs that are undertaken in developing jurisdictions, the last two questions are of considerable import. See, e.g., D. Davis, "Do You Want a Performance Audit or a Program Evaluation?" *Public Administration Review*, 1990, 50(1), pp. 35–41. *See also* **Evaluation**.

Program evaluation and review technique: A tool designed to show all the various individual tasks that need to be accomplished to complete a program, and the amount of time and resources thus required.

Program logic: *See* **Intervention logic**.

Program management: The manner in which all aspects of a particular program are coordinated, implemented, or acted upon in some way. Program management is usually more complex than project management because a program is much more extensive than a project

Program plan: A plan of all the aspects of a program that an organization is involved in, including, for example, the objectives and how they should be reached, and who is responsible for what.

Program process evaluation: A process evaluation that centers on the specific steps in an organization's performance, internal dynamics, and operations to highlight a program's strengths and weaknesses. Such an evaluation examines why certain things are happening, how the parts of the program fit together, and how external stakeholders perceive the program.

Program results audit: A review that is done of a program's results to assess whether they were realized as per *ex ante* specifications. The audit also evaluates the extent to which the organization has actively considered alternative program delivery mechanisms to better achieve the results.

Program simulation: Imitating the functioning of a program. The purpose of a program simulation is to ensure that problems that may be faced in a real situation can somehow be imitated and studied in advance of program application.

Programmed implementation: Implementation of a policy, project, or program that is done in a set manner according to a plan and timed process. While all implementation processes should ideally be programmed, the reality of policy and organizational environments is such that this will not normally be the case.

Programmed learning: Learning that is enhanced in a systematic and predetermined manner. Such a learning methodology allows the learner to progress in a structured (i.e., self-paced and self-directed) manner. Because there is considerable structure to programmed learning, there is also scope for a considerable degree of control over the process of learning. For an early discussion of the concept, see B. Skinner, "Learning Theory and Future Research," in J. Lysaught (ed.), *Programmed Learning: Evolving Principles and Industrial Applications,* Ann Arbor, MI: Foundation for Research on Human Behaviors, 1961, pp. 59–66.

Progress control: The process of determining the extent to which a project or program has progressed and how much work is still required so that consequent action will follow. Progress control is required in programmed implementation so that the progress of the project proceeds as per plan. The process of reviewing a project or program to assess the extent to which it has progressed toward the objectives set is termed a "progress review."

Progress review: *See* **Progress control**.

Progression sequences: (1) In policy formulation, this term refers to the different stages of policy development, from identification of the problem to implementation and evaluation of policy. (2) In human-resource management, it refers to the movement of an employee from a low-paying job in the organizational hierarchy to a higher-paying one farther up in the hierarchy. *See also* **Promotion**.

Progressive discipline: A penalty imposed on employees who violate organizational rules and regulations that is in keeping with the severity of the violation, and escalating in severity if the violation is repeated.

Progressive elimination: The process of solving a problem by breaking it down to its component parts. Once this is done, those parts that can be easily dispensed with are handled first in the expectation that this makes it easier to isolate those components that are difficult. The argument is that this makes even intractable problems easier to tackle. For an application of progressive elimination in the context of addressing wicked problems, see R. Bruce and N. Cote, "Taming Wicked Problems: Theory and Practice," *Public Manager,* 2002, Fall, pp. 39–42, 46.

Progressive mechanization: As used in the context of organizations, this term refers to an organization's various component systems that are rather loosely configured at first, and their interactions with the external environment are dynamic and constantly in a flux. Once fixed arrangements and protocols are established, however, such looseness and flux gradually diminish. For application, see, e.g., R. Carzo, "Some Effects of Organization Structure on Group Effectiveness," *Administrative Science Quarterly,* 1963, 7, pp. 393–424. *See also* **Equipotentiality**.

Prohibited personnel practices: Personnel actions that go against organizational principles and criteria that have been specified either by law—such as in any merit protection acts—or by internal rules and regulations. For example, undertaking reprisals against whistleblowers or coercing the political activity of an employee are considered prohibited personnel practices. In reference, section 2302(b) of title 5 (Government Organization and Employees) of the United States Code lists these and ten other prohibited personnel practices.

Project administration: *See* **Project management**.

Project beneficiaries: Individuals and others who benefit from specific projects. The benefits can be gained either directly (i.e., the project targets specific needs) or indirectly (i.e., individuals benefit by virtue of conditions that improve as a result of the project). For example, in an income-generating project targeted at poor women in rural villages, the women are the direct beneficiaries and their children could be the indirect beneficiaries.

Project categorical grant: *See* **Categorical grant**.

Project evaluation: Usually an *ex post* review of a project to ascertain whether the objectives of the project were achieved. Recommendations for improvement or a diagnosis of failure might ensue. Such evaluation is normally carried out by external entities so as to secure independent feedback.

Project management: The management of a project that has specific goals and well-defined parameters. Project management includes the following activities: acquisition of raw materials and inputs; maintenance of financial and personnel records; personnel-management activities; monitoring activities; contractual administration, if the project outsources activity; and reporting and other compliance activities. The rise of matrix organizations has led to an increased focus on project management, as organizational work increasingly tends to be done on a project basis.

Projection: (1) In group interaction, this term refers to the act of transferring to others biases and feelings of inadequacies, for example, that one may have. This has the effect of distorting reality and of conveying the wrong message to the public. (2) The term also refers to the act of forecasting and of asserting the future value of any variable.

Promotion: (1) Moving an employee up in the organizational hierarchy by virtue of the employees having met or exceeded certain criteria. (2) Making an effort to market something (a policy, program, project, etc.). (3) Encourage awareness and use of, for example, promoting public-service values and ethos in governmental agencies.

Promotion plan: A systematic way of ensuring that employees in an organization move up the hierarchy after some set standards of performance and seniority have been met or exceeded. While a promotion plan is a good tool to have, modern-day organizations rely less on such planning given flatter organizational structures and the emphasis on individual performance outcomes. The only plan that matters in this respect, then, is what the individual employee charts and seeks for himself or herself.

Prompt corrective action: Measures that are swift and that are directed at addressing the core of a problem. Prompt corrective action sends a clear signal that the organization is willing and able to tackle a problem that would have serious repercussions if left unattended. For an application, see, e.g., S. W. Kim et al., "Patterns of Bank Intermediation and Structure: A Korean Perspective," in G. de Brouwer (ed.), *Financial Markets and Policies in East Asia,* London: Routledge, 2002, p. 41.

Proof-of-concept demonstration: A requirement on bidders to show what it is that their ideas for a particular product are, how they propose the product will be developed, and how it will deliver what they say it will. A related term is proof testing, which is a method of testing whether all the required performance characteristics are evident in a particular proposal. Such proof testing is conducted by the organization that has requested bids, and includes set criteria that have been agreed to in advance and that serve to help the organization decide which bids are the most compelling. The criteria include timelines, reliability, cost, and quality levels.

Proof testing: *See* **Proof-of-concept demonstration**.

Property rights: Rights of individuals to exercise control over their properties (such as those that result from entrepreneurial efforts) in matters of purchase, sale, and usage. The existence of property rights, and ensuring that such rights are safeguarded, sits at the heart of investment decisions that those with capital make. For an early discussion, see, e.g., H. Demsetz, "Some Aspects of Property Rights," *Journal of Law and Economics,* 1966, 9(October), pp. 61–70. *See also* **Excludability**.

Proportionality: As used in the context of measures to enhance efficiency, this term denotes a micro approach to economic efficiency. It says that efficiency in the public sector between the demand for and the supply of any program services refers basically to proportionality, or to the quid pro quo equating of taxation and user fees on the one hand and the reception of services and goods on the other.

Proposal evaluation criteria: Any standards that are used to assess different proposals or bids so as to make a considered choice as to which one should be awarded a contract. The criteria generally include: management ability, technical capability, prior experience with similar projects, price, and scheduling. Different agencies will weigh the various criteria differently. While these will usually not be specified in detail in the request for bids, potential bidders will be given information on what the organization is looking for in the bids.

Proprietary information: Information that is not to be released to the public (i.e., privately owned knowledge or data). In the public sector, other than certain information that is restricted for reasons of national defense and for personal privacy, there is little proprietary information.

Prosecutorial agency: A governmental agency whose primary function is to enact criminal proceedings against those who have committed acts against the law. An example of a prosecutorial agency is the Department of Justice in the United States.

Prospect theory: Asserts that individuals are generally loss averse—that they will try to minimize their losses to the maximum possible extent even at the expense of giving up an opportunity that might yield them some benefits. That is to say, people are more sensitive to losses than they are to potential gains. Psychologists Daniel Kahneman and Amos Tversky used this theory to explain why choice for the status quo is so powerful in most individuals (it is certainly true of most governments). This further explains why those who perceive to lose from a policy or program will invest more to block policy change than those who perceive to be winners from the same. See D. Kahnemann and A. Tversky, "Loss Aversion in Riskless Choice: A Reference-Dependent Model," *Quarterly Journal of Economics,* 1991, 106(4), pp. 1039–61.

Protean career: A career that has been developed and shaped by an individual rather than by an organizational process (such as in a set career ladder). A protean career thus implies that an individual has taken charge of his/her career and is willing to shape it in ways that he/she deems appropriate and realistic.

Protective constituencies: When a program creates groups of individuals or stakeholders who become reliable defenders of the program. These protective constituencies are important for the continuation of the program since they will lobby on its behalf should the legislature or organization consider termination.

Protective regulation: *See* **Regulatory policy**.

Protest: As specifically used in contract administration, a protest refers to a complaint voiced by the agent against the principal for some perceived contravention of the contract. A protest often arises owing to a contract not having been sufficiently detailed (i.e., it is an incomplete contract). There are several mechanisms to handle protests, including a revocation of the contract if the parties cannot resolve the differences.

Prototyping: *See* **Adaptability**.

Proverbs of administration: Scholar Herbert Simon's seminal thinking on how the fundamental principles of administration could be refuted by the application of equally applicable but contradictory principles. As an example, Simon offers the principle of a scalar chain in an hierarchically oriented organization as contrasted with an equally valid principle of a matrix organization with a very flat structure. Simon's work spawned a new thinking on how organizations and administration could be viewed. See H. Simon, "The Proverbs of Administration," *Public Administration Review,* 1946, 6(4), pp. 53–67.

Provider capture: A concern raised by public-choice theorists that situating both the policy and the operational dimensions of a governmental department's work in the same place will lead to a situation where the policy advice will implicitly favor decisions to augment the interests of the department's operational aspects. *See also* **Policy-operations split**.

Proxy: Someone who is duly authorized to act on behalf of another. There can be proxy votes at board meetings when individual stakeholders cannot be present. Proxy advocacy is a situation where public officials are considered to be capable of—and favorably inclined toward—representing the interests of local citizens and groups. Proxy advocacy is ideally assumed to exist in all elected officials vis-à-vis their constituency, yet it is not always the case. See L. Koenig, *An Introduction to Public Policy,* Englewood Cliffs, NJ: Prentice Hall, 1986, p. 145.

Proxy advocacy: *See* **Proxy**.

Proxy measures: Given the difficulty oftentimes of coming up with measurable criteria for policies, proxy measures are values assigned to variables in considering policy effects. Hence, for example, the benefits of training for individual staff members may be measured by proxy by looking at the time it takes the individual to do the job after the training as compared to the time it took prior to receiving the training. The resultant difference is the impact of the training as shown by the proxy variable. Proxy measures are also known as surrogate measures.

Prudence convention: The convention of being prudent in valuing assets and operations. According to this convention, the organization, while valuing assets for balance sheet purposes, accepts the lowest of all reasonable values for an asset and also does not anticipate any unreasonable revenues in determining its financial capability. This prudence enables government officials to get a better sense of the maximum financial obligations they may need to incur to raise the capability of an organization.

Prudential regulation: A form of financial regulation that focuses on capital-asset ratios, reserve requirements, deposit insurance, and strict disclosure rules. Prudential regulation is considered to be the norm in the regulation of the financial sector because it places considerable emphasis on strict disclosure rules, which provide an accurate picture of the situation as is.

Pseudo-agenda: Refers to when policy makers accept particular issues advocated by a group or lobby having not genuinely considered the merits of the arguments put forth. This can occur especially if the policy makers are beholden to a particular group such that they are willing to accept practically anything that is propounded by the group. This distorts the situation and thus leads to an artificial (or pseudo) agenda. See L. Koenig, *An Introduction to Public Policy,* Englewood Cliffs, NJ: Prentice Hall, 1986, p. 106.

Pseudo-effectiveness: A state in an organization where no one draws attention to any particular problem but, when considered as a whole, the organization is characterized by ineffectiveness. Such a situation is not sustainable in the long run, and the organization will eventually need to make a belated effort to identify and address the underlying problem.

Pseudo-evaluation: An approach that seeks to produce reliable information about policy outcomes without critiquing the value of those outcomes on the assumption that such values are self-evident. For example, in relation to a development program on extending small-scale credits to poor women in rural areas, an evaluation might only look at the scale of such credits rather than the underlying logic of the target audience and the mode of repayment.

Psychological contract: An unwritten and implicit understanding between an employer and employee wherein each knows what is expected of the other. Given that each party comes to an employment agreement (formalized in an employment contract) with various expectations, a psychological contract will soon exist that will inform the behavior of each. For a review of the psychological contracts of contractors, see, e.g., L. Millward and P. Brewerton, "Contractors and Their Psychological Contracts," *British Journal of Management,* 1999, 10(3), pp. 253–74. *See also* **Expectancy theory**.

Psychological environment: Taken to mean any aspect of the external environment that has an impact on an individual's way of behaving and his or her attitudes toward work. A systems view of organizational action and personnel management holds that understanding the external environment is relevant because it is intrinsically related to the psychological environment of employees.

Psychological needs: The second level of needs as identified by the psychologist Abraham Maslow in his formulation of the hierarchy of human needs. Psychological needs (also known as social needs) include those of love and belonging. See A. Maslow, "A Theory of Human Motivation," *Psychological Review,* 1943, 50, pp. 370–96.

Psychological wages: A term given to any satisfaction received from work that does not have a monetary value attached to it. Psychological wages could include, for example, pleasant work conditions or prestige.

Public administration: The study of processes, systems, and institutions involved in the formulation and implementation of public policy, and associated programs designed to address and solve public problems. In the formulation of policy, bureaucracies are involved in providing advice to policy makers on what alternatives exist for the problems for which policies are being considered. The bureaucracy's involvement in the implementation of public policy is about much more than the formulation, though. The administrative dimensions of the term here come from the involvement of the bureaucracy in policy implementation: putting policies into action or administering them. In the administration of public affairs, there are three related concepts of note: (a) agency, i.e., who is engaged in the activity (in the private or public sector); (b) interest, i.e., whose interests are being served; and (c) access, i.e., who has access to the services? These have a significant bearing on the determination of various models of public administration. Recent models have tended to be centered on rational choice and on the separation between politicians and bureaucrats. For an overarching discussion of public administration, including its subfields, see, e.g., C. Hood, "Emerging Issues in Public Administration," *Public Administration*, 1995, 73(1), pp. 165–83.

Public administration, comparative: The study of public administration systems in other jurisdictions and the differences inherent in their features. The type of public administration that is evident in developing jurisdictions is more aptly termed development administration because much of the effort of the administrative machinery in these jurisdictions is on development. For some insights into this from a noted authority, see F. Riggs, "The Ecology and Context of Public Administration: A Comparative Perspective," *Public Administration Review,* 1980, 40(1), pp. 107–15.

Public administration, ecology of: A view held by system theorists that the environment in which an organization functions will have substantial impact on its performance. Hence, lesson drawing from one setting to the next should proceed with great care as the ecology of public administration is invariably different. A compelling analysis of this is contained in one of the first studies to be conducted in this area (see F. Riggs, *The Ecology of Public Administration,* New York: Asia Publishing House, 1961). See also his "The Ecology of Public Administration Theory," *Administrative Change,* 1992–1993, 20(1–2), pp. 1–27.

Public authority: A public agency that is outside the structure of government but that still provides public services to the general public. A public authority may receive funding from government and also from charges that it imposes for its services.

Public bid opening: The process of revealing all the bids that may have been made in response to a request for a proposal from a governmental agency. The law in many countries requires that all such bids have to be opened in the presence of bidders that choose to attend.

Public comment period: The amount of time given to the public to comment on a policy proposal. The length of such a period varies, but the more complex the policy, as well as the greater the degree of contestability of a policy design, the more time it is felt can be usefully spent gathering public comment. Public comment periods are considered to have opened up new horizons in citizen participation in governmental decision making. See, e.g., B. Holzinger, "Rethinking American Public Policy: The Environment, Federalism, States, and Supranational Influences," *Policy Studies Journal,* 1998, 26(3), pp. 499–511.

Public company: An entity that has a profit-maximization objective, and is privately owned but with sufficient stakeholders to require formal rules about accounts, directors, auditors, etc. A public company can also sell to the public securities in itself to generate resources for its work.

Public corporations: Legal entities that are subject to governmental control. The corporate form of public organization is selected when the organization has to be outside the ambit of the influence of politicians but still in the public domain so that it is accountable to the legislature.

Public discourse: The public debate that takes place over policy issues. Such a discourse can take place in many forums, including, for example, town-hall meetings, and select committee hearings in the legislature. See, e.g., B. Warner, "John Stuart Mill's Theory of Bureaucracy with Representative Government: Balancing Competence and Participation," *Public Administration Review,* 2001, 61(4), pp. 403–13.

Public employee: Any individual who is employed in a public-sector agency. Where the public sector is divided into various parts (such as the public service proper, state-owned enterprises, crown entities, etc.), the meaning of the term public employee may vary depending upon where exactly the individual works in these types of agencies.

Public entrepreneurship: Refers to the application of business-like and entrepreneurial values to public organizations. Such values normally include, among others, competition, customer input, outcomes-based focus, decentralization of authority, and accountability of results. For a good review of the concept, see, e.g., C. Edwards et al., "Public Entrepreneurship: Rhetoric, Reality, and Context," *International Journal of Public Administration,* 2002, 25(12), pp. 1539–54.

Public finance: A term that refers to the management and use of public funds in two different ways: (a) revenue and expenditure that accrues to, and that is incurred by, government; and (b) management of the public debt (since governments will more often than not end up borrowing to finance expenditures). In all jurisdictions, relevant legislative measures address how public finance is to be managed and where accountability lies for its proper management.

Public forums: Arenas for public discussions of policies and issues. Such forums can be town hall meetings, constituency meetings, parliamentary hearings, etc.

Public goods: Goods that are accessible to everyone. Public goods have two attributes: (a) non-exclusiveness, i.e., if they are available to one individual, they are available to all; and (b) non-rivalry (or jointness of supply), i.e., the consumption by one does not diminish the supply of the goods being potentially available for others. Ambient public goods are goods such as air and large bodies of water that are exogenously provided by nature and, therefore, are non-rivalrous in consumption (not all exogenously provided goods, however, are non-rivalrous in consumption). For a classic examination of public goods, see Mancur Olson's *The Logic of Collective Action: Public Goods and the Theory of Groups,* Cambridge, Mass.: Harvard University Press, 1965. See also, e.g., J. Sell, "Types of Public Goods and Free-Riding," in E. Lawler and B. Markovsky (eds.), *Advances in Group Processes*, vol. 5, Greenwich, CT: JAI Press, 1988, pp. 119–40. *See also* **Free-rider problem**.

Public governance: A term used to denote not only the traditional boundaries of public management but also the broader notions of legality, legitimacy, and sociopolitical environment in the study of governance. It is argued that this extension of the scope of the term enables it to better capture the reality of how societies and governments engage in meeting the needs of the public. See, e.g., W. Kickert, "Public Governance in the Netherlands: An Alternative to Anglo-American Managerialism,'" *Public Administration,* 1997, 75(4), pp. 731–52.

Public interest: A generic term that refers to the common good (i.e., something that is in the public interest). Keeping the air unpolluted, for example, is considered to be in the public interest since it benefits everyone. The notion of public interest is considered to be the guiding principle in public-sector behavior as well. For example, any decision that helps reduce the cost of and improve the timeliness of decisions related to appeals can be said to be in the public interest since it benefits those who become engaged in the judicial process. See, e.g., A. McEachern and J. Al-Arayed, "Discerning the Public Interest," *Administration and Society,* 1984, 15(4), pp. 439–53. *See also* **Public value**.

Public maladministration: Refers to the negative aspects of public administration and the inefficiencies that are evident in a public bureaucracy. See, e.g., G. Caiden, "What Really Is Public Maladministration?" *International Journal of Public Administration,* 1991, 37(1), pp. 1–16.

Public management: A generic and broad term that refers to the management and administration of public affairs. This includes the machinery that is needed to help achieve the goals of public policy. It also includes the entire processes of how public organizations are set up, function, and interact with one another. Finally, it is intricately linked to the machinery of government (including the formulation and implementation stages of public policies). *See also* **Machinery of government**.

Public management game: A game that is evident in a public bureaucracy that results from the interaction between street-level bureaucrats and their managers. The game is inherent in the different perspectives they bring to the table on matters of what works—and, therefore, what needs to be emphasized—in service delivery. See, e.g., L. Lynn, "Policy Achievement as a Collective Good: A Strategic Perspective on Managing Social Programs," in B. Bozeman (ed.), *Public Management: The State of the Art,* San Francisco: Jossey-Bass, 1993, pp. 108–33.

Public ordering: A term that refers to the contractual relationships between parties, particularly the rules of the game. The rules of the game themselves are a function of, for example, the development of the legal system and of norms in a society. Finally, public markets are also affected by the manner in which the private sector conducts its business. For a discussion of the concept, see, e.g., O. Williamson, "The Theory of the Firm as Governance Structure: From Choice to Contract," *Journal of Economic Perspectives,* 2002, 16(3), pp. 171–95. *Cf.* **Private ordering**.

Public organization: A generic term for a public agency. A public organization differs from a private one in three important respects: (a) leaders and executives who work in a public organization are less able to define an efficient course of action since they do not always have operational and programmatic independence, (b) they have little incentive to pursue an efficient course of action since they do not tend to be personally held accountable for how they manage public resources, and (c) they have less authority to impose an efficient course of action because, as unelected officers using public resources, the legislature imposes a distinct limit on their authority. See, e.g., J. Wilson, *Bureaucracy: What Government Agencies Do and Why They Do It,* New York: Basic Books, 1989, p. 349.

Public performance audit system: An approach to auditing the performance of governmental departments which analyzes and publicly discloses the *ex ante* specifications and subsequently the *ex post* performance of the departments. The underlying assumption is that when performance indicators are publicly disclosed, it increases the incentives for public officials to meet or exceed them. For an application of this system, see, e.g., S. Afsah, B. Laplante, and D. Wheeler, "Regulation in the Information Age: Indonesian Public Information Program for Environmental Management," in G. Bhatta and J. Gonzalez (eds.), *Governance Innovations in the Asia-Pacific Region: Trends, Cases and Issues,* Aldershot, UK: Ashgate, 1998, pp. 205–18.

Public personnel management: The management of all the aspects of public personnel affairs, including recruitment, compensation, training, performance management, and discipline and sanction. The primary difference between the management of personnel in the public and private sectors is that in the former, there is a direct impact of politics (in that the process is open to scrutiny by external stakeholders and citizens, and that budgets are provided by a legislature). For a description of the various components that make up public personnel management, see, e.g., D. Klingner and J. Nalbandian, *Public Personnel Management: Contexts and Strategies,* 4th edition, Upper Saddle River, NJ: Prentice Hall, 1998.

Public personnel politics: The impact of politics on the management of public personnel management and practices. One key strand here is the practice in many jurisdictions (most notably the United States) of patronage (i.e., where the executive can appoint a certain portion of public personnel positions by virtue of having been given a mandate to govern). Another strand is the tussle between merit and affirmative action, i.e., the tension between recruiting someone based on merit and the countervailing pressure to engage in recruiting based on minority representation.

Public policy: Any course of action, goals, and statements of intent enunciated and pursued by the government regarding policy. A public policy is public because the general environment in which it operates is open and contestable. In general, three types of public policies can be identified: (a) regulatory, (b) distributive, and (c) redistributive. See, e.g.,

T. Lowi, "American Business, Public Policy, Case-Studies, and Political Theory," *World Politics,* 1964, 16(4), pp. 677–715.

Public principal: Refers to any political entity that has been set up in order to accomplish certain tasks that are designed to meet the goals of government. A public principal can be created—and gets its mandate—either from a legislature or from delegated authority granted by a legislature to an existing public authority. See, e.g., J. Lane, "Incorporation as Public Sector Reform," in J. Lane (ed.), *Public Sector Reform: Rationale, Trends, and Problems,* London: Sage, 1997, pp. 286–88.

Public provision: The supply of goods to the public by governmental departments and other public-sector bodies. Until the cross-jurisdictional public-sector reforms of the past two decades, governmental departments usually enjoyed a monopoly in public provision. Such a monopoly meant that government ministers had little alternative but to use these departments to continue to provide public goods and services. The argument has thus been that such a systematic bias toward public provision has meant that departments continued to exaggerate the demand for their services, which, in turn, meant that they were also exaggerating their needed funding levels. See, e.g., D. Epple and R. Romano, "Public Provision of Private Goods," *Journal of Political Economy,* 1996, 104(1), pp. 57–84.

Public record: Any record of public activity (such as a city council meeting) that is to be made available to the general public upon request. Public records are kept in public registers whose maintenance and management are governed by administrative rules and regulations and are readily accessible to the public.

Public scrutiny: An examination by the legislature of the financial and programmatic activities of a public agency or program. Such public scrutiny can either be specified *ex ante* (such as in a requirement by law that a particular agency or program undergo a particular kind of evaluation at a set time) or be the product of intense pressure on legislators to look closely at the activities of a particular agency or program. The resultant report, however, may or may not be made public by the legislature.

Public sector: Consists of organizations owned by local, regional and central-government authorities. A subset of the public sector is the public service, which could be considered to be the core of the public sector. The public sector normally comprises the state sector (i.e., central government) and all regional and local authorities (i.e., state/provincial and local governments). *See also* **Public service**.

Public service: (1) As an activity, the term refers to what public agencies do to serve the needs of citizens and enhance the common good. (2) As a collection of entities, it comprises the various governmental departments in the public sector. For a discussion of the term in relation to recent trends, see, e.g., R. Denhardt and J. Denhardt, "The New Public Service: Serving Rather than Steering," *Public Administration Review,* 2000, 60(6), pp. 549–59.

Public trading enterprise: Nonfinancial authorities which provide services and products in the market and generally operate on a commercial or quasi-commercial basis. A government-owned corporation is an example of a public trading enterprise. *See also* **Public company**.

Public value: A result of any action that takes place in public-sector agencies that increases efficiency, effectiveness, fairness, and other such desirable values. See, e.g., M. Moore, *Creating Public Value: Strategic Management in Government,* MA: Harvard University Press, 1996, p. 10. *See also* **Public interest**.

Public-conduct theory: A theory that states that governments should act ethically since they set the standard for society. By extension, this means that public employees should also observe a common code of conduct.

Public-choice theory: The theory asserts that all public activities can be explained by looking at the economic self-interest of the individuals who are involved in them. The theory thus implies that governments and/or bureaucrats will behave so as to maximize their own utility (for example, prospects of re-election or maintenance of power). Notions of public service and altruism are absent in the theory. The theory also contends that traditional preferences for putting a range of functions together in one organization are problematic since this could lead to the possibility of some functions not being equally emphasized, or some being captured by others. This contention led, for example, to the movement to separate policy and operations from many governmental departments where previously they were housed as one. The theory thus postulates that organizational structures need to be changed so as to alter the incentive structures of those that work in them. For a reconsideration of the claims of public-choice theory, see, e.g., M. Zafirovski, "Administration and Society: Beyond Public Choice?" *Public Administration,* 2001, 79(3), pp. 665–88. *See also* **Policy-operations split**.

Public-interest group: Any organized group of individuals who seeks to help develop policies for causes that they themselves have identified as being beneficial to the general public. A public-interest group is not necessarily restricted to championing any one particular interest or group but neither does it focus—due to resource constraints—on all interests that are beneficial to society. An example of a public-interest group is the League of Women Voters in the United States.

Public-management reforms: Reforms that are evident in any sphere of the public-management domain in a jurisdiction. Such reforms could incorporate, for example, structural changes (such as a policy-operations split), functional changes (such as realigning the work that bureaucrats are expected to do), or procedural changes (such as revising the financial-management processes in governmental departments). For a discussion of the possible criteria with which such reforms can be assessed, see, e.g., J. Boston, "The Challenge of Evaluating Systemic Change: The Case of Public Management Reform," *International Public Management Journal,* 2000, 3(1), 23–46.

Public-management system: The set of various elements that constitutes the public-management sphere. It includes the following: (a) design of the public sector, i.e., how to determine the number and type of public agencies to undertake the functions of the state; (b) strategy-setting system, i.e., how governments decide and prioritize what the public sector should do; (c) accountability system, i.e., how governments hold departments accountable; (d) resource allocation system, i.e., how governments apportion resources to the various public agencies to help them fulfill their mandates; (e) values and culture, i.e., how governments develop a common set of public service values and ethos among all those who work in the public agencies; and (f) relationship between community, politicians, and public sector, i.e., how governments balance the roles and responsibilities of each. See, e.g., State Services Commission, *Statement of Intent 2002,* Wellington, New Zealand: State Services Commission, 2002, p. 25.

Public-policy analysis: A process that helps determine which public policy will deliver the goals of the government. Such an analysis looks at the nature, causes, and effects of alternative public policies. See, e.g., S. Nagel (ed.), *Handbook of Public Policy Evaluation,* London: Sage Publications, 2002, p. 155.

Public-policy making: The entirety of the process of making governmental decisions that address problems identified in society. There are two primary ways of looking at how public policies are made: (a) with the help of the rational decision-making approach, which states that policy makers use systematic, rational, and comprehensive steps to come up with the policies; and (b) with the incremental approach, which states that policy makers do not have the luxury of using such systematic, rational, and comprehensive steps to come up with policy, and that they lurch from one state of affairs to the next. Such muddling through is inherent in the notion of disjointed incrementalism. In reality, public-policy making tends to fall somewhere in between.

Public-private partnerships: Refers to the formal arrangements between government and businesses whereby the latter participate in public activities with the active support of the former. Governments will seek to enhance these partnerships because they can then locate more cost-effective ways of providing services and also of making large-scale investments. There are considered to be four types of public-private partnerships: (a) consultative arrangements (where governments merely seek the views of private organizations and do not necessarily incorporate them), (b) contributory partnerships (where governments will contribute to a private organization to carry out activities over which they have little control), (c) community-development partnerships (where governments work with groups to achieve a mutually beneficial goal), and (d) collaborative relationships (where both public and private organizations have a role to play in the decision-making process). For a discussion, see, e.g., J. Boase, "Beyond Government? The Appeal of Public-Private Partnerships," *Canadian Public Administration,* 2000, 43(1), pp. 75–92.

Public-sector termination: The deliberate ending of specific government functions, programs, policies, or organizations. Such cessation could be for various reasons, including mandate achievement, inadequate resources, or oppositional pressure from constituencies. See, e.g., G. Brewer and P. deLeon, *The Foundations of Policy Analysis,* Chicago: Dorsey Press, 1983, p. 385.

Public-service agreements: A tool used by some central agencies (such as the Treasury in the United Kingdom) to steer the prioritization and direction of public-service work toward governmental outcomes. Such an agreement focuses not only on improved priority setting but also on performance information and incentive effects for both ministers and officials alike. For a critical review of the agreement and its purported efficacy, see, e.g., O. James, "The UK Core Executive's Use of Public Service Agreements as a Tool of Governance," *Public Administration,* 2004, 82(2), pp. 397–419.

Public-service bargain: Refers to the understanding that exists in the public-management sphere in any jurisdiction between bureaucrats and elected representatives about what their roles are and what they are expected to do and not do. For example, a clear understanding of the concept of political neutrality, or of free and frank advice, can be said to be part of a public-service bargain. All too often, however, such a bargain is incomplete as is evident in, for example, a government minister asking a senior manager in a government department to furnish advice that is in consonance with the minister's own frame of reference. For a rigorous discussion of the concept of a public-service bargain, see, e.g., C. Hood, "Paradoxes of Public-Sector Managerialism, Old Public Management and Public Service Bargains," *International Public Management Journal,* 2000, 3(1), pp. 1–22.

Public-service values, modeling of: A situation where public-service leaders show by example how public service values are to be observed and made central to public work. For example, in New Zealand, the State Services Commissioner, by virtue of his position in the Public Service, is in a position to model the public-service values of responsiveness, merit, etc., to other Public Service chief executives.

Publicization: A play on the term privatization that the academician Martin Sellers coined to refer to a situation when private firms become like public agencies. The condition arises when stiff competition for government contracts leads private firms to act in a manner that pleases (act like) government so as to secure public-sector business. For his compelling argument, see "Privatization Morphs into 'Publicization': Businesses Look a Lot Like Government," *Public Administration,* 2003, 81(3), pp. 607–20.

Publicness: The degree of governmental involvement in societal matters through actions such as regulation or contracting. The term thus refers to the extent to which any particular action is in the public domain. There are three key dimensions of publicness: (a) ownership (i.e., whereas private firms are owned by shareholders, public organizations are owned collectively by the public), (b) funding (i.e., public organizations are funded largely by taxation rather than by voluntary consumer expenditures), and (c) control (i.e., public organizations are controlled more so by political than by market forces). For a discussion of these dimensions, as well as other issues related to the differences, see, e.g., G. Boyne, "Public and Private Management: What's the Difference?" *Journal of Management Studies,* 2002, 39(1), pp. 97–122.

Publicness puzzle: A term that refers to the manner in which the public aspects of organizations affect their management. Given that all organizations have some interactions with the public, the publicness puzzle focuses on an organization's relationships with customers and citizens, and how that relationship affects the way the organization works. For application of the term, see, e.g., B. Bozeman and S. Bretschneider, "The 'Publicness Puzzle' in Organization Theory: A Test of Alternative Explanations Between Public and Private Organizations," *Journal of Public Administration Research and Theory,* 1994, 4(2), pp. 197–224.

Pull-up budget: A form of bottom-up budgeting in an organization where a budget is derived from adding up the individual components of lower levels of budgets in the units and subunits of the organization.

Punctuated equilibrium: A major disruption in the manner in which an organization does its work. Such a disruption occurs not in a slow, continuous movement, but by long periods of little movement followed by short periods of rapid and radical development, because conflicts are bottled until they explode and thus put into motion major change. Such a punctuated equilibrium leads to a new paradigm that the organization subsequently embraces. See, e.g., C. Gersick, "Revolutionary Change Theories: A Multilevel Exploration of the Punctuated Equilibrium Paradigm," *Academy of Management Review,* 1991, 16, pp. 10–36. For an application of the concept, see, e.g., P. John and H. Margetts, "Policy Punctuations in the UK: Fluctuations and Equilibria in Central Government Expenditures Since 1951," *Public Administration,* 2003, 81(3), pp. 411–32.

Purchase agreement: A formal contractual arrangement entered into by a purchaser (for example, a governmental minister on behalf of the state) and a provider (for example, a governmental department) for the purchase of outputs, specifying quantity, quality, timeliness, and cost. The performance of the departmental chief executive is then assessed against the attainment or otherwise of the targets in the purchase agreement. A purchase agreement may be revised in time, often as regards its pricing or in its output specifications. See, e.g., The Treasury, *Putting It Together,* Wellington: The Treasury, 1996, p. 39.

Purchase minister: *See* **Vote minister**.

Purchase/ownership model: The concepts of purchase and ownership have been central to much thinking about the public sector in several jurisdictions. One of the initial premises has been that the public-service performance assurance system needs to achieve a better balance between purchase and ownership interests. The purchase/ownership model is useful in considering many decisions about governmental objectives. It is, for example, an effective way of prompting consideration of whether a particular service should be provided by a department or contracted out to another party.

Purchaser interest: Given that government not only owns departments but is also a purchaser (i.e., it buys their products), it is interested in output specification as well as what is actually delivered. This interest contrasts with its interest in the departments from an owner's perspective.

Purchaser-provider split: The duality of role that is evident between an entity that expresses an intent to purchase specific goods and services and another one that provides it. The reforms in public-sector management that took place in many advanced jurisdictions in the past two decades have seen to it that the same governmental department is not fulfilling both roles (to preclude having to decide which one takes precedence). For a case study of this split, see, e.g., M. Ormsby, "The Provider/Purchaser Split: A Report from New Zealand," *Governance: An International Journal of Policy and Administration,* 1998, 11(3), pp. 357–87.

Purple zone: Refers to the domain where political goals and administrative action meet, and where the rules of the game become somewhat nebulous. Purple (i.e., the relationship between politicians and public administrators) arises when in a diagram with a circle for politics, shown as blue, intersects a circle for administration, shown as red. The strategic conversation then that takes place between ministers and senior administrators is said to take place in the "purple zone." See A. Matheson, "Governing Strategically: The New Zealand Experience," *Public Administration and Development,* 1998, 18(4), pp. 349–63.

Purposive incentives: Incentives given to employees that appeal to their idealism. Such incentives are not monetary; rather, they try to instill in the employees that what they believe in is what the organization is actually doing.

Pygmalion effect: Refers to the hypothesized relationship between an individual's expectations on the job and his/her performance. If there is little expected of the individual, he/she indeed usually provides little; however, if the individual is effectively motivated and much is expected, then it could well lead to the expectations being exceeded.

Pyramidal values: Refers to how managers see values existent in organizations. The view is that as one moves up the organization pyramid, values differ, and if faced with a situation of lack of response from employees to an organizational shift (either in process or in mandate), then superiors have a tendency to use management controls to lead employees to a particular direction.

Q

Qualification review function: The assessment and review functions that organizations (such as boards) use to ascertain the equivalence of qualifications of individuals that are gained from other jurisdictions. This is an important function since it affects both the demand for, and supply of, labor in an economy. On the demand side, it determines to a large extent the willingness of local employers to consider the recruitment of candidates who have received their qualifications in a different jurisdiction. On the supply side, it serves as a decision factor for potential migrants, as well as those willing to test new labor markets, by giving them cues on what are considered appropriate and relevant qualifications. *See also* **Recognition of prior learning**.

Qualified bidder: A party that meets the general criteria to be a service contractor and that has been vetted by a governmental agency to be considered for service contracting when an opportunity arises. Such qualifications are based on, among other things, a review of financial capability, past performance, and current capabilities. The qualified bidder status, however, does not remain indefinitely. Most organizations have a rule of "refreshing" their lists so that other potential bidders are given opportunities to be considered. In order to increase transparency, agencies increasingly publish a list of their qualified bidders.

Qualified opinion: An opinion rendered by, for example, auditors on organizational processes that are based on evidence collected during an audit. Those that have been audited are encouraged to consider the opinions seriously so as to better identify ways of enhancing their internal processes. Such opinions, however, are not binding on the organizations.

Qualifying test: An examination of a candidate to determine if he/she qualifies for the particular purpose at hand (such as, for example, certification). Most such tests will measure if the individual crosses a particular threshold. The threshold will have been determined in advance and examinees will have had access to that information prior to the test. This is contrasted with a test wherein the results are comparatively ranked.

Qualities analysis: A term used to refer to the effort by organizational leaders to achieve an understanding of the potentialities that are available to them to position their organization to foster inter-agency collaboration. Each organization that is involved in forging new networks with similar entities will seek to ensure that it is a win-win situation for all parties concerned. The analysis takes into consideration the unique strengths and perceived weaknesses of the organizations concerned. See E. Bardach, *Getting Agencies to Work Together: The Practice and Theory of Managerial Craftsmanship,* Washington, DC: Brookings Institution Press, 1998, pp. 48–49.

Quality assurance: Procedures for ensuring that the right level of quality has been attained in any organizational task or production process. This refers to all activities that are related to improving the quality of the organization's work (including the processes that go into the generation of outputs). While reviews and evaluations are considered to be integral parts of quality assurance, this term is taken to imply an *ex ante* focus (i.e., assessing that quality is assured before any defects arise). Quality assurance is increasingly being used in service-delivery functions as well. For a review of quality assurance in policy shops, see, e.g., G. Bhatta, "Evidence-Based Analysis and the Work of Policy Shops," *Australian Journal of Public Administration,* 2002, 61(3), pp. 98–105.

Quality circle: A group of individuals in an organizational subunit that share ideas on the problems they face and that collectively decide on a course of action. The underlying principle in a quality circle is that those who are intimately involved with a problem will be best able to come up with workable solutions. Just as with similar measures related to quality enhancement, quality circles are effective only when staff members actively participate in them, and when management has made a demonstrable commitment to supporting the ideas generated within the circles.

Quality control: Exercising control over the production process to ensure that the good or service produced is of high quality before it is delivered to customers. Only with such control for quality can organizations assure customers that the products they are consuming are of the requisite quality. For a discussion of quality control in the context of quality management, see, e.g., J. Yong, and A. Wilkinson, "The Long and Winding Road: The Evolution of Quality Management," *Total Quality Management,* 2002, 13(1), pp. 101–21. *See also* **Total quality management.**

Quality planning: A systematic process of reformulating an organization's mission and objectives in keeping with the application of the total quality management program. Quality planning involves determining the specific needs of the organization's customers and then building those needs into well-defined service targets. Each unit within the organization is then made aware of the service targets (and may be given the opportunity to recalibrate them as well if they are not deemed particularly realistic), and management will place emphasis on ensuring that the targets are attained. For an application of quality planning, see, N. Chiu, "Service Targets and Methods of Redress: The Impact of Accountability in Malaysia," *Public Administration and Development,* 1997, 17(1), pp. 175–80.

Quality regulation: A situation where a governmental agency monitors—and seeks to ensure—quality standards for a particular product before it is marketed for public consumption. Such quality regulation centers on the enforcement of quality standards that a governmental body will have formulated and made publicly known.

Quality standards: Standards of quality that governmental agencies need to maintain in their work. For example, in the policy advice that departments provide to governmental ministers, quality standards can include: (a) timeliness (i.e., sufficient time to allow the minister to make sound decisions), (b) presentation of options (i.e., that all viable options and whole-of-government considerations are presented), (c) evidence-based analysis (i.e., all assertions are backed by evidence), and (d) scope for implementation (i.e., the policy advice specifies the parameters of how the advice may be implemented). For a more detailed discussion of what the quality standards for policy advice could include, see, e.g., *Department of Labor, Statement of Intent for the Year Ending 2004,* Wellington, New Zealand: Department of Labor, 2003, p. 71.

Quality-assurance audit: Also known as a conformity audit, this is usually conducted by an independent person or agency and serves to reassure customers that the processes used in the organization conform to some particular standards. The standards (as set by, for example, the International Organization for Standardization, which sets international industrial and commercial standards) will have been predetermined, and for transparency purposes, will have been made known in advance. A quality-assurance audit can be done at regular intervals or when a particular process is determined to be faulty. For a general discussion of this and other quality-related concepts, see, e.g., T. Conti, "A Road Map Through the Fog of Quality and Organizational Assessments," *Total Quality Management,* 2002, 13(8), pp. 1057–68.

Quango: An acronym for quasi-autonomous nongovernmental organization. Quangos are one of the varied forms of semi-autonomous bodies that are not explicitly governmental departments (and are, therefore, off-budget agencies, i.e., their expenses are not reflected in governmental budgets) but that still push a governmental agenda on specific policies. Quangos do different things, including, in some jurisdictions, regulating public utilities. Quangos have dramatically been called "government by moonlight" and "pubate organizations." For a discussion of the term, see, e.g., J. Rouse, "Performance Inside the Quangos: Tensions and Contradictions," *Local Government Studies,* 1997, 23(1), pp. 59–75.

Quantity regulation: A situation where governmental regulations restrict the quantity of any good or service (such as quantities of a particular type of fish in certain waters). Quantity regulation is often, although not exclusively, used as a means of controlling negative externalities. The determination of the level of quantity is sometimes a very protracted affair and, as such, in those instances it is likely that the limits that are set will be in effect for some years. For a discussion of quantity regulation, particularly in relation to its enforcement costs, see, e.g., E. Glaeser, and A. Shleifer, *A Case for Quantity Regulation,* Working Paper No. 8184, March 2001, Cambridge, MA: National Bureau of Economic Research. *See also* **Quota**.

Quantum reengineering: As used in the public-management context, this refers to a comprehensive restructuring of an organization that fundamentally changes it in order to make it more capable of doing its work. Quantum reengineering is thus comprehensive in nature in that it has an impact on practically all aspects of organizational life. A hypothetical example of quantum reengineering is the transformation of the role of a public-service commission from a centralized personnel-management body to one that plays mostly a brokerage and a support role to public-service departments. A frame-breaking reform effort may include elements of quantum reengineering. *See also* **Frame-breaking reform**.

Quasi-autonomous executive agency: An organization that has a mandate of delivering public services and is neither in the public sector (as a governmental department) nor in the private (as a business firm), hence also termed a hybrid organization. With the contemporary trend in public-management reforms focusing on minimizing the role of government in, among others, service delivery, such quasi-autonomous executive agencies have tended to fill the void. For a case-study application, see, e.g., W. Kickert, "Public Management of Hybrid Organizations: Governance of Quasi-Autonomous Executive Agencies," *International Public Management Journal,* 2001, 4(2), pp. 135–50.

Quasi-contractual documents: Documents that are meant to be obligations or agreements between parties but that are not necessarily framed as formal contracts. For example, there may be what is known as a job-seeker contract that governs the relationship between the governmental department that disburses unemployment benefits and the individual who receives it, but the individual may be expected to demonstrate evidence that he or she is actively seeking work. See, e.g., R. Shaw, "Rehabilitating the Public Service—Alternatives to the Wellington Model," in S. Chatterjee (ed.), *The New Politics: A Third Way for New Zealand,* Palmerston North, New Zealand: Dunmore Press, 1999, p. 191.

Quasi-corporations: Unincorporated businesses that function like public corporations because they are created for public purposes. This means that the legislature has authority over them with the public interest in mind. In many jurisdictions, for example, the education sector has seen the emergence of quasi-corporations because governments have felt the need to move away from heavily centralized administration, yet still exercise certain control over the sector. Quasi-corporations keep their own accounts, which are then audited.

Quasi-fiscal assistance: Assistance that is rendered by governments to nongovernmental organizations and private businesses not directly in money but in the form of tax concessions, loan guarantees, and the like. Providing such assistance is an important role that government plays since, among other things, it sends a strong signal to economic players that the government is willing to incur costs, or forgo revenues, in order to support particular economic endeavors.

Quasi-government: A collection of hybrid organizations (such as the National Park Foundation in the United States) that have legal characteristics of both the public and private sectors, and that are increasingly being resorted to in many advanced jurisdictions to implement public policy functions. Of interest and concern to some is the relationship between quasi-government entities and elected officials since they are not entirely within the public sector, and, therefore, accountability relationships are not always clear. Quasi-government entities are on the rise in jurisdictions because governmental agencies, given fiscal constraints, are encouraged to seek resources outside the public sector. For a review of the emergence of quasi-governments, see, e.g., A. Greer, and P. Hoggett, "Contemporary Governance and Local Public Spending Bodies," *Public Administration,* 2000, 78(3), pp. 513–29.

Quasi-independent organizations: Organizations that are linked with others in substantive ways (such as in terms of their reporting regimes) but are still rather autonomous. With the bifurcation of traditional monolithic government departments into policy organizations and operational ones, quasi-independence came to be the defining feature in the machinery of government in many advanced jurisdictions. This quasi-independence may have stemmed what is termed "producer capture," but it also left room for the separation of policy from operations. For a compelling description of this in relation to the experiences of New Zealand, see, e.g., A. Schick, *The Spirit of Reform: Managing the New Zealand State Sector in a Time of Change,* Wellington: State Services Commission and The Treasury, 1996, p. 21.

Quasi-judicial function: A task that is within the domain of such bodies as administrative tribunals, boards, or regulatory agencies that can apply law, hold hearings, and pass judgments. A quasi-judicial review is generally considered to be a highly effective method of complaint resolution since it involves the mediation and review services of an impartial public entity (such as an ombudsperson) and, therefore, gives some confidence to the complainant that the matter will be given a fair hearing. In a strict sense, a quasi-judicial review goes beyond mediation in that, in the former, a judgment is expected in favor or against the complaint that has been made, while in the latter, there could be a decision to settle the matter in an amicable manner. For an example of the quasi-judicial functions of the European Ombudsman, see K. Heede, "Enhancing the Accountability of Community Institutions and Bodies: The Role of the European Ombudsman," *European Public Law,* 1997, 3(4), pp. 587–605.

Quasi-legislative functions: The activities of agencies that center on rule making and on preparing regulations to which others must adhere. Such authority to make rules and prepare regulations is granted to the agencies by parliament (i.e., a legislature), hence the term quasi-legislative. Such functions are evident in, for example, amending a budget or a contract, or even in repealing existing regulations.

Quasi-markets: A system of ensuring that the demand for and supply of goods and services are matched not through the mechanisms of the independent forces of a market, but through the interactions of mediating agents, such as professionals and purchasing authorities, who act on behalf of consumers in choosing a precise mix of goods and services. Vouchers and contracting are usually cited as manifestations of quasi-markets. See, e.g., N. Flynn, I. Holliday, and L. Wong, "Introduction," in L. Wong, and N. Flynn (eds.), *The Market in Chinese Social Policy,* Hampshire, UK: Palgrave, 2001, pp. 1–11.

Quasi-official community groups: Community groups that are officially recognized by government to be conduits to communities in the provision of goods and services (but do not have formal recognition status to be involved in any other non-sanctioned activity). An example of a quasi-official community group is the *mahalla* in Uzbekistan, which provides child benefits and other types of social assistance to low-income families (the state gives the *mahallas* considerable autonomy to decide who deserves assistance). See, e.g., J. Conning, and M. Kevane, "Community-Based Targeting Mechanisms for Social Safety Nets: A Critical Review," *World Development,* 2002, 30(3), pp. 375–94.

Quasi-option value: The "value" that policy makers get when they put off deciding on policy options in the hope that a later decision will be better informed. When dealing with wicked problems, policy makers often generate quasi-option value since hard decisions tend to be postponed in the hope that new evidence will emerge later that might better facilitate a policy decision. See, e.g., K. Arrow and A. Fisher, "Environmental Preservation, Uncertainty, and Irreversibility," *Quarterly Journal of Economics,* 1974, 88(2), pp. 312–19.

Quasi-private organizations: Organizations that straddle the traditional boundaries between the private and the public sector. These can be found in any economic sector and perform various functions (such as provision of banking and credit services). Quasi-private organizations have functions that could be described as being in the public domain, yet their institutional arrangements can mimic private-sector ones, and they are not, for example, subject to freedom-of-information legal requirements. For a discussion of quasi-private organizations, see, e.g., M. Emmert, M. Crow, and R. Shangraw, "Public Management in the Future: Post-Orthodoxy and Organization Design," in B. Bozeman (ed.), *Public Management: The State of the Art,* San Francisco: Jossey-Bass, 1993, pp. 345–60.

Quasi-resolution: When intractable issues, which may or may not have been addressed by government before, are resolved for the time being (and the concerned parties are bound by the decision taken). But the issues are certain to resurface again in the same or another form that will have to be addressed by government. Wicked problems, if they are addressed at all, tend to have quasi-resolutions.

Quasi-senior civil service: The categorization of the civil service at the senior level by the appointment of individuals who are not technically civil servants. The fear is that the advice of special advisers (brought in by ministers for political advice) begins to supplant that of the civil service. In effect, a quasi-senior civil service is then established around the special advisers providing substantial policy advice to the government, thus bypassing the civil service (see, e.g., State Services Commission, *Annual Report of the State Services Commission, 2002,* Wellington: State Services Commission, 2002, p. 10).

Question time: Also known as the zero hour, question time is a period set out in parliament when members can ask any question of the government deemed to be in the public interest. All questions, however, are provided to governmental ministers in advance, and the ministers are expected to have a response prepared by question time. Members of parliament are allowed a set number of supplementary questions as follow-ups to the original. In parliamentary democracies, question time is viewed as a dynamic forum in which government has to publicly account for its actions, and as such the members take this session rather seriously.

Quick environment-scanning technique: A systematic—although not very rigorous—technique used by managers to provide a quick "heads-up" review of future scenarios that could affect the organization. Such scenario setting is based on whatever evidence is readily available in the organization, and it may or may not involve seeking input from stakeholders. The technique also helps managers to get a better handle on how they might want to respond to such scenarios. Much as a rigorous environmental scan is useful and must be done, time pressures and other constraints prohibit organizations from undertaking it regularly; in those instances, they resort to the quick environment-scanning technique.

Quota: (1) A form of quantity regulation, i.e., how much to produce and how much to buy. (2) In personnel management, the term refers to the fixed number of minorities who have to be hired in proportion to the majority. A quota system imposes a cost on the organization since it mandates the recruitment of individuals who may not necessarily have the required level of knowledge, skills, and abilities for the posts to which they are appointed. This requires the organization to devote resources for appropriate training and development activities for the individuals. See, e.g., R. Stryker, "Disparate Impact and the Quota Debates: Law, Labor Market Sociology, and Equal Employment Policies," *Sociological Quarterly,* 2001, 42(1), pp. 13–46.

R

Rabble hypothesis: Derived from the scientific-management movement, this concept argues that workers are incapable of responsibility, or of motivating themselves to work. It also asserts that each individual in a group setting is interested in pursuing only a narrow, rational self-interest. The argument is made that workers behave like a rabble of isolated individuals, and that they are motivated primarily by financial rewards (and conversely by the fear of being made redundant). The psychologist George Elton Mayo's work in the Hawthorne Works experiments provided the contrary view. For a case-study application, see, e.g., J. Backstrand, D. Gibbons, and J. Jones, "Who Is in Jail? A Test of the Rabble Hypothesis," *Crime and Delinquency,* 1992, 38(2), pp. 219–29.

Radius clause: Refers to the stipulation some employers have that an employee who has benefited from some organizational investment (such as training) not be able to seek employment in other (i.e., competitor) organizations in a given locale for a set period. The clause usually arises when the employer funds all or a substantial part of the employee's training, and does not wish to see a competitor benefit from it. While a radius clause may constrain an employee in terms of mobility, employers can compensate for that by drawing up more attractive conditions of service.

Raiding: (1) A situation where public officials dip into a resource base (such as surplus funds) for activities that are not productive. (2) Refers to the activities of an organization to recruit employees of competing organizations. Raiding is increasingly becoming evident in public-sector organizations, and as regards certain occupations (such as policy analysts).

Rank in person: Also termed a personal-rank system, this is a method of determining pay levels based on an employee's knowledge, skills, and abilities rather than on the nature of the employee's responsibilities (i.e., rank). On the other hand, rank in position is a method of establishing pay primarily based on the nature of the specific duties and responsibilities that an employee is to perform regardless of his or her knowledge, skills, and abilities. In a rank-in-person system, it is clearly possible for employees of the same rank to be at different levels of pay.

Rank in position: *See* **Rank in person**.

Rapid prototyping: Developing a program or policy where most of the components have been previously tested and what is left is to put them together and test their validity in a new setting. Rapid prototyping involves revisiting prior processes in iterations until a suitable and satisfactory product is in place. This includes, in the main, identifying the problem, generating alternatives, and evaluating them. Only in the last iteration will the product be "hard-coded" (i.e., constituted as the final product). The rapid-prototyping process is thus used to generate and evaluate design alternatives, and an organization needs to constantly appraise and reappraise the emerging policy or program design to see how well it fits with the criteria set at the beginning of the iteration process.

Rapid rural appraisal: A systematic, although semi-structured, method of getting information from a rural community for purposes of planning and formulating a program. The technique involves putting together a multidisciplinary team (i.e., one that has members that bring varied skills from various sectors) whose task is to collect soft data as well as tangible information. This often involves collecting information in a "quick-and-dirty" way (meaning, it does not rely wholly on scientific ways of collecting information, but still offers a rich description of community life). As the name suggests, rapid rural appraisal has had its widest application in the area of rural development. For a discussion of the concept, see, e.g., A. Ellman, "Rapid Appraisal for Rural Project Preparation," *Agricultural Administration,* 1981, 8, pp. 463–71.

Ratchet effect: An effect that is evident when a variable currently being used to determine something (for example, pay) is influenced by its own previous values. Thus, a ratchet effect is in evidence when, for example, next year's performance target is based on this year's actual performance. A downside to this is that employees obviously have a tendency to underperform this year so that they will not have to do a lot next year. See, e.g., L. Carmichael and W. B. Macleod, "Worker Cooperation and the Ratchet Effect," *Journal of Labor Economics,* 2000, 18(1), pp. 1–19.

Rate-the-rater system: A system where a board in an organization (or an independent individual) can check the tendency of supervisors and managers to inflate their evaluations of employees. This serves as a check on the tendency to reward many employees whereas only a few may actually be so deserving. At the upper levels of the organizational hierarchy, it is also possible that an external peer reviewer may be requested to review the rating results. Such a peer reviewer, however, would have to be someone who is familiar with the organizational setting, although not necessarily with the individuals who are to be evaluated.

Rational choice: (1) Used at the individual level of analysis, the term asserts that individuals' decisions can be explained in terms of goal-oriented and purposive (i.e., self-interested) behavior. Noted scholar Graham Allison posits that rational choice is one of three lenses that can be used to help explain the choices made by policy makers (the other two being organizational process and bureaucratic politics). For the original work on this by Allison, see his "Conceptual Models and the Cuban Missile Crisis," *American Political Science Review,* 1969, 63(3), pp. 689–718. (2) Rational-choice theory is used to evaluate public policy along a spectrum of areas, such as standards of policy performance as returns on investment, the notion of opportunity costs in achieving public benefits, or highlighting the superiority of market forces over governmental interventions in the economy. (3) Rational choice is also a lens for assessing public-policy situations when the environmental structure is stable and the goals of policy actors are clear (see, e.g., N. Zahariadis, "Comparing Three Lenses of Policy Choice," *Policy Studies Journal,* 1998, 26[3], pp. 434–48). For a review of the application of rational-choice theory in public administration, see, e.g., C. Hay, "Theory, Stylized Heuristic or Self-Fulfilling Prophecy? The Status of Rational Choice Theory in Public Administration," *Public Administration,* 82(1), 2004, pp. 39–62.

Rational expectations: Expectations which individuals and organizations have that—for purposes of econometric modeling—are considered to be model-consistent (i.e., their behavior in practice will be similar to what is assumed in theory). For example, according to rational expectations, we would expect to see managers rushing to spend excess funds toward the end of a financial year rather than see it reverted to the central treasury (although with suitable assumptions, it is also possible to have a rational-expectations model that does not produce such a result). The key to rational expectations is that people behave as though they have full information about the future. For an economic treatment of the concept, see, e.g., S. Grossman, "An Introduction to the Theory of Rational Expectations Under Asymmetric Information," *Review of Economic Studies,* 1981, 48, pp. 541–59.

Rational ignorance: The term is synonymous with that of the trained incapacity of bureaucrats. It implies that, given the complexity of the policy domain, bureaucrats cannot be aware of everything that affects a policy; thus, some amount of ignorance is rational and is to be expected. From the perspective of the bureaucrat, there is little incentive to seek more information because the expected benefits may be negligible (particularly if the source of that information is not independently verifiable) or that the costs for such acquisition could far outweigh benefits. See, e.g., B. Caplan, "Rational Ignorance versus Rational Irrationality," *Kyklos,* 2001, 54, pp.3–26. *See also* **Rational irrationality**.

Rational irrationality: While it is intuitive to assume that the average person has rational ignorance, a closer examination of individual behavior actually reveals that this is more irrational than rational. For example, people generally feel that even if there are only a few corruption cases in the public sector, the whole sector itself is corrupt. Such errors in judgments can be attributed to irrationality rather than ignorance. Rational irrationality thus is a counterexplanation of human behavior than that inherent in the concept of rational ignorance, and simply implies that when individuals do not have strong incentives to get accurate information, they tend to merely believe what is convenient, as opposed to what is rational. For a good review of the concept, see B. Caplan, "Rational Irrationality and the Microfoundations of Political Failure," *Public Choice,* 2001, 107, pp. 311–31. *See also* **Rational ignorance**.

Rational man: A notion that economists use to denote how human beings are naturally rational and will seek to maximize their utility in everything that they do. *See also* **Economic determinism**; **Rationality**.

Rational planning: A method of planning in organizations that has five key attributes: (a) takes a system-wide perspective; (b) has broad areas of consensus on goals, nature of problem to be addressed, most acceptable method of intervention, and priorities; (c) has capacity for rational analysis based on evidence; (d) contains suitable organizational arrangements; and (e) incorporates monitoring and evaluation mechanisms and processes, including feedback from relevant stakeholders. Rational planning is widely regarded as difficult because there are stringent requirements on credible evidence and information. For a review of an empirical test done on the problems of rational planning in public-sector organizations, see, e.g., G. Boyne et al., "Problems of Rational Planning in Public Organizations: An Empirical Assessment of the Conventional Wisdom," *Administration & Society,* 2004, 36(3), pp. 328–50.

Rational validity: Refers to the validity that a particular policy has given its basis on some legal standard and/or because it is logical and can be substantiated by irrefutable evidence. Rational validity sits at the core of the concept of evidence-based analysis (EBA) in policy formulation since in EBA the justification for recommending a policy is centered on being able to use credible empirical evidence. The rationality thus is implied in the evidence that policy analysts use in the process. *See also* **Evidence-based analysis**.

Rational-comprehensive theory of decision making: A method of decision making where technical problem-solving processes are used extensively, and where multiple alternatives are considered in pursuit of the ideal policy option. According to this theory, every time a decision has to be made policy makers need to start from the beginning: they must not assume anything. The theory was discussed at great length by the economist and political scientist Charles Lindblom (see C. Lindblom, "The Science of 'Muddling Through,'" *Public Administration Review,* 1959, 19[2], pp. 79–88). For an example of the rational-comprehensive theory of decision making in action, see D. O'Sullivan and B. Down, "Policy Decision-Making Models in Practice: A Case Study of the Western Australian 'Sentencing Acts,'" *Policy Studies Journal,* 2001, 29(1), pp. 56–70. *See also* **Crisis theory of decision making**.

Rationality: Refers simply to a process of using reasoned arguments to make claims. Rationality assumes that people understand their preferences, know which alternatives are available, know how to act on this information, and consistently apply decision criteria. Rationality can be of various types: (a) technical (i.e., a comparison of policy alternatives according to their capacity to promote effective solutions), (b) economic (i.e., a comparison of policy alternatives according to their capacity to promote efficient solutions); (c) legal (i.e., according to their legal conformity to established laws and rules), (d) social (i.e., according to their ability to maintain or improve valued social institutions), and (d) substantive (i.e., one that takes into account all four forms of rationality). Rationality can also be viewed in the context of intentions, procedures, and consequences: rationality of intentions refers to the intentions of various parties to enhance their net welfare (i.e., benefits minus costs) in all their actions; rationality of procedures refers to the ways in which net welfare is to be maximized if all relevant information is available; and rationality of consequences refers to the success achieved in maximizing net welfare. This latter from of rationality (i.e., of consequences), however, is constrained by information asymmetry and it is never possible to truly reach such rationality. See H. Simon, *Administrative Behavior: A Study of Decision-Making Processes in Administrative Organizations,* New York: Macmillan, 1947, pp. 39–41. For a comprehensive review of rationality as applied in economics, see, e.g., V. Smith, "Constructivist and Ecological Rationality in Economics," *American Economic Review,* 2003, 93(3), pp. 465–501.

Rationalization: In the organizational context, this term refers to the move to streamline the organization so that there are no excess cost areas and so that the organization is lean and efficient. The primary objective of rationalization in the public sector centers on reducing the costs of service delivery, including by reducing the size of public-sector employment. For this reason, rationalization exercises can be difficult for everyone concerned, and there is need to ideally engage in consultation with employees and other stakeholders who are impacted so that there is buy-in to the exercise. For a review of the term in relation to its application in developing jurisdictions, see, e.g., I. Hentic and G. Bernier, "Rationalization, Decentralization and Participation in the Public Sector Management of Developing Countries," International Review of Administrative Sciences, 1999, 65(2), pp. 197–210.

Rayner scrutinies: Refers to the detailed reviews that the team led by Lord (then Sir Derek) Rayner conducted in the UK civil service in the early 1980s. A small team of management advisers from the Cabinet Office's Efficiency Unit helped departmental officials identify cost savings and productivity improvements and then monitor implementation of the recommendations accepted by the relevant departmental minister. The reviews were of selected policy areas within particular government agencies. The reviews also sought to ensure that the activities of governmental agencies contributed in meaningful ways to the broader outcomes sought by the government. For a review of the results, see, e.g., National Audit Office, *Rayner Scrutiny Programs 1979 to 1983: Thirty-Ninth Report from the Committee of Public Accounts,* London: HMSO, 1986.

Reaction formation: The process of the development of often socially unacceptable behavior in employees who are frustrated in their workplace. In essence, reaction formation is the process of coming up with a new point of view concerning an old desire that has not been fulfilled. Thus, for example, employees who, due to an average performance evaluation rating, do not move ahead in the organization may develop views that are newly antagonistic of the organization. The key to note is that such a reaction from the point of view of the employee is that it is coerced (i.e., it is the actions of someone else that causes the reaction). The concept is relevant in the context of an organization since it considers the perceptions of individuals and how they see themselves in the organization. For use of the concept in relation to organizational commitment, see, e.g., J. Stanton et al., *Examining the Linkage Between Organizational Commitment and Information Security,* Proceedings of the IEEE Systems, Man, and Cybernetics Conference, Washington, DC, October 2003.

Real options analysis: Drawing from finance research, this technique of strategic planning is geared toward risk reduction through disaggregating complex issues into smaller and more manageable bits so that organization leaders can get a better handle on the contingencies that arise for each. Organizations can maximize the use of this technique by incorporating it in their strategic planning and risk-management processes. For a discussion of this tool, see, e.g., K. Miller and G. Waller, "Scenarios, Real Options, and Integrated Risk Management," *Long Range Planning,* 2003, 36(1), pp. 93–107.

Realistic job preview: Giving potential candidates a preview of the important and practical aspects of a job so that they might better understand the job and the organization. This has dual advantages: it helps the staff member get a better appreciation of the work and the environment, and it also helps the organization to assess the individual and to see where and how the organization-employee fit can be maximized. Not all organizations are able to offer a realistic job preview, however, since it may involve compromising some organizational confidentiality.

Reality leadership: Denotes a style of leadership where the leader changes his/her style in keeping with the situation that the group may be facing. Proponents of this model of leadership point to the fact that its primary focus is on actionable measures that seek to directly address the problems at hand rather than some nebulous concept of leading the organization. Since realities differ across organizations, the leadership that is exercised in each varies as well to some extent. See, e.g., C. Argyris, *Integrating the Individual and the Organization,* New York: John Wiley & Sons, 1964, p. 216.

Reallocation: When a department is permitted to reallocate funds initially agreed for other use by the funding authority or legislature. Such reallocation is possible not only of funds but also of functions and duties for which the organization need not approach the legislature unless fundamental changes to the organizational mandate are being considered.

Reasonable accommodation: The process of ensuring that both parties to a dispute make an effort to concede something in order to come to a settlement. The concept implies that both parties have certain objectives that must be compromised.

Reasonable cause: Sufficient ground for the employer to believe that an illegal act may have occurred in the organization. The employer needs to be able to demonstrate that there was reason to believe that such an act had indeed been committed and that it was detrimental to the organization in some way. The burden of proof here would lie with the employer.

Reassignment: Also called rotation, this term refers to the placing of a staff member to some other part of the organization in the same capacity and at the same level. From the organization's perspective, reassignment is relatively cost-neutral since it does not incur extra costs (particularly if the reassignment is in the same locality), although some loss in productivity is to be expected when a staff member is assigned elsewhere. For the individual, there may be costs incurred by way of adjustment to a new setting. Reassignments in the public sector are more easily carried out in centralized personnel-management systems than in those systems where each public-sector agency has control over its own human-resource management system.

Rebidding: Making firms go through a bid process again. This is done either: (a) when the received bids are inadequate in delivering the product and terms that the organization wants; or (b) in periodic exercises, which are designed to select a contractor for a subsequent contract period. Regular rebidding is favored by agencies so that they can bolster their revenue base because it forces bidders to compete with more frequency. The potential increase in such revenues is usually significantly less than the increase in any transaction costs to the agency as a result of more frequent rebidding exercises.

Reciprocal agreement: Any agreement between two jurisdictions, organizations, or programs where what is expected of one party is also expected of the other. Thus, if one jurisdiction provides tax relief to citizens of one jurisdiction then the government of that jurisdiction also provides the same relief to citizens of the first jurisdiction. While the provisions apply equally to both jurisdictions, the benefits of such agreements need not—and indeed, will generally not—be the same for both.

Reciprocal interdependencies: Is evident when the output that each unit produces serves as an input to the others in an organization and where all units depend on each other for inputs. A self-contained entity (such as, for example, a hospital) has several reciprocal interdependencies. In such a case, focusing on collective interest yields the greatest value as opposed to turf protection. See, e.g., C. Hill, "Co-operation, Opportunism, and the Invisible Hand: Implications for Transaction Cost Theory," *Academy of Management Review,* 1990, 15(3), pp. 500–13. *See also* **Pooled interdependencies; Sequential interdependencies**.

Reciprocity: (1) Refers to the methods by which an organization handles the conflicts between organizational and individual goals. In order to survive and thrive, all organizations need to ensure that this goal alignment is continually maintained. (2) Refers to the response that individuals give to stimuli that emerge externally. It is argued that, contrary to the view that people are exclusively self-interested, the concept of reciprocity implies that people will be much nicer than assumed if the stimulus is positive (such as cooperative behavior), and much more hostile than assumed if the stimulus is negative. See, e.g., E. Fehr and S. Gachter, "Fairness and Retaliation: The Economics of Reciprocity," *Journal of Economic Perspectives*, 2000, 14(3), pp. 159–81.

Recognition lag: *See* **Lag**.

Recognition of current competence: *See* **Recognition of prior learning**.

Recognition of prior learning: Also known as recognition of current competence, this term refers to the acceptance by an organization that an individual who has joined the organization may have had relevant learning from other sources outside the organization and outside his/her area of normal work (such as from voluntary work in a church). Such recognition is used as a basis for granting the individual exemption from certain requirements toward advanced standing.

Reconciliation: (1) Settlement reached between an employee and the organization subsequent to a complaint being filed by the former. (2) As used in the legislative context, and in jurisdictions where there are two chambers in the legislature in which joint assent is required, reconciliation refers to a meeting of the two chambers to agree on the specification of a particular policy.

Recruitment: The process of selecting and hiring a candidate for the organization. This starts from a needs analysis of the particular role, specification of the job description, and advertisement for candidates. This is followed by an initial review of the applicants to shortlist strong candidates, and then an interview stage to determine who is the most suitable. Recruitment can be both internal (i.e., from within the organization) and external (i.e., from outside the organization). There are merits to both types, but it is clear that for the organization to get new capabilities and new way of thinking and doing, external recruitment is preferable. External recruitment, however, is more costly, and also takes more time. Many organizations will have a rule that the first preference for filling vacancies be given to internal candidates. However, such organizations may also look externally so as to gauge the labor market.

Red tape: Refers to the lengthy delays and cumbersome procedures that bureaucracies take to get an action performed. The delay invariably arises from the bureaucracy's reliance on adherence to rules and regulations, excessive formality, and attention to routine. Red tape may result either because the staff members are not adequately skilled and so need to laboriously refer to, and follow, procedures, or because they are deliberately trying to subvert the system. See, e.g., B. Bozeman and P. Scott, "Bureaucratic Red Tape and Formalization: Untangling Conceptual Knots," *American Review of Public Administration,* 1996, 26(1), pp. 1–17.

Redeployment: *See* **Deployment**.

Redistribution: Usually refers to the reallocation of national wealth by government from the rich to the poor. Much of the activity of several governmental departments then is structured around such redistributive functions. However, it also refers to any reallocation, including through "middle-class capture," (i.e., by specifically targeting the needs of middle-class and middle-income people) which distributes from the poor to better-off groups.

Redundancy: (1) When employees are dismissed from their jobs and where the dismissal is not based on their fault. (2) The state of being not necessary. As understood thus, there are three types of redundancy: (a) clearance redundancy (i.e., the need for support from several entities before one can proceed with a decision; for example, three reviewers have to agree to funding a program before resources can be allocated), (b) backup redundancy (i.e., duplication of effort to ensure that there is backup for a function; for example, anything that is kept running/ready should something go wrong and is needed as backup), and (c) competitive redundancy (i.e., a situation that arises when different units have identical or overlapping functions that each can perform effectively).

Redundancy of functions: The basis of new organizational structures where employees have a wide repertoire of skills that they can employ to switch from function to function as the environment dictates. Such versatility means that the organization has a variety-increasing system in place that allows it to better deal with change. Redundancy of parts, on the other hand, is the basis of the traditional technocratic bureaucracy, where individual job parts are broken down so that it is easy to replace an individual, and it is inexpensive to train a new employee for that role. See, e.g., F. Emery, "The Second Design Principle: Participation and the Democratization of Work," in E. Trist and H. Murray (eds.), *The Social Engagement of Social Science—A Tavistock Anthology, Vol. II: The Socio-Technical Perspective,* Philadelphia: University of Pennsylvania Press, 1993, pp. 214–33.

Redundancy of parts: *See* **Redundancy of functions**.

Reference group: A group against which something is compared, for example, in benchmarking organizational performance. (2) A group of people with whom ideas on policy development are shared. Such reference group members only provide advice and are not empowered to approve or disapprove particular actions of the project/program team.

Reflected exclusivity: *See* **Principle of interaction**.

Reform constituencies: Those that are in support of particular aspects of any reform process. Reformists and change managers will ensure that as they push for changes to a system or organization, they also solicit support from particular constituencies so that the pressure for reform becomes tangible. The primary task for the change managers in such cases is to ensure that they have been able to convey to the reform constituencies the business case for why such reform is necessary and what benefits are to be gained.

Reform fatigue: A situation where policy makers, and the public as well, have experienced too many reform efforts and do not show the appetite for more. Reform fatigue can also set in if the initial reform efforts are extensive and the change dramatic and comprehensive. In such a situation, unless there are immediate positive results, it is difficult to sustain the reform process. Reform fatigue is inevitable if the reform constituencies also falter in their support. For a good discussion of this concept, see, e.g., E. Lora, U. Panizza, and M. Quispe-Agnoli, "Reform Fatigue: Symptoms, Reasons, and Implications," *Federal Reserve Bank of Atlanta Economic Review,* 2004, Second Quarter, pp. 1–28.

Reform sequence: The path that can be taken to reform something. For example, a country could pursue general reforms in rural and regional institutions before embarking on broad reforms in central institutions. Reforms could also proceed either in a piecemeal and ad hoc fashion or in a comprehensive manner. What sequence the reform process takes will be a function not only of the reforms themselves but also of the conditions that exist in a particular jurisdiction or organization. Thus, what is applicable in one setting will not necessarily be so in another. See, e.g., E. Lindquist, "Reconceiving the Center: Leadership, Strategic Review, and Coherence in Public Sector Reform," in OECD, *Government of the Future,* Paris: OECD, 2000, pp. 149–83.

Refresher training: Training that is offered to individuals to update their skills and competencies. Refresher training allows employees to keep their competencies current.

Regime legitimacy: The acceptance by citizens of the validity of existent laws and of the competence and rationally created rules of the bureaucracy. By extension, regime legitimacy reflects the acceptance by the general body politic of the government in place, and of the way in which successive governments are formed. For an application, see, e.g., K. Ho, *The Politics of Policy-Making in Singapore,* Singapore: Oxford University Press, 2000, p. 73.

Regime theory: A regime can be broadly taken as any principle, norm, or decision-making protocol that facilitates interactions among organizations that converge on a given issue. This convergence could take place in a formal setting (for example, an organization such as the United Nations) or an informal one (such as the coming together of interested parties to a banking crisis). Regimes facilitate cooperation among parties by drawing up the parameters, including expectations, of standards of behavior among the parties. As applied in the public-management context, regime theory argues that policy-making processes can be more usefully analyzed from the perspective of how coalitions among policy actors can be formed (i.e., focusing on social production) rather than from who exercises power over whom (i.e., merely focusing on social control). Actually, regime theory has begun to gain greater currency as jurisdictions begin to experiment with electoral systems that enable minority parties to have a presence in the legislature, thus compelling the larger parties to form electoral coalitions and policy coalitions as well. See, e.g., A. Behnke, "Ten Years After: The State of the Art of Regime Theory," *Cooperation and Conflict,* 1995, 30(2), pp. 179–97.

Regret: The difference between what can be received now for a decision and what is perceived to be the maximal value in the future. See, e.g., G. Loomes and R. Sugden, "Regret Theory: An Alternative Theory of Rational Choice Under Uncertainty," *Economic Journal,* 1982, 92(368), pp. 805–24. *See also* **Payoff function**.

Regular budget: A budget for regular (i.e., operating) expenses. A regular budget for a developing country, for example, is contrasted with a development budget (i.e., one which funds major new infrastructure projects and other activities). Most donor agencies have a policy not to provide support to the regular budget of a less-developed country since this would act as a disincentive to the government to be prudent about its regular expenses. In reality, however, governments have been known to tap into the development budgets to meet costs incurred in the regular budget.

Regulation: Refers to rules, with respect to some governmental goal, set by government and that have sanctions implied if organizations and firms do not adhere to them. These either explain certain procedures or better explain particular laws and the imposition of particular behavior on individuals and organizations. Regulation can be of three types: (a) economic (i.e., that which regulates economic activity), (b) safety (i.e., related to personal and workplace safety), and (c) information (i.e., the requirement to make certain types of information readily available). Some regulations are legislated and thus become laws, while others may be issued by public organizations. Given that there tend to be many governmental regulations (since not all are legislated and, therefore, readily available to the public at large), there is a propensity of bureaucrats to use regulations for personal gain. In addition, strict regulation may actually be counterproductive to government since it is costly to enforce. See, e.g., K. Konrad and G. Torsvik, "Dynamic Incentives and Term Limits in Bureaucracy Regulation," *European Journal of Political Economy,* 1997, 13(2), pp. 261–79.

Regulator: An agency or individual that has been given the power to regulate industries and sectors. A regulatory body is a governmental entity that has been created to administer laws that regulate any form of activity or sector (such as power and utilities) and/or supervise firms operating in that sector. *See also* **Watchdog group**.

Regulatory capture: Occurs when a regulatory body becomes more concerned about the welfare of the industries it is regulating rather than that of customers or society. Regulatory capture is likely to occur, for example, when the regulator is forced to recruit experts from the regulated industry itself (due to expertise constraints), or when the industry is very powerful economically and politically. See, e.g., J. Wilson, "The Politics of Regulation," in T. Ferguson and J. Rogers (eds.), *The Political Economy: Readings in the Politics and Economics of American Public Policy,* Armonk, NY: M.E. Sharpe, 1984, pp. 82–103.

Regulatory forbearance: Denotes the latitude that regulatory agencies may take in overseeing public-sector agencies. In other words, the oversight is not always prescriptive and regulatory agencies are flexible in their treatment of the particular regulations. Such regulatory forbearance can be either implicit or explicit. Implicit forbearance refers to an unwritten understanding that the regulatory agency will have greater latitude, while explicit forbearance signals that the latitude will be specified in writing (for example, the range of deviation that it will tolerate in performance).

Regulatory framework: The rules and system within which regulations related to a particular economic sector are formulated, monitored, and enforced. This includes processes concerning how a regulatory body (and the regulators) is determined, and what specific functions are given to the regulatory body. The framework also includes the avenues that are open to those entities being regulated should they wish to challenge any decision of the regulatory body. For a discussion of the application of a regulatory framework, see, e.g., S. Shirai, *Searching for New Regulatory Frameworks for the Intermediate Financial Market Structure in Post-Crisis Asia,* ADB Institute Research Paper 24, Tokyo: ADB Institute, 2001, pp. 55–89.

Regulatory impact analysis: One of the most commonly used tools to ensure that there has been compliance with professional and other guidelines and standards set by another party or law. According to this analysis, regulatory agencies are required to conduct a cost-benefit analysis and select the regulatory alternative that is least costly. While this tool has obvious advantages, there are also requirements on it in terms of, for example, accurate data and rigorous analysis, which are not always readily evident, particularly in developing countries (precisely the settings where the impact analysis would be the most beneficial). See, e.g., R.

Lofstedt, "The Swing of the Regulatory Pendulum in Europe: From Precautionary Principle to (Regulatory) Impact Analysis," *Journal of Risk and Uncertainty,* 2004, 28(3), pp. 237–60.

Regulatory negotiation: An alternative method to rule making that is distinct from the notice-and-comment consultation method. In regulatory negotiation (or reg-neg, as it is also known), rules are drafted by an advisory committee and then shared for comments, which are subsequently negotiated if there is no consensus among the parties. Unlike in conventional rule making, the rules in the reg-neg method are collectively drafted by the affected parties. For an application, see, e.g., L. Langbein and C. Kerwin, "Regulatory Negotiations Versus Conventional Rulemaking: Claims, Counter-Claims, and Empirical Evidence," *Journal of Public Administration Research and Theory,* 2000, 10(3), pp. 599–632.

Regulatory policy: Any policy designed to regulate an economic activity or business so that considerations of net public benefits also feature into the process. Regulatory policies can be divided into competitive regulation (i.e., designed to ensure that competition is not stifled) and protective regulation (i.e., designed to ensure that consumers are protected from unreasonable price rises). For a discussion of regulatory policy in the context of information asymmetry, see, e.g., M. Armstrong and D. Sappington, "Toward a Synthesis of Models of Regulatory Policy Design with Limited Information," *Journal of Regulatory Economics,* 2004, 26(1), pp. 5–21.

Regulatory risk: Refers to a risk faced by firms that operate in an industry that is regulated. While all firms face commercial risks, those that operate in a regulated industry have additional risks characterized by the threat of regulatory intervention, particularly if the regulations or their enforcement are not clear. This is an important risk to be considered in public-sector management because it is the government that sets up the regulatory agency and gives it its mandate. For a good discussion of this concept, see, e.g., D. Parker, "Performance, Risk, and Strategy in Privatized Regulated Industries: The UK's Experience," *International Journal of Public Sector Management,* 2003, 16(1), pp. 75–100.

Regulatory standards, convergence of: A situation where the regulatory standards of different jurisdictions begin to be uniform, i.e., they converge at a particular uniform standard. Such standards apply to products and industries that cross jurisdictional boundaries, such as regards exports and imports, where it makes sense to ensure that trading partners are applying the same rules of, for example, inspection and of quality.

Reimbursement: Funding an organization, or paying back an individual, after certain transactions have been completed. Thus, for example, a state government might meet all relevant costs of a federally mandated mental-health program from its own budget for which it would be reimbursed by the federal government.

Reinforcement: Encouragement given to someone in relation to a particular work-related behavior. Reinforcement can be positive or negative. Positive reinforcement occurs when employees are rewarded for demonstrating some desired behavior. Negative reinforcement occurs when an employee behaves as prescribed so that he/she does not get an organizational sanction.

Reinvention exercises: Efforts at public-management reforms undertaken by the Clinton administration in the United Sates which, at the federal level, sought to eliminate duplication to increase the speed with which governmental agencies responded to fast-changing public needs. Some other notable elements of the exercises included outsourcing and streamlining organizational SOPs (standard operating procedures). See, e.g., G. Caiden, "Administrative Reform—American Style," *Public Administration Review,* 1994, 54(2), pp. 123–28.

Reinvention laboratories: Resulting from the public-management reforms (i.e., the National Performance Review) undertaken by the Clinton administration in the 1990s, reinvention laboratories were instituted across the federal government as a way to give more authority to lower levels of bureaucracy to come up with innovative ways of doing things. A reinvention laboratory subscribed to the following four principles of the NPR: (a) putting customers first, (b) empowering employees to get results, (c) cutting back to basics, and (d) eliminating unnecessary bureaucracy. Key to the success in a reinvention laboratory was the delegation of authority so that decisions could be made without having to go up the hierarchical chain of command. For an analysis of the reinvention laboratory, see, e.g., J. Thompson, "The Reinvention Laboratories: Strategic Change by Indirection," *American Review of Public Administration,* 2000, 30(1), pp. 46–68.

Reinventive learning: *See* **Organizational learning**.

Relational contract: A contract between parties that does not wholly focus on a plan of action (such as delivery of goods or services) but rather on a set of general policy goals and on the criteria to be used when unforeseen contingencies arise. A relational contract has several characteristics: (a) it is generally of a long-term orientation, (b) the parameters of the relationships between the provider and purchaser are deliberately kept flexible, (c) the provider is expected to facilitate, and be much more involved in, the process of the organizational use of the services and outputs provided, and (d) the provider is expected to be actively involved in all production stages—specification, design, delivery, and monitoring and evaluation. For an economic perspective on relational contracts, see, e.g., G. Baker, R. Gibbons, and K. Murphy, "Relational Contracts and the Theory of the Firm," *Quarterly Journal of Economics,* 2002, 117(1), pp. 39–84.

Relationship capital: Goodwill that is generated for an organization as a result of frequent meetings with those outside the organization, and by sharing with them relevant experience and offering minor assistance at times. Relationship capital helps in the proper functioning of organizational networks, and is considered an aspect of the intellectual capital of the organization. See, e.g., M. Sarkar et al., "The Influence of Complementarity, Compatibility and Relationship Capital in Alliance Performance," *Journal of the Academy of Marketing Science,* 2001, 29(4), pp. 358–73. *See also* **Intellectual capital**.

Relationship letter: A written communication from a control agency (for example, a state treasury) to a governmental department setting out the expectations of financial management for the fiscal year ahead. The letter then acts as a guideline to how departments should carry out and document their transactions. The letter does not supplant any legislative arrangement that exists on financial management and reporting; what it does do is provide proper directions to departments on the administrative requirements of their resource use.

Relationship Q framework: A tool used in management development that provides a detailed picture of the relationships initiated and fostered by senior managers both within and outside the organization. This allows proper targeting of development programs to senior managers, especially in areas of interpersonal relationships. For a discussion of the framework, see, e.g., G. Lee, "The Relationship Dimension in Management Development," *Organizations & People,* 2001, 8(3), pp. 32–40.

Relative autonomy: A situation where two entities (such as institutions) have a fair degree of autonomy but are linked to some extent (such as through representation on a board of directors). For example, an organization that provides management training to senior public servants may have a relationship of relative autonomy with one that provides services to the pool of employees that feed into the senior ranks. In such a case, there would be a considerable business case to be made for, say, some overlap in the composition of the board of directors of the two organizations. See, e.g., T. Bilton et al., *Introductory Sociology,* 3rd edition, London: Macmillan, 1996, p. 668.

Relative performance evaluation: Measurement of a staff member's performance relative to peers rather than against specific *ex ante* targets set for individuals. While relative performance evaluations have some limitations, they are also very useful to organizations. For example, such evaluations help supervisors better appreciate the contributions of staff members since they can use the performance of colleagues as a benchmark. This can help in the determination of performance gaps across staff members. On the negative side, if collectively the team is not at its potential, then benchmarking individual performance against a lower team level is apt to yield lower standards of performance. *Cf.* **Absolute performance evaluation**.

Relevant capabilities: Refer to the capabilities that an organization seeks to enhance, which help it match what is being demanded by citizens, donors, and other stakeholders. This is not an insignificant issue. An organization could be so preoccupied with strengthening internal capability, for example, that it might lose sight of what it really needs to be good at doing, which is to serve clientele. The relevant capabilities come only from attempting to respond to the demands of their customers. See, e.g., A. Halachmi, "Improving Productivity Through Demographic Literacy," in A. Farazmand (ed.), *Handbook of Bureaucracy,* New York: Marcel Dekker, Inc., 1994, pp. 373–83.

Reliability: A concept that allows researchers and analysts to determine the degree to which a measure or test is reliable in determining whatever outcome is sought. The term is commonly attributed to the notion of replicability, i.e., if the measure or test were to be re-employed in another setting, how reliable would it be in explaining the impact in the new setting? For a cogent analysis of the term, see, e.g., M. Hammersley, "Some Notes on the Terms 'Validity' and 'Reliability,'" *British Educational Research Journal,* 1987, 13(1), pp. 73–81. *See also* **Validity**.

Reliability assurance: *See* **Quality assurance**.

Remediableness criterion: As used in policy analysis, this concept holds that analysts must display a superior feasible alternative to the one that they hold at any one time. Only when no such alternative can be formulated, which is also clearly implementable, will the one that has been determined be considered efficient. Economist Oliver Williamson asserts that this criterion is useful in remedying the asymmetric state of affairs that is encountered by policy analysts while formulating feasible organizational and policy alternatives. See O. Williamson, "The New Institutional Economics: Taking Stock, Looking Ahead," *Journal of Economic Literature,* 2000, 38(3), pp. 595–613.

Remedial training: Training that is given to an employee who is in need of overcoming certain deficiencies in his/her prior training (such as on numeracy skills when the job demands shift over time). Organizations may be willing to provide such training to existing staff members rather than recruit anew because the benefits could outweigh the costs.

Removal only for cause: Removal of a public employee only for a demonstrable cause such as malfeasance, dereliction of duty, and gross insubordination. Generally, however, removal only for cause is difficult to put into practice because the "for-cause" test is almost impossible to meet. See, e.g., R. Moe, *The United States: A Country Study in Organization and Governance,* Paper presented at the OECD Governance of State Agencies and Authorities Expert Meeting, Paris, 19–20 April 2001, p. 12.

Remuneration band: *See* **Salary band**.

Remuneration in kind: When an employee is paid in goods and service instead of in money (for example, fully furnished housing, paid membership in superannuation schemes, etc.). Remuneration in kind may be specified in the employment contract so that the employer gains the flexibility to manipulate it as the situation warrants.

Remuneration package: The specification of all related compensation that an employee is entitled to as part of the work he/she is to perform. The remuneration package includes specification of monetary and non-monetary rewards (if any). The package could be negotiated in a contract discussion between the employer and the employee on an individual basis (i.e., not as part of the collective-bargaining process).

Rent-seeking behavior: Refers to the tendency of firms, individuals, and even governments to not invest resources for continued growth but to extract such resources from others. In that sense, rent-seeking behavior is not considered to be productive. When the organizational leadership engages in rent-seeking behavior (such as giving themselves high fringe benefits, lucrative contract incentives, etc.), it is termed managerial rent-seeking. For a discussion of this concept, see, e.g., A. Vining, "Internal Market Failure: A Framework for Diagnosing Firm Inefficiency," *Journal of Management Studies,* 2003, 40(2), pp. 431–57.

Reorganization: The process of changing the administrative structure, formal procedures, and accountability relationships to promote bureaucratic responsiveness. Reorganization thus changes the power relationships that exist in government. Reorganizations are popular because they allow governments to tinker with organizational alignment in the public sector in a visible manner to create the impression that some action is being taken to address a particular problem. For a discussion of how reorganization shapes an agency's operating environment, see, e.g., K. Meier, *Politics and the Bureaucracy: Policy-Making in the Fourth Branch of Government,* 4th edition, Orlando, FL: Harcourt College Publishers, 2000, pp. 148–49.

Repeated relationship: Where two or more parties expect to interact repeatedly and continuously in the future. In the public sector, repeated relationships can occur, for example, between a governmental department that wishes to contract out the delivery of some services to communities and a nongovernmental organization that is active in the particular locality. Repetition would enter the picture when the organization can demonstrate that it can provide the services efficiently and effectively, and when the purchaser (i.e., the governmental department) faces greater transaction costs in seeking new providers every year.

Repetitive strain injury: *See* **Occupational overuse syndrome**.

Rephasing: Transferring any unspent monies from one financial year to the next for the same activity or project. Normally, all unspent funds in a financial year revert to the central treasury. Rephasing enables managers to better plan for multiyear budgets and activities since that will tend to cut down on the perverse incentive to spend unutilized funds rather than have it revert unspent to the treasury.

Reporting: Making available relevant information on: (a) the progress that an organization is making during the year, and (b) what the department has achieved against what was specified (*ex post* reporting). A reporting agency is a public organization that has been mandated primarily to report to the legislature and to the public about the state of affairs in a particular sector. The legislature ensures that the agency has the legal wherewithal to collect all necessary and relevant information, and the reports are made public as and when they are ready for public dissemination. Reporting costs result because all reporting requirements incur transaction costs to the organization. At the same time, reporting costs are also incurred by the control agency in relation to activities related to contract negotiations and to monitoring processes. This second strand of reporting costs tends to be underestimated in the push for greater reporting (and disclosure) provisions. *See also* **Transaction costs**.

Representative bureaucracy: The principle that the bureaucracy has to mirror certain key characteristics of society (such as the gender and/or ethnic mix). There are several types of representativeness, for example: (a) demographic or descriptive (i.e., as a proportion of the population at large), (b) substantive (i.e., as that proportion of the population would behave and think), and (c) formal (i.e., one that takes place via a general election, or a formal process). For a review of this principle in the context of the "new public management," see, e.g., R. Kelly, "An Inclusive Democratic Polity, Representative Bureaucracies, and the New Public Management," *Public Administration Review,* 1998, 58(8), pp. 201–08.

Reprioritize within baselines: A term that refers to the demand made by funding departments to other public-sector bodies to meet service demands not through increased funding but through moving funds around different line items in the fixed budget. Reliance on such a reprioritization within existing levels of funding is said to be counterproductive in the long run as it negatively affects organizational capability. See, e.g., S. Upton, "The Role of the State," *IPS Policy Newsletter, No. 56,* Institute of Policy Studies, Wellington: Victoria University, 1999.

Repudiation of contract: The refusal (or withdrawal) by a contractual party to honor contract stipulations. In such a case, the contract is considered terminated, and the matter, if serious, is forwarded to a neutral party for further action. In many cases, a repudiation of a contract is prohibited by the contract itself, and mechanisms will have been usually built in to ensure that such a situation does not arise without recourse.

Reputational risk: *See* **Risk**.

Request for proposal: A solicitation that goes out from organizations for interested and capable parties to register their interest for providing certain products or services. The request for proposal should be released in such a way that it gives reasonable time to all interested and eligible parties to submit bids. For a review of the use of request for proposals to assess the degree of competition in a jurisdiction, see, e.g., E. Savas,

"Competition and Choice in New York City Social Services," *Public Administration Review,* 2002, 62(1), pp. 82–91.

Requisite situation: *See* **Manifest situation**.

Reserved rationality, principle of: An alternate model of rational choice under uncertainty which argues that resources should be committed in the present in order to deal with potential risks in the future. The principle presumes that risks be such that should they arise, the results would be catastrophic, and it also requires policy makers to specify *ex ante* the nature of the threat and response. For a case study of this principle, see, e.g., A. Whitford, "Threats, Institutions, and Regulation in Common Pool Resources," *Policy Sciences,* 2002, 35(2), pp. 125–39.

Reserved rights doctrine: A doctrine that details the specific rights of managers as concerns the marshalling of relevant resources for, and on behalf of, the organization and the determination of how best to use them. This is not negotiable, for example, during the collective-bargaining process with unions.

Residual conflicts: Disagreements that cannot be resolved at the organizational level and need to be taken to courts of law for adjudication. Such conflicts could be between organizations or between an organization and its employees. If the latter, residual conflicts can be resource-intensive to organizations not only because there could be reparations to be made to the employees, but also because they tend to demotivate workers, and this could have an adverse impact on labor productivity.

Residual inefficiency: Any inefficiency that remains in an organizational process after efficiency drives have been put in place. Residual inefficiency is then the threshold that the organization is not able to overcome and has to bear. This provides a cue to organizational leaders as to what is attainable and what is not given a particular level of funding.

Residual liabilities: As used in a public-agency context, this refers to any existing liabilities arising from the activities of disestablished governmental departments. Examples of such liabilities may be outstanding payments to former employees or to contractors for services provided. See, e.g., State Services Commission, *Statement of Intent 2002,* Wellington: State Services Commission, 2002, p. 29.

Residual risk: The remaining level of risk that cannot be avoided and which remains even after appropriate measures have been taken. The point is to make residual risk as minimal as possible to increase its acceptability. If it is still not within the threshold of acceptability, then the organization must reconsider the activity that initiated the risk.

Resource allocation: The manner in which funds are distributed to public-sector organizations and programs. The allocation is formalized in the legislature in the first instance. A key principle of resource allocation is that, to the extent possible, there should be sustainability of resource flow for a given period (i.e., recipients should be confident that once a funding decision has been made, the allocation of resources is regular).

Resource analysis: The process of reviewing and determining the level of economic resources needed for any future course of action. Used in policy analysis, this involves translating all required physical quantities of a product or service for a policy into monetary terms, and then assessing the impact that such resource requirements will have on the general government resource base as reflected in the budget.

Resource diversion: A process whereby resources intended for a particular policy action and/or target groups and beneficiaries are diverted as a result of the need for some administrative action (such as an increased portion of the budget going to salaries and overheads). Decisions on resource diversions are taken after careful consideration of the consequences since the political backlash of resource cuts can be severe.

Resource envelope: *See* **Budget envelope**.

Resource erosion: The depletion of the worth of particular assets (such as human resources) as a result of a lack of capacity and of asset-enhancement measures. Thus, organizations that do not invest in upgrading their human-resource base, for example, can be said to face the real possibility of resource erosion down the road. For an application of this term, see, e.g., S. Newberry, "Intended or Unintended Consequences? Resource Erosion in New Zealand's Government Departments," *Financial Accountability & Management,* 2002, 18(4), pp.309–30.

Resource power: Power that an individual or party secures by virtue of control over resources or their appropriation. Resource power is usually accompanied by gaining some other power that enables the holders to make decisions regarding resource allocations.

Resource-dependence theory: A theory that asserts that organizations need to be understood in terms of their interdependence with their environments, particularly on those on which they depend for their resources. Resource-dependence theory can help explain, among others, interagency collaboration. Since the theory holds that while agencies in general value autonomy and, therefore, tend not to seek cooperation, if an agency's resource base depends on some other agency, then it is inclined toward cooperation. For a discussion of the theory in relation to organizations, see, e.g., D. Ulrich and J. Barney, "Perspectives on Organizations: Resource Dependence, Efficiency and Population," *Academy of Management Review*, 1984, 9(3), pp. 471–81.

Resource-hungry bureaucrats: A term used to denote the apparently perennial desire of bureaucrats to increase the size of their budgets, which often leads to adverse behavior. The economist William Niskanen argued forcefully that there were certain assumptions about the behavior of bureaucrats that gave rise to this phenomenon, including that bureaucrats act to maximize their organizations' budget, and that legislatures (or those who provide the funds) do not carefully monitor the proposals put forth by the bureaucrats. Niskanen was further of the view that bureaucracies tend to oversupply services, and that, unless there were external influences, they did not usually seek out efficient input combinations. For his ground-breaking work, see W. Niskanen, *Bureaucracy and Representative Government*, Chicago: Aldine-Atherton, 1971.

Responsibility accounting: For costs to be managed economically, efficiently, and effectively, it is necessary to have a costing system that identifies from where the costs arise and who was responsible for incurring them. This system is known as responsibility accounting and is based on the recognition of individual areas of responsibility, called responsibility centers. *See also* **Responsibility center**.

Responsibility center: An individual area of responsibility that organizational members have. There are four types of responsibility centers: (a) cost center (where managers are accountable only for the expenses that are under their control), (b) revenue center (where managers are primarily concerned with generating revenue for the organization), (c) profit center (where managers are accountable for revenue and expenses and for generating profits), and (d) investment center (which is similar to a profit center but the manager is also responsible for capital investment decisions. The establishment of such centers helps employees to better target the focus of their work.

Responsibility charting: The process of mapping a group or entity's work processes in an organization. To do this, there is a need to look at, among other things, workflow in the group's particular unit in the organization. Responsibility-charting also has links to competency assessment since responsibilities in organizations are normally assigned to individuals based on their competencies.

Responsible administration: A notion that refers to any management of affairs being in proper response to the elected legislature as well as to the citizens the organization serves. This duality needs to be balanced well by all public organizations, although not all of them succeed in doing so. The strain arises when organizations perceive that elected representatives are not reflecting the demands of their constituencies who are also the customers of the services provided by the organizations. In this case, the political "direction" they receive from, say, governmental ministers, is not in consonance with what they see evident on the ground.

Responsible bidder: Any bidder that an organization judges to be capable of meeting its needs for which a specific contract is to be issued. Responsible bidders draw upon their current capability and past performance (their reputation) to distinguish themselves from others. Organizations normally keep an updated list of such responsible bidders, and usually send out requests for proposals only to them rather than make a public solicitation. *See also* **Prequalification of bidders**.

Responsible minister: In some Westminster jurisdictions (such as New Zealand), each public-service department has one responsible minister who represents the owner (i.e., the state) and who exercises oversight of the government's ownership interest in the department on behalf of the public. The responsible minister also signs the performance agreement with the departmental chief executive while the vote or purchase minister signs the purchase agreements. A department may have several vote or purchase ministers but only one responsible minister (who is also a vote minister). *See also* **Vote minister**.

Responsible unionism: The type of unionism that a government considers as not opposed to its policies on, for example, workforce management, and wage determination. Responsible unionism is cited as a factor in why some countries have managed to leverage their labor laws to better align the views of unions with governmental priorities and outcomes.

Responsive competence: Refers to the ability that elected political leaders would like to see in the public bureaucracy whereby bureaucrats would capably implement policies and follow the directions that emanate from the elected leaders. Responsive competence is a key ingredient of the dichotomy between politics and administration in advanced jurisdictions. For a discussion of this concept in the context of public services in advanced jurisdictions, see, e.g., C. Campbell, "The Political Roles of Senior Government Officials in Advanced Democracies," *British Journal of Political Science,* 1988, 18(2), pp. 243–75. *See also* **Neutral competence.**

Responsive configuration: A manner of response to politicians by bureaucrats where, in order to respond to the former's articulated (as well as nonarticulated) preferences, they end up minimizing attention to both the efficiency and the effectiveness of their own work. While this may help in addressing what the politicians want, it also leads to inconsistent actions by public organizations, and inherently compromises the politics-administration dichotomy.

Responsive evaluation: A type of evaluation that is flexible in design so as to incorporate any issue that is considered to be important in judging a program's merit and impact. It is primarily used when there is no explicit mandate for the program being evaluated. See, e.g., R. Stake, "Program Evaluation, particularly Responsive Evaluation," *Evaluation Practice,* 1991, 12(1), pp. 63–76.

Responsive public service: A term that is currently much in use across practically all jurisdictions, and is taken to refer to a public service that is aware of what citizens, as well as its stakeholders, want, and delivers on them. A responsive public service is also acutely aware of what standards of services are expected of it, and it strives to attain them in a transparent manner.

Restructuring culture: The tendency of governments to apply structural solutions to policy problems. Such a culture has been particularly evident in public-sector reforms since the 1980s, with a focus, for example, on policy-operations split and the split between the commercial and noncommercial functions of governmental departments. Such a split necessarily means that new organizations need to be formed. The restructuring culture has been strong in jurisdictions such as New Zealand, where governments have tried to address public-sector performance problems by considering restructuring options. There are obvious risks to adhering to such a culture, primarily that of the fiscal and productivity costs of major restructuring. For further discussions of the restructuring culture as evident in New Zealand, see, e.g., R. Shaw, "Rehabilitating the Public Service—Alternatives to the Wellington Model," in S. Chatterjee (ed.), *The New Politics: A Third Way for New Zealand,* Palmerston North, New Zealand: Dunmore Press, 1999, p. 195.

Results: Outputs or outcomes that are a function of the organization's activities. Results can be intended or unintended. Intended results will have been specified *ex ante*, and unintended results can be either positive or negative. The causal sequence of how the desired impacts are brought about (normally categorized as inputs → process → outputs → results) is termed a results chain; and results-based management refers to a strategy that enables an organization to be more focused on meeting the results that have been specified. For a comprehensive analysis of the experiences of different countries on "managing for results," see GAO, *Managing for Results: Experiences Abroad Suggest Insights for Federal Management Reforms,* GAO/GGd-95–120, Washington, DC: US General Accounting Office, 1995, chapters 2–5.

Results framework: *See* **Intervention logic.**

Retainer: (1) A payment to have access to professional services, i.e., to maintain preferential access to a professional adviser who is paid for services rendered but cannot accept conflicting offers from elsewhere. (2) Someone who is a political appointee and retains position by virtue of that appointment rather than through a merit-based career position.

Retainer power: Power exercised in a bureaucracy by those that do not have tenure (called retainers because they retain their posts by virtue of political appointment as opposed to merit-based careerists who are tenured). See, e.g., F. Riggs, "Bureaucracy: A Profound Puzzle for Presidentialism," in A. Farazmand (ed.), *Handbook of Bureaucracy,* New York: Marcel Dekker, Inc., 1994, pp. 97–147.

Retention: The act of encouraging public servants to stay on in public service. In an environment where there is a mismatch in the scale of remuneration between the private and public sectors, public organizations face the problem not only of not getting the best and the brightest to join the service but also of not being able to retain them. Several countries have tried to come up with motivational programs, such as the "Public Service as Employer of Choice" campaign in New Zealand, to help public organizations address this problem.

Retrenchment strategies: Refers to the strategies used by management to downsize the organization as a result of the need to lower costs. In management-union relations, retrenchment strategies are agreed to in advance (for example, one such strategy may involve layoffs, the circumstances of which will have been either spelled out in the labor agreement or there will be a requirement imposed on management to inform the union at the time of consideration of implementation). For a discussion of retrenchment strategies in use, see, e.g., S. Bashevkin, "Rethinking Retrenchment: North American Social Policy during the Early Clinton and Chrétien Years," *Canadian Journal of Political Science*, 2000, 33(1), pp. 7–36. *See also* **Cutback management.**

Retroactive legislation: Any law that is applicable for a period that predates its actual legislation. While retroactive legislation is not uncommon, governments do not readily opt to pass it either. In some areas, such as in taxation, for example, the general sense is that retroactive legislation should not necessarily be opted because this could discourage compliance. On the other hand, in other areas, such as remedial pay settlements, the government may be quite willing to pass retroactive legislative provided it has the resources to sustain the claims. *See also* **Grandfather clause.**

Revealed preferences: (1) A set of preferences that are made known by stakeholders and on whose basis policy makers engage in making policies. For example, governmental ministers may explicitly make their risk preferences known to their departments so that bureaucrats know what the government will tolerate in terms of policies. (2) Refers to preferences of economic players being inferred from their conduct and not by what they actually say they prefer.

Revenue: Another term for income. A good revenue measure is characterized by: (a) yield (i.e., the volume of revenue it can generate), (b) political expediency (i.e., the extent to which it has the support of politicians), (c) ease of administration (i.e., the simplicity with which it can be put into action and maintained), (d) consistency (with the government's economic and social goals), and (e) equity (i.e., it would not unfairly increase the burden on the poorer segments of society).

Revenue center: *See* **Responsibility center**.

Revenue mobilization: The process of generating revenue (resources) for a particular program or organization. This generally implies that organizations will think of innovative ways to generate the revenue (such as new partnerships with interested parties). In some instances, international organizations (such as the World Bank and the United Nations) help in revenue mobilization for countries (such as Rwanda and Afghanistan) that face particularly severe conditions.

Revenue sharing: The distribution of revenues generated by different jurisdictions (such as local and federal government) wherein there are some legally mandated rules concerning how such monies are to be shared. See, e.g., R. Cole and D. Caputo, "The Public Hearing as an Effective Citizen Participation Mechanism: A Case Study of the General Revenue Sharing Program," *American Political Science Review,* 1984, 78(2), pp. 404–16.

Reverse delegation: *See* **Subsidiarity**.

Reverse discrimination: A term increasingly used by those who oppose affirmative action to challenge the preferential policy treatment being given to targeted minority and disadvantaged groups over members of the dominant or the majority ethnic group.

Reverse privatization: Also known as "contracting in," this concept refers to a situation when the government begins to start producing and delivering services that were once being contracted out, or when it enters the market as a competitor itself in the production and delivery of such services. Thus, if, for example, the government tax department produces a software package on tax filing that competes with a product that is in the market and that has been produced by a private firm, this may be considered to be an example of reverse privatization. Many argue that the goal of government is to help foster a good business climate, not to compete in it. To proponents of reverse privatization, this is necessary to correct problems with the contracting process itself, stem limited efficiency gains, and reverse erosion in the quality of service delivery, particularly if there is a loss of broader community values. See, e.g., M. Warner and R. Hebdon, "Local Government Restructuring: Privatization and Its Alternatives," *Journal of Policy Analysis and Management,* 2001, 20(2), pp. 315–36.

Review: *See* **Evaluation**.

Revolving door: Where the prospect of future employment in an organization outside government provides adverse incentives for bureaucrats to behave unethically. Revolving-door restrictions are those placed on government employees regarding the nature of employment they may take upon leaving government service. There are different specifications of a revolving door, ranging from a lifetime ban to a one-year "cooling off" period. For a discussion, see, e.g., S. Kelman, "What Is Wrong with the Revolving Door?" in B. Bozeman (ed.), *Public Management: The State of the Art,* San Francisco: Jossey-Bass, 1993, pp. 224–51.

Reward power: The ability to control others by virtue of being able to give rewards or by promising rewards. However, such an incentive structure works only when the organization or individual entity has the authority to actually impart rewards, rather than merely promises. In that regard, reward power stems from resource power. *See also* **Resource power**.

Rhetoric: Regarded as the most common political strategy to achieve policy outcomes, the term refers to the use of persuasive language and imagery—as opposed to tangible evidence—to garner support for a policy. See, e.g., R. Ryan, "Master Concept or Defensive Rhetoric: Evaluating Australian VET Policy Against Past Practice and Current International Principles of Lifelong Learning," *International Education Journal,* 2001, 2(3), pp. 133–47.

Rightsizing: Reducing an organization's workforce to its optimum size. This is different from downsizing, which has an objective of merely reducing the size of the organization to any level that is possibly feasible. See, e.g., R. Naiman, "'Rightsizing' the IMF, the World Bank and the WTO," *Development,* 2000, 43(2), pp. 97–100.

Rigid issues: *See* **Wicked problems**.

Risk: The chance of something happening that could adversely affect organizational goals. Risk is measured in terms of likelihood and potential impact. The element of uncertainty is the central dimension in the study of risks; while risk refers to situations where the distribution of possible outcomes is known, uncertainty means that the distribution is unknown. Risks are also viewed in relation to time, and, therefore, irreversibility; this notion of irreversibility characterizes risk-management practices that dominate organizational decision making. Risks are of several types. Systemic risks, for example, are risks affecting an industry or set of organizations (such as the general banking collapse during the Asian economic crisis of the late 1990s). Risks can also be political, economic, or reputational: political risks fall on government ministers and thus on government; economic risks have to do with the potential for monetary loss; and reputational risks can fall either on a particular public organization or on the public sector as a whole—public perception is generally such that the two are closely linked. There is also no necessary relationship between economic risk and political risk (i.e., politicians can invoke suboptimal economic decisions for many years without incurring political costs), and, on balance, the incentives on politicians are to be risk averse in a policy sense even if this means adhering to suboptimal economic policies—see I. Duncan, "SOEs and Their Place in the Enterprise Spectrum," in J. Yeabsley and A. Sundakov (eds.), *Risk and the Institutions of Government,* Wellington: Institute of Policy Studies and NZIER, 1999, pp. 75–92. *See also* **Uncertainty**.

Risk acceptance: An informed decision by a policy maker to accept a particular risk and all its subsequent consequences in relation to a specific policy option. Risk acceptance implies that policy makers have analyzed the downstream effects of undertaking the policy that carries the risk.

Risk allocation: A process of assigning risks to the various parties involved with an activity. Such an allocation is usually reflected in the amount of premium to be paid upfront or a proportion of benefits to forego in the event of the risk playing out and there being adverse effects. Within an organizational setting, risk allocation is assigned—and then monitored—by managers with a view to ensuring that individual activities and processes are suitably weighted in terms of the risks they may carry.

Risk analysis: Systematic use of available information to determine how a risk would affect relevant goals, either at the organizational level or at the systems level. Risk analysis involves a detailed examination of the potential unintended and negative consequences posed by any recommended policy, and includes the quantification of the probabilities and expected impacts of the identified risks. Risk analysis precedes application of any risk-mitigation strategies. For a description of the practical dimensions of risk analysis with respect to a governmental agency, see, e.g., B. McNab, *Risk Assessment Frameworks—Basic Principles of Risk Analysis and Decision Analysis,* Ontario Ministry of Agriculture and Food, Guelph, Ontario, Canada, 1996.

Risk appetite: Refers to the tolerance for risks and the degree of chances that any party (individual or organization) is willing to take. Each organization's appetite for risks is unique and will vary according to any one (or a combination) of several variables, but would most likely include: the extent of its legal mandate, including any fuzzy boundaries around it; the intractability of the problem it is dealing with; the strategy(ies) it pursues to meet the mandate; its organizational culture; the management style of its leaders (although it could be argued that over time, this will tend to settle at a level that is determined by the organizational culture rather than by the leaders' styles); and the responsible government minister's own tolerance for risks.

Risk assessment: Process of identifying, categorizing, and ascertaining the impact and likelihood of risks to an organization, program, etc. Tools such as a risk register and a risk profile matrix are used to describe and assess risks. *See also* **Comparative risk assessment**.

Risk aversion: Preference for not taking any risks, or when people prefer a lower level of risk for the same level of expected benefit. It is generally believed that risk aversion is higher in public organizations than in the private sector, partly because public organizations have tended to associate risk taking with increasing the possibility of something going wrong and an adverse political reaction. Risk aversion is evident not only at the political level (for example, not taking contentious decisions) but also at the managerial level (for example, not willing to experiment with new systems and processes). See, e.g., P. Bernstein, *Against the Gods: The Remarkable Story of Risk,* New York: John Wiley & Sons, Inc., 1996, p. 239.

Risk avoidance: (1) An informed decision not to become involved in a risk-generating situation. (2) The term also refers to actions taken by organizations to avoid being subject to risk that may, however, still occur in its operating environment.

Risk communication: The act of conveying to a party the nature and status of risks that an organization faces and how they can be mitigated. The communication includes the steps that others (for example, staff members) need to take to manage the risk. Risk communication is an important component of the risk-management process in the public sector as it makes transparent the entire process. See, e.g., O. Renn, "The Role of Risk Communication and Public Dialogue for Improving Risk Management," *Risk, Decision and Policy,* 1998, 3(1), pp. 5–30.

Risk control: The implementation of policies and rules that are designed to eliminate or reduce risks that an organization could face in the future. Risk control can be effected by, for example, tightening contracting policies in organizations if a substantial portion of organizational work is normally contracted out.

Risk cost-benefit analysis: A refinement to the standard cost-benefit analysis that considers notions of probability and uncertainty in estimating risks and assigning monetary values to them, which are then included as costs. While this invariably results in inflated costs vis-à-vis benefits, it is considered necessary since it better reflects the situation on the ground. See, e.g., L. Thiele, "Limiting Risks: Environmental Ethics as a Policy Primer," *Policy Studies Journal,* 2000, 28(3), pp. 540–57. *See also* **Cost-benefit analysis**.

Risk, democratizing: Refers to ensuring that all stakeholders are aware of the risks in a policy and that the eventual policy decision will reflect that level of risk awareness. Democratizing risk has the advantage of bringing in the stakeholders prior to policy implementation, and thus better informing the implementation process, particularly as it relates to any risks that the organization may face at that stage. For a case study, see, e.g., T. McDaniels, R. Gregory, and D. Fields, "Democratizing Risk Management: Successful Public Involvement in Local Water Management Decisions," *Risk Analysis,* 1999, 19(3), pp. 497–510.

Risk differential: The differences in risk appetite between principals and agents. This is an important concept since principals are inherently risk neutral while agents are typically risk averse, and this differential creates an opportunity cost for principals. This variance in the perception of what level of risk should be taken could diminish over time if the same agents are used on a continuing basis.

Risk diversification: When organizations begin to invest in or focus on different portfolios in order to spread out, and thus reduce, their risks. Public organizations are less able to diversify risks since they cannot shift their mandates (or core business) as easily as private-sector firms can. However, it is possible for them to enlarge their contractual relationships, thus effectively diversifying their risks as well.

Risk estimate: Where an agency bargains with the legislature during budget time to allot for the risks inherent in being sued by consumers in the provision of services. Given a favorable bargaining outcome, then, the organization's budget would reflect the risk estimate in its final budgetary allotment. See, e.g., R. O'Leary and J. Straussman, "The Impact of Courts on Public Management," in B. Bozeman (ed.), *Public Management: The State of the Art,* San Francisco: Jossey-Bass, 1993, pp. 189–205.

Risk evaluation: Comparing the level of risk found during the analysis process for a particular policy or program with previously established risk criteria. Risk evaluations enable organizations to manipulate their risk-tolerance levels as well as inform organizational leaders about how best to manage and mitigate future risks.

Risk exposure: The extent to which government would lose if specific public policies proved ineffective. Risk exposure is simply measured by the costs to be incurred if risks do materialize, or by the level of costs incurred to contain any risks but the risks do not materialize. Generally, the greater the degree of risk exposure, the greater the tendency to risk aversion.

Risk financing: Methods applied to fund risk treatment and the financial impact of risks. Risk financing is closely tied to the level of risk exposure to which the organization is subject.

Risk hot spot: A situation wherein an organization finds itself in need of further knowledge and where the consequence of failing to bridge the knowledge gap is serious. Risk hot spots can effectively cripple organizations if they are not treated early enough. See, e.g., R. Hall and P. Andriani, *"Managing Knowledge for Innovation," Long Range Planning,* 2002, 35(1), pp. 29–48.

Risk identification: The process of determining the nature of risks that an organization faces. A strategic approach to risk management is to identify the potential risks against the organizational objectives and to then ascertain how best to deal with them. Two commonly used tools of risk identification are: (a) a risk review, wherein a designated team (either from within or outside the organization) considers all the operations of the organization in relation to its objectives and where the associated risks may lie; and (b) a risk self-assessment, where a bottom-up approach (i.e., an assessment by staff members themselves) is used to review activities at the lowest level and then fed upward in the organizational hierarchy to determine where potential risks lie for the organization as a whole. Often, organizations will use both tools to ensure that all potential risks are identified.

Risk indifference: When managers are indifferent to the level of risks that is inherent in a policy action. This indifference could stem either from ignorance of the severity of specific risks or from the knowledge that they have risk-control processes that will suffice in identifying and mitigating risks. For a discussion of the risk indifference of superiors and how binding contracts can put an end to strategic non-cooperation, see, e.g., S. Rose-Ackman, "Reforming Public Bureaucracy Through Economic Incentives," *Journal of Law, Economics, and Organization,* 1981, 2(1), pp. 131–61. *See also* **Risk neutrality**.

Risk limit: Also known as risk threshold, this refers to the extent to which an organization is willing to go to sustain any given risk. The degree of risk appetite is positively correlated with risk limits, that is, the greater the degree of risk appetite and risk tolerance, the greater the risk limits. Different public-sector agencies will have different risk thresholds or limits for even the same potential risk; that is because even though they operate in a similar environment, they will have different access to risk-mitigation measures and resources.

Risk management: The process of identifying, ascertaining degree of intensity, and dealing with risks. The main elements in risk management include: (a) establish the context, (b) identify the risks, (c) analyze them, (d) evaluate them, (e) treat them, (f) monitor and review the actions taken, and (g) communicate and consult with stakeholders. Organizations ideally try to maintain a proactive approach to a risk-management culture where they are able to reposition themselves for risks yet to be identified; but, in reality, most organizations end up reacting to the threats that emerge. For a review of risk-management processes and experiences in the public sector, see, e.g., Privy Council Office, *Risk Management for Canada and Canadians,* Report of the ADM Working Group, Ottawa, 2000.

Risk mitigation: Refers to using controls to limit exposure to particular problems in an organization. Risk-mitigation measures can be expensive and the organization may end up committing scarce resources for backup redundancies. Issues to consider in the risk-mitigation process include, among others, decision points as to when the risk is adequately managed and how best to ensure that the risk incidence is not repeated.

Risk neutrality: When organizations care only about expected value and are indifferent to the level of risk that is inherent in a policy action. In general, the higher the level of risk tolerance, the higher also the level of risk neutrality. For a discussion of risk neutrality of superiors and how binding contracts can put an end to strategic non-cooperation, see, e.g., S. Rose-Ackman, "Reforming Public Bureaucracy Through Economic Incentives," *Journal of Law, Economics, and Organization,* 1981, 2(1), pp. 131–61. *See also* **Risk indifference**.

Risk optimization: Refers to purposive action by organizations to understand their risk limits and, through an iterative process, to settle on a risk level with which they are comfortable (as, for example, reflected in the revealed risk preferences of the board of directors). The iterative process implies that there is an initial period when organizations experiment with the appropriate level of tolerable risk.

Risk owners: Individuals and entities that are assigned responsibility and authority for the management of specific risks. Thus, for example, the human-resource department in an organization could be assigned as a risk owner for the organization's move to a bonus-based performance management system, with all its consequent risks. Owners of risks shift internally as responsibilities are reapportioned in organizational restructuring, and systematically as the machinery of government changes.

Risk perception: The presumed degree of risk that is inherent in any problem situation. Risk perception varies among different parties in keeping with their appetites (tolerance) for risks, and manifests itself in the revealed risk preferences of all relevant parties. The risk preferences of all relevant parties are assessed in the risk profiling and identification stage of risk management.

Risk pooling: The process of amalgamating several risky ventures that have uncertain return rates but where the negative incidence in one will not lead to the same in others. Large organizations can more easily engage in risk pooling because they can net out the return rates to still come out a winner.

Risk portfolio: The risks that are inherent in the activities and interests of an organization. The concept of a risk portfolio assumes that various risks share certain attributes and/or that they are interrelated. For this purpose, risks tend to be considered in groups (as in portfolios) and the degree of concern over them tends to vary with how specific risks in the portfolio are viewed. Risk-portfolio optimization is the process of determining an organization's risk appetite and seizing whatever opportunities may present themselves given such an appetite. See, e.g., KPMG, *Understanding Enterprise Risk Management: An Emerging Model for Building Shareholder Value,* New York: KPMG, 2001, p. 5.

Risk-portfolio optimization: *See* **Risk portfolio**.

Risk profiling: Detailing a specific risk that an organization faces. The profiling generally consists of: (a) determining what the specific risk is, (b) ascertaining the ownership of the risk, (c) specifying the degree of probability of risk occurrence, (d) specifying the level of impact of such risk occurrence, (e) calculating the magnitude of the risk (degree of probability times the level of impact), and (f) detailing the specific risk-mitigation measure.

Risk ratings: Ratings that are prepared for particular risks that an organization faces. The ratings can be done on individual items, such as projects and activities, to denote which ones are of less risk. The ratings are reflective of different gradations of criticality as well as of the risk perceptions of those doing the rating.

Risk reduction: Application of methods to minimize the likelihood and/or the adverse consequences of risks. Risk reduction in policy making involves, among other things, approaching lawmakers individually because group participants tend to support risky alternatives given the sense of diffusion of responsibility in a group setting.

Risk register: A register in an organization that records for each risk its: (a) source or origin, (b) nature (including its defining attributes), (c) existing controls, (d) impact and likelihood, (e) initial rating (which could be a subjective result), and (f) degree of vulnerability to factors both within and outside the organization. A risk register affords management the opportunity to best assess the particular risks that the organization faces.

Risk response: How an organization deals with the risks that it faces. Such response can be one of four types: (a) transfer—i.e., the organization can pay a premium to have a third party, such as an insurance company, bear the risks; (b) tolerate—i.e., do nothing and bear the adverse impact of the risk when, and if, it plays out; at times when the ability of the organization to do anything is minimal (or when costs are prohibitive), organizations may simply opt to tolerate the risks; (c) treat—i.e., contain the risks to an acceptable level using internal control measures; and (d) terminate—i.e., end the particular activity that is generating the risks in the first instance (not necessarily an option, however, for some public-sector agencies). *See also* **Internal control**.

Risk retention: The act of intentionally deciding to retain the responsibility or financial burden of an impending risk rather than passing it on to, say, customers. Organizations may decide to retain risks in order to protect their customer base, particularly if they feel the associated costs may be manageable in the final analysis.

Risk scanning: Refers to the process of reviewing an organization's operational environment and determining what risks loom in the horizon and their potential magnitude. Organizations use environmental-scanning techniques to get a better sense of what their environment holds for them. *See also* **Enterprise risk management**.

Risk sharing: When two or more parties decide to share the risks that are associated with a particular venture. Such a decision to share is generally formalized in a contract between the parties. Optimal risk sharing between the two parties involves balancing the costs of such sharing with the incentive gains that could potentially result. Risk sharing can be voluntary (as in two or more organizations coming together of their own volition to address a problem) or directive (as when cabinet decisions necessitate the sharing of a given risk in the public sector).

Risk shift: A result of groupthink where—due to the illusion of unanimity and certainty of action—decision makers tend to take bigger risks because of the perceived unanimity and certainty. Risk shift is possible in any group setting in the public or private sector.

Risk strategy: A strategy that an organization effects to deal with risks that it foresees in its business. A risk strategy invariably includes ways in which the organization will deal with risks in any or all combinations of avoiding, internalizing, sharing, or mitigating the identified risks. The strategy will also specify which parties are to play what part in managing the risks.

Risk structure: Refers to how an organization deals with risks, including setting up appropriate management processes. A risk structure will encompass roles and responsibilities for managing risk, accountability, and reporting lines. The structure is not necessarily rigid, though, since many risks may not be amenable for treatment just by relying on the organization's standard operating procedures.

Risk threshold: *See* **Risk limit**.

Risk tolerance: *See* **Risk appetite**.

Risk transfer: The process of shifting the responsibility and burden of dealing with the consequences of risks to another party. Such a transfer is usually done by paying a premium to another party (for example, an insurance agent). As a method of risk mitigation, risk transfer is the first option for organizations after risk avoidance.

Risk treatment schedule: A risk treatment schedule documents the management controls to be adopted to handle a potential risk that an organization may face or one that it does. The schedule includes information on: (a) the locus of responsibility for implementation of the plan, (b) the level of resources to be utilized, (c) budget allocation, (d) timetable for implementation, and (e) details of the methods and frequency of a review of compliance to appropriate standards.

Risk-adjusted net present value: In investment projects whose benefits are long term and qualitative (such as, for example, leadership development in the public service), traditional net present value (NPV) calculations are difficult and do not necessarily help in making rigorous investment decisions. To this traditional technique has been added a richer source of analysis, one that adds the notion of risk. Risk-adjusted NPV places emphasis on risks and risk management in investment decision making. It argues that if particular risks can be weighted and inserted into the derivation of the discounted costs and benefits, then decision makers get a better picture of whether or not their investments will yield a high return down the road. For a particular formulation of the concept, see C. Davis, "Calculated Risk: A Framework for Evaluating Product Development," *MIT Sloan Management Review,* 2002, 43(4), pp. 71–77.

Risk-ambiguity aversion: A term that denotes that policy makers prefer to take risks based on known—rather than unknown—probabilities. The critical missing element in this is information. This is a common occurrence in policy making and goes to some extent to explain the risk-averse nature of the public sector. A cogent discussion of the term is given in D. Ellsberg, "Risk, Ambiguity, and the Savage Axioms," *Quarterly Journal of Economics,* 1961, 75(4), pp. 643–69.

Risk-appropriate behavior: Behavior of organizations and individuals that are suitable to the risks they face. If banks, for example, face a potential problem of nonperforming loans, then they are expected to recalibrate their behavior such that they begin to look more closely at the policy of extending credit (for example, by insisting on collateral). Or, if a public agency's mandate undergoes some changes, then it may well demonstrate a changed risk behavior in keeping with its new role.

Risk-based budgeting system: A budgeting system that requires the rank ordering of projects based on their relative calculated risks. Allocation decisions are then partly based on the risk factors established for each project. See, e.g., M. Emmert, M. Crow, and R. Shangraw, "Public Management in the Future: Post-Orthodoxy and Organization Design," in B. Bozeman (ed.), *Public Management: The State of the Art,* San Francisco: Jossey-Bass, 1993, pp. 345–60.

Riskless assets: Assets that do not carry any risks in retaining them. Government bonds are an example of near-riskless assets because capital and interest payments are supported by the government's power to tax.

Risk-pooling capacity: The capacity of organizations to handle some risks when they occur by being able to net out the losses and gains that result from specific actions. The risk-pooling capacity is greater in organizations that can diversify their risk portfolios.

Risk-return trade-off: A balancing act that is done between how much risk to take in the expectation of a particular level of return. A related term, risk-reward ratio refers to the level of return that a party perceives may come out of an activity as a proportion of how much risk is perceived to be inherent in that activity.

Risk-reward ratio: *See* **Risk-return trade-off**.

Robust policy: A policy that is based on rigorous analysis and which is expected to produce most or all of the *ex ante* desirable effects. Robust policies are characterized by, among others: (a) comprehensive consideration of all aspects of the policy, (b) reliance on evidence-based analysis where the evidence is considered to be reliable, (c) consideration of the views of all stakeholders, and (d) review of all risks and unintended consequences and how they might be mitigated should they materialize.

Role ambiguity: (1) The lack of clarity in the minds of employees around just what exactly they are to do in the particular post and how that contributes to the fulfillment of an organizational mandate. Employees with role ambiguity often have a low level of intrinsic motivation. (2) The term is also used to denote social alienation among individuals in societies when, due to rapid changes in their environment, they are unsure of their roles or their place in society. The development sociologist Denis Goulet highlights this as one of the negative features of the sort of development philosophy that was evident until the 1990s when the concept of sustainable human development gained greater currency. See D. Goulet, "Development: Creator and Destroyer of Values," *World Development,* 1992, 20(3), pp. 467–75.

Role analysis: A systematic review of what a particular role in an organization hierarchy requires. Such an analysis is based on the responsibilities that the role bears and the knowledge, skills, and abilities that are required to fulfill them effectively.

Role clarification: The process of ensuring that different employees and groups in organizations understand what is expected of them so that resources are maximally employed in fulfilling organizational mandates. Role clarification becomes particularly relevant when organizational mandates shift and thus when existing role definitions within the organization are not in alignment with the new expectations of the organization.

Role conflict: When an individual or group faces contradictory demands from two or more roles in an organization. Role conflict results from role ambiguity, and from the tension between what an individual believes in and what is required of him/her in the particular role in the organization.

Role overload: When a particular role expected of an individual has so many demands that the individual fails in meeting the obligations expected of him/her. Role overload is generally associated with role extension to multiple areas of work.

Role perception: Refers to how an employee perceives his/her role, which may be different from what is actually expected of him/her. When role perceptions do not mirror the actual roles assigned, role conflicts arise. See, e.g., B. Toffler, "Occupational Role Development: The Changing Determinants of Outcomes for the Individual," *Administrative Science Quarterly,* 1981, 26(3), pp. 396–418.

Role playing: As used in the context of training, role playing is a type of simulation in which different persons act out roles as parts of the situation being analyzed. This helps in viewing a problem or a situation in a more realistic light. Role playing is a particularly constructive learning technique whereby, for instance, senior managers and potential chief executives of organizations play out various roles that mimic the reality of everyday organizational work.

Roles, separation of: The separation (or decoupling) of roles exercised by governmental departments as a result of the application of new approaches of public management. The most common roles separation that has been evident in public sectors around the world has been that of policy and operations. The other common roles separation has been that of decoupling the funder, purchaser, and provider roles of government departments. For a discussion of the latter, see, e.g., R. Shaw, "Rehabilitating the Public Service—Alternatives to the Wellington Model," in S. Chatterjee (ed.), *The New Politics: A Third Way for New Zealand,* Palmerston North, New Zealand: Dunmore Press, 1999, p. 193–97. *See also* ; **Funder/purchaser/provider split; Policy-operations split**.

Rolling budget: Also known as a continuous budget, this is a regularly updated budget where an organization has a better view of its activities as they are being executed. Rolling budgets are useful when organizations cannot reliably forecast the future costs of activities. By enabling budgets to be rolled thus, organizations achieve the flexibility to plan more confidently for the medium term.

Root-and-branch change: Any change that is comprehensive and fundamental in an organization. A root-and-branch change is disruptive to individuals' orientation to their work and to their perception of what is expected of them in the changed conditions. Root-and-branch changes also affect the working parameters of other organizations that have significant linkages with the organization undergoing the change.

Root approach: *See* **Means-end analysis**.

Rotation: *See* **Reassignment**; *see also* **Job rotation**.

Routine learning: Where there is only superficial learning and where the imitator does not internalize all the nuances of the innovation. While making innovative impulses routine learning in organizations is laudatory, unless such learning is embedded in the organization (both in the people as well as the organizational systems and processes), it cannot said to have contributed to organizational development. For a discussion of the concept, see e.g., P. Cooke and K. Morgan, *The Associational Economy: Firms, Regions, and Innovation,* New York: Oxford University Press, 1998, p. 211. *See also* **Learning**.

Routinization: The process of applying the same prescription to how a particular task is done. Routinization is important to ensure that transaction costs are minimized and to avoid uncertainties in organizational action. See, e.g., D. Hickson et al., "A Strategic Contingencies' Theory of Interorganizational Power," *Administrative Science Quarterly,* 1971, 16(2), pp. 216–29.

Rowing vs. steering: Terms coined by reinvention advocates David Osborne and Ted Gaebler to refer to the two functions that government could be involved in (goal and policy setting, i.e., "steering"; and implementing policy, i.e., "rowing"). Osborne and Gaebler argued that governments should be more involved with steering, letting the private sector and nongovernmental organizations do the rowing. They gained fame for their assertions in the 1990s when the Clinton administration applied their notions of governance in public-management reforms in the United States. For an original discussion of the concept, see, D. Osborne and T. Gaebler, *Reinventing Government: How the Entrepreneurial Spirit Is Transforming the Public Sector,* Reading, MA: Addison-Wesley, 1992.

Rubber-stamping: Approving a policy without debating or analyzing it critically. The legislature of Singapore has been said to play largely a symbolic governance role, effectively limited to rubber-stamping executive decisions—see K. Ho, *The Politics of Policy-Making in Singapore,* Singapore: Oxford University Press, 2000, p. 73.

Rule credibility: A term that refers to the degree of credibility an organization has in the eyes of the citizens that it will follow its governing rules and mandate (for example, on matters of weeding out corruption in the workplace). This is considered to be an attribute an organization needs in order to perform effectively.

Rule of law: A situation where the laws of the land are adhered to in the conduct of business and where rules are independent of the agent applying them. This adherence implies predictability, which is considered to be one of the key determinants of good governance in a country.

Rule of simplicity: A rule that stipulates that there is no purpose to making anything complex or considered as necessary without due reason. Used in policy analysis, the rule acts as a basis to ensure that the search for policy answers is based on evidence; if none exists—or cannot be located—then the analysis of problems proceeds along simpler lines.

Rule of thumb: A way of doing something that works, whether it is scientific and technically "correct" or not. A rule of thumb exists when there is no higher-order logic that explains why a particular rule exists, and when there is no set way of determining how to deal with a particular case.

Rule-making authority: The powers that governmental agencies have which allows them to make rules without having to seek the approval of the legislature. Such rules have the force of law and it is mandatory for all parties that are affected by it to adhere to them. Rulemaking authority is useful in ensuring that the legislature is not bogged down in detailed administrative work, the broad principles of which have already been debated and accepted.

Rules of the game: The basic ground rules that dictate how any activity in the public domain will take place. The rules of the game have to be adhered to by all parties. An example of the rules of the game is in contract law that stipulates how contracts need to be structured and what the adjudication process will be should any party not adhere to the contract. For a discussion of the rules of the game in relation to regulation and regulatory risks, see, e.g., D. Parker, "Performance, Risk, and Strategy in Privatized Regulated Industries: The UK's Experience," *International Journal of Public Sector Management,* 2003, 16(1), pp. 75–100. *See also* **Framework rules**.

Rules-based approach: When decision makers adhere closely to all applicable rules in the implementation of policy. For example, the government may wish to maintain a prudent fiscal policy for which adhering to the rules-based approach means that, among other things, the government sector should be kept small. A rules-based policy, then, is one that conforms to recognized rules. The essential point in the rules-based approach is that the rule is independent of the agent applying it. See, e.g., A. Husain, "Hong Kong, China in Transition," *Finance & Development,* 1997, 34(3), pp. 3–6. *Cf.* **Discretionary policy**.

Rule-utilitarianism: Refers to the rightness that is attached to an act because it is considered good for society although is not necessarily in accordance with sound economic policy. Thus, for example, giving relief to flood victims is act-utilitarianism but not necessarily rule-utilitarianism since it could lead to a moral-hazard problem. See D. Weimer and A. Vining, *Policy Analysis: Concepts and Practice,* 2nd edition, Englewood Cliffs, NJ: Prentice Hall, 1992, p. 97. *Cf.* **Act-utilitarianism**.

Rural credit systems: Arrangements in rural areas in developing countries for the granting of credits. Rural credit systems are normally characterized by: (a) a fair degree of informal lending (i.e., not through banks but through money lenders), (b) lower levels of credit extended, (c) very high interest rates since the risks of loan default tend to be high, and (d) little (or no) governmental control over the activity. Where formal mechanisms do enter the picture, the interest rates are not as high but the level of credit extended tends to be the same.

S

Sabotage: The act of deliberately seeking to derail a policy. Sabotage occurs when an individual or party does not have access to either making views known on the policy (i.e., have "voice") or opting out of it (i.e., "exit"). Thus, if any of the stakeholders to a policy do not have avenues to give expression to their views, then the result is either sabotage or exit.

Sacred-cow entitlements: Any entitlement (such as social security) that is considered to be beyond attack from any political party or group. Sacred-cow entitlements invariably lead to institutional permanence since none dares raise their voice against them.

Safe fail: An attribute of a system that can recover from failure up to a particular threshold. For this to happen, the system must have an open communication field so that all the components of the system can contribute to remedying the error.

Safety management: As applied in an organizational context, this term refers to the processes, actions, and policies that deal with how matters of safety are handled by those whose responsibility it is to ensure such in organizations. The term implies an acknowledgment on the part of the leadership of the potential for errors in organizational work and how to prevent them, the formation of intra- and cross-organizational coalitions to address any safety-related issues effectively, and a willingness to invest in whatever it takes to maintain an aggressive safety-management culture. The range of functions that is implied by this term includes communication with all stakeholders on safety issues, public relations, and even terrorism and disaster preparedness for crises. While safety management was once considered to be the primary domain of emergency response professionals, it is now taken to encompass much more, particularly in the public service, since it is expected to respond to disasters and crises. Examples of safety-management work are evident in hazardous-waste management, risk management such as for disasters (fire, storms, earthquakes, terrorist attacks), transport safety, industrial safety, accident prevention, safety culture, etc. They also include behavioral issues in dealing with safety considerations, rapid-response frameworks, chain of command and role of public agencies, among others. Safety management is a relevant concept not only in high-hazard organizations (i.e., those where the risk of error involves dire consequences) but also in those that deal with mundane affairs. *See also* **High-reliability organizations**.

Safety needs: *See* **Needs hierarchy**.

Safety nets: Assistance mechanisms that governments have in place to support the poorer segments of the population from external shocks to the economy or influential stakeholders from anticipated effects of reforms. Safety nets can include unemployment assistance, food stamps, and so forth. See, e.g., K. Chu and S. Gupta, "Social Safety Nets in Economic Reform," in K. Chu and S. Gupta (eds.), *Social Safety Nets: Issues and Experience*, Washington, DC: International Monetary Fund, 1998, pp. 7–33.

Sailing-ship effect: Refers to the tendency of organizations to become locked into a particular process or policy option, and not able to change even when a more superior alternative looks available. The concept is traditionally used in the context of organizations not being able or willing to deal with new technological innovations. See, e.g., J. Howeller, "The Response of Old Technology Incumbents to Technological Competition—Does the Sailing Ship Effect Exist?" *Journal of Management Studies*, 2002, 39(7), pp. 887–906.

Salary: Monetary compensation received by employees for work done for an organization. Salaries are differentiated from wages by the fact that the latter are based on hourly or daily rates, while salaries are given for regular, full-time work over a period of time. Salary administration refers to the processes that are involved in managing the salaries of employees. This includes keeping an eye on salary movements drawn from managers' performance evaluation of employees, and ensuring that all salary records are updated and error free.

Salary arbitration: *See* **Salary negotiations**.

Salary bands: The range of salary that employees are paid by an employer. Salary bands offer employers some room to maneuver within the band without having to consider substantial movement outside the band for a particular employee. When reporting the salaries of public officials, some organizations use salary bands so as to protect the privacy of the individuals. See, e.g., State Services Commission, *Annual Report of the State Services Commission, 2003*, Wellington: SSC, 2003, pp. 123–30.

Salary negotiations: The process of discussing the determination of a particular salary level for employees. In organizations where collective-bargaining agreements are in effect, salary negotiations take place at set periods and collectively for all employees who are members of the union. When differences arise between employee expectations and management offers, salary arbitration is conducted, which is a process of resolving the conflict. Fixed-term contracts with set schedules offer one way out of having to conduct salary arbitration.

Salary retention: A situation where an employee retains his or her salary level despite role or position reassignment within the organization.

Salary supplementation: Financial support given by external parties (for example, donor agencies) to an organization so that employees involved in project-related work receive supplementary compensation to top up their own organization-specified salaries. Salary supplementation is used as a means to reward employees involved in special activities. It is often criticized in the context of donor-assisted projects in developing countries because it is not sustainable by national governments once the donor agency stops assistance, and also because it tends to distort local market rates.

Sanctions: (1) As applied in the public-management context, a sanction is related to regulation via which government can influence a conduct of business. (2) Sanctions can also be applied by organizations against employees as punitive measures against actions that are not in consonance with organizational rules and regulations.

Sandwich course: Any training course that mixes off-workplace training with workplace training. For example, the course may have the generic and theoretical materials for a particular subject matter presented in sessions outside the organization, and the practical applications may be taught on the job.

Satisficing: When decision makers settle for a less ambitious—rather than the best—result. This search for "good enough" results is based on the philosophy that there are too many uncertainties and conflicts in values in reality, and so it may be more sensible at minimum to satisfice. In satisficing, not all possible options are considered because the organization does not have complete information. Thus, often it makes sense to satisfice since the marginal cost of searching for additional decision alternatives may exceed their marginal benefits. For an original analysis of the concept, see H. Simon, *Administrative Behavior: A Study of Decision-Making Processes in Administrative Organizations*, New York: Macmillan, 1947. *See also* **Bounded rationality**.

Scalar chain of authority: A systematic ordering of positions and duties that defines a hierarchy of authority in the organization. Generally, in organizations where the scalar chain of authority is long, decision making takes a long time. For an early discussion of this concept, see, e.g., H. Fayol, *General and Industrial Management*, translated by Constance Stores, London: Pitman Publishing, Ltd., 1949. See also, e.g., M. Fells, "Fayol Stands the Test of Time," *Journal of Management History*, 2000, 6(8), pp. 345–60. *See also* **Chain of command**.

Scalar-criterion problem: *See* **Criterion problem**.

Scalar organization: An organization that has a set hierarchy that shows how commands flow downward and accountability upward.

Scarcity formulation: The assertion that it is because of scarcity of resources that choice enters into the decision-making process; and once choice is a variable, it is the price system that serves as an effective allocative mechanism because it allows decision makers to choose one alternative/good over another. The scarcity formulation sits at the heart of economics, which also ties in with the second core element of economics, i.e., incentives. If customers make choices, then providing incentives can influence the choices that they make.

Scenario analysis: A method of reviewing different scenarios as to the future state of any particular variable or situation. Such an analysis is necessary in order to make sound policy recommendations. The analysis also offers policy makers a more structured way of viewing the medium-term future. Such an analysis is used in scenario planning, which is a qualitative method employed where current and future trends in an organization's environment are analyzed to ascertain possible futures. This allows organizational leaders to contemplate the future state of the world and to evaluate any unanticipated opportunities and trends that may be thus inherent. One key step in the scenario-planning process is to conduct a test for plausibility which checks whether the future state of the world follows logically from what is currently known—i.e., given the existing key uncertainties, how plausible is it that the future will indeed look like what emerges out of the analysis? For a good treatment of this subject matter, see, e.g., P. Schoemaker, "Multiple Scenario Development: Its Conceptual and Behavioral Foundation," *Strategic Management Journal*, 1993, 14, pp. 193–213. *See also* **Potential-problem analysis**.

Scenario writing: *See* **Formal mapping**.

Scientific management: Refers to the best way of getting something done in an organization by distinguishing the methods that are the most efficient. It was Frederick Taylor who started the movement to develop a scientific and rigorous way of managing an organization. Toward that end, he proposed four underlying principles: (a) the need for a science of work, such as in terms of linking rewards with performance; (b) the scientific selection and development of workers; (c) the first and second principle to be brought together to achieve the best results; and (d) close interaction between workers and management. See F. Taylor, *Principles of Scientific Management*, New York: Harper & Bros, 1911. See also, e.g., M. Freeman, "Scientific Management: 100 Years Old—Poised for the Next Century," *SAM Advanced Management Journal*, 1996, 61(2), pp. 35–41.

Scientific method: A method of drawing conclusions about particular assertions that is based on the following sequence of procedures: (a) define the problem that is under study, (b) gather all relevant data on the problem situation, (c) form a working hypothesis, (d) experiment to test the hypothesis, (e) interpret the results, and (f) draw appropriate conclusions regarding whether to accept or reject the hypothesis. *See also* **Rational-comprehensive theory of decision making**.

Scope of bargaining: Refers to the parameters of the collective-bargaining process that are used by unions and management to negotiate. This includes, for example, wage levels, working conditions, and method of negotiations. The scope of bargaining needs to be agreed upon by both parties before the negotiating process can begin. Both parties are expected to adhere to the scope of bargaining, but, if necessary, it is possible to have the scope widened or narrowed provided both parties agree to the change.

Scott model: Related to the concept of organizational growth, the Scott model says that an organization passes through three stages (simple, integrated, and diversified). Based on a life-cycle concept, the model puts emphasis on the interplay of structure and strategy because each of the stages has an implication for the type of strategy that the organization ought to pursue. See B. Scott, "The Industrial State: Old Myths and New Realities," *Harvard Business Review*, 1973, 51(2), pp. 133–49.

Screening interview: An interview of a pool of suitable candidates conducted by an organization to determine which should proceed to the successive rounds of the selection process. Increasingly, recruitment firms—even on behalf of public-sector organizations—conduct screening interviews.

Screening principles (of policy alternatives): There are several principles on how policy alternatives should be reviewed for further consideration. Two that are usually considered are: (a) feasibility (including economic and administrative), and (b) political acceptability. They may not necessarily be complementary, however, as often what is politically acceptable may not be economically feasible.

Sealed bid: Refers to any bid that has to be submitted unopened to the party that is seeking to purchase a particular service. This is to ensure that gaming is prevented since no bidder knows what the others are offering. For any request for such bids, there will be a public opening of the bids so that all bidders and other interested parties can see that the process is fair and transparent. Sealed bids, however, are unlikely to extract the best possible price for the seller.

Seamless service: Service that is provided to citizens by governmental agencies that work with one another in a coordinated manner. The idea of a one-stop shop is an example of seamless service. For a discussion on how seamless service ties in with government accountability, see, e.g., National Audit Office, *Joining Up to Improve Public Services*, Report by the Comptroller and Auditor General, HC 383 Session 2001–2002, London: National Audit Office, 2001, p. 69. *See also* **One-stop shop**.

Search costs: Costs incurred by an organization looking for appropriate information, technology, and markets on any aspect of its operations, including contract management. Search costs are part of the transaction costs that all organizations have to incur; many tend to contract out such work in order to lower costs but also to gain a better perspective of the information being received.

Second customer: When organizations seek to acquire a new product, there will be some individuals who will be the first ones to test the product, and after it has met their approval, the product will eventually be available to all members of the organization (or those to whom the product is relevant). The first ones to try the product are called first customers, and the rest are second customers. In other words, in the early project stages, the customer in the organization may be a manager who uses the product for purposes of testing and approving its further development, while in the latter stages of the project, the end-user is the second customer. For an application, see National Audit Office, *Ministry of Defense: Through-Life Management*, Report by the Comptroller and Auditor General, HC 698 Session 2002–2003, London: The Stationery Office, 2003, p. 26.

Second-generation reforms: Public-management reforms that focus on the capacity of the public sector to implement economic policies. The first-generation reforms, by contrast, focused on macroeconomic and broad policies and in creating the right environmental conditions for the economy to grow. For a discussion of the issues to be considered while designing second-generation reforms, see, e.g., V. Tanzi, *The Role of the State and the Quality of the Public Sector*, Washington, DC: IMF Working Paper WP/00/36, March 2000.

Second-opinion function: In the public-management context, a second-opinion function is one where any central control agency, such as a central treasury, is entitled to have a second look at the financial assumptions that governmental departments make in their budget bids and their output pricing. The purpose of the second-opinion function is not necessarily an independent opinion but an assessment of whether the first opinion is well-founded.

Second-order benefit: A benefit of a program or policy that is indirect or secondary. For example, a drug-treatment program could yield a reduced crime rate in the future. Here, the reduction in the number of drug users is a first-order benefit, while the reduced crime rate is a second-order benefit. *Cf.* **First-order benefit**.

Second-order cost: Also termed a negative externality, this refers to the cost of a program or policy that is indirect or secondary. For example, one of the second-order costs of a power plant is pollution that cannot be controlled. *Cf.* **Second-order benefit**.

Second-order effects: *See* **Second-order policy impacts**.

Second-order imitation: *See* **Imitation**.

Second-order policy impacts: The term "second order" is taken to mean small or secondary to (as contrasted with a "first-order" impact, which is significant in size and is also more overt). It also refers to an impact that is derivative rather than initial. For an example of an application in economics, see G. Akerlof, "Behavioral Macroeconomics and Macroeconomic Behavior," *American Economic Review*, 2002, 92(3), pp. 411–33.

Second-order variation: *See* **Double-loop learning**.

Secondary decision: As applied in the public-policy context, this is a decision made by an organization to solve a problem that has already been identified. Such secondary decisions center on the instrumental means to create a problem-solving environment. Decisions in organizations on how to structure internal processes to better analyze a policy problem can be seen as secondary decisions. *Cf.* **Primary decision**.

Secondary failure: Any failure that is caused by a primary failure (i.e., it is subject to something else failing first). For example, a secondary failure in a governmental agency entrusted with the social welfare of children occurs when, by virtue of neglecting to take initial calls for help seriously, the organization is suddenly faced with an unmanageable caseload of serious problems in the management of child welfare. *Cf.* **Primary failure**.

Secondary legislation: Refers to the orders and regulations that the legislature sets in relation to a specific law. Secondary legislation is much simpler and quicker to pass than primary legislation because the basis for such decisions (i.e., the law) has already been passed. Governmental ministers prefer to use secondary legislation to primary legislation since the latter can be very time consuming. A related concept is secondary regulation, which is a rule or procedure that emerges from a law that allows an oversight body to regulate a particular organization or sector. For example, in New Zealand, the Public Finance Act allows the Treasury to regulate how governmental departments report financial performance. See, e.g., S. Newberry, "Intended or Unintended Consequences? Resource Erosion in New Zealand's Government Departments," *Financial Accountability & Management*, 2002, 18(4), pp. 309–30.

Secondary regulation: *See* **Secondary legislation**.

Secondment: Placing an employee in another organization for purposes of giving the individual an opportunity to enhance his/her knowledge, skills, and abilities by learning from different environments. Secondments are often used by organizations as a leadership development tool. When the sending and receiving organizations swap employees on a secondment program, it is known as back-to-back secondments. *See also* **Experiential learning**.

Sector program evaluation: Evaluation of a group of projects or programs in one particular sector, such as health, education, etc. Sector program evaluations are designed to take into consideration the impacts of policies and programs in a more holistic manner, and are necessarily more complex and expensive to undertake.

Sectoral review: As used in the public-sector context, a sectoral review is a review of a particular sector conducted by a central control agency so as to determine how public organizations involved in the sector are managing their affairs with respect to fulfilling their mandates.

Seed money: Money that is used to start an innovative project or activity. Governments usually put up the seed money in the hope that others will follow once the viability of the activity becomes evident. Conversely, the private sector can also provide seed money for the production of public goods, particularly if they see future advantages in terms of commercially marketing the products.

Select committee: A committee of the legislature that is established for a particular purpose (such as tertiary education reform) and for a set period of time. Hearings in the select committee may be open to the public, and the committee is also empowered to call experts to give submissions.

Selection bias: As used in the context of privatization, this term denotes the fact that governments tend to select relatively healthy public companies to privatize first so as to show impressive gains and to build forward momentum. See, e.g., W. Megginson and J. Netter, "From State to Market: A Survey of Empirical Studies on Privatization," *Journal of Economic Literature*, 2001, 39(2), pp. 321–89.

Selective attention: Term used to denote the propensity of an organization to focus more attention on one or more aspects of its mission to the detriment of others. For an example of an application of selective attention, see J. Wilson, *Bureaucracy: What Government Agencies Do and Why They Do It*, New York: Basic Books, 1989, pp. 101–05.

Selective behavior: When public servants focus on only a subset of the totality of what they are required to do. This can occur either when they do not possess all the information necessary to address the totality or when they wish to undermine specific aspects of a policy. For a review of the concept, see, e.g., A. Breton and R. Wintrobe, *The Logic of Bureaucratic Conduct*, New York: Cambridge University Press, 1982, p. 37.

Selective exposure: The tendency of a group to communicate predominantly with others who share its own way of thinking. Such selective exposure necessarily diminishes the rigor of any policy analysis that is carried out by the group, and may also contribute to difficulties in communicating with a wider audience, particularly if the policy or issue under consideration has potential for systemic impact.

Selective inefficiency: A mode of action that public servants tend to pursue when they are not in agreement with a particular policy objective and seek to deter its successful implementation with deliberate inefficiencies (such as lengthening the time it takes to administer service contracts). The eventual result of selective inefficiency, they hope, will be policy termination. For a discussion of the concept, see, e.g., R. Wintrobe, "Modern Bureaucratic Theory," in D. Mueller (ed.), *Perspectives on Public Choice*, Cambridge, MA: Cambridge University Press, 1997, pp. 429–54.

Selective learning: A term that denotes the fact that an organization will monitor, engage in, and implement only those actions learnt from someone else's experiences that are appropriate to its task at hand. This is not necessarily an adverse practice, however, since selective learning provides the organization with an opportunity to best use limited organizational resources. The disadvantage is that the organization may be missing key parts of the big picture that are necessary to maximize the benefits of the learning.

Selective outsourcing: The practice of determining what services can be provided in a cost-effective manner internally and then ensuring that the rest is contracted out. What this does is enable the agency to devote its energies to enhancing its unique business and its core competencies. See, e.g., C. Snow, R. Miles, and H. Coleman, Jr., "Managing 21st Century Network Organizations," *Organizational Dynamics*, 1992, 20(Winter), pp. 5–19.

Selective perception: The tendency of managers to either ignore information they are not comfortable with or to accept information that supports their viewpoints. It also refers to the tendency by individuals to perceive only certain aspects of an issue or problem. Selective perception is compounded under conditions of information asymmetry.

Selective radical approach: An approach to public-sector reforms where the government embarks on a limited number of reforms that are well targeted and radical enough to make a real difference, if successful. This enables the government to combine the advantages of the big bang and of gradual approaches to reforms, while at the same time minimizing the risks. In a selectively radical approach, a well-thought-out policy is implemented with determination and it seeks to change the status quo quite radically. For an application to the New Zealand public-sector context, see, e.g., J. Wallis and B. Dollery, "Understanding Cultural Changes in an Economic Control Agency: The New Zealand Treasury," *Journal of Public Policy*, 2001, 21(2), pp. 191–212.

Selective retention: *See* **Principle of selective retention**.

Self-actualization needs: *See* **Needs hierarchy**.

Self-appraisal: A review conducted on oneself. Self-appraisal serves as the initial stage in the performance evaluation of an individual, and is taken into active consideration in the determination of employee performance on the job. Self-appraisal includes reporting on the measurement of self-monitored objectives.

Self-deceiving state: A term used to denote those countries whose governments continually deny that there is a particular problem or that seek to misrepresent the reality of what is actually happening in the country, and, because of such self-deception, apply inappropriate models to solve the country's problems. A brief discussion of this phenomenon is given in M. Turner and D. Hulme, *Governance, Administration and Development: Making the State Work*, London: MacMillan Press, 1997, pp. 96–97.

Self-determination theory: Asserts that individuals are motivated toward particular actions when they have a choice as to when and how they can initiate and regulate their actions. This ability to regulate action enables individuals to opt consciously for a suitable time to initiate learning gleaned from other sources.

Self-development groups: Groups whose members come together to jointly consider how they could improve their personal development. In that process, group members share analyses and observations among themselves and support each other in their own development process.

Self-directed group: A group of individuals who know what is required of them, are capable of setting their own direction, and actively work toward it. While such a group does not need to be actively managed by an outsider, it is important that the group have a definite and attainable target to work toward. Self-directed work teams are designed to improve cross-functional capabilities because team members decide for themselves which particular area they need to focus on.

Self-employed: A situation where an individual is not employed by any organization but is engaged in work that is being remunerated by others. Self-employed workers are persons who work for themselves and who are sole owners of their businesses.

Self-enforcing contract: Refers to a contract in which neither the principal nor the agent has any incentive to renege. In the ideal self-enforcing contract, long-term wages, for example, are less variable than market wages (i.e., those applicable in the spot market), and each change in the wage levels in the spot market tends to have a self-correcting effect on the wage levels in the long-term contract. For a discussion of this concept, see, e.g., J. Thomas and T. Worrall, "Self-Enforcing Wage Contracts," *Review of Economic Studies*, 1988, 55(4), pp. 541–54.

Self-evaluation: *See* **Self-appraisal**.

Self-monitored objectives: Objectives that employees are expected to monitor themselves, and to provide feedback to management in terms of the extent to which they feel they have attained them. *See also* **Self-appraisal**.

Self-paced learning: Learning that is done at a pace set by the learner. The concept of open learning is based on this concept, and self-paced learning is applicable in both face-to-face and distance learning environments.

Self-regulating system: A system that is capable of identifying any problem areas in the operational process and of fixing them (thus being able to regulate them). For an application of this concept in organizational innovation, see, e.g., S. Harkema and M. Browaeys, "Innovation and Culture Revisited: A Conceptual Approach Based on Complexity Theory," *Organizations & People*, 2003, 10(1), pp. 9–16.

Self-regulation: When a profession develops its own code of conduct to ensure that members adhere to a particular standard. Self-regulation emerges because governments often have less information than professionals about specific situations and cannot possibly regulate everything in the market. It is thus left to the professional associations to regulate the professional behavior of their members.

Self-worth: Refers to how an individual views himself/herself, and how that manifests in his/her work life. Individuals who have a high degree of self-worth tend to get more intrinsic satisfaction out of their work.

Senior civil service: All jurisdictions have a formal (or at least well-defined) cadre of employees who have the ability to manage public organizations at the most senior level, and who constitute a unifying leadership force at that level. The senior civil service usually has its own terms and conditions of employment, and members of the service are expected to be fairly mobile across the public service so that they can add value to any organization that might be in need of their expertise. For a discussion of the various issues centered on the senior civil service, see, e.g., G. Bhatta, *A Cross-Jurisdictional Scan of Practices in Senior Public Services: Implications for New Zealand*, SSC Working Paper No. 13, Wellington: State Services Commission, 2002.

Sensitivity analysis: A method of ascertaining how sensitive the various results of management decisions will be given changes in some variables. In sensitivity analysis, some assumptions are first made around what the most likely decision impact will be; this is then followed by changes in the inputs (i.e., what go into making the decisions) to determine how the output (i.e., the impact of the decision) will change.

Sensitivity training: Training designed to make managers and organizational employees aware of, and sensitive to, the various issues that affect their work. This could include, for example, gender considerations in management action, workplace safety, race relations, and so forth. Such training is constructed around: (a) identifying the various themes/attributes that make up the particular issues, (b) how to recognize those attributes when they are present in the organization, (c) how to design an appropriate response to them, and (d) how to communicate that to organizational employees. Organizations normally bring in outsiders to conduct such training so that a fresher perspective is brought to bear.

Separation interview: *See* **Exit interview**.

Separation of powers: A principle of governance in which the three branches of government—the executive, the legislative, and the judiciary—are independent of each other. This separation of powers serves as an important system of checks and balances on the work of each branch of government. The U.S. political system is considered to be a very good example of a separation of powers in government.

Sequencing: In the context of public-management reforms, sequencing refers to reforms that take place in a country step by step and one sector at a time, such that sector A is reformed before sector B. For a discussion of this with respect to public-sector innovations in service delivery, see, e.g., R. Pjnto, "Innovations in the Provision of Public Goods and Services," *Public Administration and Development*, 1998, 18(4), pp. 387–97. *Cf.* **Compatible opening**.

Sequential interdependencies: As used in the context of organizations, this term refers to the fact that one unit cannot do its job until others have done theirs (i.e., the output of one serves as the input of another). *See also* **Pooled interdependencies**; **Reciprocal interdependencies**.

Sequential spot contract: Refers to a series of short-term contracts that organizations enter into with others (governmental organizations as well as private-sector service providers) and that allow organizations to be confident about the immediate future since spot contracts are issued for the short term. See, e.g., W. Ouchi, "Markets, Bureaucracies, and Clans," *Administrative Science Quarterly*, 1980, 25(1), pp. 129–41. *Cf.* **Contingent claims contract**; **Spot contract**.

Seriability: Refers to the ability of organizations to deal with problems in whole or in parts as subcomponents of a series. The latter allows the organization to fragment problems into individual components, thus enabling it to deal with them better.

Serial processing capacity: The ability to process or focus on only one issue at a time. This obviously makes it difficult for organizations to fully appreciate the complexities of decision making in an unstable and rapidly changing environment. *Cf.* **Parallel processing capacity**.

Servant leadership: *See* **Facilitative leadership**.

Service clustering: The process of delivering services to people by grouping them around their needs. Such clustering can include a co-located information referral (where citizens can get information about the range of services available to them and how they can access them), a co-located program delivery (where the services are provided from one source), and consolidated program delivery (where one agency is responsible for providing various types of services). See, e.g., Treasury Board of

Canada Secretariat, *Getting Government Right: Governing for Canadians*, Ottawa: Treasury Board of Canada, 1997, p. 11.

Service contract: A contract that an organization signs with another that provides specialized services, such as cleaning and regular maintenance. The organization uses a service contract to get some other party with specialized labor to provide the service because it does not need the services regularly enough that it should contemplate doing the work itself.

Service delivery: The process of providing services to the public. There are several approaches to analyzing service delivery. Governmental departments could provide the services themselves or contract them out. There is also the possibility of an inclusive approach to service delivery where government departments seek to bring into a partnership those that provide services at the community level.

Service delivery game: A type of game that is evident in a public bureaucracy that results from the interaction between street-level bureaucrats and citizens. At this front-level function, the bureaucrats have a very different perception of service delivery than those who are removed from interactions with citizens. See, e.g., L. Lynn, "Policy Achievement as a Collective Good: A Strategic Perspective on Managing Social Programs," in B. Bozeman (ed.), *Public Management: The State of the Art*, San Francisco: Jossey-Bass, 1993, pp. 108–33.

Service delivery responsiveness: Focuses on assessing the extent to which clients are satisfied with the services being provided. There are four dimensions of service responsiveness that are relevant: (a) Comprehensibility—do the receivers of services understand what they are entitled to? (b) Accessibility—are they easily able to get them? (c) Relevance—do they get the services that are relevant to their needs? (d) Participatory—can they be more actively involved in service delivery?

Service enhancement: The extent to which an organization's services to citizens are enhanced (i.e., either increased or delivered more efficiently and effectively). Note, however, that generally citizens are not necessarily concerned with efficiency in the first instance; that is, as long as they receive the services they seek, they are not very occupied with the costs unless they have to pay for them, such as through user fees.

Service implementation network: *See* **Network organization**.

Service quality: The quality of a service as measured by it being: (a) appropriate and relevant, (b) available and accessible, (c) equitable, (d) acceptable in terms of quality, and (e) economic, efficient, and effective. Service quality is measured in many ways, including through citizen report cards. *See* **Citizen report card**.

Service standards: Standards that are prespecified for organizations to meet or exceed in the delivery of services to consumers. Such standards are either developed through internal benchmarking or are based on levels of performance that are evident in the private sector. Some standards are borrowed from industry benchmarks. For a review of the application of service standards, see, e.g., N. Chiu, "Service Targets and Methods of Redress: The Impact of Accountability in Malaysia," *Public Administration and Development*, 1997, 17(1), pp. 175–80.

Service/user charges: *See* **Service fee**.

Setting analysis: Refers to an analysis of the environmental setting in the organization that determines the design and delivery of a particular training method. Conducted by the training provider, a setting analysis serves as a first-level investigation of the context within which the training is to be provided to organizational members.

Settlement risk: A risk that an organization faces whereby the others that are part of an agreement are not able to fulfill their own requirements. The burden of settling the particular claim then falls on the organization.

Sex discrimination: A situation where women (almost always) are treated differently (but always negatively) because of their gender in the areas of employment, application of rules and regulations, access to credit, and such. While sex discrimination is legally prohibited in most advanced jurisdictions, women are still paid less on average than men, often because they take career breaks, and they continue to face advancement hurdles at work. *See also* **Glass ceiling**.

Shadow cabinet: *See* **Shadow government**.

Shadow government: Refers to the main opposition party in the legislature (in parliamentary systems) that has all key governmental portfolios apportioned to their members such that they form a shadow cabinet to engage government ministers with sustained portfolio expertise. Members of the shadow government are likely to hold ministerial portfolios themselves if their party forms a government.

Shadow price: Refers to a price of a good or service that needs to be calculated by proxy because no reliable market prices can be ascertained. In that case, subjective estimates of prices that people might be willing to pay are developed. For example, the shadow price of an imported product could be the exchange rate that is used in the black market, if one exists in the country.

Shadow state: A term that refers to the fact that governments increasingly permit nonprofit organizations to play a greater role in the delivery of human services through contracting arrangements. See, e.g., W. Reno, "Business Conflict and the Shadow State: The Case of West Africa," in Ronald Cox (ed.), *Business and the State in International Relations*, Boulder, CO: Westview Press, 1996, pp. 149–64. *See also* **Hollow state**.

Shadow subsidies: When costs are not associated with the use of particular resources. For example, in the conventional paradigms of development, both women and the environment were taken as given resources and their input in the production process was taken for granted. This led to a situation where policy makers did not factor in the true costs of certain production.

Shallow poverty: A type of poverty where people move frequently into and out of poverty classification depending upon how prevailing economic conditions affect their specific livelihood.

Shaping: In the context of training, this term refers to the process of making employees more aware of newer ways of doing things. Such awareness is done in several small stages rather than all at once.

Share allocation decision: In the context of privatization, this term refers to the requirement for governments to choose one group of potential investors over another. How they decide who is to be sold which public assets is contained in the share allocation decision. See, e.g., W. Megginson and J. Netter, "From State to Market: A Survey of Empirical Studies on Privatization," *Journal of Economic Literature*, 2001, 39(2), pp. 321–89.

Shared revenue: Revenue that is levied and collected by one jurisdiction but shared with others. This sharing is normally done in proportion to the amount of contribution to cost made by each jurisdiction. *See also* **Revenue sharing**.

Shared services: When two or more entities (organizations, local governments, etc.) get together to use the same source for services that they jointly need. For example, two adjacent cities may decide that they should share one ambulance service since it is efficient for both of them in terms of lowering overhead costs. *See also* **Joined-up government**.

Shared values: A notion put forth by a central agency in a country's public service that while individual departments have their own unique mandates to fulfill (hence necessitating a possibly unique organizational culture), they also share values that cut across organizations and incorporate all of the public service. It is important that organizations cultivate this sense of shared values in order to develop a proper ethos of public service in the country. See, e.g., State Services Commission, *Statement of Intent 2002*, Wellington: State Services Commission, 2002, p. 16. *Cf.* **Silo mentality**.

Shareholder activism: Refers to a situation when even minority shareholders (i.e., shareholders who do not hold the controlling interest) can have a say in the business of the firm. Shareholder activism has been on the rise in several jurisdictions as a result of conscious government policies designed to ensure that there is some internal check on how big businesses are run. For a discussion of this term in the context of the Asian economic crisis of the late 1990s, see, e.g., G. Bhatta, "Corporate Governance and Public Management in Post-Crisis Asia," *Asian Journal of Public Administration*, 2001, 23(1), pp. 1–32.

Shareholder exit: The withdrawal of shareholders from a company through the sale of their shares. This concept is used in conjunction with the notion that while shareholders can exit a company in the private sector, "shareholders" in the public sector (i.e., citizens and service users) cannot. This has implications for how public-sector organizations engage their stakeholders.

Shareholder-wealth-maximizing model: A model that argues that a firm's primary focus should be to increase the returns to its shareholders. This is something that governments are beginning to consider as well, although it is clear that they have other objectives than maximizing shareholder wealth or profit alone.

Sick-leave bank: A scheme that encourages employees to pool their sick-leave entitlements such that they may draw upon them individually if a long-term illness necessitates more time than their usual entitlements. Sick-leave banks have tended to discourage absenteeism because of peer pressure not to take sick leave unless absolutely required.

Side payments: A term used in the study of coalition formation in organizations to denote actions undertaken by coalitions to entice other individuals or groups to join them in the pursuit of certain goals. Side payments can take many forms, including offers of particular portfolios and positions should the coalition succeed in attaining its objectives. See, e.g., A. Bedeian, *Organizations: Theory and Analysis—Text and Cases*, 2nd edition, New York: Dryden Press, 1984, p. 112.

Signal-to-noise ratio: The term refers to the intricacies of the decision-making processes of organizations where decision makers need to be able to filter out the irrelevant information that will invariably be present in any decision-making scenario. A large part of arriving at the right decision revolves around how well decision makers are able to read the right cues and disregard the irrelevant information.

Silent-losers problem: A problem that arises when the vast majority of those who are affected by a particular policy (such as genetically engineered food crops) do not raise their voices (also termed "silent majority"), and thus their interests do not tend to be directly taken to heart by policy makers. For a discussion on silent losers, see, e.g., D. Weimer, and A. Vining, *Policy Analysis: Concepts and Practice*, Englewood Cliffs, NJ: Prentice Hall, 1992, pp. 100–11.

Silent majority: *See* **Silent-losers problem**.

Silo mentality: The tendency of individual organizations not to be able to think of the implications of their actions beyond their own boundaries. A silo mentality is evident in jurisdictions where the public-management model favors a more devolved system of organizations and organizational action. *Cf.* **Whole-of-government**.

Simplicity constraint: Refers to the fact that because the public generally does not have the patience—or the expertise—to digest complicated issues, governments are constrained by having to make all policy messages as simple as possible. This is easier said than done, however, and often policies are discarded—or set aside—by governments that do not wish to invest in selling an idea whose time may not yet have come. For a discussion of how this constraint manifests itself in government, see, e.g., J. Stiglitz, "The Private Uses of Public Interests: Incentives and Institutions," Distinguished Lecture on Economics in Government, *Journal of Economic Perspectives*, 1998, 12(2), pp. 3–22.

Simplifiers (of policy thinking): Those who simplify complex policy problems before dealing with them. They tend to simplify their environment and attempt to bring a problem down to the least common identifier. See, e.g., L. Koenig, *An Introduction to Public Policy*, Englewood Cliffs, NJ: Prentice Hall, 1986, p. 346. *See also* **Clarifiers (of policy thinking)**.

Simulation: Used in the context of training, simulation refers to imitating the tasks that an individual will face in a real-life work situation. Hence, in many leadership-training courses, participants will go through, for example, a mock television interview as a way of simulating a real-life environment.

Single-goal agencies: *See* **Single-purpose entities**.

Single-loop learning: *See* **First-order learning**.

Single-point accountability: The requirement that accountability for use of public funds held be to one entity. This in and of itself is not a problem, but it features as a prime reason why cross-agency collaboration (involving also the pooling of public funds) has not been very successful in place-management programs. Generally, agencies are not eager to be accountable for the usage of funds that are in the control of another agency. This makes it difficult to develop and fund joint programs. See, e.g., P. Walsh, "A Response to John Mant," *Australian Journal of Public Administration*, 2002, 61(3), pp. 117–18.

Single-purpose entities: Also known as single-goal agencies, these are organizations that are charged with fulfilling only one purpose. For example, an alcohol-counseling commission may be mandated to look only at issues surrounding alcohol-related use.

Single-stage policies: Policies that can theoretically be easily implemented (for example, the elimination of tax loopholes in legislation). Single-stage policies are generally managed by single-purpose entities although this is not a standing rule of the machinery of government. See, e.g., E. Patashnik, "After the Public Interest Prevails: The Political Sustainability of Policy Reform," *Governance: An International Journal of Policy, Administration, and Institutions*, 2003, 16(2), pp. 203–34.

Single-track appointment: When an employee in an organization is assigned one or a few related job types. What this means is that the employee's advancement in the organization will tend to take place only within that narrow job type. *Cf.* **Dual-track appointment**.

Single-use plans: Refers to plans that are good for the time period that it takes to accomplish a particular task (such as a time-bound public-works project) as opposed to a plan that can be used continuously (such as an organization's strategic plan or an equipment maintenance plan).

Single-window center: A governmental office where individuals can obtain all the permits and authorizations they need for a particular activity. Some jurisdictions allow this to happen through the Internet as well (for example, the Companies On-Line initiative in New Zealand that allows companies to register—and check their application status—through the Internet). *See also* **One-stop shop**.

Sitting next to Nellie: Also known as a work shadow, this is a method of training wherein an individual is closely associated with someone who has the competencies to perform a task and the individual learns from watching closely how the tasks get done. The assumption here is that learning will occur through observation and appropriate coaching. This is considered a practical and rather cost-effective way of developing the skills of a new employee.

Situational appraisal: The process of critically reviewing a given situation so as to determine what the nature of the particular situation is and what options it offers for how the organization should deal with any adverse eventuality. The typical steps in a situational appraisal include identifying the problem to be solved, the decision to be made, and the likely future situation that can be anticipated. Situational appraisal is a part of strategic thinking on policy making. See, e.g., L. Koenig, *An Introduction to Public Policy*, Englewood Cliffs, NJ: Prentice Hall, 1986, p. 294.

Situational approach: *See* **Contingency approach**.

Situational ethics: Refers to the application of ethical conduct and behavioral standards that vary from situation to situation (i.e., what applies in one case is not applicable in another). While situational ethics is useful for organizations to pursue, they need to be aware that making that distinction between situations is not an exact science, and any incongruity in a managerial decision sanctioning an undesirable action or behavior will need to be justified with great care to employees.

Situational theory of leadership: A theory that states that the leaders' effectiveness is determined by the situation in which they find themselves and thus that there is no one common and standard way for leaders to be effective because situations differ. Factors that differ across settings include the level of expertise, types of personality of subordinates and leaders themselves, the nature of the goal of the organization, and the unique environment within which each organization finds itself. The implications of this are that while leaders can certainly collect evidence from elsewhere about what works and what does not, ultimately they will need to develop their own ways of exercising leadership, keeping in mind the unique factors they are facing.

Size-maximizing principle: *See* **Budget-maximizing behavior.**

Skill: Ability that is either learned or inherent in individuals that enables them to perform specific tasks efficiently and effectively. Skills are at the core of what employers look for in potential employees, and remuneration levels are also largely based on the types and levels of an individual's skills. Skills can be of various types, including, for example, technical, relational, and emotional. A skills audit is a formal assessment that is done to ensure that employees have the skills required to do the job. Although this will have been ascertained initially at the recruitment stage, the organization may wish to ensure that the skills are current, for which an audit would help. Skills audits can be performed by external consultants as well as internal staff members with expertise in human-resource development.

Skill development: *See* **Training and development.**

Skills atrophy: A situation wherein skills decline due to lack of use or to obsolescence. Organizational and individual training and development plans are designed to arrest atrophy.

Skills audit: *See* **Skills.**

Skills inventory: *See* **Skills survey.**

Skills obsolescence: *See* **Skills atrophy.**

Skills survey: Also called a skills inventory, this refers to a collection of data on the existing level of skills among an organization's employees for purposes of determining where possible gaps exist so that concerted effort may be made to acquire them. A skills survey is an integral part of training needs analysis.

Skunk factory: Refers to that portion of any organization's work that not everyone is aware of, and that is occupied with conceiving new products and/or methods. It is called a skunk factory because if a so-called innovative product fails to serve its purpose, then the failure of that venture can be contained in one particular location without necessarily tainting the whole organization. Those involved in such work are termed a skunk-works group.

Slack: A term that refers to the difference between two dates (activity start up and completion) that is deliberately incorporated in project planning so as to give some leeway should something go wrong and the dates have to be adjusted. While a slack is useful to have in planning, it is not useful to have too long a slack because it implies that the preceding activity could end long before the succeeding one commences and resources would then be left sitting idle. *See also* **Organizational slack**.

Slash and burn: An approach to generating policy alternatives where draft policies are rigorously subject to critique by peer reviewers and, if time permits, by external reviewers as well. A slash-and-burn review is usually conducted anonymously, although it need not always be so. See, e.g., G. Bhatta, "Evidence-Based Analysis and the Work of Policy Shops," *Australian Journal of Public Administration*, 2002, 61(3), pp. 98–105.

Slide-rule discipline: A method of applying organizational discipline on employees not by giving management the discretion to judge the infraction on a case-by-case basis but by applying specific quantitative thresholds which automatically come into effect when an infraction occurs. While a slide-rule discipline is more transparent, it also takes away the subjective discretion that managers may wish to retain so as to be more flexible in the application of discipline.

Small-numbers bargaining: A situation caused by potential competitors not bidding for a contract because they perceive someone as having "first-mover advantage" by virtue of that bidder already having provided the service/product before. Economist William Ouchi argued that this leads to an absence of competitive pressures. See W. Ouchi, "Markets, Bureaucracies, and Clans," *Administrative Science Quarterly*, 1980, 25(1), pp. 129–41. *See also* **First-mover advantage**.

Small government: A philosophy that has been propounded by advocates of public-sector management reforms that focus entirely on reducing the size—and intervention capacity—of governments in the production and service delivery processes in a country. The argument for a small government is based on the assumption that governments are inherently inefficient and that, therefore, to reduce the overall cost of service delivery, the private sector (and, to some extent, the not-for-profit sector as well) should be encouraged to step in and fill that void. *See also* **Limited government**.

Social audit: As used in the organizational context, this term refers to a form of measurement that management takes of staff members so as to gauge their level of satisfaction with the organization, including the extent to which they feel they have achieved their personal goals at work. See, e.g., C. Medawar, "The Social Audit: A Political View," *Accounting, Organizations and Society*, 1976, 1(4), pp. 389–94.

Social benefits: *See* **Social costs**.

Social capital: Refers to the networks and shared values that encourage social cooperation and trust among members of an organization, society, or even country. Social capital encourages citizens to be more involved in policy making since they are thus more able to increase the stock of capital that comes from being a participant in the policy process. For a cogent discussion of the term, see R. Putnam, "Bowling Alone: America's Declining Social Capital," *Journal of Democracy*, 1995, 6(1), pp. 65–78. (While the concept has been popularized by Robert Putnam, he himself credits James Coleman for developing it; for Coleman's work, see, "Social Capital in the Creation of Human Capital," *American Journal of Sociology*, 1988, 94[supplement], pp. S95–S120). For an interesting counterpoint, see J. Sobel, "Can We Trust Social Capital?" *Journal of Economic Literature*, 2002, 40(1), pp.139–54.

Social contract: Refers to an unwritten contract that can be said to exist between a state and its citizens into which they voluntarily enter. The basis of the contract is trust between the citizens and the elected representatives who formulate policies. The contract also implies rights and responsibilities of each party to the contract: citizens are to take an interest in public affairs and participate in governance, while elected representatives are to steer the state toward directions expressed by the citizenry.

Social costs: Refers to the total costs of a project or program, which includes those incurred by society at large drawing from the implementation of the project. Social costs are likely to be negative externalities. Social benefits, on the other hand, refers to the total benefits of a project or program, which includes those derived by society at large drawing from the implementation of the project. Social benefits are also termed positive externalities.

Social exclusion: Refers to a situation wherein certain segments of a society (such as the very poor) are deprived of opportunities to participate meaningfully in public affairs. Social exclusion is often a product of governmental policy, which—deliberately or otherwise—does not take into consideration the needs of the marginalized populations (i.e., those who do not—rather than choose not to—have a voice in public affairs).

Social experimentation: As understood in a public-policy context, social experimentation is a process of systematically manipulating policies to bring about specific results. The term "experimentation" implies that the government is unsure how a particular policy will eventually affect the outcome that it seeks. An example of a social experimentation is the policy of a government to give more tax credits to educated married couples to encourage them to have a larger family.

Social impact: Any significant effects of a policy or program on any aspect of public life, including quality of life. While it is at the core of any public policy or program, there are serious operationalization and measurement difficulties around the term. A social-impact assessment is an evaluation that is done of any policy or program to ascertain the degree to which it will have any effect (either positive or negative) on the population. A social-impact assessment can be done either before the policy/program initiation stage (i.e., *ex ante*) or after the policy/program has been implemented (i.e., *ex post*). There are specific tools and techniques that have been developed relatively recently to rigorously conduct such an assessment.

Social judgment analysis: A form of group decision making that places appropriate weights on each piece of information related to the particular social problem being analyzed, and which develops a relation between each piece and the final social policy effected.

Social lag: Any discrepancy (or the difference in the standard of any variable) that exists between two communities/groups of people in a society. A social lag then denotes the degree of social inequity that is evident.

Social needs: *See* **Needs hierarchy**.

Social power: Power that an individual secures by virtue of his/her interactions with leaders in society, or by virtue of being a societal leader himself/herself. Social power does not necessarily imply that the individual has other forms of power as well (such as resource power). *See also* **Power**.

Social rationality: *See* **Rationality**.

Social-choice game: A type of game that is evident in a public bureaucracy that results from the interaction between those who enact legislation and policy-making executives. See, e.g., L. Lynn, "Policy Achievement as a Collective Good: A Strategic Perspective on Managing Social Programs," in B. Bozeman (ed.), *Public Management: The State of the Art*, San Francisco: Jossey-Bass, 1993, pp. 108–33.

Socialization: Formal and informal ways in which individuals and new employees are incorporated into the organization and adapt themselves to its norms and values. Such a socialization process could be something that is either coerced (as in indoctrinated) or voluntary (as in informal networks within the organization). Socialization can also be in specific domains, such as political (being imbued with political values) or cultural (being made aware of the culture of the society). See, e.g., G. Jones, "Socialization Tactics, Self-Efficacy, and Newcomers' Adjustments to Organizations," *Academy of Management Journal*, 1986, 29(2), pp. 262–79.

Soft budget constraint: *See* **Budget constraint**.

Soft institution: *See* **Institution**.

Soft pipeline: *See* **Pipeline**.

Soft policy: See **Policy**.

Soft results: Results that cannot be easily and readily quantified but that are just as important in determining the success of interventions. For example, the softer results in training in organizations can be said to include improved work practices, better organizational culture, "promotability" of workers, employees' perception of the management team, etc. Getting a better handle on such results, and incorporating them in any planning process, is critical in any organization. For a succinct review of the concept and how to operationalize it, see "Training: How to Measure 'Softer' Results," *HRFocus*, 2001, 78(4), pp. 5–6.

Soft value bias: *See* **Value bias**.

Solicitation: As used in contract administration, this term refers to a purchaser making a request for bids (i.e., soliciting proposals) from those interested in—and capable of—delivering the required services. *See also* **Request for proposal**.

Solidary incentives: Affinity-related incentives which motivate individuals. Such incentives give individuals intangible satisfaction (for example, friendship and a sense of loyalty). Organizational efforts at enhancing solidary incentives tend to be varied since different work environments call for different ways to provide the incentives.

Solutions package: The comprehensive description of a problem, and the resources (as well as the mechanisms) needed to resolve the problem. If there are several solution packages for one particular problem, decision makers tend to choose the one that has the highest cost-benefit ratio (or they apply another criterion toward making a decision). Solutions packages can either be specified in an organization's standard operating procedures or are developed specifically for emerging problems.

Span of control: A concept that is based on the notion that there is a limit to the number of employees a supervisor can supervise. The span of control thus refers to the horizontal arrangement of who reports to whom and how many employees a supervisor oversees. As first propounded by the noted administration specialist Luther Gulick in 1937, the term has at its core three variables that determine span of control relationships in organizations: (a) the degree of diversification of functions, (b) the degree of an organization's stability (measured in terms of its time horizon), and (c) size and (physical) space. For a treatment of these determinations, see, e.g., K. Meier and J. Bohte, "Span of Control and Public Organizations: Implementing Luther Gulick's Research Design," *Public Administration Review*, 2003, 63(1), pp. 61–70.

Special advisers: Individuals which governmental ministers recruit outside of civil-service regulations to help them in their functions. There is nothing wrong with ministers keeping special advisers, but critics argue that they need to be subject to some sort of a public-service code of conduct. In the UK, despite moves to institute such a code for these special advisers, their numbers doubled in the first four years of Tony Blair's Labor government. For a good review of the role of special advisers in public-sector governance, see, e.g., D. Ives, "Special Advisers for Ministers in the United Kingdom: An Update," *Canberra Bulletin of Public Administration*, 2002, No. 104, pp. 63–67.

Special audit: An audit of an organization or program that is restricted to a particular part or phase of the entity's work. The terms of reference of special audits are restrictive in that their scope of work is contained by predetermined limits.

Special committee: Also termed an ad hoc committee, this refers to a committee that is set up in the legislature for a specific purpose and for a set period of time, and asked to consider a specific problem for which the government is considering formulating a policy. See, e.g., P. Roness, "Reforming Central Government and Parliaments: Structural Recoupling and Institutional Characteristics," *International Review of Administrative Sciences*, 2001, 67(4), pp. 673–90.

Special interests: Refer to organizations/bodies that represent the interests of only a subset of the population (such as of the oil industry or dairy industry). For a case-study discussion of special interests, see, e.g., P, Keefer, *When Do Special Interests Run Rampant? Disentangling the Role in Banking Crises of Elections, Incomplete Information*, World Bank

Working Papers, No. 2543, Washington, DC: World Bank, 2001. *Cf.* **Public interest.**

Special revenue sharing: *See* **Block grant.**

Specialized task assignments: Where employees concentrate on a limited set of specialized tasks. The basis of such task assignments is the concept of the division of labor. Specialized task assignments are still prevalent in organizations because, notwithstanding the introduction of technology in the workplace and matrix work arrangements, several organizational functions (such as financial administration) continue to require individuals with specialized skills to perform highly specific tasks.

Specific capabilities: The capabilities linked to the delivery of specific objectives and the pursuit of each organization's particular mission. Technical experts in organizations are said to possess specific capabilities. *See also* **Capability.**

Specific knowledge: Knowledge that exists in an organization that is relatively expensive to transfer to other aspects (or areas of work) of the organization. This is because specific knowledge tends to be specialized to a particular area, and the marginal costs of reorienting that knowledge exceeds marginal benefits. The practice of secondments to enable staff members to acquire different knowledge, skills, and abilities is designed to enable them to access different knowledge sources.

Specific training: Also referred to as nontransferable training, this is training that is specific to a particular job in a particular organization. *Cf.* **General training.**

Specification: The act of detailing exactly what is needed or what exists. In contract administration, for example, specification refers to the purchaser specifying in great detail what it expects from the contractor. In position management, it refers to the details around what the particular position requires. In financial administration, it refers to the provision of details on financial transactions.

Specificity: A term used to denote a distinctive characteristic of organizations where a high degree of specificity of structure and coordination within organizations delineates the individual organization as a unique unit. There are two important aspects of specificity in relation to organizations: (a) specificity of both exposure to information and perception of it (i.e., the information the organization is interested in is specialized), and (b) specificity of roles (i.e., role definitions within an organization mirror the specificity of information and knowledge that the organization is interested in). See, e.g., J. March and H. Simon, *Organizations*, New York: Wiley, 1958, p. 153.

Spectator activities: *See* **Gladiatorial activities.**

Spending authority: Authority given to an organization or an individual to incur expenditures in fulfilling their mandates/responsibilities (for example, to engage contractors). Spending authority is either provided in advance by appropriation acts or granted for specific instances. Spending authority can also be withheld if the entity given the authority abuses it.

Spending caps: Limits that are imposed on organizations and programs in terms of what can be expended in a given time period. Spending caps are instituted to ensure that there are no budget blowouts in the course of program implementation. Such caps are usually set by a legislature or, less frequently, by a central treasury. See, e.g., E. Savas, *Privatizing the Public Sector: How to Shrink the Government*, Chatham, NJ: Chatham House, 1982, p. 123.

Spillover effects: Also known as externalities, spillover effects occur when the consumption, or production, of one person affects the welfare of another. There are positive spillover effects if the consumption by one person benefits another but the latter does not pay, and negative spillover effects if the consumption by one person has a negative effect on another but the former is not required to pay. Spillover effects are also evident along the following lines: (a) production to production (successful drug treatment decreases law enforcement activities), (b) production to consumption (a highway project displaces residents), (c) consumption to consumption (construction of a large mall makes it hard for citizens to find parking), and (d) consumption to production (construction of public housing improves the market for local businesses). For a case-study discussion of spillover effects, see, e.g., J. Blankenau, "The Fate of National Health Insurance in Canada and the United States: A Multiple Streams Explanation," *Policy Studies Journal*, 2001, 29(1), pp. 38–55. *See also* **Externalities.**

Spiral of silence: Refers to an organizational dysfunction in which an individual perception of what the majority of other organizational members may be thinking suppresses the willingness to speak up. When no one challenges what may well be a minority view, say of the organizational leaders', a spiral of silence emerges whereby the minority view becomes organizational decisions. The Abilene effect is considered to be a direct manifestation of the spiral of silence. See, e.g., M. Harvey et al., "The Abilene Paradox after Thirty Years: A Global Perspective," *Organizational Dynamics*, 2004, 33(2), pp. 215–26.

Spoils system: A system in which elected representatives fill positions in organizations with their own supporters. A spoils system is common practice in the United States. Those who argue in its favor assert that it is advantageous to have elected representatives bring in individuals who he/she has confidence in, while those who oppose it argue that it introduces an element of inefficiency since it does not necessarily adhere to the merit principle. *See also* **Patronage**.

Spoilt for choice: Refers to a situation where there are several choices in response to a particular problem. Employers, for example, are spoilt for choice if there are considerably more qualified candidates than before for a particular vacancy. Program objectives are at times framed informally along this concept.

Spot contract: So termed because all transactions are fulfilled on the spot. Spot contracts are also the simplest form of contract between two parties (also known as a "sales" contract). A spot contract takes place in a spot market, which is a market for goods and services where the exchange between a buyer and seller is made on the spot at the current price and no long-term commitment is made nor expected. For example, when public agencies use short-term consultants for particular work, they are said to be using the spot market. For a discussion of a spot contract, see, e.g., W. Ouchi, "Markets, Bureaucracies, and Clans," *Administrative Science Quarterly*, 1980, 25(1), pp. 129–41. *Cf.* **Contingent claims contract**; **Sequential spot contract**.

Squeaky-wheel approach to monitoring: Refers to the tendency of monitoring agencies to place emphasis on reviewing that particular component of a program, or the part of the organization, that is most in the minds of citizens and that is the most visible in the media. If it is not covered in the media or perceived to be a problem, then this approach implies that the monitoring would lessen.

Staff development: *See* **Training and development**.

Staff functions: Responsibilities that managers in organizations are expected to fulfill. Traditional staff functions include planning, budgeting, and coordination in the organization. On the other hand, line functions refer to responsibilities that employers have in the organization which carry no managerial tasks. Typical line functions include database entry, customer service, and administrative assistance, among others.

Staff principle: A principle in organization administration which asserts that individuals who support the chief executive of an organization in his/her work should ideally not be line staff but rather should be part of the office of the executive, and thus inherently involved in maintaining some form of control over the organization.

Stage-gate decision: A decision that is taken by organizations at specified stages of a project/program formulation or product development process. In a stage-gate decision process, novel ideas are considered incrementally, i.e., as they appear in each stage; this allows organizations to control for risks that may not be evident when ideas are not analyzed in stages. For a discussion of a stage-gate decision with respect to risks, see, e.g., C. Davis, "Calculated Risk: A Framework for Evaluating Product Development," *MIT Sloan Management Review*, 2002, 43(4), pp. 71–77.

Staggered schedule: Also known as glide time or flexitime, this term refers to a workplace schedule that allows employees to come in at flexible times (within bounds) so that those who start early can leave early, for example. This provides an opportunity for staff members to have a better grip on their work-life balance.

Stakeholder: An individual or group of individuals who have a stake in a policy, plan, or program of the government. Target groups are stakeholders, although not all stakeholders are target-group members. A stakeholder need not be a consumer of the product or service government produces. Stakeholder analysis is a method of ascertaining who the stakeholders of an organization or program are, how they interact with the organization, what major issues face the organization in maintaining that relationship, and finally how that can be meaningfully accomplished. A stakeholder model stipulates that in the consideration of the health of an organization or system, there should be explicit recognition of the interests of various groups (i.e., stakeholders) and that they have a long-term stake in it. For an analytical discussion of stakeholder theory, see, e.g., A. Friedman and S. Miles, "Developing Stakeholder Theory," *Journal of Management Studies*, 2002, 39(1), pp. 1–21.

Standard: A level of performance to which individuals and organizations strive to adhere. A standard could be voluntary (i.e., organizations may develop one based on best practice elsewhere) or mandatory (i.e., dictated by an external party, normally the legislature or a regulatory agency, and compulsory for the organization). For standards to be meaningful, they need to be reviewed and updated regularly. *See also* **Benchmark**.

Standard costs: *Ex ante* and benchmarked costs that managers determine to use as a basis for a comparison with actual costs. Such standard costs are useful in economy and efficiency audits.

Standard of performance: *See* **Performance standards**.

Standard operating procedures: Formalized processes that organizations have in place to handle the routine matters they face. Thus, for example, standard operating procedures can exist in how employment leave can be taken, how new employees should be inducted into the organization, and how disciplinary measures will be applied. Viewed thus, standard operating procedures are programmed sequences of actions that organizations use in general management.

Standard rating scale: A uniform scale used by an evaluator to rate employees. For a fair and equitable performance-management system, a standard rating scale is a must.

Standards letter: In many devolved public services in advanced jurisdictions, a letter is sent to all departmental chief executives by a central agency (such as a public service commission) that sets out, among other things, standards of personal behaviors which the government expects of a chief executive, and what its own goals are with which the chief executives need to be intimately familiar. The letter also sets out other standards (such as leadership of the department, and professional and personal ethics) that are used as tools for performance evaluation.

Standards of conduct: *See* **Code of conduct**.

Standing committee: Refers to a regular committee within a legislature that is mandated to review bills within a particular subject area. For a discussion of the role of standing committees in a strong parliament, see, e.g., P. Roness, "Reforming Central Governments and Parliaments: Structural Recoupling and Institutional Characteristics," *International Review of Administrative Sciences*, 2001, 67(4), pp. 673–90.

Standing orders: Refers to rules or organizations that apply to all staff members in all situations (until they are amended).

Standing plan: Also called a continuing plan, this is a plan that organizations use to address problems/issues that tend to repeat. Standard operating procedures tend to be used to give effect to standing plans.

State capability: Capability of the government to formulate, implement, and evaluate public policies. Components of state capability could include, for example, proper rules and their adherence, merit-based human-resource management practices, competition, proper and effective decentralization, and partnerships with the nongovernmental and private sectors. See, e.g., P. Evans, "The State as Problem and Solution: Predation, Embedded Autonomy, and Structural Changes," in S. Haggard and R. Kaufmann (eds.), *The Politics of Economic Adjustment: International Constraints, Distributive Conflicts, and the State*, Princeton, NJ: Princeton University Press, 1992, pp. 139–81.

State capture: The actions of individuals and others to influence the formation of laws and regulations to their own advantage. For this reason, state capture can end up as a hindrance to public-management reforms. See, e.g., J. Hellman, G. Jones, and D. Kaufmann, "Seize the State, Seize the Day: State Capture and Influence in Transition Economies," *Journal of Comparative Economics*, 2003, 31(4), pp. 751–73.

State-determined system: *See* **Path dependence**.

State-owned enterprise: State-owned enterprises (SOEs) are companies that operate as commercial businesses but are owned by the state. Every SOE has a board of directors, which is at least partly appointed by government, to take full responsibility for running the business, and they generate the bulk of their revenues from selling goods and services. They are sometimes referred to as the third, or outer, tier in the "three-tier State."

Statement of intent: A public document (i.e., intended for the legislature) that covers the most important elements of what a governmental department intends to do. In specific, the statement of intent (SOI) for an organization incorporates: (a) the context in which the organization operates; (b) where the department is heading, and what it intends to do (with the agreement and support of its governmental minister); (c) why it has chosen to do those things; and (d) what risks it foresees in this purpose and how it plans to mitigate these risks. The SOI serves as a high-level story that the department provides to the legislature, against which it will be evaluated at regular intervals. The SOI is presented in the legislature so that it becomes a public document. For a general discussion of an SOI, see, e.g., G. Bhatta, "Intent, Risks and Capability: Some Considerations on Rethinking Organizational Capability," *International Review of Administrative Sciences*, 2003, 69(3), pp. 401–18.

Statement of service performance: This is part of the financial statements that governmental departments regularly prepare (usually semi-annually). This compares the outputs proposed (i.e., *ex ante*) to the outputs actually achieved (i.e., *ex post*) by the department, and serves as a useful tool of government to monitor the performance of departments.

Statesman: A term used by the scholar Anthony Downs to denote a type of bureaucrat who gives primacy to societal values and the interests of the organization's constituencies rather than to his or her own status, power, or bureaucratic values. See A. Downs, *Inside Bureaucracy*, Boston: Little, Brown, 1967, p. 88. For a discussion of the typology of administrative roles, see, e.g., S. Selden, G. Brewer, and J. Brudney, "Reconciling Competing Values in Public Administration: Understanding the Administrative Role Concept," *Administration & Society*, 1999, 3(2), pp. 171–204.

Static complexity: *See* **Complexity**.

Status costs: Costs that are incurred by organizations to develop and maintain a distinct public image (for example, in premises or branding). With increasing pressure for governmental departments to behave like private-sector firms and compete in markets, status costs for these organizations are likely to increase in the future. Status costs can be incurred by organizational leaders as well. One such determinant of such costs is status anxiety, which is an anxiety that is developed in leaders when they worry that subordinates may be a threat to their authority.

Statute: A law enacted by legislation rather than by delegated authority. A statutory body is a public organization that is created by law (i.e., a statute). Such a body has statutory functions that are clearly spelt out in relevant laws, which may, however, allow further rules and regulations to be made by the statutory body. Statutory limits are limits that are set by law on what an organization can be involved in or how much of a budget it needs to operate within.

Steering committee: (1) A committee of the legislature which is involved in ensuring that all administrative matters are taken care of in the passage of legislation. (2) A group of individuals who are brought together with the express purpose to guide (or steer) a particular policy or program from the conceptual stage to implementation. A steering committee is different from an advisery committee.

Steering mandate: Refers to the authority and freedom given to organizations to determine how best they should link up with others so as to fulfill their mandates. Given that organizations face multidimensional problems, they also need to develop extensive relationships with other entities in their operating environment, and they need to be given the space to freely develop multirelationships in ways that are most advantageous to them without being tied to the parameters of the specific mandates they have. See, e.g., M. Considine, "The End of the Line? Accountable Governance in the Age of Networks, Partnerships, and Joined Up Services," *Governance: An International Journal of Policy, Administration, and Institutions*, 2002, 15(1), pp. 21–40.

Steering vs. rowing: *See* **Rowing vs. steering**.

Stereotyping: A term used to describe bias in perceiving peoples, which is distorted by individual perception, and is manifest most clearly in biased performance evaluations of employees. *See also* **Perceptual defense**.

Stewardship: The role of government in running the state, including, for example, strengthening public-service capability to safeguard people, government property, and interests. The concept implies that the government takes the role of a captain leading the country to prosperity and to the well being of all citizens. For a review of stewardship theory in relation to firms, see, e.g., A. Ranft and H. O'Neill, "Board Composition and High-Flying Founders: Hints of Trouble to Come?" *Academy of Management Executive*, 2001, 15(1), pp. 126–38.

Stewardship contracting: A contract given to a party that is permitted, for example, to extract from the earth but is also expected to ensure that it exercises stewardship over the property in terms of ensuring that the resource is not depleted. For example, a logging company may be awarded a contract to cut timber, but it is also expected to ensure that it does not leave forests vulnerable to, say, fires or erosion.

Stewardship reporting: As applied to risk management in organizations, stewardship reporting requires that designated individuals (usually managers) report upward on a regular basis on the actions that have been taken to ensure that control and risk procedures in their particular areas of responsibility are kept current. Stewardship reporting is used as a tool to gain assurance across the organization that risks are properly being monitored on a regular basis.

Strategic center: The concept of the centers of government (usually taken to mean the key control and coordination agencies, such as the treasury, office of the president, prime minister and cabinet, etc.) being revamped so that they can be more effective management and policy-advice coordination units. The need for a strategic center is increasingly being felt in an environment where governmental departments are given greater autonomy, which means that coordination across government is essential. See, e.g., M. Kaul, "The New Public Administration: Management Innovations in Government," *Public Administration and Development*, 1997, 17, pp. 13–26.

Strategic communities: A creative method whereby organizations learn from others' experiences and ensure that the knowledge gained from those experiences are productively tapped. Strategic communities allow organizations to collaborate with other entities that may share broadly similar environments, mandates, or risks and opportunities that would allow learning to be transferred usefully. See, e.g., J. Storck and P. Hill, "Knowledge Diffusion Through Strategic Communities," *Sloan Management Review*, 2000, 41(2), pp. 63–74.

Strategic conversations: A term that refers to the participative environment that employers can create where they can talk with employees about where the organization should be heading, and how they might get there. Strategic conversations are important in giving the employees a sense that they are involved in the direction the organization is taking. See, e.g., D. Amidon, "Leading Through Strategic Conversations," in J. Phillips, and D. Bonner (eds.), *In Action: Leading Knowledge Management and Learning*, Alexandria, VA: American Society for Training and Development, 2000, pp. 101–14.

Strategic episodes: Refer to these events and incidents that organizations encounter which allow them to test how well their organizational systems are structured and which provide lessons to them in terms of strategic planning and organizational efficiencies. Strategic episodes are set in terms of time (i.e., they have a beginning and an end), and they offer organizations learning opportunities. A strategic episode ends either when a particular goal or end situation is reached or when there is a time limitation, whichever comes first. For an excellent review of the concept of strategic episodes, see, e.g., J. Hendry and D. Seidl, "The Structure and Significance of Strategic Episodes: Social Systems Theory and the Routine Practices of Strategic Change," *Journal of Management Studies*, 2003, 40(1), pp. 175–96.

Strategic information: Information that is useful to an organization in its strategic planning work rather than at an operational level. A proposed policy change being contemplated by government can be considered to be strategic information.

Strategic learning: Refers to the presence of deeper learning, and where feedback from the organization's environment plays an important role in enhancing the learning process. Because the organization must continuously adapt to its environment, the idea that changing once will enable the organization to maintain survival is not necessarily accurate; the learning process has to be continuous. See, e.g., F. Berry, "Innovation in Public Management: The Adoption of Strategic Planning," *Public Administration Review*, 1994, 54(4), pp. 322–30. *See also* **Double-loop learning**.

Strategic management: Management of an organization that proceeds on an understanding of the long-term orientation of the organization and seeks to approach that in a purposive and logical manner. There are two general approaches to strategic management: (a) synoptic approach: rationally integrating all aspects of an organization, including rules, processes, and structures to better fit its mission; and (b) incremental approach: where there is no emphasis on the rational integration of all components and instead organizational strategy emerges from a loose amalgamation of disparate elements of the organization. For a discussion of these two approaches, see, e.g., J. Fredrickson, "Strategic Process Research: Questions and Recommendations," *Academy of Management Review*, 1983, 8(4), pp. 565–75.

Strategic planning: A systematic process by which an organization determines the desired future outcome and plans for securing the capabilities that will enable it to attain that outcome. Strategic planning is for the long term; the organization ascertains the means by which this is to be achieved and proceeds with controlled organizational change. See, e.g., W. King and D. Cleland, *Strategic Planning and Policy*, New York: Van Nostrand Reinhold, Co., 1978.

Strategic quality management: A systematic approach for striving for—and establishing—quality goals in the organization. The quality goals could refer to any number of things and will be determined by the organizational leadership and staff members, but could include such ends as improved customer satisfaction levels, fewer malfunctions in equipments, better communications with clients, etc. For a cogent analysis of strategic quality management, see, e.g., D. Leonard and R. McAdam, "Developing Strategic Quality Management: A Research Agenda," *Total Quality Management*, 2002, 13(4), pp. 507–22.

Strategic procurement: Refers to relationships that both parties to a transaction seek to enhance by avoiding an unnecessarily adversarial approach. Cooperation and collaboration are key values here and attention is placed on enhancing relational and social capital. For a good case-study application of the concept, see, e.g., A Erridge and J. Greer, "Partnerships and Public Procurement: Building Social Capital Through Supply Relations," *Public Administration*, 2002, 80(3), pp. 503–22.

Strategic resource allocation: The allocation of resources based on the identified policy priorities of a government, usually over the medium term.

Strategic results areas: Broad goals articulated by a government on a sectoral basis, which are then translated into individual key-results areas, with specific governmental departments mandated to fulfill them. See, e.g., A. Matheson, "Governing Strategically: The New Zealand Experience," *Public Administration and Development*, 1998, 18(4), pp. 349–63. *See also* **Key priorities**.

Strategic risk: Also called policy risk, this is a type of public risk that represents the fundamental basis of an organization's raison d'être. A strategic risk, if not mitigated promptly, jeopardizes the very basis of an organization's work. See, e.g., G. Scott, "Managing Operational and Policy Risks at the Center of Government," in J. Yeabsley and A. Sundakov (eds.), *Risk and the Institutions of Government,* Wellington: Institute of Policy Studies and NZIER, 1999, pp. 14–34. *Cf.* **Trading risk**.

Strategic vulnerability: Refers to weaknesses in organizations that result from a knowledge gap. Two types of strategic vulnerability can be distinguished: (a) externally vulnerable but internally safe—i.e., when the ratio of tacit knowledge to total knowledge is low (i.e., the large explicit knowledge base can be copied by competitors, but even if the employees leave, their knowledge is not lost); and (b) externally safe but internally vulnerable (i.e., the knowledge is difficult to identify and copy, but if employees leave, they take their personal knowledge with them). The process of ascertaining the degree of strategic vulnerability in an organization is termed strategic vulnerability analysis. See R. Hall and P. Andriani, "Managing Knowledge for Innovation," *Long Range Planning,* 2002, 35(1), pp. 29–48.

Strategic-choice perspective: Refers to the process by which top managers in an organization decide on which change to make to an organization's strategic direction, including how to do so. The perspective starts from the assumption that different managers interpret the organization's environment differently and thus the management team as a whole has to make a strategic decision as to how to leverage the opportunities the environment provides. Strategic-choice perspective is a response to the concept of environmental determinism. See, e.g., P. Nutt, "Making Strategic Choices," *Journal of Management Studies*, 2002, 39(1), pp. 67–96. *See also* **Environmental determinism**.

Strategy: The art of coming up with a carefully prepared plan that covers all conceivable contingencies, and that specifically helps the organization attain its mandates (i.e., specifies what tactics are to be used to attain the goals). The planning process is key to the generation of a strategy and, as such, sound intelligence (or accurate and relevant information) is considered critical in coming up with a strategy. The term "strategy creation" is used to denote the set of activities that top management and even middle- and lower-level staff members are involved in to better inform the planning process in the organization. See, e.g., P. Regner, "Strategy Creation in the Periphery: Inductive Versus Deductive Strategy Making," *Journal of Management Studies*, 2003, 40(1), pp. 57–82.

Strategy creation: *See* **Strategy**.

Strategy mapping: A technique of linking an organization's strategic objectives with appropriate performance measures. Strategy mapping draws its intellectual content and analytical methods from the balanced scorecard technique, and is similar in orientation to preparing an organizational statement of intent. It is an iterative process that seeks input from an organization's senior managers, as well as rank and file, in thinking about the organization's challenges and how they should be addressed (including how the organization's stakeholders need to be consulted). For an application of strategy mapping in a public-sector agency, see, e.g., D. Irwin, "Strategy Mapping in the Public Sector," *Long Range Planning*, 2002, 35(6), pp. 637–47.

Strawman: Refers to a first proposal that sets out the broad parameters of what a final solution might look like. It is deliberately made to be a loosely structured formulation so that it retains scope for adaptability to new ideas. The strawman is usually a response that is easily shown to be false.

Street skills: *See* **Nous capability**.

Street-level bureaucrat: A public-sector worker who is directly responsible for implementing the policies, and, thus by implication, is in the "streets" dealing with the public (the bureaucrat is also the first point of contact with the public approaching "from the street"). For a review of the nature of street-level bureaucracy, see, e.g., J. Sorg, "A Typology of Implementation Behaviors of Street Level Bureaucrats," *Policy Studies Review*, 1983, 2(3), pp. 391–406.

Stretch assignments: *See* **Job exchange**.

Strike: Action by union members against the employer that takes the form of picketing, work stoppages, or staying off work to protest some policy that the employer may have instituted, or as sympathy for members of another union in either the same organization or elsewhere. While in most jurisdictions around the world a strike is not necessarily illegal, there are only certain situations when unions can call a strike that may be considered legal (for example, when all possible steps have been taken to come to a mutual understanding, but the employer is considered to be in violation of an agreement).

"Stroke of the pen" decision: A bureaucratic decision that is made without studying the market or taking into consideration all the issues that might affect the decision. "Stroke of the pen" decisions tend to be located in the administrative domain (i.e., they do not get debated in a political forum such as the legislature, which tends to have a more visibly critical and questioning environment). See, e.g., L. White, "Interactive Policy Analysis: Process Methods for Policy Reform," in S. Nagel (ed.), *Handbook of Public Policy Evaluation*, London: Sage Publications, 2002, pp. 159–65.

Structural benchmark: Refers to those conditions which act as guides for administrators to target but which are not really critical if they cannot be attained. However, persistently failing to attain benchmarks (which presumably will be shifting downward on a year-to-year basis if not met) would mean that they would be taken as performance criteria, in which case not meeting them would have a much more personal impact on those who were responsible for them. For a discussion of the term in the organizational context, see, e.g., C. Adams and J. Gunning, "Redesigning the Aid Contract: Donors' Use of Performance Indicators in Uganda," *World Development*, 2002, 30(12), pp. 2045–56. *Cf.* **Performance criteria**.

Structural flexibility: Refers to the ability of organizations to reconfigure their internal structures so as to better deliver services and achieve their mandates in keeping with changed conditions in their operational environments. Such flexibility could result, for example, from the willingness and commitment of organizational leaders to abolish and or amalgamate various units in the organization. Structural flexibility is much more possible in an environment where organizational leaders have been delegated managerial authority to bring about such change.

Structural holes: Structural holes are disconnections between an organization and its partners, and result from gaps in information flows between them. The term also refers to the degree of diversity of an organization's partners. Structural holes are a natural consequence of the presence of information asymmetry among organizations. For a discussion of structural holes in the context of innovation, see, e.g., G. Ahuja, "Collaboration Networks, Structural Holes, and Innovation: A Longitudinal Study," *Administrative Science Quarterly,* 2000, 45(3), pp. 425–55.

Structural intervention: (1) As used in the context of organizational development, this intervention focuses on changing an organization's structural aspects. Such aspects include workplace environment and communication systems. (2) As used across the government sector, structural interventions are common when governments decide that outcomes would be better attained by instituting structural changes in the machinery of government. These changes can range from mandating the creation of new units in organizations (such as a pay and employment equity unit in a ministry of labor) to amalgamating large ministries along functional lines (such as a ministry of transport and of communications).

Structural recoupling: The actions of a government to bring together two or more organizations, or units in an organization, so as to better align objectives to means, and so as to augment organizational efficiencies. Structural recoupling is seen as a response to the general trend of the 1990s to break existing organizations into many functionally specialized entities. See, e.g., P. Roness, "Reforming Central Governments and Parliaments: Structural Recoupling and Institutional Characteristics," *International Review of Administrative Sciences*, 2001, 67(4), pp. 673–90.

Structured decisions: Refers to those decisions of organizations made in a routine fashion and which conform to (or stay within) prior organizational decisions or existing organizational policy.

Structured training: *See* **Formal training**.

Subcoalitions: Coalitions that exist within broader coalitions. Subcoalitions are likely to be evident in organizations when a particular policy or program has several components and each acquires a fair degree of criticality in terms of its contribution to organizational goals. Subcoalitions can be spatial (i.e., based in specific locations, such as headquarters versus field offices) or nonspatial (i.e., issue based). There is also more likely to be some degree of conflict among subcoalitions, which is the purpose of the creation of the subcoalition in the first place. *See also* **Coalition**.

Subcontracting: Refers to a situation where a contracting organization itself purchases some of its inputs from another contractor. Subcontracting may be used when specialized skill is necessary but not on a continuous basis, and so the contracting organization has no incentive to acquire it in-house.

Subculture: The existence of a particular type of culture in a subset of an organization that differs from other such subcultures, and also from the predominant culture of the organization. For example, the subculture in the finance section of a prisons department is likely to be different from that existing in the strategic planning division, and also different from the primary culture of the organization as a whole.

Subject civic culture: *See* **Civic culture**.

Subjective performance evaluation: Performance evaluation of employees that is based on the personal opinion of the evaluator rather than on some objective criterion. While the ideal evaluation should have almost total reliance on objective criteria, given that all evaluators bring some bias with them, it is not entirely possible to avoid a subjective performance evaluation to some degree.

Subjective responsibility: *See* **Objective responsibility**.

Submissive legislature: A legislature that cannot sufficiently exercise its watchdog functions in ensuring that the executive branch of government (particularly the bureaucracy) is accountable for the implementation of policies it passes. Bureaucracies also tend to dominate the policy-making process when the legislature is submissive. See, e.g., J. Lam, "From a Submissive to an Adversarial Legislature: The Changing Role of the Hong Kong Legislative Council," *Asian Profile*, 1994, 22(1), pp. 21–32.

Suboptimization: The process of considering logical and rational solutions to parts of a system rather than the whole. While it may appear intuitive that this, repeated several times over for all subsystems, would lead to a more rational and logical system as a whole, it is not necessarily true that this will indeed result. As a matter of fact, there may be times when it is necessary for a subsystem not to optimize in order to ensure that the system as a whole can be optimized.

Subordinate rating: *See* **Three-hundred-and-sixty-degree appraisal**.

Subsidiarity: Also known as reverse delegation, this concept refers to decentralizing the provision of public service to the lowest level of government where it can be properly carried out. Subsidiarity is considered to be at the very heart of federalism, where subjurisdictions voluntarily cede some of their powers to the center because they believe that it is a more effective way of tackling a particular problem that affects them jointly. For a discussion of subsidiarity in the context of accountability, see, e.g., E. Loffler, *Managing Accountability in Intergovernmental Partnerships*, PUMA/RD(99)4/Final, Paris: OECD, 1999, pp. 9–12.

Subsidies: Rewards or incentives that are given by governments to influence the behavior and productive capacities of individuals and other entities (for example, farmers and what the government would like them to grow on their farms). Subsidies can be demand side (such as giving vouchers to families for school education) or supply side (such as matching grants to producers of services). *Cf.* **Sanctions**.

Substantive expertise: Professional experiences of an individual that are based on demonstrable, relevant, and effective work within the organization and elsewhere. For example, when recruiting for a position in a technical assistance project on vocational training, an organization may attach some weight to a candidate's training experience but may consider the substantive experience, however, to come from the individual's work in that particular vocation.

Substantive goal: *See* **Goal**.

Substantive rationality: When the behavior of policy makers is appropriate to the achievement of outcomes that have been predetermined, and which remains within the constraints that the policy makers face. Substantive rationality is about determining the government's desired objective in relation to a particular issue. How policy makers give effect to that is captured by the concept of instrumental rationality. For a discussion of this concept by someone whose work is well noted, see H. Simon, "From Procedural to Substantive Rationality," in S. Latsis (ed.), *Methods and Appraisals in Economics*, Cambridge University Press, 1976, pp. 129–48. *Cf.* **Instrumental rationality**.

Substitutability: The ability of an organization to replace one set of activity for another but still work toward attaining its original mandate. Thus, the substitutability is not in relation to the ends but the means. See, e.g.,

D. Hickson et al., "A Strategic Contingencies' Theory of Interorganizational Power," *Administrative Science Quarterly*, 1971, 16(2), pp. 216–29.

Substitutive grant: A grant that is given so that the recipient may be able to reduce its own resources level for that particular activity and instead shift its usage to some other activity.

Substitutive knowledge: A new type of knowledge or paradigm that supplants old knowledge. While substitutive knowledge can bring vitality and vigor to an organization, it can also serve to disenchant employees since they may well have to continuously learn new procedures.

Subtractive causality: Refers to establishing cause-and-effect relationships between variables by ruling out all alternative possibilities. This ruling-out feature is often more appealing than seeking the one main rational explanation to a particular policy problem.

Succession planning: Refers to the purposive and conscious efforts by organizations to ensure that they have well-qualified individuals in place who can move up the organizational hierarchy as those in the upper echelon begin to move out. Good succession planning will have in place clear protocols on how such movements will be effectuated. For a discussion of this in the public sector, see, e.g., D. Lynn, "Succession Management Strategies in Public Sector Organizations: Building Leadership Capital," *Review of Public Personnel Administration*, 2001, 21(2), pp. 114–32.

Successive limited comparisons: Also known as the branch technique of policy analysis, this concept refers to making decisions based not on a rational means-ends analysis but on successive improvements since the sought-after ends are not distinct. The notion is also tied to the concept of decision making under bounded rationality. See, e.g., C. Lindblom, "The Science of Muddling Through," *Public Administration Review*, 1959, 19(Spring), pp 79–88. *Cf.* **Rational-comprehensive theory of decision making**.

Sufficient consensus: Refers to the notion of a workable consensus. Public policy expert Eugene Bardach describes this as the level that permits resources to be maintained at a minimally workable level or higher. See E. Bardach, *Getting Agencies to Work Together: The Practice and Theory of Managerial Craftsmanship*, Washington, DC: Brookings Institution Press, 1998, pp. 220–21. *Cf.* **Contested consensus**.

Summary discipline: Denotes a situation where the organizational leadership is compelled to discipline an employee for gross violation of an organizational rule (such as clear evidence of pilfering organizational funds). Employees thus disciplined still retain their rights to a fair and transparent process of sanctioning.

Summative evaluation: Evaluation that is done at the end of a particular project or program to ascertain if the outcomes specified *ex ante* were indeed produced, and how they were produced. Summative evaluation is thus related to studying the worth of a particular activity.

Sun-king syndrome: When supervisors and bosses overestimate their—and underestimate everyone else's—abilities to solve a problem and get things done. Delegation is progressively less evident in organizations that are led by managers who suffer from the sun-king syndrome. For an application of the term, see, e.g., *The Economist*, "The Not-So-Quiet American," March 29, 2003, p. 37.

Sunk commitments: Commitments that are made by organizations that cannot be retrieved and which may or may not lead to sunk costs. The assumption is that if organizational leaders were to have more evidence-based reasoning to defer the commitments until the very last minute, then decision making would tend to incur less sunk costs, because presumably the commitments would have been better informed. In that regard, monitoring key contingencies becomes a critical organizational activity in the decision-making process. See, e.g., K. Miller and G. Waller, "Scenarios, Real Options, and Integrated Risk Management," *Long Range Planning*, 2003, 36(1), pp. 93–107.

Sunk costs: Costs that cannot be recovered if a proposed project, program, or activity does not go ahead as planned. An example of a sunk cost is when government spends money on a prefeasibility study for a proposed project and the assessment comes back against such a project.

Sunset legislation: A requirement that a publicly funded program will end after its stipulated time period unless government wishes it to continue. Should this be the case, the legislature is required to do a comprehensive program evaluation (including formal evaluation) and pass subsequent legislation authorizing continuation. Sunset legislation ensures that there is no tendency toward unchecked proliferation of government activity.

Sunshine bargaining: Also termed goldfish-bowl bargaining, this refers to having collective bargaining done in the open with the press and public informed of all the details. This is possible in public-sector collective-bargaining processes in contrast with private firms, which are not usually subject to sunshine bargaining. *See also* **Goldfish-bowl bargaining.**

Sunshine laws: A legal provision which mandates that public organizations should provide all relevant information to the public about their work so that there is transparency of information. A good example of an application of a sunshine law is when an organization is required to publish in advance a notice on its next meeting date, the venue, and the agenda, and should allow public participation in it unless there is some confidential matter to discuss. The minutes of the meeting should also be available to the general public.

Superannuation: *See* **Pension.**

Super-bureaucrats: Refers to top bureaucrats and to those that are very powerful. Super-bureaucrats go beyond merely carrying out policy and are intimately involved in championing it to others in the organization, across government organizations, and in society at large. By the very nature of their work, they tend to be based in central agencies of government (such as the prime minister's office, the treasury, etc.). See, e.g., C. Campbell and G. Szablowski, *The Superbureaucrats: Structure and Behavior in Central Agencies*, Toronto: Macmillan, 1979, pp. 69–83. *See also* **Central agency.**

Super-citizen: A term used to denote a citizen who has several attributes of citizenship: (a) is politically informed, (b) acts rationally, and (c) is constructive in engagement. Evidence across jurisdictions tends tc show, however, that citizens generally do not exhibit all three attributes in unison. See, e.g., K. Ho, *The Politics of Policy-Making in Singapore*, Singapore: Oxford University Press, 2000, p. 206. *See also* **Super-politician.**

Super-leadership: Leadership that is successful at making group members self-directive. This ensures that the group's drive comes from within. Super-leadership is not necessarily easy to operationalize, however, and can be measured only to the extent that the group members exhibit proactive behavior in managing their tasks and delivering on their mandates.

Super-majority: When a decision has to be passed by a share of the organization's members that goes beyond the "fifty-percent-plus-one rule" (such as a two-thirds majority). A super-majority is required so as to ensure that policies that are passed are supported by a larger group of people. A super-majority requirement may also be put in place to ensure that contentious issues that have broad societal impact are widely accepted. *See also* **Fifty-percent-plus-one rule.**

Super-malimum alternatives: *See* **Lose-lose alternatives.**

Super-optimum alternatives: Alternatives for which everyone exceeds their best expectations (i.e., it is a win-win situation for all the parties). Super-optimum alternatives do not imply compromise, however, because that has a connotation of parties giving up something in return for something else. For a good discussion, see, e.g., S. Nagel, "Super-Optimum Solutions in Public Controversies," in W. Dunn and R. Kelly (eds.), *Advances in Policy Studies since 1950*, New Brunswick, NJ: Transaction Publishers, 1992, pp. 495–516. *See also* **Win-win-win policy.**

Super-politician: A term used to denote a politician who is highly qualified, well meaning, and able to undertake a considerable amount of responsibilities in a consensus-seeking manner. Super-politicians are well informed not only of the issues but also of the evidence on all facets of the issues. For a discussion of a super-politician in relation to Singapore politics and policy making, see K. Ho, *The Politics of Policy-Making in Singapore*, Singapore: Oxford University Press, 2000, p. 207. *See also* **Super-citizen.**

Super-statutes: In the public-management context, super-statutes are main legislative acts that fundamentally shape a state's public-management system. Examples of super-statutes are the 1988 State Sector Act in New Zealand and the 1966 Freedom of Information Act in the United States. The first institutionalized dramatic reforms in public-sector management, and the second provided unique avenues to citizens to access information and ensure transparency in governmental affairs.

Supplemental agreement: An agreement that is reached between principal and agent subsequent to an existing contract. A supplemental agreement becomes necessary when both parties agree to amend some prespecified contractual relationship.

Supplemental appropriation: Appropriation of funds that is made by the funding authority that is over and above what was initially made in the regular budget for the organization. Supplemental appropriation is made when the organization is successful in demonstrating to the funding authority that the extra resources are critical for attaining its mandates.

Supplementary estimates: Refers to the additional estimates for any further investment in an organization (for capital or other purposes).

Supplementary estimates are also needed to fund a changing price in outputs, or when new outputs are to be produced by the organization. The rigor of the process for assessing the need for resources remains in place; if anything, they may be viewed more critically. *See also* **Estimates of appropriation**.

Supplementary training: *See* **Refresher training**.

Supply-side moral hazard: Refers to a situation where public agencies seek to induce demand for their products and services without necessarily determining whether or not their clients are eligible for them or are in need of them (such as, for example, government-subsidized health clinics aggressively marketing their services if they get funding from government determined by the number of patients they serve). *See also* **Moral hazard**.

Supreme audit institutions: Also known as legislative audit institutions, these are agencies that specialize in controls and in enforcement of spending and revenue collection in public organizations. For a discussion of the role of supreme audit institutions in combating corruption, see, e.g., V. Sahgal and J. Burns, "Strengthening Legislative Audit Institutions: A Catalyst to Enhance Governance and Combat Corruption," in G. Bhatta and J. Gonzalez, *Governance Innovations in the Asia-Pacific Region: Trends, Cases and Issues*, Aldershot, UK: Ashgate, 1998, pp. 183–202.

Surrogate measures: *See* **Proxy measures**.

Surrogate pricing: A method of determining how much people are willing to pay for a service. In surrogate pricing, the focus is on substitutive or complementary goods that have prices (for example, expenses people are willing to pay to travel to a park as a surrogate price for the value of the recreational area). But note that, in this case, this means there is consumer surplus for those who live close by and who value the recreational area just as much.

Surveillance: Work that monitoring organizations do (often related to operation of payments system and to competition) in order to ensure that all parties are functioning the way they are supposed to. The term also refers to the role played by regulatory and oversight bodies in ascertaining how public organizations are fulfilling their mandates. Surveillance contributes to continuous monitoring of organizational processes and activities.

Suspension: Temporarily removing staff members from their positions as a result of violating some organizational rules and policies while a formal investigation is carried out. The staff member may or may not be paid wages during this suspension/investigation period.

Sustainable development: Refers to ensuring that development can continue in the long term in the economic, environmental, social, and to some extent, cultural spheres. A related concept is that of sustainable human development, which is an approach to national development formulated by the United Nations in the early 1990s to refer to development that takes into account community participation and collective modes of governance, environmentally sustainable economic activities, gender considerations, and growth with employment. See UNDP, *Sustainable Human Development—From Concept to Operation: A Guide for the Practitioner*, New York: United Nations, 1994.

Sustainable human development: *See* **Sustainable development**.

Sustainable policy regimes: Sets of policies that stand the test of time (such as policies that dwell on controlling corruption in the public sector). Such policy regimes tend to have a long-term horizon.

SWOT method: A popular method of analyzing an organization's internal and external environments by looking at the strengths and weaknesses (S-W) that are inherent in the organization, and the opportunities and threats (O-T) that it faces. By collecting evidence on these four variables, the analyst is able to derive four types of strategies that the organization can put in place to maximize its impact, (a) S-O strategies (to pursue opportunities that are a good fit with the organization's strengths), (b) W-O strategies (to overcome weaknesses to pursue opportunities), (c) S-T strategies (to find ways that the organization can use its strengths to reduce its vulnerability to threats), and (d) W-T strategies (to prevent the organization's weaknesses from making it susceptible to threats).

Symbiotic interdependency: *See* **Interdependency**.

Symbolic actions: A key element of a transformational strategy of organizational change, symbolic actions are actions that communicate new ideas and values, and that demonstrate to the outside world that the organization is undergoing a fundamental transformation. Symbolic actions may also not be very tangible in terms of policy impact, but they nonetheless send a message that importance is attached to the particular issue being addressed. For a discussion, see, e.g., L. Frost-Kumpf et al., "Strategic Action and Transformational Change: The Ohio Department of Mental Health," in B. Bozeman (ed.), *Public Management: The State of the Art*, San Francisco: Jossey-Bass, 1993, pp. 137–52.

Symbolic policies: Policies that highlight the important role that symbols play in the polity and economy. For example, a jurisdiction's policy to spend large amounts of resources on safeguarding the survival of the national bird could be considered a symbolic policy.

System capabilities: Capabilities of the state that are evident in several areas, including: (a) extraction (for example, manufacturing), (b) regulation (i.e., ensuring that the rules of the game are in place and adhered to), (c) distribution (for example, services to the rural poor), (d) symbolic output (such as defense), and (e) responsive capability (such as to deal with any emergent risks). Governments will normally not tend to have capability in all these areas to equal degree.

System integrity: (1) Refers to whether or not all components of a system are operating in the manner that they should. The systems could refer to, for example, an organization, whole of government, the public management domain, and so forth. (2) In the public-management context, it is also employed as a performance measure for a central control agency in evaluating departmental performance. The basic question being asked here is: "Is the system functioning well to achieve [these] outcomes?" See, e.g., State Services Commission, *Statement of Intent 2002*, Wellington: State Services Commission, 2002, p. 28.

System reflexivity: *See* **Double-loop learning**.

System responsiveness: As applied in the context of public management, this concept includes three strands of responsiveness: (a) on the part of governmental ministers to the public at large (or political responsiveness, i.e., responding to what the constituents want), (b) on the part of the public sector to ministers (or policy responsiveness, i.e., responding to the agenda that the government of the day has set), and (c) on the part of the central agencies to the various departments (or organizational responsiveness, i.e., responding to what the latter require in order to better fulfill their organizational mandates).

Systematic agenda: *See* **Agenda**.

Systematic risk: A risk that is evident across all projects of a certain type. Given the risk's spread, the organization cannot reduce its risk portfolio by diversifying, and managers have very little control over such risks. Systematic risks are contrasted with organization-specific risks, which, by definition, vary among organizations.

Systematic soldiering: A term coined by scientific-management theorist Frederic Taylor to refer to a situation where organizational output is low because workers are deliberately seeking to reduce their output. This is contrasted with natural soldiering, where the low output is not really a result of employees deliberately trying to do less. There are many reasons why employees may wish to be engaged in "systematic soldiering," not the least because they may wish to free up some time and energy to be engaged in other pursuits without having to be stressed from work. While this may not have been the reasoning at the time Taylor developed these constructs, they are certainly worth considering now. See F. Taylor, *The Principles of Scientific Management*, New York: Harper Bros., 1911, pp. 5–29. *Cf.* **Natural soldiering**.

Systemic crisis: A crisis that hits all aspects of a system. An example of a systemic crisis is the Asian economic fallout of the late 1990s, which started with financial troubles but quickly spread to the economic, corporate, and political domains as well.

Systemic discrimination: Discrimination of women and people of minority groups through use of employment practices. Systemic discrimination tends to be comprehensive in nature (i.e., across all aspects—and processes—of organizational work). Accordingly, responses to mitigate systemic discrimination have to ensure that they take into account all the variables that contribute to the discrimination. Thus, for example, system discrimination against older workers in organizations is addressed by focusing upon such diverse, yet related, issues as work-life balance, occupational health and safety, life transition planning and assistance, etc.

Systemic risk: *See* **Risk**.

Systems analysis: Generally refers to an explicit formal inquiry that is designed to give decision makers a better frame of reference to make effective decisions. Systems analysis is used when a problem under investigation is complex (i.e., does not lend itself to an easy solution), and there is uncertainty of the desired outcome. It focuses on an iterative process of identifying and refining the objectives, examining all possible aspects of all possible alternative solutions to the problem, and considers in an integral manner the notion of costs, benefits, and risks associated with each considered alternative. Finally, systems analysis implies clearly an interdisciplinary approach to the analysis of a problem. For a discussion of the application of systems analysis to policy making, see, e.g., J. Stewart and R. Ayers, "Systems Theory and Policy Practice: An Exploration," *Policy Sciences*, 2001, 34(1), pp. 79–94.

Systems-theory approach: An approach to organizational effectiveness that focuses on how well the organization is dealing with its environment or the system in which it operates. This contrasts with a goal approach because it does not necessarily look solely at the extent of goals attainment. For a review of systems theory as applied in the policy-problem domain, see, e.g., J. Stewart and R. Ayers, "Systems Theory and Policy Practice: An Exploration," *Policy Sciences*, 2001, 34(1), pp. 79–94. *Cf.* **Goal approach**.

T

Tabulation of bids: A process in contract administration wherein the party that has asked for bids will collate and tabulate them for further consideration. Such tabulation helps it to make a more meaningful and informed judgment about the strength of the bids received. It also enables the organization to disregard any bids that have not adhered to the bid specifications in, for example, matters of format and overall content.

Tacit knowledge: Knowledge in an organization that is acquired by experience and by learning by doing. Tacit knowledge may be held by an individual or diffused throughout an organization. In terms of knowledge management, it is more difficult for organizations to disseminate tacit knowledge as compared to explicit knowledge because tacit knowledge is not as amenable to codification. See, e.g., R. Hall and P. Andriani, "Managing Knowledge for Innovation," *Long Range Planning,* 2002, 35(1), pp. 29–48. *Cf.* **Explicit knowledge**; *see also* **Externalization**.

Tactical risk: A risk that arises from information asymmetry where decisions are made based on incomplete information. The risk is inherent in the operational aspects of organizational work as opposed to the strategic aspect. Tactical risks also tend to be specific across subunits of the organization (i.e., different units will face different tactical risks).

Talent rostering: Refers to an organization listing all the individuals in the organization and the specific talents they possess. Such a listing is helpful for many purposes, the most obvious being a ready source of reference for the organization to refer to whenever new skills are being sought as a result of an increase—or a change—in its mandate. Talent rostering also allows the organization to bring about multiskilling, where it can request individual staff members to be involved in multiple tasks (such may or may not be specified in the employment contract or the job description) but for which the employee clearly has the skills.

Tall organization: A traditional form of organizational structure, a tall organization is one where there are several hierarchies and a narrow span of control. In advanced jurisdictions, tall organizations are increasingly being replaced by flatter ones, where the chain of command is less hierarchical. *Cf.* **Flat organization**.

Tall-poppy syndrome: The tendency of individuals in organizations to belittle the achievements of high achievers. This generally arises when the organization has not been able to create a team spirit among groups. While it is expected that there will always be some evidence of this tendency in organizations, the task of the organization leadership is to ensure that it is effectively contained. The syndrome, if not corrected, can lead to organizational dysfunction.

Tame problems: Public problems where the solutions may be known but remain unaddressed because of organizational boundary and turf issues, and whose solution requires cross-agency collaboration. For a general discussion of the concept, see, e.g., H. Rittel and M. Webber, "Dilemmas in a General Theory of Planning," *Policy Sciences,* 1973, 4(1), pp. 155–69. For a discussion on how tame problems affect accountability arrangements in government, see, e.g., National Audit Office, *Joining Up to Improve Public Services,* Report by the Comptroller and Auditor General, HC 383 Session 2001–2002, London: National Audit Office, 2001, p. 69. *Cf.* **Wicked problems**.

Tandem employment: A situation where a person is job sharing, that is, where the employer knowingly permits someone to additionally work elsewhere either within the organization or outside. This is not entirely to the organization's disadvantage, however, as the employee has an opportunity to substantially widen his/her experiences and gather new skills. The disadvantages are that the employee's attention is compromised in both employment situations, and may end up not helping either employer.

Tapering of employment: A situation where an employee is permitted to gradually reduce his/her workload so as to meet personal requirements toward exiting employment. Such tapering is beneficial to the employer as well as it allows the employer to gradually seek a replacement for the person who seeks the tapered employment.

Target audience: Also known as a target group, this term refers to a selected representative collection of people for whom certain activities, projects, and programs, are intended, and for whom specific policies are designed to have an effect. Any program formulation activity will have identification of the target audience, and their needs, as the key task since that will help determine the nature of the project's work, informed as it is by what the target audience wants.

Target fee: Refers to a level of resources that the principal has agreed to pay to the agent in the form of incentives if the latter is able to perform the contract according to *ex ante* specifications. Target fees serve as a measure of ensuring that the contract is adequately fulfilled. The structure and arrangements of the fees are determined within the contract.

Target grant: Grants that are awarded by the central government for specific geographic regions and areas or for specific clientele (such as the rural poor). In all jurisdictions, the discussions around target grants center on two issues: the size of the grants and the manner in which recipients are determined.

Target knowledge: The specific knowledge set and knowledge level that an organization is targeting or hopes to attain. This is affected by the organization's predetermined outcomes and by the system and processes in place to attain those outcomes. Some proportion of the target knowledge is also a function of the sets of knowledge, skills, and abilities that individuals bring to the organization. See, e.g., R. Hall and P. Andriani, "Managing Knowledge for Innovation," *Long Range Planning,* 2002, 35(1), pp. 29–48. *See also* **Platform knowledge**.

Targeted consultation: A method of consulting with stakeholders and others about a policy by allowing those who will be affected by the policy to provide feedback on the proposed policy. Targeted consultation is differentiated from notice-and-comment consultation by the fact that only potentially affected stakeholders are targeted for consultation as opposed to opening up the comment process to everyone interested in the policy. *Cf.* **Notice-and-comment consultation**.

Targeting: (1) Being aware of the level of minority representation needed in the organization. (2) Ensuring that only selected groups of people will be subject to an organization's policy (for example, in providing certain benefits). See, e.g., J. Conning and M. Kevane, "Community-Based Targeting Mechanisms for Social Safety Nets: A Critical Review," *World Development,* 2002, 30(3), pp. 375–94.

Task analysis: *See* **Job analysis**.

Task breakdown: The main points and detailed steps specified in the performance of a task. This includes informing the employee what specific procedures need to be followed in order to complete a task.

Task competence: The ability that is expected of an individual who is given the responsibility to complete the task. Minimum levels of task competence will have been ascertained at the time of individual recruitment, but their nature and composition may change over time.

Task description: The details of what a particular task is and what it entails. When a wide range of tasks for a particular job is defined, it is known as broadbanding. This can motivate employees to pursue multiple career paths, and it benefits employers by promoting multiskilling and flexible use of labor. *See also* **Job description**.

Task environment: The context and parameters within which a particular task needs to be completed in the organization. For example, the task environment for a human-resource management adviser's work would be the corporate domain of the organization, with its associated linkages with all other divisions of the organization, as well as all the employees and relevant employment-specific legislation.

Task identity: The degree to which a job entails completion of an identifiable part that the employee can relate to as being a product of his/her own work. Increasing the task identity generally leads to greater motivation. A broad task assignment (i.e., when an employee performs a relatively large set of tasks) can also produce specific task identity as long as the tasks are clearly delineated.

Task incentives: Incentives that increase the fulfillment that employees realize from completing a task. Task incentives may or may not be tied into the organization's broad bonus reward scheme. Some task incentives are provided by the organization and some are generated from within the employees.

Task management: All aspects of managing the various processes and procedures that goes into completing a particular task. For example, toward preparing a business case for a new product or service, the task management would include, at a minimum, the collection of evidence by the research support group in the organization; preparation of the business case, which is then peer reviewed from within the organization; and then a formal submission of the business case to the treasury.

Task maturity: *See* **Life-cycle theory.**

Task-oriented activity: Any activity that is routine and can thus be planned for with a fair degree of certainty as to when and how specific procedures need to be followed and what the outcomes will be. A leadership style that is suited for carrying out task-oriented activities is termed task-oriented leadership. Such leadership is implicit, for example, in the concepts of Theory X and scientific management. In general, this kind of leadership tends to be authoritarian in nature.

Task role: A particular role that an individual needs to adopt in order to complete a particular task. Such a role could either be value neutral to the individual or the individual's value system could feature considerably in the task role. *See also* **Psychological contract.**

Task significance: The degree to which a job has a substantial impact on others (both inside and outside the organization). Generally, it can be said that the greater the degree of task significance, the greater the motivation of the employee. The variables that affect the degree of task significance can include job size, organizational outcomes, hierarchical location of the employees in the organization, etc.

Task step data: Information on the types of variables that will be considered in conducting a performance appraisal of an individual who will have been expected to have successfully completed a particular task. Such variables include timeliness, effectiveness, clarity, etc., and a premium will be placed on ensuring that such data can be operationalized.

Task variability: The degree to which an employee's work has scope for the individual to be involved in varied activities but still related to the major tasks that are expected of the particular employment position. Generally, it can be said that the greater the degree of task variability, the greater the level of intrinsic motivation of the individual.

Teach-and-test method: A method of training wherein the trainer explains the key ideas of a particular module to trainees, and then, after a period in which the trainees study the module, tests the level of comprehension in the trainees prior to moving on to a different module. The test provides the incentives for trainers to ensure that what was taught stays embedded in them.

Team building: Refers to a purposive effort to improve working relationships among an organization's staff members, particularly as it applies to groups of them who would normally be expected to work together. Here, the members of a team go through various stages in order to come to a situation where they are comfortable working with each other. With much of organizational work now rotated around teams, team building is an important development activity in an organization.

Team mania: Refers to the formation of teams to get organizational work done whether or not they are suitable. This focus on team formation stems from a desire to adhere to principles of total quality management, which emphasizes teamwork over individual work. See, e.g., J. Brickley, C. Smith, and J. Zimmerman, *Managerial Economics and Organizational Architecture,* Chicago: Irwin, 1997, p. G-9.

Team potency: Refers to a belief that group members in a team have that collectively they will be effective in fulfilling their mandates. Such a belief is self-fueling and requires that the impetus come from within the team (although votes of confidence from outside the team also help). For a brief research note on this concept, see, e.g., C. Pearce, et al., "Confidence at the Group Level of Analysis: A Longitudinal Investigation of the Relationship Between Potency and Team Effectiveness," *Journal of Occupational and Organizational Psychology,* 2002, 75(1), pp. 115–19.

Technical assistance program: A program wherein assistance to developing countries from multilateral and bilateral donors takes the form of specialized expertise. Such assistance complements any financial assistance by enabling the country to learn firsthand from the technical experts and be able to utilize the resources judiciously. Almost all donor agencies and countries have a technical assistance component in their aid programs.

Technical capacity: The capacity of governments to help establish—and then implement and manage—coherent socioeconomic policies through managerial expertise that exists in governmental departments. This implies that there are enabling authorities that can provide the necessary leadership and managerial acumen to get things done in a technical-rational way.

Technical compliance: When organizations are able to comply with a regulation technically (i.e., as the regulation specifically asks them to) but not with its underlying intent. Thus, for example, agencies could relabel posts so that it appears that they have abolished the required number of posts as per a directive.

Technical efficiency: A firm is technically efficient if it is using the minimum quantity of inputs required to produce a given output (i.e., it is a measure of the extent to which an organization is able to do what was required of it and in a manner that minimizes costs). Technical efficiency is generally measured as the ratio of the level of goal achievement to the level of effort spent on it.

Technical feasibility: A stage in project management when it is determined that the set of activities that will constitute the project can be successfully carried out with the technical expertise that is available to the organization. Such technical feasibility is a necessary precondition before financial commitments are made by project donors. Thus, for example, a proposed project on establishing a fruit-processing plant in a rather remote location will look at, among other things, the technical feasibility of having the appropriate machinery and plant in the location.

Technical rationality: *See* **Rationality**.

Technocratic elites: Individuals in high positions in government who have considerable expertise but who are confined to a narrow purview, and thus lack the softer skills of people management and have comparatively less civic spirit. Technocratic elites, for example, may be professionals at delivering services to the citizens, but may not exhibit skills of working together either among themselves or with others, or meaningfully engaging citizens. The rise of such elites can be a function of many variables, including a narrow definition of professionalism in the public sector. Individuals who bring to the organization technical expertise (for example, in project planning, decision sciences, and information and communication technology) but not necessarily strong managerial skills are known as "technocrats." For a case-study application of technocrats in governance, see, e.g., R. Gauld, "Technocrats at the Helm?: The Attitudes of New Zealand's Senior Health Officials," *International Journal of Public Administration*, 2002, 25(7), pp. 831–57.

Technological displacement: Any replacement of individuals, processes, hardware, etc., that results from the application of technology. For example, computing technology has displaced workers that were typists. Technological displacement is the negative manifestation of the application of technology, the positive one being the introduction of technology in the workplace, which has improved labor productivity measurably.

Technological imperative: An assertion that the extent of application of technology in an organization will determine its success or failure. The assumption that is made here is that technology has a central role to play in organizational processes, and the extent to which organizations can adapt their goals and alter their ways of doing things in keeping with the technology will affect that role.

Technology assessment: A systematic study of all the aspects of the impacts of technology so as to be able to determine its usefulness to any particular setting or organization. Such an assessment is essential before the organization introduces any particular technology into its processes. The assessment is similar to that for any project and encompasses considerations of the nature of the problem to be addressed by the new technology, its costs and benefits, and impact on other processes, among others.

Technology gap: (1) The difference between what is required of any new technology and the organization's given capability to adapt. (2) The differences in type and level of technology used across jurisdictions for the same function and/or in the same sector. In either case, the wider the gap, the greater the difficulty in incorporating technology in the particular organization or setting.

Technology-push type of innovation: Any innovation that is triggered in an organization by the need to grasp the opportunities offered by new technologies. Thus, for example, a public agency could use call-center technology to better address the demands and concerns of its customers, and also better market its services. See, e.g., R. Hall and P. Andriani, "Managing Knowledge for Innovation," *Long Range Planning*, 2002, 35(1), pp. 29–48.

Template: A pattern or model for something. As used in governance, it refers to a standard way that different organizations and jurisdictions apply a policy to their setting. Thus, for example, one of the templates for reducing the role of government in the economy has tended to be the disposal of public assets. *See also* **Standard operating procedures**.

Temporal specificity: Transaction-cost economists use this term to denote the importance of timing in the receipt of goods or services that are related to coordination costs. This concept is related to that of just-in-time production because there is a cost attached to the time in which either the inputs are not available or the outputs have not reached the market. See, e.g., S. Masten, J. Meehan, and E. Snyder, "The Costs of Organization," *Journal of Law, Economics, and Organization*, 1991, 7(1), pp. 1–25.

Temporary appointment: An appointment to a post that is made for a limited time. One of the main reasons for making a temporary appointment is to ensure that someone is staffing a role for which an organization seeks a suitable candidate. However, the organization could, for a period of time, merely renew the temporary appointment of the individual, and then after the individual has gained valuable on-the-job training, he/she would then be in a strong position to get the job permanently. This distorts the recruitment process since the temporary appointment will have been made on a noncompetitive basis, meaning that the individual will have secured the permanent post without having to compete for it.

Term contracting: A contract with terms of service that specify the period for which the contract is valid. While there are advantages to maintaining long-term contracts, there are also obvious advantages to specifying term contracts so that there is flexibility to not renew them if problems arise. Most contracts specify duration but some are set for indefinite periods, usually containing reconsideration options as regards conditions for both the principal and the agent.

Terminal arbitration: Arbitration that is called for in a grievance procedure that is expected to ultimately settle the matter under dispute. Under terminal arbitration, neither party has the option to challenge the ultimate decision. This is necessary in situations where the disputing parties have to work with each other but cannot find common ground on their own.

Terminal interview: An interview that is conducted with an employee just prior to the person voluntarily leaving the organization. The purpose of the interview is not only to get from the individual any impressions that might help the organization to improve in any way, but also to create goodwill that might be useful for the future (for example, in securing nominations of good candidates for future openings).

Termination: Separation of employment from an organization or the cessation of a policy. Termination of employment can be voluntary or coerced. Reasons for termination of employment as well as of policy include financial imperatives, political ideology, public outcry, etc. A termination contract is an agreement by which the organization promises to continue paying salary for a period to an employee in case of employment termination. This is designed to act as an incentive for the employee to join the organization. Payments that are made to employees whose contracts have been ended are called termination payments. The employment contract will normally broadly state the arrangements of such payments. If the termination payments appear very lucrative to employees, the term that is used to characterize such is a "golden handshake."

Terms and conditions: (1) In contract administration, the rules within which a bid needs to be submitted. (2) In employment, the details of the employment contract between the employer and the staff member that specifies issues, such as types of benefit to be given to the employee. The terms and conditions of employment for staff members who are represented by a union are handled through the collective-bargaining process; for those who are not, their terms and conditions are reviewed periodically in individual negotiations.

Terms of payment: The manner in which all bills and invoices are to be paid for services received. For example, a contractor may specify that for services rendered in helping plan an event, half the value of the contract must be paid out before the event and half upon its completion.

Terms of reference: A document that specifies the exact nature of work to be done by consultants and contractors. The terms of reference specify the following: (a) the context within which the work is to be carried out, (b) the purpose of the contract, (c) the specific work to be done, (d) reporting requirements and accountability arrangements, (e) methods of assessment, and (f) timing and costs.

Territorial departmentalization: The process of creating divisions of organizations based on their dispersal in different regions. Territorial departmentalization is appropriate for organizations whose activities are largely spread out. This gives some measure of autonomy to branches of organizations that are in other territories. A fair bit of control is still exercised by the center, however, in terms of, for example, strategic direction.

Territorial/financial equalization: The process of ensuring that the amount of funds received by territories and subjurisdictions is equal in weighted terms. In decentralization programs in developing countries, for example, the central government will have a territorial/financial equalization policy in place that ensures that the poorer regions receive a higher share of central-government revenue compared with that of the richer regions. This policy serves to augment the resource base of the poor regions.

Thematic evaluation: Evaluation of select projects and programs that focus on a common theme but which could be spread geographically or by sector. For example, programs that are designed to address poverty among a particular ethnic population would be subject to a thematic evaluation.

Theory of formal authority: States that in an organization, formal authority comes from the head of the organization and flows downward. It is the theory of formal authority that underpins the accountability locus in organizations whereby the leader is answerable to actions that are attributed to the organization.

Theory X: An assumption about human behavior that was popularized by the noted expert on Industrial Relations Douglas McGregor, which had the premise that in some individuals there was an inherent dislike of work and that, because of this, they needed to be coerced into action. He also maintained that Theory-X individuals liked to be directed, hade little or no ambition, and valued security of tenure above all. While the study of human behavior in organizations has come a long way since McGregor's work on Theory X and Theory Y, it still has considerable explanatory power in the study of the behavior of public servants in many less-developed jurisdictions. For McGregor's original work in this area, see D. McGregor, *Leadership and Motivation,* Cambridge, MA: MIT Press, 1966. For a review of how the theory can be helpful in assessing motivation, see, e.g., B. Young, S. Worchel, and D. Woehr, "Organizational Commitment Among Public Service Employees," *Public Personnel Management,* 1998, 27(3), pp. 339–48.

Theory Y: Theory-Y individuals are those who do not inherently dislike work and who do exercise self-direction. Such people do not shy from taking responsibility and from contributing creatively to organizational problem solving. In reality, organizations are not populated by people who are either Theory X or Theory Y but by people who may exhibit either of the tendencies on any given day. For a review of Theory Y and the assessment of motivation, see, e.g., B. Young, S. Worchel, and D. Woehr, "Organizational Commitment Among Public Service Employees," *Public Personnel Management,* 1998, 27(3), pp. 339–48.

Theory Z: A term used by management author William Ouchi that borrows from the Japanese style of management and emphasizes participative management and shared socioeconomic values between workers and management. Personnel policies under Theory-Z type management are characterized by trust and security of tenure. The problem of Theory-Z organizations is that it takes a long time to bring about change in them because their very culture needs to be modified before significant change can be made. See W. Ouchi, *Theory Z: How American Business Can Meet the Japanese Challenge,* Reading, MA: Addison-Wesley, 1981.

Theory-E organization: A theory that looks at how organizations concentrate on adding economic value above all else, and in that process lose out on enhancing broader organizational capability. For example, a focus on earning per share alone may not necessarily enable the organization to concentrate on enhancing all aspects of the capability that is needed to serve all stakeholders. See, e.g., M. Beer, "How to Develop an Organization Capable of Sustained High Performance: Embrace the Drive for Results-Capability Development Paradox," *Organizational Dynamics,* 2001, 29(4), pp. 233–47.

Theory-in-use: What managers actually do (as opposed to enunciate or espouse). For example, they may convey to staff members that they believe in openness of communication and a participative style of management, but may not necessarily demonstrate it with their actions. Theories-in-use are relevant to study in organizational behavior because they provide cues on actual management practices. *Cf.* **Espoused theory.**

Theory-O organization: An organization that concentrates on enhancing organizational capability and economic value (i.e., focuses on multiple variables in organizational action, such as employee welfare, work environment, work-life balance, etc.). See, e.g., M. Beer, "How to Develop an Organization Capable of Sustained High Performance: Embrace the Drive for Results-Capability Development Paradox," *Organizational Dynamics,* 2001, 29(4), pp. 233–47.

Thick-and-thin rationality: Refers to the two versions of the rationality of individual behavior. Thick rationality assumes self-interest and, as such, that behavior can be readily predicted. However, in reality, people often do not act with thick rationality; in such instances, it is more useful to consider their actions in light of thin rationality, which gives precedence to processes rather than goals. For a review of the distinction, see, e.g., B. Jones, "Bounded Rationality and Political Science: Lessons from Public Administration and Public Policy," *Journal of Public Administration Research and Theory,* 2003, 13(4), pp. 395–412.

Thickening of government: An increase in government bureaucracy resulting from new layers being added and from an increase in the number of appointees in each layer. See, e.g., P. Light, *Thickening Government: Federal Hierarchy and the Diffusion of Authority,* Washington, DC: The Brookings Institution and The Governance Institute, 1995.

Third sector: A term that refers to the alternative to the public and private sectors. The third sector is normally voluntary, not for profit, and nongovernmental in orientation. For an extensive review of third-sector organizations in the context of governance, see, e.g., E. Choudhury and S.

Ahmed, "The Shifting Meaning of Governance: Public Accountability of Third Sector Organizations in an Emergent Global Regime," *International Journal of Public Administration,* 2002, 25(4), pp. 561–88.

Third way: A term popularized by the economic sociologist Anthony Giddens to refer to the manner in which the government engages the citizenry in governance. The third way veers away from relying mostly on either the market or the statist approach. It seeks to develop a synergy between the public and private sectors, recognizing the virtues of each. Thus, the private sector's dynamism and continuous search for improvement is sought along with the public sector's noble focus on the public interest. See A. Giddens, *The Third Way: The Renewal of Social Democracy,* Cambridge, MA: Polity Press, 1998. See also, e.g., C. Scanlon, "A Step to the Left? Or Just a Jump to the Right? Making Sense of the Third Way on Government and Governance," *Australian Journal of Political Science,* 2001, 36(3), pp. 481–98.

Third-party allegations of discrimination: Allegations of discrimination against an employer made not by those against whom the discrimination may or may not have been committed but by others outside the organization. This allows the public to be more aware of any discrimination that does exist, and this public exposure enables remedial action to be taken by the employer even though there may have been no specific complaints of discrimination.

Third-party counseling: A situation where the employer takes the initiative to locate someone from outside the organization to provide counseling to employees whose performance is not up to par, or to help managers and staff members work through problems.

Third-party effects: *See* **Negative externality**.

Third-party government: A term denoted to show that the voluntary sector has begun to do most of the work intended of government. There is a clear explanation for this: as governments began to withdraw from many of their roles during the public-sector reforms of the 1980s and 1990s, this left a void in many areas, which only voluntary and nonprofit organizations were willing to enter. Over time, this resulted in their occupying a key role in service delivery. See, e.g., F. Mosher, "The Changing Responsibilities and Tactics of the Federal Government," *Public Administration Review,* 1980, 40(4), pp. 541–52. *See also* **Hollow state**.

Third-party revenue: Funds that a public organization receives from sources other than its regular budget from the legislature and its own revenue sources. Other sources could include grants and endowments. Such third-party revenue sources, however, usually do not constitute a large proportion of the organization's financial base.

Threat of reciprocity: A situation that emerges when parties are involved in long-term contractual relationships and when they often have opportunities to grant favors to—or withhold favors from—one another. The threat of reciprocity greatly reduces the need for formal enforcement mechanisms since each party has an incentive to adhere to the conditions stipulated in the contract.

Three-hundred-and-sixty-degree appraisal: A form of performance appraisal of staff members where everybody that is involved with the individual's work is asked to provide relevant feedback on his/her performance. If the individual were to be placed at the center of a circle, then above (at 90 degrees) would be the supervisor, on either side (at 180 degrees) would be peers, and below (at 360 degrees) would be subordinates. The individual is at zero degrees, which is the self-appraisal. Thus, in a 360-degree appraisal, everyone's feedback is taken into consideration. However, this is rather difficult to institute since not everyone can be familiar with all aspects of the individual's work, and individuals in many societies are also less keen to accept the critique of those who work for them. For a review of the usage of this form of appraisal, see, e.g., S. Tyson and P. Ward, "The Use of 360 Degree Feedback Technique in the Evaluation of Management Development," *Management Learning,* 2004, 35(2), pp. 205–23.

Threshold access: A situation that describes the point of access to information from governmental departments by a government that has the status of a caretaker (as when it has lost an election but the new government has not yet been formally instituted). In such a case, the caretaker government is usually limited to access to such information through one channel (in many jurisdictions, it is the commissioner for public services). See, e.g., State Services Commission, *Annual Report of the State Services Commission, 2002,* Wellington, New Zealand: State Services Commission, 2002, p. 12.

Threshold setting: Determining acceptability levels in policies. Different policies have different levels of threshold depending upon their nature and their intent. Threshold setting means policy makers are aware of what is acceptable, and what is not, in terms of policy content. For a discussion of the threshold of commitment in arriving at organizational decisions, see, e.g., M. Harvey, et al., "The Abilene Paradox after Thirty Years: A Global Perspective," *Organizational Dynamics,* 2004, 33(2), pp. 215–26.

Through-life management: An integrated approach in the acquisition process for a new product or service by an organization that deals with planning and costing activities across the whole organization, and that also takes into consideration all processes that may be necessary to manage the project for its whole life rather than just for the period during acquisition. Given the scope of coverage under through-life management, organizations need to undergo a cultural and process change in order to ensure that projects are well integrated into the overall organizational domain. For an application of this concept, see National Audit Office, *Ministry of Defence: Through-Life Management,* Report by the Comptroller and Auditor General, HC 698 Session 2002–2003, London: The Stationery Office, 2003.

Tight-loose structure: Refers to the combination of control and flexibility that characterizes effective organizations. For example, some functions (such as financial transactions) will have a tight structure so that resource planning and management is prudent and in conformance with guidelines set by law. Other transactions (such as operational matters) will have a greater degree of flexibility so as to be able to capture the innovativeness that might exist at lower levels of the organizations. For an application of the concept, see, e.g., R. Carzo, Jr., "Some Effects of Organization Structure on Group Effectiveness," *Administrative Science Quarterly,* 1963, 7, pp. 393–424.

Tilburg model: The local-government reforms that took place in this town in the Netherlands later became a model for other jurisdictions (such as in German municipal and Swiss local and cantonal reforms) in the 1990s. The model emphasizes a participatory and consultative type of governance, while at the same time incorporating business practices in the governance of local entities. The city council makes decisions about products, their quantities, and quality, and the city administration is responsible for the production at lowest possible costs. See, e.g., F. Hendriks and P. Tops, "Between Democracy and Efficiency: Trends in Local Government Reforms in the Netherlands and in Germany," *Public Administration,* 1999, 77(1), pp. 133–53.

Time span of discretion: The maximum amount of time that employees can be left alone to exercise independent judgment. The concept is used in increasing the scope of delegation in the organization. It is relevant only under the assumption that those at the lower rungs of the organizational hierarchy have a low time span of discretion, with the converse being the case for superiors.

Time-dimension model of effectiveness: Looks at effectiveness of organizations in a time horizon from short to intermediate to long run. The criteria of effectiveness in the time-dimension model are production, efficiency, satisfaction, adaptability, and development. See, e.g., J. Ivancevich and M. Matteson, *Organizational Behavior and Management,* 2nd edition, Homewood, IL: BPI Irwin, 1990, pp. 27–29.

Time-in-grade restriction: A restriction that is imposed to ensure that employees are not promoted extremely rapidly. For example, a time-in-grade restriction may be that an employee has to spend at least 18 months in a particular post before being eligible for promotion to a higher grade.

Time-inconsistency problem: Denotes a situation where due to bounded rationality (including imperfect information) as well as a future that is uncertain, agents perceive an opportunity to renege on the contracts. The only method of managing this problem is a firm precommitment that the agent will not deviate from the contract. This precommitment is important, although if the agent further perceives that the principal will not enforce the *ex ante* commitment, then the time-inconsistency problem becomes quite possible again.

TINA: An acronym that refers to "there is no alternative." It is a form of rhetoric that underlies the belief that proponents of a particular method of doing things (or of a particular policy) place on the policy/action having to be implemented. The series of reforms that practically all jurisdictions are currently involved in under "new public management" can be said to incorporate, in some sense, the notion of TINA. This is now increasingly being replaced by TANYA (the alternative not yet available).

Tipping-point leadership: Leadership that brings an organization to—and sees it through—the critical point where performance improvement tends to feed on itself, and where there is in place a virtuous cycle of learning and performance enhancement. Such change is generally possible with transformational—rather than transactional—leadership because what the organization needs to get over the performance threshold is not so much an operational focus but a focus on changing the organizational culture. See, e.g., W. Kim and R. Mauborgne, "Tipping Point Leadership," *Harvard Business Review,* 2003, 81(4), pp. 60–69.

Token bid: A bid submitted by a party as a token (i.e., without any intention of being considered seriously). Parties will do this for various reasons, to, for example, test the market, test the strength of one's own proposal, and as a collusion device with another more credible bidder.

Tokenism: Refers to paying lip service to certain principles but not really heeding those principles. For example, in the context of gendered development, tokenism would be an insincere effort by a government to create a ministry of women and development, hire a few women in top positions, and then do nothing else to help change the gendered power relationships in society. For a discussion of the concept as it applies in the public sector, see, e.g., E. Bardach, *The Implementation Game: What Happens After a Bill Becomes a Law,* Cambridge, MA: MIT Press, 1977, pp. 98–124. *See also* **Blatant resistance**; **Delayed compliance**.

Too-big-to-fail principle: The belief that some organizations cannot be allowed to fail because they are very big and their failures would send a wrong signal to the market. In South Korea in the 1990s, for example, several *chaebols* (business conglomerates) were propped up by the government based on the belief that a perceived failure in any of the conglomerates would destabilize the market. For an application of this principle in the banking industry, see, e.g., D. Morgan, "Rating Banks: Risk and Uncertainty in an Opaque Industry," *American Economic Review*, 2002, 92(4), pp. 874–88.

Tool goods: Goods for which while there is joint use, exclusion is also feasible (such as cable television, libraries).

Top-down organization: Refers to an organization in which the lines of authority, and programmatic direction, are evident as flowing downward from the organizational leadership. For a discussion of the management style in a top-down setting, see, e.g., R. Agranoff and M. McGuire, "American Federalism and the Search for Models of Management," *Public Administration Review,* 2001, 61(6), pp. 671–81.

Total compensation comparability: Refers to the comparisons that can be made in the total level of compensation received by individual workers by including the monetary equivalent of all fringe benefits that are also awarded the individuals. This presents a much more accurate picture of total compensation received, the worth of a particular job, and the organization's total wage bill.

Total institution: A term that denotes an organization such as an asylum, a prison, or even schools, which change people completely. In a total institution, all aspects of life are separated from life outside, and there is a tight schedule of daily activities. Government agencies (such as the Department Prisons) that manage total institutions need thus to have in place programs that cater to all aspects of the incarceration (including activities that will help the prison population re-enter society eventually when their sentences end). See, e.g., E. Goffman, "The Characteristics of Total Institutions," in *Symposium on Preventive and Social Psychiatry,* sponsored by the Walter Reed Institute of Research, Washington, DC: US Government Printing Office, 1957, pp. 43–84.

Total quality governance: A concept that is borrowed from total quality management to refer to governance of public-sector organizations based on stakeholder feedback. The concept is also applied to ensure that citizens are involved in the evaluation of the performance of the organizations. For an application, see, e.g., E. Bolongaita, Jr., "Total Quality Governance (TQG): A New Model for Government-Citizen Relations," in G. Bhatta and J. Gonzalez (eds.), *Governance Innovations in the Asia-Pacific Region: Trends, Cases, and Issues,* Aldershot, UK; Ashgate, 1998, pp. 103–12.

Total quality management: An organizational philosophy that focuses on efforts by everyone in the organization to continually focus on quality in all areas of operation. "Total" means that everyone is involved, and "management" implies a deliberate attempt to ensure quality. "Quality" itself has five determinants: (a) Is it as specified? (b) Does it conform to what the customer expects? (c) Is it reliable? (d) Is it affordable? (e) Is it delivered on time? For a cogent analysis of how TQM can be made sustainable in organizations, see, e.g., M. Zairi, "Beyond TQM Implementation: The New Paradigm of TQM Sustainability," *Total Quality Management,* 2002, 13(8), pp. 1161–72.

Total quality organization: Drawing from the concept of total quality management, the total quality organization is one where there are these four elements in evidence: (a) system-based management, (b) empowerment of employees, (c) quality of work life (including work-life balance), and (d) a partnership among all employees. See, e.g., C. Donald, T. Lyons, and R. Tribbey, "A Partnership for Strategic Planning and Management in a Public Organization," *Public Performance and Management Review,* 2001, 25(2), pp. 176–93.

Trading risk: As applied in the organizational context, a trading risk refers to a risk that organizations face which relates to their day-to-day activities. Management of trading risks thus centers on getting a better handle on operational fluctuations. For a discussion, see, e.g., G. Scott, "Managing Operational and Policy Risks at the Center of Government," in J. Yeabsley and A. Sundakov (eds.), *Risk and the Institutions of Government,* Wellington: Institute of Policy Studies and NZIER, 1999, pp. 14–34. *Cf.* **Strategic risk**.

Traditional public administration: A public administration where there is a dichotomy of politics and administration, and which is primarily concerned with implementing policies that have been formulated by others. In traditional public administration, administrative functions outside the policy implementation realm are not considered; thus, this form of public administration is considered passive. See, e.g., J. Skok, "Public Issue Networks and the Public Policy Cycle: A Structural-Functional Framework for Public Administration," *Public Administration Review,* 1995, 55(4), pp. 325–32.

Traditional bargain (of civil service): The implicit understanding that existed between civil servants (i.e., career officials) and governmental ministers that the former will report and be accountable to ministers. Career officials are to remain nonpartisan, loyal, and have a nonpublic identity. In return, ministers will be publicly responsible for the work of the departments and will account for them in the legislature. The nature of this bargain has begun to shift now, what with public-sector organizations with arm's-length arrangements from ministers proliferating. For a cogent discussion of this concept, see, e.g., D. Savoie, *Breaking the Bargain: Public Servants, Ministers, and Parliament,* Toronto: University of Toronto Press, 2003, pp. 40–61.

Tragedy of the commons: An assertion that common property left to the use of all inhabitants has a tendency to quickly be depleted (i.e., each seeks to maximize individual utility without regard for the public good/others). This generates from the fact that there are no incentives to sacrifice short-term gains for long-term benefits. For a discussion of the concept in detail, see G. Hardin, *Managing the Commons,* New York: Freeman, 1977. *See also* **Principle of suboptimization**.

Trained incapacity: (1) Refers to the blind spots of bureaucrats, and is synonymous with rational ignorance (they recognize that there is a problem, but if there are no resources to do anything about them, bureaucrats tend to ignore them). (2) Refers to the limitations of individuals (and organizations as well) that are trained and expert in some areas but are not capable of much in other areas. (3) The term also is applicable in settings where a wrong decision is reached by relying on past and less-relevant experience. See, e.g., R. Merton, *Social Theory and Social Structure,* Glencoe, IL: Free Press, 1957, pp. 195–206. For the original exposition of this concept, see G. Hardin, "The Tragedy of the Commons," *Science,* 1968, 162, pp. 1243–48.

Training: Refers generally to the process of enhancing the skills of staff members in an organization. Training can be work related or for individual development, and organizations will usually offer a combination of the two, with more focus obviously on the former. Training can also take many forms, such as classroom instruction, seminars, workshops, project opportunities, secondments, and so forth. For a good analysis of the relationship between training and learning, see, e.g., E. Antonacopoulou, "The Paradoxical Nature of the Relationship Between Training and Learning," *Journal of Management Studies,* 2001, 38(3), pp. 327–50.

Training and development: A process and function in personnel management whereby staff members are given opportunities to develop their skills and competencies. Such opportunities need not necessarily be only training courses; they could also be secondment opportunities, job rotations, coaching and mentoring, and project participation. Training and development is an important function in staff development, and it not only contributes to skills development in staff members but also enhances their employability, thus ultimately motivating them as well.

Training and visiting system: A system of enhancing the capacity of organizations by trainers from outside where initially some form of training is provided, and which is then followed up by a visit so as to ensure that the lessons taken from the training session are indeed being applied at the workplace. See, e.g., D. Hulme, "Enhancing Organizational Effectiveness in Developing Countries; The Training and Visit System Revisited," *Public Administration and Development,* 1992, 12(5), pp. 433–45.

Training (as embedded activity): Training is no longer taken in isolation and treated as a stand-alone activity in public organizations; rather, especially in developing jurisdictions where governments are attempting to develop a unifying culture of public service, training is seen as part of the larger political, social, and economic milieu. In this sense, it is embedded into the very fabric of administrative and bureaucratic culture. This is an important concept as it explains the nature of most training and development programs in the public sectors of developing countries. For an analysis of this embeddedness, see, e.g., M. Grindle and M. Hilderbrand,

"Building Sustainable Capacity in the Public Sector: What Can be Done?" *Public Administration and Development,* 1995, 15(5), pp. 441–63.

Training audit: An assessment of whether the right skills gaps are being addressed, and also whether the right training procedures are being followed by the trainers. Training audits are regular functions of organizations and they may either conduct the audits themselves or contract out the work. The audits contribute to the redesign and reorientation, if necessary, of the stock of training and development programs in organizations. Training audits are related to training evaluation that is a review of whether a particular training program, and/or the organization's training policy, is yielding the expected results. Training evaluations are normally conducted by someone internal to the organization although if the review encompasses the broader issue of capability enhancement, then an external evaluator is normally contracted to do the work. See, e.g., A. Hoyle, "Evaluation of Training: A Review of the Literature," *Public Administration and Development,* 1984, 4(3), pp. 275–82.

Training levy: An organizational charge that may be levied on employees to fund training sessions. A training levy could be voluntary or mandatory, although it tends to be the latter in developing jurisdictions.

Training needs analysis: Refers to the determination of what staff members need by way of training so as to enhance their competencies to perform well/better on the job. The process of conducting a training needs analysis includes several steps: first, identify what the job involves by discussing with the job holder; determine the knowledge, skills and abilities (and also attitudes) necessary to do the job (note that some of this will be "have to have," some merely "nice to have"); draw up a profile of the existing skills of the current job-holder, and; match these with the list already prepared. However, training will not always be the appropriate response to the gap—there could be issues of motivation as well that need attention, among other considerations.

Training path: The sequence of training that an individual will need to go through in order to acquire the requisite degree of competencies necessary to do the job well. Training paths are determined for staff members by a joint discussion between the employee and his/her supervisor so that the training the employee is to receive is also aligned with organizational needs. Such determination is contained in the training specification, which refers to detailing the requirements that individual employees need to meet based on their competency gaps and needs analysis.

Training policy: A policy of an organization related to the training and development (T&D) of employees. It includes not only the role that T&D plays in the organization's activities but also the assumptions and principles that various parties (such as providers) need to keep in mind in planning for, providing, and receiving training.

Training rebate: A training refund that is given to employees and organizations to offset the costs incurred for the training. This is normally a fixed proportion of the actual costs incurred but could include the total amount if it is below a predetermined threshold. A training rebate is given, for example, by a governmental agency to an organization that provides training to clientele that the government recommends (such as recently released prison inmates that the government would like to see develop some basic skills).

Training revenue: Monies received for and from the provision of training. This includes training budgets received from outside the entity (such as subsidies from government and elsewhere), fees from participants, royalty paid by external providers that use the materials developed by the organization, etc.

Trait theory: A theory of leadership that asserts that the leader's traits (i.e., characteristics) play a central role in how leadership is exercised and how subordinates are encouraged to follow the leader. The theory assumes that these traits are inherited, and that some people naturally make good leaders (that is because they have the right traits from the very beginning). See, e.g., S. Kirkpatrick and E. Locke, "Leadership: Do Traits Matter?" *Academy of Management Executive,* 1991, 5(2), pp. 48–60.

Tranches: Another word for portions. Credit is normally handed out in tranches to borrowers, not only so that the funds may be better targeted for specific purposes but also because this enables proper accounting. Loan tranches are agreed to in advance of program implementation.

Transaction costs: Costs that are incurred by agencies that are related to their interactions with other agencies and which are considered unprofitable exercises. An example of a transaction cost is the time and resource spent complying with a directive for a report from a central agency that is not going to be used for any productive purpose. A transaction-cost approach is one in which institutions are viewed as transactions between agents, and institutional behavior is an effort to minimize transaction costs. Transaction costs are incurred by organizations and individuals in gathering information, negotiating, monitoring performance, policing and enforcing compliance, reporting, etc. See, e.g., C. Dahlman, "The Problem of Externality," *Journal of Law and Economics,* 1979, 22(1), pp. 141–62. *See also* **Compliance costs**.

Transactional avoidance: Refers to the notion some organizational leaders may have which reasons that minimizing the level of transactions with external parties is useful because this minimizes the possibility of conflicts, which, in and of themselves, are not advantageous for an organization. The implicit assumption here—weak at best—is that any transaction invariably leads to conflict.

Transactional leadership: A form of leadership that succeeds in running the organization well but that cannot go beyond the operational focus, is not able to help set the vision for the organization, nor can it challenge the existing organizational culture. For that, the organization needs transformational leadership. See, e.g., J. Sarros and J. Santora, "The Transformational-Transactional Leadership Model in Practice," *Leadership and Organization Development Journal,* 2001, 22(8), pp. 383–93. *Cf.* **Transformational leadership**.

Transfer: (1) Moving an employee from one location to another either within the same organizational hierarchy or to another organization altogether (this is also known as a lateral transfer or secondment). (2) The amount of money that is shifted from the central government to subjurisdictions (also known as intergovernmental transfers), or from one entity to another. Transfer analysis refers to a systematic method of looking at the differences in various variables between two entities (programs, organizations, etc.). Such variables could include, for example, existing capabilities, administrative processes, and nature of stakeholders, among others.

Transfer payments: Direct payments to individuals with no goods and services provided to the government in return (such as in unemployment benefits). Intergovernmental transfer payments refer to the amount of funds received by one jurisdiction from another (such as from the federal government to state governments).

Transferability, degrees of: Different ways in which the successes of other jurisdictions are transferred to others; they are: copying, emulation, hybridization, synthesis, and inspiration. Copying is adoption in the manner in which it was enacted elsewhere; emulation is adoption but with adjustments to suit local circumstances; hybridization is a mixture of elements from both jurisdictions; synthesis refers to combinations of familiar elements from programs in effect elsewhere; and inspiration is when programs elsewhere are used as intellectual stimulus for a new program. See R. Rose, "What Is Lesson Drawing?" *Journal of Public Policy,* 1991, 11(1), pp. 10–26.

Transferable training: *See* **General training**.

Transference: The process whereby attitudes toward one entity are transferred to another entity. Hence, for example, citizens may see the bureaucracies as being aloof and uncaring and transfer those sentiments to the political leaders as well, or vice versa.

Transformational leadership: Refers to the type of leadership that is able to take the organization beyond just looking at the operational aspects, and to put a focus on changing the organizational culture and values and norms in the organization. Transformational leadership thus seeks to veer away from the path that others may have taken in the organization. See, e.g., J. Sarros and J. Santora, "The Transformational-Transactional Leadership Model in Practice," *Leadership and Organization Development Journal,* 2001, 22(8), pp. 383–93. *See also* **Charismatic leadership**; *cf.* **Transactional leadership**.

Transformational strategy: A strategy pursued by an organization that fundamentally alters the basis on which it operates. This includes changes in the way it deals with its external environment, including its stakeholders, and the value system it works within. A well-designed—and executed—transformational strategy leads to broad acceptance of the organization's new set of core values. For a case study of the application of transformational strategy, see, e.g., L. Frost-Kumpf et al., "Strategic Action and Transformational Change: The Ohio Department of Mental Health," in B. Bozeman (ed.), *Public Management: The State of the Art,* San Francisco: Jossey-Bass, 1993, pp. 137–52.

Transients: Transients are politically appointed individuals who come to the bureaucracy through executive appointment (i.e., through patronage). The term "transient" implies that these individuals will move out when the "patron" (i.e., the executive) leaves office at the end of the term. See, e.g., F. Riggs, "Bureaucracy: A Profound Puzzle for Presidentialism," in A. Farazmand (ed.), *Handbook of Bureaucracy,* New York: Marcel Dekker, Inc., 1994, pp. 97–147.

Transition costs: Costs that are incurred by organizations as they switch from one system, strategy, or innovative practice to another. Transition costs are part of the organization's transaction costs. While most transition costs are inevitable, and organizations plan for such contingencies, they can be minimized if the transition is well planned. In transitioning an information system, for example, transition costs can be largely avoided if the service contract with the vendor is structured in such a manner that the costs are incurred by the provider instead of the organization.

Transitional activities: *See* **Gladiatorial activities**.

Transitions-within-continuity scenario: In this scenario, while organizations are "muddling through," they will still have the opportunity to improve procedures to enhance their effectiveness. These opportunities arise in the various operational decisions that are taken by the organizational leadership, any of which, if considered in proper perspective to the desired organizational outcomes, may be able to be reoriented so as to contribute to effectiveness. See, e.g., M. Emmert, M. Crow, and R. Shangraw, "Public Management in the Future: Post-Orthodoxy and Organization Design," in B. Bozeman (ed.), *Public Management: The State of the Art,* San Francisco: Jossey-Bass, 1993, pp. 345–60. *See also* **Muddling through**.

Transparency: Refers to low-cost access to relevant and understandable information. It has to be low cost so that accessibility is not exclusive, and it has to be relevant and understandable so that users can make sense out of it. Transparency enhances the accountability of public officials and organizations to citizens. A transparent policy measure is one that is open to the public for scrutiny. The public can make use of, for example, the provisions under the jurisdiction's official information act (or something similar) to find out what the decisions are, who is taking them, how are they being made, who is gaining from them, and what are the downside risks and costs of such decisions.

Trans-organizational development: Refers to the collective picture that emerges from juxtaposing the experiences and views of the various organizations in a network to a common issue or problem being faced. While the issue or problem may be singular, the interpretations of experiences, and the intensity of involvement, will differ. Only by bringing together these disparate views will it be possible to gain a better understanding of how effective a network has become. For a review of the concept, see, e.g., D. Boje and G. Rosile, "Comparison of Socioeconomic and Other Trans-Organizational Development Methods," *Journal of Organization Change Management,* 2003, 16(1), pp. 10–20.

Trashcan management: *See* **Dumping ground of management**.

Trend-impact analysis: A systematic technique for ascertaining the impacts of various proposed actions and their likely impacts on the preferred option for a policy. The analysis also benefits from sensitivity analysis and scenario planning.

Triangulation: Use of three or more tools to substantiate an argument or assessment. Triangulation is used to ensure that any inherent bias in employing only one or two tools is minimized. It forms a key part of evidence-based policy analysis systems in organizations.

Tribunal: Refers to a body (which could be an administrative court, for example) that is empowered to make decisions on particular issues of attention in its portfolio. A tribunal has the full authority to call witnesses, and its decision is valid on the organization as well as on the employee whose case is being heard.

Trickle-down effect: The belief that impacts of policies at the macro (and central) level will eventually trickle down to the micro (and community) levels. Trickle-down effects are evident only when mechanisms that facilitate the transmission are in place. Such mechanisms include, for example, secondary markets, good communication systems, extensive interaction among the various levels, and institutions at the local level that have the capacity to receive and act upon macrolevel signals.

Trigger: Any event, decision, or action (planned or unplanned) that initiates an innovation-oriented activity or policy in an organization. The annual audit report, for example, could be a trigger for a comprehensive review of organizational processes and systems, and of how things could be done better. See, e.g., R. Cobb and C. Elder, "Issue Creation and Agenda Building," in J. Anderson (ed.), *Cases in Public Policy-Making*, 2nd edition, New York: Holt, Rinehart and Winston, 1982, pp. 3–11. *See also* **Policy window**.

Triple bottom line: Refers to the recent focus of government agencies on three key things they need to keep in mind as they go about fulfilling their mandates. The notion of a triple bottom line (TBL) is based on the assumption that organizations cannot only be focused on financial performance, or merely producing outputs efficiently and effectively; they need to take a much more holistic view of their work and how it impacts on society. In that regard, TBL centers on the performance of organizations as it affects social, economic, and environmental outcomes, and looks at three key variables: social cohesion and equity, quality of life, and ecological sustainability. For a discussion, see, e.g., P. Barrett, "Corporate Governance in the Public Sector Context," *Canberra Bulletin of Public Administration,* 2003, 107, pp. 7–27.

Trust: An institutional arrangement where one party (usually a group of people selected by government or others) legally owns assets (such as property, both physical and intellectual) that is administered in such a manner as to maximize the benefits to others (such as the public sector). Funding for trusts comes from government, although trusts will tend to have their own sources of revenue as well.

Trust effects: *See* **Momentum building.**

Turf building: The tendency of organizational leaders to seek to enhance their areas of coverage, their mandates, resources, etc. Turf protection refers to the tendency of organizations and organizational leaders to protect their mandates and domains of work (such as a particular region and/or sector). Political scientist Eugene Bardach considers turf protection to be probably the most fundamental element of bureaucratic infrastructure (more so than budgets because turf can be used to justify budgetary bids but not vice versa). See E. Bardach, *Getting Agencies to Work Together: The Practice and Theory of Managerial Craftsmanship,* Washington, D.C.: Brookings Institution Press, 1998, p. 178.

Turnkey process: Any process which has been designed by a contractor (or a party external to the organization) and which the organization then purchases back from the contractor after it has been proven to be effective/operational. Turnkey projects place the risks on the contracting party, and governments are eager to encourage such projects, especially for large infrastructure facilities.

Twinning arrangements: Institutional cooperation arrangements where organizations in different jurisdictions join hands to collaborate on various items of mutual interest. For example, a nongovernmental organization in an advanced jurisdiction that deals with problems of urban poverty might have twinning arrangements with a similar organization in a less-developed jurisdiction, and together they would try to address the problem of urban poverty in the latter country. Twinning arrangements have been promoted as an alternative to conventional technical assistance between rich and poor countries. For a discussion of the concept as applied between a donor agency and a developing country, see, e.g., M. Jones, "Sustainable Organizational Capacity Building: Is Organizational Learning a Key?" *International Journal of Human Resource Management,* 2001, 12(1), pp. 91–98.

Two-corner solution: A solution that has two extremes as a potential solution. For example, a two-corner solution to the problem of investments in management development in the senior echelons of public service might be funding entirely from the central government or entirely from governmental departments. Both are equally valid and form the two corners within which a potential solution can be found. For an application of the two-corner solution, see, e.g., M. Yoshitomi and S. Shirai, *Technical Background Paper for Policy Recommendations for Preventing Another Capital Account Crisis,* Tokyo: Asian Development Bank Institute, 2000, pp. 23–24.

Two-factor theory of motivation: *See* **Herzberg's two-factor theory**.

Two-step sealed bid: As used in contract administration, this term refers to the two steps required to select the preferred vendor. In this case, a group of selected bidders will be asked to submit their proposals and those who submit acceptable proposals will be asked to submit sealed bids. This bid process enables the organization to be surer of the quality of the bid it wishes to consider further.

U

Ubiquitous strategies: Strategies in budgeting that political scientist Aaron Wildavsky says agencies will use to be viewed favorably. Ubiquitous strategies are pervasive and used on a continuing basis, and include mobilizing clienteles and lobbies and establishing confidence in one's ability to deliver efficiently and effectively. For Wildavsky's original work on budgeting, see his *The Politics of the Budgetary Process,* Boston: Little, Brown, 1964. For application to the public sector, see, e.g., A. Fozzard, *The Basic Budgeting Problem: Approaches to Resource Allocation in the Public Sector and Their Implications for Pro-Poor Budgeting,* Working Paper 147, London: Center for Aid and Public Expenditure, Overseas Development Institute, 2001. *Cf.* **Contingent strategies**.

Ultra stability: Refers generally to the ability of a system to reconfigure and modify its internal structure to be better able to deal with environmental pressures. All organizations strive for ultra stability since it enables them to sustain their work. Internal structures and processes that are modifiable include communication mechanisms with external stakeholders, network arrangements, knowledge management system, etc.

Ultra vires: Latin for "beyond power." Used in the public sphere to describe, for example, a decision that an organization does not have the authority to make. Thus there are several ultra vires items for local governments, such as passing laws that contradict national laws.

Unappropriated budget surplus: The amount of money that is left over from a previous financial year (i.e., that was not spent) but has not yet been appropriated (i.e., allocated) in the new year's budget since it is still under consideration as to whether it should revert to the central treasury or be included in the applicable department's current budget. In most jurisdictions, funds that are not spent in a financial year automatically revert to the treasury.

Uncertainty: As applied in organizational learning, uncertainty is related to the notion of equivocality, and imposes on the organization a requirement to gather more information so that useful decisions on which directions to take can be made. All organizations face uncertainty to some extent because the external environment in which they operate is always in a state of flux. For a discussion of uncertainty and organizational learning, see, e.g., D. Gnyawali and A. Stewart, "A Contingency Perspective on Organizational Learning: Integrating Environmental Context, Organizational Learning Processes, and Types of Learning," *Management Learning,* 2003, 34(1), pp. 63–89. *See* also **Risk**.

Uncertainty avoidance: The tendency of an organization to focus on the short-term issues (of which it can be fairly certain of the directions it will take) rather than the long-term view, which has less certainty. Thus, under uncertainty avoidance, here-and-now problems are emphasized at the expense of planning for the long term. Focusing on strategic planning is one manner of addressing the tendency toward uncertainty avoidance.

Uncertainty discount: A concept that explains the decrease in utility in the future. The exact discounts for each uncertainty, of course, are not predetermined but decision makers will tend to rely on convention—and some intuition—to get a firmer grip on just how risk averse they can be. Excessive levels of uncertainty discounts clearly point to excessive risk aversion on the part of decision makers. *See also* **Certainty equivalence**.

Uncertainty principle: *See* **Principle of incomplete knowledge**.

Uncertainty reduction theory: Argues that when people encounter a situation that is uncertain they try to minimize the uncertainty by seeking more information. Thus, the higher the degree of uncertainty, the greater the motivation to seek more information. For a discussion, see, e.g., C. Berger and R. Calabrese, "Some Explorations in Initial Interaction and Beyond: Toward a Developmental Theory of Interpersonal Communication," *Human Communication Research,* 1975, 1, pp. 99–112.

Uncertainty, perception of: *See* **Perceptual uncertainty**.

Unclassified civil service: Public-service positions for which there is no need for competitive examinations, such as, for example, executive appointments. In an unclassified civil service, positions are also not rigidly determined (i.e., are not classified). Not all jurisdictions have an unclassified civil service for the senior ranks, however.

Unconstrained discretion: Refers to a situation when a party does not have any constraints on the extent of its discretion. Bureaucracies often seek unconstrained discretion in policy implementation but rarely receive it because they are usually necessarily subject to some checks or constraints (such as legal mandates, reporting and accountability requirements, etc.).

Uncontrollables: Programs (such as entitlements) that cannot be controlled (or altered) by executives. *See also* **Sacred-cow entitlements**.

Underrun: A situation where the level of actual expenditure is below what was estimated ex ante. Underruns occur when organizational planners either are not aware of the cost of inputs or have misjudged the proposed activity levels. Either way, the residuals generally revert to the central treasury in the case of under-runs in governmental agencies.

Understudy: A term for a trainee who is involved in learning the job by being coached and mentored by a more senior and experienced person.

Unencumbered appropriation: Funds that have been appropriated (i.e., set aside) but not yet committed, i.e., encumbered. Unencumbered appropriation is evident at a stage when a particular policy or program has been tentatively approved—and funding has been approved in principle—but the organization responsible for the policy or program has not fully developed it or begun implementation. On the other hand, unexpended appropriation refers to the amount of funds that have been appropriated (i.e., set aside) but have not been spent (but have been committed, i.e., encumbered). Since many expenditure items have time lags (such as payments to contractors only after they have completed the task), there is an initial discrepancy between unencumbered appropriation and unexpended appropriation.

Unexpended appropriation: *See* **Unencumbered appropriation**.

Unfair dismissal: Dismissal of an individual from employment that is not based on just cause. In such a case, the individual is entitled to file a grievance in an employment court or to a similar authority. The burden of proof, however, is on the individual to demonstrate that the dismissal was unjust.

Unfair employment practices: Activities of employers that have been deemed unfair toward employees, or toward individuals seeking employment. An example of an unfair employment practice is discrimination against an applicant based on his/her race or color. Many jurisdictions have laws that seek to ensure that organizations do not engage in such practices, although the burden of proof is on the employee/individual that he/she is being treated unfairly. *Cf.* **Fair employment practices**.

Unfreezing: A state in the organization change process to denote that change managers need to first decouple the fixed and negative mind-sets of employees before they can introduce new ideas to them. Once that is done, and employees are ready for new ideas, change managers need to help them internalize those new ideas. The process of that internalization is termed "refreezing." For the original analysis of this concept, see K. Lewin, *Field Theory in Social Science,* New York: Harper & Row, 1951. For an application of Lewin's ideas, see, e.g., R. Allen and K. Montgomery, "Applying an Organizational Development Approach to Creating Diversity," *Organizational Dynamics,* 2001, 30(2), pp. 149–61.

Unicameral legislature: A legislature that has only one house (or chamber). For example, the parliament in New Zealand is a unicameral legislature. *Cf.* **Bicameral legislature**.

Unified civil service: An institutional setup where different services (such as public service, fire, education, health, engineering, diplomatic, etc.) come under a central arrangement. A unified civil service presumably has unifying values but becomes difficult to manage as one since different components within them have unique constraints, and too large an entity becomes unwieldy. In a unified civil service, the problem usually is that specialization becomes constrained, and pay tends to be related to characteristics other than productivity.

Uniform expectations, assumption of: An assumption that is made that all parties to a particular problem or issue share the same type and level of expectations about the nature of the problem, its depth, or the proper manner in which to address it. This is an extreme assumption and is rather unrealistic.

Uniform guidelines: Standards and guidelines that apply to everyone and in all situations. For example, uniform guidelines on recruitment processes specify that when recruiting new employees, an organization must widely advertise the positions, keep detailed records of applicants and of the processes applied to select the right candidate, make public the appointment, etc.

Uniform user charge: Fees that are charged to all users at the same level regardless of the nature of the services they seek. Government-subsidized health clinics in poor rural areas, for example, often have uniform user charges applied.

Unilateral contract: A contract in which one party (the principal) seeks a service and another (the agent) provides it. There is no expectation of a reciprocal service being provided. *See* **Bilateral contract**.

Unintended consequences: *See* **Unintended distortions**.

Unintended distortions: Also known as countervailing risks, these are results that were not expected or intended when the policy was first introduced. For example, when a government decides to fund development opportunities for senior managers in the public sector, one of the unintended distortions could be the realignment of resources by individual departments toward other problems since the central government is making the commitment. For a case study, see, e.g., L. MacLean, "State Social Policies and Social Support Networks: The Unintended Consequences of State Policy-Making on Informal Networks in Ghana and Côte d'Ivoire," *International Journal of Public Administration,* 2003, 26(6), pp. 665–91.

Union: An association of employees that partake voluntarily (although this was not always so in all jurisdictions) and that seeks to represent their interests in negotiations with management over such issues as wages and working conditions. Membership to a union is voluntary, although there can be instances when the incentives are structured in such a way that employees are practically forced to join them.

Unique selling proposition: A term borrowed from the private sector that refers to the unique characteristics of a product or service that the organization seeks to provide to the public. With alternative sources of service provision, as well as policy advice, already being sought after by decision makers, many government organizations have had to think hard about their unique selling proposition in order to justify their existence.

Unity of command: This is a key concept in classic organizational theory, and refers to the premise that it is considered more efficient for an employee to report to only one superior. Being accountable to multiple superiors runs the risks of conflicting directions being given, and diminishes the effectiveness of the employee's work. *See also* **Chain of command**; **Span of control**.

Unity of direction: A concept that states that staff members engaged in similar activities should have the same objectives, and that they should all be contained in one plan. This provides the single direction that is considered effective in the organization.

Universal principles of management: Principles of management that are applicable across all settings. Such principles revolve around the following concepts: (a) division of work, (b) lines of authority, (c) responsibility and accountability, (d) span of control, (e) legitimacy, and (f) coordination. For a cross-jurisdictional discussion of the application of these principles, see, e.g., A. Negandhi, "Management in the Third World," in P. Joynt and M. Warner (eds.), *Managing in Different Cultures,* Oslo: Universeitforlaget, 1985, pp. 69–97.

Universal service provision: The requirement for a service provider (either a public-sector organization or a private firm) to provide services to all customers. Such universal services include electricity, post, water, and phone. Governments may direct private firms to ensure universal service provision, especially if the latter are under contract with governmental agencies.

Universality hypothesis: This hypothesis suggests that Western management theories, particularly those on organization, are applicable worldwide regardless of culture or of the historical experiences of a society. Implicit in this is the assumption that at some basic level, people in organizations think and act alike. See, e.g., R. Vengroff, M. Ndiaye, and M. Lubatkin, "Culture and Management: Are Western Management Styles Transferable?" in A. Farazmand (ed.), *Handbook of Bureaucracy,* New York: Marcel Dekker, Inc., 1994, pp. 253–63.

Unmeasurable uncertainty: A term used by the noted author Daniel Ellsberg to denote a situation where the unknown cannot be represented by numerical probabilities, hence it is not technically a risk. See D. Ellsberg, "Risk, Ambiguity, and the Savage Axioms," *The Quarterly Journal of Economics,* 1961, 75(4), pp. 643–69.

Unorganized complexity: A situation that features several variables interacting with one another in no particular and discernible manner. Unorganized complexity provides the organization its most complex and intractable problem scenario because of the uncertainty that is inherent in such complexity. The concept can be seen as being situated beyond organized simplicity (for example, the processes around which machines work in a preprogrammed manner) and organized complexity (for example, dynamic processes that govern the interactions among entities but which can be regulated by protocols). *Cf.* **Organized complexity**; **Organized simplicity**.

Unrestricted grants-in-aid: *See* **Grants**.

Unrevealed failure: A failure in the production process, machinery, or such, that goes unnoticed until a thorough check of procedures is done. Organizations engage in total quality management to ensure that such unrevealed failures are discernible at a very early stage of the production process. Unrevealed failures are cost-heavy because they become manifest much later in the production process, by which time organizations will have put in a considerable amount of resources to engage in production.

Unscheduled learning: (1) Any learning that takes place at the individual level that is done on one's own time and at one's own pace. Independent study modules and self-paced learning techniques are examples of unscheduled learning. (2) Any learning opportunity for a staff member that arises without it being planned; for example, having to assume a colleague's work if he/she leaves the organization unexpectedly can be termed unscheduled learning.

Unsolicited proposal: A proposal for a funding request or a bid for service that is made without there being any call for such a proposal. Many organizations allow such proposals to be made so as to ensure that they stay engaged with those that show promise of providing quality services.

Unstructured decisions: Decisions that are made which: (a) are not dependent on prior decisions, and (b) have very little structure to them which could act as cues to decision makers on how to go about formulating and implementing them. Unstructured decisions are generally made when the operating environment of the organization is very complex and volatile (such as, for a public agency, a period of political fluidity).

Unstructured training: *See* **Informal training**.

Unwritten contract: (1) The ways of doing things in an organization that are not documented. An unwritten contract "contains," for example, assumptions that different parties have about how to behave in the organization. (2) The relationship between a principal and an agent that is not put on paper largely because the two parties have worked with each other and have placed trust in their working relationships.

Up-front costs: Costs that are borne by a party at the beginning of the transaction (for example, paying the necessary administrative fees when subscribing to an investment plan). Up-front costs are transparent and allow those incurring the cost burden to make adequate provision for them in their budgets.

Up-or-out system: A career system where it is expected that employees will either keep on moving up at regular intervals or out of the organization. For an application of the concept, see, e.g., B. O'Flaherty and A. Siow, "Up-or-out Rules in the Market for Lawyers," *Journal of Labor Economics,* 1995, 13(4), pp. 709–35.

Upstream innovation interaction: An innovation that emerges away from the direct interactions between an organization and its customers, and is instead focused on being close to the originating point of the innovative idea. This "near-conception point" of innovation—while less focused on customers' stated and revealed preferences—has the advantage of drawing on more macro- and broad-level influences and ideas in the organization. See, e.g., P. Cooke and K. Morgan, *The Associational Economy: Firms, Regions, and Innovation,* New York: Oxford University Press, 1998, p. 71. *Cf.* **Downstream innovation interaction**.

Upstream integration: *See* **Backward integration**.

Upstream progress: *See* **Downstream progress**.

Upward flow of policy making: While discussing ways in which citizens can influence the decision making of public officials, the notion of an upward flow of policy making refers to how citizens exercise influence. The recent resurgence in the consideration of citizen involvement in public administration has meant that increasingly, and across practically all jurisdictions, governments and public agencies have had to consider novel ways to ensure that the upward flow of policy making will continue to remain attuned to what agencies' customer bases are really demanding. See, e.g., G. Almond and S. Verba, *The Civic Culture,* Princeton, NJ: Princeton University Press, 1963, pp. 16–18. *Cf.* **Downward flow of policy enforcement**.

Upward revenue sharing: An arrangement wherein the revenues collected by local and regional governments are shared with central government based on a formula that is agreed upon in advance. *See also* **Revenue sharing**.

Usability testing: Testing of a product prototype by potential users to assess whether or not the product is usable without problem, and to ascertain the degree of user-friendliness. All programs have to have some degree of usability testing to assess whether they show promise to be successful. Usability tests are generally done in pilot runs.

User fees: Also known as user charges, user fees are revenue that is received from payments made by individuals that use particular services. Assessing the level of user fees is a tricky affair, and several variables and considerations have to be kept in mind, including determining the right balance between service provision and meeting expenses. For a brief review of how some jurisdictions have implemented user fees for governmental services, see, e.g., GAO, *Managing for Results: Experiences Abroad Suggest Insights for Federal Management Reforms,* GAO/GGd-95-120, Washington, DC: US General Accounting Office, 1995, pp. 51–52.

User need model (of accountability): Refers to the model of instituting accountability on an organization by requiring it to provide all relevant information that users may need in making their decisions. This implies that organizations will potentially be regularly amending performance-reporting systems that seek to cater to the need for information for various users. For a review of the user need model of accountability, see, e.g., G. Boyne et al., "Plans, Performance Information and Accountability: The Case of Best Value," *Public Administration,* 2002, 80(4), pp. 691–710.

User risks: Refers to the risks that organizations face when they develop programs or products that may not be right for the customer. Such risks arise when the organization does not seek design and performance specification from eventual customers and stakeholders. See, e.g., C. Davis, "Calculated Risk: A framework for Evaluating Product Development," *MIT Sloan Management Review,* 2002, 43(4), pp. 71–77.

Using agency: Refers to an organization that facilitates and receives goods from designated purchasing agents and delivers them to the organizations that made the request for the goods. Using agencies are intermediaries, and are common in centralized planning systems and in many developing countries.

Utility theory: As applied in the organizational context, this theory asserts that the particular values that individuals have will determine their approach to problem solving. Such values will be a function of the environment within which the individuals interact with others.

Utilization analysis: An analysis that is done of the number and type of positions that exist in an organization and the extent to which they are staffed by minorities in relation to their availability. The analysis forms a key component of any diversity-enhancing programs in a jurisdiction.

V

Vacancy management: The purposive actions of organizational leadership to ensure that the organization's need for expertise is fulfilled in the most efficient and effective manner. For example, if a vacancy situation were to emerge unexpectedly (say, with an employee's resignation at short notice), then the organization—using its information base on available expertise—might decide to second someone to the vacant position while an active search is made for a more long-term replacement. *See also* **Secondment**.

Valence: The value that is placed on a reward. A positive valence has implications for values such as team spirit and sense of belonging, and a negative one for values such as withdrawal and negative competition, among others. *See also* **Expectancy theory**.

Valence-instrumentality-expectancy theory: A theory of motivation that stipulates that the expectations of reward motivate an individual to specific actions. For the employer, then, the implications are that individuals must be given the space and opportunity to see that their purposeful actions lead to specific rewards, which will motivate them to continue acting in the same manner. See, e.g., C. Pinder, *Work Motivation: Theory, Issues and Applications,* Glenview, IL: Scott, Foresman and Co., 1984, pp. 144–63.

Validation: As used in quality assurance and management, the term refers to the process by which a standard-setting agency, such as a government-established qualification authority, specifies that a particular program or institute meets the standards that have been determined to be relevant to that particular jurisdiction, and which will have been specified in advance and in a transparent manner.

Validity: The extent to which the tools used for research, or for policy development, do what they purport to do. In all the definitions provided of validity by various authors, there are two commonalities that are relevant to keep in mind: (a) the accuracy of the means of the measurement of whatever variable is under consideration, and (b) the actual measurement of what was originally sought to be measured. The notion of accuracy in the first component also ties the concept of validity with reliability. For a useful look at the terms, see, e.g., M. Hammersley, "Some Notes on the Terms 'Validity' and 'Reliability,'" *British Educational Research Journal,* 1987, 13(1), pp. 73–81. *See also* **Reliability**.

Valuational bias: The tendency of policy analysts to include in the policy-making process, and in the evaluation of alternatives, only those values that have been predetermined as sought in the particular policy being formulated. The bias could emerge from various sources, including governmental ministers, and from the government in general. See, e.g., D. McKevitt and A. Lawton, *Public Sector Management: Theory, Critique, and Practice,* London: Sage Publications, 1994, p. 45.

Value: As applied in public policy making, a value refers to a normative weight that is assigned to a particular policy objective. The public, for example, may value the fair treatment of all citizens. Values can refer to end values or instrumental values. End values are terminal values (i.e., what is eventually desired); instrumental values refer to the means of attaining end values. The latter are more easily discarded, if need be, and also more easily redefined. See L. Koenig, *An Introduction to Public Policy,* Englewood Cliffs, NJ: Prentice Hall, 1986, pp. 251–53.

Value acceptability: The degree to which the solution offered for a particular problem fits the values of policy makers and of the public. Given that these values are not likely to be uniform, the concept of value acceptability in public policy tends largely to be a subjective matter. For application of the concept, see, e.g., J. Blankenau, "The Fate of National Health Insurance in Canada and the United States: A Multiple Streams Explanation," *Policy Studies Journal,* 2001, 29(1), pp. 38–55.

Value analysis: *See* **Value assurance**.

Value assurance: A process of convincing external stakeholders that a particular product has the value that they seek and that is claimed. Value assurance is the product of, among other things, value analysis and value clarification. Value analysis is a systematic method of determining if a product or service is worth the cost/price attached to it, and, if it is, then what is the nature of the alternatives such that the value might be attained. Value clarification, on the other hand, is a procedure used when there are competing criteria for recommendations, and involves making clear all the value premises that are assumed in various policy objectives. See, e.g., W. Dunn, *Public Policy Analysis: An Introduction,* 2nd edition, Englewood Cliffs, NJ: Prentice Hall, 1994, p. 307. *See also* **Quality assurance**.

Value bias: The preference that organizational leaders exhibit with respect to how they carry out their functions, and what their basic premises are for what they do. Hard value bias refers to a preference for ensuring that for every activity there must be hard information and hard values that are measurable (and thus can be described as physical outputs). On the other hand, a soft value bias is a preference that organization leaders, as well as evaluators, have for emphasizing the subjective and intangible products of an organization. All too often, soft value bias appears in the analysis of individual project impacts. Soft values, in terms of project impacts, could be social cohesion, buy-in to project goals, etc.

Value chain: The addition of value to a product as it progresses in the production process. Thus, for example, a training program for public-sector leaders may specify its value as leading from rigorous learning experiences to better quality of decisions and to increased efficiency and effectiveness of public policy. See, e.g., R. Kaplinsky, "Globalization and Unequalization: What Can Be Learned from Value Chain Analysis?" F*Journal of Development Studies,* 2000, 37(2), pp. 116–46.

Value clarification: *See* **Value assurance**.

Value conflicts: A situation where the values of the various stakeholders to a policy are not aligned. As this can be quite common, the task of policy-making becomes centered on finding compromises such that the final policy better reflects the consensus values of the stakeholders. Such consensus, however, is not always reached, which makes the policy susceptible to attack from many sides.

Value critique: As applied in policy analysis, this refers to a set of procedures for assessing the persuasiveness of different arguments put forth in support of a particular policy objective. The value critique is not about analyzing the alternatives but about the assumptions on which the various alternatives are based. See W. Dunn, *Public Policy Analysis: An Introduction,* 2nd edition, Englewood Cliffs, NJ: Prentice Hall, 1994, pp. 308–09.

Value for money: A method of ascertaining whether a particular organizational or production process makes best use of expended resources. In particular, the method looks at three key components: economy (focused on inputs), efficiency (focused on process), and effectiveness (focused on outputs), and whether or not the organization/program is geared toward maximizing them. In recent times, a fourth component has been added to the concept of value for money, that of impact or outcomes (i.e., to what extent does the output of the organization or program effect the desired societal outcomes).

Value judgment: A subjective decision made by a consumer about the actual value to him/her of a good or service. Such determination feeds back into the production process to remedy, if necessary, the quality of the product or service. The feedback is manifest in, for example, changes in the demand for the good or service, or in the alteration of some of its features and attributes.

Value neutrality: An assumption that there is no value (or moral argument) involved in policy formulation. For example, when prices are used to determine the level of demand and supply as well as determine the nature of government involvement in the economy, the assumption is made that this is a value-neutral exercise. For an application, see, e.g., D. Johnson and G. Macy, "Using Environmental Paradigms to Understand and Change an Organization's Response to Stakeholders," *Journal of Organizational Change Management,* 2001, 14(4), pp. 314–34.

Value-added analysis: *See* **Value chain**.

Value-for-money review: A form of "clear the decks" review procedures. This implies that all aspects of the organization's work, or of the program, will come under scrutiny, including efficiency and effectiveness drivers in the items under review. A value-for-money review is done with more frequency than an output price review, and is also more searching than a conventional audit, which tells us whether the money was spent as reported. See, e.g., S. Newberry, "Intended or Unintended Consequences? Resource Erosion in New Zealand's Government Departments," *Financial Accountability & Management,* 2002, 18(4), pp.309–30. For an application example of a value-for-money review, see National Audit

Office, *Getting the Evidence: Using Research in Policy-making,* Report by the Comptroller and Auditor-General, HC 586–1 Session 2002–2003, London: The Stationery Office, 2003, pp. 35–36.

Values management: Refers to the manner in which organizations develop, institutionalize, and communicate appropriate values to staff members and others in relation to the work they perform. In public-sector organizations, a central element of values management is a clear-cut specification of the essence of public service, particularly in front-line operations where public servants interface with users of the service. Among other things, the focus has tended to be on how values can be embedded into the structures, processes, and systems in public organizations. For a comprehensive discussion of this concept, see, e.g., K. Kernaghan, "Integrating Values into Public Service: The Values Statement as Centerpiece," *Public Administration Review*, 2003, 63(6), pp. 711–19. *See also* **Code of conduct**; **Code of ethics**.

Values, public sector: Public-sector values refer, in general, not only to setting aside personal interests and working for the public good, but also having integrity in dealings with others. See, e.g., R. Gregory, "Social Capital Theory and Administrative Reform: Maintaining Ethical Probity in Public Service," *Public Administration Review,* 1999, 59(1), pp. 63–75; see also M. Brereton and M. Temple, "The New Public Service Ethos: An Ethical Environment for Governance," *Public Administration,* 1999, 77(3), pp. 455–74.

Variable budget: A budget that does not have a predetermined level. A variable budget is prepared in instances where, for example, the levels of overhead costs and levels of production change continuously. To account for the variability, managers will normally specify the budget range rather than a set level, and will establish a critical threshold point below which they perceive the budget would not be adequate to sustain operations.

Variable costs: Costs whose levels increase or decrease depending upon the size of the activity. An example of a variable cost is overtime pay given to staff members for having to work extra hours because of increased demand. *Cf.* **Fixed costs**.

Variable pay: *See* **Flexible pay**.

Vector criterion problem: *See* **Criterion problem**.

Vendor: A supplier of a good or service to an organization who does so based on the specifications of a contract that the supplier has bid for and won. Vendor evaluation is an assessment of a supplier/bidder by an organization seeking to purchase a product or service to determine that the supplier/bidder meets tender requirements.

Venture analysis: A systematic process that is employed by an organization to ensure that any plan for a new activity is rigidly constructed and consists of the following: (a) a determination of the attributes of the product and the market that it will serve, (b) an ascertainment of the costs for the venture and the possibility of any revenues being generated from it (in a public-sector agency, this might not be a relevant consideration), and (c) a determination of competitor analysis and the rigor with which any alternatives are analyzed to meet the competition. Such a venture analysis in the public sector is normally contained in a business case.

Verification: The act or process of ensuring that instructions and rules have been closely followed. This is compared with validation, where the results are compared with some standard to ensure that they are valid to a standard. Verification protocols are methods used by those conducting rules—and process—verification exercises in an organization or program. For an example of verification protocols for aid-related performance indicators, see C. Adams and J. Gunning, "Redesigning the Aid Contract: Donors' Use of Performance Indicators in Uganda," *World Development,* 2002, 30(12), pp. 2045–56. *See also* **Validation**.

Vertical accountability: A traditional approach to ensuring that entities (individuals as well as organizations) are answerable to a higher authority. For example, a governmental department will have vertical accountability to the legislature, from whence its mandate and resources emanate. Within an organization, vertical accountability is evident in the relationships between a superior and subordinates, where the latter are accountable to the former for their actions. See, e.g., M. Considine, "The End of the Line? Accountable Governance in the Age of Networks, Partnerships, and Joined Up Service," *Governance: An International Journal of Policy, Administration, and Institutions,* 2002, 15(1), pp. 21–40. *Cf.* **Horizontal accountability**.

Vertical conflict: In the organizational context, a vertical conflict refers to disagreements between entities at different hierarchical levels in an organization (for example, between call-center operators and customer-service representatives). Such conflict is normally at a low intensity and rather subdued, but if it becomes overt or very serious, then the organizational leadership will need to deal with it firmly.

Vertical coordination: Authority and control relationships that exist between the various elements of an organization whereby those below are subordinate to those above. Thus, vertical coordination refers to the interlinkages that are evident between organizational members that are placed in a hierarchy.

Vertical differentiation: Refers to the number of hierarchical levels in an organization to denote a dimension of how organizations are structured. By virtue of their being in different hierarchical levels, they are also different in terms of their functional orientation.

Vertical dyadic linkage: A term that refers to the interaction that takes place between, say, an employee and his or her immediate superior. The dyadic term implies a relationship that exists between two individuals.

Vertical equity: A notion of equity that centers on the premise that those who have more should give up more so that everyone sacrifices the same amount of utility. However, this conceals the fact that there are bound to be differences in the level of marginal utilities attached to extra resources between those who have more and those who have less. See D. Weimer and A. Vining, *Policy Analysis: Concepts and Practice,* 2nd edition, Englewood Cliffs, NJ: Prentice Hall, 1992, p. 101. *Cf.* **Horizontal equity**.

Vertical federalism: Refers to the relationships between states/provinces and the federal government (such as on assistance to state-specific programs for marginalized groups of people). *See also* **Federalism**.

Vertical fiscal imbalance: What local governments (states/provinces) cite when they are underresourced for the mandates they have been given by the central (federal) government, and that the latter should grant them greater taxing powers to generate the required resources. For obvious reasons, the federal government might not necessarily see it as such.

Vertical integration: The degree to which an upstream activity is merged with one downstream. For example, an assessment center could be involved not only in assessing public servants in terms of their competencies, but could also be involved in providing relevant training once the assessment is complete. The advantage of vertical integration is that it lets the organization get better control over the entire process as well as better control of cost drivers. The downside is that it increases administrative costs and stretches capacity. For a case study of vertical integration, see, e.g., J. Mota and L. de Castro, "A Capabilities Perspective on the Evolution of Firm Boundaries: A Comparative Case Example from the Portuguese Moulds Industry," *Journal of Management Studies,* 2004, 41(2), pp. 295–316. *Cf.* **Horizontal integration**.

Vertical job loading: A situation where an employee is given an opportunity to be involved in tasks with more responsibility but without being given a higher rank/position. Used as a job-enrichment technique, vertical loading provides employees the scope to be doing much more than what they would normally be doing, and this serves as a good training ground for future career growth. See F. Herzberg, "One More Time: How Do You Motivate Employees?" *Harvard Business Review,* 1968 (reprinted in the *HBR,* 2003 (January), pp. 87–96). *Cf.* **Horizontal job loading**; *see also* **Job enrichment**.

Vertical occupational mobility: *See* **Occupational mobility**.

Vertical training: The group training of organizational members who are at different hierarchical levels. Such vertical training has the advantage of giving an opportunity for more interactions between them that is separate from the workplace setting.

Vertical vs. horizontal tension: Refers to the pressures that organizational leadership faces in trying to find a balance between the need to deepen the level of engagement on any issue and the need to incorporate a wider view. For an example of such a tension, see OECD, *Maximizing the Impact of the OECD,* Report No. SG(2003)1, Paris: OECD, 2003, p. 25.

Vertical work group: Any working group that is established in an organization whose members come from different hierarchical levels and bring different skills to the group. A vertical work group may be established for various reasons, including to give an opportunity to those at lower levels to learn from interacting with more senior colleagues, and to develop team spirit.

Veto: Refers to the act of blocking the formalization of a policy by refusing to agree to it. There are two types of vetoes in the domain of executive-legislature interactions: a line-item veto, wherein the executive can veto individual items in a bill; and a pocket veto, wherein the executive does not sign a bill in the allotted time period and thus it expires. *See also* **Institutional veto points**.

Visible cluster: Denotes participants who are most readily seen on the public stage in relation to the search for a solution to a policy problem. An example of a visible cluster group is MADD (Mothers Against Drunk Driving).

Visible criteria: Criteria that are explicit and can be easily effected, such as amount of time spent responding to a freedom-of-information act request for contracts issued by a governmental agency. Less visible criteria might be the opportunity costs of answering such a request.

Visible hand: The term is a play on Adam Smith's "invisible hand" (i.e., the marketplace) and refers to government (more accurately, the professional management in public bureaucracy) allocating resources in an economy and, where necessary, providing services as well. While clearly the role of government has tended to diminish of late, there is no denying that it continues to play a very visible hand in all jurisdictions. *See also* **Invisible hand**.

Visible risk reduction: The process of reducing risks in the organization's work, but in such a manner that the process is transparent and visible to all. This matters considerably to organizations that rely heavily on consumer confidence that quality standards have been met and that everything is correct. The Food and Non-Food Authority in the Netherlands engages in visible risk reduction on a continuous basis by showing to the general public how it goes about raising food safety levels. See, e.g., VWA, *Visible Risk Reduction: Strategic Operational Vision for the Food and Non-Food Authority,* The Hague: Government of the Netherlands, 2002, p. 19.

Visioning: The process of keeping employees focused toward a purpose, i.e., the organization's vision of where it wants to go and what it wants to do. Visioning is an ongoing process, and requires that management continually engage employees in understanding the primary objectives and mandates of the organization. This can take place, for example, in the preparation stage of the organization's annual plan.

Vocational education: Education that is concerned with increasing the skills of individuals who wish to have a career in any vocation or occupation for which no college or university education is necessary (although vocational education can—and does—include some academic courses in law, medicine, etc.). Vocational education is provided through a combination of apprenticeships, laboratory work, classroom instruction, and on-the-job training.

Vocational guidance: Guidance and counseling that is provided to individuals who seek a vocational education. The guidance centers not only on which particular vocation to enter into, but also how to manage career expectations that may subsequently emerge.

Vocational program evaluation: Evaluation that is done of any vocational program to ensure that it meets the criteria specified and that it is effectively imparting the skills that are essential for the individuals to embark on their vocations. The evaluation is conducted by a party that has been certified by a suitable government body.

Vocational training: *See* **Vocational education**.

Voice: Refers to a manifestation of the expression given by the stakeholders to a policy or program. This is critical if the policy or program is to deliver appropriate goods and services. Voting and lobbying are considered ways of giving voice to citizens. The lack of this voice invariably leads to either sabotage or exit. For an early discussion of this concept, see A. Hirschman, *Exit, Voice, and Loyalty,* Cambridge: Cambridge University Press, 1970. For a review of voice mechanisms as applied across jurisdictions, see, e.g., D. Olowu, "Local Institutional and Political Structures and Processes: Recent Experience in Africa," *Public Administration and Development,* 2003, 23(1), pp. 41–52. *Cf.* **Exit**.

Volatility: A measure of risk or uncertainty faced by public policy makers in the political arena. The degree of volatility can be ascertained in many ways, including analyzing historical trends or imputing from current events. The greater the degree of volatility in a policy environment, the greater the difficulty in formulating suitable policies.

Voluntary arbitration: A situation where two or more parties to a dispute seek to come to a mutual understanding without the involvement of a third party as a mediating influence. Voluntary arbitration assumes that a certain amount of trust continues to be retained among the disputing parties such that they can work through their differences without the involvement of an outsider.

Voluntary compliance: A situation where those governmental agencies that are subject to specific regulations and other standards comply with them of their own accord. There is, as such, no need for control agencies to institute protocols, although there could be some monitoring and review done if doubts are raised about the degree of compliance, or whether it exists at all. Voluntary disclosure is a form of voluntary compliance, and refers to the act of making an organization's information public on a voluntary basis. A bank, for example, may decide to make a voluntary disclosure about its reserves to stem public concerns about its strengths.

Voluntary contributions: Refer to the amount of funds that donors and funding agencies commit to an organization/program that is over and above their mandated contributions. Not all funding agencies make voluntary contributions, however, but for those that do, it shows the extent of interest that they have on issues and themes that are of importance to them. Voluntary contributions are also good proxies for the revealed preferences of organizational members.

Voluntary disclosure: *See* **Voluntary compliance**.

Voluntary organization: An organization whose members voluntarily support its work, including partly or wholly funding its activities. When voluntary organizations bid for—and receive—contracts from any level of government, they are at times seen as just another agent, but in reality, voluntary organizations carry a different connotation than the for-profit organizations that competitively bid for government contracts. This is because voluntary organizations—by virtue of their raison d'être—are deemed to possess more caliber to foster social capital. See, e.g., S. Puffer and J. Meindle, "The Congruence of Motives and Incentives in a Voluntary Organization," *Journal of Organizational Behavior,* 1993, 13(4), pp. 425–34.

Voluntary sector: *See* **Civil society**.

Vote: (1) An exercise in ascertaining the preferences of citizens on, for example, who should be their representatives in the legislature, or who should be represented on an organization's board. (2) An amount of money appropriated by parliament for various activities and functions, which becomes the responsibility of one governmental minister and which is administered by one governmental department.

Vote minister: The governmental minister responsible for a vote (i.e., one which groups one or more appropriations). A vote minister, also called a purchase minister, buys the delivery of outputs (goods and services) from a department, using funds approved by parliament. A vote minister signs the purchase agreement with a department while the responsible minister signs the chief-executive performance agreement. While a department has only one responsible minister, it may have several vote ministers. *See also* **Responsible minister**.

Voter apathy: The lack of interest exhibited by citizens in the electoral process. The eventual impact of this on public-sector management is a growing sense among public administrators that the policies that are formulated do not necessarily reflect the true wishes of the majority of the stakeholders. *See also* **Democratic deficit**.

Voting with one's feet: When citizens (or consumers) apply pressures on governments by moving to areas that are more favorable (for example, wealthier individuals moving to suburbs from inner cities if local taxes are too high in the city). This serves as strong feedback to governments on the policies they have in place.

Vulnerability (in interagency collaboration): Vulnerability in interagency collaboration is caused by factors such as: (a) turnover in personnel (such that institutional knowledge that could provide the proper context is lost), (b) failures of competent leaders to be straightforward (such that trust among participants is lost), and (c) a high level of turf protection (such that a silo mentality becomes entrenched).

Vulnerability assessment: An assessment that is done to ascertain how susceptible an organization is in terms of the extent to which processes and the systems in place ensure adequate controls on the risks that can emerge in its operations. The assessment is an integral part of the organization's risk-management process, and it determines the extent to which the organization will be involved in particular programs and activities.

W

Wage: Refers to recompense given regularly by an employer to employees either in cash or in kind. While they are often used interchangeably, wages technically differ from salaries—wages are normally meant to refer to payments for work done by casual or temporary workers; salary is used for long-term and contract workers. Wage incentives are inducements, over and above the regular wages, given to employees to do better work. A bonus is an example of a wage incentive.

Wage administration: Refers to all the activities associated with determining and administering wages and salaries in an organization. This includes regularly assessing: (a) relevant market rates, (b) job sizes, (c) employees' competencies in relation to their responsibilities, and (d) adhering to any changes that result from collective-bargaining processes.

Wage arbitration: A method of reaching an understanding between management and unions on the level of wages to be paid to employees. While such an understanding may be reached amicably, at times it necessitates arbitration, that is, the parties refer their respective cases to a neutral third party for a decision. The decision is known as a wage award.

Wage award: *See* **Wage arbitration**.

Wage ceiling: *See* **Wage structure**.

Wage criteria: The standards (both specific to the organization and external to it) that are used in configuring the wage and salary structure in an organization. Generic criteria of setting wages and salaries include job responsibilities, ability to pay of the employer, market conditions, skills levels of employees, etc.

Wage floor: *See* **Wage structure**.

Wage incentive: *See* **Wage**.

Wage parity: *See* **Parity**.

Wage range: *See* **Wage structure**.

Wage resistance: A situation that arises when an employer faces pressures against scaling back wages in the face of increases in cost of living. In those organizations and industries where collective bargaining is required, union demands further exacerbate such pressures.

Wage structure: The details of an organization's compensation rates and schedule. Wage structures are revised regularly to: (a) ensure that they reflect the true value of the work performed by employees, and (b) align the organization's wage structure to the prevalent market rates. Wage structures have wage ranges embedded in them. In the range, a wage floor refers to the lowest level of compensation that an organization is required to give to its employees as established by contract or law. On the other hand, a wage ceiling is the highest level of compensation that the organization is willing and/or able to give its staff members for a particular job or function. Wage ceilings are determined by internal organization planning processes or from market rates.

Wage survey: A survey taken regularly by an organization of similar employers in the region to determine what the level of wages should be in that organization. A wage survey is essential to document to the employees that the organization is committed to providing wages that are competitive.

Waiting period: (1) The amount of time (usually two weeks) a new employee and the employer need to wait in order to allow reasonable contests of the appointment. This ensures that the recruitment and selection process is transparent. (2) The amount of time before a strike can officially commence.

Waiver of bids: A situation where an organization seeking a service does not seek bids from service providers because of any number of reasons (such as uniqueness of circumstances). However, such circumstances must be duly recorded in the interest of transparency since public organizations are subject to the requirements of an official information act or other acts of that nature. The waiver also applies automatically when the budget for the service being sought does not exceed some preset level.

Waiver of mistake: A situation where an organization seeking bids from service providers disregards some competing bids' omissions and errors if they do not substantially affect the competition among the bids (i.e., if the mistakes are fairly superficial). A "waiver of mistake," however, may affect the final decision of who is awarded the contract if none of the competing bids contain serious errors and omissions but some do have superficial ones and are still considered based on the "waiver of mistake" principle.

Want objective: *See* **Must objective**.

Warrant: As used in policy analysis, a warrant is a form of policy argument that qualifies an assertion. The warrant serves as the basis on which the policy claim rests for it allows the analyst to move from policy-relevant information to a policy claim. For a discussion of warrants and argumentation theory in the context of public management, see, e.g., M. Barzelay, "How to Argue About the New Public Management," *International Public Management Journal,* 1999, 2(2[A]), pp. 183–216.

Washington consensus: Policy advice of the international financial institutions based in Washington, DC—namely the International Monetary Fund and the World Bank—that are based on market-fundamentalist policies. The view argues that states need to cut back the size of government and open up many government services for private-sector provision, among others. In fact, though never more than an informal term, it goes beyond statecraft to include fiscal discipline, opening economies to international competition, etc. See, e.g., J. Williamson, "What Washington Means by Policy Reform," in J. Williamson (ed.), *Latin American Adjustment: How Much Has Happened?* Washington, DC: Institute of International Economics, 1990, pp. 7–20.

Washminster system: Refers to the juxtaposition of the characteristics of the Westminster system of government and the U.S. model of government (i.e., as evident, for example, where there is a strong system of checks and balance in government and where patronage exists in the senior civil service). Australia can be considered to be characterized by a Washminster system of government. For a discussion of the term in relation to the senior civil service, see, e.g., J. Uhr, "Rethinking the Senior Executive Service: Executive Development as Political Education," *Australian Journal of Public Administration,* 1987, 46(1), 20–36.

Waste maximization (of bureaucracies): The assertion that in cases where the bureaucracy is the only provider of services (i.e., a monopoly), there is a tendency for it to maximize its waste for any given quantity of service it chooses to provide. Raising salaries (but not improving the quality of the service) is considered by critics to be an example of the waste maximization of bureaucracies. See, e.g., R. McKenzie and G. Tullock, *Modern Political Economy: An Introduction to Economics,* New York: McGraw-Hill, 1978, pp. 414–15.

Watchdog group: Any group that is concerned with ensuring that public welfare and safety is maintained in the work of governmental agencies and that all organizations involved in a particular industry and sector are playing by the rules. For example, the Center for Public Integrity in the United States reports on relations between government officials and the private sector. Its main purpose is to make sure that private, commercial interests do not capture public policy. A watchdog group could well be a governmental agency itself (such as the Environmental Protection Agency in the United States). See, e.g., "Public Office and Private Interest: The Suits Inside the Battle Dress," *The Economist,* April 19, 2003, pp. 52–53. For the different functions that a watchdog group could be involved in, see, e.g., A. Kakabadse, N. Korac-Kakabadse, and A. Kouzmin, "Ethics, Values, and Behaviors: Comparison of Three Case Studies Examining the Paucity of Leadership in Government," *Public Administration,* 2003, 81(3), pp. 477–508.

Watching brief: Refers to the act of keeping an eye on emerging developments in relation to an issue under investigation. Any updated information is then fed back to relevant decision makers so that proper decisions can be made. Watching briefs are kept by all governmental departments on their particular areas of mandate.

Welfare management: As used in organizational human-resource practices, this term refers to the management of those activities in the organization that are designed to enhance the welfare of employees. Examples of welfare management in an organization include a work-life balance program or a wellness program. While it is possible that organizations may transfer the costs of these services to employees (by, for example, deducting an amount from their regular pay), more often than not they will internalize these costs.

Well pay: Payment by the employer to employees if they have not used their sick leave entitlement during a particular time period. This is designed to motivate the employees to stay healthy. Normally, employees cannot cash out their sick-leave entitlements; hence, well pay serves as an inducement for them.

Wellington model: Alludes to the type of public-sector reforms that were pursued in New Zealand in the 1980s and 1990s. The Wellington model is overwhelmingly characterized by the existence of contractual relationships among the various participants in the public sector (including, for example, between departmental chief executives and ministers) and efficiency (for example, in service delivery) emphasized over effectiveness (for example, better results for citizens). The Wellington model is also based on the applications—and draws from the intellectual rigor—of agency theory and public-choice theory. For a description of the model, see, e.g., R. Shaw, "Rehabilitating the Public Service—Alternatives to the Wellington Model," in S. Chatterjee (ed.), *The New Politics: A Third Way for New Zealand,* Palmerston North, New Zealand: Dunmore Press, 1999, p. 187–218. For an example of a discussion of the contractual nature of relationships in the New Zealand public sector, see A. Schick, "Why Most Developing Countries Should Not Try New Zealand's Reforms," *World Bank Research Observer,* 1998, 13(1), pp. 123–31.

Westminster system: *See* **Parliamentary system**.

What-if analysis: *See* **Contingency analysis**.

Whistle-blowing: An act of bringing to the open unethical, wrongful conduct, or criminal activities ongoing in an organization. Such exposure can be made either by an individual or staff members, and while such exposure is usually made in the media for maximum publicity, the accusations, if merited, will be investigated by the appropriate watchdog agency or law enforcement officials. Whistle-blowing legislation in many jurisdictions gives whistleblowers protection against retaliatory measures taken by the organization. See, e.g., G. Brewer and S. Selden, "Whistle Blowers in the Federal Civil Service: New Evidence of the Public Service Ethic," *Journal of Public Administration Research and Theory,* 1998, 8(3), pp. 413–39.

White elephant: A public-sector project that is grand in scale and resource requirements but is of little value. A big and glistening airport in a city that has very little air-traffic potential is an example of a white elephant. The costs of such white-elephant projects are immense, not only in terms of the actual expenses but also in relation to the opportunity costs of the resources so expended.

White paper: A government publication that is intended as a precursor to the introduction of a bill in the legislature. A white paper puts forth the evidence and the argument that the government wishes to make with reference to a particular proposed policy measure (i.e., it deals with the government's stated policy intentions). For an example, see Government of Singapore, *Competitive Salaries for Competent and Honest Government: Benchmarks for Ministers and Senior Public Officers: White Paper,* Cmd.13 of 1994, Singapore: Prime Minister's Office, October 21, 1994. *See also* **Green paper**.

Whitehall model (of civil service): A model of civil service that exists in the United Kingdom and that has the following three attributes: (a) the civil service tends to be recruited extensively on the basis of merit (i.e., based on the knowledge, skills, and abilities of candidates), which is ascertained through various tests and assessment mechanisms; (b) the civil service is (in theory, at least) a single entity and movement within it is seamless; and (c) elected representatives are dependent on permanent civil servants for policy advice and policy implementation. With the increasing pressure to find a happy medium between a neutral and technocratic civil service and the predilection of governmental ministers to retain political advisers, this traditional model of civil service in the UK has come under increasing strain. For a compelling analysis of the relationships between bureaucrats and politicians in the context of the Whitehall model, see, e.g., G. Wilson and A. Barker, "Bureaucrats and Politicians in Britain," *Governance: An International Journal of Policy, Administration, and Institutions,* 2003, 16(3), pp. 349–72.

Whole-job ranking: One of two most common methods of job evaluation, whole-job ranking merely involves taking the entire job into consideration and ranking it with other jobs. As such, there is no effort made to delineate the specifics of the job and attach weights to different components; as such, whole-job ranking is simplistic.

Whole-life cost: Refers to the total resources that are necessary to acquire and sustain any level of capability in an organization. For example, if an organization were to be planning to acquire a new machine to increase its efficiency of operations, then the costs of acquiring it, operating it, and maintaining it (as well as the associated costs of staff time to be trained to use it) could be considered to constitute the whole-life cost of that particular capability enhancement measure.

Whole of government: A whole-of-government view means taking into consideration the impact of any action or issue on all parts of government operation. This is done, for example, by: (a) seeking opportunities for cross-departmental initiatives, (b) brokering information and good practices across the public service, and (c) increasing collaboration among governmental agencies. See, e.g., A. Thurley, "Whole-of-Government Outcomes," *Canberra Bulletin of Public Administration,* 2003, 106, pp. 30–35.

Wicked problems: Problems that are not clearly defined and are not confined to a conventional policy area and, therefore, for which there is no easy solution. Because there are no rules on when and where to stop, wicked problems tend not to be solved at all. These problems consist of two different types: (a) those that are situation dependent and cannot be easily tackled, i.e., they are intractable; and (b) those that can only be solved by working across organizational boundaries, but, because of the difficulties of such crossover, tend not to be addressed at all. For one of the earliest discussions of the concept, see C. Churchman, "Wicked Problems," *Management Science,* 1967, 4(14), pp. 141–42.

Wider state sector: Refers to public agencies and other autonomous governmental bodies that have the following attributes: (a) they are part of central government, (b) they have been given some autonomy from the governmental ministries that they are associated with; and (c) they are subject to different management and financial rules from traditional government ministries.

Willful violation: An act on the part of an employee that goes against the norms and regulations of the organization he/she works for, done deliberately by the individual, knowing well that sanctions will be warranted.

Window dressing: (1) The simulation of a public-sector manager that he/she or the organization is performing well (for example, as described in the organization's annual report) when, in fact, matters are not well. (2) How policy issues are presented to all stakeholders and general citizenry. This occurs when government presents a façade that it is doing something about a problem, for example, on minimizing income inequalities, by talking of grand policies but not acting on such.

Window of opportunity: A usually limited time frame when decisions can be made to make the best of a particular situation, and when there is room for new policies to be developed (or new interpretations of the same policy to emerge). For example, the presence of a sizable third party in parliament may make for windows of opportunity for their policy efforts by compelling the major parties to compromise on long-held—but narrow—views on particular issues. See, e.g., J. Blankenau, "The Fate of National Health Insurance in Canada and the United States: A Multiple Streams Explanation," *Policy Studies Journal,* 2001, 29(1), pp. 38–55.

Win-lose game: *See* **Zero-sum game**.

Win-lose style (of policy leadership): A style of leadership that is aggressive in its approach to attaining organizational mandates (winning), but it also loses by making enemies in its aggressive pursuit of self-interests. See, e.g., L. Koenig, *An Introduction to Public Policy,* Englewood Cliffs, NJ: Prentice Hall, 1986, p. 49. *See also* **Lose-leave style (of policy leadership); Yield-lose style (of policy leadership)**.

Winner takes all: A situation where the winning party receives all associated claims or benefits (or inversely, incur all costs)—there is no consolation prize. The winner-takes-all notion leads to a zero-sum game, where someone's gain is someone else's loss. *See also* **Zero-sum game**.

Winner tortoise: A term used to denote something done slowly and methodically but which ultimately results in success. For example, it is argued that while the clean-air policy in Sweden took a long time to be effected, it was successful because a consensus emerged in the various issues surrounding the policy. See, e.g., L. Lundqvist, *The Hare and the Tortoise: Clean Air Policies in the United States and Sweden,* Ann Arbor: University of Michigan Press, 1980). *See also* **Loser hare**.

Winner's curse: A situation where the eventual winner of a bid ends up paying too much for the contract. This scenario occurs when a bidder—relatively uninformed due to information asymmetry—presumes that winning will come only when the bid is high. See, e.g., R. Wilson, "Competitive Bidding with Disparate Information," *Management Science,* 1969, 15(7), pp. 446–48. *See also* **Post-purchase regret**.

Win-win bargaining: Bargaining that takes place between two parties where there are mutual-gains negotiations. Such negotiations focus on consensus and mutual interests, and often include direct bargaining between the parties themselves rather than through agents and/or lawyers.

Win-win situation: *See* **Super-optimum alternatives**.

Win-win-win policy: A particular policy that brings about a winning (or successful) result in several dimensions at the same time (such as, for example, on equity, efficiency and environmental protection). For an application, see, e.g., J. Nugent and C. Sarwa, "The Three E's—Efficiency, Equity and Environmental Protection—In Search of 'Win-Win-Win' Policies: A CGE Analysis of India," *Journal of Policy Modeling,* 2002, 24(1), pp. 19–50.

Within-role conflict: A tension that exists in an employee as a result of different roles that he or she is expected to play. For example, an employee may have some societal values that may be at odds with the values he/she is expected to model in the workplace.

Women-friendly policies: Policies that employers pursue that are considered to be especially targeted at creating an environment in the organization and workplace where women feel safe and are encouraged to belong. Such policies revolve around issues such as flexitime, training and development, maternity entitlements, anti-sex discrimination, positive equal opportunities, and formalized human-resource management. For a case-study application, see, e.g., C. Ng and W. Chiu, "Managing Equal Opportunities for Women: Sorting the Friends from the Foes," *Human Resource Management Journal,* 2001, 11(1), pp. 75–88.

Work enrichment: *See* **Job enrichment**.

Work environment: All the factors and situations that affect the manner in which an individual does his or her work. A work environment can be positive or negative. If the former, the employee has an inducement to perform better; if the latter, the performance suffers.

Work improvement teams: Groups of employees who are charged with seeking to identify and solve the problems they face at the workplace. Such a group consists of staff members who generally work together and who face a common work environment. Work improvement teams are a part of the total quality management approach in organizations.

Work-in-progress: Development of a particular product (for example, a policy analysis paper) that is not released beyond the group members who are involved in it. The purpose of disseminating a work-in-progress document is to gather relevant peer review and feedback, and, if necessary, strengthen the analysis contained in it. Work-in-progress documents are, however, subject to freedom-of-information requirements and the organization is mandated to cite them if they are deemed relevant to the information being requested.

Work-life balance: The distribution of an employee's time and commitment in such a manner that neither work nor private life is compromised by the other. Work-life balance is a product of family-friendly policies instituted by organizations, and is an increasingly accepted concept in organizations that seek to motivate employees by letting them know that the organization recognizes—and values—that the employee has differing commitments to meet. In the end, the purpose of instituting a policy of work-life balance in the organization is to create an environment where the employee is inherently motivated. For a comprehensive review of the issues, see, e.g., A. Saltzstein, et al., "Work-Family Balance and Job Satisfaction: The Impact of Family-Friendly Policies on Attitudes of Federal Government Employees," *Public Administration Review,* 2001, 61(4), pp. 452–67.

Work premium: That component of a wage that is paid to an employee which seeks to compensate the individual's exposure to something difficult or inconvenient in relation to work. For example, the hazardous-duty allowance that staff members of the United Nations receive when based in war-torn countries is a work premium.

Work redesign: *See* **Work structuring**.

Work-related training: Training offered to staff members that is related to their work. Some training opportunity that is offered to staff members, however, has to do with non-work-related aspects (such as planning for retirement). In the elite Administrative Service of Singapore, for example, work-related training constitutes about 60 percent of the total training budget for a senior public servant; the rest is set aside for individual development.

Work rescheduling: *See* **Work structuring**.

Work shadow: *See* **Sitting next to Nellie**.

Work sharing: The act of dividing—and reconfiguring—the work in an organization in such a manner that all individuals that are currently in employment will continue to be engaged in some work. The purpose of work sharing is to minimize the chances of an employee being laid off. Three types of work sharing may be identified: (a) reduction in hours, (b) division of work, and (c) rotation of employment. The first is the most common. For a good analysis of this concept in a jurisdictional setting, see, e.g., J. Hunt, "Has Work-Sharing Worked in Germany?" *Quarterly Journal of Economics,* 1999, 114(1), pp. 117–48.

Work structuring: Refers to the process by which work for a particular employee is designed. This includes, for example, setting the hours of work, method of salary payment, types and amounts of pay deductions, if any, etc. While some of these (such as hours of work) tend to be standard for other employees, others are not (such as deductions). Work rescheduling is also a form of work structuring, and refers to providing flexibility to employees to manage their work around some constraints they may be facing, such as at home with child care. However, such flexibility can only be accommodated up to a point, and the employee will still have to complete the tasks assigned and also work the minimum number of hours required. Another related concept is work redesign, which is changing some or all of the aspects of the work in order to create variety to motivate an employee. Such work redesign can include, for example, changing the workplace seat plan, adding responsibilities, or changing the mix of duties, etc.

Workable consensus: *See* **Sufficient consensus**.

Workbench audit: A process of observing workers at work to assess what factors affect their performance. Such an audit helps management to come up with measures that more accurately reflect what might have the most impact when implemented.

Worker participation: The involvement of employees in the decision-making system in an organization. Such participation can be minimal (as in being asked to provide some feedback to organizational policies that have already been decided by management) or extensive (as in employee groups coming up with ideas of their own that are expressed, developed, and implemented together with management). One vehicle of worker participation is a workers' council, which refers to a joint labor-management body that is considered an improvement to the collective-bargaining process since the participation of workers in such a council is formalized, and it helps give voice to employee sentiments and concerns. Workers' councils thus play a critical role in resolving problems of mutual interest to both labor and management.

Workflow bureaucracies: Large organizations that are highly structured, although not all workflow bureaucracies have the same concentration of authority. The term comes from a typology of organizations first determined in the UK in the early 1960s. The group proposed that any organization could be characterized by its degree of specialization of functions, standardization of procedures, formalization of documentation, and centralization (or concentration) of authority.

Workflow chart: Also known as a work activity chart, this is a graphic depiction of what the organization's activities are, when they are to be completed, and the status of resources (time, money, effort) thus spent. Workflow charts are used extensively in project management within organizations.

Workforce analysis: Analysis done of the workforce in an organization that involves: (a) the listing of each job, (b) a ranking by salary paid, and (c) a ranking by the level of supervision required for each position. Compliance requirements necessitate such an analysis from time to time (such as reporting on compliance with equal employment opportunity requirements). Workforce analysis is an important component of job evaluation. *See also* **Job evaluation**.

Working climate: Refers to the environment in which an individual works in an organization. It consists of all the factors that affect how an employee does his/her work, and includes factors such as lighting, work routines, peer relationships, team culture, etc. The working climate in an organization is an important determinant of employee motivation. *See also* **Herzberg's two-factor theory**.

Working conditions: (1) The conditions of service that are specified in an employment contract (such as on work hours, benefits received, etc.). (2) *See also* **Working climate**.

Working group: A group of people formed to work on a particular problem or issue. Working groups can have representation from outside the organization and their methods of work are normally fairly informal, although their work will be based on set terms of reference. Once the particular piece of work is complete, the working group is disbanded.

Working paper: A paper that is prepared which results from research that revolves around some themes/areas that the organization is involved in, and which presents tentative conclusions that are meant to be debated and discussed by relevant parties (such as other government organizations, think tanks, academicians, etc.). Opinions expressed in the working paper are, however, attributed to the author(s) and not to the entity that commissions or publishes the work.

Workmen's compensation: Refers to a scheme that provides income and medical coverage to workers in case they meet with an accident or suffer an injury while on duty. In many jurisdictions, workmen's compensation is mandated by law. Schemes around workers' compensation, however, have stringent controls instituted to ensure that they are not abused.

Workplace bargaining: *See* **Collective bargaining**.

Workplace diversity: The presence of a diverse workforce in an organization that reflects the diversity that exists in society. In many jurisdictions, employers are mandated/encouraged to ensure that they work toward enhancing workplace diversity. Defining such diversity, and getting a handle on the specific parameters of just how diversity is to be improved, is a difficult process. For example, what should the comparator be for, say, the senior executive service: total population, total number of senior managers, total employees in the public sector, or any other variable?

Workplace practices: Activities that are related to how the work of the organization is carried out. This includes, for example, the organization's recruitment practices, use of training and development opportunities such as job rotations and secondments, employee involvement in organizational decision making, management-union relations (if there is a union), method of learning and knowledge management, etc. It is workplace practices that are cited and that serve as the base when claims are made against employers for discrimination, harassment, etc.

Workshop: A method of imparting training and knowledge whereby participants are given problems and case studies to tackle in small groups. A workshop has a much more hands-on approach to training than the traditional classroom-type instruction or seminar.

Worst-case analysis: A method of determining the possible outcomes of specific actions based on the least favorable conditions. Such an analysis provides decision makers with information on resource requirements that are the maximum and on the possible outcomes that are the least desired. This combination of maximum resource loss and least desired outcome constitutes the worst case for the organization for the particular issue/problem at hand.

Wrap-up clause: *See* **Zipper clause**.

Written warning: Refers to a warning that is more severe than a verbal warning in relation to unacceptable behavior or performance of an employee. A written warning is of more consequence to the employee because it may be placed on a formal personal record.

Wrongful dismissal: *See* **Unfair dismissal**.

X

X-efficiency analysis: As used in the application of employee motivation, this is a tool designed to ascertain why one particular style of management results in greater efficiency than any other. For an example of an application of the analysis in relation to the operation of performance indicators, see J. Taylor and R. Taylor, "Performance Indicators in Academia: An X-Efficiency Approach?" *Australian Journal of Public Administration,* 2003, 62(2), pp. 71–82.

X-efficiency theory: As used in the context of organization dynamics, this term looks at the causes and effects of relationships between efficiency and inefficiency. The theory makes several assertions, for example, that organizations that are owner operated are more efficient than those that are not; or that in the main, organizations do not necessarily operate at their most optimal level. In economist Harvey Leibenstein's original work in this area, X-efficiency related to measures that ensured that an organization or economy moved to the production possibility frontier (and allocative efficiency ensured that it chose a point on the frontier in accordance with price signals). See H. Leibenstein, "Allocative Efficiency vs. 'X-Efficiency,'" *American Economic Review,* 1966, 56(3), pp. 392–415.

X-inefficiency: Denotes a situation where an organization is producing the right outputs but is not economizing on the level of inputs. X-inefficiency is said to be possible in public agencies where, due to a monopoly situation, a higher price can be charged to consumers, and where the lack of competitive pressures means that public organizations tend not to invest adequately in research and development. Finally, there are likely to be wasteful expenditures on expensive executive benefits, and so forth. For a jurisdictional analysis of the concept, see, e.g., L. White, "Appropriate Technology, X-Inefficiency, and a Competitive Environment: Some Evidence from Pakistan," *Quarterly Journal of Economics*, 1976, 90(4), pp. 575–89. *See also* **Organizational slack**.

Y

Yardstick: Any standard or benchmark used by organizations or individuals as comparators to measure performance or targets. **See also Benchmark.**

Yardstick competition: Refers to the comparison of jurisdictions in terms of the extent to which they have achieved results. The concept is useful when considering that at times it is not meaningful to look at policy results without putting them into context of what others have achieved. For a discussion of the concept, see, e.g., T. Besley and A. Case, "Incumbent Behavior: Vote-Seeking, Tax-Setting, and Yardstick Competition," *American Economic Review,* 1995, 85(1), pp. 25–45.

Yes-no decision variable: *See* **Zero-one decision variable.**

Yield-lose style (of policy leadership): A style of leadership that places more emphasis on maintaining collegial relationships with others than on targeting goal achievement. This yielding nature of leadership ultimately does nothing for the organization, hence the term. *See also* **Win-lose style (of policy leadership); Lose-leave style (of policy leadership).**

Young Turks: Young staff members who are ambitious and want to push through change and reforms aggressively. At times, though, their enthusiasm for change eclipses their political acumen and they become sidelined by more entrenched interests in the organization.

Z

Zairean disease: A term used in relation to aid and aid dependence, and refers to the notion that foreign aid to developing countries can worsen the quality of governmental institutions there. This can happen in many ways, for example, by (a) reducing governmental reliance on its own internal revenue sources (such as taxes), (b) weakening the state bureaucracies by taking what little skilled human resource there may be in the country, (c) hindering the development of administrative capacity by implementing projects that governments would have otherwise undertaken, and (d) generally fostering a dependency syndrome in government. See, e.g., M. Godfrey et al., "Technical Assistance and Capacity Development in an Aid-Dependent Economy: The Experience of Cambodia," *World Development,* 2002, 30(3), pp. 355–73.

Zealot: A term used by the renowned scholar Anthony Downs to denote a type of bureaucrat who is extremely partisan in what he/she does but is also very committed to the work and mission at hand. See A. Downs, *Inside Bureaucracy,* Boston: Little, Brown, 1967, p. 88.

Zero contribution thesis: An argument that rational self-interested individuals will not necessarily always act in their own interest unless there is coercion from an external source. This further implies that individuals will not always agree to collective action even when there is societal benefit, and thus public policy will have to be designed in such a way as to facilitate such collective action. For a cogent review of the thesis, see, e.g., E. Ostrom, "Collective Action and the Evolution of Social Norms," *Journal of Economic Perspectives,* 2000, 14(3), pp. 137–58.

Zero hour: *See* **Question time**.

Zero-based budgeting: Also called priority-based budgeting, this form of budgeting starts from a systematic consideration of an organization's objectives, strategies, and tactics. It also requires that the allocation of resources be based on the organization revisiting its basic assumptions and calculations every time a budget request is made. For this, the organization must periodically re-evaluate the need for all of its programs and justify the continuance of each program in the budget proposal.

Zero-defect culture: Derived from total quality management, this term refers to an organizational policy to not tolerate any defects (also known as continuous improvement). While such culture may not be often realistic, the drive toward zero defects characterizes the concept of total quality in the organization.

Zero-infinity problem: Refers to the probability of a problem that is very small yet whose potential impact is enormous. This means governments cannot be complacent about problems that have a very low likelihood of occurrence if the consequences are likely to be severe. See, e.g., P. Clough, "Environmental Risks in Public and Corporate Policy," in A. Sundakov and J. Yeabsley (eds.), *Risk and the Institutions of Govern-*

ment, Wellington: Institute of Policy Studies, and New Zealand Institute of Economic Research (NZIER), 1999, pp. 35–45.

Zero-one decision variable: A problem-solving algorithm whose values are zero or one (i.e., it is a binary variable). The former refers to a negative value and the latter to a positive one. Thus, a problem whose response set can only be yes or no is a zero-one decision variable. In public policy making, however, few situations contain the zero-one decision variable. *See also* **Wicked problems.**

Zero-sum game: A situation where the gains of one party are at the expense of another, however, not correspondingly on a one-to-one basis. This means that a party losing something has a level of marginal costs that is higher than the marginal benefits of the party that is winning. See, e.g., P. Bernstein, *Against the Gods: The Remarkable Story of Risk,* New York: John Wiley & Sons, Inc., 1996, p. 113. *See also* **Games.**

Zipf's law: An assertion that people will use as little effort as possible and will choose the easiest way and means to complete a task. In this regard, Zipf's law has similarities to a Theory-X type of individual. The law derives its name from George Kingsley Zipf, a linguistic professor. *See also* **Principle of least effort.**

Zipper clause: Also called a wrap-up clause, this term refers to a provision in a contract among parties that everything that has been agreed to has been specified in the written contract. As such, nothing else should be assumed from the contract that is not written therein.

Z-management: *See* **Theory Z.**

Zone of acceptance: Realms within which employees accept the directions and orders given by organizational leaders. A zone of acceptance thus refers to a situation in which an individual questions, understands, accepts, and then complies with the directives that are given. *See also* **Zone of indifference.**

Zone of discretion: *See* **Administrative discretion.**

Zone of independent judgment: *See* **Administrative discretion.**

Zone of indifference: A situation in which an individual does not consciously question the directives that are given and complies with them even though he/she may be inherently indifferent to them. Proponents of the dichotomy between politics and administration prefer that bureaucrats exhibit such a zone of indifference.

Zone of uncertainty: As applied in the context of the performance management of employees, the zone of uncertainty refers to the range of values (or degree of goal attainment) within which it is difficult for organizational leadership to determine whether the employee has actually attained the desired level of performance. It is intuitive that staff members will be asked to be as specific as possible about what they feel are their achievements and to cite critical incidents to substantiate their claims in a performance appraisal exercise. In reality, however, managers will continue to face the zone of uncertainty in their interactions with staff members since it is not possible that all will be known about every issue or incident. The greater the degree of zone of uncertainty, the more difficult it is for managers to make a firm decision on the individual's mobility and reward levels.

Z-organization: An organization that has characteristics of traditional Japanese organizations, including: (a) long-term employment, (b) slow evaluation and promotion, and (c) low reliance on job rotation as a developmental and learning tool. Lifetime tenure, however, is now slowly becoming less evident in the public service, even in Japan. See, e.g., W. Ouchi and A. Jaeger, "Type Z Organization: Stability in the Midst of Mobility," *Academy of Management Review,* 1978, 3(2), pp. 305–14.

About the Author

Gambhir Bhatta joined the Asian Development Bank in August 2005 as a Senior Governance Specialist. Prior to this, he was affiliated with the School of Government at Victoria University of Wellington, where he was on leave from his position as a Senior Advisor at the New Zealand State Services Commission in Wellington. The Commission—along with the Treasury, and the Department of Prime Minister and Cabinet—forms a triage of central agencies in the New Zealand Public Service.

In his professional career, Dr. Bhatta has been involved with various organizations in different sectors across numerous countries. He has also been a consultant to the United Nations, Asian Development Bank, and Singapore Civil Service College, among others. This is his third book, and his essays have appeared in several international journals, including the *International Review of Administrative Sciences*, *Public Personnel Management*, *Public Performance and Management Review*, *Policy Studies Journal*, and *International Journal of Training & Development*.

Dr. Bhatta has dual master's degrees in economics and political science from Bowling Green State University, Ohio, and a Ph.D. in public and international affairs from the University of Pittsburgh, with a specialization in applied policy analysis.